# **Peru** Handbook

*South American Handbook*, the longest running guidebook in the English language, has provided generations of travellers with comprehensive coverage of the entire continent. This Handbook is in Footprint's series of new guides to the individual countries of Latin America. The first to be published are Handbooks to Peru, Chile and Ecuador & Galápagos. These will be followed by guides to Brazil, Colombia, Bolivia, Argentina and Venezuela.

# You won't find a country with more culture than Peru.

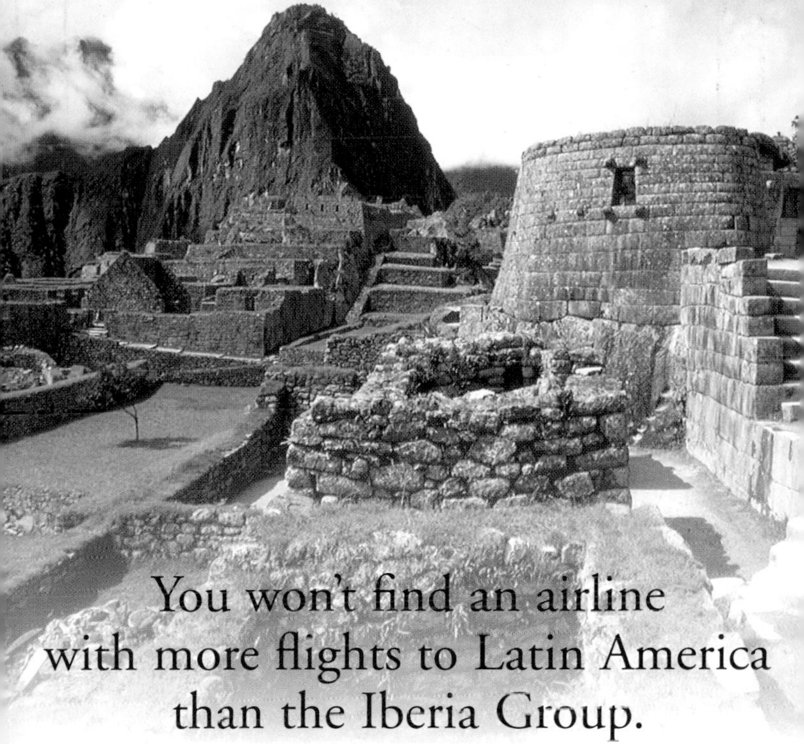

# You won't find an airline with more flights to Latin America than the Iberia Group.

When you can discover a hidden Inca city amidst uncharted jungle, wonder over stones inscribed in a pre-Colombian age and observe the floating islands of reeds on the highest lake in the world, you can appreciate that few countries have more to offer than Peru.

And of course, with our Circular Fares which give you the freedom to travel throughout Latin America as you please, no one proves a better travelling companion than the Iberia Group.

To book, call Iberia Group Reservations on **0171-830 0011**
or contact your specialist travel agent.

VIASA
VENEZUELAN INTERNATIONAL AIRWAYS

IBERIA

Leading the way to Latin America.

# Peru Handbook

Alan Murphy

Latin America series editor: Ben Box

**Footprint** Handbooks

*For my part, I travel not to go anywhere, but to go. I travel for travel's sake. The great affair is to move.*

Robert Louis Stevenson

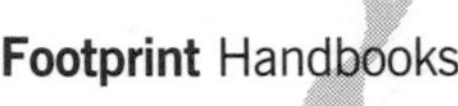


6 Riverside Court, Lower Bristol Road
Bath BA2 3DZ England
T 01225 469141 F 01225 469461
E mail handbooks@footprint.cix.co.uk
www.fooprint-handbooks.co.uk

ISBN 0 900751 82 7 ISSN 1363-738x
CIP DATA: A catalogue record for this book is available from the British Library

In North America, published by

4255 West Touhy Avenue, Lincolnwood
(Chicago), Illinois 60646-1975, USA
T 847 679 5500 F 847 679 24941
E mail NTCPUB2@AOL.COM

ISBN 0-8442-4914-9
Library of Congress Catalog Card
Number: 96-72519

1st Edition
January 1997



**Every effort has been made to ensure that the facts in this Handbook are accurate. However travellers should still obtain advice from consulates, airlines etc about current travel and visa requirements and conditions before travelling. The authors and publishers cannot accept responsibility for any loss, injury or inconvenience, however caused.**

Cover design by Newell and Sorrell; cover photography by Phil Dolby, Tony Morrison/ South American Pictures and Dave Saunders

Production: Design by Mytton Williams; Typesetting by Jo Morgan, Ann Griffiths and Melanie Mason-Fayon; Maps by Sebastian Ballard, Alasdair Dawson and Kevin Feeney; Charts by Ann Griffiths; Original line drawings by Andrew Newton; Proofread by Rod Gray and David Cotterell.

Printed and bound in Great Britain by Clays Ltd., Bungay, Suffolk

# Contents

# The Editors

## Alan Murphy

Like Scott of the Antarctic 100 years before, Alan Murphy's 'Voyage of Discovery' originated in the Scottish city of Dundee. Having ended a career in journalism with local publishing giant, DC Thomson in order to put some letters after his name, Alan then left his native Scotland for the steamy jungles of South America, informing family and friends that he "might be gone for some time". He travelled extensively throughout the continent, particularly in Peru. Despite frequent and painful reminders of Scotland's 1978 World Cup debacle, Alan developed a deep and lasting affection for the country and its people, finally leaving to take up residence in La Paz and a job writing for the fledgling Bolivian Times newspaper. Now living in London, Alan's growing involvement with Footprint Handbooks means that he can continue his relationship with this most fascinating of countries.

## Ben Box

A doctorate in medieval Spanish and Portugese studies provided very few job prospects for Ben Box, but a fascination for all things Latin. While studying for his degree, Ben travelled extensively in Spain and Portugal. He turned his attention to contemporary Iberian and Latin American affairs in 1980, beginning a career as a freelance writer at that time. He contributed regularly to national newspapers and learned tomes, and after increasing involvement with the *South American Handbook*, became its editor in 1989. Although he has travelled from the US/Mexico border to southern Chile (not all in one go) and in the Caribbean, Ben recognises that there are always more places to explore. He also edits the *Mexico and Central American Handbook* and is series editor for Footprint Handbook's Latin American titles. To seek diversion from a household immersed in Latin America, he plays village cricket in summer and cycles the lanes of Suffolk.

## Specialist contributors

Peter Pollard for geography; Dr Nigel Dunstone (University of Durham) for flora and fauna; Ben Box for literature; Dr Valerie Fraser (University of Essex) for fine art and sculpture; Nigel Gallop for music and dance; Sarah Cameron for the economy section; Mark Eckstein for responsible tourism; Mark Duffy and Simon Harvey for adventure tourism; Paul Davies of Journey Latin America for details of air transport; Richard Robinson for world wide radio information; Dr David Snashall for health.

For specific contributions to the text: Richard Elgar and Bill Glick (South American Explorers Club, Lima); Robert and Daisy Kunstaetter (Latin American Travel Consultants, Quito); Peter Frost (Cusco); Nicholas Asheshov (Urubamba and the Sacred Valley); Lucy Davies and Mo Fini (Tumi) for permission to use material from *Arts and Crafts of South America*.

# Introduction and hints

SEVERAL YEARS ago, while wandering around Trujillo, on the north coast of Peru, I was approached by a group of school children, eager to know what I thought of their country, extolling its virtues and, finally, pleading with me to tell everyone back home to come and visit. This is not an unusual occurrence in a country where practically everyone you meet sees themselves as an ambassador, whose duty it is to gauge foreign opinion and promote their own town or village as a prime tourist destination. It's an attitude that permeates the national psyche of a country relieved to see an end to international isolation.

Peruvians have good reason to be proud. Their country's main attractions are known, even to the most geographically-challenged – Machu Picchu, Cusco, the Nasca Lines – but these are only the tip of a vast, unexplored iceberg. Now, though, areas which were once well and truly off the beaten track are opening up to tourism as access, infrastructure and information improve.

In the Southern Andes, for instance, Ayacucho was once the centre of one of the most influential pre-Incan cultures – and has the ruins to prove it. The city also has 33 colonial churches and hosts one of the most impressive Semana Santa festivals in the entire continent. High in the mountains is the Mantaro Valley, an area which produces the finest handicrafts and where each village is renowned for its own particular product.

More remote parts include the Cotahuasi Canyon. This is not a name on the tip of everyone's tongue, but it has recently been calculated to be the deepest canyon in the world, deeper even than its better-known neighbour, the Colca Canyon. Here, you will encounter people who may never have set eyes on a pair of hiking boots or a fleece jacket. Further north, in the high cloud forest, lie countless precolumbian sites, built by a mysterious people considered by some to be of Viking descent. The most visited of the sites, Kuelap, is of such immense proportions as to make the Great Pyramid at Giza seem like something out of Legoland. Many of these ancient citadels are lost and uncharted, buried deep in the tropical forests, possibly waiting for the next Hiram Bingham to stumble across them.

New forms of tourism are also developing to cope with the increasing demand of pioneering travellers hungry for a new and exciting challenge. One of the fastest growing is 'adventure tourism', which covers everything from mountain biking to hang-gliding from desert cliffs. Less physical, but more spiritually rewarding, the burgeoning field of 'mystical tourism' offers the chance to study ancient Andean philosophy, learn the dark secrets of witchcraft, or have a shaman interpret your hallucinatory visions deep in the Amazonian jungle.

Those young ambassadors in Trujillo may have been understating their case. More people should visit Peru, certainly, but they should visit now. In fact, get on the next flight to Lima, for what was once one of Peru's problems, a lack of tourists, is now, ironically, one of its great assets. Many of those hidden treasures are waiting to be 'discovered'.

Alan Murphy

Peru
Not to Scale
ECUADOR
COLOMBIA
BRAZIL
BOLIVIA
CHILE
Pacific
Ocean
To Quito
Guayaquil
Machala
Cuenca
Tumbes
Loja
Macará
Talara
Paita
Sullana
Piura
Sechura
Jaén
Moyobamba
Yurimaguas
Chachapoyas
Celendín
Tarapoto
Cajamarca
Chiclayo
Pacasmayo
Trujillo
Caraz
Huaraz
Chimbote
Casma
Pativilca
Chancay
Callao
LIMA
Iquitos
Río Amazonas
Leticia
Río Marañón
Río Ucuyali
Río Huallaga
Cruzeiro do Sul
Pucallpa
Tingo María
Huánuco
Cerro de Pasco
La Merced
Satipo
La Oroya
Tarma
Jauja
Huancayo
Huancavelica
Ayacucho
Andahuaylas
Quillabamba
Manu
Río Madre de Dios
Puerto Maldonado
Brasiléia
Iñapari
Machu Picchu
Cuzco
Abancay
Urcos
Sicuani
Cañete
Pisco
Ica
Nasca
Chala
Huancane
Juliaca
Lake Titicaca
Puno
Copacabana
Juli
LA PAZ
Arequipa
Matarani
Mollendo
Moquegua
Ilo
Tacna
Arica
N
To Santiago

Colca, Apurímac and Urubamba. By the same author, 'Diarios de Cotahuasi', in *Caretas* magazine, 6 July 1995, and 'Rio Cotahuasi: the World's Deepest Canyon – Really!' in *South American Explorer*, Spring 1996 edition. Kurt Casey, 'Cotahuasi Canyon – an Ultimate Peruvian Adventure', in *American Whitewatwer*, July/Aug, 1995. Joe Kane, *Running the Amazon*.

## SURFING

Peru is a top internationally renowned surfing destination. Its main draws are the variety of wave and the all year round action. Point Break, Left and Right Reef Break and waves up to 6m can all be found during the seasons; Sept to Feb in the N and Mar to Dec in the S, though May is often ideal S of Lima.

Ocean swells are affected by two currents; the warm El Niño in the N and the cold Humboldt current in the S arriving from Antartica. Pimentel, near Chiclayo, is the dividing point between these two effects but a wet suit is normally required anywhere S of Piura.

The biggest wave is at Pico Alto (sometimes 6m in May), S of Lima, and the largest break is 800m at Chicama, near Trujillo. There are more than 30 top surfing beaches. North of Lima these are: Chicama and Cabo Blanco (both highly rec); Pimentel; Pacasmayo/El Faro; and Mancora. South of Lima the best beaches are: Punta Hermosa, Punta Rocas (right reef break) and Pico Alto (best in May), the pick of the bunch; Señoritas (left reef break); San Bartolo; Caballeros (right reef break); La Isla (point break); El Huaico (left reef break); Los Muelles; Cerro Azul.

International competitions are held at Pico Alto (Balin Open in May) and Punta Rocas (during the summer months). A surfing magazine *Tablista* is published in Dec and July and there are forecasts in the US *International Surf Report* (see **Lima Sports** section, page 114).

## DIVING

The chill of the Humboldt current puts many people off diving in the Peruvian waters. Diving off the Paracas peninsula is rewarding, as is the warmer tropical ocean off Tumbes with larger fish. It is also practiced in the Bahía de Pucusana. The best season for visibility is Mar to Nov because the rivers from the mountains don't deposit silt in the sea. It can be cheap to do a PADI course in Peru; less than US$200 for a month's course, 2 weeks of theory, 4 dives in a pool, 4 in the ocean (see **Lima Sports** page 114).

## CAVE DIVING

This is not yet widely known in Peru, but there is an organization which can provide information; *Centre of Subterranean Explorations of Peru (CEESPE)*, Av Brasil 1815, Jesús María, Lima, T 463-4722, Sr Carlos Morales is very helpful.

A cave which has attracted international expeditions is the *Gruta de Huagapo*, or 'The Cave that Weeps', located in the Valle de Palcaymo 30 km NW of Tarma in the Department of Junín, at 3,572m.

## YACHTING

Yacht clubs in Lima are: *Club Regatas de Lima*, 494 García y García, T 429-2994; *Yacht Club Ancón*, Malecón San Martín, T 488-3071; *Club Regatas Unión*, Gálvez s/n, T 429-0095

# How to go

## GETTING AROUND

Few nationalities require more than a valid passport and a ticket home to visit Peru. Among those who do need a visa are Australians and New Zealanders. There are direct flights from several European capitals (but not London), from the USA (Miami is the main departure point) and from all over Latin America. With tourism a major force in the economy, the authorities are attracting more international airlines and foreign investors to ensure the sector's continued growth and thus ever easier access for foreigners.

Once in Peru, if you decide to fly around the country during your visit, the three major national airlines operate airpasses, which may be the best value to suit your itinerary. For overland travellers, the road network, as said elsewhere, is being upgraded and better roads mean better bus services and improved conditions for drivers. Peru, however, is no different from other Latin American countries in that travelling by road at night or in bad weather should be treated with great care. It is also true that there are many more unpaved than paved roads, so it is unwise to have too tight a schedule.

## PRACTICALITIES

The unit of currency is the new sol, normally referred to as just the sol. If you take your spending money in US dollars, you will have no difficulty acquiring soles through banks, exchange houses, or with a credit card. It is not a cheap country, especially for the budget traveller, but compared with North America or Europe visitors will find some things good value (eg local food, handicrafts, mid-range accommodation, public transport). Upper class restaurants, on the other hand, are very expensive and Lima is much more costly than the provinces.

Accommodation is plentiful throughout the price ranges, with a great deal of money being invested, especially at the expensive end of the market. Basic hotels are usually just that, but there is also a good choice of mid-range establishments, many catering for tourists, or backpackers and climbers in regions which attract this type of visitor. Camping is only a surprise to the local inhabitants in the remotest of areas. The authorities have recategorized hotels, paying special attention to the security provided. Peru's reputation in this regard was not good, but much has been done to improve the situation. Complacency should not be encouraged, yet. Common sense and seeking local advice should see you through OK, on most occasions.

After privatization, the phone service is getting better and, with it, communications via the Internet are expanding. Parcel post is very expensive and, like its letter equivalent, not always reliable.

Do not take preconceived ideas to Peru. It is a big country in many senses, "broad and alien" the writer, Ciro Alegría, called it. He was referring to the Sierra Indians experience of their own country, but Pe-

foot of the mountains where the river flow is greatest and high sunshine levels ensure good crop production.

The climate of this region depends almost entirely on the ocean currents along the Pacific coast. Two bodies of water drift northwards, the one closest to the shore, known as the Humboldt Current, is the colder, following the deep sea trench along the edge of the Pacific Plate. The basic wind systems here are the South-East Trades crossing the continent from the Atlantic, but the strong tropical sun over the land draws air into Peru from the Pacific. Being cool, this air does no more than condense into mist (known as the *garúa*) over the coastal mountains and that mostly in the N. This is sufficient to provide moisture for some unusual flora but virtually never produces rain, hence the desert conditions. The mixing of the two cold ocean currents, and the cloud cover which protects the water from the strongest sunlight, creates the unique conditions favourable to fish, notably sardines and anchovy, giving Peru an enormous economic resource. In turn, the fish support vast numbers of seabirds whose deposits of guano have been another very successful export for the country. This is the normal situation; every few years, however, it is disrupted by the phenomenon known as '*El Niño*' (see page 29).

## The Highlands

The Highlands, or *la sierra*, extend inland from the coastal strip some 250 km in the N, increasing to 400 km in the S. The average elevation is about 3,000m and 50% of Peruvians live there. Essentially it is a plateau dissected by dramatic canyons and dominated by some of the most spectacular mountain ranges in the world.

**Mountains** The tallest peaks are in the Cordillera Blanca (Huascarán; 6,768m) and the neighbouring Cordillera Huayhuash (Yerupajá; 6,634m). Huascarán is often quoted as the second highest point in South America after Aconcagua, but this is not so; there are some five other peaks on or near the Argentina-Chile border over 6,770.

The snowline here, at 9° S, is between 4,500m and 5,000m, much lower than further S. For example, at 16° S, permanent snow commences at 6,000m on Coropuna (6,425m). The reasons for this anomaly can be traced again to the Humboldt current. The Cordillera Balnca is less than 100 km from the coast, and the cool air drawn in depresses temperatures at high altitudes. Precipitation comes also from the E and falls as snow. Constant high winds and temperatures well below freezing at night create an unusual microclimate and with it spectacular mountain scenery, making it a mecca for snow and ice mountaineers. Dangers are heightened by the quite frequent earthquakes causing avalanches and landslides which have brought heavy loss of life to the valleys of the region. In 1970, 20,000 people lost their lives when Yungay, immediately W of Huascarán, was overwhelmed.

**Canyons** Equally dramatic are the deep canyons taking water from the high mountains to the Pacific. The Colca Canyon, about 100 km N of Arequipa, has been measured at 3,200m from the lower rim to the river, more than twice as deep as the Grand Canyon. At one point it is overlooked by the 5,227m Señal Yajirhua peak, a stupendous 4,150m above the water level. Deeper even than Colca is the Cotahuasi Canyon, also in Arequipa Department, whose deepest point is 3,354m. Other canyons have been found in this remote area yet to be measured and documented. There is no doubt that in recent geologic history, there was much greater precipitation and heavy ice-age glaciation has assisted the erosion process to create these dramatic features.

In spite of these ups and downs which cause great communications difficulties, the presence of water and a more temperate climate on the plateau has attracted people throughout the ages. Present day important population centres in the Highlands include Cajamarca in the N, Huancayo in central Peru and Cusco in the S, all at around 3,000m. Above this, at around 4,000m, is the 'high steppe' or *puna*, with constant winds and wide day/night temperature fluctuations. Nevertheless, fruit and potatoes (which originally came from the *puna* of Peru and Bolivia) are grown at this altitude and the meagre grasslands are home to the ubiquitous llama.

**Volcanoes** Although hot springs and evidence of ancient volcanic activity can be seen almost anywhere in Peru, the southern part of the *sierra* is the only area where there are active volcanoes. These represent the northernmost of a line of volcanoes which stretch 1,500 km S along the Chile-Bolivia border to Argentina. Sabancaya (5,977m), just S of the Colca canyon, is currently active, often with a dark plume downwind from the summit. Beyond the Colca canyon is the Valle de los Volcanes, with 80 cinder cones rising 50-250m above a desolate floor of lava and ash. There are other dormant or recently active volcanoes near the western side of Lake Titicaca – for example Ubinas – but the most notable is El Misti (5,822m) which overlooks Arequipa. It is perfectly shaped, indicating its status as active in the recent geologic past. Some experts believe it is one of the most potentially dangerous volcanoes in South America. Certainly a major eruption would be a catastrophe for the nearby city.

**Lake Titicaca** The southeastern border with Bolivia passes through Titicaca, with about half of the lake in each country. It is the largest lake in South America (ignoring Lake Maracaibo in Venezuela which is linked to the sea) and at 3,812m, the highest navigable body of water in the world. It covers about 8,300 square km, running 190 km NW to SE, and is 80 km across. It lies in a 60,000 square km basin between the coastal and eastern Andes which spread out southwards to their widest point at latitude 18° S. The average depth is over 100m, with the deepest point recorded at 281m. 25 rivers, most from Peru, flow into the lake and a small outlet leaves the lake at Desaguadero on the Bolivia-Peru border. This takes no more than 5% of the inflow, the rest is lost through evaporation and hence the waters of the lake are slightly brackish, producing the *totora* reeds used to make the mats and balsa boats for which the lake dwellers are famed.

The lake is the remnant of a vast area of water formed in the Ice Age known as Lake Ballivián. This extended at least 600 km to the S into Bolivia and included what is now Lake Poopó and the Salar de Uyuni. Now the lake level fluctuates seasonally, normally rising from Dec to Mar and receding for the rest of the year but extremes of 5m between high and low levels have been recorded. This can cause problems and high levels in the late 1980s disrupted transport links near the shoreline. The night temperature can fall as low as -25°C but high daytime temperatures ensure that the surface average is about 14°C.

The shores of Titicaca have attracted settlers since early times, and good agricultural prospects and water availablity make for a population concentration around Puno and most of the Peruvian sector of the basin. The name 'Titicaca' has been variously interpreted as relating to the *titi* (a native wild cat), the 'rock of the puma' and the 'crag of lead'.

## The Montaña and the Amazon basin

Almost half of Peru is on the eastern side of the Andes and about 90% of the country's drainage is into the Amazon system. It is an area of heavy rainfall with cloud-forest above 3,500m and tropical rainforest lower down. There is little savanna, or natural grasslands, characteristic of other parts of the Amazon basin.

Inevitably, there is dispute on the Amazon's source. Officially, the mighty river begins as the Marañon, whose longest tributary rises just E of the Cordillera Huayhuash. However, the longest journey for the proverbial raindrop, some 6,400 km, probably starts in southern Peru, where the headwaters of the Apurímac (Ucayali) flow from the snows on the northern side of the Nevado Mismi, near Cailloma.

With much more rainfall on the eastern side of the Andes, rivers are turbulent and erosion dramatic. Although vertical drops are not as great – there is a whole continent to cross to the Atlantic – valleys are deep, ridges narrow and jagged and there is forest below 3,000m. At 1,500m the Amazon jungle commences and water is the only means of surface transport available, apart from three roads which reach Borja (on the Marañon), Yurimaguas (on the Huallaga) and Pucallpa (on the Ucayali), all at about 300m above the Atlantic which is still 4,000 km or so downstream. The vastness of the Amazon lowlands becomes apparent and it is here that Peru bulges 650 km NE past Iquitos to the point where it meets Colombia and Brazil at Leticia.

In the past, minerals found in the eastern Cordilleras, for example Cerro de Pasco, created road and rail links with the Pacific, later extended to the fringes of the lowlands where rich agricultural lands were developed. More recently, oil and gas have been found in various places in this huge area. New finds are made every year nowadays and no doubt pipelines and roads will eventually link more places to the Pacific coast.

## CLIMATE

Each of Peru's geographical zones has its own climate. On the coast summertime is from Dec to April, when temperatures range from 25° to 35°C and it is hot and dry. Wintertime is May-Nov, the temperature drops a bit and it is cloudy.

The coastal climate is determined by the cold sea-water adjoining deserts. Prevailing inshore winds pick up so little moisture over the cold Humboldt current, which flows from Antartica, that only from May to Nov does it condense. The resultant blanket of cloud and sea-mist (called *garúa*) extends from the S to about 200 km N of Lima. The other major factor to affect the coastal climate periodically is El Niño, described above.

**In the sierra**: from April to Oct is the dry season. It is hot and dry during the day, around 20°-25°C, and cold and dry at night, often below freezing. From Nov to April is the wet season, when it is dry and clear most mornings, with some rainfall in the afternoon. There is a small temperature drop (18°C) and not much difference at night (15°C).

**The selva**: April-Oct is dry season, with temperatures up to 35°C. In the jungle areas of the S, a cold front can pass through at night. Nov-April is the wet season. It is humid and hot, with heavy rainfall at any time.

## FLORA AND FAUNA

The neotropical realm is a land of superlatives, it contains the most extensive tropical rainforest in the world; the Amazon has by far the largest volume of any river in the world and the Andes are the longest uninterrupted mountain chain. The fauna and flora are to a large extent determined by the influence of those mountains and the great rivers, particularly the Amazon and Orinoco. There are also huge expanses of open terrain, the pampas – a great temperate grassland, tree-covered savannahs, dry deserts and

## El Niño

The climate of the western coast of South America is dominated by what is happening in the Pacific Ocean. Warm currents off the coast N of the Equator bring rains to the coasts of Colombia and Ecuador, and prevailing westerlies bring temperate rains to mid Chile and southwards. At the same time, all the way across the Pacific from Indonesia towards Peru along the Equator there is a huge body of warm water. Most of the time, this warm water is kept away from the shoreline by the prevailing easterly trade winds. This allows the cold currents flowing northwards up the coast of northern Chile and Peru to produce the very dry conditions for 2,000 km. The Atacama desert is normally as dry as any in the world.

From time to time, however, the whole cycle is disrupted by the phenomenon known as El Niño. The immediate cause of the dramatic weather change is that the warm water which normally reaches the coast of South America only from 10° N to 5° S of the Equator extends S, sometimes as far as northern Chile. This brings devastating windstorms and torrential rains to places which are normally without any rain at all. An extreme example was in Trujillo, which recorded an average of 5 mm of rain for the 7 years from 1917 to 1924. In March 1925, 394 mm of rain fell – 226 mm of it in only 3 days. More recently, in 1982-83, over 2,000 mm of rain fell in some coastal localities of Peru during a 6 month period.

The economic damage on land can be enormous, but there is also the effect on the ocean itself. The food cycle is disrupted, the fish disappear and the seabirds starve. It takes time for all these human and natural dislocations to get back to normal. These 'events' seem to be on a 3-7 year cycle, and there is historical evidence to suggest that they have been around since the time of the Incas. There is a belief that they are becoming more frequent. El Niño, when it happens, makes itself felt in Dec to Feb, most often near Christmas, hence the name, which means 'Christ-child'.

southern tundras. It is this immense range of habitats which makes South America one of the greatest regions of biological diversity.

This diversity arises not only from the wide range of habitats available, but also from the history of the continent. South America has essentially been an island for some 70 million years joined only by a narrow isthmus to Central and North America. Land passage played a significant role in the gradual colonisation of South America by species from the N. When the land-link closed these colonists evolved to a wide variety of forms free from the competitive pressures that prevailed elsewhere. When the land-bridge was re-established some 4 million years ago a new invasion of species took place from North America, adding to the diversity but also leading to numerous extinctions. Comparative stability has ensued since then and has guaranteed the survival of many primitive groups like the opossums.

### The Coast

The coastal region of Peru is extremely arid, partly as a result of the cold Humboldt current. Warm moisture laden air over the tropical oceans moves eastward towards the coast where it condenses when in contact with the colder temperatures above the Humboldt current. The resultant fogbank moves inland where it is heated and eventually vaporises, only condensing again as it rises over the Andes. Thus the area between the coast and the mountains receives little or no rain accounting for the paucity of animal life here. In some areas, intermittent oases (lomas) develop where winter snows distribute moisture annually. The plants

other predators are also much in evidence; although rarely seen their paw marks are commonly found along the forest trails. Rare bird species are also much in evidence, including fasciated tiger-heron and primitive hoatzins.

In the (very) early-morning good views of peccaries, brocket deer and tapir may be obtained at mineral licks (*collpa*). Macaw and parrot lick are found along the banks of the river. Here at dawn a dazzling display arrives and clamber around in the branches overhanging the clay-lick. At its peak there may be 600 birds of up to six species (including red and green macaws, and blue-headed parrots) clamouring to begin their descent to the riverbank where they jostle for access to the mineral rich clay. A necessary addition to their diet which may also neutralise the toxins present in the leaf and seed diet. Rare game birds such as razor billed curassows and piping guans may also be seen.

A list of over 600 bird species has been compiled. Particularly noteworthy species are the black-faced cotinga, crested eagle, and the spectacular Harpy eagle, perhaps the world's most impressive raptor, easily capable of taking an adult monkey from the canopy. Mixed species flocks are commonly observed containing from 25 to 100+ birds of perhaps more than 30 species including blue dacnis, blue-tailed emerald, bananaquit, thick-billed euphoria and the paradise tanager. Each species occupies a slightly different niche, and since there are few individuals of each species in the flock, competition is avoided. Mixed flocks foraging in the canopy are often led by a white-winged shrike, whereas flocks foraging in the understorey are often led by the bluish-slate antshrike.

# History

Three major obstacles restrict our knowledge of ancient Peru. First, the very terrain of the country is a challenge to present, let alone, past inhabitants. The Andes are the most seismically active mountain range on Earth; devastating earthquakes and landslides have damaged or destroyed whole cities. The tropical lowlands have defied exploration and remains of the past may still be hidden in the undergrowth. Flashfloods unleashed by the El Niño current sweep down the N coast at intervals, driving away the fish and washing away the adobe houses and irrigation canals. Fortunately the coastal desert from Lambayeque department S to Paracas has revealed an 'American Egypt' for archaeologists, although this has meant a bias towards the coastal region and a reliance on the contents of tombs for information.

Secondly, the lack of the written word has deprived us of any firsthand record of the everyday lives of the earliest settlers. The Spanish chroniclers based their accounts on the Incas' own version of the past, but this was inevitably coloured with propaganda, myth and folklore. The third problem is looting, incited by demand from the international antiquities market. Gangs of *huaqueros* plunder sites too numerous to be policed or protected by archaeologists. In spite of these handicaps, Peru has revealed a precolumbian history of highly advanced societies that prevailed against awesome odds.

| YEAR | Epoch and Period | | | North Coast | North Mountains | Central Coast | South Coast | Central Mountains | Lake Titicaca-Altiplano |
|---|---|---|---|---|---|---|---|---|---|
| 1,500 | Centralized Urban Societies | Military Status | Inca Empire | Inca | Inca | Inca | Inca | Inca | Inca |
| | | | Regional States | Chimú | | Chancay | Inca-Chincha | Chancas | Aymara Kingdoms |
| 1,000 | | | Wari Empire | Northern Wari | Local Wari Kingdoms | Pachacamac | Southern Wari | Wari | |
| 500<br>0 | | Theocratic Kingdoms and Chiefdoms | Regional States | Moche and Gallinazo | Cajamarca and Recuay | Lima | Nazca | Huarpa | Tiwanaku and Pucara |
| 1,000 | | | Formative Period | Salinar<br>Cupisnique | Huaras<br>Chavín | Ancón | Paracas | Rancha<br>Chupas<br>Wichqana | Kalasasaya<br>Chiripa<br>Wankarani |
| 5,000 | | Village-based farmers | Archaic Period | Huaca Prieta | ? | Paraiso<br>Encanto | Otuma<br>Chilca | Cachi<br>Piki | ? |
| 10,000<br>20,000 | | Hunter-gatherers | Lithic Period | Paiján | Lauricocha<br>Guitarrero | Canario<br>Arenal<br>Chivateros<br>Oquendo | ? | Jaywa<br>Fuente<br>Ayacuchco<br>Pacaicasa | Visachani |

The development of Andean Societies from 20,000 BC to the Conquest

Source: María Rostworowski (1988) *Historia del Tahuantinsuyu* Instituto de Estudios Peruanos, Lima

## PRECOLUMBIAN HISTORY

The Incas told the Spaniards that before they established their Tawantinsuyo Empire, the land was overrun by primitives constantly at war with one another.

There were, in fact, many other civilized cultures dating back as far as 2000 BC. The most accomplished of these were the Chavín-Sechín (c 900-200 BC), the Paracas-Nasca (c 200 BC-500 AD), the Huari-Tiahuanaku (c 750 BC-1000 AD), and the Moche-Chimú (200 BC-1400 AD).

### Early settlement

It is generally accepted that the earliest settlers in Peru were related to people who had crossed the Bering Straits from Asia and drifted through the Americas from about 20,000 BC. Theories of early migrations from across the Pacific and Atlantic have been rife since Thor Heyerdahl's raft expeditions in 1947 and 1969-70.

Human remains found in a cave in Lauricocha, near Huánuco, have a radiocarbon date of c 7500 BC, but the earliest signs of a village settlement in Peru, were found on the central coast at Pampa, dating from 2500 BC. Between these two dates it is thought that people lived nomadically in small groups, mainly hunting and gathering but also cultivating some plants seasonally. Domestication of llamas, alpacas and guinea pigs also began at this time, particularly important for the highland people around the Titicaca basin.

The abundant wealth of marine life produced by the Humboldt Current, especially along the N coast, boosted population growth and settlement in this area. Around 2000 BC climatic change dried up the *lomas* ('fog meadows'), and drove sea shoals into deeper water. People turned more to farming and began to spread inland along river valleys.

### Origins of Andean civilization

From the second millenium BC to around the first century BC is known as the Formative Period when the first signs of the high culture of Andean society appeared. During this period sophisticated irrigation and canal systems were developed, farming productivity increased and communities had more time to devote to building and producing ceramics and textiles. The development of pottery also led to trade and cultural links with other communities. Distribution of land and water to the farmers was probably organized by a corporate authority, and this may have led to the later 'Mit'a' labour system developed by the Incas.

Above all, this period is characterized by the construction of centres of urban concentration that promoted labour specialization and with it the development of cultural expression. The earliest buildings constructed were *huacas*, adobe platform mounds, centres of some cult or sacred power. Huaca Florida was the largest example of this period, near the Río Rimac, later replaced by Huaca Garagay as a major centre for the area. Many similar centres spread along the N coast, most notably Aspero and Piedra Parada.

During this period, however, much more advanced architecture was being built at **Kotosh**, in the central Andes near Huánuco. Japanese archaeological excavations there in the 1960s revealed a temple with ornamental niches and friezes. Some of the earliest pottery was also found here, showing signs of influence from southern Ecuador and the tropical lowlands, adding weight to theories of Andean culture originating in the Amazon. Radiocarbon dates of some Kotosh remains are as early as 1850 BC.

### Chavín-Sechín

For the next 1,000 years or so up to c 900 BC, communities grew and spread inland from the N coast and S along the northern highlands. Farmers still lived in simple adobe or rough stone houses but built increasingly large and complex ceremonial centres, such as at Las Haldas in the Casma Valley. As farming became more productive and pottery more advanced, commerce grew and states began to develop throughout central and North-central Peru, with the associated signs of social structure and hierarchies.

Around 900 BC a new era was marked by the rise of two important centres; **Chavín de Huantar** in the central Andes and **Sechín Alto**, inland from Casma on the N coast.

**Chavín** takes its name from the site of Chavín de Huantar in the northern highlands. This was the first of several 'horizon styles' that were of the greatest importance in Peru and had very widespread influence. The other later ones, the Huari-Tiahaunaco and the Inca, were pan-Peruvian, affecting all parts of the country. The chief importance of Chavín de Huantar was not so much in its highly advanced architecture as in the influence of its cult coupled with the artistic style of its ceramics and other artefacts. The founders of Chavín may have originated in the tropical lowlands as some of its carved monoliths show representations of monkeys and felines.

Objects with Chavín traits have been found all along the coast from Piura to the Lurin valley S of Lima, and its cult ideology spread to temples around the same area. Richard L Burger of Yale University has argued that the extent of Chavín influence has been exaggerated. Many sites on the coast already had their own cult practices and the Chavín idols may have been simply added alongside. There is evidence of an El Niño flood that devastated the N coast around 500 BC. Local cults fell from grace as social order was disrupted and the Chavín cult was snatched up as a timely new alternative.

**The Chavín cult** was paralleled by the great advances made in this period in textile production and in some of the earliest examples of metallurgy. The origins of metallurgy have been attributed to some gold, silver and copper ornaments found in graves in Chongoyape, near Chiclayo, which show Chavín-style features. But earlier evidence has been discovered in the Andahuaylas region, dating from 1800-900 BC. The religious symbolism of gold and other precious metals and stones is thought to have been an inspiration behind some of the beautiful artefacts found in the central Andean area. The emergence of social hierarchies also created a demand for luxury goods as status symbols.

The cultural brilliance of Chavín de Huántar was complemented by its contemporary, Sechín. This huge granite-faced complex near Casma, 370 km N of Lima, was described by JC Tello as the biggest structure of its kind in the Andes. According to Michael Moseley of Harvard University, Chavín and Sechín may have combined forces, with Sechín as the military power that spread the cultural word of Chavín, but their influence did not reach far to the S where the Paracas and Tiahuanaku cultures held sway.

### The Upper Formative Period

The Chavín hegemony, which is also known as the Middle Formative Period, broke up around 300 BC. The 'unity' of this period was broken and the initial phase of the regional diversification of Andean cultures began. The process of domestication of plants and animals culminated in the Upper Formative Period. Agricultural technology progressed leading to an economic security that permitted a considerable growth in the centres of population. Among the many diverse stylistic/cultural groups of this period are: the Vicus on the N coast; Salinar in the Chicama valley; Paracas Necrópolis on the S coast; and Huarás in the Ancash highlands.

**Paracas Necrópolis** is the early phase of the Nasca culture and is renowned for the superb technical quality and stylistic variety in its weaving and pottery. The

War-scene depicted on a Moche vessel (AD 200-750)

*mantos* (large, decorated cloth) rank amongst the world's best, and many of the finest examples can be seen in the museums of Lima. The extreme dryness of the desert here has preserved remarkably the textiles and ceramics in the mummies' tombs which have been excavated.

Paracas Necrópolis is, in fact, a cemetery located on the slopes of Cerro Colorado, in the Department of Ica, from which 429 funerary bundles were excavated. Each bundle is a mummy wrapped in many fine and rough textiles. Paracas Necrópolis corresponds to the last of the 10 phases into which Paracas ceramics have been divided. The previous ones, known as Paracas Cavernas, relate to the Middle Formative Period and were influenced by the Chavín cult.

## The Nasca culture

The Regional Development Period up to about 500 AD, was a time of great social and cultural development. Sizable towns of 5-10,000 inhabitants grew on the S coast, populated by artisans, merchants, government administrators and religious officials.

One of the most famous cultures of this period, or indeed of precolumbian history was the Nasca. The famous Nasca Lines are a feature of the region. Straight lines, abstract designs and outlines of animals are scratched in the dark desert surface forming a lighter contrast that can be seen clearly from the air. There are many theories of how and why the lines were made but no definitive explanation has yet been able to establish their place in Peruvian history. There are similarities between the style of some of the line patterns and that of the pottery and textiles of the same period. It is clear from the sheer scale of the lines and the quality of the work that, whatever their purpose, they were very important to the Nasca culture.

In contrast to the quantity and quality of the Nasca artefacts found, relatively few major buildings belonging to this period have been uncovered in the southern desert. Dos Palmas is a complex of rooms and courtyards in the Pisco Valley and Cahuachi in the Nasca Valley is a large area including adobe platforms, a pyramid and a 'wooden Stonehenge' cluster of preserved tree trunks. As most of the archaeological evidence of the Nasca culture came from their desert cemeteries, little is known about the lives and social organization of the people. Alpaca hair found in Nasca textiles, however, indicates that there must have been strong trade links with highland people.

## The Moche culture

Nasca's contemporaries on the N coast were the militaristic Moche who, from about 100-800 AD built up an empire whose traces stretch from Piura in the N to Casma, beyond Chimbote, in the S. The Moche built their capital in the middle of the desert, outside present day Trujillo. It features the huge pyramid temples of the Huaca del Sol and Huaca de la Luna. The Moche roads and system of way stations are thought to have been an early inspiration for the Inca network. The Moche increased the coastal population with intensive irrigation projects. Skilful engineering works were carried out, such as the La Cumbre canal, still in use today, and the Ascope aqueduct, both on the Chicama river.

The Moche's greatest achievement, however, was its artistic genius. Exquisite ornaments in gold, silver and precious stones were made by its craftsmen. Moche pottery progressed through five stylistic periods, most notable for the stunningly lifelike portrait vases. A wide variety of everyday scenes were created in naturalistic ceramics, telling us more about Moche life than is known about other earlier cultures, and perhaps used by them as 'visual aids' to compensate for the lack of a written language.

A spectacular discovery of a Moche royal tomb at Sipán was made in Feb 1987 by Walter Alva, director of the Bruning Archaeological Museum, Lambayeque. Reports of the excavation in the *National Geographic* magazine (Oct 1988 and June 1990), talked of the richest unlooted tomb in the New World. The find included semi-precious stones brought from Chile and Argentina, and seashells from Ecuador. The Moche were great navigators.

The cause of the collapse of the Moche Empire around 600-700 AD is unknown, but it may have been started by a 30 year drought at the end of the 6th century, followed by one of the periodic El Niño flash floods (identified by meteorologists from ice thickness in the Andes) and finished by the encroaching forces of the Huari Empire. The decline of the Moche signalled a general tipping of the balance of power in Peru from the N coast to the southern sierra.

## Huari-Tiahuanaku

The ascendant Huari-Tiahuanaku movement, from c 600-1000 AD, combined the religious cult of the Tiahuanaku site in the Titicaca basin, with the military dynamism of the Huari, based in the central highlands. The two cultures developed independently but, as had occurred with the Chavín-Sechín association, they are generally thought to have merged compatibly.

Up until their own demise around 1440 AD, the Huari-Tiahuanaku had spread their empire and influence from Cajamarca and Lambayeque in the N and across much of southern Peru, northern Bolivia and Argentina. The Huari introduced a new concept in urban life, the great walled urban centre, the best example of which is their capital city, 22 km N of Ayacucho. They also made considerable gains in art and technology, building roads, terraces and irrigation canals across the country.

The Huari-Tiahuanaku ran their empire with efficient labour and administrative systems that were later adopted and refined by the Incas. Labour tribute for state projects had been practised by the Moche and was further developed now. But the empire could not contain regional kingdoms who began to fight for land and power. As control broke down, rivalry and coalitions emerged, and the system collapsed.

## The Chimú culture

After the decline of the Huari empire, the unity that had been imposed on the Andes was broken. A new stage of autonomous regional or local political organizations began. Among the cultures corresponding to this period were the Kuelap, centred in the Chachapoyas region (see **Northern Peru**, page 183), and the Chimú.

The Chimú culture had two geographical foci. To the N was Lambayeque, near Chiclayo, while to the S, in the Moche valley near present-day Trujillo, was the great adobe walled city of Chan Chán. Covering 20 sq km, this was the largest pre-Hispanic Peruvian city.

Chimú has been classified as a despotic state that based its power on wars of conquest. Rigid social stratification existed and power rested in the hands of the great lord *Siquic* and the lord *Alaec*. These lords were followed in social scale by a group of urban couriers who enjoyed a certain degree of economic power. At the bottom were the peasants and slaves. In 1450, the Chimú kingdom was conquered by the Inca Túpac Yupanqui, the son and heir of the Inca ruler Pachacuti Inca Yupanqui.

## THE INCA DYNASTY

The origins of the Inca Dynasty are shrouded in mythology and shaky evidence. The best known story reported by the Spanish chroniclers talks about Manco Capac and his sister rising out of Lake Titicaca, created by the Sun as divine founders of a chosen race. This was in approximately AD 1200. Over the next 300 years the small tribe grew to supremacy as leaders of the largest empire ever known in the Americas, the four territories of Tawantinsuyo, united by Cusco as the umbilicus of the Universe (the four quarters of Tawantinsuyo, all radiating out from Cusco, were 1 – Chinchaysuyo, North and North-West, 2 – Cuntisuyo, South and West, 3 – Collasuyo, South and East, 4 – Antisuyo, East.

**At its peak**, just before the Spanish Conquest, the Inca Empire stretched from the Río Maule in central Chile, N to the present Ecuador-Colombia border, containing most of Ecuador, Peru, western Bolivia, northern Chile and NW Argentina. The area was roughly equivalent to France, Belgium, Holland, Luxembourg, Italy and Switzerland combined, 980,000 sq km.

The first Inca ruler, Manco Capac, moved to the fertile Cusco region, and established Cusco as his capital. Successive generations of rulers were fully occupied with local conquests of rivals, such as the Colla and Lupaca to the S, and the Chanca to the NW. At the end of Inca Viracocha's reign the hated Chanca were finally defeated, largely thanks to the heroism of one of his sons, Pachacuti Inca Yupanqui, who was subsequently crowned as the new ruler.

From the start of Pachacuti's own reign in 1438, imperial expansion grew in earnest. With the help of his son and heir, Topa Inca, territory was conquered from the Titicaca basin S into Chile, and all the N and central coast down to the Lurin Valley. The Incas also subjugated the Chimú, a highly sophisticated rival empire who had re-occupied the abandoned Moche capital at Chan Chán. Typical of the Inca method of government, some of the Chimú skills were assimilated into their own political and administrative system, and some Chimú nobles were even given positions in Cusco.

Perhaps the pivotal event in Inca history came in 1532 with the death of the ruler, Huayna Capac. Civil war broke out in the confusion over his rightful successor. One of his legitimate sons, Huáscar, ruled the southern part of the empire from Cusco. Atahualpa, Huáscar's half-brother, governed Quito, the capital of Chinchaysuyo. In the midst of the ensuing battle Francisco Pizarro arrived in Tumbes with 179 men. When Atahualpa got wind of their presence there was some belief that Pizarro and his *conquistadores* on horseback were Viracocha and his demi-gods predicted in Inca legend. In need of allies against the Cusco faction, Atahualpa agreed to meet the Spaniards at Cajamarca.

**Francisco Pizarro's** only chance against the formidable imperial army he encountered at Cajamarca was a bold stroke. He drew Atahualpa into an ambush, slaughtered his guards, promised him liberty if a certain room were filled with treasure, and finally killed him after receiving news that another Inca army was on its way to free him. Pushing on to Cusco, he was at first hailed as the executioner of a traitor: Atahualpa had killed Huáscar after the battle of Huancavelica 2 years previously. Panic followed when the *conquistadores* set about sacking the city, and they fought off with difficulty an attempt by Manco Inca to recapture Cusco in 1538.

For the whole period of the Conquest John Hemming's *The Conquest of the Incas* is invaluable; he himself refers us to Ann Kendall's *Everyday Life of the Incas*, Batsford, London, 1978. Also *Oro y tragedia* by Manuel Portal Cabellos, excellent on the division of the empire, civil war, the conquest and *huaqueros*.

## Inca Society

The people we call the Incas were a small aristocracy numbering only a few thousand, centred in the highland city of Cusco, at 3,400m. They rose gradually as a small regional dynasty, similar to others in the Andes of that period, starting around 1200 AD. Then, suddenly, in the mid-1400s, they began to expand explosively under Pachacuti, a sort of Andean Alexander the Great, and later his son, Topa. Less than a hundred years later, they fell before the rapacious warriors of Spain. The Incas were not the first dynasty in Andean history to dominate their neighbours, but they did it more thoroughly and went further than anyone before them.

## Empire building

Enough remains today of their astounding highways, cities and agricultural terracing for people to marvel and wonder how they accomplished so much in so short a time. They seem to have been amazingly energetic, industrious and efficient – and the reports of their Spanish conquerors confirm this hypothesis.

They must also have had the willing cooperation of most of their subject peoples, most of the time. In fact, the Incas were master diplomats and alliance-builders first, and military conquerors only second, if the first method of expansion failed. The Inca skill at generating wealth by means of highly efficient agriculture and distribution brought them enormous prestige and enabled them to 'out-gift' neighbouring chiefs in huge royal feasts involving ritual outpourings of generosity, often in the form of vast gifts of textiles, exotic products from distant regions, and perhaps wives to add blood ties to the alliance. The 'out-gifted' chief was required by the Andean laws of reciprocity to provide something in return, and this would usually be his loyalty, as well as a levy of manpower from his own chiefdom.

Thus, with each new alliance the Incas wielded greater labour forces and their mighty public works programmes surged ahead. These were administered through an institution known as *mit'a*, a form of taxation through labour. The state provided the materials, such as wool and cotton for making textiles, and the communities provided skills and labour.

*Mit'a* contingents worked royal mines, royal plantations for producing coca leaves, royal quarries and so on. The system strove to be equitable, and workers in such hardship posts as high altitude mines and lowland coca plantations were given correspondingly shorter terms of service.

## Organization

Huge administrative centres were built in different parts of the empire, where people and supplies were gathered. Articles such as textiles and pottery were produced there in large workshops. Work in these places was carried out in a festive manner, with plentiful food, drink and music. Here was Andean reciprocity at work: the subject supplied his labour, and the ruler was expected to provide generously while he did so.

Aside from *mit'a* contributions there were also royal lands claimed by the Inca as his portion in every conquered province, and worked for his benefit by the local population. Thus, the contribution of each citizen to the state was quite large, but apparently, the imperial economy was productive enough to sustain this.

Another institution was the practice of moving populations around wholesale, inserting loyal groups into restive areas, and removing recalcitrant populations to loyal areas. These movements

Spanish overseer and an indigenous weaver, from a 16th century chronicle by Felipe Guaman Poma de Ayala

of *mitmakuna*, as they were called, were also used to introduce skilled farmers and engineers into areas where productivity needed to be raised.

## Communications

The huge empire was held together by an extensive and highly efficient highway system. There were an estimated 30,000 km of major highway, most of it neatly paved and drained, stringing together the major Inca sites. Two parallel highways ran N-S, along the coastal desert strip and the mountains, and dozens of E-W roads crossing from the coast to the Amazon fringes. These roadways took the most direct routes, with wide stone stairways zig-zagging up the steepest mountain slopes and rope suspension bridges crossing the many narrow gorges of the Andes.

Every 12 km or so there was a *tambo*, or way station, where goods could be stored and travellers lodged. The *tambos* were also control points, where the Inca state's accountants tallied movements of goods and people. Even more numerous than *tambos*, were the huts of the *chasquis*, or relay runners, who continually sped royal and military messages along these highways.

**The Inca state kept records** and transmitted information in various ways. Accounting and statistical records were kept on skeins of knotted strings known as *quipus*. Numbers employed the decimal system, and colours indicated the categories being recorded. An entire class of people, known as *quipucamayocs*, existed whose job was to create and interpret these. Neither the Incas nor their Andean predecessors had a system of writing as we understand it, but there may have been a system of encoding language into *quipus*.

Archaeologists are studying this problem today. History and other forms of knowledge were transmitted via songs and poetry. Music and dancing, full of encoded information which could be read by the educated elite, were part of every major ceremony and public event information was also carried in textiles, which had for millenia been the most vital expression of Andean culture.

## Textiles

Clothing carried insignia of status, ethnic origin, age and so on. Special garments were made and worn for various rites of passage. It has been calculated that, after agriculture, no activity was more important to Inca civilization than weaving. Vast stores of textiles were maintained to sustain the Inca system of ritual giving. Armies and *mit'a* workers were partly paid in textiles. The finest materials were reserved for the nobility, and the Inca emperor himself displayed his status by changing into new clothes every day and having the previous day's burned.

Most weaving was done by women, and the Incas kept large numbers of 'chosen women' in female-only houses all over the empire, partly for the purpose of supplying textiles to the elite and for the many deities, to whom they were frequently given as burned offerings.

These women had other duties, such as making *chicha* – the Inca corn beer which was consumed and sacrificed in vast quantities on ceremonial occasions. They also became wives and concubines to the Inca elite and loyal nobilities. And some may have served as priestesses of the moon, in parallel to the male priesthood of the sun.

## Religious worship

The Incas have always been portrayed as sun-worshippers, but it now seems that they were just as much mountain-worshippers. Recent research has shown that Machu Picchu was at least partly dedicated to the worship of the surrounding mountains, and Inca sacrificial victims have been excavated on frozen Andean peaks at 6,700m. In fact, until technical climbing was invented, the Incas held the world altitude record for humans.

Human sacrifice was not common, but every other kind was, and ritual attended every event in the Inca calendar. The main temple of Cusco was dedicated to the numerous deities: the Sun, the Moon, Venus, the Pleiades, the Rainbow, Thunder and Lightning, and the countless religious icons of subject peoples which had been brought to Cusco, partly in homage, partly as hostage. Here, worship was continuous and the fabulous opulence included gold cladding on the walls, and a famous garden filled with life-size objects of gold and silver. Despite this pantheism, the Incas acknowledged an overall Creator God, whom they called Viracocha. A special temple was dedicated to him, at *Raqchi*, about 100 km S-E of Cusco. Part of it still stands today

## The Military Forces

The conquering Spaniards noted with admiration the Inca storehouse system, still well-stocked when they found it, despite several years of civil war among the Incas. Besides textiles, military equipment, and ritual objects, they found huge quantities of food. Like most Inca endeavours, the food stores served a multiple purpose: to supply feasts, to provide during lean times, to feed travelling work parties, and to supply armies on the march.

Inca armies were able to travel light and move fast because of this system. Every major Inca settlement also incorporated great halls where large numbers of people could be accommodated, or feasts and gatherings held, and large squares or esplanades for public assemblies.

Inca technology is usually deemed inferior to that of contemporary Europe. Their military technology certainly was. They had not invented iron-smelting, and basically fought with clubs, palmwood spears, slings, wooden shields, cotton armour and straw-stuffed helmets. They did not even make much use of the bow and arrow, a weapon they were well aware of. Military tactics, too, were primitive. The disciplined formations of the Inca armies quickly dissolved into melees of unbridled individualism once battle was joined.

This, presumably, was because warfare constituted a theatre of manly prowess, but was not the main priority of Inca life. Its form was ritualistic. Battles were suspended by both sides for religious observance. Negotiation, combined with displays of superior Inca strength, usually achieved victory, and total annihilation of the enemy was not on the agenda.

## Architecture

Other technologies, however, were superior in every way to their 16th century counterparts: textiles; settlement planning; and agriculture in particular with its sophisticated irrigation and soil conservation systems, ecological sensitivity, specialized crop strains and high productivity under the harshest conditions. The Incas fell short of the Andean predecessors in the better-known arts of ancient America – ceramics, textiles and metalwork – but it could be argued that their supreme efforts were made in architecture, stoneworking, landscaping, road-building, and the harmonious combination of these elements.

These are the outstanding survivals of Inca civilization, which still remain to fascinate the visitor: the huge, exotically close-fit blocks of stone, cut in graceful, almost sensual curves; the astoundingly craggy and inaccessible sites encircled by great sweeps of Andean scenery; the rhythmic layers of farm terracing that provided land and food to this still-enigmatic people.

### The ruling elite

The ruling elite lived privileged lives in their capital at Cusco. They reserved for themselves and privileged insiders certain luxuries, such as the chewing of coca, the wearing of fine vicuña wool, and the practice of polygamy. But they were an austere people, too. Everyone had work to do, and the nobility were constantly being posted to state business throughout the empire. Young nobles were expected to learn martial skills, besides being able to read the *quipus*, speak both Quechua and the southern language of Aymara, and know the epic poems.

The Inca elite belonged to royal clans known as *panacas*, which each had the unusual feature of being united around veneration of the mummy of their founding ancestor – a previous Inca emperor, unless they happened to belong to the *panaca* founded by the Inca emperor who was alive at the time. Each new emperor built his own palace in Cusco and amassed his own wealth rather than inheriting it from his forebears, which perhaps helps to account for the urge to unlimited expansion.

This urge ultimately led the Incas to overreach themselves. Techniques of diplomacy and incorporation no longer worked as they journeyed farther from the homeland and met ever-increasing resistance from people less familiar with their ways. During the reign of Wayna Capac, the last emperor before the Spanish invasion, the Incas had to establish a northern capital at Quito in order to cope with permanent war on their northern frontier. Following Wayna Capac's death came a devastating civil war between Cusco and Quito, and immediately thereafter came the Spanish invasion. Tawantisuyo, the empire of the four quarters, collapsed with dizzying suddenness.

## CONQUEST AND AFTER

Peruvian history after the arrival of the Spaniards was not just a matter of *conquistadores* versus Incas. The vast majority of the huge empire remained unaware of the conquest for many years. The Chimú and the Chachapoyas cultures were powerful enemies of the Incas. The Chimú developed a highly sophisticated culture and a powerful empire stretching for 560 km along the coast from Paramonga S to Casma. Their history was well-recorded by the Spanish chroniclers and continued through the Conquest possibly up to about 1600. The Kuelap/Chachapoyas people were not so much an empire as a loose-knit 'confederation of ethnic groups with no recognized capital' (Morgan Davis 'Chachapoyas: The Cloud People', Ontario, 1988). But the culture did develop into an advanced society with great skill in roads and monument building. Their fortress at Kuelap was known as the most impregnable in Tawantinsuyo. It remained intact against Inca attack and Manco Inca even tried, unsuccessfully, to gain refuge here against the Spaniards.

In 1535, wishing to secure his communications with Spain, Pizarro founded Lima, near the ocean, as his capital. The same year Diego de Almagro set out to conquer Chile. Unsuccessful, he returned to Peru, quarrelled with Pizarro, and in 1538 fought a pitched battle with Pizarro's men at the Salt Pits, near Cusco. He was defeated and put to death. Pizarro, who had not been at the battle, was assassinated in his palace in Lima by Almagro's son 3 years later.

For the next 27 years each succeeding representative of the Kingdom of Spain sought to subdue the Inca successor state of Vilcabamba, N of Cusco, and to unify the fierce Spanish factions. Francisco de Toledo (appointed 1568) solved both problems during his 14 years in office: Vilcabamba was crushed in 1572 and the last reigning Inca, Túpac Amaru, put to death.

For the next 200 years the Viceroys closely followed Toledo's system, if not his methods. The Major Government – the Viceroy, the *Audiencia* (High Court), and *corregidores* (administrators) – ruled through the Minor Government – Indian chiefs put in charge of large groups of natives: a rough approximation to the original Inca system.

### Towards independence

The Indians rose in 1780, under the leadership of an Inca noble who called himself Túpac Amaru II. He and many of his lieutenants were captured and put to death under torture at Cusco. Another Indian leader in revolt suffered the same fate in 1814, but this last flare-up had the sympathy of many of the locally-born Spanish, who resented their status, inferior to the Spaniards born in Spain, the refusal to give them any but the lowest offices, the high taxation imposed by the home government, and the severe restrictions upon trade with any country but Spain.

Help came to them from the outside world. José de San Martín's Argentine troops, convoyed from Chile under the protection of Lord Cochrane's squadron, landed in southern Peru on 7 September 1820. San Martín proclaimed Peruvian independence at Lima on 28 July 1821, though most of the country was still in the hands of the Viceroy, José de La Serna. Bolívar, who had already freed Venezuela and Colombia, sent Antonio José de Sucre to Ecuador where, on 24 May 1822, he gained a victory over La Serna at Pichincha. San Martín, after a meeting with Bolívar at Guayaquil, left for Argentina and a self-imposed exile in France, while Bolívar and Sucre completed the conquest of Peru by defeating La Serna at the battle of Junín (6 August 1824) and the decisive battle of Ayacucho (9 December 1824). For over a year there was a last stand in the Real Felipe fortress at Callao by the Spanish troops under General Rodil before they capitulated on 22 January 1826. Bolívar was invited to stay in Peru, but left for Colombia in 1826.

Following independence Peru attempted a confederation with Bolivia in the 1830s but this proved temporary. Then, in 1879 came the disastrous War of the Pacific, in which Peru and Bolivia were defeated by Chile and Peru lost its southern territory. A long-standing legacy of this was the Tacna-Arica dispute, which wasn't settled until 1929.

## POST-INDEPENDENCE PERU

### Economic change

Peru's economic development since independence has been based upon the export of minerals and foodstuffs to Europe and the United States. Guano, a traditional fertilizer in Peru and derived from the manure of seabirds, was first shipped to Europe in 1841. In the three decades that followed it became an important fertilizer in Europe and by the early 1860s over 80% of the Peruvian government's revenues were derived from its export. Much of this income, though, went to pay off interest on the spiraling national debt. By the 1870s the richer deposits were exhausted and cheaper alternatives to guano were being discovered. One of these was nitrates, discovered in the Atacama desert, but Peru's defeat by Chile in the War of the Pacific ensured that she would lose her share of this wealth.

After the decline of guano Peru developed several new exports. In the 1890s the demand in Europe and USA for Amazonian rubber for tyres and for use in electrical components led to a brief boom in both the Brazilian and Peruvian Amazon, the Peruvian industry being based on the Amazon port of Iquitos. This boom was short-lived as cheaper rubber was soon being produced from plantations in the East Indies.

Peru's colonial mineral exports, gold and silver, were replaced by copper, although ownership was mainly under control of foreign companies, particularly the US-based Cerro de Pasco Copper Corporation and Northern Peru Mining. Oil, discovered near the coast, became another important product, amounting to 30% of Peruvian exports by 1930. The role of the main oil company, International Petroleum Company (IPC – a subsidiary of Standard Oil) was to become a major political issue,

## The War of the Pacific

One of the major international wars in Latin America since independence, this conflict has its roots in a border dispute between Chile and Bolivia: the frontier between the two in the Atacama desert was ill-defined.

There had already been one conflict: in 1836-1839, when Chile defeated Peru and Bolivia, putting an end to a confederation of the two states. The discovery of nitrates in the Atacama complicated relations: in the Bolivian Atacama province of Antofagasta nitrates were exploited by Anglo-Chilean companies.

In 1878 the Bolivian government, short of revenue, attempted to tax the Chilean-owned Antofagasta Railroad and Nitrate Company. When the company refused to pay, the Bolivians seized the company's assets. The Chilean government claimed that the Bolivian action broke an 1874 agreement between the two states. When Peru announced that it would honour a secret alliance with Bolivia by supporting her, the Chilean president, Aníbal Pinto, declared war on both states.

None of the three states was prepared; they lacked skilled officers and adequate weapons. Control of the sea was vital, and ironclad ships were far superior to wooden vessels. The Chileans blockaded the Peruvian nitrate port of Iquique with two wooden ships, the *Esmeralda* and the *Covadonga*. Peru, meanwhile, sent her two best ironclads, the *Huáscar* and the *Independencia*, to Iquique. In the Battle of Iquique, 21 May 1879, the *Esmeralda* was sunk, but in the course of the battle the *Independencia* ran aground and was captured, thus altering the balance of forces between the two navies. Later, in October 1879 off Angamos near Antofagasta, the two Chilean ironclads, *Blanco Encalada* and *Cochrane*, cornered the *Huáscar* and captured her.

Rather than attack the Peruvian heartland as they had done in the 1836-1839 war, the Chileans invaded the southern Peruvian province of Tarapacá and then landed troops N of Tacna, seizing the town in May 1880 before capturing Arica, further S. In Jan 1881 fresh Chilean armies seized control of Lima.

Despite these defeats and the loss of their capital, Peru did not sue for peace, although Bolivia had already signed a ceasefire, giving up her coastal province. Under the 1883 peace settlement Peru gave up Tapapacá to Chile. Although the provinces of Tacna and Arica were to be occupied by Chile for 10 years, it was not until 1929 that an agreement was reached under which Tacna was returned to Peru, while Chile kept Arica. Apart from souring relations between Chile and her two northern neighbours to this day, the War gave Chile a monopoly over the world's supply of nitrates and enabled her to dominate the southern Pacific coast.

with critics claiming that its profit-levels were exorbitant. Further exports came from sugar and cotton, which were produced on coastal plantations.

## Social change

Independence from Spanish rule meant that power passed into the hands of the Creole elite with no immediate alternation of the colonial social system. The *contribución de indíginas*, the colonial tribute collected from the indians was not abolished until 1854, the same year as the ending of black slavery.

Until the 1970s land relations in the sierra changed very little, as the older landholding families continued to exert their traditional influence over 'their' peones. The traditional elite, the so-called '44 families', were still very powerful, though increasingly divided between the coastal aristocracy with their interests in plantation agriculture and trade, and the serrano elite, more conservative and inward-looking.

The pattern of export growth did, however, have major effects on the social structure of the coast. The expansion of plantation agriculture and mining led to the growth of a new labour force; this was supplied partially by Chinese indentured labourers, about 100,000 of whom arrived between 1855 and 1875, partly by the migration of Indians from the sierra and partly by the descendants of black slaves.

## Political developments

For much of the period since independence Peruvian political life has been dominated by the traditional elites. Political parties have been slow to develop and the roots of much of the political conflict and instability which have marked the country's history lie in personal ambitions and in regional and other rivalries within the elite.

The early years after independence were particularly chaotic as rival caudillos (political bosses) who had fought in the independence wars vied with each other for power. The increased wealth brought about by the guano boom led to greater stability, though political corruption became a serious problem under the presidency of José Rufino Echenique (1851-1854) who paid out large sums of the guano revenues as compensation to upper class families for their (alleged) losses in the Wars of Independence. Defeat by Chile in the War of the Pacific discredited civilian politicians even further and led to a period of military rule in the 1880s.

Even though the voting system was changed in 1898, this did little to change the dominance of the elite. Voting was not secret so landowners herded their workers to the polls and watched to make sure they voted correctly. Yet voters were also lured by promises as well as threats. One of the more unusual presidents was Guillermo Billinghurst (1912-1914) who campaigned on the promise of a larger loaf of bread for 5 cents, thus gaining the nickname of "Big Bread Billinghurst". As president he proposed a publically-funded housing programme, supported the introduction of an 8-hr day and was eventually overthrown by the military who, along with the elite, were alarmed at his growing popularity among the urban population.

**The 1920s** were dominated by Augusto Leguía. After winning the 1919 elections Leguía claimed that Congress was plotting to prevent him from becoming president and induced the military to help him close Congress. Backed by the armed forces, Leguía introduced a new constitution which gave him greater powers and enabled him to be re-elected in 1924 and 1929. Claiming his goal was to prevent the rise of communism, he proposed to build a partnership between business and labour. A large programme of public works, particularly involving building roads, bridges and railways, was begun, the work being carried out by poor rural men who were forced into unpaid building work. The Leguía regime dealt harshly with critics: opposition newspapers were closed and opposition leaders arrested and deported. His overthrow in 1930 ended what Peruvians call the "Oncenio" or 11 year period.

The 1920s also saw the emergence of 2 political thinkers who would have great influence in the future, not only in Peru but elsewhere in Latin America. Juan Carlos Mariátegui, a socialist writer and journalist, argued that the solution to Peru's problems lay in the reintegration of the Indians through land reform and the breaking up of the great landed estates.

Víctor Raúl Haya de la Torre, a student exiled by Leguía in 1924, returned after the latter's fall to create the Alianza Popular Revolucionaria Americana, a political party which called for state control of the economy, nationalization of key industries and protection of the middle classes, which, Haya de la Torre argued, were threatened by foreign economic interests. In 1932 APRA seized control of Trujillo; when the army arrived to deal with the rising, the rebels murdered about 50 hostages, including 10 army officers. In reprisal the army murdered about 1,000 local residents suspected of sympathizing with APRA. APRA eventually became the largest and easily the best-organized political party in Peru, but the distrust of the military and the upper class for Haya de la Torre ensured that he never became president.

**A turning point in Peruvian history** occurred in 1948 with the seizure of power by General Manuel Odría, backed by the coastal elite. Policies encouraging increased exports were pursued at a time when other Latin American states such as Mexico and Argentina were attempting to reduce their dependence on the world market and to promote their own industries. Odría outlawed APRA and went on to win the 1950 election in which he was the only candidate. He also tried to build up working class support by public works projects in Lima. Faced with a decline in export earnings and the fall in world market prices after 1953, plus increasing unemployment, Odría was forced to stand down in 1956.

## MODERN PERU

In 1962 Haya de la Torre was at last permitted to run for the presidency; although he won the largest percentage of votes he was prevented from taking office by the armed forces who seized power and organized fresh elections for 1963. In these the military obtained the desired result: Haya de la Torre came second to Fernando Belaúnde Terry. Belaúnde attempted to introduce reforms, particularly in the landholding structure of the sierra; when these reforms were weakened by landowner opposition in Congress, peasant groups began invading landholdings in protest.

At the same time under the influence of the Cuban revolution, guerrilla groups began operating in the sierra. Military action to deal with this led to the deaths of an estimated 8,000 people. Meanwhile Belaúnde's attempts to solve a long-running dispute with IPC resulted in him being attacked for selling out to the unpopular oil company and contributed to the armed forces' decision to seize power in 1968.

### The 1968 coup

This was a major landmark in Peruvian history. Led by General Juan Velasco Alvarado, the Junta had no intention of handing power back to the civilians. A manifesto issued on the day of the coup attacked the 'unjust social and economic order' and argued for its replacement by a new economic system 'neither capitalist nor communist'. Partly as a result of their experiences in dealing with the guerrilla movement, the coup leaders concluded that agrarian reform was a priority.

In launching a wide-ranging land reform in 1969 Velasco declared "Peasants: the landlords will no longer eat from your poverty." Large estates were taken over and reorganized into cooperatives. By the mid-1970s 75% of productive land was under cooperative management. The government also attempted to improve the lives of shanty-town dwellers around Lima, mainly by providing them with legal titles to their homes. A further set of measures attempted to increase the influence of workers in industrial companies: all firms had to have worker representatives on the board of directors.

At the same time attempts were made to reduce the influence of foreign companies. Soon after the coup IPC was nationalized, to be followed by other transnationals including ITT, Chase Manhattan Bank and the two mining giants Cerro de Pasco and Marcona Mining. After a dispute with the US government, compensation was

## Sendero Luminoso (Shining Path)

Initially conceived in the San Cristóbal de Huamanga University in Ayacucho by Abimael Guzmán, a professor in Philosophy, in 1970, Shining Path spent years selecting recruits and preparing its strategy before launching its armed struggle in July 1980.

The full name of the organization is the Communist Party of Peru – for the Shining Path of José Carlos Mariátegui. Mariátegui (1895-1930) was the founder of Peruvian communism. It spread from its original base in Ayacucho to operate in most of the country's departments. By the mid-1980s it was believed to have 2-3,000 regular fighters with many more in part-time militia and urban cells. Shining Path believes in 'prolonged popular war' (which could last 50 years) in which the cities will be surrounded from the countryside, and that the Indians should once more rule Peru. Ideologically, it is closest to the traditional Maoism of the 'Gang of Four', though in principal it derides all foreign communist governments.

The operations of Shining Path have included sabotage, kidnapping and the murder of local officials and members of the security forces. Suspected informers have been mutilated and sometimes killed. Government counter-insurgency forces responded with great brutality. Indeed, alleged terrorist massacres have sometimes been shown to be the work of these forces. Of some 15,000 deaths attributed to this struggle up to mid-1988, most are said by human rights organizations to be the work of security forces.

In the early 1980s Shining Path also established a presence in the upper Huallaga valley, Peru's main coca growing region. After a series of pitched battles, it succeeded in driving out the police, army, other guerrilla groups and even the drug traffickers' gunmen and was then able to collect an estimated US$40 million a year in taxes on the cocaine trade.

Shining Path showed no interest in a negotiated peace, preferring to fight for an eventual total victory, however high the cost. Their strategy, though, had to be reconsidered after the arrest of their leader,Abimael Guzmán, in September 1992, who was sentenced to life imprisonment. Although Sendero did not capitulate, many of its members in 1994-5 took advantage of the Law of Repentance, which guaranteed lighter sentences in return for surrender, and freedom in exchange for valuable information. The military meanwhile, continued

agreed.

Understandably, opposition to the Velasco government came from the business and landholding elite. The government's crack-down on expressions of dissent, the seizure of newspapers and taking over of TV and radio stations all offended sections of the urban middle class. Trade unions and peasant movements found that, although they agreed with many of the regime's policies, it refused to listen and expected their passive and unqualified support.

As world sugar and copper prices dropped, inflation rose and strikes increased. Velasco's problems were further increased by opposition within the armed forces and by his own ill-health. In Aug 1975 he was replaced by General Francisco Morales Bermúdez, a more conservative officer, who dismantled some of Velasco's policies and led the way to a restoration of civilian rule.

**Belaúnde returned to power in 1980** by winning the first elections after military rule. His government was badly affected by the 1982 debt crisis and the 1981-1983 world recession; inflation reached over 100% a year in 1983-1984. His term was also marked by the growth of the Maoist guerrilla movement **Sendero Luminoso** (Shining Path) and the smaller Túpac Amaru (MRTA).

## APRA victory

In 1985 APRA, in opposition for over 50 years, finally came to power. With Haya de la Torre dead, the APRA candidate **Alan García Pérez** won the elections and was allowed to take office by the armed forces. García attempted to implement an ambitious economic programme intended to solve many of Peru's deep-seated economic and social problems. He cut taxes, reduced interest rates, froze prices and devalued the currency. However, the economic boom which this produced in 1986-1987 stored up problems as increased incomes were spent on imports. Moreover the government's refusal to pay more than 10% of its foreign debt meant that it was unable to borrow. In 1988 inflation hit 3,000% and unemployment soared. By the time his term of office ended in 1990 Peru was bankrupt and García and APRA were discredited.

## Peru under Fujimori

In presidential elections held over two rounds in 1990, **Alberto Fujimori** of the Cambio 90 movement defeated the novelist **Mario Vargas Llosa**, who belonged to the Fredemo (Democratic Front) coalition. Fujimori, without an established political network behind him, failed to win a majority in either the senate or the lower house. Lack of congressional support was one of the reasons behind the dissolution of congress and the suspension of the constitution on 5 April 1992. President Fujimori declared that he needed a freer hand to introduce market reforms and combat terrorism and drug trafficking, at the same time as rooting out corruption. Initial massive popular support, although not matched internationally, did not evaporate.

In elections to a new, 80-member Democratic Constituent Congress (CCD) in Nov 1992, Fujimori's Cambio 90/Nueva Mayoría coalition won a majority of seats. Earlier that month a coup designed to remove Fujimori by retired military officers was foiled. Three major political parties, APRA, Acción Popular and the Movimiento de Libertad, boycotted the elections to CCD. In municipal elections held in Feb 1993 the trend against mainstream political groups continued as independent candidates won the lion's share of council seats. The elections to the CCD satisfied many aid donor's requirements for the resumption of financial assistance.

A new constitution drawn up by the CCD was approved by a narrow majority of the electorate in Oct 1993. Among the new articles were the immediate re-election of the president (previously prohibited for one presidential term), the death penalty for terrorist leaders, the establishment of a single-chamber congress, the reduction of the role of the state, the designation of Peru as a market economy and the favouring of foreign investment. As expected, Fujimori stood for re-election on 9 April 1995 and the opposition chose as an independent to stand against him former UN General Secretary, Javier Pérez de Cuéllar. Fujimori was re-elected by a resounding margin, winning about 65% of the votes cast. The coalition that supported him also won a majority in Congress.

The government's success in most economic areas did not appear to accelerate the distribution of foreign funds for social projects. Furthermore, rising unemployment and the austerity imposed by economic policy continued to cause hardship for many. Alleviating this poverty was the administration's stated aim, but how it would be implemented was an early question in Fujimori's second term. Of similar concern was whether there would be any relaxation in the concentration of power in the president's hands and whether this would alter his populist approach. In Aug 1996, Fujimori persuaded Congress that the constitutional changes regarding the president's term of office approved in 1993 do not apply to the years prior to 1993. It has therefore been accepted in law that Fujimori may stand for reelection in the year 2000; the constitution has been interpreted to state that this would be his second (not third) term, if elected.

## Túpac Amaru

The name of Túpac Amaru, the last Inca ruler to be assassinated by the Spaniards (1572), has become associated with insurrection. In the late 18th century, Túpac Amaru II's rebellion against Spanish colonial rule culminated in his very public, horrific execution in 1781. 201 years later, the Movimiento Revolucionario Túpac Amaru (MRTA) adopted the name for its Cuban-inspired insurgency.

After the detention of MRTA's leader, Victor Polay, in 1992, believed that the group had been effectively silenced. Any complacency on that front was shattered on 17 December 1996 when a cocktail party at the Japanese ambassador's residence in Lima, to celebrate the Emperor of Japan's birthday, was infiltrated by 30 MRTA rebels. They took 490 people hostage, including Peruvian ministers (among them Foreign Minister Francisco Tudela), many ambassadors and prominent business people. Had President Fujimori not been delayed, he too might have been among the hostages. The women captives were released immediately and the danger of a massive, televised bloodbath was steadily reduced as the guerrillas continued to set hostages free under various pretexts. The MRTA's central demands were: release from jail of all MRTA prisoners; improvement of prison conditions throughout Peru; redistribution of government resources to alleviate poverty; and a 'war tax' payable to MRTA. As the hostage crisis was played out in full view of the world's TV and press, President Fujimori made few public announcements. He ruled out the use of force as long as the MRTA had down their arms and freed the hostages to a guarantor commission. Néstor Cerpa Cartolini, the guerilla leader, invited the media into the residence for an interview on New Year's Eve. This raised the propaganda stakes, but prompted the Red Cross to withdraw as mediators. While the rebels' action dented the president's claim almost to have rid Peru of terrorism, it was too early to tell at the time of going to press what repercussions would be felt in investment, tourism and trade, let alone the future of the 74 hostages and their captors inside the ambassador's residence.

After the dissolution in the 1820s of Gran Colombia (largely present-day Venezuela, Colombia and Ecuador), repeated attempts to determine the extent of Ecuador's eastern jungle territory failed. While Ecuador claimed that its territory has been reduced from that of the old Audiencia of Quito by gradual Colombian and especially Peruvian infiltration, Peru has insisted that its Amazonian territory was established in law and in fact before the foundation of Ecuador as an independent state. The dispute reached an acute phase in 1941 when war broke out between Ecuador and Peru; the war ended with military defeat for Ecuador and the signing of the Rio de Janeiro Protocol of 1942 which allotted most of the disputed territory to Peru. Since 1960 Ecuador has denounced the Protocol as unjust (because it was imposed by force of arms) and as technically flawed (because it refers to certain non-existent geographic features). According to Peru, the Protocol demarcated the entire boundary and all the features are provable to US aerial photographic maps. Ecuador's official policy remains the recovery of a sovereign access to the Amazon. In Peru's view, the Protocol gives Ecuador navigation rights, but does not and cannot return land that Ecuador never had in the first place.

Sporadic border skirmishes continued throughout recent decades and in Jan 1995 these escalated into an undeclared war over control of the headwaters of the Río Cenepa. Argentina, Brazil, Chile and the USA (guarantors of the Rio de Janeiro Protocol) intervened diplomatically and a ceasefire took effect after 6 weeks of combat, during which both sides made conflicting claims of military success. A multinational team of observers was dispatched to the region in Mar 1995 to oversee the disengagement of forces and subsequent demilitarization of the area of the conflict. In 1996 the bases for negotiations to end the dispute were being sought.

# People

At the time of the Spanish conquest, there were an estimated 9 mn indigenous inhabitants of the region that is now Peru. In the subsequent hundred years, this figure fell to 600,000. By the time of independence from Spain, out of a total population of 1.2 mn, the Indian population had remained static, still at about 600,000. According to some statistics, the proportion of indigenous to non-indigenous inhabitants of Peru is roughly the same now as it was in the early $19^{th}$ century: 47.1% was classed as Quechua in the 1981 census, 32% mestizo, 12% white, 5.4% Aymara, 1.7% Amerindian and 1.8% other. There is, however, a wide variation in the estimates given for indigenous Peruvians. Some figures put the Quechua and Aymara people as low as 3 mn, with 200,000-250,000 Amazonian Indians from 40-50 ethnic groups. *The Gaia Atlas of First Peoples* (1990) says that Highland Indians total 8 mn and Amazonian Indians 600,000. These discrepancies notwithstanding, Peru has a substantial indigenous population, only smaller as a percentage of the total than Bolivia and Guatemala of the Latin American republics.

The first immigrants were the Spaniards who followed Pizarro's expeditionary force. Their effect, demographically, politically and culturally, has been enormous. Like most of Latin America, Peru received many emigrés from Europe seeking land and opportunities in the late 19th century. The "other" category above includes a sizable contingent of Asian immigrants. Chinese labourers were introduced in the 1860s to work the guano on the Pacific coast. The Japanese community, numbering some 100,000, established itself in the first half of the 20th century. Alberto Fujimori, one of its members, is the first president of Japanese descent outside Japan anywhere in the world. During Fujimori's presidency, many other Japanese Peruvians have taken prominent positions in business, central and local government. Despite the nickname 'chino', which is applied to anyone of Oriental origin, the Japanese and Japan are respected for their industriousness and honesty.

Peru has a small black community, based mainly in Chincha, S of Lima. Their forefathers were originally imported into Peru as slaves.

The structure of Peruvian society, especially in the coastal cities, has been radically altered by internal migration. This movement began most significantly in the 1950s and 1960s as people from the Highlands sought urban jobs in place of work on the land. It was a time of great upheaval as the old system of labour on large estates

## Day of the dead

One of the most important dates in the indigenous people's calendar is the 2nd of November, the 'Day of the Dead'. This tradition has been practised since time immemorial. In the Incaic calendar, November was the eighth month and meant *Ayamarca*, or land of the dead. The celebration of Day of the Dead, or 'All Saints' as it is also known, is just one example of religious adaptation in which the ancient beliefs of ethnic cultures are mixed with the rites of the Catholic Church.

According to Aymara belief, the spirit (*athun ajayu*) visits its relatives at this time of the year and is fed in order to continue its journey before its reincarnation. The relatives of the dead prepare for the arrival of the spirit days in advance. Among the many items necessary for these meticulous preparations are little bread dolls, each one of which has a particular significance. A ladder is needed for the spirit to descend from the other world to the terrestrial one. There are other figures which represent the grandparents, great grandparents and loved ones of the person who has 'passed into a better life'. Horse-shaped breads are prepared that will serve as a means of transport for the soul in order to avoid fatigue.

Inside the home, the relatives construct a tomb supported by boxes over which is laid a black cloth. Here they put the bread, along with sweets, flowers, onions and sugar cane. This latter item is an indispensable part of the table as it symbolizes the invigorating element which prevents the spirit from becoming tired on its journey towards the Earth. The union of the flowers with the onion is called *tojoro* and is a vital part of the preparations. It ensures that the dead one does not become disoriented and arrives in the correct house.

The tomb is also adorned with the dead relative's favourite food and drink, not forgetting the all-important glass of beer as, according to popular tradition, this is the first nourishment taken by the souls when they arrive at their houses. Once the spirit has arrived and feasted with its living relatives, the entire ceremony is then transported to the graveside in the local cemetery, where it is carried out again, beside the many other mourning families.

This meeting of the living and their dead relatives is re-enacted the following year, though less ostentatiously, and again for the final time in the third year, the year of the farewell. It does not continue after this, which is just as well as the costs can be crippling for the family concerned.

was threatened by the peasant majority's growing awareness of the imbalances between the wealthy cities and impoverished sierra. The process culminated in the agrarian reforms of the government of Gen Juan Velasco (1968-75). Highland-to-city migration was given renewed impetus during the war between the state and Sendero Luminoso in the 1980s. Many communities which were depopulated in that decade are now beginning to come alive again.

## Peru's indigenous people

The literacy rate of the indigenous population is the lowest of any comparable group in South America and their diet is 50% below acceptable levels. The conflict between Sendero Luminoso guerrillas and the security forces has caused the death of thousands of highland Indians. Many indigenous groups are also under threat from colonization, development and road-building projects. Long after the end of Spanish rule, some indigenous peoples continue to be dispossessed and exploited for their labour.

## The Quechua people

According to Inca legend, the Quechuas were a small group who originally lived near Lake Titicaca. They later moved to Cusco, from where they expanded to create the Inca empire. Their language and culture soon spread from Quito in the N through present-day Ecuador, Peru and Bolivia to northern Chile. Predominantly an agricultural society, growing potatoes and corn as their basic diet, they are largely outside the money economy. Today, there remain two enduring legacies of Inca rule; their magnificent architecture and their unwritten language, Quechua, which has given its name to the descendants of their subjects. About 2 million Indians speak no Spanish, their main tongue being Quechua.

## The Aymara people

High up in the Andes, in the southern part of Peru, lies a wide, barren and hostile plateau, the *altiplano*. Prior to Inca rule Tihuanaco on Lake Titicaca was a highly-organized centre for one the greatest cultures South America has ever witnessed: the Aymara people. Today, the shores of this lake and the plains that surround it remain the homeland of the Aymara. The majority live in Bolivia, the rest are scattered on the south-western side of Peru and northern Chile. The climate is so harsh on the *altiplano* that, though they are extremely hard-working, their lives are very poor. They speak their own unwritten language, Aymara.

## The Amazonian peoples

Just as the Amazon landscape is not homogeneous, neither are its original cultures. Before the arrival of the Europeans, an estimated 6 million people inhabited the Amazon basin, comprising more than 2,000 tribes or ethnic-linguistic groups who managed to adapt to their surroundings through the domestication of a great variety of animals and plants, and to benefit from the numerous nutritional, curative, narcotic and hallucinogenic properties of thousands of wild plants.

It's not easy to determine the precise origin of these aboriginal people. The high humidity and other characteristics of the area have meant the deterioration of much of the archaeology. What is known, however, is that since the beginning of colonial times this population slowly but constantly decreased, mainly because of the effect of western diseases such as influenza and measles. This demographic decline reached dramatic levels during the rubber boom of the late 19th and early 20th centuries, as a result of forced labour and slavery.

Today, at the basin level, the population is calculated at no more than 2 million inhabitants making up 400 ethnic groups, of which approximately 200-250,000 live in the Peruvian jungle. Within the basin it is possible to distinguish at least three large conglomerates of aboriginal societies: the inhabitants of the *varzea*, or seasonally flooded lands alongside the large rivers (such as the Omagua, Cocama and Shipibo people); the people in the interfluvial zones or firm lands (such as the Amahuaca, Cashibo and Yaminahua) and those living in the Andean foothills (such as the Amuesha, Ashaninka and Matziguenga).

It is worth noting that, while the Amazon rainforest began to suffer massive deforestation and depredation only this century, the natives began to be decimated very much earlier, in the 16th century. In

## Andean mysticism

In the 1990s Andean shamanism and mysticism have attracted increasing attention. Ceremonies to the Apus – mountain spirits – have become so mainstream in Peru, that a 1996 international conference on terrorism hosted by the Peruvian government featured a ritual peace offering at Pachacamac, a pre-Inca pilgrimage site near Lima.

In highland cities, especially, it is common to engage a ritual specialist, called an *altomisayoq*, to perform a *pago*, or offering, when laying the foundations of a house or starting a business venture. Ritual objects for use in these ceremonies are sold at specialized stands in the local markets. Another type of ritualist, called a *curandero*, is summoned when someone is ill.

Some of these healers are experts in the use of dozens of medicinal plants, while others invoke spirit powers to expel illness. Sometimes eggs or guinea pigs are passed over the patient's body, and then cracked, or killed, in order to read the innards and diagnose the illness. Inevitably this field has its share of charlatans, but there are also *curanderos* who have many attested cures to their credit.

One thing shamans from all the Andean regions have in common is the use of a *mesa* – a layout of ceremonial power objects – which is thought to attract spirit power and channel it to the shaman. Another feature running through all strains of Andean mysticism, despite the usual presence of Christian elements, is a living connection, via innumerable practices and associations, to Peru's precolombian past.

Those ritualists who seek to communicate with 'the other side' in their ceremonies often use psychoactive plants. These vary according to the region. On the coast, *curanderos* often take an infusion of the San Pedro cactus, a form of mescaline. The highland shamans invariably chew coca leaf, a much milder psychoactive, but with broader uses. Coca is burned with every offering, and many ritualists cast the leaves to read the fortunes of their clients. These shamans usually invoke the power of the mountain deities in their ceremonies. In the rainforest regions shamans use the powerful psychedelic vine, ayahuasca (vine of the dead – so called because it is believed to transport the user to the spirit world), as they have for millenia.

Foreigners have recently shown great interest in this traditional substance, and ayahuasca is currently enjoying a vogue in the USA. User reactions vary immensely, according to individual sensitivity. Anyone thinking of trying it should exercise great caution, especially in selecting the shaman.

There is a dark side to Andean shamanism, since many people seek out shamans for the purpose of putting harmful or deadly spells on their enemies, and many shamans are happy to oblige if the price is right. Some recent books have called attention to the exotic mysticism of Peru, notably the bestselling *Celestine Prophecy*, by James Redfield. But, whatever the merits of his ideas, the author merely uses 'Peru' as a very unconvincing and inaccurate backdrop for his tale, which really has nothing to do with Andean mysticism.

this way, the first endangered species of the jungle were the native people.

## RELIGION

The Inca religion (described on page 41) was displaced by Roman Catholicism from the 16th century onwards, the conversion of the inhabitants of the 'New World' to Christianity being one of the stated aims of the Spanish *conquistadores*. Today, official statistics state that 92.5% of the population declares itself Catholic, 5.5% Protestant. One million or more people belong to some 27 different non-Catholic denominations. It is worth noting here that one of the first exponents of Liberation Theology, under which the Conference of Latin American Bishops in 1968 committed themselves to the 'option for the poor', was Gustavo Gutiérrez, from Huánuco. This doctrine caused much consternation to orthodox Catholics, particularly those members of the Latin American church who had traditionally aligned themselves with the oligarchy. Gutiérrez, however, traced the church's duty to the voiceless and the marginalized back to Fray Bartolomé de las Casas (see *The Peru Reader*, pages 293-96; reference under **Literature**, below).

Among the other religions making up the remaining 2% of the population are the surviving beliefs of some Indian groups and Japanese faiths which have adherents in some Lima circles. There is a growing interest in Andean and Amazonian mysticism (see the box **Andean mysticism**, page 53), which is being exploited by the tourist trade.

## EDUCATION

Education is free and compulsory for both sexes between 6 and 14. There are public and private secondary schools and private elementary schools. There are 32 State and private universities, and two Catholic universities. A new educational system is being implemented as too many children cannot complete secondary school.

# Culture

## ARTS AND CRAFTS

Peru is exceptionally rich in handicrafts. Its geographic division into four distinct regions – coast, mountains, valleys and Amazon basin – coupled with cultural differences, has resulted in numerous variations in technique and design. Each province, even each community, has developed its own style of weaving or carving.

The Incas inherited 3,000 years of skills and traditions: gold, metal and precious stonework from the Chimu; feather textiles from the Nasca; and the elaborate textiles of the Paracas. All of these played important roles in political, social and religious ceremonies. Though much of this artistic heritage was destroyed by the Spanish conquest, the traditions adapted and

> The information on arts and crafts in this Handbook has been adapted from *Arts and Crafts of South America*, by Lucy Davies and Mo Fini, published by Tumi, 1994. Tumi, the Latin American Craft Centre, specializes in Andean and Mexican products and produces cultural and educational videos for schools: at 8/9 New Bond Street Place, Bath BA1 1BH (T 01225 462367, F 01225 444870), 23/2A Chalk Farm Road, London NW1 8AG (F 0171-485 4152), Little Clarendon St, Oxford OX1 2HJ (T/F 01865-512307), 82 Park St, Bristol BS1 5LA (T/F 0117 929 0391). Tumi (Music) Ltd specializes in different rhythms of Latin America.

### A belt for every occasion

The belt plays a particularly important role in the lives of the indigenous peoples. The Incas developed a range of belts, or *chumpis*, of ritual and spiritual significance which are still used today.

*Chumpis* are believed to have protective and purifying qualities. In the Cusco area, some communities place *chumpis* on sacred mountain tops, or *apus*, in order to communicate with the gods. Traditionally women give birth lying on a *chumpi* and the baby is wrapped in a softer version, known as a *walt'ana*, which ensures he or she will grow up properly. From adolescence, women wear a *chumpi* under their skirt to encourage a lover or deter an unwanted suitor. It is even common practice for the bridegroom to lasso his bride with one. And the age-old tradition of burying the dead with the family *chumpi* is still occasionally observed.

evolved in numerous ways, absorbing new methods, concepts and materials from Europe while maintaining ancient techniques and symbols.

### Textiles and costumes

Woven cloth was the most highly-prized possession and sought after trading commodity in the Andes in precolumbian times. It is, therefore, not surprising that ancient weaving traditions have survived.

In the 9th century BC camelid fibre was introduced into weaving on the S coast. This allowed the development of the textiles of the Paracas culture which consist of intricate patterns of animalistic, supernatural and human forms embroidered onto dark backgrounds. The culture of the Chancay valleys cultivated cotton for white and beige dyed patterned cloth in preference to the camelid fibres used by the Paracas and Nasca cultures.

**The Incas** inherited this rich weaving tradition. They forced the Aymaras to work in *mitas* or textile workshops. The ruins of some enormous *mitas* can be seen at the temple of Raqchi, S of Cusco (see page 327). Inca textiles are of high quality and very different from coastal textiles, being warp-faced, closely woven and without embroidery. The largest quantities of the finest textiles were made specifically to be burned as ritual offerings – a tradition which still survives. The Spanish, too, exploited this wealth and skill by using the *mitas* and exporting the cloth to Europe.

**Prior to Inca rule** Aymara men wore a tunic (*llahua*) and a mantle (*llacata*) and carried a bag for coca leaves (*huallquepo*). The women wore a wrapped dress (*urku*) and mantle (*iscayo*) and a belt (*huaka*); their coca bag was called an *istalla*. The *urku* was fastened at shoulder level with a pair of metal *tupu*, the traditional Andean dress-pins.

**The Inca men** had tunics (*unkus*) and a bag for coca leaves called a *ch'uspa*. The women wore a blouse (*huguna*), skirts (*aksu*) and belts (*chumpis*), and carried foodstuffs in large, rectangular cloths called *lliclla*s, which were fastened at the chest with a single pin or a smaller clasp called a *ttipqui*. Women of the Sacred Valley now wear a layered, gathered skirt called a *pollera* and a *montera*, a large, round, red Spanish type of hat.

Textiles continue to play an important part in society. They are still used specifically for ritual ceremonies and some even held to possess magical powers. One of the most enduring of these traditions is found among the Aymara people of Taquile island on Lake Titicaca.

### Textile materials and techniques

The Andean people used mainly alpaca or llama wool. The former can be spun into fine, shining yarn when woven and has a lustre similar to that of silk, though sheep's wool came to be widely used following the Spanish conquest.

A commonly used technique is the drop spindle. A stick is weighted with a wooden wheel and the raw material is fed through one hand. A sudden twist and drop in the spindle spins the yarn. This very sensitive art can be seen practiced by women while herding animals in the fields.

Spinning wheels were introduced by Europeans and are now prevalent owing to increased demand. In Ayacucho and San Pedro de Cajas, centres of the cottage textile industry, the wheel is the most common form of spinning. Precolumbian looms were often portable and those in use today are generally similar. A woman will herd her animals while making a piece of costume, perhaps on a backstrap loom, or waist loom, so-called because the weaver controls the tension on one side with her waist with the other side tied to an upright or tree. The precolumbian looms are usually used for personal costume while the treadle loom is used by men for more commercial pieces.

**The skills of dyeing** were still practiced virtually unchanged even after the arrival of the Spanish. Nowadays, the word *makhnu* refers to any natural dye, but originally was the name for cochineal, an insect which lives on the leaves of the nopal cactus. These dyes were used widely by precolumbian weavers. Today, the biggest centre of production in South America is the valleys around Ayacucho.

Vegetable dyes are also used, made from the leaves, fruit and seeds of shrubs and flowers and from lichen, tree bark and roots.

## Symbolism

Symbolism plays an important role in weaving. Traditionally every piece of textile from a particular community had identical symbols and colours which were a source of identity as well as carrying specific symbols and telling a story. One example is on the island of Taquile where the *Inti* (sun) and *Chaska* (Venus) symbols are employed as well as motifs such as fish and birds, unique to the island.

Animal figures dominated the motifs of the Chavín culture and were commonly used in Paracas textiles. Specimens of cotton and wool embroidery found in Paracas graves often show a puma as a central motif. Today, this and other precolumbian motifs are found on many rugs and wall-hangings from the Ayacucho region. Other symbols include Spanish figures such as horses and scenes depicting the execution of Túpac Amaru.

## Pottery

The most spectacular archaeological finds in South America have been made in Peru. The Nasca culture (100 BC-AD 900) excelled in polychrome painting of vessels with motifs of supernatural beings, often with strong feline characteristics, as well as birds, fish and animals. Many of the Nasca ceramic motifs are similar to those found in Paracas textiles.

**Moche or Mochica** vessels combined modelling and painting to depict details of Moche daily life. Human forms are modelled on stirrup spout vessels with such precision that they suggest personal portraits. The Moche also excelled in intricate linear painting often using brown on a cream base.

**Inca ceramic decoration** consists mainly of small-scale geometric and usually symmetrical designs. One distinctive form of vessel which continues to be made and used is the *arybola*. This pot is designed to carry liquid, especially chicha, and is secured with a rope on the bearer's back. It is believed that *arybolas* were used mainly by the governing Inca élite and became important status symbols. Today, Inca-style is very popular in Cusco and Pisac.

With the Spanish invasion many indigenous communities lost their artistic traditions, others remained relatively untouched, while others still combined Hispanic and indigenous traditions and techniques. The Spanish brought three innovations: the potter's wheel, which gave greater speed and uniformity; knowledge of the enclosed kiln; and the technique of lead glazes. The enclosed kiln made temperature regulation easier and allowed higher temperatures to be maintained, producing stronger pieces. Today, many communities continue to apply pre-Hispanic techniques, while others use more modern processes.

## Jewellery and metalwork

Some of the earliest goldwork originates from the Chavín culture – eg the *Tumi* knife found in Lambayeque. These first appeared in the Moche culture, when they were associated with human sacrifice. Five centuries later, the Incas used *Tumis* for surgical operations such as trepanning skulls. Today, they are a common motif.

The Incas associated gold with the Sun. However, very few examples remain as the Spanish melted down their amassed gold and silver objects. They then went on to send millions of Indians to their deaths in gold and silver mines.

**During the colonial period** gold and silver pieces were made to decorate the altars of churches and houses of the élite. Metalworkers came from Spain and Italy to develop the industry. The Spanish preferred silver and strongly influenced the evolution of silverwork during the colonial period. A style known as Andean baroque developed around Cusco embracing both indigenous and European elements. Silver bowls in this style – *cochas* – are still used in Andean ceremonies.

**False filigree**, as it is termed, was practiced by some pre-Hispanic cultures. The effect of filigree was obtained with the use of droplets or beads of gold. True filigree work developed in the colonial period. Today, there are a number of centres. Originally popular in Ayacucho, the tradition continues in the small community of San Jerónimo de Tunan, near Huancayo. Here, silversmiths produce intricate filigree earrings, spoons and jewellery boxes among other things. Catacaos near Piura also has a long tradition of filigree work in silver and gold.

**Seeds, flowers and feathers** continue to be used as jewellery by many Amazonian peoples. Pre-Hispanic cultures also favoured particular natural materials; eg the sea shell spondylus was highly revered by the Chavín and Moche. It was found only along part of the Ecuadorean coast and must have been acquired through trade. The western fashion for natural or ethnic jewellery has encouraged production, using brightly-coloured feathers, fish bones, seeds or animal teeth.

## Woodcarving

Wood is one of the most commonly used materials. Carved ceremonial objects include drums, carved sticks with healing properties, masks and the Incas' *keros* – wooden vessels for drinking chicha. *Keros* come in all shapes and sizes and were traditionally decorated with scenes of war, local dances, or harvesting coca leaves. The Chancay, who lived along the coast between 100 BC and AD 1200, used *keros* carved with sea birds and fish. Today, they are used in some Andean ceremonies, especially during *Fiesta del Cruz*, the Andean May festival.

**Glass mirrors** were introduced by the Spanish, although the Chimú and Lambayeque cultures used obsidian and silver plates, and Inca *chasquis* (messengers) used reflective stones to communicate between hilltop forts. Transporting mirrors was costly, therefore they were produced in Lima and Quito. Cusco and Cajamarca then became centres of production.

In Cusco the frames were carved, covered in gold leaf and decorated with tiny pieces of cut mirror. Cajamarca artisans, meanwhile, incorporated painted glass into the frames.

### Gourd-carving

Gourd-carving, or *máte burilado*, as it is known, is one of Peru's most popular and traditional handicrafts. It is thought even to predate pottery; engraved gourds found on the coast have been dated to some 3,500 years ago. During the Inca empire gourd-carving became a valued art form and workshops were set up and supported by the state.

Gourds were used in rituals and ceremonies and to make *poporos* – containers for the lime used while chewing coca leaves. Today, gourd-carving is centred around the small communities of Cochas Grande and Chico, near Huancayo.

## LITERATURE

### Quechua

The fact that the Incas had no written texts in the conventional European sense and that the Spaniards were keen to suppress their conquest's culture means that there is little evidence today of what poetry and theatre was performed in pre-conquest times. It is known that the Incas had two types of poet, the *amautas*, historians, poets and teachers who composed works that celebrated the ruling class' gods, heroes and events, and *haravecs*, who expressed popular sentiments. Greater understanding of the *quipus* which survived Spanish destruction indicate that the knots made by the *quipucamayocs* (archivists) recorded not just numbers of state production, but also set phrases and formulae of history, law and poetry. There is strong evidence also that drama was important in Inca society. The Spanish *Tragedia del fin de Atawallpa* is possibly a 16th century version of a play performed before the Spaniards conquered Cusco, while *Ollantay*, the best known Quechua drama, is held by some to be genuinely precolumbian, whereas others claim it was written in the colonial period.

Written Quechua even today is far less common than works in the oral tradition. Although Spanish culture has had some influence on Quechua, the native stories, lyrics and fables retain their identity, infused since the 16th century with, on the one hand, the despair of defeat and the loss of the familiar world and, on the other, a sense that the proper order will eventually be restored, with European domination overthrown. Not until the 19th century did Peruvian writers begin seriously to incorporate indigenous ideas into their art, but their audience was limited. Nevertheless, the influence of Quechua on Peruvian literature in Spanish continues to grow.

### The Colonial Period

The Spanish officials in 16th-century Lima, headquarters of the Viceroyalty of Peru, concentrated their efforts on the religious education of the new territories, banning the diffusion of novels and encouraging only doctrinal theatre. Lyric poetry was less restricted, but literary output was mainly histories and letters. Chroniclers such as Pedro Cieza de León (*Crónica del Perú*, published from 1553) and Agustín de Zárate (*Historia del descubrimiento y conquista del Perú*, 1555) were written from the point of view that Spanish domination was right. Their most renowned successors, though, took a different stance. Inca Garcilaso de la Vega was a mestizo, whose *Comentarios reales que tratan del origen de los Incas* (1609) were at pains to justify the achievements, religion and culture of the Inca empire, not as superior to the Christian, but as one which was neither pagan nor barbaric. He also commented on Spanish society in the colony. A later work, *Historia general del Perú* (1617) went further in condemning Viceroy Toledo's suppression of Inca culture. Through his work, written in Spain, many aspects of Inca society, plus poems and prayers have survived.

Writing at about the same time as Inca Garcilaso was Felipe Guaman Poma de Ayala, whose *El primer nueva corónica y buen gobierno* (1613-15) is possibly one of the most reproduced of

Latin American texts (eg on T-shirts, CDs, posters and carrier bags). Guaman Poma was a minor provincial Inca chief whose writings and illustrations, addressed to King Felipe III of Spain, offer a view of a stable pre-conquest Andean society (not uniquely Inca), in contrast with the unsympathetic colonial society that usurped it. The poor quality of his Spanish (because it was not his first language) is amply compensated by the 456 vividly expressive pictures which provide a visual history of precolonial and colonial life in the Andes.

In the years up to Independence, the growth of an intellectual elite in Lima spawned more poetry than anything else. As criollo discontent grew, satire increased both in poetry and in the sketches which accompanied dramas imported from Spain. The poet Mariano Melgar (1791-1815) wrote in a variety of styles, including the *yaraví*, the love-song derived from the precolumbian *harawi* (from *haravek*). That he sought expression in Indian styles and that he died in an uprising against the Spanish ensured Melgar a place in the Peruvian struggle from freedom from the colonial imagination.

## After Independence

After Independence, Peruvian writers imitated Spanish *costumbrismo*, sketches of characters and life-styles from the new Republic. The first author to transcend this fashion was Ricardo Palma (1833-1919), whose inspiration, the *tradición*, fused *costumbrismo* and Peru's rich oral traditions. Palma graduated through romanticism and politics to the world of letters, being the librarian who restocked the Biblioteca Nacional, sacked by the Chileans after the War of the Pacific. Palma's *Tradiciones peruanas* is a collection of pieces which celebrate the people, history and customs of Peru through sayings, small incidents in mainly colonial history and gentle irony. His precise prose style and his art in storytelling made Palma immensely popular.

**The affectionate tone of Palma's** *tradiciones* seems lightweight compared with the soul-searching that followed Peru's defeat in the War of the Pacific. Manuel

### The Jesuits' chocolate

A good example of a *tradición* by Ricardo Palma is "El chocolate de los jesuitas". One day, in congress, Palma heard one deputy refer to another as a man of substance, "like the chocolate of the 'teatinos'" (a name given to the clerics of the Order of San Cayetano and later to the Jesuits). The phrase stuck in his brain and he investigated its origin. Rather than an insult, implying indigestibility, it turned out to be a compliment because it referred to the "riquísimo" chocolate, flavoured with cinnamon and vanilla, sent by the Jesuits from Cusco to the Court of King Carlos III of Spain in the 18th century.

The Superior Jesuit in Lima in 1765 wished to combat the growing influence of Governor Manuel Amat y Juniet with the Court. He therefore got permission to send the chocolate, free of duty, to Spain. These gifts won praise for the Jesuits in all quarters; only the Conde de Aranda, an enemy of the Superior, failed to succumb to the delicacy. And all this was soon after a hot theological debate over whether taking chocolate constituted breaking one's fast. The Jesuits had decreed that it did not.

One day, Viceroy Amat was informed that a case of Cusco chocolate weighed so much that it appeared to be full of stones. The Viceroy inspected said box at Callao. It indeed contained chocolate, but even the Viceroy was smart enough to realise that it was indigestible. Each ball of chocolate contained an ounce of gold.

González Prada (1844-1918), for instance, wrote essays fiercely critical of the state of the nation: *Páginas libres* (1894), *Horas de lucha* (1908). José Carlos Mariátegui, the foremost Peruvian political thinker of the early 20th century, said that González Prada represented the first lucid instant of Peruvian consciousness. He also wrote poetry, some Romantic, some, like his *Baladas peruanas*, an evocation of indigenous and colonial history, very pro-Indian, very anti-White. See "El Mitayo", an interchange between a son and his father who has to leave home to work in the "fatal" mines, according to "the unjust law of the white man". Questions such as "When will the llama of the puna love the desert sands? – When the tiger of the forest drinks the water of the sea" end with "Son, the breast of the White Man will never be moved" to pity and tenderness.

## 20th century

Mariátegui himself (1895-1930), after a visit to Europe in 1919, considered deeply the question of Peruvian identity. His opinion was that it could only be seen in a global context (either we save ourselves together, or we disappear together) and that the answer lay in Marxism. With this perspective he wrote about politics, economics, literature and the Indian question (see *Siete ensayos de interpretación de la realidad peruana*, 1928). Already, after González Prada, writers had continued this theme. For instance Clorinda Matto de Turner (1854-1909) intended to express in *Aves sin nido* (1889) her "tender love for the indigenous people" and her indignation at clerics and the civil authorities. She hoped to improve the living conditions of the Indians; she wished to relieve their exploitation in "the night of ignorance", end their martyrdom and, at the same time, create Peruvian literature. Regardless of the debate over whether the novel achieves these aims, she was the forerunner by several years of the 'indigenist' genre in Peru and the most popular of those who took up González Prada's cause. Other prose writers continued in this vein at the beginning of the 20th century, but it was Ciro Alegría (1909-67) who gave major, fictional impetus to the racial question. Like Mariátegui, Alegría was politically committed, but to the APRA party, rather than Marxism. Of his first three novels, *La serpiente de oro* (1935), *Los perros hambrientos* (1938) and *El mundo es ancho y ajeno* (1941), the last is the most famous, a panoramic study of an Indian community's struggle to maintain its way of life in the face not only of natural hardship, but also of the encroachment of landowners and the state.

**Contemporary with Alegría** was José María Arguedas (1911-1969), whose novels, stories and politics were also deeply-rooted in the ethnic question. Arguedas' singularity came from the fact that, though not Indian, he had a largely Quechua upbringing and trying to reconcile this with the hispanic world in which he worked was a source of trauma. The inner conflict, which echoed the Indians' fight of national recognition, was one of the main causes of his suicide. His books include *Agua* (short stories – 1935), *Yawar fiesta* (1941), *Los ríos profundos* (1958) and *Todas las sangres* (1964). They portray different aspects of the confrontation of Indian society with the changing outside world that impinges on it. *Los riós profundos*, being much more autobiographical, contains a broader spectrum of Quechua culture than his other works.

**In the 1950s and 1960s**, there was a move by prose writers away from a predominantly rural, indigenist to an urban setting. At the forefront were, among others, Mario Vargas Llosa, Julio Ramón Ribeyro, Enrique Congrains Martín, Oswaldo Reynoso, Luis Loayza, Sebastián Salazar Bondy and Carlos E Zavaleta. Taking their cue from a phrase used by both poet César Mora and

Salazar Bondy (in an essay of 1964), "Lima, la horrible", they explored all aspects of the city, including the influx of people from the Sierra. As Vargas Llosa pointed out, to most Limeños, a novel by Ciro Alegría would be as distant as a French novel and the new aim was to demonstrate that the city, too, was equally alien and alienating. These writers incorporated new narrative tech-

## Mario Vargas Llosa

Vargas Llosa was born in 1936 in Arequipa and educated in Cochabamba (Bolivia), from where his family moved to Piura. After graduating from the Universidad de San Marcos, he won a scholarship to Paris in 1958 and, from 1959 to 1974, lived first in Paris then in London in voluntary exile. Much has been written about his personal life, how first he had an affair with an aunt and then married a cousin. Similarly, his political opinions have been well documented, changing from a socialist and supporter of the Cuban Revolution to an opponent of any form of authoritarian government, to become presidential candidate in 1990, losing to Alberto Fujimori. He subsequently took up Spanish citizenship. Even more critical space has been devoted to his novels, as befits an author of the highest international standing and one of the leading figures in the so-called 'Boom' of Latin American writers in the 1960s. He has also written short stories, plays, journalism, academic studies (eg on Flaubert and García Márquez) and autobiography (see *El pez en el agua* – 1994).

It is for his novels that Vargas Llosa the writer is best known: *La ciudad y los perros* (1963); *La casa verde* (1966); *Conversación en la Catedral* (1969); *Pantaleón y las visitadoras* (1973); *La tía Julia y el escribidor* (1977); *La guerra del fin del mundo* (1981); *Historia de Mayta* (1984); *¿Quién mató a Palomino Molero?* (1986); *El hablador* (1987); *Elogio a la madrastra* (1988); *Lituma en los Andes* (1994). The first three, with their techniques of flashback, multiple narrators and different interwoven stories, are an adventure for the reader. Meanwhile, the humorous books, like *Pantaleón* and *La tía Julia* cannot be called lightweight. *La guerra del fin del mundo* marked a change to a more direct style and an intensification of Vargas Llosa's exploration of the role of fiction as a human necessity, extending also to political ideologies. With this, the assuredness shown in his first novels has declined. This does not mean that his mastery of the art has diminished, more that the contradictions of art have become an increasingly important element in the art itself.

Vargas Llosa has always maintained that in Peruvian society the writer is a privileged person who should be able to mix politics and literature as a normal part of life. "How can a writer turn his back on reality? How can he write and live at the margins of actuality? The writer has an ethical duty, a moral obligation: to intervene with the continuous and free exercise of criticism. The writer must not be militant, but must be authentic." This drive for authenticity led to his excursion into national politics, but it could be said to have been at odds with the role of the storyteller: "You will never cease to marvel at the strange birth of stories. They build themselves up with things you thought you had forgotten and which memory rescues when you least expect it, only for the imagination to betray them. But you must know that, instead of a lawyer, diplomat or poet, I ended up dedicating myself to the role that I learnt best from you: telling stories. Look, perhaps that's it: to repay a debt. As I didn't know the true story, I had to add things that I remembered, others that I made up as I went along, stealing from here and there" (taken from the last speech of his play, *La señorita de Tacna* – 1981).

niques so that the urban novel presented a discontinuous, impersonal world, operating on many levels; a world where popular culture and speech were rich sources of literary material, despite the difficulty in transcribing them.

This should not imply that Lima became the sole topic of novels after the 1950s. Many broadened their horizons, such as Vargas Llosa whose novels after *La ciudad y los perros* encompassed many different parts of the country. An additional factor was that several writers spent many years abroad, Vargas Llosa himself, for instance, and Ribeyro (born 1929), whose short stories, especially, are masterful. The tales, less experimental technically than some of his contemporaries, are mostly set in Lima, but embrace universal themes of delusion and frustration. The title story of *Los gallinazos sin pluma* (1955), a tale of squalor and greed amid the city's rubbish tips, has become a classic, even though it does not contain the irony, pathos and humour of many of his other stories or novels.

It is only possible to add a few names to those already mentioned: Manuel Scorza (1928-83) wrote a series of five novels under the general title of *La guerra silenciosa* (including *Redoble por Rancas*, *El jinete insomne*, *La tumba del relámpago*). The principal theme of the novels is the efforts of Indian communities in the central Andes to recover their lands in the 1950s and 1960s. In one sense the books follow the indigenist tradition of the Indians' struggle in the face of insuperable difficulties, but they also emphasize that their society and myths do and will continue to survive, if necessary with growing militancy. In 1983 Scorza published *La danza inmóvil*, the first volume of a trilogy which was never complete because he died in a plane crash.

Alfredo Bryce Echenique (born 1939) has enjoyed much popularity following the success of *Un mundo para Julius* (1970), a satire on the upper and middle classes of Lima. His other novels include *Tantas veces Pedro* (1977), the two-volume *Cuaderno de navegación en un sillón Voltaire* (1981, 1985), *La última mudanza de Felipe Carrillo* (1988), *No me esperen en abril* (1995) and various collections of short stories. In all Bryce's writing, humour is an important element. To round off this incomplete list of prose writers, one should mention Miguel Gutiérrez (born 1940, *El viejo saurio se retira*, the three-volume *La violencia del tiempo*), Alonso Cueto (born 1954, *El vuelo de la ceniza*, *La batalla del paraíso*), Fernando Ampuero (born 1949, *Miraflores' melody*, *Bicho raro*), and Eduardo González Viaña (born 1941, *Los peces muertos*, *Batalla de Felipe en la casa de palomas* – a collection of dreamlike stories).

## 20th-century poetry

At the end of the 19th century, the term Modernism was introduced in Latin America by the Nicaraguan Rubén Darío, not to define a precise school of poetry, but to indicate a break with both Romanticism and Realism. In Peru one major exponent was José Santos Chocano (1875-1934), who labelled his poetry "mundonovismo" (New Worldism), claiming for himself the role of Poet of South America (as counterpart of Walt Whitman in North America). His verse, grand, heroic, extolling the virtues of all that is South American (see, for example, *Alma América*, 1906), won him the international fame that he sought, but his star soon waned. A much less assuming character was José María Eguren (1874-1942) who, feeling alienated from the society around him, sought spiritual reality in the natural world (*Simbólicas*, 1911; *La canción de las figuras*, 1916; *Poesías*, 1929). James Higgins (see below) asserts that with Eguren the flourishing of Peruvian 20th-century poetry began.

Without doubt, the most important poet in Peru, if not Latin America, in the first half of the 20th century, was César

## César Vallejo

Me moriré en París con aguacero,
un día del cual tengo ya el recuerdo.
Me moriré en París -y no me corro-
talvez un jueves, como es hoy, de otoño.
...
César Vallejo ha muerto, le pegaban
todos sin que él les haga nada...

*I shall die in Paris with heavy rain,*
*One day which I already remember.*
*I shall die in Paris – I shan't budge on that-*
*Perhaps on a Thursday, like today, in autumn.*
...
*César Vallejo has died, they hit him*
*everyone without him doing anything to them...*

"Piedra negra sobre una piedra blanca" from *Poemas humanos*.

Before Vallejo had reached such a sorry state he had published *Trilce*, whose title is untranslatable: it could be a mixture of 'triste' and 'dulce' (sad and sweet), a noun suggesting trinity, or meaningless. The poems themselves vary from the very peculiar (No XXXII):

999 CALORIAS
Rumbbb Trraprrrr rrach chaz
Serpentínica u del biscochero
engirafada al tímpano...
Y hasta la misma pluma
con que escribo por último se troncha.
Treinta y tres trillones trescientas treinta
y tres calorías.

*The serpentine-like u of the biscuit-seller*
*giraffed to the timpany...*
*and even the pen itself*
*with which I write ultimately splits.*
*Thirty three trillion three hundred and thirty*
*three calories.*

to the poignant (No III):

LAS PERSONAS MAYORES
¿a qué hora volverán?
Da la seis el ciego Santiago,
y ya está muy oscuro.
Madre dijo que no demoraría.

*The grown-ups*
*when will they return?*
*blind Santiago is striking six,*
*and already it is very dark.*
*Mother said she would not be long.*

and despairing (No XVIII):

OH LAS CUATRO PAREDES DE LA CELDA
Ah las cuatro paredes albicantes
que sin remedio dan al mismo número.

*Oh the four walls of the cell.*
*Ah the four whitening walls*
*which remorselessly come to the same number.*

Gordon Brotherston calls *Trilce* "an inexhaustible book". Indeed, the interpretations of Vallejo's preoccupations with numbers, everyday events (like meals and rain), childhood and family, imprisonment, love and hope are endless. For all its apparent modernity, Vallejo stressed that "The new poetry based on new sensibility is simple and human and, at first glance, might be taken for old, or not even invite speculation as to whether it is or is not modern." When he was in Europe the need for this humanity was obvious to him:

Un hombre pasa con un pan al hombro
¿Voy a escribir, después, sobre mi doble?
...
Otro busca en el fango huesos, cascaras
¿Cómo escribir, después, del infinito?

Un albañil cae de un techo, muere y ya
no almuerza
¿Innovar, luego, el tropo, la metáfora?
...
Alguien pasa contando con sus dedos
¿Cómo hablar del no-yó sin dar un grito?

*A man passes with a loaf on his shoulder*
*Shall I then write about my double?*
...
*Another looks for bones, rinds in the mud*
*How to write, then, about the infinite?*

*A mason falls from a roof, dies and no longer*
*eats lunch*
*To innovate, later, the trope, the metaphor?*
...
*Someone passes counting on his fingers*
*How to speak of the not-I without giving a yell?*
(*Poemas humanos*)

Vallejo. Born in 1892 in Santiago de Chuco (Libertad), Vallejo left Peru in 1923 after being framed and briefly jailed in Trujillo for a political crime. In 1928 he was a founder of the Peruvian Socialist Party; he joined the Communist Party in 1931 in Madrid; from 1936 to his death in Paris in 1938 he opposed the fascist takeover in Spain. His first volume was *Los heraldos negros* in which the dominating theme of all his work, a sense of confusion and inadequacy in the face of the unpredictability of life, first surfaces. *Trilce* (1922), his second work, elaborates on that theme but the means of expression becomes completely individual, unlike anything before it in the Spanish language. The poems contain (among other things) made-up words, distortions of syntax, their own internal logic and rhythm, graphic devices and innovative uses of sounds, clichés and alliterations. But this poetic reinvention of language is not used to the extent that form overwhelms content. On the contrary, it is precisely because meaning in the world is so hard to find that the poet has to go to extreme lengths to find an authentic means of communication. In turn, the reader is forced to reevaluate his/her view of reality. *Poemas humanos* and *España, aparta de mí este cáliz* (written as a result of Vallejo's experiences in the Spanish Civil War) were both published posthumously (1939). They broaden the perspective of *Trilce*, adding the dimension of human suffering to the personal insecurities of the earlier work.

There is no space to detail all the poets of worth since Vallejo, but James Higgins' comprehensive study outlines the careers of many who developed through the avant-garde (eg César Moro, 1903-56, a surrealist painter and poet), then the so-called 'pure', or introspective movement of the 1940s (eg Martín Adán, 1908-85), to the wider social realities of man or woman's place in a (still) unyielding world (eg Carlos Germán Belli, born 1927; Blanca Varela, born 1926).

In the 1960s, writers began to reflect the broadening horizons of that increasingly liberal decade, politically and socially, which followed the Cuban Revolution. One poet who embraced the revolutionary fervour was Javier Heraud (born Miraflores 1942). His early volumes, *El río* (1960) and *El viaje* (1961) are apparently simple in conception and expression, but display a transition from embarking on the adventure of life (the river) to autumnal imagery of solitude. In 1961 he went to the USSR, Asia, Paris and Madrid, then in 1962 to Cuba to study cinema. He returned to Peru in 1963 and joined the guerrilla Ejército de Liberación Nacional. His last poems reveal the next stage of his transition to political commitment. In 1960 he had written "I do not laugh at death. It happens simply, but I am not afraid to die among birds and trees". On 15 May 1963 he was shot by government forces near Puerto Maldonado.

Other major poets who began to publish in the 1960s were Luis Hernández (1941-77), Antonio Cisneros (born 1942), Rodolfo Hinostroza (born 1941) and Marco Martos (born 1942). In the 1970s, during the social changes propelled by the Velasco regime (1968-75), new voices arose, many from outside Lima, eg the Hora Zero group (1970-73 – Enrique Verástegui, Jorge Pimentel, Juan Ramírez Ruiz), whose energetic poetry employed slang, obscenities and other means to challenge preconceptions. Other poets of the 1970s and after include José Watanabe, Tulio Mora, Abelardo Sánchez León, Giovanna Pollarda (poet and screenwriter) and Carmen Ollé, whose *Noches de adrelina* (1981) "marks the beginning of a forthrightly feminist yet unabashedly erotic school of Peruvian poetry" (*The Peru Reader*, page 482).

• **Many sources** have been used in the preparation of this survey; special acknowledgement must be given to: James Higgins, *A History of Peruvian Literature* (Liverpool monographs in Hispanic studies 7, 1987); *The Peru Reader*, ed Orin Starn, Carlos Iván Degregori and Robin Kirk (Duke University Press, 1995); Jean Franco, *Spanish American Literature since Independence* (London and New York, 1973); Gerald Martin, *Journeys through the Labyrinth* (London and New York, 1989); Gordon Brotherston, *The Emergence of the Latin American Novel* and *Latin American Poetry* (Cambridge University Press, 1977 and 1975); Darío Villanueva and José María Viña Liste, *Trayectoria de la novela hispanoamericana actual* (Madrid, 1991). Thanks are also due to Anja Louis of Grant and Cutler Ltd, London.

## FINE ART AND SCULPTURE

The Catholic Church was the main patron of the arts during the colonial period. The innumerable churches and monasteries that sprang up in the newly-conquered territories created a demand for paintings and sculptures, met initially by imports from Europe of both works of art and of skilled craftsmen, and later by home-grown products.

### The Colonial period

An essential requirement for the inauguration of any new church was an image for the altar and many churches in Lima preserve fine examples of sculptures imported from Seville during the 16th and 17th centuries. Not surprisingly, among the earliest of these are figures of the crucified Christ, such as those in the Cathedral and the church of La Merced by Juan Martínez Montanés, one of the foremost Spanish sculptors of the day, and that in San Pedro, by his pupil Juan de Mesa of 1625. Statues of the Virgin and Child were also imported to Lima from an early date, and examples from the mid 16th century survive in the Cathedral and in Santo Domingo by Roque de Balduque, also from Seville although Flemish by birth.

Sculptures were expensive and difficult to import, and as part of their policy of relative frugality the Franciscan monks tended to favour paintings. In Lima, the museum of San Francisco now houses an excellent collection of paintings imported from Europe, including a powerful series of saints by Zubarán, as well as other works from his studio, a series of paintings of the life of Christ from Ruben's workshop and works from the circles of Ribera and Murillo. The Jesuits commissioned the Sevillian artist Juan de Valdés Leal to paint a series of the life of St Ignatius Loyola (1660s) which still hangs in San Pedro. The Cathedral museum has a curious series from the Bassano workshop of Venice representing the labours of the monks and dating from the early 17th century. Another interesting artistic import from Europe that can still be seen in Lima are the gloriously colourful painted tile decorations (*azulejos*) on the walls of the Dominican monastery, produced to order by Sevillian workshops in 1586 and 1604.

Painters and sculptors soon made their way to Peru in search of lucrative commissions including several Italians who arrived during the later 16th century. The Jesuit Bernardo Bitti (1548-1610), for example, trained in Rome before working in Lima, Cusco, Juli and Arequipa, where examples of his elegantly Mannerist paintings are preserved in the Jesuit church of the Compañia. Another Italian, Mateo Pérez de Alesio worked in the Sistine Chapel in Rome before settling in Peru. In Lima the Sevillian sculptor Pedro de Noguera (1592-1655) won the contract for the choirstalls of the Cathedral in 1623 and, together with other Spanish craftsmen, produced a set of cedar stalls decorated with vigorous figures of saints and Biblical characters, an outstanding work unmatched elsewhere in the Viceroyalty.

European imports, however, could not keep up with demand and local workshops of creole, mestizo and Indian craftsmen flourished from the latter part of the 16th century. As the Viceregal capital and the point of arrival into Peru, the art of Lima was always strongly influenced by European, especially Spanish models, but the old Inca capital of Cusco became the centre of a regional school of painting which developed its own characteristics.

A series of paintings of the 1660s, now hanging in the Museo de Arte Religioso, commemorate the colourful Corpus Christi procession of statues of the local patron saints through the streets of Cusco. These paintings document the appearance of the city and local populace, including Spanish and Inca nobility, priests and laity, rich and poor, Spaniard, Indian, African and mestizo. Many of the statues represented in this series are still venerated in the local parish churches. They are periodically painted and dressed in new robes, but underneath are the original sculptures, executed by native craftsmen. Some are of carved wood while others use the pre-conquest technique of maguey cactus covered in sized cloth.

A remarkable example of an Andean Indian who acquired European skills was Felipe Guaman Poma de Ayala whose 1,000 page letter to the King of Spain celebrating the Andean past and condemning the colonial present is discussed above (see page 58).

One of the most successful native painters was Diego Quispe Tito (1611-1681) who claimed descent from the Inca nobility and whose large canvases, often based on Flemish engravings, demonstrate the wide range of European sources that were available to Andean artists in the 17th century. But the Cusco School is best known for the anonymous devotional works where the painted contours of the figures are overlaid with flat patterns in gold, creating highly decorative images with an underlying tension between the two- and three-dimensional aspects of the work. The taste for richly-decorated surfaces can also be seen in the 17th and 18th century frescoed interiors of many Andean churches, as in Chinchero, Andahuaylillas and Huaro, and in the ornate carving on altarpieces and pulpits throughout Peru.

**Andean content** creeps into colonial religious art in a number of ways, most simply by the inclusion of elements of indigenous flora and fauna, or, as in the case of the Corpus Christi paintings, by the use of a specific setting, with recognizable buildings and individuals.

Changes to traditional Christian iconography include the representation of one of the Magi as an Inca, as in the painting of the Adoration of the Magi in San Pedro in Juli. Another example is that to commemorate his miraculous intervention in the conquest of Cusco in 1534, Santiago is often depicted triumphing over Indians instead of the more familiar Moors. Among the most remarkable 'inventions' of colonial art are the fantastically over-dressed archangels carrying muskets which were so popular in the 18th century. There is no direct European source for these archangels, but in the Andes they seem to have served as a painted guard of honour to the image of Christ or the Virgin on the high altar.

## Independence and after

Political independence from Spain in 1824 had little immediate impact on the arts of Peru except to create a demand for portraits of the new national and continental heroes such as Simón Bolívar and San Martín, many of the best of them produced by the mulatto artist José Gil de Castro (d Lima 1841). Later in the century another mulatto, Pancho Fierro (1810-1879) mocked the rigidity and pretentiousness of Lima society in lively satirical watercolours, while Francisco Laso (1823-1860), an active campaigner for political reform, made the Andean Indian into a respectable subject for oil paintings.

It was not until the latter part of the

19th century that events from colonial history became popular. The Museo de Arte in Lima has examples of grandiose paintings by Ignacio Merino (1817-1876) glorifying Columbus, as well as the gigantic romanticized 'Funeral of Atahualpa' by Luis Montero (1826-1869). A curious late flowering of this celebration of colonial history is the chapel commemorating Francisco Pizarro in Lima cathedral which was redecorated in 1928 with garish mosaic pictures of the conqueror's exploits.

**Of the modern movements** Impressionism arrived late and had a limited impact in Peru. Teofilo Castillo (1857-1922), instead of using the technique to capture contemporary reality, created frothy visions of an idealized colonial past. Typical of his work is the large 'Funeral Procession of Santa Rosa' of 1918, with everything bathed in clouds of incense and rose petals, which hangs in the Museo de Arte, in Lima. Daniel Hernández (1856-1932), founder of Peru's first Art School, used a similar style for his portraits of Lima notables past and present.

## The 20th century

During the first half of the 20th century, Peruvian art was dominated by figurative styles and local subject matter. Political theories of the 1920s recognized the importance of Andean Indian culture to Peruvian identity and created a climate which encouraged a figurative *indigenista* school of painting, derived in part from the socialist realism of the Mexican muralists. José Sabogal (1888-1956) is the best known exponent of the group which also included Mario Urteaga (1875-1957), Jorge Vinatea Reinoso (1900-1931), Enrique Camino Brent (1909-1960), Camilo Blas (1903-1984) and Alejandro González (1900-1984).

The Mexican muralist tradition persisted into the 1960s with Manuel Ugarte Eléspuru (1911) and Teodoro Núñez Ureta (1914), both of whom undertook large-scale commissions in public buildings in Lima. Examples of public sculpture in the indigenist mode can be seen in plazas and parks throughout Peru, but it was in photography that indigenism found its most powerful expression. From the beginning of the century photographic studios flourished even in smaller towns, and Martín Chambi (1891-1973) maintained studios in Cusco, Puno and Arequipa.

**From the middle of the century** artists have experimented with a variety of predominantly abstract styles and the best-known contemporary Peruvian painter, Fernando de Szyszlo (1925) has created a visual language of his own, borrowing from Abstract Expressionism on the one hand and from precolumbian iconography on the other. His strong images, which suggest rather than represent mythical beings and cosmic forces, have influenced a whole generation of younger Peruvian artists. Other leading figures whose work can be seen in public and commercial galleries in Lima include Venancio Shinki, Elda di Malio, Ricardo Weisse, Julia Nabarrete and Leoncio Villanueva. With the more stable economic and political conditions of recent years, young artists have been encouraged to stay in Peru rather than head for Miami. Art schools are flourishing in a number of provincial centres and although quality is variable the future looks bright.

## MUSIC AND DANCE

Peru is the Andean heartland. Its musicians, together with those of Bolivia, have appeared on the streets of cities all over Europe and North America. However, the costumes they wear, the instruments they play, notably the *quena* and *charango*, are not typical of Peru as a whole, only of the Cusco region. Peruvian music divides at a very basic level into that of the highlands ('Andina') and that of the coast ('Criolla').

## The Highlands

The highlands are immensely rich in terms of music and dance, with over 200 dances recorded. Every village has its fiestas and every fiesta has its communal and religious dances. Those of Paucartambo and Coylloriti (Q'olloriti) in the Cusco region moreover attract innumerable groups of dancers from far and wide. The highlands themselves can be very roughly subdivided into some half dozen major musical regions, of which perhaps the most characteristic are Ancash and the N, the Mantaro Valley, Cusco, Puno and the Altiplano, Ayacucho and Parinacochas.

There is one recreational dance and musical genre, the **Huayno**, that is found throughout the whole of the Sierra, and has become ever more popular and commercialized to the point where it is in danger of swamping and indeed replacing the other more regional dances. Nevertheless, still very popular among Indians and/or Mestizos are the Marinera, Carnaval, Pasacalle, Chuscada (from Ancash), Huaylas, Santiago and Chonguinada (all from the Mantaro) and Huayllacha (from Parinacochas). For singing only are the mestizo Muliza, popular in the Central Region, and the soulful lament of the Yaravi, originally Indian, but taken up and developed early in the 19th century by the poet and hero of independence Mariano Melgar, from Arequipa (see page 59).

The Peruvian Altiplano shares a common musical culture with that of Bolivia and dances such as the Auqui-Auqui and Sicuris, or Diabladas, can be found on either side of the border. The highland instrumentation varies from region to region, although the harp and violin are ubiquitous. In the Mantaro area the harp is backed by brass and wind instruments, notably the clarinet. In Cusco it is the *charango* and *quena* and on the Altiplano the *sicu* panpipes.

Two of the most spectacular dances to be seen are the **Baile de las Tijeras** ('scissor dance') from the Ayacucho/Huancavelica area, for men only and the pounding, stamping **Huaylas** for both sexes. Huaylas competitions are held annually in Lima and should not be missed. Indeed, owing to the overwhelming migration of peasants into the barrios of Lima, most types of Andean music and dance can be seen in the capital, notably on Sun at the so-called 'Coliseos', which exist for that purpose.

Were a Hall of Fame to be established, it would have to include the Ancashino singers La Pastorcita Huaracina and El Jilguero del Huascarán, the *charango* player Jaime Guardia, the guitar virtuoso Raul García from Ayacucho and the Lira Paucina trio from Parinacochas. However, what the young urban immigrant from the Sierra is now listening to and, above all, dancing to is 'Chicha', a hybrid of Huayno music and the Colombian Cumbia rhythm, played by such groups as Los Shapis.

## Música Criolla

The music from the coast could not be more different from that of the Sierra. Here the roots are Spanish and African. The immensely popular **Valsesito** is a syncopated waltz that would certainly be looked at askance in Vienna and the **Polca** has also suffered an attractive sea change.

Reigning over all, though, is the **Marinera**, Peru's national dance, a splendidly rhythmic and graceful courting encounter and a close cousin of Chile's and Bolivia's Cueca and the Argentine Zamba, all of them descended from the Zamacueca. The Marinera has its 'Limeña' and 'Norteña' versions and a more syncopated relative, the Tondero, found in the northern coastal regions, is said to have been influenced by slaves brought from Madagascar. All these dances are accompanied by guitars and frequently the *cajón*, a resonant wooden box on which the player sits, pounding it with his hands. Some of the great names of 'Música Criolla' are the singer/composers Chabuca Granda and Alicia Maguiña, the female singer Jesús Vásquez and the groups Los Morochucos and Hermanos Zañartu.

**Also on the coast** is to be found the music of the small black community, the 'Música Negroide' or 'Afro-Peruano', which had virtually died out when it was resuscitated in the 50s, but has since gone from strength to strength. It has all the qualities to be found in black music from the Caribbean – a powerful, charismatic beat, rhythmic and lively dancing, and strong percussion provided by the *cajón* and the *quijada de burro*, a donkey's jaw with the teeth loosened.

Some of the classic dances in the black repertoire are the Festejo, Son del Diablo, Toro Mata, Landó and Alcatraz. In the last named one of the partners dances behind the other with a candle, trying to set light to a piece of paper tucked into the rear of the other partner's waist. Nicomedes and Victoria Santa Cruz have been largely responsible for popularizing this black music and Peru Negro is another excellent professional group.

Finally, in the Peruvian Amazon region around Iquitos, local variants of the Huayno and Marinera are danced together with the Changanacui, to the accompaniment of flute and drum.

The music and dance of the forest indians has not been included in this survey because it tends to exist only in its isolated cosmos, rarely relating to, or connecting with, national or regional cultures.

# Economy

## Structure of production

Agriculture, forestry and fishing account for only 7% of gdp, but employ about a third of the labour force. In 1995 a new agriculture law abolished the land reform law imposed by the military régime and eliminated limits on land holding. It is hoped to encourage large scale investment in agroindustry and export crops.

The Costa is the most productive area of the country and has traditionally been the dominant economic region. Occupying 11% of the total land area, most of the export crops are grown here, with excellent crops of cotton, rice, sugar and fruit where the coastal desert is irrigated. Irrigation is, however, costly and the Government is hoping to substitute luxury fruit and vegetables for export instead of the thirsty sugar cane and rice.

Most food production is in the Sierra, where revitalization of agriculture is a government priority, with the aim of returning to the self-sufficiency of Inca times. Pacification in the highlands and good weather have helped food supply, and there have been improvements in living standards, although two thirds of the inhabitants of the Sierra still live in poverty.

Fishing suffered a dramatic decline in 1983 as the Niño current forced out of Peruvian waters the main catch, anchovy, whose stocks were already seriously depleted by overfishing in the 1970s. Peru lost its position as the world's leading fishmeal exporter to Chile, but by the 1990s was exporting

## Peru : Fact File

### Geographic

| | |
|---|---|
| Land area | 1,285,216 sq km |
| forested | 53.2% |
| pastures | 21.2% |
| cultivated | 2.7% |

### Demographic

| | |
|---|---|
| Population (1995) | 23,489,000 |
| annual growth rate (1990-95) | 1.7% |
| urban | 71.8% |
| rural | 28.2% |
| density | 18.3 per sq km |
| Religious affiliation | |
| Roman Catholic | 92.5% |
| Birth rate per 1,000 (1990-95) | 29.0 (world av 25.0) |

### Education and Health

| | |
|---|---|
| Life expectancy at birth, | |
| male | 62.7 years |
| female | 66.6 years |
| Infant mortality rate per 1,000 live births (1990-95) | 75.8 |
| Physicians (1992) | 1 per 1,116 persons |
| Hospital beds | 1 per 509 persons |
| Calorie intake as % of FAO requirement | 80% |
| Population age 25 and over with no formal schooling | 12.3% |
| Literate males (over 15) | 92.9% |
| Literate females (over 15) | 81.7% |

### Economic

| | |
|---|---|
| GNP (1993) | US$33,973mn |
| GNP per capita | US$1,490 |
| Public external debt (1993) | US$16,123mn |
| Tourism receipts (1992) | US$237mn |
| Inflation (annual av 1990-94) | 746.7% |
| Radio | 1 per 4.4 persons |
| Television | 1 per 12 persons |
| Telephone | 1 per 28 persons |

### Employment

| | |
|---|---|
| Population economically active (1993) | 7,109.527 |
| Unemployment rate (1993) | 7.1% |
| % of labour force in | |
| agriculture | 33.0 |
| mining | 2.4 |
| manufacturing | 10.4 |
| construction | 3.7 |
| Military forces | 115,000 |

**Source** *Encyclopaedia Britannica*

high quality fishmeal again, helped by rising fish catches and the abolition of the state monopoly, which encouraged private investment in new technology. Pescaperú began selling its assets in 1994 and seven fishmeal plants were sold in a year.

**Manufacturing** contributes 28% of gdp. After high growth rates in the early 1970s, manufacturing slumped to operating at 40% of its total capacity as purchasing power was reduced and the cost of energy, raw materials and trade credit rose faster than inflation. A consumer-led recovery in 1986 led to most of manufacturing and the construction industry working at full capacity, but the boom was followed by a severe slump in 1988-90. Growth returned in the 1990s and the areas of greatest expansion were food processing, fishmeal and transport equipment, while those sectors still adjusting to increased competition from imports, such as electrical appliances, remained stagnant or declined.

**Although mining** has traditionally been important in Peru since pre-Conquest times, the sector contracted sharply in the 1980s because of poor world prices, strikes, guerrilla activity in mining areas, rising costs and an uncompetitive exchange rate. The Fujimori Government passed a new Mining Law in 1992 to attract private investment, both domestic and foreign, and growth in mining has boomed in the 1990s with over 80 mining companies operating in the country. Copper and iron deposits are found on the S coast, but the Sierra is the principal mining area for all minerals, including silver, gold, lead and zinc.

Centromín and Mineroperú, the state mining companies, are having their assets sold off to private mining companies. Mines sold to US companies include Tintaya, a high-grade copper deposit between Cusco and

## Tourists invade as terrorists retreat

Tourism is booming in Peru after several years of decline. Numbers of foreigners entering Peru fell from 359,300 in 1988 to 216,534 in 1992, but with the elimination of the terrorist threat and greater security visitors began to return. The Fujimori Government privatized the many state-owned hotels and introduced new tax benefits for investors. Services have subsequently improved and the number of airlines and flights to Peru have increased. In 1995 485,000 tourists generated income of US$520mn, making tourism the third largest foreign exchange earner in Peru. 1996 arrivals were forecast at 600,000, with income of US$700mn, and were projected to increase by about 20% a year until 2005. Market surveys show that tourists' average length of stay has risen to 21 days and they are less likely to be including Peru as part of a whistle-stop tour of South America. Although niche tourism, such as ecotourism or adventure tourism, is flourishing, large international hotel chains are also moving in. Management contracts have been signed with big players such as Marriott, Hilton and Sheraton for new hotels in the Cusco area, where there is a shortage of rooms in the four and five star category. Nationwide the basic infrastructure is lacking to cope with greater numbers of visitors and the extra demand is putting strain on the supply of transport, guides, restaurants and entertainment for both the small, special interest groups and traditional tours.

Arequipa, and Cerro Verde, an open pit copper mine in the S. Many under-capitalized Peruvian mining companies have joined forces with foreign companies to develop concessions. The largest locally-controlled company is Compañía de Minas Buenaventura, which in a joint venture owns the largest gold mine in Latin America, Yanacocha, in Cajamarca, which produces 554,000 oz a year.

The US-owned Southern Peru Copper Corporation (SPCC) was the only major mining company not to be nationalized by the military in the 1970s, and it now produces some two thirds of all Peru's copper at its Cuajone and Toquepala mines. The company invested over US$500mn in the early 1990s in modernization and environmental improvements after vociferous public criticism for its lack of pollution control and the need for greater efficiency and competitiveness.

Official estimates for exploration, development and expansion of existing projects start at investment of US$8.7bn in 1993-2003; new projects will push up investment still further and call for spending on energy generation, roads and other infrastructure, together with housing, health and education facilities for employees. In the same period the value of metals production is forecast to rise from US$2bn to US$5bn a year with exports doubling to US$4bn. Copper output will increase from 400,000 to 900,000 tonnes a year and gold will double to 2 million troy oz.

**Oil production** comes from the northeastern jungle, although some is produced on and off the NW coast. No major new reserves have been found since 1976 and proven oil reserves have declined to 380 million barrels. Oil output fell from a peak of 195,000 b/d in 1982 to about 130,000 b/d in the mid-1990s. However, the Camisea gas and condensates field in the southeastern jungle is huge, with reserves in two deposits estimated at 12 trillion cu ft of natural gas and 700 million barrels of condensates, equivalent to 2.4 billion barrels of oil, more than six times current reserves. The field was discovered by Royal Dutch Shell in the 1980s and development of the field by the company was eventually agreed in 1996. Since the passing of new legislation in 1993, several contracts have been signed with private oil companies for exploration and development. The privatization of the state oil company, Petroperú, began piecemeal in 1996.

## Recent trends

Growing fiscal deficits in the 1980s led to increasing delays in payments to creditors and as arrears accumulated to both official agencies and commercial banks, the IMF declared Peru ineligible for further loans in 1986. President García limited public debt service payments to 10%

of foreign exchange revenues but reserves continued to fall. By 1987 the free-spending policies had pushed the country into bankruptcy and inflation soared as the Government resorted to printing money.

**President Fujimori** inherited an economy devastated by financial mismanagement and isolationist policies, with Peruvians suffering critical poverty, high infant mortality, malnutrition and appalling housing conditions. His Government had to deal with hyperinflation, terrorism and drug trafficking, compounded in 1991 by a cholera epidemic which affected hundreds of thousands of people, cut food exports and sharply curtailed tourism revenues.

An economic austerity package introduced in 1990 raised food and fuel prices and was the first stage of sweeping reforms. Monetary and fiscal control was accompanied by liberalization of the financial system, foreign investment rules, capital controls and foreign trade; the tax code, ports and customs and labour laws were reformed, monopolies eliminated and state companies privatized. Successful negotiations with creditors reinstated Peru in the international community and investors returned, but the *auto golpe* in 1992 rocked confidence and international aid was suspended until after the elections at the end of the year.

**Arrears to the IMF and World Bank** were repaid in 1993 and the Paris Club of creditor governments rescheduled debts due in 1993-94. The reform programme remained on course with emphasis put on control of inflation and tight control of the money supply. Exports and imports grew strongly and the new economic and political stability also encouraged foreign tourists to return.

In 1994 Peru registered the highest economic growth rate in the world, as gdp expanded by 12.7%. An agreement with commercial bank creditors was signed in 1995 when Peru became the last major Latin American debtor nation to convert loans at a discount into bonds, known as Brady bonds. Servicing of the new debt was deemed possible because of a steep rise in tax receipts from 4% of gdp in 1990 to 14% in 1995 and forecast to grow further to 20% of gdp by 2000. The pace of privatization was slowed because of fears of overheating and inflation, and the Government's limited capacity to spend all the proceeds on poverty reduction as required by law, but it was planned that no state companies would remain by the end of the decade.

## GOVERNMENT

Under a new constitution (approved by plebiscite in Oct 1993), a single chamber, 80 seat congress replaced the previous, two-house legislature. Men and women over 18 are eligible to vote; registration and voting is compulsory until the age of 60. Those who do not vote are fined. The President, to whom is entrusted the Executive Power, is elected for 5 years and may, under the constitution which came into force on 1 January 1994, be re-elected for a second term. In 1987 Congress approved a change in the administration of the country, proposing a system of 13 Regions to replace the 24 Departments (divided into 150 Provinces, subdivided into 1,321 Districts). The proposal remained nothing more than that until 1990, when it was renewed. It has still not been implemented, except for the Inca region, which includes the Departments of Cusco, Apurímac and Madre de Dios.

## TRANSPORT

### RAIL

Several roads and two railways run up the slopes of the Andes to reach the Sierra. These railways, once British owned, run from Lima in the centre and the ports of Matarani and Mollendo in the S. From

Lima a railway runs to La Oroya, at which point it splits, one section going to Cerro de Pasco and the other to Huancavelica, via Huancayo. Passengers are carried on the railway from Arequipa to Juliaca; here again the line splits, to Cusco and to Puno. A separate part links Cusco with Quillabamba via Machu Picchu. There are in all 2,121 km of railway (1993).

## ROAD

There are three main paved roads: the Pan-American Highway runs N-S through the coastal desert and is in good condition, though annual improvement work make parts of it a mess for months and pot holes are a problem in parts. A spur runs N-E into the Sierra to Arequipa, with a partially paved continuation to Puno on Lake Titicaca which then skirts the lake to Desaguadero, on the Bolivian frontier, a total of 3,418 km. The road to Arequipa is much improved (1995); that to Puno is not good. Similarly poor is the stretch Puno-Cusco. These routes are more usually travelled by train.

The Central Highway from Lima to Huancayo is mostly well-paved; it continues (mostly paved) to Pucallpa in the Amazon basin. Also paved and well-maintained is the direct road from Lima N to Huaraz.

All other roads in the mountains are of dirt, some good, some very bad. Each year they are affected by heavy rain and mud slides, especially those on the eastern slopes of the mountains. Repairs are limited to a minimum because of a shortage of funds. Note that some of these roads can be dangerous or impassable in the rainy season. Check beforehand with locals (not with bus companies, who only want to sell tickets) as accidents are common at these times. Total road length in 1993 was 69,942 km.

# Responsible Tourism

Much has been written about the adverse impacts of tourism on the environment and local communities. It is usually assumed that this only applies to the more excessive end of the travel industry such as the Spanish Costas and Bali. However it now seems that travellers can have an impact at almost any density and this is especially true in areas "off the beaten track" where local people may not be used to western conventions and lifestyles, and natural environments may be very sensitive.

Of course, tourism can have a beneficial impact and this is something to which every traveller can contribute. Many National Parks are part funded by receipts from people who travel to see exotic plants and animals, the Galápagos (Ecuador) and Manu (Peru) National Parks are good examples of such sites. Similarly, travellers can promote patronage and protection of valuable archaeological sites and heritages through their interest and entrance fees.

However, where visitor pressure is high and/or poorly regulated, damage can occur. It is also unfortunately true that many of the most popular destinations are in ecologically sensitive areas easily disturbed by extra human pressures. This is particularly significant because the desire to visit sites and communities that are off the beaten track is a driving force for many travellers. Eventually the very features that tourists travel so far to see may become degraded and so we seek out new sites, discarding the old, and leaving someone else to deal with the plight of local communities and the damaged environment.

Fortunately, there are signs of a new awareness of the responsibilities that the travel industry and its clients need to endorse. For example, some tour operators fund local conservation projects and travellers are now more aware of the impact they may have on host cultures and environments. We can all contribute to the success of what is variously described as responsible, green or alternative tourism. All that is required is a little forethought and consideration.

It would be impossible to identify all the possible impacts that might need to be addressed by travellers, but it is worthwhile noting the major areas in which we can all take a more responsible attitude in the countries we visit. These include, changes to natural ecosystems (air, water, land, ecology and wildlife), cultural values (beliefs and behaviour) and the built environment (sites of antiquity and archaeological significance). At an individual level, travellers can reduce their impact if greater consideration is given to their activities. Canoe trips up the headwaters of obscure rivers make for great stories, but how do local communities cope with the sudden invasive interest in their lives? Will the availability of easy tourist money and gauche behaviour affect them for the worse, possibly diluting and trivialising the significance of culture and customs? Similarly, have the environmental implications of increased visitor pressure been considered? Where does the fresh fish that feeds the trip come from? Hand caught by line is fine, but is dynamite fishing really necessary, given the scale of damage and waste that results?

Some of these impacts are caused by factors beyond the direct control of travellers, such as the management and operation of a hotel chain. However, even here it is possible to voice concern about damaging activities and an increasing number of hotels and travel operators are taking "green concerns" seriously, even if it is only to protect their share of the market.

**Environmental Legislation** Legislation is increasingly being enacted to control damage to the environment, and in some cases this can have a bearing on travellers. The establishment of National Parks may involve rules and guidelines for visitors and these should always be followed. In addition there may be local or national laws controlling behaviour and use of natural resources (especially wildlife) that are being increasingly enforced. If in doubt, ask. Finally, international legislation, principally the Convention on International Trade in Endangered Species of Wild Fauna and Flora (CITES), may affect travellers.

CITES aims to control the trade in live specimens of endangered plants and animals and also "recognizable parts or derivatives" of protected species. Sale of Black Coral, Turtle shells, protected Orchids and other wildlife is strictly controlled by signatories of the convention. The full list of protected wildlife varies, so if you feel the need to purchase souvenirs and trinkets derived from wildlife, it would be prudent to check whether they are protected. Every country included in this Handbook is a signatory of CITES. In addition, most European countries, the USA and Canada are all signatories. Importation of CITES protected species into these countries can lead to heavy fines, confiscation of goods and even imprisonment. Information on the status of legislation and protective measures can be obtained from Traffic International, UK office T (01223) 277427, e-mail traffic@wcmc.org.uk.

**Green Travel Companies and Information** The increasing awareness of the environmental impact of travel and tourism has led to a range of advice and information services as well as spawning specialist travel companies who claim to provide "responsible travel" for clients. This is an expanding field and the veracity of claims needs to be substantiated in some cases. The following organizations and publications can provide useful information for those with an interest in pursuing responsible travel opportunities.

**Organizations** **Green Flag International** Aims to work with travel industry and conservation bodies to improve environments at travel destinations and also to promote conservation programmes at resort destinations. Provides a travellers' guide for "green" tourism as well as advice on destinations, T (UK 01223) 890250. **Tourism Concern** Aims to promote a greater understanding of the impact of tourism on host communities and environments; Southlands College, Wimbledon Parkside, London SW19 5NN, T (UK 0181) 944-0464, e-mail tourconcern@gn.apc.org). **Centre for Responsible Tourism** CRT coordinates a North American network and advises on N American sources of information on responsible tourism. CRT, PO Box 827, San Anselmo, California 94979, USA. **Centre for the Advancement of Responsive Travel** CART has a range of publications available as well as information on alternative holiday destinations. T (UK – 01732) 352757.

**Publications** *The Good Tourist* by Katie Wood and Syd House (1991) published by Mandarin Paperbacks; addresses issues surrounding environmental impacts of tourism, suggests ways in which damage can be minimised, suggests a range of environmentally sensitive holidays and projects.

# Will you help us?

Our authors explore and research tirelessly to bring you the most complete and up-to-date package of information possible. Yet the contributions we receive from our readers are also **vital** to the success of our Handbooks. There are many thousands of you out there making delightful (and sometimes alarming!) discoveries every day.

So important is this resource that we make a special offer to every reader who contacts us with information on places, experiences, people, hotels, restaurants, well-informed warnings or any other features which could enhance the enjoyment of our travellers everywhere. When writing to us, please give the edition and page number of the Handbook you are using.

So please take a few minutes to get in touch with us - we can benefit, you can benefit and all our other readers can benefit too!

**Please write to us at:**

Footprint Handbooks,
6 Riverside Court, Lower Bristol Road, Bath BA2 3DZ England
Fax: +44 (0)1225 469461 E Mail travellers@footprint.cix.co.uk

# Lima



PERU'S capital city tends to elicit an extreme response from even the most casual of acquaintances – you either love it or hate it. The 8 million inhabitants of this great, sprawling metropolis will defend it to the hilt and, in their next breath, tell you everything that's wrong with it.

The well-established cliché is to call Lima a city of contradictions, but it's difficult to get beyond that description. Here you'll encounter grinding poverty and conspicuous wealth in abundance. If the grim squalour of the poorer districts and constant begging of street children gets too much at least the visitor has the option of heading for Miraflores or San Isidro, whose chic shops, bars and restaurants would grace any major European city.

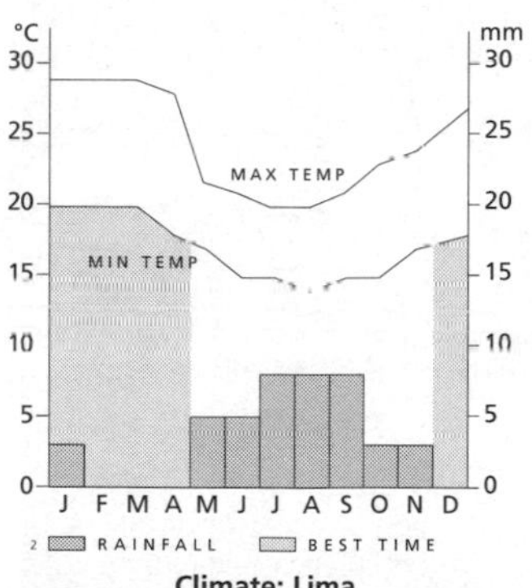

Climate: Lima

Lima's image as a place to avoid or quickly pass through is enhanced by the thick grey blanket of cloud that descends in May and hangs around for the next seven months, seemingly perched on top of the many skyscrapers. If the visitor, however, could hang around until the blanket is pulled aside in November to reveal bright blue skies, they would see a very different place. This is beach weather for all Limeños, when weekends become a raucous mix of sun, sea, salsa and ceviche and your average sardine would feel claustrophobic at the city's more popular coastal resorts.

While Lima has the ability to incite frustration, fear and despair in equal measure it can also, given the chance, entertain, excite and inform. It boasts some of the finest museums and historical monuments in the country and the best cuisine and nightlife. Scratch beneath that coating of grime and decay and you'll find one of the most vibrant and hospitable cities anywhere.

## HISTORY

Lima, originally named *La Ciudad de Los Reyes*, The City of Kings, in honour of the Magi, was founded on Epiphany in 1535 by Francisco Pizarro. From then until the independence of the South American republics in the early 19th century, it was the chief city of Spanish South America. The name Lima, a corruption of the Quechua name *Rimac* (speaker), was not adopted until the end of the 16th century.

At the time of the Conquest, Lima was already an important commercial centre. It continued to grow throughout the colonial years and by 1610, the population was 26,000, of whom 10,000 were Spaniards. This was the time of greatest prosperity. The commercial centre of the city was just off the Plaza de Armas in the Calle de Mercaderes (1st block of Jr

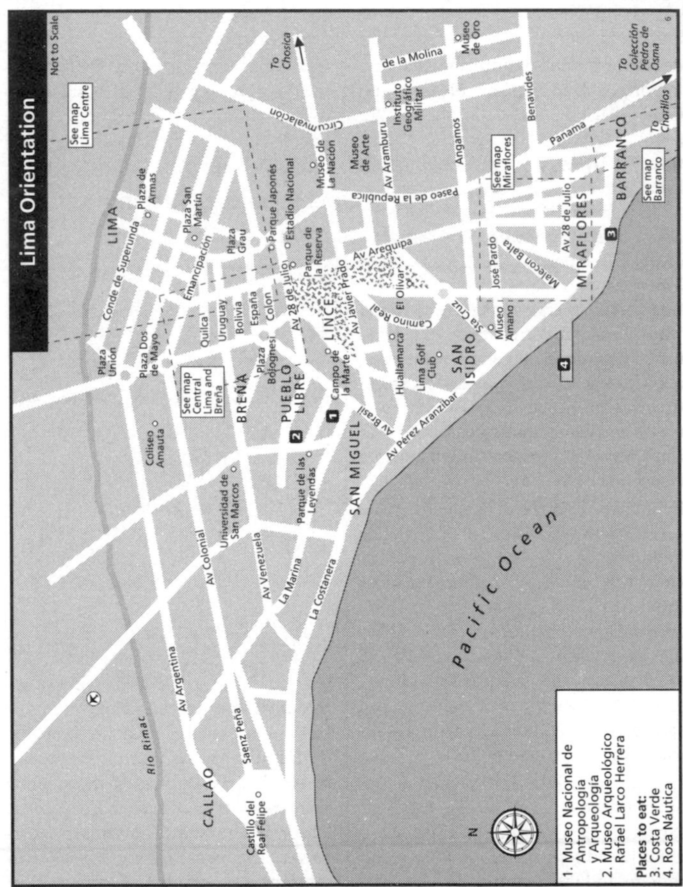

### 'At the time of going to press ...'

Lima was the site of the first printing press in South America (presses had been established earlier in Mexico). Probably the first document to come off the Lima press of Antonio Ricardo was *Pragmática sobre los diez días del año*, ordering that 10 days in Oct be skipped in order to bring South America into line with the new Gregorian calendar. The only known copy is in the John Carter Brown Library, Providence, Rhode Island. Most probably the second product was the trilingual (Spanish/Quechua/Aymara) *Doctrina Cristiana* published in 1584. A scholar called Rodríguez Buckingham speculates that Antonio Ricardo would have had to make a living from the time of his arrival in Lima (in the early 1580s) until he had official permission to begin printing. Ricardo may therefore have produced illicit playing cards and religious pictures.

Monica Barnes, editor of the journal, *Andean Past*.

de la Unión) and was full of merchandise imported from Spain, Mexico and China. All the goods from the mother country arrived at the port of Callao, from where they were distributed all over Peru and as far away as Argentina.

At this time South American trade with Spain was controlled by a monopoly of Sevillian merchants and their Limeño counterparts who profited considerably. It wasn't until the end of the 18th century that free trade was established between Spain and her colonies, allowing Peru to enjoy a period of relative wealth. Much of this wealth was reinvested in the country, particularly in Lima where educational establishments benefitted most of all.

**Ever since Francis Drake** made a surprise attack on Callao on the night of 13 February 1579, plans were made to strengthen the city's defences against the threat from English pirates. However, an argument raged over the following century between Spain and Lima as to what form the defences should take and who should pay. Finally, it was agreed to encircle the city with a wall, which was completed by 1687.

Life for the white descendents of the Spaniards was good, although *criollos* (Spaniards born in the colonies) were not allowed to hold public office. The Indians and those of mixed blood were treated as lesser citizens. Their movements were strictly controlled. They weren't allowed to live in the city centre; only in areas allocated to them, referred to as *reducciones*.

### Earthquakes and wars

There were few cities in the Old World that could rival Lima's wealth and luxury, until the terrible earthquake of 1746. The city's notable elegance was instantly reduced to dust. Only 20 of the 3,000 houses were left standing and an estimated 4,000 people were killed. Despite the efforts of the Viceroy, José Manso de Velasco, to rebuild the city, Lima never recovered her former glory.

During the 19th century man-made disasters rather than natural ones wreaked havoc on the the capital and its people. The population dropped from 87,000 in 1810 to 53,000 in 1842, after the wars of Independence, and the city suffered considerable material damage during the Chilean occupation which followed the War of the Pacific.

### Towards the 20th century

Lima was built on both banks of the Rimac river. The walls erected at the end of the 17th century surrounded three sides while the Rimac bordered the fourth. By the time the North American railway engineer, Henry Meiggs, was contracted to demolish the city walls in

1870, Lima had already begun to spread outside the original limits. Meiggs reneged on his contract by leaving much of the wall intact in the poor area around Cercado, where the ruins can still be seen.

By the beginning of the 20th century the population had risen to 140,000 and the movement of people to the coastal areas meant that unskilled cheap labour was available to man the increasing numbers of factories. Around this time, major improvements were made to the city's infrastructure in the shape of modern sanitation, paved streets, new markets and plazas. For the entertainment of the burgeoning middle classes, a modern race track was opened in what is now the Campo de Marte, as well as the municipal theatre, the Teatro Segura. At the same time, the incumbent president, José Pardo, dramatically increased government expenditure on education, particularly in Lima.

Large-scale municipal improvements continued under the dictatorship of Augusto Leguía and the presidency of Oscar Benavides, who focussed on education for the masses, housing facilities for workers and low cost restaurants in the slum areas which were now growing up around Lima.

## MODERN LIMA

Lima (*Phone code* 01) continues to struggle to live up to its former reputation as the City of Kings. It is now very dirty and seriously affected by smog for much of the year, and is surrounded by 'Pueblos Jóvenes', or shanty settlements of squatters who have migrated from the Sierra. Villa El Salvador, a few miles SE of Lima, may be the world's biggest 'squatters' camp' with 350,000 people building up

### Impressions of Lima

Ever since the earthquake of 1746 all but razed the city to the ground, descriptions of Lima have tended towards the unfavourable.

Take the German naturalist and traveller, Alexander Von Humboldt, for instance, who considered life in the city to be tedious with few diversions and described driving round the capital in 1802 thus: "_the filthyness of the streets, strewn with dead dogs and donkeys, and the unevenness of the ground make it impossible to enjoy." Charles Darwin, who made a short visit in 1839 during his historic research trip on the *Beagle*, was no less graphic in his appraisal. He found it "in a wretched state of decay; the streets are nearly unpaved and heaps of filth are piled up in all directions where black vultures pick up bits of carrion."

Rather more complimentary was Jean Jacques Tschudi, the Swiss naturalist who made extensive explorations in Peru. He wrote: "The impression produced at first sight of Lima is by no means favourable, for the periphery, the quarter which the stranger first enters, contains none but old, dilapidated and dirty homes; but on approaching the vicinity of the principal square, the place improves so greatly that the miserable appearance it presents at first sight is easily forgotten."

The French feminist, Flora Tristan, who was Paul Gauguin's grandmother, came to Peru in 1834. She travelled extensively in the country and wrote a fascinating account of her experience, *Peregrinaciones de una Paria*, in which she painted Lima in a most favourable light: "The city has many beautiful monuments", she wrote, "The homes are neatly constructed, the streets well marked out, are long and wide." Paul Gauguin himself spent his early formative years in Lima, where he was brought by his parents who were fleeing Napoleon Bonaparte's France. Towards the end of his life Gauguin wrote a collection of memoirs in which he included his impressions of Lima.

an award-winning self-governing community since 1971. They pay no taxes to the government but when a school is built the government will pay for the roof.

Over the years the city has changed out of recognition. Many of the hotels and larger business houses have moved to the fashionable seaside suburbs of Miraflores and San Isidro, thus moving the commercial heart of the city away from the Plaza de Armas. Among the traditional buildings which still survive soar many skyscrapers which have changed the old skyline.

Half of the town-dwellers of Peru now live in Lima. The metropolitan area contains eight million people, nearly one third of the country's total population, and two-thirds of its industries.

### Climate

Only 12° S of the equator, one would expect a tropical climate, but Lima has two distinct seasons. The winter is from May to Nov, when a damp *garúa* (Scotch mist) hangs over the city, making everything look greyer than it is already. It is damp and cold, 8° to 15°C. The sun breaks through around Nov and temperatures rise as high as 30°C. Note that the temperature in the coastal suburbs is lower than the centre because of the sea's influence. Also protect against the sun's rays when visiting the beaches around Lima, or elsewhere in Peru.

## PLACES OF INTEREST IN CENTRAL LIMA

**Street names**: several blocks, with their own names, make up a long street, a *jirón* (often abbreviated to Jr). The visitor is greatly helped by the corner signs which bear both names, of the *jirón* and the name of the block. The new and old names of streets are used interchangeably: remember that Colmena is also Nicolás de Piérola, Wilson is Inca Garcilaso de la Vega, and Carabaya is also Augusto N Wiese. The city's urban motorway is often called 'El Zanjón' (the ditch) or Via Expresa.

**The traditional heart of the city**, at least in plan, is still what it was in colonial days. Even though many of the buildings are run down, there being no money to restore them, it is still worth visiting the colonial centre to see the fine architecture and works of art. Most of what the tourist wants to see is in this area.

### Plaza de Armas

One block S of the Río Rímac lies the Plaza de Armas, which has been declared a World Heritage by Unesco. The Plaza used to be the city's most popular meeting point and main market. Before the building of the Acho bullring in the 1760s, bullfights were traditionally held here.

Around the great Plaza de Armas stand the **Palacio de Gobierno**, the **Cathedral**, the **Archbishop's Palace**, the **Municipalidad** and the **Club Unión**. The **Correo Central** (Post Office) is opposite the visitors' entrance to the Government Palace. Running along two sides are arcades with shops: Portal de Escribanos and Portal de Botoneros. In the centre of the Plaza is a bronze fountain dating from 1650.

**The Palacio de Gobierno** (Government Palace), on the N side of the Plaza, stands on the site of the original palace built by Pizarro. When the Viceroyalty was founded it became the official residence of the representative of the crown. Despite the opulent furnishings inside, the exterior remained a poor sight throughout colonial times, with shops lining the front facing the Plaza. The facade was remodelled in the second half of the 19th century, then transformed in 1921, following a terrible fire. In 1937, the palace was totally rebuilt.

The visitors' entrance is on Jr de la Unión. There are no set schedules for visiting, only private tours. Visits are organized by Lima Tours (see below). The ceremonial changing of the guard is at 1145.

**The Cathedral** stands on the site of two previous buildings. The first, finished in

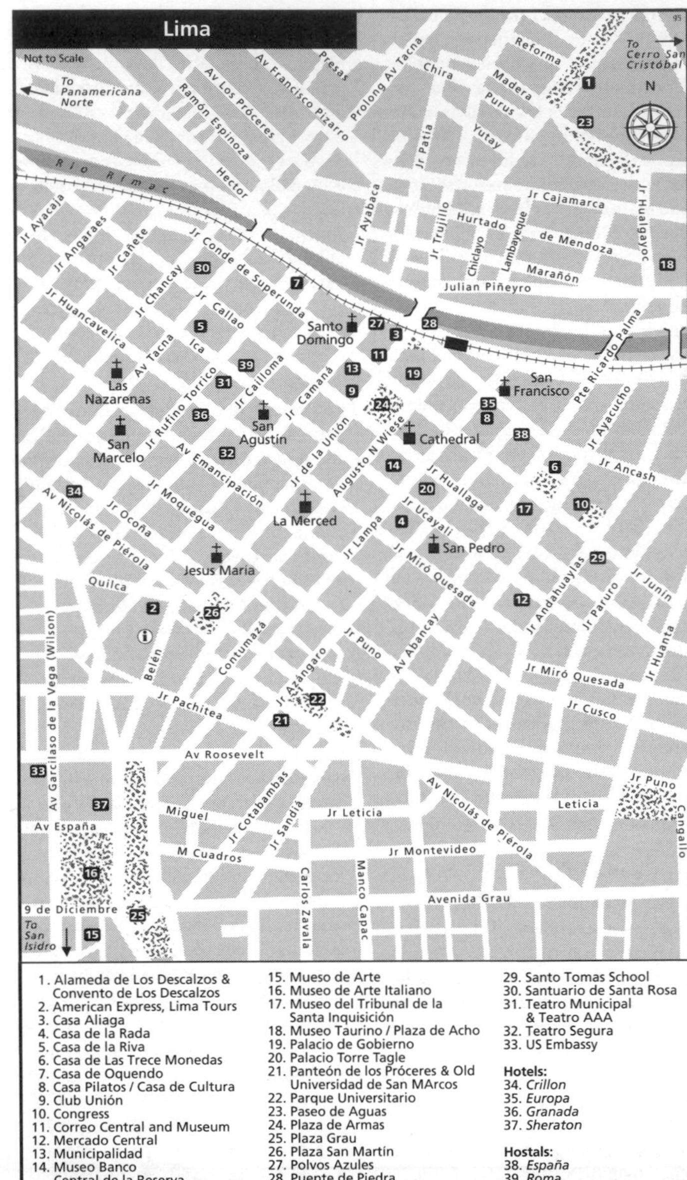
Lima
Not to Scale
To Panamericana Norte
To Cerro San Cristóbal
N
Río Rímac
Av Los Próceres
Ramón Espinoza
Av Francisco Pizarro
Presas
Prolong Av Tacna
Chira
Reforma
Madera
Purus
Yutay
Jr Patia
Hector
Jr Ayabaca
Jr Trujillo
Hurtado
Jr Cajamarca
de Mendoza
Chiclayo
Lambayeque
Marañón
Jr Hualgayoc
Julian Piñeyro
Jr Ayacaja
Jr Angaraes
Jr Cañete
Jr Conde de Superunda
Jr Chancay
Jr Huancavelica
Jr Callao
Av Tacna
Ica
Santo Domingo
Pte Ricardo Palma
San Francisco
Jr Ayacucho
Jr Ancash
Las Nazarenas
Jr Rufino Torrico
Jr Cailloma
Jr Camaná
San Agustín
Jr de la Unión
Augusto N Wiese
Cathedral
San Marcelo
Av Emancipación
Jr Huallaga
Jr Ucayali
Av Nicolás de Piérola
Jr Moquegua
Jr Ocoña
La Merced
Jr Lampa
San Pedro
Jr Miró Quesada
Jesus Maria
Quilca
Jr Andahuaylas
Jr Paruro
Jr Junín
Av Garcilaso de la Vega (Wilson)
Belén
Contumazá
Jr Azángaro
Jr Puno
Av Abancay
Jr Miró Quesada
Jr Huanta
Jr Pachitea
Jr Cusco
Av Roosevelt
Av Nicolás de Piérola
Jr Puno
Cangallo
Miguel
Jr Cotabambas
Jr Sandia
Jr Leticia
Leticia
Av España
M Cuadros
Jr Montevideo
Carlos Zavala
Manco Capac
Avenida Grau
9 de Diciembre
To San Isidro
1. Alameda de Los Descalzos & Convento de Los Descalzos
2. American Express, Lima Tours
3. Casa Aliaga
4. Casa de la Rada
5. Casa de la Riva
6. Casa de Las Trece Monedas
7. Casa de Oquendo
8. Casa Pilatos / Casa de Cultura
9. Club Unión
10. Congress
11. Correo Central and Museum
12. Mercado Central
13. Municipalidad
14. Museo Banco Central de la Reserva
15. Mueso de Arte
16. Museo de Arte Italiano
17. Museo del Tribunal de la Santa Inquisición
18. Museo Taurino / Plaza de Acho
19. Palacio de Gobierno
20. Palacio Torre Tagle
21. Panteón de los Próceres & Old Universidad de San MArcos
22. Parque Universitario
23. Paseo de Aguas
24. Plaza de Armas
25. Plaza Grau
26. Plaza San Martín
27. Polvos Azules
28. Puente de Piedra
29. Santo Tomas School
30. Santuario de Santa Rosa
31. Teatro Municipal & Teatro AAA
32. Teatro Segura
33. US Embassy
Hotels:
34. Crillon
35. Europa
36. Granada
37. Sheraton
Hostals:
38. España
39. Roma

1555, was partly paid for by Francisca Pizarro on the condition that her father, the *Conquistador*, was buried there. A larger church, however, was soon required to complement the city's status as an Archbishopric. In 1625, the three naves of the main building were completed while work continued on the towers and main door. The new building was reduced to rubble in the earthquake of 1746 and the existing church, completed in 1755, is a reconstruction on the lines of the original.

The interior is immediately impressive, with its massive columns and high nave. Also of note are the splendidly carved stalls (mid-17th century), the silver-covered altars surrounded by fine woodwork, mosaic-covered walls bearing the coats of arms of Lima and Pizarro and an allegory of Pizarro's commanders, the 'Thirteen Men of Isla del Gallo'. The assumed remains of Franscisco Pizarro lie in a small chapel, the first on the right of the entrance, in a glass coffin, though later research indicates that they reside in the crypt.

There is a Museo de Arte Religioso in the cathedral, free guided tours (English available, give tip), ask to see the picture restoration room. The cathedral is open to visitors Tues-Sun 1000-1800; all-inclusive entrance ticket, US$2, students US$1.

Next to the cathedral is the **Archbishop's Palace**, rebuilt in 1924, with a superb wooden balcony.

**The Municipalidad de Lima** is worth visiting to see the collection of paintings by the Peruvian artist, Ignacio Merino (1817-1876), who left all his pieces to the State. Some are kept here and the others in the Museo de Arte (see below). The library has some impressive woodwork. There is also a miniature replica of the boat *La Victorieuse*, which was successfully commanded by the French Admiral du Petit Thouars in the War of the Pacific. Open 0800-1500, Mon-Fri, free admission.

### Around the centre

The Jr de La Unión, the main shopping street, runs to the Plaza de Armas. It has been converted into a pedestrian precinct which teems with life in the evening. In the two blocks S of Jr Unión, known as C Belén, several shops sell souvenirs and curios. The shops nearer to the best hotels are more expensive.

From the Plaza, passing the Government Palace on the left, straight ahead is the **Desamparados** Station of the Central Railway. The name, which means "the helpless ones", comes from the orphanage and church that used to be nearby.

**The Puente de Piedra**, behind the Palacio de Gobierno is a Roman-style stone bridge built in 1610. Until about 1870 it was the only bridge strong enough to take carriages across the river Rimac to the district of the same name. Though this part of the city enjoyed considerable popularity in Colonial times, it could no longer be considered fashionable.

The **Alameda de los Descalzos** was designed in the early 17th century as a restful place to stroll and soon became one of the most popular meeting places. People of all social classes would gather here for their Sunday walk, some up to the cross at the top of **Cerro San Cristóbal**. Travellers today would be ill-advised to follow in their footsteps as this can be a dangerous area to wander around alone. Worth visiting on the Alameda de los Descalzos, though, is the **Convento de los Descalzos** (see under **Churches** below). Near the Alameda is the **Paseo de Aguas**, which was also popular for a Sunday stroll in days gone by

On Jr Hualgayoc is the bullring in the **Plaza de Acho**, famous for once being the largest in the world and the first in the Spanish America, inaugurated on 20 January 1766. Limeños have always been great enthusiasts of bullfighting and in 1798 a royal decree had to be passed forbidding fights on Sundays as people were failing to attend mass. Next to the bullring is the **Museo Taurino** (see **Museums** below).

July is the month when the most famous fighters come from Spain for the *Fiestas Patrias*. The season is also from Oct to the first week of Dec. Famous *toreros* practise in the Lima ring, the oldest in the Americas, and fighting bulls are of Spanish stock.

Wedged between Av Abancay and Jr Ayacucho is **Plaza Bolívar**, from where General José de San Martín proclaimed Peru's independence. The plaza is dominated by the equestrian statue of the Liberator. Behind lies the Congress building which occupies the former site

## A fashion for passion

A unique form of women's dress worn by Lima's upper class *mestizas* – women born in the colonies of Spanish origin – in the 18th century was the *saya* and *manto*. Both were of Moorish origin. The *saya* was an overskirt of dark silk, worn tight at the waist with either a narrow or wide bottom. The *manto* was like a thick, black veil fastened by a band at the back of the waist where it joined the *saya*. It was brought over the shoulders and head and drawn over the face so closely that only a small, triangular space was left uncovered, sufficient for one eye to peep through. This earned them the title *Las Tapadas*, or "covered ones".

The fashion was created by Lima's *mestizas* in order to compete in the flirting stakes with their Spanish-born counterparts, whose tiny waists and coquettish fan-waving was turning men's heads. The *tapadas*, though veiled, were by no means modest. Their skirts were daringly short, revealing their appealingly tiny feet, and necklines plunged to scandalously low levels. The French feminist, Flora Tristan, was much taken with this brazen show. She commented: "I am sure it needs little imagination to appreciate the consequences of this time-honoured practice."

One consequence of this fashion, which ensured anonymity, was that Lima's *mestizas* could freely indulge in romantic trysts with their lovers. Often, however, they were content with some playful flirting – sometimes with their unwitting husbands. Another consequence of their anonymity was political. Many *tapadas* used their afternoon strolls to pass notes and messages to the organizers of the independence movement. This romantic and political intrigue usually took place on the Paseo de Aguas, a popular walkway of pools and gardens built by the Viceroy.

"Tapado con saya y manto"
(After a Bonnafé lithograph)

of the **Universidad de San Marcos**, the first University in the Americas. Founded by the Dominicans in 1551, students first began to use this building in 1574. The University now occupies other premises away from the city centre.

The newer parts of the city are based on **Plaza San Martín**, S of Jr de la Unión, with a statue of San Martín in the centre. One and a quarter km W is the **Plaza Dos de Mayo**. About 1 km due S of this again is the circular **Plaza Bolognesi**, from which many major *avenidas* radiate.

## Colonial Mansions

At Jr Ucayali 363, is the **Palacio Torre Tagle**, the city's best surviving specimen of secular colonial architecture. It was built in 1735 for Don José Bernardo de Tagle y Bracho, to whom King Philip V gave the title of First Marquis of Torre Tagle. The house remained in the family until it was acquired by the government in 1918. Today, it is still used by the Foreign Ministry, but visitors are allowed to enter courtyards to inspect the fine, Moorish-influenced wood-carving in balconies, wrought iron work, and a 16th-century coach complete with commode. During working hours, Mon-Fri, visitors may enter the patio only.

Another historic mansion worth visiting is the late 16th century **Casa de Jarava** or **Pilatos** opposite the San Francisco church, Jr Ancash 390, open 0830-1645, Mon-Fri. **Casa La Riva**, Jr Ica 426, T 428-2643, is open 1000-1300, 1400-1600, it has an 18th century porch and balconies, a small gallery with some 20th century paintings. It is run by the Entre Nous Society. **Casa de Oquendo** or **Osambela** is at Conde de Superunda 298. It is said that José de San Martín stayed here after proclaiming independence from Spain. The house is typical of Lima secular architecture with two patios and a broad staircase leading from the first to the upper floor. Art exhibitions are staged here; open 0900-1300.

**Casa Negreiros**, at Jr Azángaro 532, once belonged to Don José Balta, one time president of Peru. The patio with Ionic columns is one of the best Neoclassical examples of its type in Lima. The house is now run as a restaurant. **Casa de las Trece Monedas** at Jr Ancash 536 was built in 1787 by Counts from Genoa, it still has the original doors and window grills.

The **Casa Aliaga**, Unión 224, is still occupied by the Aliaga family but has been opened to the public. Lima Tours has exclusive rights to include the house in its tours; T 424-5110/7560/9386. The house contains what is said to be the oldest ceiling in Lima and is furnished entirely in the colonial style. Don Jerónimo de Aliaga was one of the 13 commanders to arrive with Francisco Pizarro, and all 13 were given land around the main square to build their own houses when Lima was founded in 1535.

**Casa Barbieri**, Jr Callao, near Jr Rufino Torrico – is a fine old 18th-century town house in the Sevillian style. Ring the bell in the entrance hall for permission to look at the patios. **Casa Museo Prado**, Jr Cusco 448, visitable when Sr Prado is in residence, is a beautifully maintained house with early 19th-century front and, apparently, a 17th-century patio. **Casa de Riva Agüero**, Jr Camaná 457, has the library and archives of the Universidad Católica on the 1st floor; the 2nd floor has a small folk art museum. A special appointment is needed to visit the rest of the house.

**AAA Theatre** (Amateur Artists' Association), Jr Ica 323, is in a lovely 18th-century house with an *azaguán*, a covered area between the door and patio, a common feature in houses of this period. **Casa de la Rada**, or **Goyoneche**, Jr Ucayali 358, opposite Palacio Torre Tagle, is an extremely fine mid-18th-century town house in the French manner which now belongs to a bank. The patio and first reception room are open occasionally to the public.

## Churches

**La Merced** Church and Monastery are in Plazuela de la Merced, Unión y Huancavelica. The first mass in Lima was said here on the site of the first church to be built. At independence the Virgin of La Merced was made a Marshal of the Peruvian army. The restored colonial façade is a fine example of Baroque architecture. Inside are some magnificent altars and the choir stalls and the vestry's panelled ceiling are also noteworthy. A door from the right of the nave leads into the Monastery where you can see some 18th century religious paintings in the sacristy. The cloister dates from 1546. The church is open 0700-1230, 1600-2000 every day and its monastery 0800-1200 and 1500-1730 daily.

**Santo Domingo** Church and Monastery is on the 1st block of Jr Camaná. Built in 1549, the church is still as originally planned with a nave and two aisles covered by a vaulted ceiling, though the present ceiling dates from the 17th century. The Cloister is one of the most attractive in the city and dates from 1603. The second Cloister is much less elaborate. A chapel, dedicated to San Martín de Porres, one of Peru's most revered saints, leads off from a side corridor. Between the two cloisters is the Chapter House (1730), which was once the premises of the Universidad de San Marcos. Beneath the sacristy are the tombs of San Martín de Porres and Santa Rosa de Lima (see below). In 1669, Pope Clement presented the alabaster statue of Santa Rosa in front of the altar.

Entrance, US$2.75, students US$1.25; monastery and tombs open 0900-1300, 1500-1800 Mon-Sat; Sun and holidays am only. Basilica de La Veracruz is open lunchtimes. The main hall has some interesting relics.

**San Francisco** Church and Monastery, stand on the first block of Jr Lampa, corner of Ancash. The baroque church, which was finished in 1674, was one of the few edifices to withstand the 1746 earthquake. The nave and aisles are lavishly decorated in the Moorish, or Mudejar, style. The Choir, which dates from 1673, is notable for its beautifully-carved seats in Nicaraguan hardwood and its Mudejar ceiling. There is a valuable collection of paintings by the Spanish artist, Francisco de Zuburán (1598-1664) which depict the apostles and various saints.

The monastery is famous for the Sevillian tilework and panelled ceiling in the cloisters (1620). The 17th century *retablos* in the main cloister are carved from cedar and represent scenes from the life of San Francisco, as do the paintings. A broad staircase leading down to a smaller cloister is covered by a remarkable carved wooden dome dating from 1625. Next to this smaller cloister is the Capilla de la Soledad where a café is open to the public. The Catacombs under the church and part of the monastery are well worth seeing. This is where an estimated 25,000 Limeños were buried before the main cemetery was opened in 1808.

The church and monastery are open 0930-1745, entry US$1.80, US$0.70 students, US$0.50 children, only with guide, Spanish and English (recommended), last groups start at 1245 and 1745 daily.

**San Pedro** Church and Monastery is on the 3rd block of Jr Ucayali. The church, finished by Jesuits in 1638, has an unadorned facade, different from any other in the city. In one of the massive towers hangs a 5-ton bell called *La Abuelita* (the grandmother), first rung in 1590, which sounded the Declaration of Independence in 1821. The contrast between the sober exterior and sumptuous interior couldn't be more striking. The altars are marvellous, in particular the high altar, attributed to the skilled craftsman, Matias Maestro. The church also boasts Moorish-style balconies and rich, gilded wood carvings in the choir and vestry, all tiled throughout. The most important paintings in the church are hung near the main entrance.

In the monastery, the sacristy is a beautiful example of 17th century architecture. Also of note are La Capilla de Nuestra Señora de la O and the penitentiary. Several Viceroys are buried below. The church and monastery are open 0700-1300, 1740-2030 every day.

**Santuario de Santa Rosa** is on Av Tacna, 1st block. Santa Rosa is the first Saint of the Americas and Patron Saint of Lima. Born on 20 April 1586, Rosa of Lima became a member of the third Order of St Dominic and established an infirmary for destitute children and old people in her family home. She died at the age of 31 on 23 August 1617 and was beatified on 16 December 1668. 30 Aug is her day.

The small but graceful church was built in 1728 and contains the "Little Doctor" image of Jesus who helped Rosa cure the sick. Beyond the church is a sanctuary where she was born and lived. There is a tiny room where she would allow herself only 2 hrs' sleep each night on a bed of 2 tree trunks with stones as pillows. A chapel was later built on the site.

The hermitage in the garden was built by Rosa herself and she would retire there to pray alone. The well, into which she threw the key to the padlocked chain around her waist, now receives petitions from the faithful for forgiveness and thanksgivings. The sanctuary is open 0930-1300, 1500-1800 daily; entrance to the grounds is free.

The 18th century **Las Nazarenas Church**, on Av Tacna, 4th block, was built around an image of Christ Crucified painted by a liberated slave in the mid 16th century. In the earthquake of 1655, the church collapsed but the painting on the wall remained intact. This was deemed a miracle and the painting became the most venerated image in Lima. Together with an oil copy of El Señor de los Milagros (Lord of Miracles), the image is encased in a gold frame and carried on a silver litter – the whole weighing nearly a ton – through the streets on 18, 19, and 28 Oct and again on 1 Nov (All Saints' Day). The church is open 0700-1130 and 1630-2000 daily.

**San Agustín** is on Jr Ica, 251, W of the Plaza de Armas. Its façade (1720) is a splendid example of churrigueresque architecture. There are carved choir stalls and effigies, and a sculpture of Death, said to have frightened its maker into an early grave. Open 0830-1200, 1530-1730 daily, ring for entry. Since being damaged in the last earthquake the church has been sensitively restored, but the sculpture of Death is in storage.

The 18th century **Jesús María** on Jr Moquegua, 1st block, contains some of the finest paintings and gilded Baroque altars in all of Lima. The church of **Magdalena Vieja**, built in 1557, but reconstructed in 1931, with altar pieces of gilded and carved wood, is particularly fine. It can be seen during a visit to the Museum of Archaeology on Plaza Bolívar in Pueblo Libre (see **Museums** below).

Another church worth seeing for its two beautiful colonial doors is **San Marcelo**, at Av de la Emancipación, 4th block. The interior is also remarkable, particularly the 18th century gold leaf high altar and pulpit and the religious paintings sited above attractive Sevillian tiles.

The **Convento de Los Descalzos** on the Alameda de Los Descalzos in Rímac was founded in 1592 and contains over 300 paintings of the Cusco, Quito and Lima schools which line the four main cloisters and two ornate chapels. The chapel of El Carmen was constructed in 1730 and is notable for its baroque gold leaf altar. A small chapel dedicated to Nuestra Señora de la Rosa Mística has some fine Cusqueña paintings. Opposite, in the chapel dedicated to Señora de los Angeles, Admiral Grau made his last confession before the battle of Angamos.

The museum shows the life of the Franciscan friars during colonial and early republican periods. The cellar, infirmary, pharmacy and a typical cell have been restored. The library has not yet been incorporated into the tour (researchers may be permitted to see specific books on request). The convent is open daily 0930-1300, 1500-1745, except Tues, entrance US$1. Guided tour only, 45 mins in Spanish, but worth it.

The church of **Santo Tomás**, on Junín y Andahuaylas, is now a school – Gran Unidad Escolar 'Mercedes Cabello de Carbonera'. It is said to have the only circular cloister in the world apart from St Peter's in Rome, and a fine 17th-century Italian-designed baroque library. Ask the doorman on Andahuaylas to see inside.

**NB** Churches are open between 1830 and 2100 unless otherwise stated. Many are closed to visitors on Sun.

## MUSEUMS

There are two museums of anthropology and archaeology, the original and a new one opened in 1990. The former contains the original pottery collection but the latter has a much bigger display and many activities. The old museum is **Museo Nacional de Antropología y Arqueología**, Plaza Bolívar in Pueblo Libre, not to be confused with Plaza Bolívar in the centre. On display are ceramics of the Chimú, Nasca, Mochica and Pachacámac cultures, various Inca curiosities and works of art, and interesting textiles. The museum houses the Raimondi Stela and the Tello obelisk from Chavín, and a reconstruction of one of the galleries at Chavín. It also has a model of Machu Picchu.

Open Tues-Sat 0900-1800, admission US$1.50; T 463-5070. Guides are available. To get there take bus 12 or colectivo along Av Tacna or Av Venezuela, get off at Av Vivanco and walk two blocks; or any bus or colectivo going along Av Brasil, get off at block 22, Av Vivanco, and walk seven blocks. Taxi US$2.

**Museo de la Nación**, on Javier Prado Este 2465, San Borja, T 476-9875/476-9878, in the huge Banco de la Nación building. This is the new anthropological and archaeological museum for the exhibition and study of the art and history of the aboriginal races of Peru. There are good explanations in Spanish on Peruvian history, with ceramics, textiles and displays of almost every ruin in Peru. There is an excellent copy of the tomb of the Señor de Sipán and a display of the discoveries. Another exhibition shows artefacts from Batán Grande near Chiclayo (Sicán culture). The museum holds a concert every Sun and most evenings there is a lecture, or an event in the theatre (see the monthly programme, or newspaper).

Open Tues-Fri 0900-1700, Sat/Sun 1000-1700, entry US$1.50. Take a colectivo from Miraflores or the centre to the Universidad de Lima and get out at block 24 on Javier Prado; taxi US$2-3.

**Museo Peruano de Ciencias de la Salud**, now part of the Museo de la Nación, has a collection of ceramics and mummies, plus an explanation of precolumbian lifestyle, divided into five sections: *micuy* (Quechua for food), *hampi* (medicine), *onccoy* (disease), *hampini* (healing) and *causay* (life).

**Museo de Oro** (Gold Museum) is the private collection of Miguel Mujica Gallo, in the 18th block of Prolongación Av Primavera (Av de Molina 1110), Monterrico (T 435-0791). An underground museum contains items which have been exhibited in the world's leading museums. This excellent collection includes precolumbian gold, silver and bronze, ceramics, weavings, mummies, etc. Allow plenty of time to appreciate it fully. The catalogues cost US$20 or US$40 and the complete book US$70. Upstairs is a remarkable arms collection with an impressive exhibition from Spanish colonial times. In the garden are high quality, expensive craft shops.

Open daily (including Sun and holidays) 1200-1900. Admission US$5, children half price. No photography allowed. Take a colectivo from the centre to the corner of Av Arequipa y Av Angamos (you can walk to Av Angamos from Miraflores) and take bus 11, 72, 112 or 985, or a colectivo, to the 18th block of Av Primavera. Taxi US$3-4.

**Museo Arqueológico Rafael Larco Herrera**, Av Bolívar 1515, Pueblo Libre, T 461-1312, is the Chiclín pottery museum brought from Trujillo. The greatest number of exhibits stem from the Mochica period (AD 400-800). The Cupisnique period, dating back to 1000 BC, and the Nasca, Chimú, and Inca periods are also well represented. There is an erotica section in a separate building. This is a museum for the pottery specialist and it gives an excellent overview on the development of Peruvian cultures. It is more like a warehouse than a museum with few explanations, but the general visitor will enjoy the excellent collection of precolumbian weaving, including a sample of two-ply yarns with 398 threads to the inch. There are also several mummified weavers buried with their looms and a small display of gold pieces.

Admission US$5 (half price for student-card holders), open Mon-Sat 0900-1800, Sun 0900-1300. Photography not permitted. Take Bus 23 or colectivo from Av Abancay, any bus or colectivo to the 15th block of Av Brasil, and another one on Av Bolívar. Taxi US$2-3.

**Museo Arqueológico Amano** is on C Retiro 160, 11th block of Av Angamos, Miraflores. This very fine private collection of artefacts from the Chancay, Chimú and Nasca periods, owned by the

Mochica culture

late Mr Yoshitaro Amano, boasts one of the most complete exhibits of Chancay weaving. It is particularly interesting for pottery and precolumbian textiles, all superbly displayed and lit.

Visits are by appointment Mon-Fri in afternoons only, T 441-2909. Admission free (photography prohibited). Take bus or colectivo to the corner of Av Arequipa y Av Angamos and another one to the 11th block of Av Angamos, or bus 1, 73, or colectivo from Av Tacna y Av La Vega to corner Av Comandante Espinar y Av Angamos and walk to the 11th block.

**Museo Banco Central de Reserva**, Av Ucayali 291 and Lampa, one block from San Pedro Church, on same side as Torre Tagle Palace, T 427 6250, ext 2657. This is a large collection of pottery from the Vicus or Piura culture (AD 500-600) and gold objects from Lambayeque, as well as 19th and 20th century paintings. Both modern and ancient exhibitions are highly recommended.

Open Tues-Fri 1000-1600, Sat-Sun 1000-1300. Photography prohibited.

**Museo Nacional de la Cultura Peruana**, Av Alfonso Ugarte 650, Lima, T 423-5892. This extraordinary mock Tiahuanako façade houses a rather disjointed collection of precolumbian and modern artefacts, including *mate burilado* (carved gourds), *retablos*, textiles, *keros* and *huacos*. There are examples of ceramics and cloth from some Amazonian tribes and a set of watercolours by Pancho Fierro, the 19th century *costumbrista* artist. Open Tues-Fri 1000-1630, Sat 1000-1400. Admission US$1, free guide in Spanish.

**Poli Museum**, Lord Cochrane 466, T 422-2437, Miraflores, is one of the best private collections of precolumbian and colonial artefacts in Peru, including material from Sipán. Guided tours (not in English) by Sr Poli cost US$50 irrespective of the size of the group; allow 2 hrs.

**Museo de Arte**, 9 de Diciembre 125, T 423-4732, in the Palacio de la Exposición, built in 1868 in Parque de la Exposición. There are more than 7,000 exhibits, giving a chronological history of Peruvian cultures and art from the Paracas civilization up to today. It includes excellent examples of 17th and 18th century Cusco paintings, a beautiful display of carved furniture, heavy silver and jewelled stirrups and also precolumbian pottery.

Between April and Oct, and with special programmes in the holiday season, the cinema shows films and plays almost every night (cheap); see the local paper for details, or look in the museum itself. Free guide, signs in English. Open Tues-Sun 1000-1700, entry US$1.50.

**Museo de Arte Italiano**, Paseo de la República, 2nd block, T 423-9932, is in a wonderful neo-classical building, given by the Italian colony to Peru on the centenary of its independence. Note the remarkable mosaic murals on the outside. It consists of a large collection of Italian and other European works of art, including sculpture, lithographs and etchings. The museum now also houses the Instituto de Arte Contemporáneo, which has many exhibitions. Open Mon-Fri 0900-1630, US$1.

**Contemporary Folk Art Museum**, on Saco Olivero 163, between Arenales and 3rd block of Arequipa, is recommended. There is a shop in the museum grounds. Open Tues-Fri, 1430-1900; Sat 0830-1200.

**Pinacoteca Municipal**, housed in the Municipal Building on the Plaza de Armas, contains a large collection of paintings by Peruvian artists. The best of the painters is Ignacio Merino (1817-1876). The rooms and furnishings are very ornate. Open Mon-Fri, 0900-1300.

**Colección Pedro de Osma** is on Av Pedro de Osma 421, Barranco. This is a private collection of colonial art of the Cusco, Ayacucho and Arequipa schools; T 467-0915/0019 for an appointment. Take bus 2, 54 or colectivo from Av Tacna. The number of visitors is limited to ten at any one time. Admission US$3.

**Museo Nacional de Historia**, Plaza Bolívar, Pueblo Libre, T 463-2009, is in a mansion built by Viceroy Pezuela and occupied by San Martín (1821-1822) and Bolívar (1823-1826). It is next to the old Museo de Antropoligía y Arqueología. Take the same buses to get there (see above). The exhibits comprise colonial and early republican paintings, manuscripts, portraits, uniforms, etc. The paintings are mainly of historical episodes. Open daily 0900-1700. Admission US$1.50.

**Museo del Tribunal de la Santa Inquisición** stands on Plaza Bolívar, C Junín 548, near the corner of Av Abancay. The main hall, with a splendidly carved mahogany ceiling, remains untouched. The Court of Inquisition was first held here in 1584, after being moved from its first home opposite the church of La Merced. From 1829 until 1938 the building was used by the Senate. In the basement there is an accurate recreation

## Guilt by inquisition

Established by Royal Decree in 1569, the Court of Inquisition was soon to prove a particularly cruel form of justice, even in the context of Spanish rule.

During its existence, the Church meted out many horrific tortures on innocent people. Among the most fashionable methods of making the accused confess their "sins" were burning, dismemberment and asphyxiation, to name but a few. The most common form of punishment was public flogging, followed by exile and the not so appealing death by burning. Up until 1776, 86 people are recorded to have been burned alive and 458 excommunicated.

Given that no witnesses were called except the informer and that the accused were not allowed to know the identity of their accusers, this may have been less a test of religious conviction than a means of settling old scores. This Kafkaesque nightmare was then carried into the realms of surreal absurdity during the process of judgement. A statue of Christ was the final arbiter of guilt or innocence but had to express its belief in the prisoner's innocence with a shake of the head. Needless to say, not too many walked free.

The Inquisition was abolished by the Viceroy in 1813 but later reinstated before finally being proscribed in 1820.

*in situ* of the gruesome tortures. The whole tour is fascinating, if a little morbid. A description in English is available at the desk. Admission free. Students offer to show you round for a tip; good explanations in English. Mon-Fri 0900-1300, 1430-1700.

**Museo Histórico Militar**, Parque Independencia, in Real Felipe Fortress, Callao, T 429-0532. There are many interesting military relics such as: a cannon brought by Pizarro, a cannon used in the War of Independence, the flag that flew during the last Spanish stand in the fortress, portraits of General Rodil and of Lord Cochrane, and the remains of the small Bleriot plane in which the Peruvian pilot, Jorge Chávez, made the first crossing of the Alps from Switzerland to Italy. He was killed when the plane crashed at Domodossola on 23 September 1910. Open 0930-1400, US$2 including guide, no cameras allowed. Take bus 25, 74, 94 or colectivo from Av La Vega.

**Museo Naval**, Av Jorge Chávez 121, off Plaza Grau, Callao, T 429-4793, contains a collection of paintings, model ships, uniforms, etc. Open Mon-Fri 0900-1400. Admission free

**Museo de los Combatientes del Morro de Arica**, Cailloma 125, Lima, T 427-0958, gives the Peruvian view of the famous battle against the Chileans during the War of the Pacific. Open Tues-Sat 1000-1500, admission US$0.50.

**Museo Miguel Grau**, Jr Huancavelica 170, Lima, T 428-5012, is the house of Admiral Grau and has mementoes of the War of the Pacific. Open daily 0900-1400, admission free.

**Museo de Historia Natural Javier Prado**, Av Arenales 1256, Jesús María, T 471-0117, belongs to Universidad de San Marcos. The exhibits comprise Peruvian flora, birds, mammals, butterflies, insects, minerals and shells. Open Mon-Sat 0900-1800; admission US$1 (students US$0.50). Take a colectivo from Av Tacna.

**La Casa O'Higgins**, Unión 550, is an interesting colonial house which holds temporary exhibitions from the Universidad de Lima (entry US$1). Bernardo O'Higgins, president of Chile from 1817-23, died here on 24 October 1842.

**Museo Taurino**, Hualgayoc 332, Plaza de Acho Bull Ring (see above), Rímac, T 482-3360. Apart from matadors'

relics, the museum contains good collections of paintings and engravings – some of the latter by Goya. Mon-Sat 0800-1600. Admission US$1; students US$0.50, photography US$2.

**Philatelic Museum**, at the Central Post Office, off Plaza de Armas, T 427-5060, ext 553. Contains an incomplete collection of Peruvian stamps and information on the Inca postal system. There is a stamp exchange in front of the museum every Sat and Sun, 0900-1300. You can buy stamps here as well, particularly commemorative issues. Shop hours, Mon-Fri 0800-1200, 1400-1500; museum open 0915-1245, Mon-Fri., L

**Museo Numismático**, Banco Wiese, 2nd floor, Cusco 245, T 427-5060 ext 2009. Displays Peruvian coins from the colonial era to the present.

**Museo Teatral**, Teatro Segura, Jr Huancavelica 251, Lima, T 427-7437, open during performances. Contains a collection of mementoes and photographs of people who have appeared on the Lima stage.

**NB** Some museums are only open between 0900 and 1300 from Jan to Mar, and some close altogether in January. Many are closed at weekends and on Mon; some close early if there are few visitors.

## PARKS AND ZOOS

**Parque las Leyendas**, is on the 24th block of Av de La Marina, Pueblo Libre, between Lima and Callao, T 452-6913. It is arranged to represent the three regions of Peru: the coast, the mountainous Sierra, and the tropical jungles of the Selva, with appropriate houses, animals and plants, children's playground. Elephants and lions have been introduced so the zoo is no longer purely Peruvian. It gets very crowded at weekends. The Park is open daily 0900-1700, entrance US$2. There is a handicrafts fair (Feria Artesanal) at the entrance to the park; particularly good insect specimens can be bought here. Take bus 23 or colectivo on Av Abancay, or bus 135A or colectivo from Av La Vega.

## SUBURBS OF LIMA

The Av Arequipa connects the centre of Lima with Miraflores. It was the opening of this thoroughfare in 1921 that transformed the districts of San Isidro and Miraflores into popular residential areas. Parallel to Av Arequipa is the Vía Expresa, a highway carrying fast traffic to the suburbs (six lanes for cars, two for buses). San Isidro, Pueblo Libre, Miraflores and parts of Lince have some good examples of Art Deco and Estilo Barca residential architecture.

### SAN ISIDRO

To the E of Av La República, down C Pancho Fierro, is **El Olivar**, an old olive grove planted by the first Spaniards which has been turned into a delightful park (best visited in daylight). Beyond this is the Lima Golf Club and the Country Club, primarily a hotel, which incorporates the Club Real with swimming pools, tennis courts, etc (open to members only). This is an 8 km taxi ride from the centre of Lima. There are many good hotels and restaurants in San Isidro; see main Lima lists, hotels page 102 and restaurants page 104.

Between San Isidro and Miraflores, at C Nicolás de Rivera 201, is **the Pan de Azúcar**, or **Huallamarca**, a restored adobe pyramid of the Maranga culture, dating from about AD 100-500. There is a small site museum, open daily, 0900-1700. Take bus 1 from Av Tacna, or minibus 13 or 73 to Choquechaca, then walk.

West of San Isidro is the rundown seaside resort of **Magdalena del Mar**, inland from which is **Pueblo Libre** (formerly Magdalena Vieja), where the **Museo de Antropología y Arqueología**, the **Museo Arqueológico Rafael Larco Herrera** and the **Museo Nacional de Historia** are found (see under Museums, page 90). In Pueblo Libre is the church of **Santa María Magdalena**, on Jr San Martín, whose plain exterior conceals some fine ornamentation and art inside.

## MIRAFLORES

Av Arequipa continues past San Isidro to the coast at **Miraflores**, the largest, most important suburb of Lima, with well stocked shops and many first class hotels and restaurants (see main Lima lists: hotels, page 100, Youth Hostel, page 103 and restaurants, page 104). Together with San Isidro this is now the social centre of Lima.

There is a handsome park in the middle of the shopping centre and at the end of Av Mcal Benavides, which is commonly called Av Diagonal, you can get the best view of the whole Lima coastline from Chorrillos to La Punta. The Mcal Necochea clifftop park, or Parque de los Amantes, as it is more commonly known, overlooks the Waikiki Club, a favourite with Lima surfers.

The **Parque Salazar** is a great place to listen to a concert in the summer, while overlooking the bay. Several walkways and roads (also the highway from the centre, the Vía Expresa) work their way down to the ocean, where a beach road runs around the entire bay. There are several beaches, popular with surfers and sun lovers, and a number of beach clubs (for members only). At night the clubs become discos, where the Limeños come to dance salsa until the early hours. There are plenty of seafood kiosks along the beach and two expensive restau-

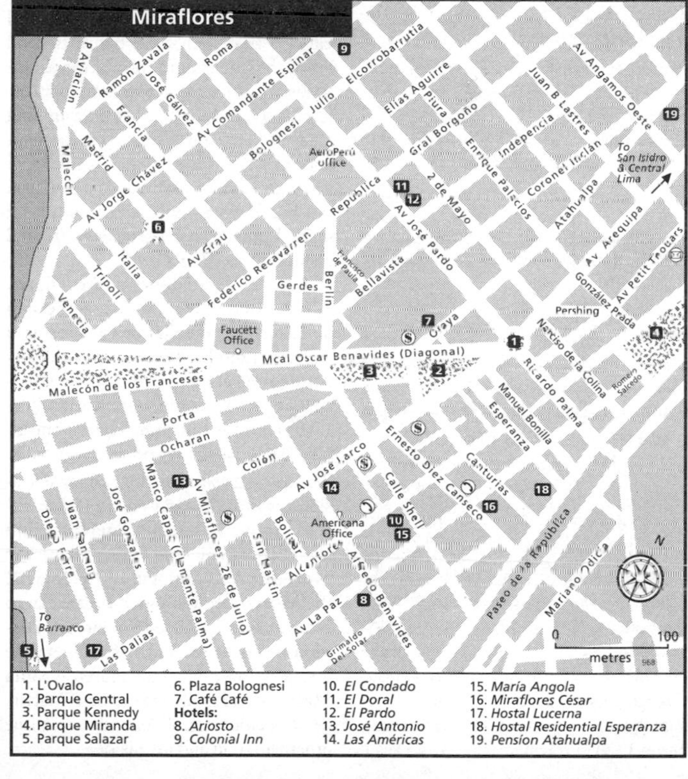

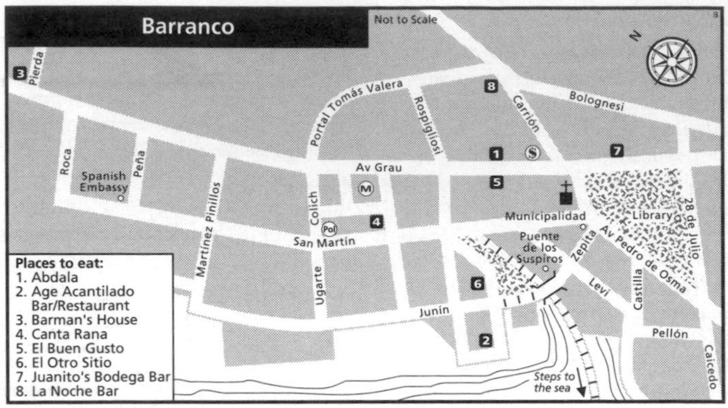


rants, *Costa Verde* and *Rosa Náutica*. The latter, on a pier, is one of the nicest in Lima.

In **Parque Kennedy** is an artists' and craftsmen's market, most evenings of the week, and concerts Thur-Sun. Calle San Ramón, opposite Parque Kennedy off Av Diagonal, is closed to traffic and lined with many pizzerias, hence its nickname of Pizza Street.

The house of the author, poet and historian **Ricardo Palma** is at Gral Suárez 189. He is one of Peru's most famous literary figures, best known for his work *Tradiciones Peruanas*, which covers the country's colonial period. The house where he lived and died is now a museum, open to the public, Mon-Fri 0930-1230, 1330-1800, small entrance fee, T 445-5836.

The Miraflores branch of **Banco Wiese** has an exhibition of finds from El Brujo archaeological site N of Trujillo. Open Mon-Fri, 0900-1230, free admission.

At Borgoña, 8th block s/n, turn off Av Arequipa at 45th block, is **Huaca Pucllana**, a pre-Inca site which is under excavation. This adobe pyramid is also associated with the Maranga culture. The site can be visited by guided tours only (give tip). There is a small site museum; admission free.

## BARRANCO

South of Miraflores is **Barranco**, which was already a seaside resort by the end of the 17th century. During the republic it was a holiday centre for rich Limeños and many British and Germans built opulent country houses there. Nowadays, Barranco is something of an intellectual haven where a number of artists have their workshops.

The attractive public library, formerly the town hall, stands on the delightful plaza. Nearby is the interesting *bajada*, a steep path leading down to the beach, where many of Lima's artists live. The old houses are in state of disrepair and many are under restoration. **The Puente de los Suspiros** (bridge of sighs), leads towards the Malecón, with fine views of the bay.

Barranco is a quiet, sleepy suburb during the day but comes alive at night when the city's young flock here to party at weekends. Squeezed together into a few streets are dozens of good bars and restaurants (see main Lima list). No visit to Lima would be complete without a tour of Barranco's "sights".

Take a colectivo to Miraflores then another. Some run all the way to Barranco from Lima centre; check on the front window or ask, same fare. It is a 45 mins walk from Miraflores to Barranco along the Malecón with lovely sunsets in summer.

## CHORRILLOS

The next development on the coast is at **Chorrillos**, a fashionable resort with a cliff promenade, and boating. At Hacienda La Villa, an old Spanish *hacienda* worth visiting, there is occasionally open air dancing to *salsa* music. Down the beach from Chorrillos is the fish market, with several seafood stalls (the fish is fresh, but is caught in polluted water), the clean beach of Playa Agua Dulce, and the Club Regatas de Lima. Overlooking the beach is *Café Suizo* – beware of overcharging in seaside restaurants.

Beyond Chorrillos is **La Herradura**, another bathing resort with several restaurants. The private Club Unicornio is open to tourists.

## CALLAO

Founded in 1537, Callao quickly became the main port for Spanish colonial commerce in the Pacific. Despite its proximity to Lima, Callao has a distinct character and its inhabitants will not take kindly to being called Limeños.

### History

During much of the 16th century Spanish merchants were plagued by threats from English pirates such as Sir Francis Drake and Richard Hawkins who were all too willing to relieve the Spanish armada of its colonial spoils. The harbour was fortified in 1639 in order to prevent such attacks.

In 1746, the port was completely destroyed by a massive wave, triggered by the terrible earthquake of that year. According to some sources, all 6,000 of Callao's inhabitants were drowned. The watermark is still visible on the outside of the 18th century church of Nuestra Señora del Carmen de la Legua which stands near the corner of Av Oscar Benavides and the airport road, Av Elmer Faucett.

In 1850, the first railway in South America was opened between Lima and Callao. It was used not only as a passenger service but, more importantly, for the growing import-export trade, transporting ore from the mines in the Central Highlands and manufactured goods from the disembarking ships.

### Modern Callao

Callao (*Pop* 588,600) is now contiguous with Lima. The road between the two is lined by factories. Shipyards, far from sea, load the fishing vessels they build on huge lorries and launch them into the ocean at Callao. The port is still very much a commercially active place. It handles 75% of the nation's imports and some 25% of its exports. San Lorenzo island, a naval station, protects the roadstead from the S and inland stretches the Rímac valley. The market is between Sáenz Peña and Buenos Aires.

The port's few attractions include **The Club**, the oldest English club on the W coast, at Pasaje Ronald, C Constitución, Callao. There is also an English cemetery.

The **Castillo del Real Felipe** is still a military post, and tourists are allowed to

Callao in the early 17th century as drawn by Huaman Poma de Ayala

### The fortress of Real Felipe

Work on the fortress of Real Felipe was begun following the disastrous earthquake and flood of 1746 and finally completed in 1774. The fortress guns, manned by Spanish Royalists, kept at bay Admiral William Brown in 1816 and the independence fighter, Lord Cochrane, 2 years later. However, they were unable to prevent Cochrane from entering the harbour one dark, misty night, on 5 November 1820, and capturing the Spanish frigate *Esmeralda* after a bloody struggle in which he was wounded.

The following year, the independence fighters, the Patriots, captured the fort and, in 1823, President Riva Aguero took refuge there after the Royalists had taken temporary control of Lima. The Royalist Brigadier, José Ramón Rodil took the fortress with the help of some mutinous Patriots and held it throughout a 2-year siege. He was finally forced to surrender after nearly half the garrison and many of the families who had fled there for protection died of starvation and disease.

visit it. The **Museo Histórico Militar** is in the old barracks. There is also the **Museo Naval** (see page 93 for both).

The Naval College is at **La Punta**, just beyond Callao, served by municipal buses and colectivos through Callao from Lima. La Punta is on a spit of land stretching out to sea. It was once a fashionable beach resort and is still a pleasant enough residential area, but the water is cool. A yacht club is on the N side. The walk along the seafront between Callao and La Punta has its charms.

• **Transport** Lima is at least 20 mins by car, colectivos US$0.30, bus US$0.25, taxi US$3-4 to the centre or Miraflores.

**Warning** Callao has a serious theft problem, avoid being there in the evening.

## LIMA BEACHES

Lima is situated on the Pacific Ocean, somewhat protected by an open bay, with its two points at La Punta (Callao) and Salto de Fraile (Chorrillos). A Malecón runs along the coast, giving a good view. In summer (Dec-April) the city's beaches get very crowded at weekends and lots of activities are organized. Even though the water of the whole bay has been declared unsuitable for swimming, Limeños see the beach more as part of their culture than as a health risk. Do not camp on the beaches as robbery is a serious threat and for the same reason, take care on the walkways down. Don't take any belongings with you to the beach, only what is really necessary.

**Beaches S of Lima** can be very dangerous because of the strong Pacific current. Every year people are drowned. The following beaches are considered to be safe: Santa María and Naplo (near Pucusana). All the other famous beaches have a strong current and swimming should be treated with caution or avoided: Las Señoritas, Los Caballeros, Punta Hermosa, Punta Negra, San Bartolo, Chilca and León Dormido.

## EXCURSIONS

### CIENEGUILLA

Cieneguilla, about 20 km E of Lima, on the Lurín river, is a small village in the country, an easy escape from the city and cloud cover of Lima. It is a popular place on Sun, with good restaurants with gardens and swimming pools. The valley of Lurín is good for birdwatching in the early morning.

### PACHACAMAC

Pachacámac is in the Lurín valley, 31 km from Lima. When the Spaniards arrived, Pachacámac was the largest city and ceremonial centre on the coast. It was a vast complex of palaces and temple-pyramids, to which pilgrims went to pay homage to the creator-god Pachacámac, a wooden statue of whom is in the site museum.

Hernando Pizarro came to Pachacámac in 1533, having been sent by his brother to speed the delivery of gold from the coast for Atahualpa's ransom. However, great disappointment awaited Pizarro as there was no store of riches. In their desperate search for the promised gold the Spaniards destroyed images, killed the priests and looted the temples. The ruins encircle the top of a low hill, whose crest was crowned with a **Temple of the Sun**, a large pyramid built in 1350 of sun-baked bricks, now partially restored. Slightly apart from the main group of buildings and hidden from view is the reconstructed **House of the Mamaconas**, where the 'chosen women' were taught to weave and spin fine cloth for the Inca and his court. Further to the N the **Temple of Urpi-Huachac**, who was reputed to be the wife of Pachacámac, is in a state of total ruin.

An impression of the scale of the site can be gained from the top of the Temple of the Sun, or from walking or driving the 3 km circuit.

The site is open 0900 to 1700; closed 1 May. Entrance US$1.25, includes the small site museum which sells soft drinks.

• **Transport Bus or colectivo from Lima**: from Av Montevideo y Ayacucho. The buses (US$0.40, 1 hr) and colectivos (US$0.60) go via Chorrillos; tell the driver you are going to the *ruinas* or he will leave you in Pachacámac town further on. A yellow Enatru bus marked Lurín-Pachacámac No P1 leaves from Parque Campo de Marte along Av Grau to Pachacámac. Taxi, round trip with a few hours at the site, US$25. Several travel agencies offer 3 hrs excursions including English-speaking guide for US$35; Lima Tours run daily trips, about 3½ hrs, for about US$15 pp.

## PURUCHUCO

On the way to Chosica, up the Rímac valley, turn off at Km 4½ to Puruchuco, to see the reconstructed palace of a pre-Inca Huacho noble. There is a small museum with ceramics and textiles from the lower Rímac or Lima valley and a selection of indigenous plants and animals.

Open 0900-1700, Tues-Sun (closed 1 May and 28 July). Entrance US$1; transport as for Chosica.

## CAJAMARQUILLA

This large adobe pre-Inca city can also be visited. The turnoff (left, at Huachipa) is about 6 km on from the Puruchuco turn. The site cannot be seen from the road; look for a sign 'Zona Arqueológica' in the middle of a brick yard. Keep on driving through the yard, and Cajamarquilla is at the end of an ill-kept dirt road. Open daily 0900-1700.

## PUCUSANA

Pucusana, 60 km S of Lima, is a pleasant, relaxed fishing village with some good restaurants serving seafood, not cheap, and some basic hotels (in our E range). All are very popular with Limeños from Dec to Mar, school holidays, and at weekends. There are plenty of buses from the bus station area in Lima. Robbery is common on the beaches and you are advised to sit on your clothes and other possessions. Do not leave anything unattended when swimming.

## ANCON

In the 19th and early 20th centuries, this was the smart seaside resort in Peru, but has now been deserted by the wealthy and in summer is crowded with daytrippers. It has a mix of elegant 19th century houses with wooden balconies and modern apartment blocks. Also bathing, tennis, and a yacht club. The beaches are very small and crowded during Jan-Mar holidays.

On the way to Ancón is the pleasant Santa Rosa beach (entrance fee). Beyond Ancón is a Chancay cemetery, from which has come much Chancay weaving and pottery (as seen in the Museo Amano). In the valley of Chillón, N of Callao, are several interesting pre-Inca and Inca ruins; the Templo de la Media Luna y El Paraíso and **Chuquitanta.** For more information contact Dr Richard Holmberg at the Instituto Nacional de Cultura, Callao.

● **Accommodation & places to eat** **D** *Hostal del Pirata*, antique furniture, good views, excellent seafood; *Restaurant Cinco Luches*, has rooms to rent, **E**; *Los 5 Tenedores*, is a rec restaurant on the Corniche.

● **Transport** 30 km NW of Lima, reached by a double-lane asphalted highway. Colectivo from Plaza 2 de Mayo in Lima, US$0.60, returns 1 block from Ancón Cathedral.

## LOCAL FESTIVALS

18 Jan, Founding of Lima. The whole of Feb is Carnival during which time there is water-throwing on Sun. Some 'jokers' mix paint, oil, etc, with the water, so watch out. Semana Santa, or Holy Week, is a colourful spectacle with processions. 28-29 July is Independence, with music and fireworks in the Plaza de Armas on the evening before. October is the month of Our Lord of the Miracles with impressive processions (see *El Comercio* for dates and routes). The Pacific International Fair is held every other year in November. See also **Public Holidays** in Information for travellers.

## LOCAL INFORMATION

**Hotel prices**

| | | | |
|---|---|---|---|
| L1 | over US$200 | L2 | US$151-200 |
| L3 | US$101-150 | A1 | US$81-100 |
| A2 | US$61-80 | A3 | US$46-60 |
| B | US$31-45 | C | US$21-30 |
| D | US$12-20 | E | US$7-11 |
| F | US$4-6 | G | up to US$3 |

● **Accommodation**

All hotels and restaurants in the upper price brackets charge 18% VAT and 10% service on top of prices (neither is included in prices below). In cheaper hotels water may be scarce in the middle of the day. The more expensive hotels charge in dollars according to the parallel rate of exchange at midnight. More visitors stay in the Miraflores area than in the centre, as it is more organized, cleaner and safer, but more expensive. Backpackers prefer the cheaper *hostales* in the centre, which has more theft problems, is more chaotic, but which, with care and attention to your belongings, is OK. Consult the general **Security** section in the **Information for travellers** and see also the **Warning** under **Buses** below. Note that many parks are used as meeting places for drug pushers, thieves and couples. They are also home to street people.

**Miraflores**: **L2** *Las Américas*, Av Benavides 415, T 445-9494, F 444-1137, 5-star, commercial centre, pool, gym, restaurant; **L2** *María Angola*, Av La Paz 610, T 444-1280, F 446-2860, rec; **L2** *Miraflores César*, La Paz y Diez Canseco, T 444-1212, F 444-4440, luxury, pool, gym, sauna, facilities for the handicapped; **L2/3** *El Condado*, Alcanfores 465, T 444-3614, F444-1981, deluxe, casino, parking; **L2/3** *El Pardo*, Independencia 141, T 444-2283, F 444-2171, a/c, satellite TV, fax and telex service, pool, gym, good restaurant, rec.

**A2** *Ariosto*, Av La Paz 769, T 444-1414, F 444-3955, friendly, rec; **A2** *La Hacienda Resort*, 28 de Julio 511, T 444-4346, F 444-1942, English spoken, excellent 5-star service, breakfast inc; **A2** *Grand Hotel Miraflores*, Av 28 de Julio 151, casino, disco, very pleasant, T 447-9641; **A2** *José Antonio*, 28 de Julio 398, T/F 445-6870, clean, friendly, good restaurant, rec.

**A3** *El Doral*, Av José Pardo 486, T 447-6305, F 446-8344, nice rooms with lounge and kitchenette, safe, friendly, pool, rec; **A3** *Hostal Miramar Ischia*, Malecón Cisneros 1244, overlooking Pacific, inc breakfast, good value restaurant, friendly, rec.

**B** *Colonial Inn*, Cmdte Espinar 310, T 446-6666, F 445-7587, colonial style, parking, inc breakfast; **B** *Hostal El Ejecutivo*, Av 28 de Julio 245, T 447-6310, F 444-2222, inc breakfast, payment in dollars, overpriced but clean, tariff negotiable for long stay, safe, luggage can be left; **B** *Hostal Huaychulo*, Av Dos de Mayo 494, T 445-1195, safe, helpful, excellent (German owner-manager, speaks English too), rec; **B** *Hostal La Castellana*, Grimaldo del Solar 222 (nr US consulate), T 444-3530/4662, F 446-8030, pleasant, good value, nice garden, safe, restaurant, laundry, English spoken,

15% discount for South American Explorers Club (SAEC) members, rec; **B** ***Hostal Lucerna***, Las Dalias 276 (parallel with 12th block of Larco), T 445-7321, F 446-6050, friendly, safe, quiet, cosy, rec; **B** ***Hostal El Patio***, Diez Canseco 341a, T 444-2107, inc breakfast, reductions for long stays, clean, comfortable, friendly, English and French spoken; **B** ***Hostal Res Esperanza***, Esperanza 350, T 444-2411/4909, F 444-0834, café, bar, TV, phone, pleasant, secure; **B** ***Hostal Palace***, Av 28 de Julio 1088, T 445-6040, F 440-0450, inc breakfast, very clean, comfortable, friendly, keeps luggage, English-speaking reception; **B** ***Hostal Qosqo***, Malecón Cisneros 1070, T/F 992-6596, with bath, hot water, TV, inc breakfast, simple rooms, nice location, bar with ocean views; **B** ***Hostal Res Torreblanca***, Av José Pardo 1453, T/F 447-9998/3363, inc breakfast, quiet, safe, laundry, restaurant and bar, friendly, cosy rooms, will help with travel arrangements, rec; **B** ***Hostal San Antonio Abad***, Ramón Ribeyro 301, T 447-6766, T/F 446-4208, quiet, secure, very friendly and helpful, free airport transfer, highly rec; **B** ***Hostal Señorial***, José González 567, T 445-7306, inc breakfast, comfortable, friendly, nice garden, rec; **B** ***Res Alemán***, Arequipa 4704, T 445-6999 (no sign), comfortable, clean, friendly, quiet, excellent breakfast, laundry service extra; **B** ***Suites Eucaliptas***, San Martín 511, T 445-8594, F 444-3071, European-style, kitchenette, sauna, jacuzzi, pool, safety deposit, laundry, credit cards accepted.

**C** ***Armendariz***, Av Armendariz 375 (between Miraflores and Barranco), on No 2 bus line, T 445-4565, inc breakfast, rec.

**D** ***Pensión José Luis***, Paula de Ugarriza 727, San Antonio district, T 444-1015, apartments in private house, small kitchen, reservation required, laundry facilities, very clean and friendly, English-speaking owner, highly rec; **D-C** ***Pensión Yolanda***, Domingo Elias 230, T 445-7565, clean, use of kitchen, owner speaks English, family house, quiet, safe, reservation required, highly rec; **D** ***Res El Castillo Inn***, Diez Canseco 580, T 446-9501, family home, use of kitchen and lounge; **D** ***Hospedaje Atahualpa***, Atahualpa 646c, T 447-6601 (C with private bath), inc breakfast, friendly, parking, hot water, cooking and laundry facilities, clean, taxi service, rec; **D** pp Sra Jordan, Porta 724, T 445-9840, inc break-

fast, 5 rooms, family home, friendly, quiet; **D** *Pensión San Antonio*, Paseo de la República 5809, T 447-5830, shared bath, clean, comfortable, friendly, helpful, hot water on first floor, rec; **E** *Hostal Andalucia*, Jr Tacna 472, T 445-8717, with bath, clean, good value, helpful, quiet.

**San Isidro**: **L3** *El Olivar de San Isidro*, Pancho Fierro 194, T 441-1454, F 441-1382, luxury, modern, restaurant, coffee shop, garden, swimming pool, quiet, popular with business visitors.

**A2** *Country Club*, Los Eucaliptos, T 440-4060, F 440-8912, all services, restaurant and coffee shop, quiet, helpful, reasonable rates (except for overseas faxes), gaming room; **A2** *Garden*, Rivera Navarrete 450, T 442-1771, good, large beds, shower, small restaurant, rec.

**A3** *Hostal Beech*, Los Libertadores 145, T 442-8713, F 442-8716, with bath, inc breakfast, noisy, but rec; **A3** *Regina's*, Av Dos de Mayo, T442-8870, inc breakfast, pool, rec.

**B** *Hostal Limatambo*, Av Aramburú 1025, T 441-9615, 24-hr snack bar, won the 'América-86' award for good service and quality; **B** *Residencial Francia*, Samuel Velarde 185, 11th block of Av Ejército, T 461-7054, price inc taxes and breakfast, bath, hot water, laundry facilities, swimming pool, gardens, very friendly and helpful; **B** *Sans Souci*, Av Arequipa 2670, T 422-6035, F 441-7824, clean, safe, friendly, good services, garden, garage.

**C** *Hostal Santa Mónica*, Av Pezet 1419, T 441-9280, rec.

In **Santa Beatriz**, between San Isidro and Centre: **C-D** *Hostal Mont Blanc*, Jr Emilio Fernández 640, T 433-8055, with bath, inc breakfast, quiet area, safe (video monitoring), 15 mins walk or 5 mins by minibus to centre, owner arranges excursions; **D** *Res Los Petirrojos*, Petirrojos 230, Corpac (Sra Miri), T 441-6044, clean, spacious, inc breakfast.

In **Lince** is **D** *Hostal Ambassador*, Julio C Tello 650, T 470-0020, clean, safe, hot water, changes money for guests, highly rec.

In **central Lima**, rec in the upper price brackets: **L2** *Lima Sheraton*, Paseo de la República 170, T 433-3320, F 433-6344, *Las Palmeras* coffee shop good, daily buffet breakfast, all you can eat for US$15 pp, casino.

**L3** *Crillón*, Av Nicolás de Piérola, or Colmena 589, T 428-3290, F 432-5920, good food and service in *Skyroom* (open 1200-2400 Mon-Sat, Peruvian/international cuisine, buffets and live music at weekends, great view over Lima).

**A1** *Grand Bolívar*, Unión 958, Plaza San Martín, T 427-2305, F 433-8626 (may be negotiable to C out of season), palatial old building, good ambience, helpful, excellent restaurant, have a pisco on the terrace overlooking plaza, highly rec.

**B** *El Plaza*, Nicolás de Piérola 850, T 428-6270, very noisy at the front but quiet at the back (except Sat), convenient, good, safe for luggage (cheaper in low season), inc breakfast; **B** *Grand Castle*, Av Carlos Zavala Loayza 218, T 428-3181, opp Ormeño bus station, inc breakfast (poor), hot water, comfortable, good service, Japanese restaurant, rec; **B** *Kamana*, Jr Camaná 547, T 426-7204, F 426-0790, modern, TV, phone, comfortable, safe, restaurants, French and some English spoken; **B-C** *Hostal San Martín*, Av Nicolás de Piérola 882, p 2, Plaza San Martín, T 428-5337, a/c, inc breakfast served in room, friendly, helpful, safe, rooms on street noisy, money changing facilities, Japanese run, good restaurant, good service, rec; **B** *Savoy*, Cailloma 224, T 428-3520, F 433-0840, comfortable, but has seen better days.

**C** *Hostal Los Virreyes*, Jr Cañete 826, T 431-2733, comfortable, clean, hot water, central position, rec; **C-B** *Hostal Renacimiento*, Parque Hernán Velarde 52, T 433-2806, nice rooms, quiet, parking, colonial building, very close to national stadium, not all rooms with bath, clean, helpful.

**D** *Granada*, Huancavelica 323, T 427-9033, inc breakfast, clean, hot water, English spoken, safe, friendly, safety deposit, washing facilities; **D** *Res Kori Wasi*, Av Washington 1137, T 433-8127, with bath, pleasant, safe, friendly; **D-C** *Res Roma*, Jr Ica 326, T 427-7576, 426-0533, F 427-7572, hot water all day unless full, safe to leave luggage, friendly, basic but clean, often full, motorcycle parking, highly rec (*Roma Tours*, helpful for trips, reservations, flight confirmations, Dante Reyes speaks English).

**E** *Gran*, Av Abancay 546, T 428-5160, enormous hotel, old house, popular with locals, friendly; **E** *Hostal Belén*, Belén 1049, just off San Martín, T 427-8995, discount for groups of 3 or more but give prior notice, Italian spoken, basic breakfast extra, hot water, basic, clean, friendly; **E** *Hostal de las Artes*, Jr Chota 1454, T433-0031, Dutch owned, English spoken, clean, safe luggage store, friendly, nice colonial building, usually hot water, good restaurant, close to SAEC, rec; **E** *Hostal Iquique*,

Jr Iquique 758, Breña, round corner from SAEC (discount for members), T433-4724, clean, friendly, use of kitchen, hot water, storage facilities; **E** pp *Hostal Wilson*, Jr Chancay, T 424-8924, a bit run down but friendly and safe for luggage deposit; **E** *Pensión Ibarra*, Av Tacna 359, Apt 162, p 15 and 16, T 427-1035, no sign, breakfast extra, discount for longer stay, use of kitchen, balcony with views of the city, clean, friendly, very helpful owner, hot water, full board available, highly rec; **E** *Hostal España*, Jr Azángaro 105, no sign (G pp in dormitory), fine old building being restored, T 428-5546, shared bath, friendly, hot water if you're quick, run by a French-speaking Peruvian painter and his Spanish wife, English spoken, motorcycle parking, luggage store (free), laundry service reported as unreliable, roof garden with some animals in tiny cages, mixed reports on security, always busy, good café, rec; **E** *Familia Rodríguez*, Av N de Piérola 730, 2nd floor, T 423-6465, with breakfast, clean, friendly, popular, some rooms noisy, will store luggage, dormitory accommodation with only one bathroom, transport to airport US$9.50.

**F** pp *Hostal Samaniego*, Av Emancipación 184, Apto 801, reservation required, 15 spaces available (4 rooms), noisy, use of kitchen, will store luggage for foreigners.

**Outside Lima** is the 5-star, **A2** *El Pueblo*, Santa Clara, Km 11.2, Vitarte (along the Central Highway), huge luxurious complex in the country, with restaurants, bars, discos, swimming pool, tennis, shows, shops; you can visit for the day and use the facilities for a small fee, reservations T 494-1616/170. Next door is *La Granja Azul*, Carretera Central (turn off between Km 13 and 14 of Carretera Central, buses from Parque Universitario every 15 mins, last bus back leaves 2000 but a minibus leaves the hotel for Lima at 2200), restaurant specializing in exotic cocktails and chicken dishes, dancing every night, rec.

About 1 km from airport **E** *Hostal Salvatore*, Jr Salaverry 440, clean, TV, restaurant, and *Hostal Aeropeurto*, safe, clean, rec.

If arriving by air, especially at night, you can try the tourist office at the airport (beyond passport control) if you want to arrange a hotel room, but they are not always helpful. **Hotel reservations** for Lima and elsewhere in Peru can be made through Reservaciones Central, a travel agency, Av Panamericana 6251, San Antonio/Miraflores, T 446-6895; it charges a small commission, also offers all usual services.

**Youth hostel**: *Albergue Turístico Juvenil Internacional*, Av Casimiro Ulloa 328, San Antonio between San Isidro and Miraflores, T 446-5488, F 444-8187, basic cafeteria, travel information, cooking (minimal) and laundry facilities, US$9 members, US$10 non-members, dormitory, more for double room, swimming pool often empty, extra charge for kitchen facilities, clean and safe, situated in a nice villa, rec. 20 mins walk from the beach. Bus No 2 or colectivos pass Av Benavides to the centre; taxi to centre, US$2.50.

**Camping**: under no circumstances camp on or nr the beach at Miraflores, theft and worse is rife in these areas. Camping gas (in small blue bottles) available from any large hardware store or bigger supermarket, about US$3. Backpack makers and repairers, *Ursus* (Alberto

Abalero), Av El Ejército 1982, Miraflores, T 422-6678. *Alpamayo*, Larco 345, sells camping equipment.

## ● Places to eat

Check all restaurant prices before ordering as prices have soared since 1990 in upper and middle class establishments. Menu prices fail to show that 18% government tax and 10% service will be added to your bill in this class of restaurant. A cheap *menú* (set lunch) still costs US$1.30-3, while a meal in a moderate café/bistro will cost US$15-20; in middle-range restaurants a meal costs US$25-30, rising to US$60-80 at the upper end of the range. Chinese is often the cheapest at around US$5 inc a drink. Unless stated otherwise, prices of places listed below are in the moderate range.

In **Miraflores** we recommend the following: ***Rosa Náutica***, T 447-0057, built on old British-style pier (Espigón No 4), in Lima Bay, nr Miraflores, not to be missed, delightful opulence, finest fish cuisine, experience the atmosphere by buying an expensive beer in the bar, sunset rec, open 1230-0200 daily; ***La Costa Verde***, on Barranquito beach, T 441-4084, excellent fish and wine, pecan pie highly rec, very expensive, Amex accepted, open 1200-2400 daily, Sun buffet.

**Other seafood**: *San Marino*, José Gálvez 618, T 446-7545, expensive; ***Canta Rana***, Figari 121, Blvd San Ramón, T 445-0498, open Mon-Sat 1300-1700; ***Bahía Blanca***, Benavides 2514, T 447-7123; ***Don Beta***, José Gálvez 667, T 446-9465, open 0800-2200 daily; ***Carlín***, La Paz 646, T 444-4134, open 1200-1600, 1900-2400 daily, cosy, international, expensive; ***Pizzería Restaurant Erik***, Av Benavides 1057, cheap local and international food, highly rec, try the *salsas*; ***Don Rosalino***, Juan Figari 135, pizzas; ***Stefanos***, Av José Pardo 779, T 446-9646, open 1300-2200 Tues-Sun, pastas and pizzas; ***Las Tejas***, Diez Canseco 340, T 444-4360, open 1100-2300 daily, good, typical Peruvian food; ***El Señorío de Sulco***, Malecón Cisneros 1470, at the end of Av Pardo, T 445-6640, authentic Peruvian dishes; ***Rincón Chami***, Esperanza 1st block, *comida criolla*, very good value; ***C'est Si Bon***, Cdte Espinar 663, T 446-9310, open 1000-2200 daily, French-style.

*El Alamo*, La Paz y Diez Canseco, open 1230-1500, 1900-2400, cosy spot for wines, raclettes and fondues, expensive; ***Cheese and Wine***, Av La Paz 552, good fondues, raclette, salads and wines, warm, cosy atmosphere, excellent service; ***Oriental***, José de San Martín 561, T 444-4018, open 1130-1500, 1900-2300 Mon-Sat, 1130-1500 Sun, great Chinese food; ***Asia Garden***, Diez Canseco 493, T 444-2313, Chinese; ***Palachinke***, Shell 120, T 447-9205, open 1200-2300 daily, excellent, large pancakes; ***The Steak House***, La Paz 642, T 444-3110, 1200-1500, 1800-2400, steaks and salads, another branch in San Isidro (Las Camelias 870); ***La Tranquera***, Av Pardo 285, T 447-5111, steaks, open 1200-2400 daily; ***El Rodizio***, Ovalo Gutiérrez y Santa Cruz, T 445-0889, open 1300-0100, good meats and salad bar; ***Martín Fierro***, Malecón Cisneros 1420, T 446-3992, Argentine, good Sun buffet; ***El Rincón Gaucho***, Parque Salazar, T 447-4778, open 1200-2400 Tues-Sat, grills and steaks, and ***El Otro Gaucho***, Rep Panamá 6488, T 446-1842, 1200-2400 daily.

***Manolo***, Av Larco 608, T 444-2244, 0800-2230 daily, good food, popular, expensive; ***New York Pizza Company***, Av Larco 1145, open 1200-2400, tasty, English spoken; ***Whatta Burger***, Grau 120, American-style hamburgers; ***Mediterráneo Chicken***, Av Benavides block 420, T 447-9337, open 1200-2300 daily, chicken and salads (branch in San Isidro); next door is ***Silvestre***, good fresh juices and vegetarian sandwiches, fairly expensive; ***Tomas***, 2nd floor of Santa Isabel Supermarket, Benavides 486, open 24 hrs, good, cheap, fast food; ***Varsovia 2000***, Esperanza 135, good set lunch; ***La Tasca***, Espinar 300, good value *menú*; ***Rebecca***, Jr Atahualpa 192, good, cheap *menú*.

The 'Pizza Street', located on Diagonal (1 block from Shell), popular on Fri-Sat nights for drinks, discos, meeting spot.

Best ice cream, ***Quattro D***, Angamos Oeste 408, open 1000-0100 daily; second best at ***Fragola***, Av Benavides 468. Best yoghurt ***Mi Abuela***, Angamos 393, 0900-2100 daily; ***Media Naranja***, Shell 130, good for breakfast, Brazilian owner. ***Pastelería Sueca***, Av Larco 759, good hamburgers, pastries, salads; ***Brenchley Arms***, Atahualpa 174, T 445-9680, British pub, British owner, typical food, informal and relaxed, tourist information, expensive (US$10 for bar snacks), darts.

**Vegetarian**: *Bircher Berner*, Av Shell 598, T 444-4250, closed Sun, with store, slow service, good cheap *menú*; ***Govinda***, Shell 630, good; ***La Huerta del Sol***, El Alamo precinct, La Paz y Diez Canseco, T 444-2900, lunch menu US$3, main dishes US$5, good food, pleasant setting; ***Rincón Vegeteriano***, Los Pinos 173, entre 2 y 3 de Benavides, cheap lunch US$1.75.

**Cafés**: ***Vivaldi***, Ricardo Palma 258, 0800-0200 daily, also snacks and drinks, good cappucinos; ***Haiti***, Diagonal 160, 0700-0200 daily, drinks, café snacks, expensive, popular meeting place; ***Café Suisse***, Av Larco 111, on main square, for very good cakes, coffee, European-style food and delicatessen, expensive; ***Café Café***, Martir Olaya 250, nr Ovalo, very popular, good atmosphere.

In **San Isidro**: ***La Réserve***, Las Flores 326, T 440-2786, open 1200-1530, 1930-2400, expensive, French cuisine; ***Aquarium*** (at the *Country Club Hotel*), T404060, open 1130-1500, 1900-2300 daily, expensive, rec. **Seafood**: ***Punta Sal***, Conquistadores 948, T 441-7431, 0900-1700 daily, expensive; also ***La Caleta***, D Deteano 126, T 442-3835, 1200-1600, 1930-2400 daily, expensive; ***La Otra Alea***, Av Aramburu 511, T 441-2608, ***Puerto Azul***, Conquistadores 1018, T 441-0193, 1000-1800 daily; similar is ***El Pirata***, Av Dos de Mayo 674, T 422-3114, 1100-2300 Thur-Sat, 1100-1800 Sun-Wed; also ***Cebiches El Rey***, Av Aramburu 975, T 442-1809, 1000-2400 Mon Sat, until 1800 Sun, with branches in Miraflores, Callao and Barranco.

***Valentino's***, M Bañón 215 (nr Camino Real and Av Javier Prado), T 441-6174, open 1200-1500, 1930-2400, great Italian food; ***Fredos***, Conquistadores 512, excellent homemade pastas, ***Los Años Locos***, Conquistadores 430, T 442-4960, 1000-2400 Mon-Sat; ***José Antonio***, B Monteagudo 200, T 461-9923, 1300-1600, 1930-2400 Mon-Sat, creole and Peruvian dishes, expensive; ***Mi Casa***, Augusto Tamayo 150, T 440-3780, Japanese, 1200-1500, 1900-2300 Mon-Sat; ***Lung Fung***, Av Rep de Panamá 3165, T 422-6382, 1200-1500, 1900-2400 daily, Chinese; ***El Dorado***, Av Arequipa 2450, T 422-1080, 1100-1500, 1900-2300, Chinese, good views of Lima, expensive; ***La Casa de España***, Conquistadores 331, T 440-0114, 1000-1600, 1900-2300 Mon-Sat, 1000 1600 Sun, Spanish; ***La Carreta***, Rivera Navarrete 740, T 440-5424, open 1200-2400 daily, Peruvian and international, good steaks; ***Don Alfredo***, M Bañón 295, T 422-6681, 1200-1600, 1900-0100 Mon-Sat, 1200-1500 Sun, expensive, excellent, helpful, friendly; ***La Ronda***, Las Begoñas y Andrés Reyes, excellent value, US$10-15. La Plaza de Miguel Dazzo is a place for nightlife, restaurants, bars and discos, popular with Limeños.

In **Barranco**: ***El Otro Sitio***, Sucre 317, T 477-2413, open 1230-1600, 1900-2400, Mon-Sat, in a fine 18th century house, excellent creole buffet, expensive with live music; ***Manos Morenas***, Av Pedro de Osma 409, T 467-0421, open 1230-1630, 1900-2300, creole cuisine with shows some evenings (cover charge for shows); ***El Buen Gusto***, Av Grau 323, good for atmosphere, service, selection of meat dishes and desserts; ***El Cortijo***, Rep de Panamá 675, T 445-4481, 1200-2400 daily, Peruvian; ***El Florentino***, Av Grau 680, bar/restaurant/peña; ***Abdala***, Av Grau 340, German owner, good; ***La Ermita***, Bajada de Baños 340, Puente de Suspiros, T 467-1791, open 1230-2400, international cuisine, romantic, expensive. **Seafood**: ***Canta Rana***, Génova 101, T 445-0498, daily 1200-1700, good, also for *ceviche*; ***El Catamarán***, Av Rep de Panamá 258, T 477-1657, lunch only. Around the main plaza are several good bars and pizza restaurants; also good *peñas* and night-life.

In **Magdalena del Mar**: ***Waco***, Félix Dibos 1087, T 461-9432, open 1100-1500, 1900-2300, Mon-Sat, rec. **Pueblo Libre**: ***Taberna Quierolo***, Av San Martín 1090, 2 blocks from Museo Nacional de Antropología y Arqueología, old bar, good seafood and atmosphere, not open for dinner; ***Puerto Coral***, La Marina 1004, friendly, huge dishes (try *parihuela*).

In **Monterrico**, nr the Gold Museum: ***Pabellón de la Caza***, Alonso de Molina 1196, T 437-9533, 1200-1500, 1900-0100 Mon-Sat, Sun brunch 1030-1600, expensive, very good food and service, delightful surroundings; ***Puerto Fiel***, Av Primavera 1666, 3 blocks from Gold Museum, seafood, rec

**Lince**: ***Blue Moon***, Pumacahua 2526, T 470-1190, open 1030-0200 daily, expensive Italian bistro. **Chorrillos**: ***El Salto del Fraile***, Herradura Beach, T 442-6622, 1200-2300 daily, Peruvian and seafood; ***El Encuentro Otani***, San Pedro 182, La Campina, T 467-7668, 0900-1700 daily, excellent seafood, creole and oriental, very good value. **San Borja**: ***El Piqueo Trujillano***, Av San Luis 1956-58, T 476-1993, 1130-1830 Mon-Thur, 1200-2100 Fri-Sun, creole cooking; ***Shanghai***, Av San Luis 1988, T 435-9132, 1200-1500, 1900-2300 daily, Chinese. **Surco**: ***El Mono Verde***, Av Vicus F-56, Urb La Capullana, T 448-7288, 1300-1900 daily, evening by reservation only, good creole and Peruvian cuisine; ***Punta Pez***, Camino del Inca 398, T 442-6272, seafood.

**Jesús María**: ***El Centro Cultural Peruano Japonés***, Gregorio Escobedo 803, T 463-0606, good, cheap Japanese food.

In **central Lima**: ***L'Eau Vive***, Ucayali 370, T 427-5712, across from the Torre Tagle Palace, run by nuns, open Mon-Sat, 1245-1430, 2030-2230, fixed-price lunch menu (+ taxes and couvert), Peruvian-style in interior dining room, or à la carte in either of dining rooms that open on to patio, excellent, profits go to the poor; ***El Mesón del Frayle***, in the cloisters of San Francisco, very good, pleasant ambience, 1200-1800 (later by arrangement); ***Maury***, Ucayali 201, T 427-6210, Peruvian/international, good pisco sours; ***Chifa Cai***, Carabaya y Ucayali, clean, cheap, good fish dishes, ask about vegetarian if they're not too busy; ***Casa Vasca***, Colmena 734, T 423-6690, 1000-2300 daily, Spanish; ***Daruma***, Nicolás de Piérola 712, T 423-8209, 1000-1500, 1830-2200, Mon-Sat, Japanese; ***Gigi's***, Uruguay 411, good chifa, open for lunch; ***Raimondi***, Quesada 110 (no sign), T 427-7933, 1300-1600 daily, Peruvian, good (especially *ceviche*); ***Buena Muerte***, Junín y Abancay, Plaza Bolívar, lunch only, good *cevichería*; ***Hedi***, Puno 367, good, cheap seafood, lunch only, popular; ***Rolando's***, Washington 988, good seafood/*ceviche*; ***Lucky Star***, N de Piérola 733 (3 blocks from Plaza San Martín), 1000-2400, good, Peruvian; ***El Damero de Pizarro***, Jr de la Unión 543, huge helpings, popular with locals, loud music; ***El Pan Nuestro***, Ica 129, T 428-9931, 2 blocks from *Res Roma*, open 0800-2100 Mon-Sat, good value, good food; ***Machu Picchu***, nr *Hostal España* on Jr Azángaro, excellent set menus for breakfast (US$1.50, but ask as it's not on the menu) and lunch, huge portions; ***Casa del Cappelletti***, Av Tacna, block 7, open 1100-2200, cheap, good Italian; ***Nuevo Siglo***, Jr Moquegua 585, good menú US$1.30. The restaurant/bar opp the railway station serves good food, old-world atmosphere, good pisco sours. Very close to SAEC on Jr Breña is ***La Choza Náutica***, excellent ceviche and friendly service. Also nr SAEC is ***Nakasone***, good chicken, fries and salad for US$2.75, good service.

**Vegetarian restaurants**: ***Natur***, Moquegua 132, rec, some English spoken; ***Govinda***, Av Callao 480 y Tacna, good value lunch and at Av Arenales 674, Jesus María; ***Centro Aplicación Naturista Sebastián Kneipp***, Jr Loreto 379, Rímac, highly rec; ***Centro de la Salud 'La Naturaleza'***, Jr de la Unión, 819, No 107, or Jr Lampa 440, T 427-3832, 1000-1900, Mon-Fri; ***San Juan***, Camaná 949. In Jesús María, ***Comedor Vegetariano Nuevo Mundo***, Camillo Carrillo 159, cheap, acceptable.

A good coffee bar for snacks and sandwiches is ***Googies*** in Plaza San Martín; also ***Sandwich Tacna***, Tacna 327, popular and crowded at lunchtime. Good coffee at ***Café de Paso***, Carabobo y Cusco (stand-up coffee shop); ***Café Azzurra***, Jr Unión 574, for coffee and ice cream, also serves food during the day and breakfasts; ***Bar Edén***, Huancavelica 285, good strong expresso served from a 1950s Italian machine, male clientèle meet to discuss the day's events; ***Pastelería Lobatón***, Jr Unión 672, good *churros*. There are plenty of other cafés and snackbars in the centre of Lima.

## ● Bars

In **Barranco**: ***Johann Sebastian Bach***, Av Grau 687, classical music, has concerts nightly; ***Pizzelli Latina***, Pedro de Osma, great local bar; ***Barman's House***, Piérola 109, cheap takeaway cocktails; ***Juanito's Bodega Bar***, on the plaza, rec for local colour; ***La Noche***, popular, video bar. There are many others by the plaza in Barranco, also on the pedestrian street (Sánchez Carrión) leading from Barranco plaza to Av Bolognesi and others nr Puente de los Suspiros, eg ***El Age Acantilado***, great view, nice atmosphere. ***Video Pub***, Conquistadores, block 5, San Isidro, modern.

In **Miraflores**: ***Medi Rock***, Benavides 420, good live rock music, US$2.50 cover charge, US$2 for a small beer; ***Phantom Video y Café***, Diagonal 344, open weekends 2000-0400, music videos, good record shop downstairs; ***Nautilus***, Ricardo Palma 130, open late till dawn for food and drink.

In **central Lima** there are many good discos and video bars on and around Jr de la Unión.

## ● Airline offices

Peruvian airlines with international and national flights: **Faucett**, Garcilaso de La Vega 865, Lima, T 433-6364; Av Diagonal 592, Miraflores, T 446-3444; reservations, T 464-3322. **AeroPerú**, head office at Av Pardo 601, Miraflores, T 241-1797; reservations, T 241-0606; Av Garcilaso de la Vega 870, T 447-8255. Peruvian airlines with national flights only: **Americana**, Av Larco 345, p 5, Miraflores, T 447-1902, F 444-2761; reservations and reconfirmation, T 447-1919; Av Benavides 439, Miraflores, T 444-1246, F 444-3950; also at Jr Belén 1015, Lima, T 428-0474. **Expreso**

**Aéreo**, Av Larco 101, edif Caracol, of 303, Miraflores, T 444-9984. **Aero Cóndor**, Jr Juan de Arona 781, San Isidro, T 442-5215/441-8484. **Aero Continente**, Francisco Masias 528, p 8, San Isidro, T 442-8770/7829. **Imperial Air**, Av J Prado Este, San Isidro, T 476-3642; reservations, T 476-4542. **Aero Ica**, Tudela y Varela 150, San Isidro, T 421-6653, F 440-1030. **Grupo Ocho**, military airline, T 452-9560, at airport (desk not always staffed).

**International airlines**: **Aeroflot** 444-8710; **Air France** 470-4702; **Alitalia** 442-8506; **American Airlines** 442-8555/475-6161; **Avianca** 470-4232; **Iberia** 428-3833; **KLM** 447-1394; **Lan Chile** 446-6958/6995; **LAB** 447-3292; **Varig** 442-4031/4148; **Viasa** 241-4519; **Servivensa** 447-2694; **Saeta**, Andalucía 174, Miraflores, block 42 of Av Arequipa, T 422-4526/27/28; **Lacsa** 446-0758 (often have cheaper flights from USA).

● **Banks & money changers**

Most banks at their main branch change TCs without commission into soles, but will charge 2-3% for changing cheques into dollars cash. Banco de Crédito and Interbanc give the best rates. There are especially large queues on Mon. Banks are the best place to change TCs and *casas de cambio* for cash. Open Mon-Fri 0900-1300, 1500-1700, unless stated otherwise, many also open Sat am. **Citibank**, Las Begoñas 580, San Isidro, charges no commission on its own TCs, open 0830-1245 in summer. **Bank of America**, Augusto Tamayo 120, San Isidro, will change Bank of America TCs into local currency, 1.5% commission. **Interbanc**, Jr de la Unión 600, esq Huancavelica changes cash and Amex TCs, no commission into soles, open 0900-1500, and Sat 0900-1200; Av Larco 5th block, Miraflores, US$5 commission on TCs up to US$1000; R Navarrete 857, San Isidro, open Sat am, no commission into soles; cash against Visa card. **Banco de Crédito**, Av Lampa 499, Larco y Shell, Miraflores; Amex and Citicorp TCs, no commission; cash against Visa card, US$300/day max; **Banco Wiese**, Diagonal 176, Miraflores, 1% commission on Amex and Citicorp TCs, cash against Mastercard. **Banco Continental**, at Lampa y Emancipación; República de Panamá 3055, San Isidro; Larco 467, Miraflores; 1% commission to soles or dollars, min US$5. **Banco Mercantil**, Ucayali y Carabaya, changes Amex and Citicorps TCs (soles only, no commission) and gives cash on Visa and Mastercard; also branches in Miraflores and San Isidro. **LAC Dolar**, Jr Camaná 779, 1 block from Plaza San Martín, p 2, T 428-8127, T/F 427-3906, open Mon-Sat 0900-1900, Sun and holidays 0900-1400, good rates, very helpful, safe, fast, reliable, 2% commission on cash and TCs (Amex, Citicorp, Thomas Cook, Visa), will come to your hotel if you're in a group, repeatedly rec. **P & P Cambios**, N de Piérola 805, Mon-Fri 0900-1700, Sat 0900-1200; Av Benavides 735, Miraflores, Mon-Fri 0900-1300, 1500-1700; 2% commission on TCs in soles or dollars, **Cambios MFB**, Jr Camaná 825, T 428-7102/0004, one block from Plaza San Martín, friendly and reliable, will change Thomas Cook TCs. Lima Sheraton Casino changes TCs into dollars, no commission. Always check your money in the presence of the cashier, particularly bundles of pre-counted notes. The banks which deal with credit cards are very efficient in replacing stolen cards; similarly the American Express office (see **Travel Agents** below) in replacing stolen cheques (police report needed). **Diners Club**, Canaval y Moreyra 535, San Isidro, T 441-4272, Mon-Fri 0900-1330, 1430-1800.

The **gold dealers** on Pasaje Los Pinos, Miraflores, give good street rates. Many money changers at corner of Plaza San Martín and Jr de la Unión, in the streets behind *Hotel Bolívar*, and nr L'Ovalo in Miraflores, identified by their calculators and hiss of 'dollars', change money at the parallel rate; some change other South American currencies (see **Warning** under **Currency** in **Information for travellers**). Double-check amounts shown on calculators.

● **Cultural centres**

**Peruvian-British Cultural Association**, Av Arequipa 3495, San Isidro, T 470-5577, with reading room and British newspapers (bus 1, 2, 54A). For other offices, library and film shows, Jr Camaná 787, T 427-7927, classes only; theatre, Av Benavides 620, Miraflores, T 445-4326. **British Council**, Alberto Lynch 110, San Isidro 27, T 704-350. The theatre of the British Cultural Association is the **Teatro Británico** (amateur productions of plays in English), C Bella Vista, Miraflores, T 445-4326. **Cámara de Comercio Peruano-Británico**, Av Rep de Panamá 3563, of 202, San Isidro, T 441-3268, F 442-2135. **Instituto Cultural Peruano y Norteamericano**, Cusco 446, T 428-3530, in centre, with library (one can take the US graduate school GRE exam here); branch at Av Arequipa 4798, Miraflores, T 446-0381. Language tuition, US$80 for 4 weeks, Mon-Fri, 2 hrs a day. **The American Society of Peru**, Av Angamos 1155, Miraflores, T 441-4545. **Goethe-Institut**, Jr Nasca 722, Jesus María, Lima 11, T 433-3180, Mon-Fri, 1100-1200, 1500-2000, library, theatre, German papers, tea and cakes, you will need your passport. **Alliance Française**, Av Garcilaso de la Vega 1550, T 423-0139, also in Miraflores, Av Arequipa 4598, T 446-8511. **Euroidiomas**, Juan Fanning 520, Miraflores, T 445-7116, English papers, tea room, Ciné Club.

**American Schools**: Colegio Franklin Roosevelt, the American School of Lima, Monterrico, co-educational: Villa María, La Planicie (for girls); María Alvarado, Lima (girls). **British Schools**: Markham College, for boys, is one of only four Headmasters' Conference Schools outside the Commonwealth. Colegio San Andrés, for boys, run by the Free Church of Scotland. Colegio San Silvestre, a school for girls at Miraflores, is represented in the Association of Headmistresses. Colegio Peruano-Británico, San Isidro, co-educational. In La Molina, Colegio Newton offers the international baccalaureate. **German School**: Colegio Peruano Alemán Von Humbolt, Av Benavides 3081, Miraflores, T 448-7000.

## ● Embassies & consulates

**Argentine Consulate**, Pablo Bermúdez 143, p 2, Jesús María, T 433-5709, open 0800-1300. **Bolivian Consulate**, Los Castaños 235, San Isidro, T 422-8231 (0900-1330), 24 hrs for visas. **Brazilian Consulate**, José Pardo 850, Miraflores, T 446-2635, Mon-Fri 0930-1300. **Chilean Consulate**, Javier Prado Oeste 790, San Isidro, T 440-7965, open 0900-1300, need appointment. **Ecuadorean Consulate**, Las Palmeras 356, San Isidro (6th block of Av Javier Prado Oeste), T 442-4184. **Colombian Consulate**, Natalio Sánchez 125, p 4, T 433-8922/3, Mon-Fri 0900-1300. **Paraguayan Consulate**, Los Rosarios 415, San Isidro, T 441-8154, open 0900-1300. **Uruguayan Consulate**, Av Larco 1013, p 2, Miraflores, T 447-9948, open 0930-1330. **Venezuelan Consulate**, Av Salaverry 3005, San Isidro, T 441-5948.

**US Embassy**, Av Encalada block 17, Monterrico, T 434-3000, F 434-3065, for emergencies after hours T 434-3032, the Consulate is in the same building. **Canadian Embassy**, Libertad 130, Casilla 18-1126, Lima, T 444-4015. **New Zealand Embassy**, contact British Embassy. **South African Consulate**, contact Swiss Embassy.

**British Embassy and Consulate**, Edif Pacífico-Washington, Plaza Washington, corner of Av Arequipa (5th block) and Natalio Sánchez 125, p 11 (Casilla de Correo 854), T 433-5032/4839/4932/5137, open Mon-Thur 0830-1700, Fri 0830-1315, good for security information and newspapers (yellow bus No 2 passes the Embassy). **Irish Consulate**, Santiago Acuña 135, Urb Aurora, Miraflores T 445-6813. **Austrian Embassy**, Av Central 643, p 5, San Isidro, T 442-8851. **German Embassy**, Av Arequipa 4202, Miraflores, Casilla 18-0504, T 445-7033. **French Consulate**, Arequipa 3415, San Isidro, T 470-4968. **Belgian Consulate**, Angamos 380, Miraflores, T 446-3335. **Spanish Embassy**, Jorge Basadre 498, San Isidro, T 470-5600/78, open 0900-1300. **Swiss Embassy**, Av Salaverry 3240, Magdalena, Lima 17 (Casilla 378, Lima 100), T 264-0305/0719. **Swedish Embassy**, Camino Real 348, p 9, Torre del Pilar, San Isidro, T 440-6700. **Norwegian Consulate**, Canaval Moreyra 595, T 440-4048. **Danish Consulate General**, at Bernardo y Monteguido, San Isidro, T 462-1090. **Netherlands Consulate**, Av Principal 190, Santa Catalina, La Victoria, T 476-1069, open Mon-Fri 0900-1200. **Italian Embassy**, Av G Escobedo 298, Jesús María, T 463-2727. **Israeli Embassy**, Natalio Sánchez 125, p 6, same building as British Embassy, Santa Beatriz in Lima, Aptdo 738, T 433-4431. **Japanese Embassy**, Av San Felipe 356, Jesus María (postal address: Apdo 3708, Lima), T 463-0000.

**NB** During the summer, most embassies only open in the morning.

## ● Entertainment

**Cinemas**: some *Ciné Clubs* are: ***El Cinematógrafo***, Pérez Roca 196, Barranco; *Filmoteca de Lima*, Museo de Arte, closed Mon; ***Cooperativa Santa Elisa***, Jr Cailloma 824; ***Euroidiomas***, Juan Fanning 520, Miraflores; ***La Otra Vía***, Valdelomar 665, Pueblo Libre; ***Melies***, Av Bolívar 635, Pueblo Libre; ***Raimondi***, Alejandro Tirado 274, Lima. Free films also at Banco Central, Lampa y Ucayali, Wed at 1630, arrive early. Also the cultural institutions (see above) usually show a film once a week (often Thur). Entry about US$1. The section 'C' (Cultural) in *El Comercio* is good for checking film and theatre programmes. Many good cinemas throughout the city. Most films are in English with Spanish subtitles; US$2 in the centre, US$4.50 in Miraflores. Cinemas in centre tend to have poor sound quality. ***Ciné Pacífico***, at L'Ovalo in Miraflores, is the best for comfort and sound quality and shows the latest movies, but you pay US$5.50 for the priviledge.

**Discotheques**: good nightlife in Miraflores nr Parque Diagonal and Av Larco, with discos, video-pubs and pizzerías. All discos have a cover charge of between US$8 and US$20 pp or couple, including one drink. In most discos only couples are allowed in; most are expensive for drinks, and open from 2100 till 0400. ***Keops***, Camino Real 149, San Isidro, is very popular with young Limeños. ***Casablanca***, P Fierro 117, San Isidro, cheaper, casual; ***Amadeus***, close to the Gold Museum, Lima's most expensive and luxurious disco, US$20 cover; ***La Rosa Naútica***, above restaurant of same name, young crowd, US$10 cover; ***Casa Vieja***, San Martín y La Paz, Miraflores, casual, US$10 cover; ***Psicosis***, Bella Vista, 1st block, Miraflores, expensive, young clientele, US$15/couple; ***Nirvana***, Shell y Paseo de la República, Miraflores, modern, casual, US$8/couple; ***Bizzaro***, Lima y Diez Canseco facing Parque Kennedy, Miraflores, 2nd Floor Edif D'Anafrio, US$5 cover, New York-style, dancing and billiards; similar is ***Bauhaus***, on Bellavista. In Surquillo, ***Africa***, Av Tomás Marsano 826, and ***El Zalonazo***, C Uno 157, both rec. There are several discos along the beach in Miraflores, most of them are *salsatecas*, where only salsa is played, cover charge about US$10 pp. ***Bartlotto***, up the Malecón in San Miguel, at end of Av Brasil, *salsateca*, US$6 pp.

**Folklore**: every Sun at the ***Coliseo Cerrado***, Av Alfonso Ugarte. Also at the ***Teatro Municipal***, Jr Ica (tickets US$0.60-3.60), Tues 2000. ***Cooperativa Santa Elisa***, Cailloma 824, p 3, has a folk group every Wed, 2000. The ***Museo de Arte*** has seasons of Peruvian folklore on Wed, at 2000, US$1.20 entrance. *Peñas* are generally cheap, tavern-like places with Peruvian music, much dancing and audience participation; ***Huluchay Peña***, Trujillo 228 (across the bridge past the Post Office), Fri, Sat, 2100, entrance US$3, inexpensive, crowded, good, but take a taxi there and back; ***Las Brisas de Lago Titicaca***, just off Plaza Bolognesi, US$4.50 entry, rec; ***Peña El Ayllu***, Jr Moquegua 247, open every night, entrance free, rec; *La Palizada*, Av del Ejército 800, Miraflores; ***Kerygua***, Central Park, Diagonal, Miraflores, good folk music on Fri and Sat, entrance US$2.50; ***La Casa de Edith Barr***, Ignacio Merino 250, Miraflores; ***Taberna 1900***, Av Grau 268, Barranco, folklore and creole; ***El Buho Pub***, Sucre 315, Barranco, creole music; ***La Casona de Barranco***, Grau 329, modern music, creole and jazz. Many others in Barranco around Plaza Grau and Puente de los Suspiros, eg *Los Balcones* on Av Grau; ***La Estación de Barranco***, at Pedro de Osma 112, good, family atmosphere, varied shows, live music at weekends, US$14 cover charge, and ***Latinoamericano*** on same street; ***Mit-Uns***, Av Bolognesi opp *La Noche*, similar to *La Estación*, US$7; ***Nosferatu*** next to Puente de los Suspiros.

**Theatre**: most professional plays are put on at the **Teatro Segura**, C Huancavelica, block 2, Lima, T 427-7437; **Teatro Municipal** (Jr Ica, block 3, Lima, T 428-2303 – also orchestral and ballet performances); **Teatro Arequipa**, Av Arequipa, block 8, Lima, T 433-6919; **Teatro Marsano**, Av Petit Thouars, Miraflores, T 445-7347. Open air theatre in Parque Salazar, Miraflores (end of Av Larco) between Nov and April; check press for programme. Others are produced by amateur and university groups. **Teatro Cabaña** in the Parque de la Exposición puts on a strong programme of progressive theatre, take student card. **AAA Theatre Workshop**, Jr Ica 323. English speaking theatre occasionally by the Good Companions at **Teatro Británico**, details in *Lima Times*. The Sun edition of *El Comercio* publishes all cinema and theatre details

## ● Health, hospitals & medical services

**Baths**: Baños Pizarro, Unión 284, steam rooms, US$3, cold showers only, café and swimming pool. Windsor Turkish Baths, on Miguel Dasso, San Isidro, separate facilities for men and women, steam, sauna, cold pool and whirlpool, US$4. See Yellow Pages for other addresses.

**Dentists**: *Dr Zuelei Cornejo*, Octavio Espinoza 443, San Isidro, T 422-9638. *Ribamar Camacho Rodríguez*, Clínica Los Pinos, Miraflores, T 446-4103/2056, speaks a little English, highly rec. *Víctor Melly*, Av Conquistadores 905, San Isidro, T 422-5757. *Dr Víctor Aste*, Antero Aspillaga 415, San Isidro, T 441-7502. *Dra Ada Lucía Arroyo Torres*, Jr Laredo 196, Centro Comercial Monterrico, T 436-0942.

**Doctors**: *Dr Augusto Saldarriaga Guerra*, Clínica Internacional, T 433-4306. *Dr Alejandro Bussalleu Rivera*, Instituto Médico Lince, León Velarde 221, Lince, T 471-2238, speaks

English, good for stomach problems. Also good for stomach or intestinal problems, *Dr Raul Morales*, Clínica Padre Luis Tezza, Av del Polo 570, Monterrico, T 435-6990/6991 (no English spoken). *Dr Jorge Mejía*, Analisisclínicos, Av J Pardo Oeste 910, T 440-0643, stool analysis.

**Hospitals**: *Anglo-American Hospital*, Av Salazar, 3rd block, San Isidro, T 221-3656, rec for injections, but not typhoid; stocks gamma globulin, US$45/consultation. *Instituto de Medicina Tropical*, Universidad Particular Cayetano Heredia, Av Honorio Delgado, Urb Ingeniería, San Martín de Porres, T 482-3903/3910, for tropical diseases, or any medical help or advice, very good, cheap, for check-ups after a long jungle trip. *Hospital del Niño*, Av Brasil, vaccination centre for yellow fever, tetanus and typhoid at the side. *Clínica Internacional*, Jr Washington 1475, Lima, T 428-8060, US$30 per consultation; *Clínica San Borja*, Av del Aire 333, San Borja, T 475-3141/4997; *Clínica de Fracturas San Francisco*, Av San Felipe 142, Jesus María, T 463-9855/6202. *Policlínico Japonés*, Av Gregorio Escobedo 783, Jesús María, T 461-9291, X-rays, check-ups and analysis, reasonable prices. All clinics have 24-hr emergency service and most of them have English-speaking doctors. A consultation costs between US$25 and US$45, not inc any medicines. *Centro Especializado de Diagnóstico*, Av Arequipa 1840, Lince, T 471-8506, for x-rays, analyses, etc, no English. *Centro Anti-Rabia*, Jr Austria, Chacra Rios, Lima, T 431-4047.

**Pharmacy**: ***Botica Inglés***, Jr Cailloma 336, sells Dr Scholl foot supplies for those contemplating or recovering from the Inca Trail, among others in the centre. Tampons are available everywhere.

### ● Language schools

Most institutes have standard packages for 1 month, 2 hrs a day from Mon to Fri, about US$80; you can arrange for 2, or 3 weeks, or private tuition (about US$10/hour). **Instituto de Idiomas Pontífica Universidad Católica del Perú**, Jr Camaná 956, Lima, T 431-0052; **La Católica Universidad Instituto de Idiomas**, Camino Real 1037, San Isidro, T 441-5962; **Centro de Idiomas de Lima**, Av Manuel Olguín 215, Monterrico, T 435-0601, F 435 5970 (PO Box 772, Lima 100), US$12/hour, classes suited to students' travelling schedules, full board accommodation can be arranged with families US$120/week. See also Instituto Cultural Peruano y Norteamericano above. **Quechua Classes** Señora Lourdes Gálvez, Los Insurgentes 154, Urb Santa Constanza de Monterrico, opposite Javier Prado Oeste 41 in Surco, T 435-3910, gives 3 month courses for US$6/hr; at the same address is Señora Llorgelina Savastizagal, T 438-2676. **Universidad San Marcos**, T 452-4641, dept of Idiomas, Sats only, 4½ hrs, US$15.

### ● Laundry

Most of the better class hotels have a laundry service and there are many laundries in Lima, but they are very expensive as they charge per item (eg US$3-4 for a pair of trousers). There are some laundries in Miraflores and San Isidro which charge per kilo, about US$1.50-2. Mostly next day service. ***Continental***, Callao 422, same-day and next-day laundry and dry-cleaning, good, charge per item. ***Burbujitas***, Porta 293, Miraflores, 4 kg wash and dry for US$4.50. ***Lavaquik***, Av Benevides 604, Miraflores; ***Lava Center***, Víctor Maurtúa 140, San Isidro, T 440-3600, US$0.50/kg; ***Tokai***, Cantuarias 380, Miraflores, Mon-Sat 0900-1900, rec, US$1.10 kg; coin laundromat at Berlin 315, US$4.35 per load, same day service, reliable, rec.

### ● Places of worship

**Non-catholic**: the ***Union Church of Lima*** (Interdenominational), Av Angamos 1155, Miraflores, Worship Sun 1030, T 441-1472. ***Trinity Lutheran Church of Peru***, Las Magnolias 495, Urb Jardín, San Isidro. ***Church of the Good Shepherd***, Av Santa Cruz 491, Miraflores (Anglican) T 445-7908, Sun 0800 Holy Communion, 1000 morning service. ***International Baptist Church of Lima***, Col Inclán 799, Miraflores, T 475-7179, Worship Sun 1000. ***Christian Science Society***, 1285 Mayta Capac (nr Av Salaverry), Jesús María. ***English Benedictine Monastery***, Jr Olivares de la Paz, Las Flores (57M minibus from Plaza de Acho); Sunday Mass 0900, weekdays 1900. ***Synagogue***, Av 2 de Mayo 1815, San Isidro, T 440-0290. **Catholic Mass in English**, La Iglesia de Santa María Reina, Ovalo Gutiérrez, Av Santa Cruz, Miraflores, T 424-7269, Sun 0930.

### ● Post & telecommunications

**Air freight**: most companies are in Callao (see Yellow Pages under 'Agencias de Carga'). They all charge about the same and only handle large amounts: by air about US$15/kg, surface US$3-5/kg. You can deal direct with the airlines, all have a cargo office at the airport. KLM is best. UPS, Paseo de la República 6299, Miraflores, T 446-0444, documents or freight to USA US$37/kg, to Europe US$96.

**Post Offices**: central office is on Pasaje Piura, 1 block from the Plaza de Armas, T 427-5592, hours: Mon-Sat 0800-2000, Sun 0800-1400. *Poste restante* is in the same building, but on the other side (unreliable). In Miraflores, Av Petit Thouars 5201, Mon-Sat 0800-2000. There are many sub-post offices in all districts of Lima, but sending a letter from the suburbs takes longer. Express letters can be sent from the Central Post Office or at the airport (mail posted at the airport reaches Europe in 5 days). There are private companies for express letters, eg: EMS, T 432-3950/278531; DHL, T 451-8587/452-1278; Letter Express, T 444-4509; Peru Express, T 431-1769; VEC, T 442-0830/0866; Skyway, T 422-9225/440-2353. When receiving a package of over 1 kg, it must be collected from the Aduana post office, Av Tomás Valle, nr the airport, open Mon-Fri 0830-1400, or from Teodoro Cárdenas 267, Lince, T 471-6877. For parcels see page 444, **Mail**.

**Telecommunications**: Telefónica del Perú, Jr Carabaya 933, Plaza San Martín, T 433-1616, open daily 0800-2200; also at Diez Canseco y La Paz, Miraflores, opp *Hotel César*, open daily 0730-2100; Tarata 280, off Larco, Miraflores, open Mon-Sat 0830-2130, Sun 0830-1300. Payphones on the street, and at airport, can be used for national and international calls with coins or phonecards. Telefónica offices can be found all over Lima; phone and fax. For full details on phone operation, see **Telephones** in **Information for travellers**, page 444.

### ● Shopping

Since so many artesans have come from the Sierra to Lima, it is possible to find any kind of handicraft in the capital. The prices are the same as in the highlands, and the quality is high. Silver and gold handicrafts of all kinds; Indian hand-spun and hand-woven textiles; manufactured textiles in Indian designs; llama and alpaca wool products such as ponchos, rugs, hats, blankets, slippers, coats, sweaters, etc; *arpilleras*, appliqué pictures of Peruvian life (originated in Chile with political designs), made with great skill and originality by women in the shanty towns; fine leather products mostly hand made. The *mate burilado*, or engraved gourd found in every tourist shop, is cheap and a genuine expression of folk art (cheaper in villages nr Huancayo). For handicrafts produced by cooperatives, with benefits going directly to the producers, contact the non-profit organization ***Minka***, Av Grau 266, Edif El Portal, p 2, Barranco, open Tues-Sat 1100-1900, good selection of handicrafts; for further information contact Norma Velásquez. ***Silvania Prints***, Colmena 714 (nr *Hotel Bolívar*), Conquistadores 905 (San Isidro), sell modern silk-screen prints on Pima cotton with precolumbian designs. On Av Nicolás de Piérola vendors sell oil paintings of Andean scenes, bargains abound. ***Centro Artesanal 'El Arte Peruano'***, Av Alfonso Ugarte 901-925, T 424-1978, open 0900-2000, ask for Carlos Ramos for especially fine retablos, or Guillermo Arce for fine Cajamarca mirrors in colonial style; they also sell rugs from Ayacucho and San Pedro de Cajas, ceramics from Ayacucho and Cusco and other items (there is a nationwide handicraft association of this name). ***Artesanías Perú SA*** government store for Peruvian handicrafts in San Isidro (Av Jorge Basadre 610, T 440-1925/228847). ***La Casa de la Mujer Artesana***, Av Perú 1550 (Av Brasil cuadra 15), Pueblo Libre, T 423-8840, F 423-4031, cooperative run by Movimiento Manuela Ramos, excellent quality work mostly from *pueblos jóvenes*.

Miraflores is the best place for high quality, pricey handicrafts; there are many shops on and around Av La Paz, and on Petit Thouars, blocks 53/54. Rec is ***Kuntur Wasi***, Ocharan 182, T 444-0557, high quality, English-speaking owner very knowledgeable about Peruvian textiles, frequently has exhibitions of fine folk art and crafts; ***Antisuyo***, Jr Tacna 460, Miraflores, Mon-Fri 0900-1930, Sat 1030-1830, an indigenous cooperative run by an Englishwoman, sells high-quality handicrafts from all regions, reasonable prices, T 447-2557 (another outlet in Cusco). ***Agua y Tierra***, Diez Canseco 337b, excellent fine crafts and indigenous art. ***Centro Comercial El Alamo***, La Paz (close to *César Hotel*), Miraflores, 0900-2000, *artesanía* shops with good choice. ***Las Pallas***, Cajamarca 212, 5th block of Av Grau, Barranco, T 477-4629, Mon-Sat 0900-1900, good quality handicrafts. Antiques available in Miraflores on Av La Paz. See ***H Stern's*** jewellery stores at *Hotels Miraflores César*, *Bolívar* and *Sheraton*, and at the International Airport.

**NB** It is better to buy pullovers in the Sierra. However, although Lima is more expensive, it is often impossible to find the same quality of goods elsewhere; geniune alpaca is odourless wet or dry, wet llama 'stinks'. Alpaca cloth for suits, coats, etc (mixed with 40% sheep's wool) can be bought cheaply from factories: ***Cinsa***, Av Argentina 2400, microbus 93, 70 or 84 from Plaza Castilla; ***Lanificio***, Nicolás Arriola 3090, San Luis, T 432-0859, better quality in their Arequipa factory (see page 265) (gives 10% discount to foreigners attached to their embassies). Alpaca wool for knitting or weaving from ***Alpaca III***, Av Larco 859, Miraflores. Made-to-measure cotton shirts in 24 hrs from Sr Hurtado, 'Sir', Jr Carabaya 1108, and in 48 hrs from Luz Manrique, Cailloma 328, T 427-9472. A good tailor is ***Navarro Hermanos***, in Belén, below the Tourist Office. Another is ***Creaciones Vargas***, Jr Ica 380, T 427-8680, good value. Export quality jeans are made by ***Sombrería Palacio***, Unión 214. There are bargains in clothing made from high quality Pima cotton.

**Bookshops**: fair selection of foreign-language books at ***Librería Delta***, N de Piérola 689, Lima; and at ***ABC Bookstores*** Av Paseo de la República 3440, No 32B, San Isidro, also by *Cine El Pacífico*, Miraflores. ***Librería Studium***, Plaza Francia 1164 (with several branches), sells history/travel books in English. *Studium* and *Librería de la Universidad de San Marcos* give student discounts. Books in English, French and German also available from ***Librería Ayza***, Jr Unión 560, rec, will supply works in Quechua. ***Librería Internacional***, Jr Unión (corner of Plaza San Martín) has a wide selection of books on South America in all languages, good for regional maps. Good English selection at ***Epoca***, on Belén in the centre, on José Pardo in Miraflores and other branches, T 445-7430/0282. ***Portal*** on the plaza in Barranco has good selection, with a gallery, excellent handicrafts for sale and coffee shop. ***Librería El Pacífico*** in Miraflores has a good selection of English books. Rare books, many shops on Av Azángaro. **NB** Foreign language books are subject to a high tax (US$12) and there are no guidebooks for sale. International newspapers, from newstands, Block 6, Av N de Piérola, or in the Parque Central, Miraflores (taken from aircraft).

Secondhand books are found in the 5th to 6th block of Av Grau in the centre, some English books are sold, but poor selection. Also around Plaza Francia on the pedestrian street that runs to block 10 of Garcilaso de la Vega.

**Film**: Agfa distributor at E Diez Canseco 176; for cheap film try at the black market at Feria Polvos Azules, at Puente de Piedra. Many developers using Kodak equipment offer same-day service; all at similar prices. Many on Jr Unión and Plaza San Martín; also Av Larco, Miraflores. Good but expensive place for developing photos and slides at Grimaldo del Solar 275, between Shell and Benavides, Miraflores, T 444-2304, open Mon-Fri 0945-1300, 1400-1830, Sat 0945-1300. *Profesa*, Av Petit Thouars 3231, San Isidro, T 442-3542, specialist shop for photographic equipment. **Camera repairs**: *Camera House*, Larco 1150, Office 39, p 2, Miraflores, Mon-Fri 1530-1900, ask for Clemente Higa, who is often there later in pm. ***Frankitec***, Jr Lampa 1115, oficina 104, Lima 1, T 428-4331, Swiss technician, better for mechanical cameras.

**Maps**: a good map of the Lima area is available from street sellers in the centre of Lima, or in better bookshops (published by Lima 2000, US$10, or US$14 in booklet form). A cheaper, less accurate, and less discreet map is published by Cartográfica Nacional for US$3-4. The **Instituto Geográfico Nacional** (Av Aramburu 1198, Surquillo, Lima 34, T 475-9960, F 473-3075), sells a standard map of Peru (1:2,200,000), US$10, department maps, US$7, a Peru road map, US$10 and a beautiful 4-sheet map of Peru, 1:1,000,000, US$30; at the same size and for the same price is a geological map; topographical maps, 1:100,000, which only cover Peru from the coast to the highest mountains and most of the Department of Loreto, cost US$7. Satellite map of most of the jungle area, 1:100,000, is US$8; black-and-white aerial photos available at US$8. Passport is needed to enter; they are open 0900-1700, Mon-Fri. Maps of N and S border areas are not sold. If you submit a letter to the IGN, giving your credentials and adequate reasons, plus a photocopy of your passport, you may be able to obtain maps of the border regions. Aerial photographs are available at **Servicio Autofotográfico Nacional**, Las Palmas airforce base, Chorrillos, T 467-1341, open Mon-Fri 0800-1300, 1330-1545. **Ingement**, Pablo Bermúdez 211, Jesus María, T 433-6234, open 0730-1400, has information on geology and sells some maps. **Senamhi**, República de Chile 295, Jesus María, T 433-7624, open 0830-1345, has good information on Peruvian meteorology. Petroperú maps for town centres rec.

**Markets**: Parque Diagonal/Kennedy, Miraflores (by *Restaurant Haiti*): secondhand books, jewellery, sandals made to measure, paintings and other handicrafts, Dec-June, Wed to Mon, in winter Sat and Sun only; **Feria Artesanal**, Av de la Marina 790 and Av Sucre Oeste, in Pueblo Libre, the biggest crafts market in Lima, but expensive, bargaining is expected; take any colectivo that says Brasil/La Marina from Plaza Bolognesi or Ugarte; taxi US$2-3; watch your possessions, as thieves are numerous. Extensive market selling woollen goods, leatherwork, bric-a-brac and Peruvian goods and souvenirs on sidestreets off **Lampa**; for hardware, sidestreets off **Av Colmena**: for books, **Parque Universitario. Polvos Azules**, behind Central Post Office, 1 block from Plaza de Armas, sells just about anything (including stolen cameras), small handicraft section (ask directions) which sells the best and cheapest earrings, including the parts for making them; the market is generally cheap and very interesting, it doesn't get going until around 1000; beware pickpockets. The handicrafts markets in Miraflores on Av Petit Thouars, blocks 52-54, have a good selection. Flowers are sold at the Estadio Nacional, 8th block of Paseo de la República, open daily.

In every suburb you can find one or more food market. Some of the bigger supermarkets are **Wong** (at Benavides y Panama, nr Youth Hostel) and **Santa Isabel** (24-hr supermarket at Benavides y La Paz – excellent stock).

## ● Sports

**Association football matches** and various athletic events take place at the National Stadium, in the centre of the city on ground given by the British community on the 100th anniversary of Peru's Declaration of Independence. The local soccer derby is Universitario against Alianza Lima (tickets US$2.50-25).

**Bull fighting**: there are two bullfight seasons: Oct to first week in Dec and during July. They are held in the afternoons on Sun and holidays. Tickets can be bought at Plaza Acho from 0930 1300 (T 481-1467), or Farmacia Dezza, Av Conquistadores 1144, San Isidro, T 440-8911/3798. Prices range from US$14 to US$90 (see page 85).

**Clubs**: there are many private sports clubs but you have to be a member to get in; some will allow visitors for a small fee (US$3-6), even though most only allow visitors with a member, for a small fee.

**Cockfights**: are frequently organized and advertised: the Plaza de Gallos is at C Sandía 150, nr Parque Universitario.

**Cycling**: popular, without yet becoming a serious sport: ***Bike Touring Club*** meets every Sun at 0730 outside *Cine Orrantia*, Javier Prado y Av Arequipa, T 463-1747 (planning meetings at Cabo Gutarra 613, Pueblo Libre), contact Tito López and Mónica Miranda (Tito repairs bikes, but does not have spares). ***Mountain Bike Club***, at *Cicling* shop, Av Benavides 2997, Miraflores, president Gustavo Prado. *Centro Comercial de Bicicletas*, Av San Juan de Miraflores 1281, Miraflores, T 446-0228. Hard to find 28" tyres, try ***Casa Okuyama***, Jr Montevideo, Lima. Good shop is ***Biclas***, Av Los Conquistadores, San Isidro.

**Golf**: the Lima (T 426006), Inca, Granja Azul and La Planicie golf clubs and the Country Club de Villa all have 18-hole courses. The Santa Rosa, Cruz de Hueso and Huampani golf clubs have 9-hole courses.

**Horse racing**: Hipódromo Monterrico, on Tues and Thur evenings (1900) and Sat and Sun (1400) in summer, and in winter on Tues evening and Sat and Sun afternoons. Foreigners must bring their passport. Preferred seating US$2, first class US$0.75, second class US$0.20; T 436-5677 or 435-1035 ext 2316/2317. For Caballos de Paso, which move in four-step amble, extravagantly paddling their forelegs, National Paso Association, Miraflores, T 447-6331. Races are held at the Peruvian de Paso breeding farm in Lurin, S of Lima, T 435-6574.

**Lima Cricket and Football Club**: Justo Vigil 200, Magdalena del Mar, T 461-0080/4030. The club has extensive sports facilities, as well as football, rugby (training at 1700 on Thur, May-Oct) and cricket, squash, swimming, snooker, etc. Also restaurant, pub and friendly place to meet people. If you play cricket get in touch, December-February.

**Mountaineering**: the information provided by the informal mountaineering clubs is questionable. *Club Andino*, Av Paseo de la República 932, Santa Beatriz, contact Lucho Shernela, T 463-7319, meetings Thur 1900-2200; ***Asociación de Andinismo de la Universidad de Lima***, Pabellón F (Bienestar Universitario), Universidad de Lima, Javier Prado Este s/n, T 437-6767 ext 2107/2134, F 437-8066, meetings Wed 1800-2000; ***Club de Montañeros Américo Tordoya***, Jr Tarapacá 384, Magdalena, T 460-6101, meetings Thur 1930, contact Gonzalo Menacho. ***Aso-***

*ciación Andes Perú*, Av Larco 853, of D, Miraflores, T 445-6055, contact Pedro Marchetti.

**Trekking and backpacking**: for information contact Percy Tapiá, *Trek Andes*, Av Benavides 212, of 1203, Miraflores, PO box 01-3074, Lima 100, T/F 447-8078, good information. *Instituto Nacional de Recreación*, Educación Física y Deportes (Inred), has an Andean specialist, César Morales Arnao, at the Estadio Nacional, Tribuna Sur, door 4, p 3, T 433-4192, ext 42, rec. *Trekking and Backpacking Club*, Jr Huáscar 1152, Jesus María, Lima 11 (T 423-2515), run by Miguel Chiri Valle, free information on Peru and South America, storage and gas cylinders available. *Meiggs Trekking Club*, Casilla 41-0091, Lima 41, T/F 446-3493, runs trips once a month, contact Fernando Pinto. Good advice from Richard Hidalgo, T 448-2691. Good climbing and hiking equipment shop, *Alpamayo*, at Av Larco 345, Miraflores, T 445-1671, F 445-0370; owner Sr Enrique Ramírez speaks fluent English.

**Parapenting, Hangliding, Ballooning**: contact Sr José Bustamante, *High Flight Peru*, Parque San Carlos 217, Lima 21, just off 14th block of Av Bolívar, T 463-4199 (Sr Bustamante is opening a new Youth Hostel, E, at Los Sauces 418, Chaclacayo, Km 24, T 497-2343, F 462-7998).

**Diving**: for information and equipment contact; *Mundo Submarino*, Av Conquistadores 791, San Isidro, T 441-7602, Sr Alejandro Pez Z is a professional diver and arranges trips; *Kailua Dive Shop*, Av Conquistadores 969, San Isidro, T/F 441-4057, owner Paolo is Italian, also runs PADI diving course.

**Surfing**: *Federación Peruana de Tabla* is located at Club Waikiki, Costa Verde s/n, Bajada Baños, Miraflores, PO Box 180007, T/F 442-3830; several surf shops, best is *O'Neills*, Av Santa Cruz 851, Miraflores, T 445-0406, contact Gino, very knowledgeable, speaks English; the surfing magazine '*Tablista*' is published in Dec and July, available at kiosks in Lima.

### ● Tour companies & travel agents

Most of those in Lima specialize in selling air tickets, or in setting up a connection in the place where you want to start a tour. Shop around and compare prices; also check all information carefully. It is best to use a travel agent in the town closest to the place you wish visit; it is cheaper and they are more reliable.

Those listed below are divided into the following groups: a) standard tours, well-organized but expensive; b) standard tours, less expensive; c) adventure tours; d) specialized tours.

a) *Lima Tours*, Jr Belén (or extension of Unión) 1040 (PO Box 4340), Lima, T 424-5110/7560/9386, F 426-3383, highly rec; in the same building is the American Express agent, which will not change TCs into dollars cash but is the only place to give TCs against an Amex card; also at Los Rosales 440, San Isidro, T 442-0750, F 441-1405; Av Pardo 392, Miraflores, T 241-7551, F 446-8716. *Cóndor Travel*, Mayor Armando Blondet 249, San Isidro, T 442-7305, F 442-3634; *Kinjyo Travel*, Las Camelias 290, San Isidro, T 442-4000, F 442-1000; *Solmartur*, Av La Paz 744, Miraflores, T 444-1313, F 444-3060; *Perú Chasqui*, Mariana de los Santas 198-201, San Isidro, T 441-1455, F 441-1459; *Panorama*, Bella Vista 210, of A, Miraflores, T 446-9578, F 445-0910; *Hada Tours*, 2 de Mayo 529, Miraflores, T/F 446-2714.

b) *Nuevo Mundo*, Jr Camaná 702, Lima, T/F 427-0635; *Turismo Pacífico*, Alcanfores 373, Miraflores, T 444-3363; *Setours*, Cdte Espinar 229, Miraflores, T 446-7090, F 446-7129; *Tecnitur*, Manuel Freyre y Santander 282, Miraflores, T/F 447-1289; *Julia Tours*, Francia 597, Miraflores, T 447-9798, F 447-3021; *Peruvian's Life*, Diez Canseco 332, Miraflores, T/F 444-8825.

c) *Explorandes*, Bellavista 518, Miraflores, T 445-0532, F 445-4486; *Andean Tours*, Jr Shell 319, of 304, Miraflores, T 447-8430; *Hirca*, Bellavista 518, Miraflores, T/F 447-3807; *Alpamayo Tours*, Emilio Cavanecia 160, of 201, San Isidro, T/F 442-3886, Duilio Vallutino and 'Pepe' López are two of the most experienced rafters and kayakers in Peru and led the first ascent of the Río Cotahuasi nr Arequipa, rec for river rafting; *Irré Tours*, Av Boulevard 1012, T 475-8808, Julio speaks good English, arranges trips and guides for small groups.

d) *CanoAndes*, Av San Martín 455, Barranco, T 477-0188, F 474-1288, rafting and kayaking trips; *Viento Sur Expediciones*, Av La Molina 400, Ate-Vitarte, T 435-6226, sailing tours to Paracas and day tours from Lima.

**Useful addresses**: *Apavit*, Asociación Peruana de Agencias de Viajes y Turismo, Antonio Roca 121, Santa Beatriz, T 433-7610; *Apta*, Asociación Peruana de Operadores de Turismo de Aventura, Benavides 212, of 1203, Miraflores, T 447-8078; *Agotur*, Asociación de Guías

Oficiales de Turismo, Jr Belén 1030, Lima, T 424-5113.

**Private guides**: Rolando Peceros, contact Lima Tours, T 427-6720 or 448-5562 (home), specialist in Peruvian archaeology from Chiclayo to Nasca, charges US$25/day. Tino Guzmán Khang, T/F (home) 429-5779, 24-hr cellphone 997-7060, or South American Explorers Club, cultural tours, especially Pachacámac, museums, special interest tours, English and French speaking, US$10/hour up to 3 people, highly rec.

**NB** We have received complaints about agencies, or their representatives at bus offices or the airport arranging tours and collecting money for companies that either do not exist or which fall far short of what is paid for. Do not conduct business anywhere other than in the agency's office and insist on a written contract.

### ● Tourist offices

Tourist offices throughout Peru are operated by the Ministerio de Industria, Comercio, Turismo e Integración, C 1 Oeste, Corpac, p 14, F 442-9280. In Lima, the tourist office is Infotur, Jr Unión (Belén) 1066, Oficina E-2, T 431-0117, Mon-Fri 0930-1730, Sat 1000-1300; they give out tourist information, make reservations and are very helpful, including on which parts of the country it is safe to visit. Copetur (Corporación Peruana de Turismo), Schell 120 of 25, Miraflores, T 445-3083, F 446-1593. There is a tourist booth at the airport which will make local reservations, or you can call the hotel direct. There are several representatives of travel agencies at the airport, but they are rather pushy; better to take your time and arrange trips once settled in your hotel, or shop around later. Ask for the helpful, free, *Peru Guide* published in English by Lima Editora, T 444-0815, available at travel agencies or other tourist organizations.

There now exists a 24-hr hotline for travellers' complaints, T 224-7888 (dial 01 first from outside Lima), or toll free on 0-800-4-2579 (not from pay phones); this is run by the Tourist Bureau of Complaints and will help with complaints regarding customs, airlines, travel agencies, accommodation, restaurants, public authorities or if you have lost, or had stolen, documents.

**South American Explorers' Club**: Av Rep de Portugal 146 (Breña – on the 13th block of Alfonso Ugarte), T/F 0051 (01151 from USA)-1-

425-0142, email montague@amauta.rcp.net, is a non-profit, educational organization which functions primarily as an information network for Peru and South America. Membership is US$40 a year (US$60/couple), plus US$7 for postage of its quarterly journal, *The South American Explorer* (outside the US) and numerous member services such as access to files of travel information, equipment storage, personal mail service, trip planning, etc. Open 0930-1700 Mon to Fri; non-members are welcome, but asked to limit their visits, staff very helpful. The clubhouse is attractive and friendly; it is not necessary to 'explore' to feel at home here. They will sell used equipment on consignment (donations of used equipment, unused medicines etc, are welcome). Their map of the Inca Trail is good (US$4), and they sell an excellent map of the Cordillera Huayhuash. Other useful dyeline trekking maps inc the Llanganuco-Santa Cruz trek in the Cordillera Blanca, and the Cordillera Vilcanota (Auzangate). There is a good library and they sell travel books (inc this one) and guides (at a discount to members), book swap facilities are available, and some excellent handicrafts. For further information, and the most recent views on where and how to travel safely, write to: Casilla 3714, Lima 100, Peru; 126 Indian Creek Rd, Ithaca, NY 14850, USA (T 607-277-0488, F 607-277-6122, E-mail explorer@samexplo.org); or Apdo 21-431, Eloy Alfaro, Quito, Ecuador (T/F 225-228, E-mail explorer@saec.org.ec). The US office can supply books, maps and trip-planning services; book and maps can be shipped worldwide. Online information http://www.samexplo.org.

**Tourist and archaeological information**: Federico Kaufmann-Doig is a great source of information on Peruvian archaeology, for serious students and archaeologists. He has worked on various sites in Peru and is currently engaged on a 3-year project in the Kuelap area. He is the director of the Instituto de Arqueología Amazónica, T 449-0243, or (home) 449-9103. His book, *Historia del Perú: un nuevo perspectivo*, in 2 volumes (*Pre-Inca*, and *El Incario*) is available at better bookshops. The Instituto Nacional de Cultura, in the Museo de la Nación, should be contacted by archaeologists for permits and information. The Museo Nacional de Antropología y Arquelogía in Pueblo Libre (address above) is the main centre for archaeological investigation and the Museo de la Nación holds exhibitions.

**The Peruvian Touring and Automobile Club**: Av César Vallejo 699 (Casilla 2219), Lince, Lima (T 403270), offers help to tourists and particularly to members of the leading motoring associations. Good maps available of whole country; regional routes and the South American sections of the Pan-American Highway available (US$2.10).

### ● Useful addresses

**Tourist Police**, Museo de la Nación, J Prado 2465, p 5, San Borja, T 476-9896, F 476-7708, friendly, helpful, English and some German spoken, open 0800-2000; rec to visit when you have had property stolen. **Dirección General de Migraciones**, España 700, Breña, open 0900-1300; if passport stolen can provide new entry stamps, also for visa extensions, given same day. **Intej**, Av San Martín 240, Barranco, can extend student cards, T 477-4105. **YMCA**, Av Bolívar 635, Pueblo Libre, membership required. **Biblioteca Nacional**, Av Abancay (cuadra 4) y Miró Quesada, T 428-7690, open 0830-2000.

### ● Transport

**Local Bus**: the bus routes are shared by buses and colectivos (small vans); the latter run from 0600-0100, and less frequently through the night, they are quicker and stop wherever requested. Bus fares US$0.30, colectivos US$0.35-0.45, depending on length of journey. The principal routes are from the centre of Lima to Miraflores, San Isidro, Pueblo Libre, central market and airport. The centre, between Tacna, Abancay and Nicolás de Piérola is now free of buses. Look for route names on bus windscreen, but check that the bus is going in the direction you want.

**Buses to Miraflores**: plenty of colectivos run the route between the centre and Miraflores, along Tacna, Garcilaso de la Vega, Arequipa and Larco, 24 hrs, US$0.30 by day, US$0.35 on Sun, US$0.45 after midnight. Routes are displayed on the windscreen. Some buses also run this route for US$0.30; check the route before you get in. On Vía Expresa, buses can be caught at Avs Tacna, Garcilaso de la Vega and Ugarte (faster than Av Arequipa, but watch for pickpockets). The main stop for Miraflores is Ricardo Palma, 4 blocks from Parque Kennedy. Taxi US$2.30.

**Car rental**: all rental companies have an office at the airport, where you can arrange everything and pick up and leave the car. Cars can be hired from **Hertz**, Rivera Navarrete 550, San

## Beetling around Lima

Anyone taking a taxi in Lima will experience the ubiquitous VW Beetle. The famous German car, much-loved the world over, has a reputation as a tough, durable little character, but Lima's taxi drivers take this claim to extreme and often ridiculous lengths. If some of the city's Beetles were supermarket food, they wouldn't be so much past the sell-by date as a serious health hazard.

The first clue to your taxi's age and roadworthiness may be the complete lack of paintwork on the exterior, leaving a nice rust finish. A quick glance at the windscreen can also help determine the expected degree of comfort and safety. Chances are, it's been shattered so many times it'll resemble the work of some crazed, hyperactive spider, meaning the driver has to lean out the side window in order to see where he's going.

The seemingly simple matter of getting into the car can be deceptively tricky. This usually involves a stream of shouted instructions which are impossible to decipher, followed by the driver rushing out to do it himself. The brave or foolhardy may attempt to open the passenger door unaided, but be warned: this will invariably leave you standing on the pavement with an entire car door in your hands.

Those travelling at night or through one of Lima's frequent grey drizzles will quickly find out that lights and windscreen wipers are seen as luxury extras rather than an essential prerequisite to accident-free driving. This can be viewed as yet another reason to abandon all hope of arriving at your destination or as a blessing in disguise. Half the time you won't want to see where you're going anyway, especially as you rush headlong down a pot-hold backstreet, strewn with piles of rubbish, roaming livestock and dead dogs.

To take your mind off the perils of your taxi journey you could strike up a conversation with the driver, or just close your eyes, grit your teeth and think of the money your saving.

Isidro, T 442-4475; **Budget**, Francisco de Paula Camino 231-A, Miraflores, T 445-1266; **Avis**, Av Camino Real 1278, San Isidro, T 441-9760; **Dollar**, Av La Paz 438, Miraflores, T 444-4920; **National**, Av España 449, Lima, T 433-3750; **Thrifty**, Aristides Aljovin 472, Miraflores, T 444-4441; **VIP**, Conquistadores 697, San Isidro, T 441-3705. Prices range from US$40 to US$60 depending on type of car. The condition of vehicles is usually very poor. Beware of deep street potholes. Make sure that your car is in a locked garage at night. Russian-made 4WD Niva vehicles are often rented; they are up to the conditions of Andean driving, but Lada saloon cars are not. Note that it can be much cheaper to rent a car in a town in the Sierra for a few days than to drive all the way from Lima. Also, if there are any problems with the rental car, companies do not have a collection service.

**Cycling**: into or out of Lima is not rec, difficult and dangerous.

**Taxis**: no taxis use meters and anyone can operate as a taxi driver. You must bargain the price beforehand and insist on being taken to the destination of your choice, not the driver's. Fares: within city centre US$1.50-2; to Miraflo res and most suburbs US$2-3.50; from outside airport to centre US$4-5, San Isidro/Miraflores US$6-7, Breña US$3.50; from inside airport gates to centre US$8-9, Miraflores US$12-13. After dark and on holidays, 35%-50% surcharge. Always have exact fare ready. Licensed taxis are blue and yellow, but there are many other types. VWs are cheapest, the bigger black taxis charge US$15-20 from centre to suburbs. Licensed and phone taxis are safest. There are several reliable phone taxi companies, which can be called for immediate service, or booked in advance; prices are 2-3 times more than ordinary taxis; eg to the airport US$12, to suburbs US$7-8. Some are *Taxi Real*, T 470-6263; *Taxi Metro*, T 437-3689; *Lady's* T 470-8528; *Taxi Phono*, T 422-6565; *Taxi*

*Seguro*, T 448-7226. Paco, T 461-6394, is dependable for phone hiring, similarly Willy, T 452-7456, speaks perfect English, highly rec, works with SAEC. Jaime Torres, Los Algarrobos 1634, Urb Las Brisas, T 462-9400, has been rec as honest and reliable, speaks excellent English. Drivers don't expect tips; give them small change from the fare. If hiring a taxi for over 1 hr agree on price/hour beforehand. To Callao, La Punta, San Miguel, Magdalena, Miraflores (US$4), Barranco, Chorrillos, by agreement, basis US$5/hour. Rec, knowledgeable driver, Hugo Casanova Morella, T 485-7708 (he lives in La Victoria), for city tours, travel to airport, etc. 'Trici-Taxis', 3-wheel cycle carts, can be hired for moving about with heavy baggage.

**Air** Jorge Chávez Airport, 16 km from the centre of Lima. There is control of people entering and leaving the airport; tourists have to show passports. Luggage may be checked several times, so arrive 2-3 hrs before your departure (1½ hrs for domestic flights).

Strict controls at the airport may mean that an official will demand to search your luggage. Legally they cannot ask for money and this also applies on arrival. This is not true if you are importing goods or bringing a large quantity of new merchandise, when taxes are charged. Taxes cannot be charged on new personal possessions. At the customs area, insist that you are a tourist and that your personal effects will not be sold in Peru; if necessary ask them to stamp in your passport that you are bringing a bicycle, stereo, whatever, and will leave with it.

Only official Corpac porters are allowed in the customs area. Do not give your bags to unofficial porters who are desperate to carry your luggage (they will expect a tip if you even so much as look at them). 24-hr left luggage costs US$3/item/day (make sure luggage is locked, or use the US$1 plastic loop to seal bags).

**Banco Mercantil** and **Banco del Comercio** in Departures change TCs (Amex and Citicorp), no commission and give cash advance on Visa or Mastercard, open 24 hrs; the latter handles airport tax along with Banco Continental; also Visa ATM in Departures. **Casa de Cambio** in Arrivals changes cash and TCs, open 24 hrs. Avoid getting left with soles at the airport when leaving; changing them back into dollars can take a lot of time, and you need to show the official exchange slips. **Post Office** upstairs in Departures, open 24 hrs. **Telefónica del Perú** has a 24-hr office; lots of payphones. **Information** on arrivals and departures: international T 452-3135; national T 452-9570. The **Prohotel** agent at the airport is very helpful with hotel bookings of all classes; there is a second hotel booking agency. Taxi drivers also tout for hotel business, offering discounts – don't let yourself be bullied.

There are several cafes, restaurants and shops and a duty-free shop in the Departure lounge which will accept Amex cards. Prices on some items higher than at supermarkets. Safe to stay all night in 24-hr expresso-snack bar upstairs but expensive. You can also sleep on the 1st floor above the check-in area. There is an airport workers' canteen 'comedor de los trabajadores' also open to the public, just beyond the perimeter fence to the right of the main terminal. For those in transit, refreshment options are expensive, although temporary access to shops in the main lobby of the terminal building is possible.

Taxi from desk outside Arrivals, US$8-9 to centre, US$12-13 to Miraflores. See above for other taxi fares. The gate for cars leaving the airport is in the middle of the parking area; for pedestrians it is at the lefthand corner of the parking area, from where you can catch a cheaper taxi to the city (US$4 to centre, US$7 to Miraflores). There is a service called Airport Express, every 20 mins to Miraflores from the national exit, comfortable micro buses, US$4.50 pp, only during the day. Local buses and colectivos run between the airport perimeter and the city centre and suburbs, their routes are given on the front window ('Tacna' for the centre, 'Miraflores' for Miraflores, 'Brasil' for South American Explorers Club). Outside the pedestrian exit are the bus, colectivo and taxi stops, but there is more choice for buses at the roundabout by the car entrance. Luggage is not allowed on buses. Colectivo service from Av Tacna y Colmena (N de Piérola) 733, from 0600 to 2000, colectivos wait until they have 5 passengers, US$0.75 pp, and US$0.25 for luggage. The big hotels have their own buses at the airport, and charge US$6.

**Internal air services**: the domestic airlines serve the following places: Andahuaylas, Arequipa, Ayacucho, Cajamarca, Chiclayo, Cusco, Huánuco, Iquitos, Juanjui, Juliaca, Moyobamba, Piura, Pucallpa, Puerto Maldonado, Rioja, Tacna, Talara, Tarapoto, Tingo María, Tocache, Trujillo, Tumbes and Yurimaguas. Expreso Aéreo also serves the following places on an irregular basis: Bellavista, Chachapoyas, Chimbote and Saposoa. Aéro Cóndor has a small plane for flights to northern destinations and jungle areas: Cajamarca, Chimbote, Huánuco, Palmapampa, San Francisco, Tingo María, also tourist flights to Ica and Nasca. Grupo Ocho's flights to selected destinations are fixed schedule, but must be booked well in advance, at least 10 days (Cusco, Pucallpa, Andahuaylas, Chachapoyas). To most destinations there are daily flights, but flights may cancelled in the rainy season.

**Train** There has been no passenger service to La Oroya or Huancayo since 1991, although trains are running from Huancayo to Huancavelica. Check South American Explorers Club for information. For all these destinations there are bus and colectivo services. Central Railway of Peru maintains freight service to La Oroya (with an extension N to Cerro de Pasco) and SE to Huancayo (with an extension to Huancavelica): Desamparados station, behind Palacio de Gobierno. (For description of line see page 352). On Sun in the dry season there is a train to San Bartolomé at 0830, returning at 1600.

**Bus companies**: there are many different bus companies, but the larger ones are better organized, leave on time and do not wait until the bus is full. For approximate prices, frequency and duration of trip, see destinations. Bus companies which serve all Peru (in Lima unless stated otherwise): *Ormeño*, Carlos Zavala 177, T 427-5679, also at J Prado Este 1059, more expensive luxury service to Trujillo and Chiclayo, well-organized and rec; *Cruz del Sur*, Quilca 531, T 427-1311/423-5594, expanding network, good buses, rec; *Expreso Sudamericano*, Montevideo 618, T 427-6548/6549, fewer buses, cheaper, older buses.

Companies with routes to the N: *Perú Express*, Guillermo Dansey 235, T 424-8990, luxury buses to Chimbote, Trujillo, Chiclayo; *Chiclayo Express*, Av Grau 653, T 428-5072, to Chiclayo direct; *Expreso Panamericano*, Av Alfonso Ugarte 951, T 424-9045, to Chimbote, Trujillo, Chiclayo. *Transporte Cinco*, Jr Sandia 205, T 428-1915, to Barranca, Paramonga; *Olano/Oltursa*, Jr Apurimac 567 y Av Grau 617, T 428-2370, to Chiclayo, Piura, Jaén, Bagua, Tumbes; *Atahualpa*, Jr Sandia 266, T 427-5838, to Chimbote, Cajamarca, Celendín; *Fortaleza*, Leticia 515, T 428-2577, similar routes. *Rodríguez*, Av Roosevelt 354, T 428-0506, to Huaraz and Caraz, rec; *Movil Tours* and *Paradise Tours*, both at Abancay 947, to Huaraz, both rec (as is Ormeño); *Cóndor de Chavín*, Montevideo 1039, T 428-8122, to Chavín. *Cruz de Chalpón*, Montevideo 809, T 427-0981, to Chimbote, Trujillo, Piura; *Espadín*, Carlos Zavala 140, T 428-5857, to Churín; *Turismo Chimbote*, Huarochiri 785 (2 blocks off 2 de Mayo), T 424-0501, Chimbote direct and Caraz; *Chinchaysuyo*, Av Grau 525, T 427-5038, to Casma, Caraz, Chimbote, Trujillo, Pacasmayo and Piura; *Antisuyo*, Av Abancay 947, T 428-1414, to Trujillo; *Las Dunas*, Paseo de la República 821, La Victoria, T 431-0235, to Chimbote, Trujillo, Chiclayo, luxury. *Transporte Piura*, Montevideo 801, to Trujillo, Chiclayo, Piura, Tumbes; *Transtysa*, Av Montevideo 724, T 428-0412, to Chiquián and Pachapaqui; *Civa Cial*, Carlos Zavala 217 y Montevideo 500 (opp Ormeño), T 432-4926, to Trujillo, Chiclayo, Piura, Tumbes, Huaraz, Chachapoyas (the only direct service) and Bagua, good service, if a little too fast at times. In the same terminal is an office selling tickets for Cruz del Sur, whose buses leave from Jr Quilca (see above), and an office for *Mariscal Cáceres*, whose buses leave from here and from 28 de Julio (see below).

Companies with routes to the S: *Cañete*, Av Grau 427, T 428-2729, to Cañete direct; *General de San Martín*, Montevideo 552, T 428-1423, to Pisco and Ica; *Señor Luren*, Av Abancay 1165, T 428-0630, to Ica and Nasca; *Cóndor Aymaraes*, Jr Condesuyos 477, T 428-6618, to Ica, Nasca and Abancay; *Plateados del Sur*, Montevideo 517, T 427 9485, to Ica and Nasca; *Victoria del Sur*, Montevideo 762, T 428-8682, to Arequipa and Tacna; *Morales Moralitos*, Av Grau 141, T 427-6310, to Abancay and Cusco; *Señor de Animas Apurímac*, Av Luna Pizarro 453, La Victoria, T 431-0904, to Apurímac, Abancay, Cusco; *Expreso Jacantaya*, Av Grau 486, T 432-8987.

Companies to the centre: *Huaytapallana*, Jr Cotabambas 321, T 428-4286, similar; also *Mariscal Cáceres*, Av 28 de Julio 2195, La Victoria, T 474-7850, good 'Imperial' service to Huancayo (similarly Cruz del Sur, address above). *León de Huánuco*, Av 28 de Julio 1520, T 432-9088, to Huánuco, Tingo María, Pucallpa, *Chanchamayo*, Av Luna Pizarro 453, La Victoria, T 432-4517, to Tarma, San Ramón, La Merced, rec; *Nuestra Señora de la Merced*, Av 28 de Julio 1535, La Victoria, similar route; *Satipo Expreso*, Av Luna Pizarro 488, La Victoria, T 423-9272, to La Merced; *Transmar*, Av 28 de Julio 1511, La Victoria, T 433-7440, to Tingo María and Pucallpa, also *Etposa*, Av José Gálvez 1121, Lince, T 472-1402; *Trans Rey*, Av

28 de Julio 1192, La Victoria (terminal), Av Luna Pizarro 398, La Victoria (ticket office), T 431-9808, luxury bus to Pucallpa.

*Comités* are small vans which run on some routes throughout Peru; they are quicker, more comfortable, but double the price of buses. They only leave when full. In Lima unless otherwise stated: *Comité No 14*, Leticia 604, T 428-6621, to Huaraz; *No 25*, Jr Azángaro 839, T 428-7524, to Chimbote; *No 12*, Montevideo 736, T 427-3327, to Huancayo and Huánuco; *No 30*, Av Bolívar 1335, La Victoria, T 432-9459, and *No 22*, Ayacucho 997, T 428-9082, to Huancayo; *No 1*, Luna Pizarro 377, T 431-0652, to Tarma; *No 18*, Av N de Piérola 1470, T 428-8143, to Huacho and Barranca. Colectivos to Huacho and Huaral leave from Plaza de Acho.

**International buses**: to enter Peru, a ticket out of the country may be required. If you have to buy a bus ticket, be warned: they are not transferable or refundable.

*Ormeño* international buses leave from Javier Prado 1059, T 472-1710, no change of bus at border: to Guayaquil (US$60) and Quito (US$70) twice a week; Cali (US$130) and Bogotá (US$145) once a week; Cúcuta (US$185) and Caracas (US$195) once a week; Santiago (US$70) on Tues and Sat, 2½ days, 3 meals inc; Mendoza (US$130) and Buenos Aires (US$140) twice a week, 3½ days, inc 3 meals and hotel in Santiago, good buses. *Caracol* (in Cruz del Sur building) to Guayaquil (US$40), Quito (US$50), Cali (US$100), Bogotá (US$120), Cúcuta (US$145) and Caracas (US$150), same bus all the way, no food inc. Also to Santiago (US$91), Buenos Aires (US$180), Mendoza (US$137), Montevideo (US$190), Asunción (US$218) and Rio de Janeiro (US$248), inc meals, have to change bus in Santiago. *El Rápido*, Av Carlos Zavala Loayza 177, T 428-3181, weekly to **Mendoza** and **Buenos Aires**, fare inc meals and one night in a hotel, takes 4 days. Connecting twice weekly services to **Guayaquil** and **Quito** (although there are no through buses; you can buy through tickets but they are very expensive and give no priority), leaving Lima on Wed and Sun at 0845. The trip takes 2½ days; often long frontier delays. Bear in mind that international buses are more expensive than travelling from one border to another on national buses.

**Warning** The area around the bus terminals is very unsafe; thefts and assaults are more common in this neighbourhood than elsewhere in the city. You are strongly advised to consider taking a taxi to and from your bus. Make sure your luggage is well guarded and put on the right bus. It is also important not to assume that buses leave from the place where you bought the tickets.

In the weeks either side of 28/29 July (Independence), and of the Christmas/New Year holiday, it is practically impossible to get bus tickets out of Lima, unless you book in advance. Prices for bus tickets double at these times.

# Lima to Callejón de Huaylas



THIS IS A region of geographic and cultural contrasts, covering the entire department of Ancash and the northern part of Lima. A vast sweep of relentless grey coastal desert runs North to the smelly fishing port of Chimbote. Inland a series of roads snake their way up to high mountain passes before dropping into the spectacular Callejón de Huaylas. This area of jewelled lakes and sparkling white mountain peaks attracts mountaineers, hikers, cyclists and rafters in their thousands. Even the archaeologist is catered for: the pre-Inca ruins at Chavín de Huantar and Sechín are two of the most important sites in Peru.

## LIMA TO CHIMBOTE

Between Lima and Pativilca there is a narrow belt of coastal land deposited at the mouths of the rivers and, from Pativilca to the mouth of the Río Santa, N of Chimbote, the Andes come down to the sea. Between Lima and Pativilca cotton and sugar-cane are grown, though the yield of sugar is less than it is further N where the sunshine is not interrupted by cloud. Much irrigated land grows vegetables and crops to supply Lima and Callao. Between June and Oct, cattle are driven down from the Highlands to graze the *lomas* on the mountain sides when the mists come.

The Pan-American Highway parallels the coast all the way to the far N, and feeder roads branch from it up the various valleys. Just N of Ancón (see page 99), the Pasamayo sand dune,

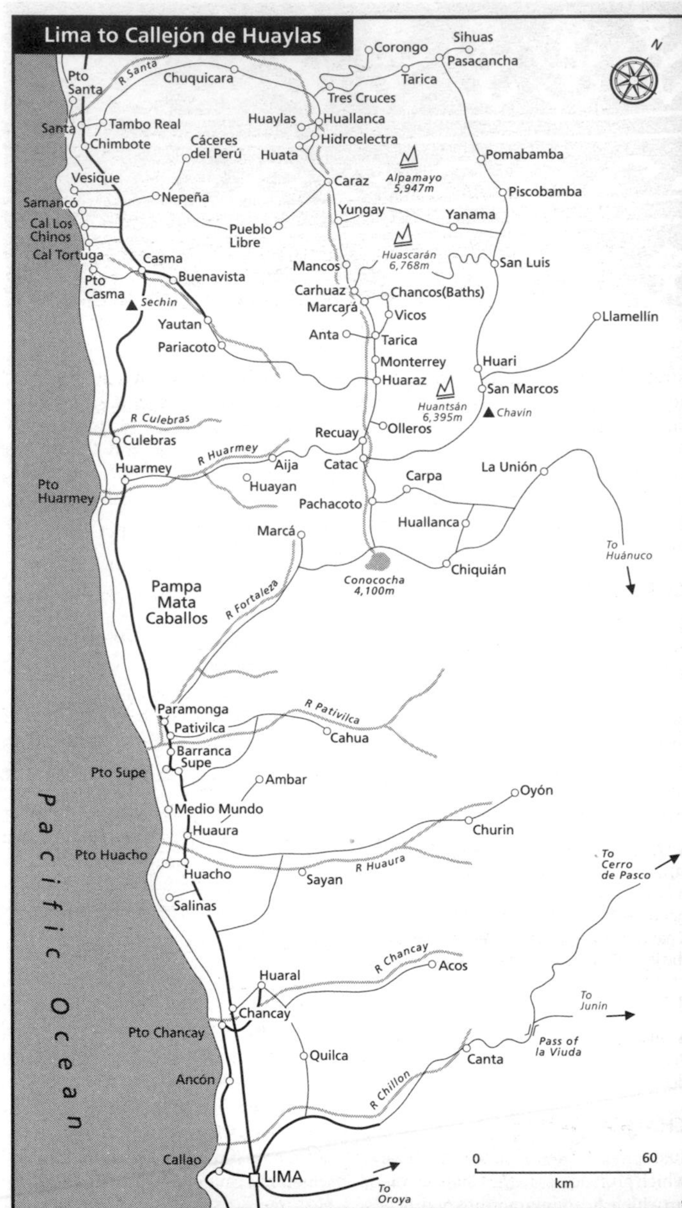
Lima to Callejón de Huaylas
N
R Santa
Pto Santa
Santa
Tambo Real
Chimbote
Chuquicara
Corongo
Sihuas
Pasacancha
Tarica
Tres Cruces
Huaylas
Huallanca
Hidroelectra
Huata
Cáceres del Perú
Vesique
Samancó
Cal Los Chinos
Cal Tortuga
Nepeña
Pueblo Libre
Caraz
Alpamayo 5,947m
Pomabamba
Piscobamba
Yungay
Yanama
Huascarán 6,768m
San Luis
Mancos
Casma
Buenavista
Pto Casma
Sechin
Carhuaz
Marcará
Chancos(Baths)
Vicos
Yautan
Pariacoto
Anta
Tarica
Monterrey
Huaraz
Llamellín
Huari
San Marcos
Huantsán 6,395m
Chavín
R Culebras
Culebras
Olleros
Recuay
R Huarmey
Huarmey
Aija
Catac
La Unión
Huayan
Carpa
Pto Huarmey
Pachacoto
Huallanca
Marcá
To Huánuco
Chiquián
Conococha 4,100m
Pampa Mata Caballos
R Fortaleza
Paramonga
R Pativilca
Pativilca
Cahua
Barranca
Supe
Pto Supe
Ambar
Oyón
Medio Mundo
Pacific Ocean
Huaura
Churin
Pto Huacho
Huacho
Sayan
R Huaura
To Cerro de Pasco
Salinas
R Chancay
Acos
Huaral
Chancay
To Junín
Pto Chancay
Pass of la Viuda
Quilca
Canta
Ancón
R Chillon
Callao
LIMA
To Oroya
0
60
km

Chancay textile

stretching for 20 km, comes right down to the seashore. The old road which snakes along the base beside the sea is spectacular, but is now closed except to commercial traffic. The new toll road (US$0.85), which goes right over the top, is much safer and you get spectacular views over the nearby coast and valleys.

## CHANCAY

Lying on the coast, Chancay suffers from severe water shortages, but there is a fresh water source on the beach. The sea here can be dangerous and heavily polluted, and if that doesn't put you off, then the awful smell from the fish processing factories certainly will. There is no bus terminal but it's easy to catch long distance buses on the Pan-American Highway.

• **Accommodation** C *Hostal Villa de Arnedo*, clean and friendly, pool open in summer, restaurant, rec; **E** ***Hostal Chancay***, safe, good beds, can wash clothes. The 'castle' at Chancay, a pseudo-medieval summer house (built 1922-42) on the beach, is planned to be converted to a 220-bed hotel, open to visitors (US$1), café, playground.

• **Places to eat** *Pizzería Donatello* on Plaza, expensive and *Costa Azul*, with gardens, overlooking sea; both good.

## CHANCAY VALLEY

Just inland from Chancay is **Huaral**, which gives access to the Chancay Valley, up which are the extraordinary, little-visited ruins of **Chiprac**, **Rupac** and **Añay**.

Chiprac is a 2½ hrs climb from Huascoy (see below). The Salvador family have accommodation and Carlos is a recommended guide for the ruins, though a guide is not strictly necessary. It is a good day's walk there and back with time to take photographs and eat. Huascoy celebrates the Fiesta de San Cristóbal in the week before Independence (28 July), with a procession, masses, dancing, fireworks and football matches.

Rupac is best reached from La Florida. Its ruins are the best preserved of the group, though less extensive than Chiprac. All the ruins have complete roofs, which is unique in Peru.

For Añay, go to Huaral as for the other ruins, then get transport to Huayopampa (basic accommodation) or La Perla from where the ruins can easily be reached. Get a guide to show you up from either village.

• **Transport** Take a bus from Lima to Huaral; from Plaza de Acho, by the bullring – beware of thieves. Then take the Juan Batista bus, Tues and Fri, to Huascoy US$2, 2 km beyond San Juan, which is up beyond Acos. This is described as "A hair-raising, breath-taking and bone-shaking ride, up to 3,500m above sea-level."

Turn right 1 km N of turn off to Sayán (see below) where, a further 3 km, there is a national reserve, **Loma de Lachay**, which has thousands of snail shells, locust-trees and much bird life. In Sept-

Oct the plants are in bloom and very beautiful. There is a visitors centre, trails, camping and picnic areas. The reserve is very popular with Lima residents at the weekend.

## HUACHO

North on the dual carriageway to Km 101, the port of **Huacho** (*Pop* 35,900) is 120 km from Lima (bus 2½ hrs, US$2, or Comité 18, daily colectivos, US$2.50). It is the outlet for cotton and sugar grown in the rich Huaura valley. There is a cemetery near Huacho where mummies may be found. There are cotton-seed oil and other factories. The port and sea are sometimes alive with huge jellyfish.

• **Accommodation** **C** *Hostal Villa Sol*, clean, pleasant, restaurant, pool, playground; **E** *Hostal Maury*, basic but friendly; **E** *Italia*, communal bathrooms, clean; **F** *El Pacífico*, safe, dirty, water problems, inadequate clothes-washing facilities; *Hostal de Milagritos*, comfortable. Camping is possible at El Paraíso beach.

## CHURIN

The journey inland from Huacho, up the Huaura valley, is splendid. Beyond Sayán are terrific rock formations, then the road passes through subtropical vegetation around **Churín**, one of Peru's best-known spas, with hot, sulphurous springs which are used to cure a number of ailments. The climate is dry, temperatures ranging from 10° to 32° C; the area is heavily forested. It is famous for its cheeses.

• **Accommodation** *Hostal San Juan de Churín*, Av Victor Larco Herrera 315, Local T 12, with bath, hot water, restaurant, bar, TV, clean; *Hostal La Meseta* (member of Peruvian Youth Hostel Association), contact in Lima at Paul Harris 367, San Isidro, T 422-7619; *Internacional*, Av Victor Larco Herrera 410, T 15, with bath, hot water, clean, moderately priced.

• **Transport** Buses from Lima go to Churín, Oyón (between Churín and Raura) and Huamahuanca; Espadín y Hnos (see Lima, **Bus Companies**), 2 daily, 6½ hrs, US$3.50. Only travel to this area in daylight, and check with locals on villages beyond Churín as there has been terrorist acitivity in the past.

Near here, at **Chiuchín**, is **C** *Albergue San Camilo*, excellent. From Chiuchín, there are buses to nearby villages, such as **Huancahuasi**, where one can buy woven goods, see interesting churches, and spot *vicuña* in lovely surroundings. Above 4,000m is a chain of lakes which reflect the Cordillera Raura (up to 5,800m). The road ends at Raura mine, one of several coal mines in the area.

## HUACHO TO SUPE

Just across the river from Huacho, is **Huaura** where the balcony is still preserved from which San Martín declared the country's independence from Spain. Try *guinda*, the local cherry brandy.

We pass from the wide valley of Mazo through the irrigated valley of San Felipe. Midway between Huaura and Supe, on the coast road, is **Medio Mundo**, with a lake between the village and the sea. It is a good camping spot, with tents for rent, which is guarded at weekends. Bring food and water – there is none for bathrooms or drinking. The turnoff is outside the village on the Pan-American Highway, to the left, look for the sign, 'Albufera de Medio Mundo'. It is hot and busy in summer.

## SUPE

There is more desert and then the cottonfields of San Nicolás lead to **Supe** at Km 187, a small busy port shipping fishmeal, cotton, sugar and minerals.

• **Accommodation & places to eat** **F** *Hostal Supe*. Better is **F** *Hostal Grau*, basic, clean, safe, comfortable, laundry, good value. Next door is *El Norteño*, a good restaurant.

At **Aspero**, near Supe, is one of the earliest prehistoric sites in Peru (see History section, page 38).

## BARRANCA

At **Barranca** (Km 195; *Phone code* 034) the beach is long, not too dirty, though windy.

• **Accommodation & places to eat** E *Hostal Casablanca*, on the beach front; E *Hotel Chavín*, with bath, warm water, clean, good value, rec, front rooms are noisy, also restaurant on 1st floor for lunch and dinner (try *arroz con conchas*), breakfast bar and café opens onto street by main entrance; F *Hotel Casanova*, on main street, with bath, clean, unwelcoming, safe motorcycle parking; F *Jefferson*, Lima 946, clean, friendly; G *Pacífico*, with bath, clean, good value; G *Colón*, Jr Gálvez 407, friendly, basic. There are many other hotels on the main street, and plenty of bars and restaurants. Here and in Supe try the *tamales*.

• **Banks & money changers** Banco de la Nación, Barranca, accepts TCs, although at poor rates.

• **Transport** Buses stop opp the service station (*el grifo*) at the end of town. From **Lima to Barranca**, 3½ hrs, US$3; to **Pativilca**, 3½ hrs, US$3.50; see Lima, **Bus Companies** with routes to the N. As bus companies have their offices in Barranca, buses will stop there rather than at Pativilca or Paramonga. Bus from Barranca to **Casma** 155 km, several daily, 3 hrs, US$3. From Barranca to **Huaraz**, 4 hrs, US$6, daily buses or trucks.

The straggling town of **Pativilca** (Km 203), has a small museum. Just beyond Pativilca, a good paved road turns E for Huaraz in the Cordillera Blanca. *Cornejo*, is a good, cheap restaurant.

## PARAMONGA

4 km beyond the turn-off to Huaraz, beside the Highway, are the well preserved ruins of the Chimú temple of **Paramonga**. Set on high ground with a view of the ocean, the fortress-like mound is reinforced by eight quadrangular walls rising in tiers to the top of the hill; admission US$1.20. It is well worth visiting. Not far from the fortress, the Great Wall (La Muralla) stretches across the Andes. Paramonga is a small port, 3 km off the Pan-American Highway, 4 km from the ruins and 205 km from Lima, shipping sugar.

• **Transport** No buses run to the ruins, only to the port (about 15 mins from Barranca). Taxi from Paramonga and return after waiting, US$4.50, otherwise take a Barranca-Paramonga port bus, then a 3 km walk.

## NORTH TO CASMA

Between Pativilca and Chimbote the mountains come down to the sea. The road passes by a few very small protected harbours in tiny rock-encircled bays – Puerto Huarmey, Puerto Casma, and Vesique. Between Paramonga and Huarmey there are restaurants at Km 223 and 248.

• **Accommodation** At **Huarmey** town, on the Pan-American Highway is **C-D** *Hotel de Turistas*, small, clean, good service, restaurant, noisy from traffic on highway; and **D** *Hostal Santa Rosa*, on plaza.

## CASMA

The town, largely destroyed by the 1970 earthquake, has since been rebuilt, partly with Chilean help. It has a pleasant Plaza de Armas, several parks and two markets including a good food market. The weather is usually sunny, hence its title *Ciudad del Sol Eterno* (City of Eternal Sun).

### Excursions

About 15 km SE of Casma are the ruins of **Chanquillo**. There is a cemetery with pottery on the ground, and a Chimú castle of four concentric rings, with three towers in the middle. Visible from Chanquillo is a large wall with 13 towers atop a ridge. The ruins were damaged by the 1970 earthquake.

• **Access** Take a truck going to San Rafael and ask for Castillo de Chanquillo (irregular departures from the E end of town, before bridge over Río Sechín; ask when last truck returns to Casma). After alighting, walk 2 km uphill to the cemetery.

Alternatively, take a southbound bus and alight at Km 361 on the Pan-American, 15 km S of Casma. 100m N of the milestone a rough track runs E into the desert; it crosses under the high-tension power line and becomes impassable af-

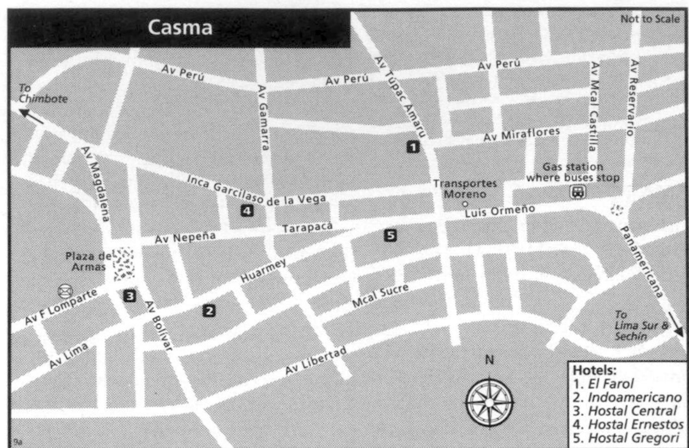


ter about 1.5 km. A mountain bike or 4WD can continue on the hard-packed sand. If walking follow a heading of about 45 degrees for almost 1 km, passing 2 hills to your left, and climbing a low sand ridge from which the ruins are finally visible. The trek through the desert is interesting; start early and take water and sun protection. If you know there will be a truck returning from San Rafael in the afternoon, walk down to the oasis to make a round trip, but it can be easy to get lost.

There are several other sites around Casma: Pallka, Pampa de las Llamas, Mojeque (by the town of Santa Matilde), La Cantina (by San Rafael), Taucach (W of Sechín Alto) and Manchán (at Km 370 on the Pan-American Highway).

## Local information

### ● Accommodation

**D** *Hostal El Farol*, Tupac Amaru 450, T/F 711064, ask for cheaper rate in low season, best in town, with bath, includes continental breakfast, hot water in most rooms, good restaurant, pleasant garden setting, parking, rec; **D** *Hostal* Ernesto's, Garcilaso de la Vega y Gamarra, T 711475, modern, clean, with bath, hot water, bakery downstairs.

**E** *Gregori*, Luis Ormeño 579, T 711073, cheaper without bath, clean but noisy, restaurant downstairs; **E** *Indoamericano*, Av Huarmey 130, T711395, cheaper without bath, hot water, clean, good, front rooms noisy, changes cash dollars.

**F** *Hostal Central*, Plaza de Armas 140, dirty, cold water, very basic, friendly, helpful.

### ● Places to eat

*Sechín*, Nepeña esq Mejía, nr plaza, friendly, good set meal and chicken; *Tío Sam*, Huarmey 138, Chinese and *criollo*; *El Farol*, at the hotel, good set meal and à la carte. There are several *cevicherías* on Av Ormeño 600 block and cheap restaurants on Huarmey. *Heladería El Pibe*, Gamarra 466, is good for ice-cream.

### ● Banks & money changers

Good rates for cash and TCs, no commission, at **Banco de Crédito**, Bolívar 181; *Hotel Indoamericano*, cash only.

### ● Entertainment

*Discoteca Las Terrazas*, Av Lima, nr plaza; *Discoteca Flamenco*, Av Nepeña.

### ● Post & telecommunications

**Post Office** at Fernando Loparte, 1 block from Plaza de Armas. National and International **phone** and **fax** at *Sonia's*, Huarmey 302; and *Luz*, Av Ormeño 118.

### ● Transport

Buses from **Lima**, 370 km, several buses daily, 6 hrs, US$5 (see Lima, **Bus Companies**); to **Lima**, Turismo Chimbote, Ormeño 544, at 1000 and 2400; Chinchaysuyo, Ormeño 526, at 0100. To **Chimbote**, 55 km, several buses and colectivos daily, 1 hr, US$1. To **Trujillo**, 175 km, daily buses, 3 hrs, US$2.50. Most buses N pass Casma 0400-0600; buses S 0900-1200; wait by gas station at E end of Av Ormeño. At other times, take a bus to Chimbote.

## CASMA TO HUARAZ

From Casma a road runs inland over the **Callán pass** (4,224m) 150 km to Huaraz. A difficult but beautiful trip, worth taking in daylight. Not all buses take this route, so check before leaving. From Casma the first 30 km are paved, a good dirt road follows for 30 km to **Pariacoto**. From here to the pass the road is rough (landslides in rainy season), but once the Cordillera Negra has been crossed, the wide, gravel road is better with spectacular views of the Cordillera Blanca.

• **Accommodation & places to eat In Pariacoto**: **F** *Hostal Eddier*, on plaza, basic but nice; **G** *Alojamiento Saenz Peña*, Gonzalo Salazar, cuadra 5, basic; *Restaurant Iris* is good.

• **Transport** Bus to **Huaraz**, 150 km, via Pariacoto, 6-7 hrs, US$6, Transportes Moreno, 0800 and 2100 daily, or trucks; via Pativilca, US$6.60, Turismo Chimbote at 2200, Chinchaysuyo at 2330.

## SECHIN

This is one of the most important ruins on the Peruvian coast. It consists of a large square temple completely faced with carved stone monoliths – probably over 500 of them – representing two lines of warriors marching towards the principal entrance from opposite sides. Between each warrior are carvings of men being eviscerated, heads with blood gushing from eyes or mouths, dismembered legs, arms, torsos, ears, eyes and vertebrae. The mural is thought to narrate the results of a battle, with the fates of the conquerors and the conquered graphically depicted. The style is unique in Peru for its naturalistic vigour. The importance of the site lies in the fact that it is one of the oldest centres in the country to demonstrate the development of warlike activity and to show the extent to which extreme violence was a part of life.

Within the stone temple is an earlier, pre-ceramic mud temple with painted walls. The complex as a whole forms a temple-palace associated with the development of the local pre-Chavín Sechín culture, dating from about 1500 BC. Three sides of the large stone temple have been excavated and restored. You

Section of the wall at Sechín

cannot see the adobe buildings inside the stone walls, which belong to an earlier period. They were later covered up and used as a base for a second storey which unfortunately has been completely destroyed. Some experts think the temple and surroundings were buried on purpose. Others believe it was engulfed by natural disaster. The latter theory is supported by finds of human skeletons. Tombs have been found in front and at the same level as the temple. A wall of a large adobe building under excavation can be seen and runs round the sides and back of the temple.

The site is open to tourists, 0830-1830 daily, photography best around midday (US$2.25, children half price); ticket also valid for museum and Pañamarca (see page 129), and there is an attractive, shady picnic garden. The Max Uhle Museum by the ruins has an interesting display of Sechín artefacts and replica of the facade of the inner adobe temple. If you require a guide enquire in advance for Wilder León or Carlos Cuy, who speaks English and French. Outside the museum is an orientation map showing the location of the different archaeological sites in the Casma area.

2 km further along is Sechín Alto, two pyramids of the late Chavín period, but these have not yet been excavated.

• **Access** It is quite easy to walk to the ruins from Casma. Follow Av Ormeño E, at the circle turn right and follow the Pan-American Highway, walk about 3 km S to a well posted sign showing a left turn for Huaraz (this is at Km 370), then simply follow the road for 2 km to the ruins. Frequent colectivos leave from in front of the market in Casma, US$0.30 pp, or taxi US$0.50 pp, but leave early in the morning; Transportes Moreno 0800 service to Huaraz might take you as far as the turnoff for the ruins.

## PLAYA TORTUGAS

Located 2 km E of the Pan-American Highway at Km 391, 18 km N of Casma, Playa Tortugas is a fishing village on a nice bay with calm water and a rocky beach. Watch out for spiny sea urchins along the shore. Many small fish restaurants line the main road. There is electricity only at weekends and during the high season (Dec to Mar). It is popular with Limeños during vacation but deserted at other times of the year.

• **Accommodation C** *Hostal El Farol*, at S end of the bay, T 711064 (Casma), 424-0517 (Lima), perched on a hill by the ocean with great views, nice rooms, private bath, has its own electricity generator, playground, restaurant open in season, open all year; **D** *Hospedaje Gabriela*, just N of the access road, with bath, cold water, open Dec to April; *Hostal Oasis*, 250m S of access road, T 334693 (Chimbote), with bath, open high season only; *Suizo*, at N end of the beach.

• **Transport** Taxi from Casma US$3.50; colectivos from Plaza de Armas in Casma, daily at 0600, several 1000-1400, 1800, Mon-Fri only, US$0.70.

From the N end of the bay the road continues to **Playa Huayuna**, a windy, closed bay with a sandy beach and a scallop farm. From the S end of Tortugas a road goes to **Rincón de Piños**, a beach with wild surf. To the S of Casma, at Km 345, are the sandy beaches of **La Gramita** and **Las Aldas**.

## CHIMBOTE

In one of Peru's few natural harbours, a port has been built to serve the national steel industry. Chimbote (*Pop* 296,600; *Phone code* 044) is also Peru's largest fishing port; fishmeal is exported and the smell of the fishmeal plants is very strong. There are no tourist attractions as such, but the city will become increasingly important as an access to the Cordillera Blanca once paving is completed on the road through the Cañon del Pato (estimated late 1996).

Chimbote is not a clean place and carries the dubious honour of being the spot where Cholera first landed in South America in 1991. The city was damaged by the 1970 earthquake. Today, it has a

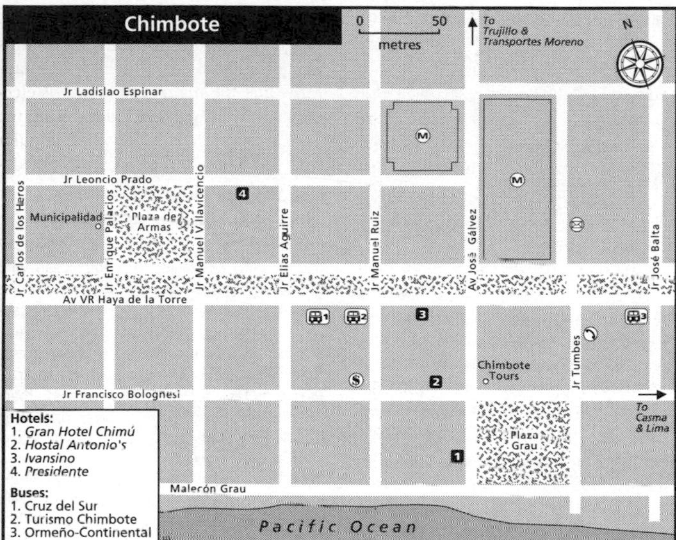


spacious Plaza de Armas, the cathedral and several public buildings have since been rebuilt, and the modern Municipal building has a small art gallery downstairs (open 0900-2000). Bathing is forbidden on the bay, though there is a public swimming pool at Vivero Forestal. Flocks of brown pelicans and masked boobies may be seen from the beach. **NB** The main street, Av Victor Raul Haya de la Torre was formerly known as José Pardo and both names are used interchangeably.

## Excursions

About 25 km S of Chimbote, at Km 405 on the Pan-American Highway, a paved road leads E to the Nepeña valley, where several precolumbian ruins including Cerro Blanco, Pañamarca and Paredones can be found.

The village of Capellanía is 11 km from the crossroads; just beyond are the ruins of **Pañamarca**. The site includes a 2-storey stone structure, built on a hill, dating from the formative period (2000 BC-100 AD) and many adobe structures from the Mochica period, including three pyramids. Remains of polychromatic murals and animal sculptures can also be seen. The Nepeña valley is believed to have been conquered by the Mochicas in the 5th century, when it became the southern limit of their empire.

20 km from Pañamarca, via the villages of San Jacinto and Moro, is the site of **Paredones**, a large stone structure, with 4m high granite walls and a very impressive gateway known as 'Portada de Paredones' or 'Puerta del Sol'. It is believed to have been a Chavín palace.

In the same valley is another site with similar characteristics known as **Siete Huacas**. A large carved monolith (Monolito de Siete Huacas), reminiscent of the Sechín carvings was found at the site.

## Local information

**Warning** Chimbote is not a safe city; layoffs at both the steel mill (operating at 10% capacity in 1995) and the fishing industry (owing to rapidly dwindling stocks) have resulted in high unemployment and a good deal of street crime. Avoid the shanty towns which have burgeoned around the city and be especially careful nr the market and bus stations, day or night. Also note that water shortages can be a problem, so make sure your hotel has a tank before taking a room.

## ● Accommodation

**A1** *Gran Hotel Chimú*, ex-State Tourist Hotel, José Gálvez 109, T/F 321741, inc breakfast, minibar, safe parking.

**B** *Hostal Antonio's*, Bolognesi 745, T/F 325783, clean, hot water, minibar; **B** *Ivansino Inn*, Haya de la Torre 738, T 331395, F 321927, inc breakfast, comfortable, clean, modern, cable TV, minibar; **B** *Presidente*, L Prado 536, T 322411, F 321988, with bath, clean, friendly, hot showers, safe parking (extra), poor snack bar, rec.

**C** *Hostal Karol Inn*, Manuel Ruiz 277, T/F 321216, clean, with bath, hot water, a good place to stay, family run, laundry service, cafeteria; **C-D** *Residencial El Parque*, E Palacios 309, on plaza, T 323963, converted old home, with bath, hot water, clean, nice, friendly.

**D** *Augusto*, Aguirre 265, T 324431, with bath, clean, fornt rooms noisy, water intermittent as elsewhere in town, overpriced; **D** *Felic*, Haya de la Torre 552, T 325901, **E** without bath, clean, quiet, rec; **D** *San Felipe*, Haya de la Torre 514, T 323401, with bath, hot water, clean, friendly, comfortable, restaurant; **D** *Venus*, Haya de la Torre 675, T 321339, with bath, dirty but friendly, nr bus stations, useful if you arrive at night.

**E** *Hostal Playa*, Malecón Miguel Grau 185, OK, safe, clean; **E** *Hostal Paraíso*, Haya de la Torre 1015, T 323718, cheaper without bath, basic, clean, nr Ormeño bus station.

**F** *Hostal El Santa*, Espinar 671, basic.

## ● Places to eat

*Pollo Gordo*, Prado y Aguirre, good chicken and cold beer; *Buenos Aires*, Aguirre nr the beach, popular lunch place; *Marisquito*, Bolognesi nr Palacios, good local food, disco at night; *Chifa Cantón*, Bolognesi, Chinese, good; *La Fogata Inn*, Villavicencio, good grilled food; *Aquarius*, Haya de la Torre 360, vegetarian. There are several cheap restaurants on Haya de la Torre by the plaza. An excellent bakery is *Delca*, at Haya de la Torre 568.

## ● Banks & money changers

**Banco de Crédito** and **Interbanc**, both on Bolognesi and M Ruiz, for TCs and cash; **Casa Arroyo**, M Ruiz 292, cash only. There are other *casas* and street changers along M Ruiz between Bolognesi and VR Haya de la Torre.

## ● Post & telecommunications

**Post**: Serpost, Jr Tumbes behind market. **Telecommunications**: Telefónica main office, Tumbes 356, national and international fax and phone; also at Haya de la Torre 420 and M Ruiz 253.

## ● Tour companies & travel agents

**Chimbote Tours**, Bolognesi 801, T 325341, F 324792, helpful and friendly, English spoken.

## ● Transport

**Local Taxis**: radio taxis from T 334433; T 327777; and T 322005.

**Air** Airport is at the S end of town. It was undergoing renovations in late 1995; more flights expected in the future. To **Lima**, 45 mins, Aerocóndor, daily 0930 (from Lima 0800), US$53; Expreso Aéreo, Mon, Wed, Fri at 1630, Tues, Sat 1000 (from Lima Mon-Sat 0700). To **Cajamarca**, Expreso Aéreo, Mon-Sat 0800 (from Cajamarca Tues and Sat 0900), US$30.

**Buses** from **Lima**, to Chimbote, 420 km, 6 hrs, US$7-9, several buses daily inc: Turismo Chimbote, VR Haya de la Torre 670, T 321400, 9 daily, rec; Cruz del Sur, Haya de la Torre 636; Continental (Ormeño), J Balta 289, esq Haya de la Torre (see Lima, **Bus Companies** with routes to the N). To **Trujillo**, 130 km, 2½ hrs, US$2.50, several buses and colectivos daily. To **Tumbes**, 889 km, 13 hrs, US$11, Continental at 1630, Cruz del Sur at 2200. It is 8-10 hrs to **Huaraz** via the Santa Valley (for a description of this route, see page 147), US$6; daily buses (Transportes Moreno, J Gálvez 1178, T 321235, 0800, rec), book the previous day. To Huaraz via Casma and Pariacoto, with Moreno, 0645 and 2000, US$6; via Pativilca, Cruz del Sur at 2145 and Turismo Chimbote at 2100, US$7.

## THE CORDILLERA BLANCA AND THE CALLEJÓN DE HUAYLAS

Apart from the range of Andes running along the Chile-Argentina border, the highest mountains in South America are along the Callejón de Huaylas and are perfectly visible from many spots. From the city of Huaraz alone, one can see over 23 snow-crested peaks of over 5,000m, of which the most notable is Huascarán (6,768m), the highest mountain in Peru. Although the snowline is now at the 5,000m level, it was not long ago (geologically speaking) that snow and ice covered the Callejón at 3,000m.

Despite its receding snowline, the Cordillera Blanca still contains the largest concentration of glaciers found in the world's tropical zone. From the retreating glaciers come the beauty and the plague of the Callejón. The turquoise-coloured lakes which form in the terminal moraines are the jewels of the Andes and visitors should hike up to at least one during their stay. At the same time these *cochas* (glacial lakes) have caused much death and destruction when dykes have broken, sending tons of water hurtling down the canyons wiping out everything in their path. The levels of some high mountain lakes have been artificially lowered for flood control and to feed the huge Cañon del Pato dam. The result has improved safety but has marred some of the area's great scenic beauty.

### Routes to the Callejón de Huaylas

Probably the easiest way to see the Santa Valley and the Callejón de Huaylas, is to take the paved road which branches E off the Pan-American Highway N of Pativilca (see page 125), 187 km from Lima.

The road at first climbs gradually from the coast. At Km 48, just W of the town of **Chasquitambo** (*Restaurante Delicias*) it reaches *Rumi Siki* (Rump Rock), with unusual rock formations, including the one that gives the site its name. Beyond this point, the grade is steeper and at Km 120 the chilly pass at 4,080m is reached. Shortly after, Laguna **Conococha** comes into view, where the Río Santa rises. Delicious trout is available in Conococha village. A dirt road branches off from Conococha to **Chiquián** (see page 160) and the **Cordilleras Huayhuash** and **Raura** to the SE.

After crossing a high plateau the main road descends gradually for 47 km until **Catac** (see page 140), where another road branches E to Chavín and on to the **Callejón de Conchucos** (see page 140). Huaraz is 36 km further on and the road then continues N through the Callejón de Huaylas, where it runs between the towering Cordillera Negra, snowless and rising to 4,600m, and the snow-covered Cordillera Blanca. Farms appear at about 4,000m; potatoes and barley are grown at the higher altitudes and maize, alfalfa and fruits lower down. The valley has many picturesque villages and small towns, with narrow cobblestone streets and odd-angled house roofs.

The alternative routes to the Callejón de Huaylas are via the Callán pass from Casma to Huaraz (see page 127), and from Chimbote to Caraz via the Cañón del Pato (page 151). The former is a rough but interesting dirt road through the heart of the Cordillera Negra. The latter was being widened and paved in 1995/6 and will become an important access to the area once work is completed. Views of the Cañon del Pato are magnificent.

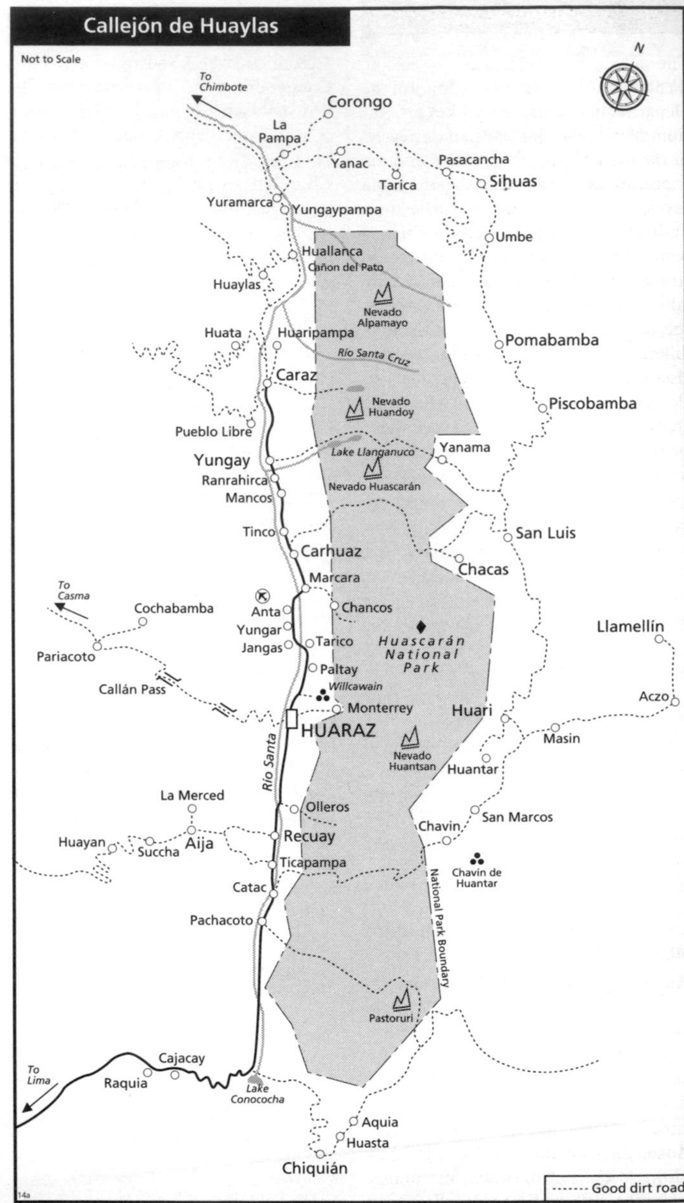
Callejón de Huaylas
Not to Scale
N
To Chimbote
Corongo
La Pampa
Yanac
Tarica
Pasacancha
Sihuas
Yuramarca
Yungaypampa
Umbe
Huallanca
Cañon del Pato
Huaylas
Nevado Alpamayo
Huata
Huaripampa
Pomabamba
Río Santa Cruz
Caraz
Nevado Huandoy
Piscobamba
Pueblo Libre
Yanama
Lake Llanganuco
Yungay
Ranrahirca
Nevado Huascarán
Mancos
Tinco
San Luis
Carhuaz
Chacas
Marcara
To Casma
Cochabamba
Anta
Chancos
Llamellín
Yungar
Jangas
Tarico
Huascarán National Park
Pariacoto
Paltay
Callán Pass
Willcawain
Aczo
Monterrey
Huari
HUARAZ
Masin
Nevado Huantsan
Huantar
Río Santa
La Merced
Olleros
San Marcos
Chavin
Recuay
Huayan
Succha
Aija
Ticapampa
Chavín de Huantar
Catac
National Park Boundary
Pachacoto
Pastoruri
Cajacay
To Lima
Raquia
Lake Conococha
Aquia
Huasta
Chiquián
------ Good dirt road
14a

## HUARAZ

The valley's focus is **Huaraz** (*Pop* 80,000; *Alt* 3,091m; *Phone code* 044), capital of the Department of Ancash, 420 km by road from Lima. The city was half destroyed in the earthquake of May 1970 so don't expect red-tiled roofs or overhanging eaves. The Plaza de Armas has been rebuilt, except for the Cathedral, which is being resited elsewhere. What the reconstructed city lacks in colonial charm, however, it more than makes up for by its spectacular setting at the foot of the Cordillera Blanca. The peaks of Huascarán, Huandoy, and San Cristóbal loom so close as to seem almost a part of the architecture. For good panoramic views go to the *Mirador Rataquenua* at the cross (visible from Huaraz) 1 hr walk from the town (turn left past the cemetery and head uphill through a small forest). It is best to go early in the day and women are not advised to go alone. To get a truly amazing view of the whole valley, continue past the *Mirador* up to *Pukaventana*.

On first impressions Huaraz may seem a bit of a one-horse town, but it is a tourist centre as well as a busy commercial hub, especially on market day (Thur). It is brim full of hotels of all categories and the main thoroughfare, Avenida Luzuriaga, is bursting at the seams with travel agencies, climbing equipment hire shops, *pizzerías*, cafés and bars. This is quite obviously a prime destination for hikers and a mecca for international climbers.

### MUSEUMS

**Museo Regional de Ancash**, Instituto Nacional de Cultura, on Plaza de Armas, containing stone monoliths and *huacos* from the Recuay culture, well labelled and laid out; open Tues-Sat 0800-1900, Sun-Mon 0800-1500; entry US$1.80, includes entry to Willkawain ruins on same day. **Museo de Miniaturas del Perú**, Jr Lúcar y Torre 460, models of Huaraz and Yungay before the earthquake, plus a collection of Barbie dolls in Peruvian dress, strange but interesting. Open Mon-Sat, 0800-1300, 1500-2200, US$0.85.

### EXCURSIONS

#### Willkawain

About 8 km to the NE is the Willkawain archaeological site. The ruins date from AD 700 to 1000, which was the second and imperial phase of the Huari empire. During this period, the Huari influence spread N from the city of the same name near Ayacucho. The Huari empire was remarkable for the strong Tiahuanacu influence in its architecture and ceramics. The Huari introduced a new concept in urban life, the great walled urban centre.

The site consists of 3 large 2-storey structures with intact stone slab roofs and several small structures. The windowless inner chambers can be explored with the help of a flashlight, though most of the rooms are inaccessible. A few, however, have been opened up to reveal a sophisticated ventilation system and skilful stone craftsmanship. Entrance to the site; US$1.25.

Even if you're not an archaeology buff, the trip is worth it for a fascinating insight into rural life in the valley. A good grasp of Spanish will greatly enhance the pleasure of this experience as the locals are very welcoming. A recommended trip is to take a colectivo up to the ruins and walk back down to Huaraz ($1\frac{1}{2}$-2 hrs).

• **Access** Take a colectivo N along Luzuriaga (or walk) past the *Hotel Huascarán*. After crossing a small bridge take a second right marked by a blue sign, it is about 2 hrs uphill walk; ask frequently as there are many criss-crossing paths. About 500m past Willkawain is Ichiwillkawain with several similar but smaller structures. Beware of dogs en route (and begging children). Take a torch. The ruins are along the road to Laguna Llaca, colectivos leave from Jr Caraz above Fitzcarrald (US$0.45 to Willkawain); there is also an alternative road from the ruins to Monterrey.

#### Monterrey

North of Huaraz, 6 km along the road to

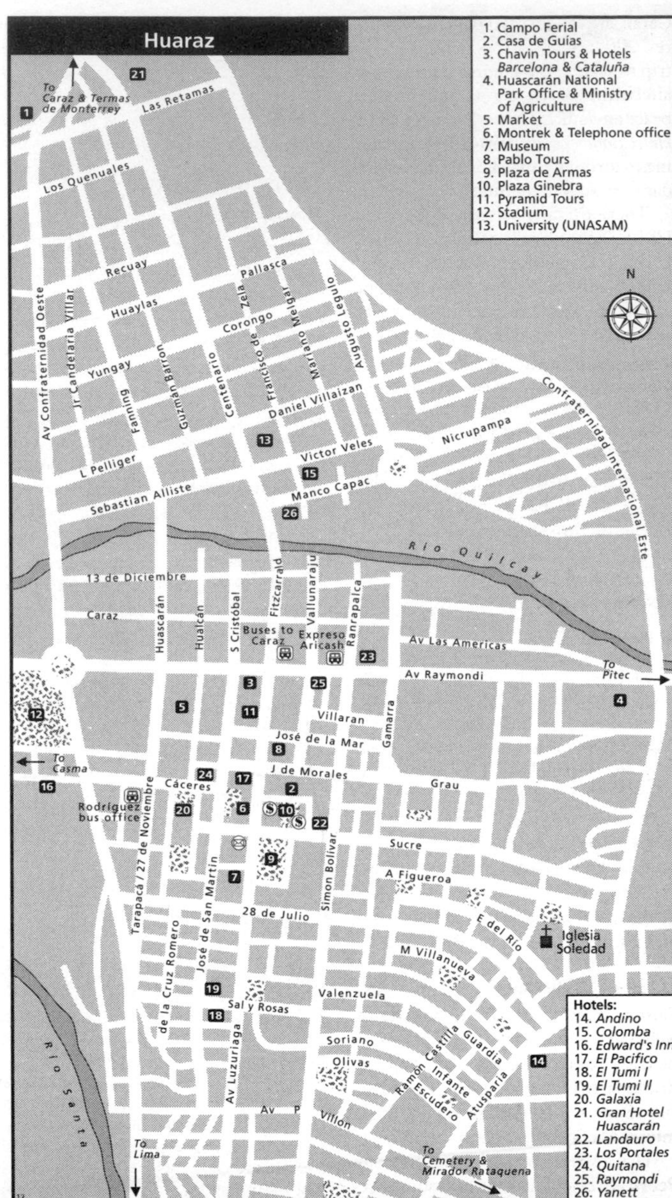
Huaraz
1. Campo Ferial
2. Casa de Guías
3. Chavin Tours & Hotels Barcelona & Cataluña
4. Huascarán National Park Office & Ministry of Agriculture
5. Market
6. Montrek & Telephone office
7. Museum
8. Pablo Tours
9. Plaza de Armas
10. Plaza Ginebra
11. Pyramid Tours
12. Stadium
13. University (UNASAM)
Hotels:
14. Andino
15. Colomba
16. Edward's Inn
17. El Pacifico
18. El Tumi I
19. El Tumi II
20. Galaxia
21. Gran Hotel Huascarán
22. Landauro
23. Los Portales
24. Quitana
25. Raymondi
26. Yanett
To Caraz & Termas de Monterrey
Las Retamas
Los Quenuales
Recuay
Huaylas
Yungay
Pallasca
Corongo
Daniel Villaizan
Victor Veles
Manco Capac
Nicrupampa
L Pelliger
Sebastian Alliste
Av Confraternidad Oeste
Jr. Candelaria Villar
Fanning
Guzmán Barron
Centenario
Zela
Francisco de
Mariano Melgar
Augusto Leguio
Confraternidad Internacional Este
Río Quilcay
13 de Diciembre
Caraz
Huascarán
Hualcán
S Cristóbal
Fitzcarrald
Vallunaraju
Ranrapalca
Buses to Caraz
Expreso Aricash
Av Las Americas
Av Raymondi
To Pitec
Villaran
José de la Mar
Gamarra
J de Morales
Grau
To Casma
Cáceres
Rodríguez bus office
Sucre
A Figueroa
28 de Julio
Tarapacá / 27 de Noviembre
José de San Martín
Simon Bolívar
E del Río
Iglesia Soledad
M Villanueva
Valenzuela
Sal y Rosas
de la Cruz Romero
Soriano
Olivas
Ramón Castilla
Guardia
Infante
Escudero
Atusparia
Av Luzuriaga
Av P Villon
Río Santa
To Lima
To Cemetery & Mirador Rataquena
N

Caraz, are the thermal baths at Monterrey (*Alt* 2,780m). A good place for a day trip to soak in the thermal baths and an alternative place to stay for those seeking peace and quiet. The baths are run by the *Hotel Baños Termales Monterrey* and, owing to the high iron content, the water is dark brown but not dirty.

There are two pools: the lower pool is US$0.90; the upper pool, which is nicer, US$1.35; also individual and family tubs US$1.35 pp for 20 mins. The upper pool is closed Mon for cleaning. It gets crowded at weekends and holidays.

● **Accommodation** **B** ***Baños Termales Monterrey***, Av Monterrey, at top of hill, T/F 721717, slightly run down but classic old spa (under new management in 1995), price includes breakfast and use of pools, restaurant, bar, good location for walking, there is a rock face behind the hotel which is used for climbing practice; **B** ***El Patio***, Av Monterrey, 250m down hill from baths, T/F 01-437-6567 (Lima), inc breakfast, meals on request, bar, friendly, colonial-style, rec; **C** ***El Nogal***, on side street off Av Monterrey across from El Patio, new, modern.

● **Places to eat** There are several country style restaurants in Monterrey which are popular with locals and busy at weekends, serving trout, *pachamanca* and other regional specialities. Along the Huaraz-Caraz road at Km 7 is ***Las Terrazas***; at Km 6.5 is ***El Cortijo***; at Km 5.5 ***El Viejo Molino***, T 721268, along the Río Santa. There are several cheaper restaurants and stands along Av Monterrey.

● **Transport** City buses along Av Luzuriaga go as far as Monterrey (US$0.22), until 1900; taxi US$2-3.

To the E of Huaraz, off the road to Unchus and Pitec, are the ruins of **Huahullac**.

## LOCAL FESTIVALS

Patron saints' day, **El Señor de la Soledad**, week starting 3 May, parades, dancing, music, fireworks and much drinking. Independence celebrations, 28 July. **Semana del Andinismo**, in June, international climbing and skiing week.

The festivals of **San Juan** and **San Pedro** are celebrated throughout the region during the last week of June. On the eve of San Juan fires are lit throughout the valley to burn the chaff from the harvest. The following day the entire valley is thick with smoke. **Semana Santa**, or Holy Week, is widely celebrated and always colourful and lively.

## LOCAL INFORMATION

### ● Accommodation

Hotels are plentiful but fill up rapidly during high season (May-Sept), especially during public holidays and special events when prices rise (beware overcharging). Lodging in private homes is common during these periods.

**Out of town**: **C** *Complejo Turístico Eccame*, in Yungar nr the airport, Km 18 on the road to Caraz, T 721933, country setting, horse riding.

**In town**: **A2-3** *Hostal Andino*, Pedro Cochachín 357, some way SE from centre, T 721662, T/F 722830, includes breakfast, best in town, restaurant (fondue expensive), safe parking, Swiss run, beautiful view of Huascarán, climbing and hiking gear for hire, rec.

**A3** *Gran Hotel Huascarán*, Av Centenario block 10, at the N end of town, T 721640, F 722821, uninspiring ex-state hotel, large rooms, poor restaurant, **C** for camping in courtyard with use of facilities.

**B** *Hostal Saxofón*, Cascapampa 250, 1 block from *Gran Hotel Huascarán*, T/F 721722, pleasant with garden, parking.

**C** *El Tumi I*, San Martín 1121, T 721784, with bath, good restaurant (serves huge steaks), fairly good; **C** *Hostal Colomba*, Francisco de Zela 210, on Centenario across river, T 721422, lovely old hacienda, bungalow, family-run (German), garden, friendly, safe car parking; **C** *Hostal Los Portales*, Raymondi 903, T 721402, F 721247, with bath, hot water, parking, a pleasant place to stay; **C** *Hostal Montañero*, Plaza Ginebra 30-B (ask at Casa de Guías), T/F 722306, hot water, very clean, modern, comfortable, friendly, good value, climbing equipment rental and sales.

**D** *Casablanca*, 27 de Noviembre/Tarapacá 138, T 722602, F 721970, clean, pleasant modern, nr market; **D** *Edward's Inn*, Bolognesi 121, T/F 722692, cheaper without bath, clean, not always hot water, laundry, friendly, food available, insist on proper rates in low season, popular, Edward speaks English and knows a lot about trekking and rents gear (not all guides share Edward's experience), highly rec; **D** *El Tumi II*, San Martín 1089,

T 721784, with bath, reasonable value, beds not too comfortable; **D** pp ***Familia de Alcides Ames***, 27 de Noviembre 773, T 723375, with breakfast, very friendly, Sr Ames is an expert on glaciers, his son is a climbing and rafting guide; **D** ***Hostal Oscar***, La Mar 624, T 721145, with bath, hot water, cheap breakfast, good beds, **E** out of season, rec; **D** ***Hostal Raymondi***, Raymondi 820, T 721082, central, with bath, hot water (am only in ground floor shower), comfortable, charges for left luggage, café serves good breakfast; **D** ***Hostal Rinconcito Huaracino***, Fitzcarrald 238, T 725665, cheaper without bath, modern, clean, front rooms are noisy; **D** ***Hostal Yanett***, Av Centenario 164, at N end of town across river, T 721466, friendly, hot water, clean, large rooms, restaurant for breakfast, rec.

**E** ***Alojamiento Belenita***, D Antúnez 772, 1 block from Plaza Belén, T 721896, price includes breakfast, shared bath, hot water, courtyard, cooking and laundry facilities, friendly; **E** ***Alojamiento Norma***, Pasaje Valenzuela 837, nr Plaza Belén, T 721831, inc breakfast, cheaper without bath, hot water, rec; **E** ***Hostal Chong Roca***, J de Morales 687, T 721154, with bath, very clean, friendly, hot water 24 hrs, huge rooms, rec; **E** ***Hostal Continental***, 28 de Julio 586 nr Plaza de Armas, clean, hot water, friendly, cafeteria, rec, avoid rooms overlooking street as there are two noisy *peñas* nearby; **E** ***Hostal Copa***, Jr Bolívar 615, cheaper without bath, limited hot water, laundry facilities, clean, owner's son, Walter Melgarejo is a well-known guide, popular with trekkers, restaurant; **E** ***Hostal Estoico***, San Martín 635, T 722371, cheaper without bath, friendly, clean, safe, hot water, laundry facilities, rec; **E** ***Hostal Galaxia***, Jr de la Cruz Romero 688, T 722230, cheaper without bath, hot water, laundry facilities, basic, friendly, rec; **E** ***Hostal Los Andes***, Tarapacá 316, T 721346, cheaper without bath, hot water, clean, friendly, laundry facilities, attractive but noisy, hard beds; **E** ***Hostal Maguiña***, Av Tarapacá 643, opposite Rodríguez bus terminal, noisy in am, hot water, laundry facilities, breakfast available, luggage stored, clean, English and French spoken, helpful in arranging trekking and equipment hire, rec; **E** ***Hostal Quintana***, Mcal Cáceres 411, T 726060, cheaper without bath, hot shower, laundry facilities, clean, basic, stores luggage, friendly, popular with trekkers, some beds are new and comfortable, others less so; **E** ***Hostal Tany***, Lúcar y Torre 468, T 722534, with bath, hot water at night, spotlessly clean; **E** ***Hostal Virgen del Carmen***, Jr de la Cruz Romero 664, T 721729, or 481-5311 (Lima), cheaper without bath, hot water, run by a lovely, friendly and helpful old couple from Lima, homely atmosphere, nice clean rooms, cheap laundry service, highly rec; **E** ***Residencial Cataluña***, Av Raymondi 822, T 721117, with bath, basic, restaurant open only in season, clean, safe, noisy, tepid water.

**F** ***Albergue El Tambo***, Confraternidad Internacional Interior 122-B, clean, laundry and cooking facilities, 3 rooms with 12 beds, friendly; **F** ***Alojamiento María Gloria***, Pasaje Valenzuela 854 nr Plaza Belén, T 722112, cheaper without bath, hot water, meals available; **F** ***Alojamiento San Martín de Porres***, Pasaje San Martín de las Porres off Las Américas 300 block, T 721061, clean, friendly, rec; **F** pp ***Alojamiento Alpes Andes***, at Casa de Guías, Plaza Ginebra 28-g, T 721811, member of Peruvian Youth Hostel Association, nice dorms for up to 6 people, with rec restaurant *Alpes Andes*, muesli, yoghurt in am, pastas and pizzas in evening, guided tours organized; it also houses the guide association of Huaraz, Casa de Guías, T 721811, F 722306, provides climbing and trekking information, good meeting place for climbers, notice board for messages; **F** pp ***Hostal López***, behind *Edward's Inn*, ask nr Estadio just off Av Bolognesi at Santa river end, lukewarm showers, washing facilities for clothes, beautiful garden and restaurant, good views, luggage stored, very friendly.

**G** pp ***Alojamiento El Rey***, Pasaje Olivera 919 nr Plaza Belén, T 721917, dormitory style, shared bath, clean, cooking and laundry facilities, family run, friendly and charming people, meals available; **G** pp ***Casa de Jaimes***, C Alberto Gridilla 267, T 722281, two blocks from main plaza, clean, hot showers, washing facilities, maps and books of region, use of kitchen, popular, rec; **G** ***Casa Jansy's***, Jr Sucre 948, hot water, meals, laundry, owner Jesús Rivera Lúcar is a mountain guide, rec; **G** ***Familia Sánchez***, Jr Caraz 849, clean, basic, warm water, helpful, cheap breakfast. There are usually people waiting at the bus terminals offering cheap accommodation in their own homes.

**Youth Hostels** See *Alojamiento Alpes Andes* above; ***Hostal la Montañesa***, Av Leguía 290, Centenario, T 721287.

### ● Places to eat

Restaurant and bar at ***Ebony 86***, Plaza de Armas, friendly, clean; ***Monttrek Pizza Pub***, Luzuriaga 646, T 721124, good pizzas and pastas, indoor climbing wall, shows videos; ***Chez Pepe***, Luzuriaga 570, good pizza, chicken, meat, run by Pepe from *Residencial Cataluña*; ***La Familia*** at Luzuriaga 431, popular with gringos, vegetarian dishes, good food but slow service; ***Créperie Patrick***, Luzuriaga 424 y Raymondi, excellent crêpes, fish, quiche, spaghetti and good wine; ***Chifa Jim Hua***, Luzuriaga 643, large, tasty portions for US$2-3; ***Monte Rosa***, Av Luzuriaga 496, good pizzería, reasonable prices, open 1830-2300, Swiss owner is Victorinox representative, offering knives for sale and repair service; ***Café Central***, Luzuriaga 808, good for breakfast; ***Miski Huasi***, Jr Sucre 476, small, cheap, some vegetarian; ***Las Puyas***, Morales 535, good cheap meals and breakfasts, popular with gringos; ***Pío Pío***, Av Centenario 329, rec; ***Sihuasino***, above the San Francisco church, good for *pachamanca* and *chicha*; ***Pizza Bruno***, Luzuriaga 834, T 725689, French-owned, good meals, especially crêpes, open from 1830, pricey, owner Bruno Reviron also organizes treks; ***Querubín***, Jr J de Morales 767, clean, friendly, traditional dishes, also vegetarian, cheap, rec; ***Huaraz Querido***, Jr Huascarán 184, excellent *cevicheria*, rec. Also good for *ceviche* is ***Warmi Juicio***, Pasaje Octavio Hinostroza 522, 2 blocks from Plaza de Armas; and ***Cevichería Tito's***, on the 5th block of Lúcar y Torre. ***La Fontana***, Av Tarapacá 561, excellent pancakes and juices, cheap, very friendly, ***La Estación***, Luzuriaga 928, a video pub which serves a good lunch for US$1, also good steaks for US$2, good food and atmosphere, very friendly owner, rec; ***Faby Star***, on Sucre, serves good, cheap local dishes, try their "huge" *milaneza*. On Calle Francisco, parallel to Centenario, is ***Tejas***, a good example of a *Recreo*, a restaurant that specializes in typical local dishes, the *cuy* is especially recommended, open only at weekends, like many other *Recreos*.

Note that middle and high-class restaurants charge a 31% tax on top of the bill.

## ● Banks & money changers

**Banco de Crédito**, on Plaza de Armas, closed 1300-1630, changes cash, no commission on TCs into soles, good rates, into cash dollars 5% commission, cash advance on Visa; **Interbanc**, on Plaza de Armas, 5% commission on TCs, cash advance on Visa. Casa de Cambio *Oh Na Nay*, across from Interbanc, cash only, good rates. Street changers on Luzuriaga (be careful). Travel agents also change dollars and TCs, but generally offer poor rates.

## ● Entertainment

***Imantata***, Luzuriaga 424, disco and folk music; ***La Cueva del Oso***, Luzuriaga 674, taverna-style, good peña; ***Taberna Tambo***, José de la Mar, folk music daily, disco, open 1000-1600, 2000-0200, rec, knock on door to get in; ***Amadeus***, Parque Ginebra, bar-disco; ***Bad Boy Pub Disco***, Jr J de la Mar 661, live rock groups; ***Monttrek Disco***, just off Plaza de Armas, in converted cinema, reasonable prices.

## ● Laundry

***Fitzcarrald***, Fitzcarrald, close to bridge; ***Lavandería Liz***, Bolívar 711, US$2/kg; another at San Martín 732. Also at the Casa de Guías (see above).

## ● Post & telecommunications

**Post**: Serpost, Luzuriaga opp Plaza de Armas, open 0800-2000 daily.

**Telecommunications**: Telefónica del Perú, Luzuriaga esq Sucre, national and international phone and fax, open 0700-2300 daily.

## ● Shopping

Daily market (1600-2000) in covered sidewalks of Luzuriaga for local sweaters, hats, gloves, etc, wall hangings, good value. Souvenirs inc ceramics from stalls on Mcal Cáceres nr the market. *Andean Expressions*, Jr J Arguedas 1246, near La Soledad church, T 722951, run by Lucho, Mauro and Beto Olaza, rec for hand-printed clothing and gifts. For camping supplies: ***Bodega Rosa Rosita***, San Martín 617; ***Bodega Chong Roca***, Jr J de Morales 661; ***Comercial Anita***, Jr San Cristóbal 369; ***Bodega Ortíz***, Luzuriaga 400 block, nr Raymondi.

**Camping gear**: several shops of the trekking agencies sell camping gaz cartridges. White gas is available from *ferreterías* on Raymondi below Luzuriaga and by Parque Ginebra. The following agencies are rec for hiring gear: ***Andean Sport Tours*** (see address below); ***Casa de Guías*** rents equipment and sells dried food; ***Monttrek*** (see address below); ***Chavín Tours*** (Willy Gordillo at *Hostal Casablanca*, address above, T 722602); ***Lobo***, Luzuriaga 557, T 724646, ***Pablo Tours*** (see below). Check all camping and climbing equipment before taking it. Gear is usually of poor quality, mostly second hand, left behind by others. Best to bring your own. All prices standard, but not cheap, throughout town. All require payment in advance, passport or air ticket as deposit and will only give 50% of your money back if you return gear early.

## ● Sports

**Climbing and trekking**: the Cordillera Blanca is the main climbing and hiking centre of Peru. The season is from May to Sept, although conditions vary from year to year (see **Climbing and Trekking in Peru**, page 15). See also under **Tourist Information** below and in the same paragraph for *Casa de Guías*. Recommended mountain guides are: Hugo Cifuentes Maguiña and his brother César (speaks English and French), Av Centenario 537; also in *Casa de Guías*; Augusto Ortega, Jr San Martín 1004, T 724888, the only Peruvian to climb Everest. Several of the agencies and *Casa de Guías* run rock climbing courses at Monterrey (behind *Hotel Baños Termales Monterrey*) and Huanchac (30 mins walk from Huaraz). Ask for details from *Casa de Guías* and tour agencies below; US$7.50-10 pp/day, inc guide and transport. See under **Travel agents** for organized trips.

**Mountain biking**: contact Julio Olaza at ***Mountain Bike Adventures***, Lúcar y Torre 538, T 721203, Julio speaks excellent English, US$15 for 5 hrs, various routes (see page 17). Julio also rents rooms, **F** pp, comfortable, luggage stored, discount for bikers. See also tour companies below.

**River rafting and canoeing**: contact Carlos Ames *River Runners*, Calle 27 de Noviembre 773 y La Mar 661, T 723375, F 724888 (see page 18); see also tour companies below.

## ● Tour companies & travel agents

All agencies run conventional tours to Llanganuco, Pastoruri (both US$9 pp) and Chavín (US$11 pp). Many hire equipment (see above) and also offer rafting on Río Santa (US$15/half day), climbing and trekking tours and ski instruction. Most agencies provide transport, food, mules and guides. Prices are generally 20% lower during low season (Oct-April). **NB** Tour agencies shouldn't recommend Pastoruri as a first trip. Best to go to Llanganuco first to acclimatize.

The following are recommended: ***Pablo Tours***, Luzuriaga 501, T 721145; ***Chavín Tours***, Luzuriaga 502, T 721578; ***Hiroshanka Sport***, Julián de Morales 611, T 722562, climbing, trekking, horse riding, 4WD hire (also rents rooms, **E** pp, with bath, hot water, breakfast). ***Monttrek***, Luzuriaga 640, T 721124, good trekking and climbing information, advice and maps, also run ice and rock climbing courses (at Monterrey), tours to Lago Churup and 'spectacular' *Luna Llena* tour; also mountain bike hire, ski instruction and trips, river rafting. Upstairs in Pizzería is a climbing wall, good maps, videos and slide shows. For new routes and maps contact Porfirio Cacha Macedo, 'Pocho', at *Monttrek* or at Jr Corongo 307, T 723930. ***Andean Sport Tours***, Luzuriaga 571, T 721612, basic practice wall behind office, also organizes mountain bike tours, ski instruction and river rafting. On the 2nd floor of the ***Hotel Residencial Cataluña***, Av Raymondi, T 72117, José Valle Espinosa, 'Pepe', hires out equipment (pricey), organizes treks and pack animals, sells dried food, and is generally helpful and informative.

## ● Tourist offices

Basic tourist information from OPTUR (Oficina de Promoción Turística) on Luzuriaga by Plaza de Armas, Mon-Fri 0900-1300, 1600-1900, Sat 0900-1300.

**Casa de Guías**: Plaza Ginebra, T 721811, climbers and hikers' meeting place, useful with information, arrangements for guides, *arrieros*, mules, etc. The Dirección de Turismo issues qualified guides and *arrieros* a photo ID, check for this when making arrangements. Prices for specific services are set so enquire before hiring someone. Prices in late 1995: *arriero*, US$7/day; mule, US$3/day; basic guide (who knows the area but has no special qualifications) without pack animals, US$9/day. Qualified trekking guides cost US$30/day; climbing guides US$40-60/day, depending on the difficulty of the peak. In the low season guides' prices are about 20-30% less. You are required to provide or pay for food for all porters and guides. **NB** Some guides speak English and are friendly but lack technical expertise; others have expertise but lack communicative ability. You may have to choose between the former and the latter.

## ● Transport

**Air** No regular service; private charter from AeroCóndor from Lima. Taxi to airport (at Anta) about 23 km from town, 20 mins, US$3. All transport N to Carhuaz goes past the airport; minivan, 40 mins, US$0.50.

**Buses to Lima**: Huaraz-**Lima**, 420 km, 7 hrs, US$5-9. The road is in good condition. See Lima **Bus companies** for bus lines and their addresses. There is a large selection of buses to Lima, both ordinary service and luxury coaches; departures throughout the day. Many of the companies have their offices along Fitzcarrald and on Av Raymondi. Some rec companies are: *Cruz del Sur*, Lúcar y Torre 573, T 723532; *Transportes Ro-*

*dríguez*, Tarapacá 622, T 721353; *Expreso Ancash* (Ormeño), Raymondi 845, rec; *Civa Cial*, San Martín 508, T 721947; *Movil Tours*, Raymondi 616, T 722555.

**Other buses**: to **Casma** and Chimbote via the Callán pass (150 km) 6-7 hrs, US$6, sit on left for best views: Transportes Moreno, Raymondi 892, T 721344, daily 0830 and 2000; Transportes Huandoy, Fitzcarrald 261, T 722502, daily 0800. To **Chimbote**, 185 km: Transportes Moreno, daily 0700, US$6, 8-9 hrs via Caraz and Cañón del Pato, see under Chimbote, sit on the right for the most exciting views (see page 147). Other companies go to Chimbote via Pativilca; Turismo Chimbote, Raymondi 815, T 721984, US$7, 6 hrs. To **Pativilca**, 160 km, 4 hrs, US$3.50. To **Trujillo**: Cruz del Sur, Chichaysuyo (Fitzcarrald 369), Rodríguez, Turismo Chimbote, Empresa de Transportes 14 (Fitzcarrald 216, T 721282), all buses go at night, 8-9 hrs, US$7. Several buses and minivans run daily, 0500-2000, between Huaraz and **Caraz**, 2 hrs, US$1.10. They stop at all the places in between; depart from Fitzcarrald esq Jr Caraz. To **Chavín**, 110 km, 4 hrs, US$3, and on to Huari, 150 km, 6 hrs, US$4.50 from Huaraz: Chavín Express, Mcal Cáceres 338, T 724652, daily 0900, 1100 and 1300; Cisper Tours, Tarapacá 621, T 722025, daily 0900 and 1300; Lanzón de Chavín, Tarapacá 602, daily 1000 to Huari, to Llamellín, Tues and Sat 1000, US$8. To **Chacas** (US$7) and **San Luis** (US$7.60), Transportes Huandoy, 7 hrs (also to Llamellín). To **Huallanca**, via Pachacoto (see below), US$3.50; some trucks and buses run this route, continuing to La Unión and Huánuco. Colectivos to Recuay, Ticapampa and Catac daily 0500-2000, US$0.65, from Mcal Cáceres y Tarapacá.

**Taxi**: standard fare in town is about US$0.90; radio taxis T 721482 or 722512.

## HUASCARAN NATIONAL PARK

Established in July 1975, the park includes the entire Cordillera Blanca above 4,000m. It covers a total area of 3,400 sq km and is 180 km from N to S and 20 km from E to W. It is a UNESCO World Biosphere Reserve and part of the World Heritage Trust. The park's objectives are to protect the unique flora, fauna, geology, archaeological sites and extraordinary scenic beauty of the Cordillera. Please make every attempt to help by taking all your rubbish away with you when camping. The park administration officially charges visitors US$1/day to enter the park but this was not always enforced in 1995. The park office is in the Ministry of Agriculture, at the E end of Av Raymondi in Huaraz, open am only, T 722086; limited general information but useful for those planning specific research activities.

### A blooming century

The giant *Puya Raimondi*, named after Antonio Raimondi, the Italian scholar who discovered it, is a rare species, considered to be one of the oldest plants in the world.

Often mistakenly referred to as a cactus, it is actually the largest member of the Bromeliad family and is found in only a few isolated areas of the Andes. One of these areas is the Huascarán National Park, particularly the Ingenio and Queshque gorges, the high plateaus of Cajamarquilla and along the route leading to Pastoruri in the Pachacoto gorge.

At its base, the *Puya* forms a rosette of long, spiked, waxy leaves, 2m in diameter. The distinctive phallic spike of the plant can reach a height of 12m during the flowering process. This takes its entire lifespan – an incredible 100 years – after which time the plant withers and dies.

As the final flowering begins, usually during May for mature plants, the spike is covered in flowers. As many as 20,000 blooms can decorate a single plant. During this season, groups of *Puya Raimondi* will bloom together, creating a spectacular picture against the dramatic backdrop of the Cordillera Blanca.

# A CIRCUIT OF THE CALLEJON DE HUAYLAS

## HUARAZ TO CHAVIN

South of Huaraz, on the main road, is **Recuay**, one of the few provincial capitals which survived the 1970 earthquake and conserves its colonial features (27 km, 30 mins).

The road passes **Olleros** at 3,450m. Some basic meals and food supplies available, but no accommodation. The famous, easy 3-day hike to Chavín, along a precolumbian trail, with spectacular views of snow-covered peaks, starts from Olleros. See below for a description.

An alternative trek from Olleros is to **Quebrada Rurec** via **Huaripampa**, a small village with a few *bodegas* which will sell or prepare food. Public transport is available to Huaripampa. There are granite walls of up to 600m at Rurec, the highest in the Cordillera Blanca; they are recommended for rock climbing. The trek itself is also worthwhile.

• **Transport** You can get off at the main road and walk the 2 km to Olleros, or catch a truck or minibus from Tarapacá y Jr Cáceres, nr *Edward's Inn*, to the village, 29 km, US$0.30.

The main road continues from Recuay to **Catac**, 11 km, where a good dirt road branches E for Chavín.

• **Accommodation & places to eat** *Hostal Central* and one other, both basic. *Restaurant La Familia*, good.

7 km S of Catac on the main road is **Pachacoto** from where a road goes to **Huallanca** on the other side of the Cordillera Blanca (133 km, 6-7 hrs). There is not a lot of local transport on this route. In this S part of the Cordillera there are few high, snow-covered peaks, but the glacier of **Pastoruri** is used as the only skiing area in Peru. It is nothing compared to other skiing areas in South America, there aren't even ski lifts, but it is a place to get in a little practice. Tours and private transport can be arranged in Huaraz; US$80 for a van up to 10 people.

A good place to see the impressive Puya Raimondi plants is the Pumapampa valley. Hike up the trail from Pachacoto to the park entrance, 2½ hrs, where there is a park office. You can spend the night here. Walking up the road from this point, you will see the gigantic plants.

From Catac to Chavín is a magnificent, scenic journey, if frightening at times. The road passes Lago Querococha, has good views of the Yanamarey peaks and, at the top of the route, is cut through a huge rock face, entering the Cauish tunnel at 4,550m. On the other side it descends the Tambillo valley, then the Río Mosna gorge before Chavín.

Along the E side of the Cordillera Blanca, which is known as the **Callejón de Conchucos**, runs a good, but narrow, dirt road, subject to rapid deterioration when it rains. Public transport is less frequent and less reliable here than in the Callejón de Huaylas, with some towns getting only 2 buses per week, direct from Lima. Private vehicles, usually large trucks, are few and far between. The region has also seen less foreign tourists and some discretion, as well as responsible behaviour, is called for. If you plan to travel in this area, allow plenty of time, especially in the rainy season.

## OLLEROS TO CHAVIN TREK

Note that the numbers in the text relate to the numbers on the map.

**1.** If you take a Huaraz-Catac minibus, get off at the cross before the Bedoya bridge. As you start uphill take the shortcut to Olleros to avoid the main road.

**2.** About 50m past the main plaza in Olleros take the street on the right heading towards the bridge.

**3.** When you reach Canray Chico, turn right to keep on the road which follows the Río Negro. Keep the river on the left. The track is not always clear but it's

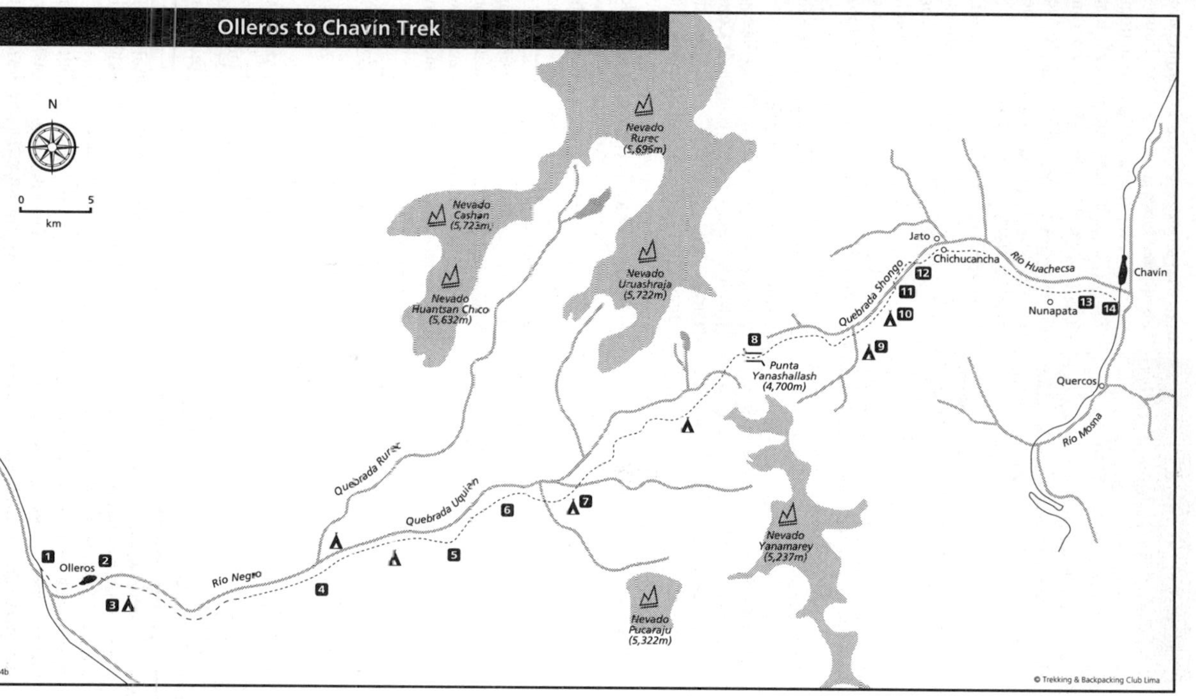
Olleros to Chavín Trek
N
0
5
km
Nevado Rurec (5,696m)
Nevado Cashan (5,723m)
Nevado Huantsan Chico (5,632m)
Nevado Uruashraja (5,722m)
Jato
Chichucancha
Río Huachecsa
Chavín
Quebrada Shongo
Nunapata
Punta Yanashallash (4,700m)
Quercos
Río Mosna
Quebrada Rurec
Quebrada Uquian
Nevado Yanamarey (5,237m)
Olleros
Río Negro
Nevado Pucaraju (5,322m)
1
2
3
4
5
6
7
8
9
10
11
12
13
14
014b
© Trekking & Backpacking Club Lima

difficult to get lost.

**4.** At this point a track branches off to the left into the Quebrada Rurec (see above); continue straight ahead.

**5.** Here you'll see a corral and, on the right, 2 small hills with houses. Head for the houses; don't follow the road with the bridge.

**6.** Once you pass the swamps and the corrals you'll climb up to some houses. A big stick would be useful here to fend off the resident canines.

**7.** Head towards the trees, at which point you start the climb towards the pampas that will lead to the **Punta Yanashallash**. This is a good spot to camp for the night. At the top of the valley, it divides into 4 valleys. The path swings right to avoid the marsh then heads up the second valley on the left, often with a ridge between the path and the river, to the highest point. It is quite easy to lose the track here, but keep heading in the direction of the pass and you'll pick it up eventually. It's a slow, gradual climb to the pass.

**8.** Here you reach the **Punta Yanashallash**, which is marked by great piles of rocks. From here you start going downhill.

**9.** Here you'll find a collection of houses or huts and a good camping spot.

**10.** Cross the swampy area and river before the trail starts again.

**11.** Follow the narrow trail which takes you down to another swampy area. Stay on the right side of the swamp and cross a small wooden bridge with some houses at the other end.

**12.** Follow the river until a large wooden bridge; cross it to continue the trail, which leads to the village of **Chichucancha**. Note that the valley leading down to Chavín is much more cultivated and populated. It may be better to camp near the foot of the descent from the pass in order to avoid beggars.

**13.** Head down into the Quebrada Huachecsa till you reach Punta Huancayo where you can see the ruins of **Chavín de Huantar**.

**14.** Go through the village of Nueva Florida to reach the road. The town of Chavín is on the left and the archaeological ruins are straight ahead.

(Thanks to the Trekking & Backpacking Club, Huascar 1152, Jesús María, Lima, for the above information.)

## CHAVIN DE HUANTAR

Chavín de Huantar, a fortress temple, was built about 600 BC. It is the only large structure remaining of the Chavín culture which, in its heyday, is thought to have held influence in a region between Cajamarca and Chiclayo in the N to Ayacucho and Ica in the S. In Dec 1985, UNESCO designated Chavín a World Heritage Trust site.

The site is in good condition despite the effects of time and nature. The easternmost building was damaged in 1993 when the Mosna river burst its banks, while in 1945 a major landslide along the Huachecsa river completely covered the site with mud. It took many years to remove the rubble and some structures remain hidden.

The main attractions are the marvellous carved stone heads and designs in relief of symbolic figures and the many tunnels and culverts which form an extensive labyrinth throughout the interior of the structures.

The carvings are in excellent condition, though many of the best sculptures are in Huaraz and Lima. The famous Lanzón dagger-shaped stone monolith of 800 BC is found inside one of the temple tunnels. John Streather writes: "There is only one carved head *in situ* on the walls of Chavín now. The best things are the finely-drawn stone reliefs of condors, pumas and priest-warriors. These are by far the finest examples of stonework of any Peruvian, or indeed Andean, culture of any period. The lines are outstanding for their fluidity, sinuousness,

## The stone gods of Chavín

Archaeologists have been able to learn very little about the Chavín culture, whose architecture and sculpture had a strong impact on the artistic and cultural development of a large part of the coast and central highlands of Peru. Based on physical evidence from the study of this 17-acre site, the temple of Chavín de Huantar is thought to have been a major ceremonial centre.

What first strikes visitors upon arrival at Chavín is the quality of the stonework found in the temple walls and plaza stairways. Three major classes of sculpture have been found: one has an architectural function; the second has an ornamental function; and the third is cult sculpture. The architectural stonework includes the cornices, roofs and columns, decorated with feline motifs. The ornamental group consists of small, quadrangular or rectangular slabs carved with mythical designs and tenoned heads set into the external wall of the temple. The purely cultist sculptures include the *Lanzón*, the Tello obelisk and the Raimondi stela. The latter two currently grace the Museum of Anthropology and Archaeology in Lima.

At 5m high, the *Lanzón* is the crowning glory of the Chavín religion. It stands at the heart of the underground complex, at the junction of two narrow passageways. Its Spanish name comes from the lance, or dagger-like shape of the monolith which appears to be stuck in the ground. Carved into the top of the head are thin, grooved channels and some speculate that animals, or even humans, may have been sacrificed to this god. Others, however, disclaim the sacrificial theory and suggest that the *Lanzón* was merely the dominant figure for worship.

Named after the Peruvian scientist, Julius C Tello, the Tello obelisk belongs to the earliest period of occupation of Chavín (ca 100 BC). It represents a complex deity – perhaps a caiman-alligator – connected with the earth, water and all the living elements of nature. Carved on the body are people, birds, serpents and felines which the divine beast has consumed.

The Raimondi stela was named after the Italian naturalist, who also gave his name to the famous plant, not to mention a fair percentage of the streets in the region. It shows a feline anthropomorphic divinity standing with open arms and holding some sort of staff in each hand.

Together, the figures carved on the stones at Chavín indicate that the resident cult was based principally on the feline, or jaguar, and secondarily on serpents and birds.

The Raimondi Stela

Measurements: 1.95m high by 0.76m wide

Material: diorite (Drawing: Hamilton Arce)

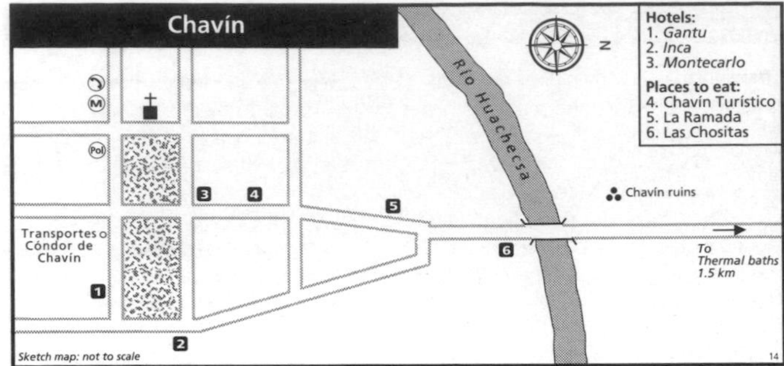


complexity and precision. Nothing like them seems to have existed either before or after them. The earliest Sechín art is clearly an inspiration, but looks very clumsy when compared with the delicate exactitude of the Chavín. In many ways it resembles early Chinese art more than anything Andean in its spirit and manner, though not in its symbolism, which is entirely Andean and American."

In order to protect the site some areas are closed to visitors. Although some of the halls have electric lights, take a torch. The guard is also a guide and gives excellent explanations of the ruins; Marino González is another knowledgeable guide. There is a small museum at the entrance, with carvings and some Chavín pottery. Entry US$2.25, students US$1.35; open 0800-1600 Mon-Sat, 1000-1600 Sun and holidays. Camping is possible with permission from the guard.

You will receive an information leaflet in Spanish at the entrance. The guard also sells other reference material including *Chavín de Huantar* by Willhelm and Nancy Hoogendoorn, an English/Spanish guide to the ruins which includes a description of each building and an historical overview.

## CHAVIN TOWN

The town of Chavín (*Alt* 3,140m), just N of the ruins, is the commercial centre for the nearby potato and corn growing area. Carved stone replicas are produced for the tourist trade. It has a pleasant plaza with palm and pine trees. The shops are well stocked with basic supplies and there is a small, basic market. There is nowhere to change money in town. The local *fiesta* takes place on July 13-20.

There are hot sulphur baths (Baños Termales de Chavín) about 2 km S of Chavín at Km 68 in the village of Quercos. They consist of 1 small pool and 4 individual baths in a pleasant setting by the Río Mosna. Camping is possible here. Buy detergent in the shop above baths and scrub your tub before bathing; entry US$0.45.

• **Accommodation** There are 3 very basic hostals around the plaza, some of which are very dirty. The best is **E** ***Inca***, Wiracocha 160, with bath, F without, good beds, hot water on request, nice garden, friendly; **F** ***Montecarlo***, 17 de Enero S, shared bath, cold water, cold at night; **F** ***Gantu***, Huayna Capac 135, very basic, shared bath, cold water; unsigned *Hostal* at 17 de Enero 831N, at N end of town, past police checkpoint.

• **Places to eat** From S to N along the main street, 17 de Enero, are: ***Las Chositas***, with garden setting, serves trout; ***La Ramada***, regional dishes, also trout and set lunch; ***Sr de Murhuay***, basic set meal; ***Chavín Turístico***, 439S, best in town, good *menú* and á l carte, clean, nice courtyard, friendly; ***Mi Ranchito***, Plaza de Armas, regional dishes, OK; ***El Lanzón de Chavín***, 216N, regional dishes, set lunch, friendly.

• **Post & telecommunications** Post office

and telephone service at 17 de Enero 365N; open 0630-2200.

• **Transport** Buses to Huaraz, 110 km, 4 hrs, US$3, see under Huaraz. Buses to Huaraz from Huari pass through Chavín between 0400-0600 daily but are often full; trucks go in the afternoon. There is plenty transport to **Catac**, 2½ hrs, US$2; many buses or trucks from there to Huaraz, 1 hr, US$0.50. Huaraz travel agencies organize daily tours to the ruins; sometimes you can hitch a ride back with them. Taxi, 4 hrs, US$20. To **Lima**, 438 km, 14 hrs, US$9 with Cóndor de Chavín twice a week, see Lima **Bus Companies** with routes to the N. Most buses from Lima go on to Huari and Pomabamba. Perú Andino and Solitario pass through Chavín, daily except Thur, en route to Lima; more frequent service Wed and Sun. From Chavín to **Huari**, 38 km, 2 hrs, in pm, **San Luis**, a further 61 km, 3 hrs, and **Piscobamba**, 62 km, 3 hrs: several buses and trucks serve this route as far as Huari on quite a good dirt road. The scenery is very different from the other side of the Cordillera Blanca, very dry and hot. Gasoline is available at N end of Chavín.

## CHAVIN TO POMABAMBA

From Chavín one circuit by road back to Huaraz is via Huari, San Luis, Yanama and Yungay (see page 152) but travel along this route can be very slow as the bus service is infrequent.

The road N from Chavín descends into the dry Mosna river canyon. After 8 km it reaches **San Marcos**, a small, friendly town with a nice plaza.

• **Accommodation & services** There are a few basic restaurants and *hostales*, inc **F** *Familia Luis Alfaro*, across from the church. Gasoline is available 24 hrs.

**ROUTES** 20 km beyond San Marcos, at the junction of the Huari and Mosna rivers, is the village of **Pomachaca** (Las Tunas), where a road branches NE to **Llamellín**. The main road continues N and climbs, criss-crossing the Huari river amid dry hills, to reach Huari 12 km further on.

### HUARI

The town, perched on a hillside at 3,150m, has steep streets and enjoys good views of the surrounding mountains. The Plaza de Armas and cathedral are modern, having been rebuilt after the 1970 earthquake. It has a small fruit and vegetable market, which is quite busy on Sun, and well-stocked shops. The water supply can be intermittent. The local *fiesta* of *Nuestra Señora del Rosario* is held during the first 2 weeks of Oct.

• **Accommodation F** *El Dorado*, Bolívar 341, basic, comfortable, sunny patio, shared bath, hot water; **F** *Añaños*, Alvarez 437, next to market, very basic but clean. There are a few others which are very basic, all **F**.

• **Places to eat** *Los Angeles*, Ancash 669, off main plaza, chicken, popular; ***Rinconcito Huaracino***, Bolívar 530, good *menú*, open till 2100; ***Centro Virgen del Rosario***, San Martín by Parque Vigíl, coffee, sweets and snacks, very clean and friendly, open evenings and Sun, run by an Italian nun and her students.

• **Post & telecommunications** The post office is at Luzuriaga 324 by Parque Vigíl. Telephone at Libertad 940, open 0700-2200 daily.

• **Transport** Bus companies have their offices around Parque Vigíl. To **Huaraz**, 5-6 hrs, US$4.50, all companies depart daily 0200-0400, also on Fri at 1500. To **San Luis**, on Tues and Sat; El Solitario at 0600, Perú Andino at 0830; buses headed N pass through Huari between 2200 and 2400. To **Lima**, 13 hrs, US$10, Turismo Huari on Sun, Wed and Fri at 0630, Perú Andino on Sun and Wed at 0800; on the other days, except Thur, buses bound for Lima originating further N pass Huari between 1000 and 1200.

## HUARI TO CHACAS

There is a spectacular 2-3 days walk from Huari to Chacas via Laguna Purhuay, as described by John Myerscough from Derbyshire in England: "The route is clearly shown on the IGM map, sheet 19. The walking is very easy, over a 4,500m pass and through two of the best valleys I've ever been in. Plenty of streams and lots of good places for camping. Amazing rock strata."

**To get to Laguna Purhuay**, climb the

stairs at the end of Jr Luzuriaga, in Huari, to the main road, turn right, or N, and walk for about 3 km to the village of Acopalca, which has a fish farm where you can buy trout. Turn left after crossing the bridge in town (ask directions). It is a 1½-hr walk up to the lake. The path to Chacas forks left just before the lake. Another good trail crosses the outflow and climbs above the eastern shore to a good lookout, then divides: the left fork descends to the inflow, which is a narrow gorge called *La Cola* (the tail); the right fork climbs to the village of Cachitzin (no facilities). There are no good trails along the shore of the lake.

Alberto Cafferata of Lima writes: "The Purhuay area is beautiful. It has splendid campsites, trout, exotic birds and, at its N end, a 'quenoal' forest. This is a microclimate at 3,500m, where the animals, insects and flowers are more like a tropical jungle, fantastic for ecologists and photographers." A day walk to Laguna Purhuay is recommended for those who don't want the longer walk to Chacas.

## CHACAS

10 km S of San Luis, off the main road, is Chacas, with its fine church. The local *fiesta patronal* is in mid-Aug, with bullfights, a famous *carrera de cintas* and fireworks. Seek out the Taller Don Bosco, a woodcarving workshop run by an Italian priest.

• **Accommodation & places to eat** There are a few basic shops, restaurants, a small market and two or three basic hostals, inc *Hostal de Pilar*.

It is a 2-day hike from Chacas to Marcará (see page 156) via the Quebradas Juytush and Honda (lots of condors to be seen). The Quebrada Honda is known as the Paraíso de las Cascadas because it contains at least seven waterfalls (Alberto Cafferata, Caraz).

## SAN LUIS

From Huari the road climbs to the Huachacocha pass at 4,350m and descends to San Luis at 3,130m. There is accommodation at **G** *Hostal Rotta*, also a few basic restaurants, shops and a market.

• **Transport** Buses run to **Chavín** on Wed and Sun, 5 hrs, US$6; to **Huaraz**, 8 hrs, via Yanama and the pass at 4,730m under Huascarán; and **Pomabamba**. Trucks also provide transport in this area.

A large sanctuary to Nuestra Señor de Pumayukay, built by Italian priests, is due to be completed in 1996. It is a 15-min ride from San Luis towards Pomabamba and then a turnoff to the E.

## YANAMA

28 km N of San Luis, a road branches left to Yanama, 50 km from San Luis, at 3,400m. It has one marked hotel outside and one unmarked hotel, **G**, on the plaza; ask at the pharmacy. Food is available, but no electricity in the village, which is beautifully surrounded by snow-capped peaks. A day's hike to the ruins above the town affords superb views.

• **Transport** Daily bus between Yungay and Yanama, US$4.50, 5 hrs, continuing to Pomabamba Tues, Sat (returning twice a week, US$11). Trucks also go along this route.

The route from Yungay to Yanama is particularly spectacular. Eckhart Harm of Germany writes: "The 70 km stretch from Yanama to Yungay is the most exciting of roads. If you leave early in the morning, you will always have the sun in the right place for taking photos. Between snow-capped peaks you ascend to the Portachuelo de Llanganuco pass from where you have an overwhelming view of Huascarán, Huandoy, Laguna de Llanganuco and other mountains, and the endless serpentines of the road winding down to the lake."

A longer circuit to Huaraz can be made by continuing from San Luis 62 km to **Piscobamba**. There is a basic, but clean and friendly hotel, and one other, both **F**;

also a few shops and small restaurants.

## POMABAMBA

Known as "City of the Cedars", though none can be seen, Pomabamba is 22 km beyond Piscobamba. The town is worth a visit on several counts. There are very hot natural springs there, the furthest are the hottest. There is a small museum opposite the restaurant on the corner of the main plaza, which the people in the courtyard offices will open free on request.

• **Accommodation & places to eat** F *Hostal Pomabamba*, on main square, basic, safe for luggage; *Alpamayo*, plaza, basic; *San Martín de Porres*, off the smaller plaza, basic. Rooms above the Marino agency. The restaurant on the corner of the main plaza is friendly and good (cold though); *Canela*, rec.

• **Tour companies & travel agents** *One Pyramid Travel*, Huaraz 209, T 721283, run by Victor Escudero, who speaks English, he specializes in archaeological tours, inc some little known, unspoilt places, recommended.

• **Transport** Occasional buses run from San Luis. Bus to Lima twice a week via San Luis and Chavín. To Chimbote twice a week via Sihuas.

### Treks from Pomabamba

Several good walks into the Cordillera Blanca start from near Pomabamba. You can go via Palo Seco or Laurel to the Lagunas Safuna, from which one can go on, if hardy, to Nevado Alpamayo, dubbed 'the most beautiful mountain in the world'. The glacier of Alpamayo is an incredible sight. From there, continue down to Santa Cruz and Caraz for several days' hard walking in total.

For the less energetic, it is a good 4½-5 hrs walk up to the quite large and extensive, though sadly dilapidated, ruins of **Yaino**, on top of a very steep mountain and visible from the main plaza of Pomabamba.

Ask directions in the village and on the way, too. The walls are beautifully built and there are two very large buildings, a square one and a circular one. The site commands excellent views of the many peaks of the Cordillera. The walk to Yaino and back to Pomabamba can be done in a day if you start early. Take food and lots of water; you can get very dehydrated climbing and perspiring in the thin dry air. It's also very cold high up if the sun goes in, so go with warm, waterproof clothes.

## POMABAMBA TO CAÑON DEL PATO

From Pomabamba the road goes N through cold, wild mountains and valleys, passing in 23 km Palo Seco and Andeymayo. The mining town of **Pasacancha** (hotel and restaurant), 56 km beyond Palo Seco, is the junction for a road N to Sihuas (expensive, basic hostales). Buses twice a week from Pomabamba via Sihuas to Chimbote, 16 hrs.

Daytime trucks run from Pasacancha, through Tarica and Yanac, past pre-Inca *chullpas* to Tres Cruces (basic friendly restaurant, no accommodation). Transportes Moreno buses from Tres Cruces go to Yuramarca, before the Cañon del Pato, and on to Caraz (and from there to Yungay and Huaraz). A detour from Yuramarca is along a frightening road to **Corongo**. There is a bus from Caraz once a week with Empresa Callejón de Huaylas from the main plaza, but only travel in the summer or you may be stuck for a considerable time.

Places like San Luis, Piscobamba, Pomabamba and Sihuas were on the royal Inca Road, that ran from Cusco to Quito.

## CAÑON DEL PATO TO HUARAZ

**The route from Chimbote via the Santa Valley**: just N of Chimbote, a road branches NE off the Pan-American Highway and, joining another road from the town of Santa, goes up the Santa valley following the route, including tunnels, of the old Santa Corporation Railway. This used to run as far as **Huallanca** (not to be confused with the town SW of Huaraz), 140 km up the valley, but the track was largely destroyed by the 1970 earthquake. At Huallanca is an impressive hydroelectric plant, built into a mountain, which can not be visited. *Hotel Huascarán*, good, friendly; everything closes early. At the top of the valley the road goes through the very narrow and spectacular **Cañón del Pato** before reaching the Callejón de Huaylas and going on S to Caraz and Huaraz. The Cañon section was closed in 1995 for widening and paving and traffic detoured via Huaylas; due to be completed in 1996.

An alternative road for cyclists is the private road known as the 'Brasileños', used by a Brazilian company which is building a water channel from the Río Santa to the coast. The turn-off is 15 km S of the bridge in Chao, on the Pan-American Highway.

## CARAZ

Now almost totally restored after the 1970 earthquake, this pleasant town (*Alt* 2,250m) is a good centre for walking, parasailing and the access point for many excellent treks and climbs. It is increasingly popular with visitors as a more tranquil alternative to Huaraz. The town enjoys splendid views of Huandoy and Huascarán as well as the northern Cordilleras in July and August. In other months, the mountains are often shrouded in cloud. Caraz has a milder climate than Huaraz and is more suited to day trips. The sweet-toothed will enjoy the excellent locally-produced *manjar blanco*, a sort of toffee, from which it derives its nickname, *Caraz dulzura*.

It is expected that tourism will further increase once the paving of the road through the Cañon del Pato is completed. Five new hotels were under construction in 1995.

### Museums

**Museo Arqueológico de Caraz** is at 1 de Mayo y Mcal Cáceres, open 0800-1400, free; small but interesting collection of ceramics and artefacts from the region; also a good place to ask about the ruins of **Tunshukaiko** (see below).

### Excursions

The ruins of **Tunshukaiko** are in the suburb of Cruz Viva, to the N before the turn-off for Parón. This is a poor area so be discrete with cameras etc.

There are 7 platforms from the Huaraz culture, dating from around BC 500. Minimal excavations have taken place and only the tops of a couple of the structures are accessible, some of which are estimated to have been up to 50m in height.

• **Access** From the plaza, follow San Martín uphill, turn left on 28 de Julio, continue past the bridge over the Río Llullán; at the level of the turn-off for Parón ask the way as the ruins are behind some houses to the left. There isn't much to see at this time, but walking around will give you some idea of just how large these structures are.

### Local festivals

Virgen de Chiquinquirá, 20 Jan; Semana Turística, last week in July, with sports festivals, canoeing, parasailing and folkloric events.

### Local information

**● Accommodation**

**D** *Hotel Restaurant Chamanna*, Av Nueva Victoria 185, T 791223, 25 mins walk from centre of town, from the plaza follow San Martín up hill, turn left at 28 de Julio, continue past the turnoff to Lago Parón, run by Germans Ute Baitinger and Reiner Urban, clean cabañas set in beautiful gardens and good food, European and local; **D** *Regina*, Los Olivos s/n y Gálvez, at S end of town 1 block W of road to Yungay, T 791520, modern, with bath, hot water, clean, good value; **D** *Chavín*, San Martín 1135 just off Plaza, T 791171, with bath, sometimes hot water, owner can arrange trips to Lago Parón.

**E** *El Cafetal*, San Martín 307, T 791137, 7 blocks from the plaza, friendly, very basic, 2 rooms with bath, hot water; **E** *Hostal La Casona*, Raymondi 319, 1 block from plaza, T 791334, **F** without bath, cold water, clean, lovely little patio; **E** *Morovi*, Luzuriaga 3a cuadra, at S end of town, T 791409, F without

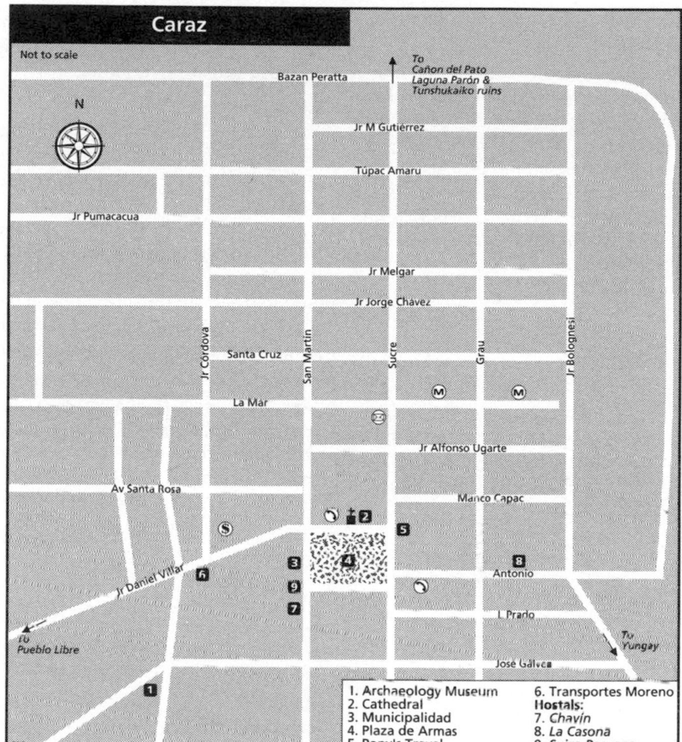


bath, clean, friendly, helpful, hot water.

**F** ***Ramírez***, D Villar 407 above Moreno terminal, T 791368, basic, shared bath, cold water, helpful.

**In private homes**: **F** pp ***Familia Caballero***, D Villar 485, enquire at Pony's Travel on plaza, shared bath, basic, friendly; **F** ***Familia Aguilar***, San Martín 1143, T 791161, basic, shared bath, friendly, Prof Bernardino Aguilar Prieto has good information on the Cordillera Negra.

## ● Places to eat

***La Boca del Lobo***, San Martín 1029, off main plaza, fish, seafood and *menú*, good, Dutch, English and French spoken; ***Jeny***, on plaza, good food and prices; also on plaza, ***El Mirador***, Sucre 1202, nice view from terrace, good for afternoon coffee, and ***Café Heladería El Portal***, on San Martín, good snacks and sweets; ***La Punta Grande***, D Villar, inexpensive local meals; ***Esmeralda***, Av Alfonso Ugarte 404, good meat and local food, friendly, good value, rec; ***La Capullana***, 3 km from town along the road to Cañon del Pato, pleasant garden setting, good food, expensive, poor service; ***La Olla de Barro***, Sucre 1004, good, English spoken; ***Palmira***, 500m S of town, E of main road, serves excellent trout, reasonably priced (open 1200-1800), pleasant outdoor setting; ***Añanu Caraz***, Sucre 1107, *menú*, popular with locals.

## ● Banks & money changers

**Banco de Crédito**, D Villar 217, cash and TCs at good rates, no commission; **Interbanc**, Sucre 903, cash only, poor rates; *Comercial Fournier*, Sucre 907, cash only, daily 0800-1330, 1600-2000; *Pony's Travel* (see below) cash only; *Importaciones América*, Sucre 721,

T 791479 (Esteban), good rates and service, open weekends and evenings.

**● Entertainment**

*Taberna Discoteca Gato Negro*, 28 de Julio s/n, on the way to Parón, good atmosphere, reasonable prices; *Taberna Discoteca Alpamayo Inn*, Bolognesi, moderate prices, a bit impersonal; *Taberna Disco Huandy*, Mcal Cáceres 119.

**● Post & telecommunications**

**Post Office**: at San Martín.
**Telecommunications**: national and international phone and fax service at Raymondi y Sucre.

**● Shopping**

The best shop for camping supplies is *Kike*, at Sucre 918. Some dehydrated food is available from *Pony's Travel* (see below).

**● Sports**

**Swimming**: there is a cold water pool at the S entrance to town; adults US$0.45, children US$0.20.

**● Tour companies & travel agents**

*Pony's Travel*, Sucre 1116, Plaza de Armas, T/F 791580/791529, or Lima 447-4696, open daily 1000-2100, English, French and Quechua spoken, excellent and reliable information about the area, owners Alberto and Haydée Cafferata are very knowledgeable about treks and climbs; local tours and trekking arranged, equipment for hire; also mountain biking to Lago Parón (5 hrs, moderate difficulty) and Portachuelo de Llanganuco (10 hrs, difficult), bike hire US$10/day, US$1/hour, maps and guides included, helmets and gloves available, recommended. Another trekking guide is Mariano Araya, who is also keen on photography and archaeology.

**● Tourist offices**

At Plaza de Armas, in the municipality, T 791029, limited information.

**● Transport**

**Buses** From Caraz to **Lima**, 470 km; buses go via Huaraz. Most buses on the Lima-Huaraz route continue to Caraz (see Lima, **Bus Companies**). Several buses (6 companies) daily, fares ranging from US$6 (eg Chinchaysuyo) to US$10 (Expreso Ancash), 14 hrs. From Caraz to **Huaraz**, several buses and many colectivos daily, 0500-2000, 2 hrs, US$2.25, road in good condition; taxi US$15. To **Yungay**, 12 km, 30 mins, US$0.45. To **Chimbote**, Transportes Moreno, US$5.80, via Huaraz and Casma at 0600 and 1730 daily; via Huallanca 0830 daily (see under Chimbote). To village of **Parón** (for trekking in Laguna Parón area) pickups from corner Santa Cruz and Grau by market, 0500 and 1300, 1 hr, return from Parón 0600 and 1400; to **Cashapampa** (Quebrada Santa Cruz) buses from Santa Cruz between Grau and Sucre by market, 1000, 1100, 1200 and 1500, 2 hrs, US$1.35.

## TREKS FROM CARAZ

### Pueblo Libre

A good day hike with good views of the Cordillera Blanca is to Pueblo Libre. Follow Jr D Villar E across the Río Santa bridge and turn S to Tunaspampa, an interesting desert area with cacti and hummingbirds. Continue through the villages of Shingal, Tocash and Rinconada on to Pueblo Libre. It is about 4 hrs round trip, or you can take a colectivo back to Caraz.

A longer day walk – about 7 hrs in total – with excellent views of Huandoy and Huascarán follows the foothills of the Cordillera Blanca, from Caraz South. To leave town, follow Bolognesi up to 28 de Julio, turn right, go past the 2 de Mayo (Markham) High School and climb Cerro San Juan; 45 mins. Continue S towards the eucalyptus forest (1 hr 20 mins). After climbing a steep hill, where you get to a small house, take the smaller branch to the left. This leads to the main local summit in an area known as Ticrapa (2 hrs). Head down to Punyan on the Caraz-Yungay road (3 hrs), where you can take transport back to Caraz.

### Lago Parón

From Caraz a narrow, rough road goes E 32 km to Lago Parón, in a cirque surrounded by several, massive snow-capped peaks, including Huandoy, Pirámide Garcilazo and Huaraz. The water level has been lowered to protect Caraz, and the water from the lake is used for the Cañon del Pato hydroelectric scheme. The gorge leading to it is spectacular.

It is about a 2-day trek (25 km) up to the lake at 4,150m, or a 5-6 hrs walk from the village of Parón. Where possible follow the walking trail which is much shorter than the road. By climbing up the slippery moraine to the S of the lake towards Huandoy, you get a fine view of Artesonraju. If there is room, you can stay at the refuge run by Hidrandina (kitchen, bathroom) ask guard for permission, no charge, but any food used should be replaced.

A trail follows the N shore of the lake to a base camp on the N side of the inflow, about 2 hrs past the refuge. Beyond this point, the trail divides, one branch goes towards Pirámide Garcilazo (5,885m) and Pisco (5,752m), another to Laguna Artesoncocha at the base of an enormous glacier, and a third towards Artesonraju (6,025m).

There are camping possibilities along these trails; try to find shelter in the quenual stands or behind a ridge, as the wind can be very strong and the nights are cold. The views are magnificent as you are always surrounded by many beautiful peaks. When you ford a river, remember that the flow increases significantly in the afternoon with the meltdown, so make sure you can get back to your camp early. On the route to Artesonraju there is a morraine camp, just before reaching the glacier. You will need a map if you are going past Laguna Parón.

• **Transport** From Caraz, colectivos go to the lake if there are enough passengers and only in the dry season, US$3-4 pp. Taxi from Caraz US$15, or from Huaraz, US$30 return. Travel agencies in Huaraz and Caraz organize day-trips to the lake (about US$50 pp from Huaraz).

## Santa Cruz Valley

The famous Llanganuco-Santa Cruz hike is done most easily starting in the Santa Cruz valley. Take a truck from Caraz in the morning up to Cashapampa (see transport above). It takes about 4 days, up the Santa Cruz Valley, over the pass of Punta Unión, to Colcabamba or Vaquería (see Llanganuco to Santa Cruz trek below for details). In this direction the climb is gentler, giving more time to acclimatize, and the pass is easier to find. You can hire an *arriero* and mule for about US$8/day.

3 km N of Cashapampa, 1-2 hrs hike, are the hot-baths of Huancarhuas. It is almost impossible to hitch from the end of the trail back to Yungay. Be on the road by 0800 to catch the daily truck or bus coming from Yanama. Travellers describe this journey down to Yungay as exhilerating and terrifying.

## The Alpamayo valley

This offers a beautiful, but difficult, 10 day trek from Cashapampa to Pomabamba; for the experienced only. From Cashapampa head up to the Cullicocha lake, passing the first pass at Los Cedros (4,850m), down the Mayobamba valley and up the third pass at 4,500m. Then into the Tayapampa valley, on to the village of Huillca, up the fourth pass at 4,280m and down to Collota, Yanacollpa and Pomabamba. **NB** Please carry out *all* your rubbish.

## Cordillera Negra

For hikes in the Cordillera Negra, a truck leaves from Caraz market at 1000 to Huata at 2,700m, where there is a religious sanctuary and a dirty hotel, **F**. From here you can climb to the Quebrada de Cochacocha (3,500m) at the top of which is the Inca ruin of Cantu (excellent views), and on to the Inca lookout, **Torreón Andino** (5,006m). Take water, food and tent with you. Allow 3 days for the hike; there are lagoons near the peak. 6 km down a track off the Caraz-Huata road are the Inca ruins of Chonta

Seek advice from Prof Bernardino Aguilar Prieto in Caraz, San Martín 1143, T 791161; refer to his Torreón Andino Information book before climbing it.

A large stand of **Puya Raimondi**, said to

be more impressive than those by Pastoruri, can be seen in the Cordillera Negra W of Caraz, along the road to Pamparomas. Take a truck or bus from the market as far as the Yuashtacruz pass at 4,300m, from where the plants are visible.

• **Transport** To Pamparomas pickups leave from the corner of Grau and Lamar by the market, on Mon, Wed and Fri at 0830, US$3, returning the same afternoon; also buses from Campo Ferial behind the market, at 0900 on the same days, returning in the afternoon. Check times in advance. To hire a pickup, US$25-35.

## YUNGAY

The main road goes on to **Yungay**, 12 km S of Caraz. Yungay was completely buried during the 1970 earthquake by a massive mudslide caused when a piece of Huascarán's glacier was pried loose by the quake and came hurtling towards the town; a hideous tragedy in which 20,000 people lost their lives. The earthquake and its aftermath are remembered by many residents of the Callejón de Huaylas and the scars remain part of the local psyche.

The original site of Yungay, known as Yungay Viejo, has been consecrated as a *camposanto* (cemetery). It is a desolate, haunting place, utterly barren save for four palm trees from the old Plaza de Armas. Nearby, atop a hill, is the old cemetery with a large statue of Christ, where a handful of residents managed to escape the disaster. There are a few monuments marking the site of former homes.

The new settlement is on a hillside just N of the old town, and is growing gradually. It has a pleasant modern plaza and a concrete market, good on Thur and Sun, which is good for stocking up on supplies for hiking.

**Local fiestas**: on Oct 17 is Virgen del Rosario; on Oct 28 is the anniversary of the founding of the town, celebrated with parades, fireworks and dances.

• **Accommodation E** pp *COMTURY*, Complejo Turístico Yungay, Prolongación 2 de Mayo 1019, 2.5 km S of the new town, 700m E of main road in Aura, the only neighbourhood of old Yungay that survived, T 722578, nice bungalows with space for up to 10, pleasant country setting, hot water, fireplace, friendly, restaurant with regional specialities, camping possible; **E** ***Hostal Gledel***, Av Arias Graziani, N past plaza, T 793048, a few cheaper rooms available, owned by Sra Gamboa, who is hospitable and a good cook, very clean, shared bath, hot water, excellent meals prepared on request, nice courtyard, highly rec; **E** ***Hostal Yungay***, Jr Santo Domingo on plaza, T 793053, clean, basic, shared bath; **F** ***Hostal Blanco***, follow the hospital street at N end of plaza and continue up hill, there are signs, T 793115, shared bath, basic, nice views.

• **Places to eat** *Alpamayo*, Av Arias Graziani s/n, at N entrance to town, good; ***El Portal***, by the market, fair. There are several small *comedores* in and around market and by the plaza.

• **Transport** Buses, colectivos and trucks run the whole day to Caraz, 12 km, US$0.45, and Huaraz, 54 km, 1½ hrs, US$1.10. To Yanama, via the Portachuelo de Llanganuco pass at 4,767m, 58 km: buses and trucks leave Yungay daily from in front of the Policía Nacional, 1 block S of plaza, at around 0800 but you may have to wait until they are full, 4-5 hrs, US$4.50. Some buses and trucks continue to San Luis, a further 61 km, 3 hrs, US$2.50, Huari (61 km) and Chavín (38 km, 6 hrs, US$3.50); on Tues and Sat the bus continues N to Piscobamba and Pomabamba (US$11 Yungay-Pomabamba). Buses or colectivos will do the route to the Llanganuco lakes when there are enough people, and only in the dry season, 1½ hrs; colectivo US$4.50, bus US$2.50. Huaraz travel agencies organize trips to Llanganuco for about US$8.

## EXCURSIONS FROM YUNGAY

A day walk from Yungay to **Mirador de Atma** gives beautiful views of Huascarán, Huandoy and the Santa valley. From town, follow a new dirt road E for 3 km (about 1 hr). You can return via the Quebrada Ancash road which runs further N, between the Río Ancash and Cerro Pan de Azucar. This will bring you to the Yungay-Caraz road about 1 km N of Yungay. It is about a 3 hrs round trip.

**Matacoto**, 6 km from Yungay, is in the Cordillera Negra at 3,000m, with excellent views of Huascarán, Huandoy and other major peaks. The turn-off is at Huarazcucho (Km 251), 3 km S of new Yungay; it is another 3 km W from here, across the bridge over the Río Santa to Matacoto. Camping possible, kitchen and hot baths, US$6, ask for Susana Scheurich (German, she also speaks English, French and Italian). Horse hire in Matacoto US$3/half day, ask for Pachamanca, recommended. Trucks go on Wed and Sun 0700-1300, US$0.50; on other days transport costs US$8. Matacoto can also be reached from Mancos (3 hrs trekking; see below).

## LLANGANUCO TO SANTA CRUZ TREK

For trekkers this is one of the finest walks in the Cordillera Blanca. The following numbers correspond to the numbers on the map.

**1.** Arrive in Yungay early for transport to Yanama (see above).

**2.** Entry point to the Huascarán National Park. The Park office is situated here below the lakes at 3,200m, 17 km from Yungay. Accommodation is provided for trekkers who want to start from here, US$2 pp. The entrance fee to the park is US$1/day, but is based purely on trust. Although you can start hiking up the Llanganuco valley from the park office, most hikers continue by bus or truck to María Huayta (see below), where the Llanganuco-Santa Cruz trail starts. From the park office to the lakes takes about 5 hrs (a steep climb).

There is a *refugio* at the lakes. From the lakes to the pass will take a further 2-3 hrs, with perfect views of the surrounding peaks. Just before the zig-zag climb up to the pass, there is a trail, very difficult to find, heading N, up to the Pisco base camp and the Demanda valley where, to the left, Laguna 69 is situated and, to the right, the Broggi glacier. There is a doorless *refugio* by the Broggi glacier, so one can spend the night after hiking up from the lakes, continue next day to Laguna 69 and return in time to catch a truck to Yanama.

**3.** This is the military control point. About 50m before the control is a moraine which is the short-cut to the Portachuelo pass.

**4.** From the Portachuelo de Llanganuco down to **Vaquería** at 3,700m, about 9 km. However, get off here, at **María Huayta** (Km 66). From this point you will find a trail beside the house that takes you down to the trail to Colcabamba, 4 km, 3 hrs. If you don't get off here, the truck or bus will leave you in Vaquería, which is 3 kms up in the valley.

**5.** **Colcabamba** is a small village with basic lodging and food, should you decide to stay there. Familia Calonge is recommended, friendly, good meals. You can arrange an *arriero* and mule for about US$9/day.

**6.** From Colcabamba the trail goes up the Huaripampa valley. As you enter the valley, you cross a bridge. There is a trail to the left which you should not follow. As you climb up to a curve you'll see another trail leading off to the right; do not follow this.

**7.** Push open the gates and continue through.

**8.** The trail starts again but it is best to keep close to the river to avoid the swamps. There are good camping spots from here to Punta Pucaraju.

**9.** Quebrada Paría: here you'll see a signpost. The trail continues up to the right.

**10.** From Paría you'll find a forest of quenoales. The trail crosses the river here; look for a wide spot which has rocks to use as stepping stones.

**11.** After 15 mins you'll reach some large boulders on your right. Here you'll find the trail on your left. Start climbing and look for markers (piles of stones) on the way.

**12.** Once you reach the wall of the morraine begin the climb to the highest point at Punta Unión, 4,750m. The views from here are wonderful. Look for the markers.

**13.** Go through the pass and a few metres ahead you'll see a marker to the right. Follow the track down to the pampa. From here it is downhill through the Santa Cruz valley to Cashapampa. You can camp anywhere on the way.

**14.** Cross the pampa and you'll reach a swamp from where you can see a signpost across the river. Follow the river; on the right you'll see a quenoal forest. In the middle of the river is a large rock. 5m before the rock is a natural bridge to cross the river. A bit further on is a good side trek up to the Alpamayo base camp.

**15.** Recrossing the river, you'll see a signpost. Follow the trail until you reach a large boulder. On the left is a cave; head towards it to get back on the right trail,

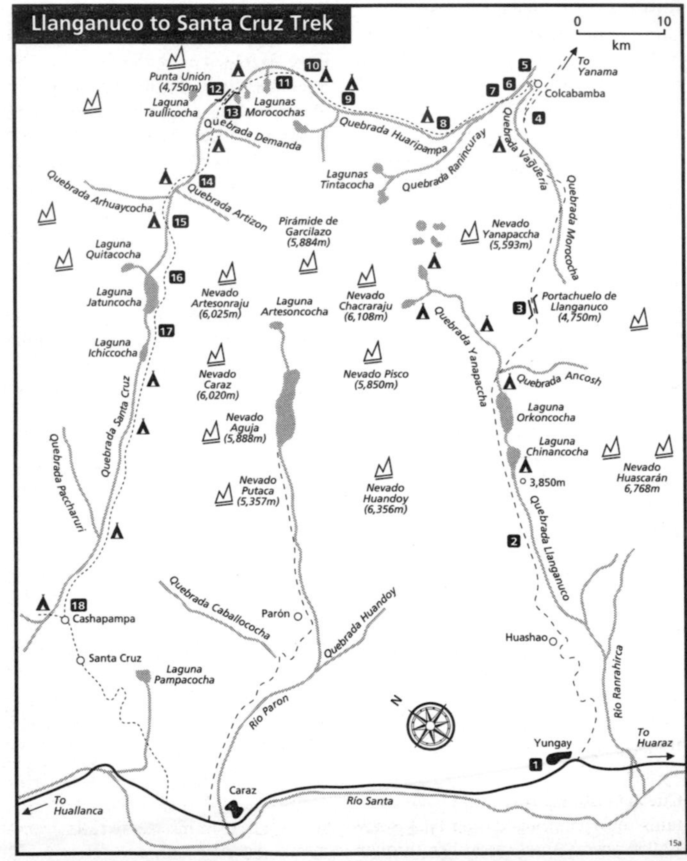

otherwise you'll end up in the middle of the swamp.

**16.** Once you reach Jatuncocha, the trail goes up to the left through the rock avalanche.

**17.** About 45 mins further on you reach a another swamp. The trail continues on the left.

**18.** At the end of the Santa Cruz valley you reach a eucalytptus forest. Don't cross the bridge but follow the trail and in 15 mins you'll be in Cashapampa. Trucks from Cashapampa to Caraz leave at 0600, 1200, 1300 and 1400, 2 hrs, US$1.35. Alternatively, hike via the little village of Santa Cruz to Caraz, about 5 hrs. You can stay overnight in a private house in Cashapampa for US$1. Some people recommend starting the hike at the Santa Cruz end, see Caraz excursions for details. The trek takes 4 days on average. **Please take all your rubbish with you.**

Thanks to the Trekking & Backpacking Club, Huascar 1152, Jesús María, Lima, for the above information.

## MANCOS

After Yungay, the main road goes to Mancos (8 km S, 30 mins) at the foot of Huascarán. There is one hostal, some basic shops and restaurants.

Climbers of Huascarán can go to Musho to reach the base camp. You can do a strenuous 30 km, 1-day walk which gives great views of Huascarán. From Mancos follow the road E and take the branch for Tumpa, about 13 km away; ask directions as the road branches several times. Continue N to Musho about 1 km. You can descend via Arhuay to Ranrahica, which is between Mancos and Yungay on the main road. There are daily colectivos from Mancos to Musho; transport to Ranrahica and Arhuay is on Wed and Sun only.

**Cueva Guitarreros** is a cave which contains rock paintings dating back some 12,000 years. Access is either through Mancos, from where it is about 30 mins walking along an overgrown trail (with many spines!), or through Tingua and Shupluy further S, from where it takes about 1 hr.

The **Chirpas thermal springs**, which have a high Lithium content, are near the caves. There are good views of Huascarán from around this area.

## CARHUAZ

From Mancos to Carhuaz is 14 km. It is a friendly, quiet mountain town with a pleasant plaza with tall palm trees and lovely rose bushes. There is very good walking in the neighbourhood (see below). Market days are Wed and Sun (the latter is much larger) when *campesinos* bring their produce to town. Good peaches are grown locally, among other crops. The local fiesta in honour of the *Vírgen de las Mercedes* is celebrated from Sept 14 to 24 and rated as the best in the region. The locals are renowned for their livley celebrations, hence the town's nickname, *Cahuaz alegría*.

• **Accommodation D** pp *Casa de Pocha*, 1 km out of town towards Hualcán, at foot of Nevado Hualcán, ask directions in town, T celular 613-058 (Lima 462-1970), price includes all meals, nice country setting, entirely solar and wind energy powered, hot water, sauna, home-produced food (vegetarian available), horses for hire, camping possible; **E** ***Hostal Residencial Carhuaz***, Av Progreso 586, T 794139, just off plaza, cheaper without bath, varying standards of rooms (check first), basic but pleasant, hot water, nice courtyard and garden; **F** ***Hostal La Merced***, Ucayali 600, T 794327, excellent, clean, friendly, hot water, rec. Due to open in 1997 is ***Casa Blanca***, in Acopampa, 3 km S of town, T 794149, country setting, ask at *Heladería El Abuelo* on the plaza.

• **Places to eat** ***Los Pinos***, Av Amazonas 645, good typical food and set meals, rec; ***El Palmero***, Av Progreso 490, good value, friendly. There are several other restaurants on the plaza. ***Café Heladería El Abuelo***, Plaza de Armas, D'Onofrio and local ice-cream, sweets, clean and friendly, also sells regional maps and guides.

• **Transport** There are trucks (only 1 or 2 a day) and one minivan (0800) going up the Ulta valley to Chacas (see page 146), 87 km, 4-5 hrs, US$4.50. The road works its way up the Ulta valley to the pass at Punta Olímpica from where there are excellent views. The dirt road is not in a very good condition owing to landslides every year (in the wet season it can be closed). The trucks continue to San Luis (see page 146), a further 10 km, 1½ hrs. Each Thur, a bus (Transportes Huandoy) does the trip from Carhuaz to Chacas and returns, US$6 one way, 5 hrs. To Huaraz, colectivos and buses, 0500-2000, US$0.65, 1 hr; to Caraz, 0500-2000, US$0.90, 1 hr.

## TREKS FROM CARHUAZ

The trek up to the **Ulta valley** over the Punta Yanayacu pass to Yanama is little used but offers impressive views of Huascarán and other peaks. It takes 3 days. If you catch a truck up the valley to where the road begins to zig-zag up to the pass, it will shorten the trek by one day. If not, start hiking from Shilla, 13 km E of Carhuaz, or Huaypan. There is a bus Carhuaz-Shilla-Huaypan.

A shorter trek in the same direction is to Laguna Auquiscocha at 4,319m. From where the trail begins by the road, to some beautiful waterfalls below Aquiscocha, it is a hard 3 hrs walk. You can camp or make a day trip.

**Baños de La Merced**, 7 km E of Carhuaz, near the village of Hualcán, were badly damaged by a landslide in 1993. The hot springs can be seen bubbling between the rocks by the river's edge and there are some small rock pools in which the enthusiastic can bathe.

• **Access** From the plaza follow Comercio to the top of the hill, turn right as far as *cinco esquinas* (five corners), turn left and follow the road uphill. When you reach the bridge, cross it left to Hualcán and ask directions from there. There is transport to Hualcán leaving from behind the church in Carhuaz on weekends only.

If you don't cross the bridge to Hualcán but continue along the S bank of the river, you will reach the **Baños de Pariacaca** on the left side of the road; 1½ hrs from Carhuaz. There is a small pool behind a wall, used by the locals for washing. Move the stones to change the water if you plan to bathe.

Half an hour beyond is the village of **Pariacaca** (no facilities) from where a trail coninues into the mountains. In 3 hrs you can reach **Laguna Rajupaquinan** and, 45 mins beyond, the imaginatively named **Laguna 513**, with beautiful views of the surrounding peaks. If you continue, you will see the Auquiscocha lakes which you can reach in another 2½ hrs. Laguna 513 can also be reached directly from Hualcán in about 4 hrs, along the N side of the river. This latter trail has fewer rocks to negotiate. Make sure to take adequate gear and a map if you plan to go beyond Pariacaca.

## CARHUAZ TO HUARAZ

The main road goes on from Carhuaz 6 km to **Marcará**; **E** *Alojamiento Restaurant Suárez*, Leguia 144, basic, shared bath, and other basic restaurants and shops.

Pick-ups and colectivos go from here E along a branch road 3 km to **Chancos**, a little settlement with hot baths. There is accommodation in the shape of two very basic *alojamientos*, including *Bonilla*, ½ km W of town, and several basic restaurants and food stalls.

There is an uninviting lukewarm pool (US$0.45); none too clean private tubs (US$0.90) and very popular natural steam baths in caves (US$1.35 pp). The caves are interesting and worth a try, with locked changing rooms (cave 5 is the smallest and hottest). Buy eucalyptus leaves and other aromatic herbs from the local children to add some fragrance to your steam bath.

From Marcará the road and transport continue to **Vicos**, 3 km further up the Huandoy valley (7 km, from Marcará, 1½ hrs, US$1.50). Vicos is in superb surroundings with views of Nevados

Tocllaraju and Ranrapalca. To hike from Chancos to Vicos takes about 2 hrs up the valley through farmland. A trail leads from Vicos to Laguna Lejíacocha (4 hrs).

There are archaeological sites at Copa, Kekepampa and Joncopampa; the latter is considered to be second only to Chavín in the region. From Vicos, cross the river on a footbridge, it is about 1 hr further to Joncopampa.

From Vicos, one can walk through the Quebrada Honda, over the Portachuelo de Honda at 4,750m, to Chacas; about 4 days, an excellent, not difficult hike.

The main Carhuaz-Huaraz road goes on to **Taricá**, where there is a home pottery industry (good value purchases from Francisco Zargosa Cordero) and thence to Huaraz, 26 km from Marcará, 1 hr, US$0.50.

• **Accommodation** **F** *Hostal Sterling*, no hot water, food, friendly.

## TREKKING IN THE CORDILLERA BLANCA

**Hilary Bradt writes**: The Cordillera Blanca offers the most popular backpacking and trekking in Peru, with a network of trails used by the local people and some less well defined mountaineers' routes. Most circuits can be hiked in 5 days. Although the trails are easily followed, they are rugged and the passes very high – between 4,000 and nearly 5,000m – so backpackers wishing to go it alone should be fit and properly acclimatized to the altitude, and carry all necessary equipment. Essential items are a tent, warm sleeping bag, stove, and protection against wind and rain (climatic conditions are quite unreliable here and you cannot rule out rain and hail storms even in the dry season). Trekking demands less stamina since equipment can be carried by donkeys.

**The South American Explorers' Club** writes that this area is a mecca for climbing and hiking, but get information before you start. The Club publishes a good map with additional notes on the popular Llanganuco to Santa Cruz loop, and the Instituto Geográfico Nacional has mapped the area with its 1:100,000 topographical series. These are more useful to the mountaineer than hiker, however, since the trails marked are confusing and inaccurate.

Apart from the book by Hilary Bradt (see Information for travellers), a useful guide to the area currently in print is *Peruvian Andes* by Philipe Beaud, costs US$24, available through Cordee in the UK, some shops in Huaraz and the South American Explorers' Club. A new edition of *Callejón de Huaylas y Cordillera Blanca*, a good guide to the area, by Felipe Díaz, in Spanish, English and German, is due to be published in 1996.

● **Maps**

An excellent map of the Callejón de Huaylas and Cordillera Huayhuash, by Felipe Díaz, is available in many shops in Huaraz and at Casa de Guias. Maps of the area are available from the IGN in Lima. Hidrandina, the state hydroelectric company, at 27 de Noviembre 773, has dye-line maps of the Cordillera Blanca, open in morning only. Several guides and agencies have their own sketch maps of the most popular routes. Maps are also available by mail-order from Latin American Travel Consultants, PO Box 17-17-908, Quito, Ecuador, F (593-2) 562566, Internet: LATC@pi.pro.ec.

### Advice to climbers

The height of the Cordillera Blanca and the Callejón de Huaylas ranges and their location in the tropics create conditions different from the Alps or even the Himalayas. Fierce sun makes the mountain snow porous and the glaciers move more rapidly. The British Embassy advises climbers to take at least 6 days for acclimatization, to move in groups of four or more, reporting to the Casa de Guías or the office of the guide before departing, giving the date at which a search should begin, and leaving the telephone number of your Embassy with money. Rescue operations are very limited; insurance is essential (cannot be purchased locally), since a guide costs US$40-50 a day and a search US$2,000-2,500 (by helicopter, US$10,000).

Be well prepared before setting out on a climb. Wait or cancel your trip when weather conditions are bad. Every year climbers are killed through failing to take weather conditions seriously. Climb only when and where you have sufficient experience.

**NB** Check locally on political conditions. A few robberies of hikers have taken place; do not camp near a town or village, never leave a campsite unattended and always hike with others when heading into the remote mountain districts.

On all treks in this area, respect the locals' property, leave no rubbish behind, do not give sweets or money to children who beg and remember your cooking utensils, tent, etc, would be very expensive for a campesino, so be sensitive and responsible.

## CORDILLERA HUAYHUASH AND RAURA

The **Cordillera Huayhuash** lying S of the Cordillera Blanca, is perhaps the most spectacular in Peru for its massive ice faces which seem to rise sheer out of the contrasting green of the Puna. Azure trout-filled lakes are interwoven with deep quebradas and high pastures around the hem of the range. You may see tropical parrokeets in the bottom of the gorges and condors circling the peaks. The circuit is very tough; allow 12 days. There are up to eight passes over 4,600m, depending on the route. Both ranges are approached from Chiquian in the N, Oyun in the S or Cajatambo to the SW.

### THE HUAYHUASH CIRCUIT

The trek starts in **Chiquian**. From there, descend to the **Río Pativilca** and down the scorched canyon to the confluence of the **Río Llamac**. Head eastwards up river to **Llamac**, the last opportunity to buy supplies. Only potatoes can be found beyond – if you're lucky.

A must is a side trip to **Laguna Jahuarcocha**, which lies beneath **Yerupajá** (Peru's second highest peak at 6,634m) and Nevados **Jirishanca** and **Rondoy**. The lake offers the most idyllic campsite in the Cordillera. It is reached over a pass at 4,700m SE of Llamac; first head SW along a path just beneath the cemetery and zig-zag up above the town.

The main circuit trail is regained over a 4,800m pass beneath Rondoy. From Rondoy village, the **Punta Cacanan** (the first pass on the main circuit trail, at 4,700m) is the northernmost point on the trek and gives access to the village of **Janca**, **Laguna Mitacocha** and the eastern flank of the Cordillera.

A very steep short cut on scree is through the gap in the northern spur of the range above Rondoy village and Janca village on the other side. This could save 2-3 hrs.

The eastern side of the Cordillera is a chain of passes, lakes and stunning views of **Jirishanca Chico**, **Yerupajá Chico**, **Yerupajá** and **Siula Grande**. From Janca, a small side valley leads off **Quebrada Mitacocha** to **Punta Carhuac** (4,650m) and beyond to **Laguna Carhuacocha**. Following on from there are **Punta Carnicero** (4,600m), the twin lakes of **Azulcocha** and **Atogshayo** (just beyond the pass) and **Huayhuash village**.

The next pass, **Portachuela** (4,750m) overlooks the superb southward line of pyramidal peaks and rounded ice caps of the **Cordillera Raura**. A path leads from **Laguna Viconga** below (near the dam), over a pass and hugs the western flank of the Raura all the way to **Oyun**. Four days away from Oyun is **Churin**, which boasts the "best thermal baths in Peru".

If you are bailing out at **Cajatambo**, it is downhill all the way from Laguna

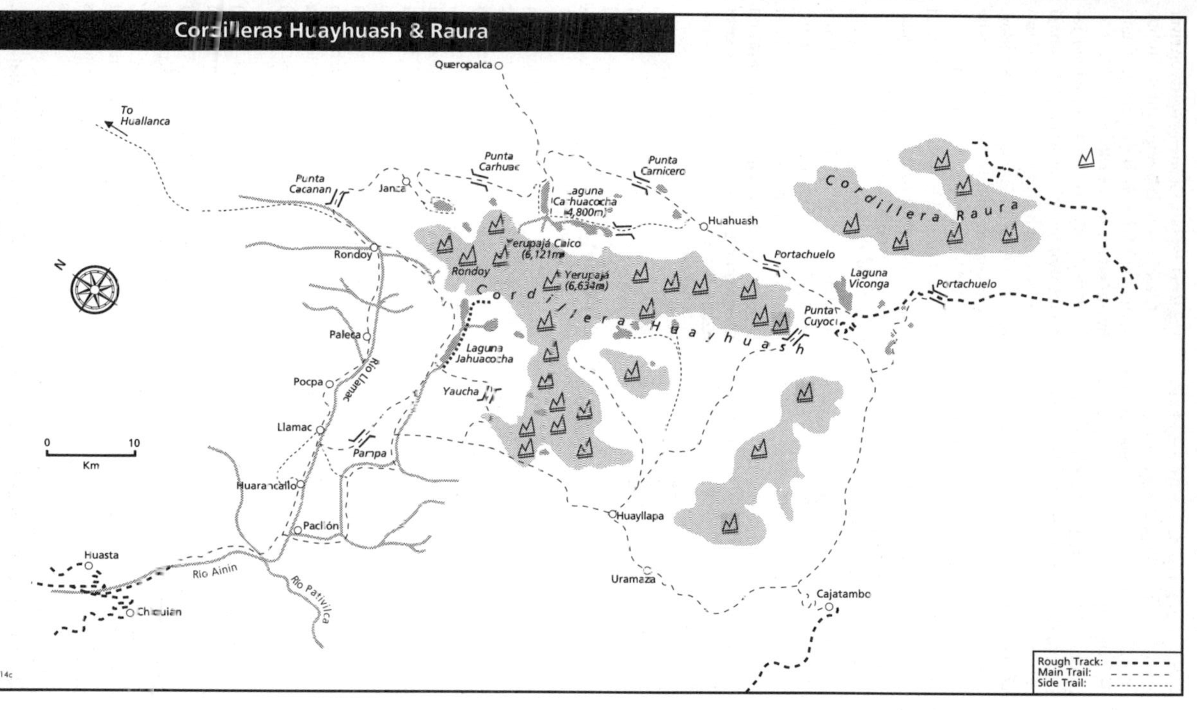
Cordilleras Huayhuash & Raura
Queropalca
To Huallanca
Punta Cacanan
Janca
Punta Carhuac
Laguna Carhuacocha (4,800m)
Punta Carnicero
Huahuash
Cordillera Raura
Rondoy
Yerupajá Chico (6,121m)
Rondoy
Yerupajá (6,634m)
Portachuelo
Laguna Viconga
Portachuelo
Punta Cuyoc
Cordillera Huayhuash
N
Paleta
Laguna Jahuacocha
Pocpa
Río Llamac
Yaucha
Llamac
0
10
Km
Pampa
Huarancallo
Pacllón
Huayllapa
Huasta
Río Ainin
Río Pativilca
Uramaza
Cajatambo
Chiquian
014c
Rough Track:
Main Trail:
Side Trail:

Viconga, apart from a short sting in the tail at the end. Those continuing the circuit must cross the **Pasa Puyoc** (5,000m) above Laguna Viconga (sometimes snowbound). It is another 3-4 days back to Chiquian in the N.

## CHIQUIAN

This is usually the starting point for the Huayhuash circuit. It is a town of narrow streets and overhanging eaves. An interesting feature is a public television mounted in a box on a pedestal which sits proudly in the Plaza de Armas.

• **Accommodation & places to eat** **F** *Hostal San Miguel*, Jr Comercio 233, nice courtyard and garden, many rooms, popular, rec; **F** *Hostal Inca*, 1 block from plaza, not as big as *San Miguel*. A good, basic restaurant is *Yerupajá*, Jr Tarapacá 351. Buy all your food and supplies in Huaraz as there is little in Chiquián.

• **Transport** Three daily buses run from Huaraz to Chiquián (El Rápido, between Raymondi and Tarapacá, Huaraz, Virgen del Carmen and one other), 120 km, 3-4 hrs, US$2, dep Huaraz about 1400, Chiquián 0500. There are also trucks on the route, leaving from the market, not daily. It is not well-travelled. Direct buses go from Chiquián to Lima, 353 km, 8 hrs, US$5.25, with Tubsa, Firesa and Cavassa overnight. There is also a connection from Chiquián to Huallanca, some trucks and buses doing this route, not daily. Trucks and buses go on to La Unión and Huánuco.

**Mule hire** It is sometimes a problem in the high climbing/trekking season to hire mules straightaway. This is because all the ones from Chiquián are kept at Llamac and Pocpa, where they are most needed as there is no connecting road. It may take a day to bring the mules to Chiquián.

A guide for the Huayhuash is Sr Delao, ask for him in Chiquián.

## CAJATAMBO

The southern approach to the Cordillera Huayhuash is a small, developing market town. The plaza is being rebuilt.

• **Accommodation & places to eat** **F** *Hostal Miranda*, Jr Tacna 141, homely, friendly, small rooms, rec; **G** *Hostal Cajatambo*, on plaza, basic, cheap, not for the squeamish, the courtyard is a chicken slaughterhouse; **G** *Hostal Trinidad*, Jr Raimondi 141, basic. *Restaurant Andreita*, is at Av Grau 440.

• **Transport** Buses to Lima leave Tues, Wed, Sat and Sun at 0600, US$8.80, with Empresa Andina (office on plaza next to *Hostal Cajatambo*).

# Northern Peru



An area of great and diverse interest, Northern Peru is poised for major tourist development. Here stand elegant colonial cities such as the restored Trujillo and ruined Saña. The former indigenous settlements of Cajamarca, Chiclayo and Piura have been transformed into commercial centres but still retain much of their quaint charm. There are mountain villages with local customs and on the coast, deep-sea fishing, surfing, and the 'caballitos de totora' reed rafts at Huanchaco and Pimentel. Above all, the region is famous for its many monumental ruins of highly-skilled pre Inca cultures. Among the best known are Chan Chán, Kuelap, Tucumé, Sipán, Batán Grande and El Brujo. Between the oases, all the way to Ecuador, runs the desert. The sweeping grey dunes and dusty cliffs contain rare flora and fauna, including the iguana and the *huerequeque*, the long-legged bird portrayed on prehispanic pottery.

## NORTH TO TRUJILLO

North of the mouth of the Río Santa the Andes recede, leaving a coastal desert belt 8 to 16 km wide containing the three great oases of Northern Peru – the areas of Trujillo, Chiclayo and Piura.

North of Chimbote the Highway crosses the valleys of Chao and Virú, and after 137 km reach the first great oasis of Northern Peru, Trujillo. In the valley there is an abrupt line between desert and greenery. Cultivation requires irrigation ditches which take their water from far up in the mountains.

## TRUJILLO

**Trujillo** (*Pop* 750,000; *Phone code* 044), capital of the Department of La Libertad, disputes the title of second city of Peru with Arequipa. The greenness surrounding the city is a delight against the

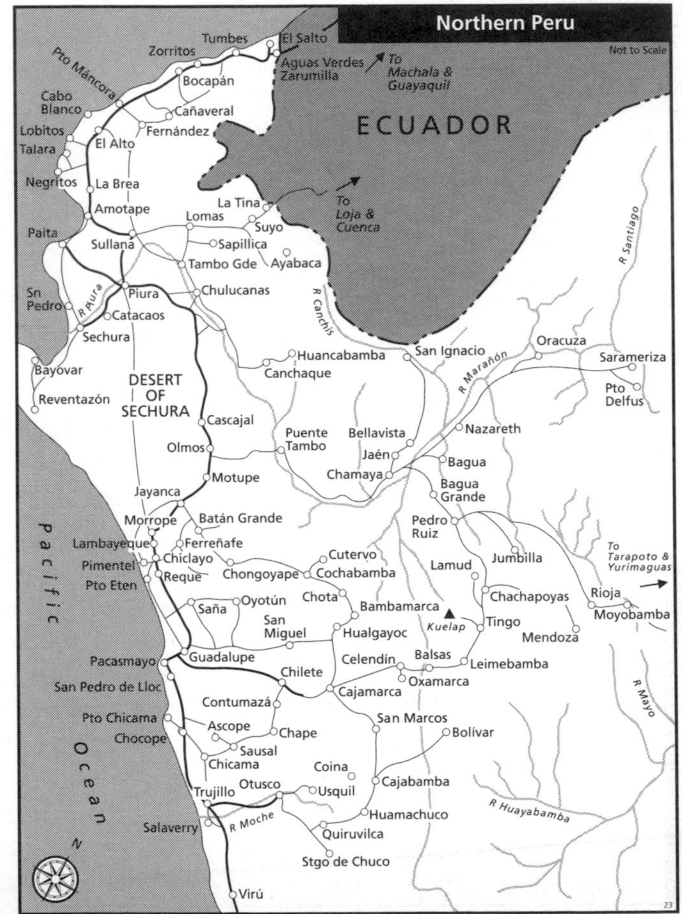

backcloth of brown Andean foothills and peaks. Founded by Diego de Almagro in 1534 as an express assignment ordered by Francisco Pizarro, the city was named after the latter's native town in Spain.

There is enough here to hold the attention for several days. The area abounds in precolumbian sites, there are beaches and good surfing within easy reach and the city itself still retains many old churches and graceful colonial homes built during the reigns of the viceroys. With its compact colonial centre and mild, spring-like climate, Trujillo is best explored on foot. Besides the Cathedral it has 10 colonial churches as well as convents and monasteries.

## Economy

La Libertad was once the foremost producer of sugar in Peru but is still struggling to recover from an economic crisis brought on by social changes in the 1970s and 80s. Other agricultural products are rice, fruit, potatoes and cereals.

**Mining** is important to the region's economy. 18 km by road from Trujillo is the area's port, **Salaverry**, exporting sugar and minerals and importing consumer goods and machinery. The Quiruvilca copper mines are 120 km inland by road from Salaverry. The concentrating plant at Shorey is connected with the mines by a 3 km aerial cableway, and with its coal

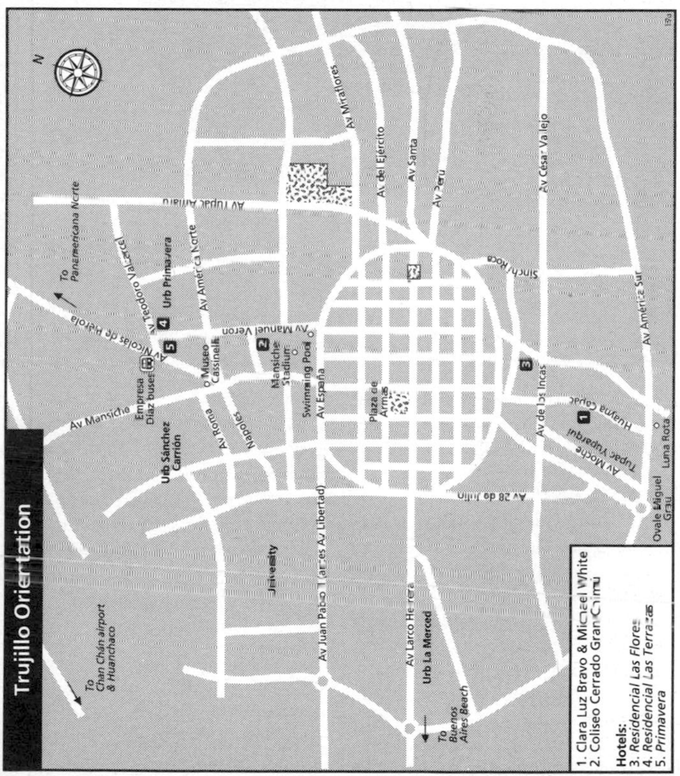

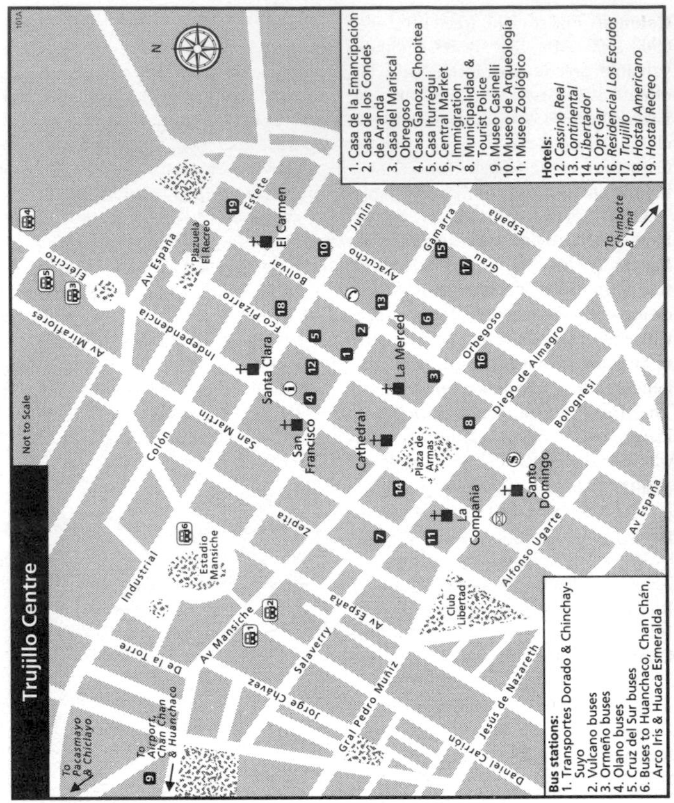


mine by a further 8 km. The ore is then taken by a 40 km cableway to Samne and from there it is sent by road to Salaverry.

## PLACES OF INTEREST

The focal point is the pleasant and spacious **Plaza de Armas**. The prominant sculpture represents agriculture, commerce, education, art, slavery, action and liberation, crowned by a young man holding a torch depicting liberty. Fronting it is the **Cathedral**, dating from 1666, with its museum of religious paintings and sculptures next door. Also on the Plaza are the *Hotel Libertador*, the colonial style Sociedad de Beneficencia Pública de Trujillo and the Municipalidad.

The **Universidad de La Libertad**, second only to that of San Marcos at Lima, was founded in 1824. Near the Plaza de Armas, at Jr Pizarro 688, is the spacious 18th century **Palacio Iturregui**, now occupied by the **Club Central**, an exclusive and social centre of Trujillo, open 1100-1300 and 1600-2000. Exhibitions of local ceramics are often held.

### Colonial houses

Two other beautiful colonial mansions on the Plaza have been taken over by the Banco Central de Reserva. One is the Republican-style **Casa Urquiaga (or**

**Calonge)**, Pizarro 446, free entry, open 0900-1600 Mon-Sat, which contains valuable precolumbian ceramics. The other is **Casa Bracamonte (or Lizarzaburo)**, Independencia 441, now closed. Also on the Plaza, next to the Cathedral, is the **Lynch House**, boasting the oldest facade in the city.

Other mansions, still in private hands, include **Casa del Mayorazgo de Facalá**, Pizarro 314, now Banco Wiese, free entry when bank is open. Its former owner was Don Pedro de Tinoco whose wife embroidered the first Peruvian flag to be hoisted following Trujillo's independence from Spanish rule in 1820. The **Casa de la Emancipación**, Jr Pizarro 610 (Banco Continental), is where independence from Spain was sworn, open daily 0900-1300 and 1700-2000. The **Casa del Mariscal de Orbegoso**, Orbegoso 553, named after the ex-President, General Luis José de Orbegoso, is a museum, owned by Banco Internacional, open daily 0900-1300 and 1600-1900, free entry. **Casa Ganoza Chopitea**, Independencia 630 opposite San Francisco church, is architecturally the most representative house in the city and considered the most outstanding of the viceroyalty. It combines Baroque and Rococo styles.

### Churches

Many churches were damaged in the 1970 earthquake. One of the best, the 17th century **La Merced** at Pizarro 550, with picturesque moulded figures below the dome, is being restored, but part of the dome has collapsed because of building work next door. **El Carmen** church and monastery at Colón y Bolívar, has been described as the 'most valuable jewel of colonial art in Trujillo'. Next door is the Pinacoteca Carmelita. **La Compañía**, near Plaza de Armas, is now an auditorium for cultural events. In **San Francisco,** on the corner of Gamarra and Independencia, is the still-preserved renaissance pulpit which survived the earthquake of Saint Valentine's Day that destroyed the city in 1619. Other old churches include: **Belén** on the 6th block of Almagro; **Santa Clara** on the 4th block of Junín; **San Agustín** on the 6th block of Mcal Orbegoso; **Santa Ana** on the 2nd block of the same street; and **Santo Domingo** on the 4th block of Bolognesi.

**Plazuela El Recreo**, at the N end of Pizarro, was known as El Estanque during the colonial period as it housed a pool from which the city's water was distributed. A marble fountain now stands in the square, transferred from the Plaza de Armas in 1929, fronted by several open-air restaurants. There are two markets, one on Gamarra, the Mercado Central, and the Mercado Mayorista on Calle Roca.

## MUSEUMS

**Museo de Arqueología**, Casa Risco, Junín y Ayacucho, open 0800-1300 (entrance, US$1), houses a large and interesting collection of pottery.

The basement of the **Cassinelli** garage on the fork of the Pan-American and Huanchaco roads contains a superb private collection of Mochica and Chimú pottery, recommended. Demonstrations of the whistling *huacos* are given; entry,

Huaco from Moche period

US$2.50, open 0830-1130, 1530-1730.

**Museo de Zoología de Juan Ormea**, Jr San Martín 349 (0800-1400); interesting displays of Peruvian animals, entrance free (but donations welcome, and needed).

## EXCURSIONS

**Las Delicias**, a clean beach with good surf, is about 20 mins by bus (US$0.35) and 15 mins by taxi from Trujillo.

**• Accommodation & places to eat**

**F** *Hostal Zlang*, shared bath, small, clean, quiet, rec. Breakfast is available in ***Bar-café*** next door; other meals available from other members of the family; the owner is very knowledgeable and his son runs tours to Chan Chán. Round the corner is a good restaurant serving traditional food.

## LOCAL FESTIVALS

The two most important festivals are the **National Marinera Contest** and the **Festival Internacional de La Primavera**. The former is held in the last week of Jan and consists of hundreds of couples competing in six categories, from children to seniors (see **Música criolla**, page 68). This event is organized by the Club Libertad and has taken place since 1960.

The Festival de la Primavera is held in the last week in September. Organized by the Club de Leones, it is a celebration of the arrival of Spring and has grown over the years to become one of Peru's most important tourist events. The festival is not for the politically sensitive as it is basically a massive beauty pageant with beauty queens from South and North America participating. Also featured are Trujillo's famous *Caballos de Paso*, a fine breed of horses with a tripping gait that has made them renowned worldwide. These horses, a Spanish legacy, have been immortalized in Peruvian waltzes. Riders still compete in their own form of the Marinera dance and buyers from around the world congregate to see them shown at the Spring Festival.

In the first week of May is the Festival del Mar, a celebration of the disembarkation of Taycanamo, the leader of the Chimú period. A procession is made in Totora boats.

## LOCAL INFORMATION

**NB** Trujillo has confusing double street names: the smaller printed name is that generally shown on maps, in guide books and in general use.

**● Accommodation**

**A1** *Libertador*, Independencia 485 on Plaza de Armas, T 232741, F 235641, ex-Turistas, price inc tax, pool, full of character, cafeteria and restaurant, continental breakfast US$5, excellent buffet lunch on Sun, rec; **A2** *El Gran Marqués*, Díaz de Cienfuegos 145-147, Urb La Merced, T/F 249582, price inc tax and breakfast, modern, pool, restaurant, rec.

**A3** *Cassino Real*, Pizarro 651, T 257034, F 257416, inc tax and American breakfast, car rental provided; **A3** *Los Conquistadores*, Diego de Almagro 586, T 244505, F 235917, price inc tax and American breakfast, bar, restaurant, very comfortable, upgraded late 1995.

**C** *Continental*, Gamarra 663, T 241607, F 249881, opp market, inc tax, clean, good, safe, restaurant rec; **C** *Hostal Residencial Las Terrazas*, Av Manuel Vera Enríquez 874, Urb Primavera, behind Hotel Primavera, T 232437, with bath, hot water, TV, phone, garage, cafeteria, garden, pool, good value, friendly; **C** *Opt Gar*, Grau 595, T 242192, with bath and TV, good, friendly, excellent restaurant (lunch only for non-guests) and snack bar, rec; **C** *Residencial Los Escudos*, Orbegoso 676, T 255961, with bath, make sure you ask for the hot water to be switched on, small garden, expensive laundry service, friendly, door locked at night, secure, rec; **C** *San Martín*, San Martín 743-749, T 234011, with bath, good value, small restaurant, good for breakfast, clean but noisy, rec; **C** *Vogi*, Ayacucho 663, T 243574, inc tax, with bath, TV, clean, safe, quiet, rec.

**D-E** *Hostal Chan Chán*, Huayna Cápac 201 esq Sinchi Roca 304, T 242964/251301, with bath, hot water, TV, cafeteria; **D** *Hostal Recreo*, Estete 647, T 246991, with bath, TV, clean, friendly, safe, restaurant, rec; **D-E** *Hostal Residencial Las Flores*, Atahualpa 282-284, T 242527, clean, big rooms, good value; **D-E** *Primavera*, Av N de Piérola 872, Urb Primavera, nr Empresa Díaz bus terminal,

T 231915, F 257399, with bath, hot water, restaurant, bar, pool; **D-E** ***Roma***, Nicaragua 238, next to El Aguila bus station, T 259064, clean, secure, friendly, helpful, luggage stored, rec; **D** ***Sudamericano***, Grau 515, T 243751, with bath, hot water, phone, laundry service, parking, bar-restaurant, clean, reasonable value; **D-E** ***Trujillo***, Grau 581, T 243921, with bath, clean, good value, rec.

**E** ***Grau***, Grau 631, T 242332, with bath, clean, good value; **E** ***Hostal Americano***, Pizarro 792, T 241361, a vast, rambling old building, next to cinema, rooms without bath are noisy and very basic, most rooms without window (Nos 134 and 137, and those either side of 303, have windows, balconies and good views), safe, good meeting place; **E** ***Hostal Royers***, Av Los Incas 687, T 257095, with bath, hot water, friendly but dirty, basic, comfortable, hot water 1200-1400, 3rd floor is best for water.

There are several cheap hotels on Ayacucho, all of which are decaying and very basic: **E** ***Hostal Central***, 728, T 246236, basic but clean, friendly, bargaining possible; **F** ***Hostal Lima***, 718, T 244751, popular with gringos, dirty, baths terrible; **F** ***Hostal Internacional***, Bolívar 646, T 245392, cheaper without bath, very basic. Familia Moreno, Huáscar 247, **E**, nr centre, clean, quiet, safe, or Catrina Castillo, Pedro Muñiz 792 (10 blocks from the Plaza de Armas) **F**, friendly.

**Youth hostel**: **E** *Hostal Rossel*, Av España 252, T 253583, F 256282.

### ● Places to eat

Typical restaurant with good reputation and higher prices is ***El Mochica***, Bolívar 462. ***Chifa Oriental***, Gamarra 735, rec; ***El Pesquero***, Junín 118, good fish; ***Pollería El Bolívar***, Pizarro 501 y Plaza de Armas, good chicken and salad for US$2.50; ***24 Horas***, Jr Gamarra 700 block, reasonably priced meals, always open; ***ABC***, Orbegoso y San Martín, good for chicken; ***De Marco***, Pizarro 725, good, especially the ice creams and coffee, set menu US$2.50, desserts and cakes, good source of information for passing cyclists; ***El Sol***, Pizarro 660, good, cheap set meals, vegetarian dishes; ***Romano***, Pizarro 747, good *menú*, breakfasts, coffee and cakes, slow service, pricey; ***Juguería San Agustín***, Pizarro 691, good juices, good *menú*, popular, excellent value; ***La Nonna***, Pizarro 722, good, cheap local food; ***Pizzería Valentino***, Orbegoso block 2, very good; ***Reyno del Sol***, Bolívar 438, good breakfasts and vegetarian meals, friendly, nice rooftop setting, open 0800; ***La Selecta***, Pizarro 870, set lunch for US$1.75, good value; ***La Pizza Nostra***, Pizarro 568, Italian dishes, cheap chicken and fries. Good, cheap seafood restaurants at Plazuela El Recreo, at the end of Pizarro, outdoor seating, pleasant atmosphere. Wholewheat bread at ***Panadería Chalet Suizo***, Av España e Independencia. Cheap meals in the market at Grau y Gamarra. It's difficult to find a meal before 0800. A Mon speciality is *shambar*, a thick minestrone made with ham.

### ● Airline offices

***Americana***, Pizarro 486, T 261687; ***Faucett***, Pizarro 532, T 232771, F 232689; ***AeroPerú***, Pizarro 470, T 234241/242727; ***Aero Continente***, Av España 307, T 248174, T/F 244592.

### ● Banks & money changers

**Banco de Crédito**, Gamarra 562, no commission on cash or TCs (Amex) into soles only, good rates, Visa cash advance; **Interbanc**, Pizarro y Gamarra, good rates for cash, no commission on TCs, reasonable rate, Visa cash advance; **Banco Wiese**, Pizarro 314, *Casa de Mayorazgo de Facalá*, good rates for TCs, no commission into soles, cash on Mastercard. Banks close 1300-1615, they give same rate for cash dollars as street changers, *casas de cambio* and travel agencies. Unicard cashpoint at **Extebandes**, works for Royal Bank of Canada cardholders.

### ● Embassies & consulates

**British**, Honorary Consul, Mr Winston Barber, Jesús de Nazareth 312, T 235548; **Finnish**, Bolívar 200, T 276122; **German**, Honorary Consul, Dr Guillermo Guerra Cruz, C Estados Unidos 105-107, Urb El Recreo, T 245903, F 261922.

### ● Entertainment

***Las Tinajas***, Pizarro y Almagro, on Plaza de Armas, pub-disco, live rock music and *peña* on Sat; ***Luna Rota***, América Sur 2119, at end of Huayna Capac, *Crack* disco very popular with locals; ***La Taberna***, Av Húsares de Junín 350, Urb La Merced, good for Andean folk music; ***Camana Video Pub***, San Martín 791, good at weekends. There are 3 cinemas: *Cine Perú* is at Pizarro 748, US$1.50; *Cine Ideal*, Orbegoso 530; *Cine Star*, Orbegoso 739, US2.

### ● Hospitals & medical services

**Hospital**: *Clínica Peruana Americana*, Av Mansiche 702, T 231261, English spoken, good.

## ● Post & telecommunications

**Post Office**: Independencia y Bolognesi. **Telecommunications**: Telefónica del Perú, Bolívar 658, national and international phone calls and faxes.

## ● Security

The city is generally safe but be especially careful at bus stations when arriving or leaving; guard your laggage very carefully. Also take care beyond the inner ring road, Av España, towards the hill and in the Sánchez Carrión district at night.

## ● Shopping

**Camera repairs**: *Laboratorios de Investigación Científica*, San Martín 745, over Fuji shop opp *Hotel San Martín*, good. Hugo Guevara, *G&M Color*, Ayacucho 825, T 255387, and España 2787, T/F 259483, 1 hr developing service and electrical repairs.

**NB** Tourists may be approached by vendors selling *huacos* and necklaces from the Chimú period; the export of these items is strictly illegal if they are genuine, but they almost certainly aren't. For **old car freaks**, look for the funeral director's premises, just off the main plaza, where there are hearses as old as a 1910 Chevrolet with wooden coachwork and wheelspokes; the proprietor is happy to show you around.

## ● Sports

Outdoor swimming pool next to Mansiche stadium, where buses leave for Chan Chán and Huanchaco; open 0900-1300 and 1600-1800, US$0.50.

## ● Tour companies & travel agents

*Muchik*, Pizarro 555, T 253225, T/F 258932; *Chacón Tours*, Av España 106-112, T 255212, rec; *Trujillo Tours*, San Martín y Almagro 301, T 233091, F 257518, work with Lima Tours; *Cóndor Travel*, Pizarro 547, T/F 244658; *Sigma Tours*, Pizarro 570, T 201335, F 201337, rec; *Guia Tours*, Independencia 519, T 245170, T/F 246353. Prices vary and competition is fierce so shop around for best deal. Few agencies run tours on Sun and often only at fixed times on other days. To Chan Chán, El Dragón and Huanchaco, US$15 pp; to Huacas del Sol and de la Luna, US$13 pp; to El Brujo, US$20-25 pp; city tour US$6.50 pp (minimum of 2 people; discounts for 4 or more).

**Guides**: Clara Bravo, Huayna Capac 542, T 260003/243347, is an experienced official tourist guide with her own transport; she speaks Spanish, English, German and understands Italian. She takes tourists on extended circuits of the region and is good for information (archaeological tour US$16 for 6 hrs, city tour US$7 pp). She also offers accommodation in Trujillo and Huanchaco, US$5 pp. Another rec official guide is José Soto Ríos, who can be contacted at the Tourist Police office on Independencia (see below) or at Atahualpa 514,

T 251489, he speaks English. Pedro Puertas, English speaking, not an official guide but very knowledgeable, often unavailable, at Km 560 on the Panamericana Norte, 2½ km from the Plaza de Armas, he can also be contacted through *Hostal Americano*. Other experienced guides are Oscar and Gustavo Prada Marga, Miguel Grau 169, Villa del Mar. The tourist office has a list of official guides; average cost US$7/hour.

### ● Tourist offices

***Caretur***, Independencia 628, T/F 258216, private organization, helpful, free information. Maps available from ***Touring and Automobile Club***, Argentina 278, Urb El Recreo, T 242101; also from ***Librería Ayacucho***, Ayacucho 570. **Tourist Police** have an office at Pizarro 402, on the corner of Plaza de Armas, open daily 0800-2000; also at Independencia 630, Casa Ganoza Chopitea. They are very helpful, provide useful information, and most of the staff speak English. They will negotiate a good price for taxis to visit sites; expect to pay around US$24 per car for 3-4 hrs. Any complaints about tourist services should be addressed to the Ministerio de Industria y Turismo, Av España 1801, T 245345/245794.

### ● Useful addresses

**Immigration**: Av Larco 1220, Urb Los Pinos. Gives 30-day visa extensions, US$20 (proof of funds and onward ticket required), plus S/2 for *formulario* in Banco de la Nación (fixers on the street will charge more).

### ● Transport

**Local Bus and colectivos**: on all routes, US$0.20-0.35; colectivos are safer as there are fewer people and fewer pick-pockets. **Taxi**: town trip, US$1. Chan Chán, airport US$5; Huanchaco, US$6.50. Beware of overcharging, check fares with locals. Taxi from *Hotel Libertador*, US$7/hour, or contact Tourist Police (see above). Taxi driver Jorge Enrique Guevara Castillo, Av del Ejército 1259, Altos 1, rec. Another taxi driver, Félix Espino, T 232428, reliable, good value. English chartered accountant Michael White (speaks fluent Spanish and a useful amount of German) provides transport, plus translation and business services, very knowledgeable about tourist sites, he also produces and sells t-shirts with local motifs; see under **Guides** above, Clara Bravo, for address.

**Air** To Lima, 1 hr, US$53, daily flights with Faucett, AeroPerú, Americana and Aero Continente; to Chiclayo 30 mins, US$12, Faucett, Americana; to Piura, 45 mins, US$30, AeroPerú, Americana; to Tarapoto, US$58, Aero Continente, Americana; to Pucallpa and Iquitos, AeroPerú. Check flight times as they change frequently. Taxi to airport, US$5; or take bus or colectivo to Huanchaco and get out at airport turn-off (US$0.25).

**Buses** To **Lima**, 548 km, 8-9 hrs on good road. There are many bus companies doing this route, among those rec are: Ormeño, Av Ejército 233, T 259782, normal service 4 daily, US$7.50, super especial (meal, drinks included), US$19.50; Cruz del Sur, Av Ejército 285 and Av Mansiche 331, T 261801, US$8.70; Empresa Díaz, Nicolás de Piérola 1079 on Panamericana Norte, T 232476, US$6.50, at 2130. Trans Olana (Oltursa), Av Ejército 342, T 2603055, offer a *bus cama* service to Lima, with full reclining seats, a/c, heating, meals and drinks, US$22.50, dep 2300; connection at Lima for Arequipa. Cheaper buses tend to arrive at night and do not have terminals, dropping passengers in the street. To **Pacasmayo**, 120 km, 2 hrs, US$1.50, several buses and colectivos a day; similarly to **Chiclayo**, 209 km, 3 hrs, US$3-3.50; and on to **Piura**, 278 km, 6 hrs, US$6.50 (Transportes Dorado, Daniel Carrión y Av Mansiche, T 242880, at 1830, 1930; Chinchay-Suyo, González Prada 337, also at Carrión, T 246818, US$5.30, at 1215, 2220); and **Tumbes**, 282 km, US$9, 10-12 hrs (Cruz del Sur at 2000); to **Huaraz**, 319 km, via Chimbote and Casma (169 km), direct, 9 hrs (Cruz del Sur, US$6.50, Chinchay-Suyo, US$7.85, both at 1930) several buses and colectivos to **Chimbote**, El Sol/LitPerú/América Express from Tupac Yupanqui 300, 135 km, 2 hrs, US$2.50. To **Cajamarca**, 300 km, 7-8 hrs, US$6.50; Trans Vulcano, Mansiche 299, T 235847, at 1030, 2130 (also to Chiclayo); Trans Mercurio, Av Mansiche 403, at 2230; Empresa Díaz at 1300, 2200. Transportes Guadalupe, Av Mansiche 331, has buses to **Tarapoto**, via Jaén, Chachapoyas and Moyobamba, departing at 1000 daily, 24 hrs, US$20. To **Tayabamba** (see page 176) with Emp Huancapata (Sucre, s/n) Sun only, dep 1800, arrives Tues 1200, 40 hrs, US$5, very rough road. Bus returns Wed only at 0800.

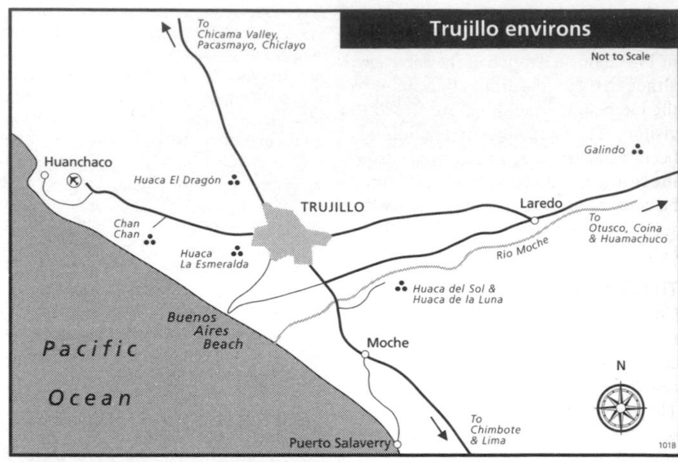


## ARCHAEOLOGICAL SITES NEAR TRUJILLO

### CHAN CHAN

The crumbling ruins of the imperial city of the Chimú domains and largest adobe city in the world are about 5 km from the city. The ruins consist of nine great compounds built by Chimú kings. The 9m high perimeter walls surrounded sacred enclosures with usually only one narrow entrance. Inside, rows of storerooms contained the agricultural wealth of the kingdom, which stretched 1,000 km along the coast from near Guayaquil to Paramonga.

Most of the compounds contain a huge walk-in well which tapped the ground water, raised to a high level by irrigation higher up the valley. Each compound also included a platform mound which was the burial place of the king, with his women and his treasure, presumably maintained as a memorial. The Incas almost certainly copied this system and transported it to Cusco where the last Incas continued building huge enclosures. The Chimú surrendered to the Incas around 1471 after 11 years of siege and threats to cut the irrigation canals.

The dilapidated city walls enclose an area of 28 sq km containing the remains of palaces, temples, workshops, streets, houses, gardens and a canal. What is left of the adobe walls bears well-preserved moulded decorations showing small figures of fish, birds and various geometric motifs. Painted designs have been found on pottery unearthed from the debris of

Section of wall of Tschudi Palace, Chan Chán

a city ravaged by floods, earthquakes, and *huaqeros*. Heavy rain and flooding in 1983 damaged much of the ruins and although they are still standing, many of the interesting mouldings are closed to visitors. The **Ciudadela of Tschudi** has been reconstructed (15 mins walk from the road), open 0900 to 1700 (but it may be covered up if rain is expected). Museum on the main road, US$1, 100m before the turn-off to the site.

### The Chimú culture

Chimú was a despotic state which based its power on wars of conquest. Rigid social stratification existed and power rested in the hands of the great lords. These lords were followed in the social scale by a group of urban courtiers who enjoyed a certain amount of economic power. At the bottom were the peasants and slaves. The Chimú economy was based on agriculture supplemented by fishing, hunting and craft production; they were renowned metalsmiths, working mainly with gold. Chan Chán was not looted. The Spaniards, however, despoiled its burial mounds of all the gold and silver statuettes and ornaments buried with the Chimú nobles.

• **Access to Chan Chán** A ticket which covers the entrance fees for Chan Chán, Huaca El Dragón and Huaca La Esmeralda (for 2 days) costs US$2.50. A guide costs US$6-7; map and leaflet in English US$0.75. Buses and kombis leave from José Gálvez 394, corner of Los Incas, near market, or corner of España and Industrial; nos 114A or B and 6B, US$0.35, 20 mins; US$0.25 to Chan Chán entrance; taxi, US$5. Tourist police are on duty at the turn-off on the Trujillo-Huanchaco road and at Chan Chán. It is relatively safe to walk on the dirt track from turn-off to site, but go in a group and don't stray from the road as robberies have occurred; a mototaxi can be taken from the turn-off, US$1. If alone, contact the Tourist Police in Trujillo to arrange for a policeman to accompany you. On no account walk the 4 km to, or on Buenos Aires beach near Chan Chán as there is serious danger of robbery, and of being attacked by dogs.

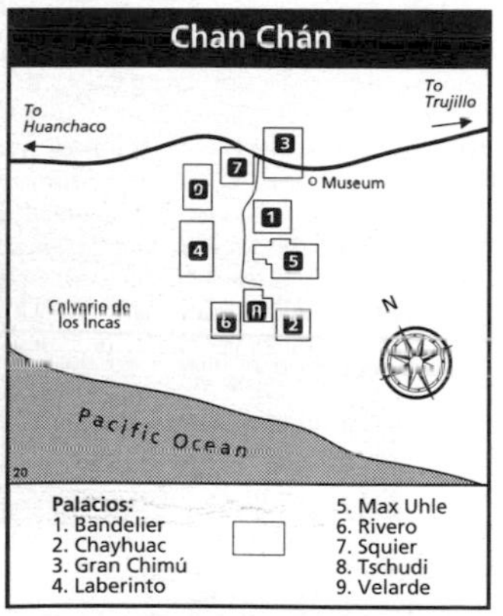


## OTHER SITES NEAR CHAN CHAN

The restored temple, **Huaca El Dragón**, dating from Huari to Chimú times (1000-1470 AD), is also known as **Huaca Arco Iris** (rainbow), after the shape of friezes which decorate it. It is on the W side of the Pan-American Highway in the district of La Esperanza; taxi costs US$2; open 0800-1700.

The poorly restored **Huaca La Esmeralda** is at Mansiche, between Trujillo and Chan Chán, behind the church (not a safe area). Buses to Chan Chán and Huanchaco pass the church at Mansiche. The tour to Chan Chán includes a visit to these ruins.

## HUACAS DEL SOL AND DE LA LUNA

A few kilometres S of Trujillo are the huge Moche pyramids, the **Huaca del Sol** and the **Huaca de la Luna** (open 0900-1300, entry US$1). The interior passageways of the Huaca de la Luna are not open to visitors, though a guided tour from on-site archaeologists may be possible; the site is under the control of the tourist police; interesting friezes are being excavated by students from the University (five discovered since 1992). The Trujillo Pilsen brewery is currently sponsoring excavations.

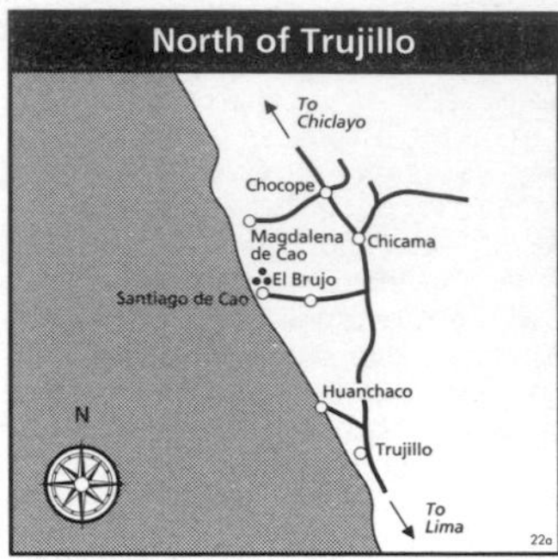


• **Access** Taxi about US$8 return; bus or colectivo marked Mayorista or Huacas, 20 mins, US$0.25 from corner of Zela near Mercado Mayorista, or colectivos about hourly from C Suárez y Los Incas. If you want a walk, get out at Bodega El Sol on the right hand side of the road; opposite is a huge Pilsen sign. Here starts a path to Moche, about an hour's interesting walk through farmland; it is inadvisable to walk unless in a large group.

North of Trujillo is the sugar estate of **Hacienda Cartavio**, in the Chicama valley (43 km). One of the biggest sugar estates in the world, also in the Chicama valley, is the Casa Grande cooperative. It covers over 6,000 ha and employs 4,000 members. Visits (guided) are only possible before 1200; US$0.75 by bus.

## EL BRUJO

60 km N of Trujillo, is considered one of the most important archaeological sites on the N coast. The complex, covering 2 square km, consists of Huacas Prieta, Cortada and Cao Viejo. This complex is collectively known as **El Brujo** and was an important Moche ceremonial centre.

Huaca Cortada (or El Brujo) has a wall decorated with high relief stylized figures. Huaca Prieta is, in effect, a giant rubbish tip dating back 5,000 years, which once housed the very first settlers to this area. In front of Cao Viejo are the remains of one of the oldest Spanish churches in the region. It was common practice for the Spaniards to build their churches near these ancient sites in order to counteract their religious importance.

### Moche culture

The Moche culture (100-700 AD)influenced an area of 600 km from Piura in the N to Nepeña in the S. There was a high degree of social differentiation and a strong military hierarchy. Warrior-priests held power and organized society for expansionist wars of conquest.

Human sacrifices were frequently carried out and one of the most important murals of Huaca Cao Viejo is of a Moche executioner with a spider-like lower body holding a human head in its left hand. Other murals depict scenes of ritual combat and a line of bound prisoners showing signs of genital mutilation. The murals of Cao Viejo, in high relief and polychromated, are perhaps one of the most important discoveries in South America in recent years.

• **Access to El Brujo** You can reach the complex from Cartavio (possibly combining with a visit to the rum factory). Taxis and mototaxis are available from Cartavio market; better to pay them to wait at the site and take you back. Alternatively take a bus to Chocope on the Pan-American Highway N; from there take a Kombi to Magdalena de Cao and walk 8 km to the site, or ask a Kombi to take you to El Brujo and wait or drop you off and return later (don't pay full fare in advance, US$5 each way from Chocope). It is better to go in the morning as there are more people around. There is a better chance of finding transport in Cartavio. Buses to Cartavio and Chocope leave Trujillo from González Prada y Los Incas and pass along Av Mansiche. It may be easier to hire a car if you're in a group, or take a guided tour. Clara Bravo (see **Guides** above) charges US$53/car (4 people) to El Brujo for the 4-5 hrs round trip (extension to Sipán, Tucumé, Brüning museum possible). For more information, ask the Tourist Police (see above).

The ruins of **Caballo Muerto** are located in the Laredo cooperative, E of Trujillo. The 1,000 year-old site consists of 8 mounds, the most important of which is the Burial Ground of the Kings, a U-shaped platform with a ceremonial patio

## The Moche: master craftsmen

One of the most remarkable pre-Inca civilizations was the Moche people, who evolved during the first century AD and lasted until around AD 750. Though these early Peruvians had no written language, they left a vivid artistic record of their life and culture in beautifully modelled and painted ceramics.

Compared with the empires of their successors, the Chimú and Inca, the realm of the Moche was very small, covering less than 250 miles of coast from the valleys of Lambayeque to Nepeña, south of present-day Chimbote. Though a seemingly inhospitable stretch of coast, the Moche harnessed rivers spilling from the Andean cordillera, channelling them into a network of irrigation canals that watered the arid coastal valleys. The resultant lush fields produced plentiful crops, which, along with the sea's bountiful harvest of fish and seafood, gave the Moche a rich and varied diet. With the leisure allowed by such abundant food, Moche craftsmen invented new techniques to produce their artistic masterpieces. It is these ancient pottery vessels that have made the greatest contribution to our understanding of this great civilization.

These masters of sculpture used clay to bring to life animals, plants and anthropomorphic deities and demons. They recreated hunting and fishing scenes, combat rituals and elaborate ceremonies. They depicted the power of their rulers as well as the plight of their sick and invalid.

The violence and death of war is a common theme in their work; prisoners of war are apparently brought before tribunals where their throats are cut and their blood consumed by those present. Decapitation and dismemberment are also shown.

Moche potters were amazingly skilled at reproducing facial features, specializing in the subtle nuances of individual personality. In addition to these three-dimensional sculptures, the Moche potter was skilled at decorating vessels with low-relief designs. Among the most popular scenes are skeletal death figures holding hands while dancing in long processions to the accompaniment of musicians. The potters also developed a technique of painting scenes on ceramic vessels. Over a period of several centuries the painters became increasingly skillful at depicting complex and lively scenes with multiple figures. Because of their complexity and detail, these scenes are of vital importance in reconstructing Moche life.

The early introduction of moulds and stamps brought efficiency to the production of Moche ceramics. By pressing moist clay into the halves of a mould, it was possible to produce an object much more rapidly than modelling it by hand. Similarly, the use of stamps facilitated the decoration of ceramic vessels with elaborate low-relief designs. Mould-making technology thus resulted in many duplications of individual pieces. Since there were almost no unique ceramic objects, elaborate ceramics became more widely available and less effective as a sign of power, wealth and social status of the elite.

Although among the most sophisticated potters in Spanish America, the Moche did not use ceramics for ordinary tableware. Neither do their ceramics show many everyday activities, such as farming, cooking and pottery making. This is because Moche art expresses the religious and supernatural aspects of their culture and nothing of everyday life is illustrated for its own sake.

(Extracted from *National Geographic*, Vol 177, No 6, June 1990.)

surrounded by the polychrome heads of feline gods.

## HUANCHACO

Narrow pointed fishing rafts, known as *caballitos* (little horses), made of totora reeds and depicted on Mochica and Chimú pottery are still a familiar sight in many places along the northern Peruvian coast. Unlike those used on Lake Titicaca, they are flat, not hollow, and ride the breakers rather like surfboards (you can rent one on the beach, beware of rocks in the surf). You can see fishermen set off in their reed rafts at around 0500, returning to shore about 0800 when they stack the boats upright to dry in the fierce sun.

The village, now developed with the beach houses of the wealthy of Trujillo, is overlooked by a huge church from the

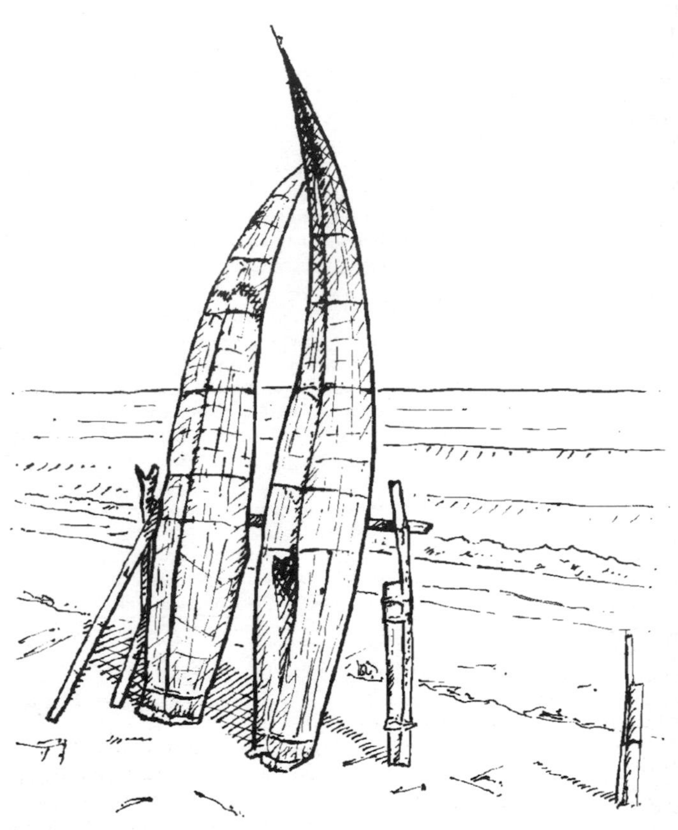

Caballitos de Totara, Huanchaco

belfry of which are extensive views. Children sell imitation precolumbian *objets d'art* and beads. It's cheaper to stay in Huanchaco than Trujillo but the choice of restaurants is more limited. Entry to pier, US$0.10.

**NB** The strength of the sun is deceptive; a cool breeze off the sea reduces the temperature, but you can still be badly sunburned.

**Local festivals** Several times a year, especially at Easter, Festival del Mar (the biggest *fiesta* in Huanchaco), the annual Olímpidas Playeral and El Festival Internacional de la Primavera, there are surf competitions. See under Trujillo.

• **Accommodation** **C** *Caballito de Totora*, Av La Rivera 219, T 351828, inc taxes, D in low season, pool, friendly, nice garden, clean, restaurant, parking, good value, rec; **C** *Hostal Bracamonte*, Los Olivos 503, comfortable, good, chalets with private bath, or converted caravans, you can camp on the grass, pool, own water supply, emergency generator, rents bicycles, secure, good restaurant, English spoken, highly rec.

**D** *Hostal Sol y Mar*, Los Pinos 571, T 245524, pool, restaurant, friendly owner, garden, rec; **D** *Hostal Huanchaco*, Larco 287 on Plaza, T 230813, shared bath, cold water, clean and friendly, pool, expensive cafeteria with home-made cakes and other good meals, video, pool table, rec; **D** *Hostal Los Esteros*, Av Larco 618, T 230810, with bath, hot water, restaurant, friendly, safe motorcycle parking.

**E** *Casa de los Amigos*, Las Gardineras 373, nr *Hotel Bracamonte*, German-owned, basic, intermittent cold water supply, kitchen facilities, sun terrace, **F** to camp in garden.

**F** pp *Golden Club*, Av La Rivera 217, T 241189, 8 rooms, gym, pool, restaurant, use of kitchen, popular with surfers, laid back, excellent value, rooms on first floor cheaper, rec; **F** pp *La Casa Suiza*, run by Heidi and Oscar Stacher, Los Pinos 451, 3 blocks from beach, clean, shared bath, 3 rooms with private bath, cold water, nice roof balcony, excellent breakfast US$1, friendly, highly rec.

Basic accommodation at the house of the very friendly Señora Lola, Manco Capac 136, **G** pp, noisy at weekends. Opposite is Sr Carlos Sánchez Leyton, **G**, good, safe, cold water. Señora Nelly Neyra de Facundo offers accommodation at Las Palmeras 425, **G**, very friendly, rec. Accommodation, inc food, with families is easy to find, US$2-3 a day, such as friendly English-speaking Sra Mabel Díaz de Aguilar, nr the football ground.

• **Places to eat** Good fish restaurants on the sea front, eg Malecón Larco 602; ***Violetta***, a private house – 4 blocks directly inland from the pier (good meals provided for US$1) and Familia Flores, popular; ***El Tramboyo***, near the pier, good, helpful, friendly; ***Lucho del Mar***, excellent sea food, check the bill; next door is ***Estrella Marina***, good fish, great value; ***Piccolo***, 5 blocks from plaza, cheap, friendly, live folk music weekend evenings, excellent; ***Club Colonial***, on plaza, run by Belgians, fish, chicken or meat, excellent but expensive, rec. Good fish also at *Pisagua*, just past the pier, and *La Esquina*, C Unión 299, opposite the pier. ***Arroyitos Chickens***, C Atahualpa 135, excellent roast chicken, fries and salad for US$2. Try *picarones*, people come from Trujillo at weekends especially to eat them. Do not eat fish in the hut-like restaurants on the way into town from Trujillo as they aren't hygienic.

• **Post & telecommunications** Post Office at Manco Kapac 306, open 0900-1445.

• **Shopping** *Artesanías del Norte*, opp *Hotel Bracamonte* on Olivos, sells local pottery, hats, t-shirts with local motifs and balsa wood products. Food in shops is no more expensive than Trujillo. There is a small fresh fruit market.

• **Transport** Kombis between Trujillo and Huanchaco are 114A or B; they both do a clockwise circuit of Huanchaco and run to the Cassinelli museum, then A goes round the W side of Trujillo onto Av 28 de Julio and Av Vallejo/Los Incas as far as Zela, while B goes round the E side on Av Industrial, España and Vallejo/Los Incas also to Zela. At night B goes only to España y Grau; both run till 2300 (later at weekends). Fare US$0.35, 20 mins. 'Micros' follow similar routes to Los Incas, but in daylight only; colectivos and some radio taxis run at night. Taxi US$6.50.

## PUERTO CHICAMA

Puerto Chicama, 70 km N of Trujillo is known by surfers as the best surf beach in Peru, claiming that it has the longest left-hand point-break in the world. There are a few basic places to stay and eat; it's a real surfers' hang-out. Friendly locals.

# FROM THE COAST TO CAJAMARCA

## 1. FROM TRUJILLO

To the NE of Trujillo is Cajamarca, which can be reached either from Trujillo or from Pacasmayo (paved throughout). The old road NE to Cajamarca is terrible and (for cyclists especially) lonely, taking 12-15 hrs (as opposed to 8 hrs via Pacasmayo – see below), but it is more interesting, passing over the bare puna before dropping to the Huamachuco valley. Off it lies **Otusco**, an attractive Andean town with narrow cobbled streets. In **Agallpampa** there is one, unsigned *hostal*. Further on, at the mining town of Shorey, a road branches off to **Santiago de Chuco**, birthplace of the poet César Vallejo, where there is the annual festival of Santiago El Mayor in the second half of July. The main procession is on 25 July, when the image is carried through the streets. Close to Yancabamba is *Hostería El Viajero* and in Quiruvilca there is one hotel.

## HUAMACHUCO

The road runs on to this colonial town, 181 km from Trujillo, formerly on the royal Inca Road. It has a huge main plaza and a controversial modern cathedral. There is a colourful Sun market. A 2-hr walk (take the track which goes off to the right just after crossing the bridge on the road to Trujillo) takes you to the extensive ruins of hilltop pre-Inca fortifications, **Marcahuamachuco** (car US$5 pp). Nearby, beyond the local radio station, 1 hr's walk, are the pre-Inca ruins of **Viracochabamba**.

Worth seeing in the Huamachuco area are **Laguna Sausacocha** (with Inca ruins nearby) and *haciendas* Yanasara and Cochabamba, deep down in the valley of the Río Chusgón, about 2-3 hrs by truck E of the town. **Yanasara**, noted for its fighting bulls, is still in the hands of its long-term owner, Francisco Pinillos Montoya. There is a guest house at Cochabamba, which used to be the Andean retreat of the owners of the Laredo sugar plantation, near Trujillo. The climate, at about 2,300m, is mild.

- **Accommodation** **F** *Hostal San Francisco*, Sánchez Carrión 380, clean, hot shower; **G** *Fernando*, Bolívar 361, good value, clean; **G** *La Libertad*, not rec, rooms and bathrooms filthy; and others.

- **Places to eat** On main plaza; *El Cairo*, Sánchez Carrión 754, good food and service, rec.

- **Buses** Transportes Quiroz **from Trujillo** (T 247011), US$5, 12 hrs, at 1530, 1700, 1800, take warm clothing; Antisuyo **to Trujillo** three daily, US$4, 10 hrs. There are also colectivos from Trujillo. Buses to **Cajamarca**, US$1.80. Direct bus to Lima, 24 hrs.

From Huamachuco buses (Empresa Huancapata which start in Trujillo) run SE to **Tayabamba**, on the far bank of the Marañón, passing through the old gold-mining centres of Pataz province, such as Parcoy and Buldibuyo. This journey takes a good 18 hrs in 'normal' conditions.

Reached from **Pataz** itself (a friendly gold-mining town, about 100 km from Huamachuco) are the unique circular ruins of El Gran **Pajatén** (pre-Inca); ask at Tourist Office in Cajamarca for details. A national park, Río Abiseo, incorporating Gran Pajatén and four other sites – La Playa, Las Papayas, Los Pinchudos and Cerro Central – is planned. Only archaeologists and researchers are allowed there to visit El Gran Pajatén.

## CAJABAMBA

From Huamachuco the road runs on 48 km through impressive eucalyptus groves to **Cajabamba**, which lies in the high part of the sugar-producing Condebamba valley. It has an attractive Plaza de Armas.

- **Accommodation** **F** *Flores*, toilet, friendly, clean, on the Plaza de Armas. Other hotels and restaurants.

- **Buses** Several buses daily to Huamachuco;

Quiroz, Antisuyo, about 3 hrs, US$2.20, also trucks. Two direct buses a day from Trujillo, 12 hrs. To Cajamarca, via San Marcos (below) with Empresa Díaz (unreliable) and Empresa Atahualpa, 0500, US$3.

Cajabamba can also be reached in a strenuous but marvellous 3-4 days hike from **Coina**, 132 km E of Trujillo at 1,500m in the Sierra Alto Chicama. The first day's walk brings you to Hacienda Santa Rosa where you stay overnight. Then you cross the mountains at about 4,000m, coming through Arequeda to Cajabamba. The ruins at Huacamochal may be seen en route; the scenery is spectacular. It is advisable to hire a guide, and a donkey to carry the luggage. A map of the route is available from the Post Office in Coina.

• **Accommodation D** *Hostería El Sol*, full board or bed only, built by the late Dr Kaufmann, who opened a hospital for local people here; details from *Hostería El Sol*, Los Brillantes 224, Santa Inés, Trujillo, T 231933, Apdo 775.

## SAN MARCOS

The road continues from Cajabamba through **San Marcos** to Cajamarca. San Marcos is important for its Sun cattle market; both it and Cajabamba are on the Inca Road.

• **Accommodation & transport** There are 3 hotels inc **G** pp *Nuevo*, with bath, water shortages, but clean and quiet. Bus to Cajamarca (124 km), Atahualpa and Empresa Díaz leaving early in the morning, takes 6 hrs US$3.60.

## 2. PACASMAYO TO CAJAMARCA

**Pacasmayo** (*Pop* 12,300), port for the next oasis N, is 142 km N of Trujillo, and is the main road connection from the coast to Cajamarca. The paved 180 km road to Cajamarca branches off the Pan American Highway soon after it crosses the Río Jequetepeque. The river valley has terraced rice fields and mimosas may often be seen in bloom, brightening the otherwise dusty landscape.

A few kilometres N on the other side of Río Jequetepeque are the ruins of **Pacatnamú** comparable in size to Chan Chán – pyramids, cemetery and living quarters of nobles and fishermen, possibly built in the Chavín period. Evidence also of Moche tribes. Micro bus to Guadelupe, 10 km from ruins, and taxi possible from there (Ortiz family, Unión 6, T 3166), US$20. Where the Pan-American Highway crosses the Jequetepeque are the well-signed ruins of **Farfan** (separate from those of Pacatnamú, but probably of the same period).

• **Accommodation E** *Ferrocarril*, 1½ blocks from Pacasmayo seafront on small plaza, quiet and clean, no hot water (ask for water anyway); **F** *Panamericano*, Leoncio Prado 18, with private cold shower, good value, friendly, clean, safe, reasonable restaurant downstairs; **F** *San Francisco*, opp *Panamericano*, basic, OK. Several cheap restaurants on the main street.

103 km E of Pacasmayo is the mining town of **Chilete**. 21 km from Chilete, on the road N to San Pablo, are the stone monoliths of **Kuntur Wasi**. The site is undergoing new development under a Japanese archaeological team.

• **Accommodation** *Hotels Amazonas* and *San Pedro*, **G**, filthy bathrooms. Rooms are hard to find on Tues because of Wed market.

40 km S of Chilete is the attractive town of **Contumazá** on an alternative route from Trujillo to Cajamarca. This passes through the cane fields and rice plantations of the Chicama valley before branching off to climb over the watershed of the Jequetepeque. Further along the road to Cajamarca is **Yonán,** where there are petroglyphs.

## CAJAMARCA

**Cajamarca** (*Pop* 70,000; *Alt* 2,750m; *Phone code* 044), is a beautiful colonial town and the most important in the northern mountain area. This was one of the biggest cities in the Inca empire and was where the Indians and Spanish had their first showdown. Here Pizarro ambushed and captured Atahualpa, the Inca emperor. Despite their huge numerical inferiority, the heavily-armed Spaniards took advantage of an already divided Inca kingdom to launch their audacious attack. The Indians attempted to save their leader by collecting the outrageous ransom demanded by Pizarro for Atahualpa's release. This proved futile as the Spanish, of course, executed the Inca once the treasure had been collected.

The city's violent past is belied by today's provincial calm. Cajamarca is now better known as a producer of delicious cheese, of intricately worked mirrors (see **Shopping** below) and as the home of artist Andrés Zavallos, one of the founding fathers of the city's community of poets, writers, painters and musicians. Most notable of these was Mario Urteaga, the only Peruvian artist to have his work in the permanent collection at New York's Metropolitan Museum of Art.

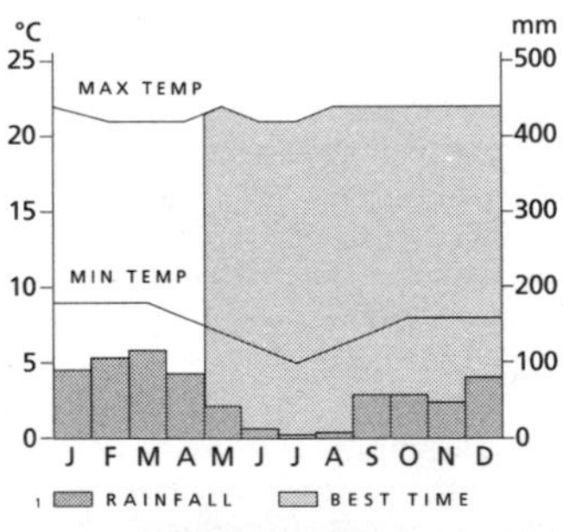


**Climate: Cajamarca**

## PLACES OF INTEREST

The **Cuarto de Rescate** is not the actual ransom chamber but in fact the room where Atahualpa was held prisoner. It is open 0900-1300, 1500-1745, 0900-1245 Sat and Sun, closed Tues, US$1.35, entrance on Amalia Puga beside San Francisco church (ticket also valid for Belén church and nearby museums). A red line on the wall is said to indicate where Atahualpa reached up and drew a mark, agreeing to have his subjects fill the room to the line with gold and silver treasures. The room was closed to the public for centuries and used by the nuns of Belén hospital. The chamber also has two interesting murals.

The Plaza where Atahualpa was ambushed and the stone altar set high on **Santa Apollonia hill** where he is said to have reviewed his subjects can also be visited (small entrance fee). There is a road to the top, or the physically fit can walk up from C 2 de Mayo, using the steep stairway. The view from the top, over red-tiled roofs and green fields, is worth the exertion, especially very early in the morning for the beautiful sunrises.

The **Plaza de Armas**, where Atahualpa was executed, has a 350-year-old fountain, topiary and gardens. The impressive **Cathedral,** opened in 1776, is still missing its belfry. Many belfries were left half-finished in protest against a Spanish tax levied on the completion of a church. On the opposite side of the Plaza is the 17th century **San Francisco Church**, older and more ornate than the Cathedral and home to the **Colonial Art Museum** which is filled with typically gruesome colonial pantings and icons. A guided tour of the museum includes entry to the church's spooky catacombs.

The **Complejo Belén** comprises the Institute of Culture, a museum, art gallery and a beautifully ornate church, considered the city's finest. Connected to the church is the **Pinacoteca**, a gallery of local artists' work, which was once the

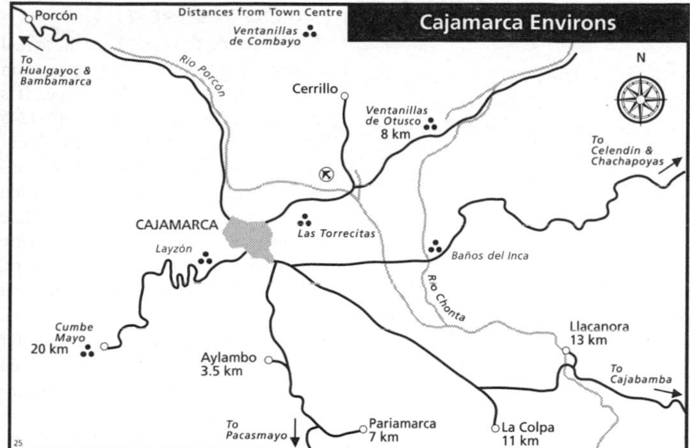


kitchen of an 18th century hospital for men. Across the street is a maternity hospital from the same era, now the **Archaeological Museum** (see **Museums** below). The **Cultural Institute** sells Spanish language books and good postcards and handicrafts are for sale in the cloisters of the church.

Other churches well worth seeing are **San Pedro** (Gálvez y Junín), **San José** (C M Iglesias y Angamos), **La Recoleta** (Maestro y Casanova) and **Capilla de La Dolorosa**, close to San Francisco.

The city has many old colonial houses with garden patios, and 104 elaborate carved doorways. See the **Bishop's Palace**, next to the Cathedral; the **palace of the Condes de Uceda**, now occupied by the Banco de Crédito on Jr Apurímac 719; the house of **Toribio Casanova**, Jr José Gálvez 938; the house of the **Silva Santiesteban family**, Jr Junín 1123; and the houses of the **Guerrero** and **Castañeda** families.

## MUSEUMS

The **Education Faculty of the University** has a museum at Del Batán 283 with objects of the pre-Inca Cajamarca culture, not seen in Lima; the attendant knows much about Cajamarca and the surrounding area. Open 0800-1200, 1500-1700 in winter, and 0800-1200 in summer, US$0.20 (guided tour). The University maintains an experimental **arboretum** and agricultural station. The **Museo de Arte Colonial**, at the Convento de San Francisco, is also worth a visit (see above). The **Archaeological Museum**, one block from Belén church at Junín y Belén has a wide range of ceramics from all regions and civilizations of Peru, samples of local handicrafts, costumes used during the annual carnival celebrations and an informative curator. All museums are closed on Tues but open at weekends.

## EXCURSIONS

The surrounding countryside is splendid. Look out for the local building method called Tapial, made of compressed adobe alternating with layers of stones or wood.

**Aylambo** is a village which specializes in ceramics. These are produced in workshops which are run on ecologically sound principles. Money from sales of products pays those working in the studios. The village is 1½ hrs walk, 3½ km,

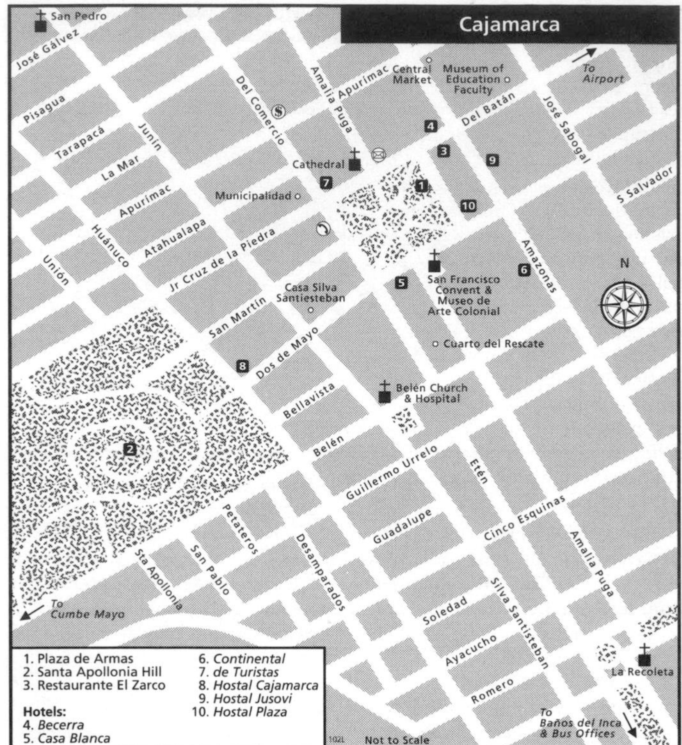


from Av Independencia. You can visit the *Escuela/Taller* where children learn pottery, open Mon-Fri 0730-1200, 1300-1700, Sat 0730-1230.

6 km away are the warm sulphurous thermal springs known as **Los Baños del Inca**, where there are baths whose temperature you can control. The baths are cleaned after each user; open 0500-2000 daily, public bath US$0.65, private bath US$0.90, swimming pool US$0.45 (take your own towel). Atahualpa tried the effect of these waters on a festering war wound. Buses and Kombis marked Baños del Inca every few minutes from Amazonas, US$0.25, 15 mins.

Other excursions include **Llacanora**, a typical Andean village in beautiful scenery. **La Colpa**, a *hacienda* which is now a cooperative farm of the Ministry of Agriculture, breeds bulls and has a lake and gardens. The cows are hand-milked at 1400, not a particularly inspiring spectacle in itself, but the difference here is that the cows are called by name and respond accordingly.

**Ventanillas de Otusco**, part of an old pre-Inca cemetery, has a gallery of secondary burial niches (US$0.90 entry). A 1-day round trip can be made, taking a bus from Del Batán to Ventanillas de Otusco (30 mins) or colectivos leaving hourly from Revilla 170, US$0.15, walk to Baños del Inca (1½ hrs, 6 km); walk to Llacanora (1 hr, 7 km); then a further hour to La Colpa.

A road goes to **Ventanillas de Combayo**, some 20 km past the burial niches of Otusco. These are more numerous and more spectacular, being located in a rather isolated, mountainous area, and are distributed over the face of a steep 200m high hillside.

**Cumbe Mayo**, a *pampa* on a mountain range, is 20 km SW of Cajamarca. It is famous for its extraordinary, well-engineered pre-Inca channels, running for several kilometres across the mountain tops. It is said to be the oldest man-made construction in South America. The sheer scale of the scene is impressive and the huge rock formations are strange indeed but do take with a pinch of salt your guide's explanations, which can range from the humorous to the positively psychedelic. It is worth taking a guided tour since the area offers a lot of petroglyphs, altars and sacrificial stones from pre-Inca cultures. On the way to Cumbe Mayo is the Layzón ceremonial centre.

• **Access to Cumbe Mayo** There is no bus service; guided tour prices are about US$7 pp; taxi US$15. The *hostal* at the site is **F** pp. A milk truck goes daily to Cumbe Mayo leaving at 0400 from C Revilla 170. Ask Sr Segundo Malca, Jr Pisagua 482; small charge, dress warmly. To walk up takes 4 hrs. The trail starts from the hill of Santa Apollonia (Silla del Inca), and goes to Cumbe Mayo straight through the village and up the hill; at the top of the mountain, leave the trail and take the road to the right to the canal. The walk is not difficult and you do not need hiking boots. Take a strong torch. The locals use the trail to bring their goods to market.

## LOCAL FESTIVALS

The **pre-Lent Carnival** is very spectacular and regarded as one of the best in the country. Not for the faint-hearted, however, as it is also one of the most raucous. Accommodation is virtually impossible to find at this time. In Porcón, 16 km to the NW, **Palm Sunday** processions are worth seeing. **Corpus Cristi** is held in May or June and is a solemn religious affair. On 24 June is **San Juan** in Cajamarca, Chota, Llacanora, San Juan and Cutervo. An agricultural fair is held in July at Baños del Inca; on 28/29 July is Independence; on the first Sun in Oct is the **Festival Folklórico** in Cajamarca.

## LOCAL INFORMATION

**Hotel prices**

| | | | |
|---|---|---|---|
| L1 | over US$200 | L2 | US$151-200 |
| L3 | US$101-150 | A1 | US$81-100 |
| A2 | US$61-80 | A3 | US$46-60 |
| B | US$31-45 | C | US$21-30 |
| D | US$12-20 | E | US$7-11 |
| F | US$4-6 | G | up to US$3 |

● **Accommodation**

**A2** *Laguna Seca*, at Baños del Inca, in pleasant surroundings, recently refurbished, private hot thermal baths in rooms, swimming pool with thermal water, restaurant, bar, disco, horses for hire, rec.

**B** *Continental*, Jr Amazonas 760, T 922758, very clean, hot water, good restaurant, noisy, rec; **B-C** *Hostal Cajamarca*, in colonial house at Dos de Mayo 311, T 922532, F 928813, clean, hot water, TV, phone, food excellent, good local music, travel agency next door, rec; owners also run **A3-B** *Albergue San Vicente*, outside the town at Santa Apollonia, T 922644, in an old hacienda (both places in Peruvian Youth Hostel Association); **B-C** *Hostal Los Pinos*, Jr La Mar 521, T/F 925992, price inc breakfast, rooms with TV, a lovely colonial-style house.

**C** *Turistas* (60 rooms) on Plaza de Armas, T 922470/71, T 922472, with bath, laundry service, 2 restaurants, bar, parking extra; **C** *Casa Blanca*, Dos de Mayo 446 on Plaza de Armas, T/F 922141, room service, clean, safe, nice building and garden, good.

**D** *Hostal Amazonas*, Amazonas 528, T 922620, modern, clean, no hot water, friendly; **D** *Hostal Atahualpa*, Pasaje Atahualpa 686, T 922157, hot water in mornings only, clean, good value; **D** *Hostal Becerra*, Del Batán 195 (unsigned), T 923496, intermittent tepid water, modern, clean, friendly, possible to leave luggage until late buses depart; **D** *Hostal Jusovi*, Amazonas 637, T 922920, with bath, comfortable, hot water only in am, safe; **D** *Hostal José Gálvez*, Av Manco Capac 552, at Baños del Inca, T 920203, with private thermal bath, good value; **D** *Hostal Prado*, Jr La Mar 582, T 923288, F 924388, without bath, no heating; **D** *Hostal San Lorenzo*, Amazonas 1070, T 922909,

T/F 926433, with bath, hot water, clean, friendly, helpful; **D** ***Hostal Turismo***, Dos de Mayo 817, T 923427, clean, can be noisy at weekends, rec.

**E** ***Hostal Delfort***, Apurímac 851, nr market, with bath, clean, spacious, good value; **E** ***Hostal Dos de Mayo***, Dos de Mayo 585, T 922527, shared bath, hot water am and evening, rec; **E** ***Hostal Plaza***, Plaza de Armas 669, T 922058, old building with handmade wood furnishings, mainly large rooms with many beds, private bath and balcony (F without bath), hot water but poor water supply, quiet, rec (especially rooms 4 and 12), with new annex (dirty but is open at 0200); **E** ***Hostal Sucre***, Amalia Puga 815, T 922596, with toilet and wash basin in each room, water am only, good value, sometimes noisy, not very safe, poor restaurant upstairs.

**F** ***Hostal San José***, Angamos 358, T 922002, shared bath, basic, clean, cheap, hot water. Rooms to rent at *Restaurant Encuentro Tupanakuy*, Huánuco 1279, **G** pp, very friendly; also at *Restaurant Carimbó,* Dos de Mayo 712, **E** pp inc meals.

## ● Places to eat

***Los Faroles***, Jr Dos de Mayo 311, in *Hostal Cajamarca*, local specialities, friendly, informal, rec, *peña* in the evening; ***Salas***, on Plaza, fast service, good, cheap local food, best *tamales* in town; ***El Zarco***, Jr Del Batán 170, very highly rec, much frequented by local residents, inexpensive, try the *sopa fuchifú*, *humitas de maíz*, also has short *chifa* menu, good vegetarian dishes, excellent fish; ***El Real Plaza***, Jr Dos de Mayo 569, good food, excellent hot chocolate; ***Las Rocas***, Dos de Mayo 797, excellent sandwiches, cheap; ***La Namorina***, on edge of town on road to Baños del Inca, opp Ché service station, renowned for its speciality, *cuy frito*; ***Cajamarquesa***, Amazonas 770, very good, not cheap, tables in garden of colonial building; ***Rocco's Pizza Bar***, Jr Cruz de Piedra 653, 1500-0030, good pizza, popular with local kids; ***Om-Gri***, San Martín, nr Plaza de Armas, Italian dishes; ***Christian***, Del Comercio 719, snacks, juices, set lunch for $1.10; ***Michelangelo***, on the corner of Del Batán y Amazonas, fast food, pizza, chifa. The restaurant at *Hotel Continental* serves an excellent *cuy frito* with rice, salad and potatoes for US$5; *Los Maderos*, Amazonas 807, local specialities and *peña*, open 2100-0300 Mon-Sun; ***Bananas***, Dos de Mayo on Plaza, good juices, fruit salads, yoghurt, sandwiches, pizza, good music. For early breakfasts go to the market.

**Food specialities**: *Queso mantecoso* (full-cream cheese); *manjar blanco* (sweet); *humitas* (ground maize with cheese); *cuy frito* (fried guinea pig); eucalyptus honey (sold in the market on C Amazonas; said to be a cure for rheumatism). Try the flaky pastries filled with apple or *manjar blanco* from the street sellers. The area is renowed for its dairy produce; many shops sell cheese, *manjar blanco*, butter, honey, etc: try *La Pauca* at Amazonas 713, or *Manos Cajamarquiñas* at Tarapacá 628.

## ● Banks & money changers

**Banco de Crédito**, Jr del Comercio y Apurímac, changes TCs without commission, cash advance on Visa; **Banco Continental**, Tarapacá 721, changes TCs US$5 commission minimum. Dollars can be changed in most banks, travel agencies and the bigger hotels; better rates from **street changers** on Jr Del Batán and Plaza de Armas.

## ● Hospitals & medical services

**Hospital**: Av Mario Urteaga.

## ● Laundry

Jr Amalia Puga 545, expensive.

## ● Post & telecommunications

**Post Office**: Serpost at Del Batán 133 on Plaza de Armas, 0800-2045.

**Telecommunications**: Telefónica del Perú main office on Plaza de Armas, Jr Del Comercio s/n; also at Amalia Puga 1022, and Amazonas 518; for national and international calls.

## ● Shopping

Handicrafts are cheap, but bargain hard. Specialities inc cotton and wool saddlebags (*alforjas*). Items can be made to order. The market on Amazonas is good for *artesanía*.

Cajamarca is famous for its gilded mirrors. The *Cajamarquiña* frames are not carved but decorated with patterns transferred onto pieces of glass using the silkscreen process. This tradition lapsed during the post-colonial period and present production goes back less than 20 years. (Lucy Davies and Mo Fini, Tumi).

## ● Tour companies & travel agents

*Cajamarca Tours*, Dos de Mayo 323, T 922813. A group of local guides has formed ***Cumbemayo Tours***, Amalia Puga 635 on Plaza, T/F 922938, highly rec, with tours to Ventanillas de Otusco (US$5 pp), Cumbe Mayo (US$6.50 pp), Kuelap and Gran Vilaya (US$30 pp a day, 7 day tour). ***Inca Atahualpa Tours***, Amazonas 770, T 922495. ***Aventuras Cajamarca***, office next to *Hotel Casa Blanca*, T/F 923610, run by Jorge Caballero, rec. ***Inca Baths Tours***, Amalia Puga 807, rec for Cumbe Mayo (US$7 pp)

Several travel agenices around the Plaza de Armas offer trips to local sites and further afield (eg Kuelap, normally a 5-day trip, US$200 pp). A rec tour guide is Edwin Vásquez, ask for him in the *Cuarto de Rescate* or *Hostal Dos de Mayo*.

● **Tourist offices**

At Belén 650, T 922834, helpful. Also tourist information at the Museum at Del Batán 283.

● **Transport**

**Air** Expreso Aéreo flies Lima-Cajamarca daily, direct or via Chimbote, US$71 one way, 1½ hrs; also Cajamarca-Chachapoyas US$42, twice a week; office at Jr Del Comercio 700, T/F 923419. Aero Continente, daily except Tues, to/from Lima, US$75 one way; also with Aero Cóndor. **NB** Check schedules as they change frequently. Airport 3 km from town; taxi US$3.

**Buses** To **Lima**, 856 km, 17-19 hrs, US$9-11; the road is paved, several buses daily; see under Lima **Bus Companies**. To **Pacasmayo**, 189 km, 5-6 hrs, US$8, several buses and colectivos daily. To **Trujillo**, 296 km, 7½ hrs, US$5-7, 10-12 buses daily, 1200-2230; most continue to Lima. To **Chiclayo**, 260 km, 7 hrs, US$6, several buses daily, most continuing to Piura (US$11.15) and Tumbes. To **Celendín**, 112 km, 5 hrs, US$4.35, at 0630 and 1300; the route follows a fairly good dirt road through beautiful countryside. Also to **Cajabamba**, 75 km, US$4.35, 5 hrs, several daily. Some buses and trucks do the route Hualgayoc, Bambamarca, Chota, Cochabamba, Cutervo and on to Batán Grande but not a well-travelled route. Among the bus companies are: Expreso Sudamericano, Atahualpa 300, T 923270 (to Lima, Chiclayo, Piura, Sullana and Trujillo); Palacios Transporte, Atahualpa 322, T 925855 (Lima, Trujillo, Celendín, Cajabamba and Bambamarca); Trans Vulcano, Atahualpa 318, T 921090 (Chiclayo and Chepen); Nor Peru, Atahualpa 302, T 924550 (Lima, Trujillo, Celendín, Cajabamba); Empresa Díaz, Ayacucho 753, T 923449 (to Trujillo); Empresa Trans Mercurio, Juan XXIII s/n, T 925630 (to Trujillo and Chiclayo); Atahualpa, Jr Atahualpa 299, T 923060 (Lima, Celendín, Cajabamba, Chota, Trujillo and Chiclayo); Turismo Civa, Independencia 321, T 922377 (to Lima, luxury service inc meals, toilet, US$13.50); Expreso Cajamarca, Independencia 319, T 923337; TEPSA, Sucre y Reina Farje, T 923306; Turismo Arberia, Atahualpa 315, T 926812 (to Chiclayo).

## THE CHACHAPOYAS REGION

Cajamarca is a convenient starting point for the trip E to the province of Amazonas, which contains the almost embarrassing archaeological riches of the Chachapoyans, also known as Sachupoyans. Here lie the great pre-Incan cities of Gran Vilaya, Cerro Olán and the immense fortress of Kuelap (also spelt Cuelap), among countless others.

● **Recommended reading** The whole area is full of largely unexplored remains; some of them have been studied by the Swiss archaeologists Henri and Paula Reichlen (who surveyed 39 sites in 1948 – see *Récherches archaeologiques dans les Andes du haut Utcubamba*, in *Journal des Américanistes*, which includes an accurate map), and the American archaeologist Gene Savoy (who went further than the Reichlens; see his book *Antisuyo*); Kaufmann Doig refers to them as the "12 Cities of the Condors"; his map showing their location is in his *Arqueología Peruana*. In 1992 he started a new project in the area. Ask if he is in Chachapoyas as he is worth contacting. See also Morgan Davis' book, *The Cloud People, an Anthropological Survey*. Also the booklet on Kuelap, available in Chachapoyas, very informative (ask Carlos Torres Mas, see below).

## CELENDIN

East from Cajamarca, the first town of note is **Celendín,** where there is a cinema and cock fighting Sun night in the local arena. Festival 16 July (Virgen del Carmen). There is also an interesting local market on Sun where you can buy cheap sandals and saddlebags. The town has electricity from 1800 to 0100.

3 hrs SE from Celendín by bus (US$2.25) is the village of **Oxamarca**. From here it is 10 km, or a 2½ hrs walk, to the ruins of **La Chocta**. Strategically placed atop a steep ridge, the most notable feature of the fortress is the collection of small, square stone burial houses, known as *Chullpas*, many of which have been torn down by farmers and looted by *huaqueros*. Morgan Davis writes that the *Chullpas* are thought to date from the

Cajamarca II period, beginning after AD 100. There is also evidence of Inca occupation. There are no hotels or restaurants in Oxamarca. Ask Gregorio Sánchez Junio in Celendín. He has a private museum at Jr San Martín 423 and is very helpful with maps and information about local ruins.

• **Accommodation** A few basic *hostales*, all on Jr 2 de Mayo: **E** *Hostal Celendín*, with bath, on the plaza, good, clean, friendly, good restaurant; **E** *Amazonas*, OK, clean, helpful.

• **Places to eat** *Santa Isabel*, Jr José Gálvez 512, clean, OK; *Bella Aurora*, good but not open in evenings; the market is OK as well.

• **Transport** To **Cajamarca**, 107 km, 4½ hrs, see under Cajamarca **Buses**. Atahualpa dep at 0500, continue to Chiclayo, 3 hrs stop in Cajamarca, US$11.40, arrive early to get a seat. Bus to **Balsas**, 55 km, 5 hrs, US$3. Trucks daily. On to **Leimebamba**, 89 km, 7 hrs, US$5.20. It is almost impossible to get transport from Balsas to Leimebamba, except the one pick-up a week from Celendín; probable waiting time 2-3 days. On to **Tingo**, 45 km, 8 hrs, US$6; several buses and trucks daily. On to **Chachapoyas**, 38 km, 1½ hrs, US$1.75; several buses and trucks daily. To **Chachapoyas**, 227 km, once a week, 20-25 hrs (35 or more in the rainy season, US$12). **NB** It is common for buses to leave later than the set time, to break down and to suffer long delays (up to several days) in the wet season. Always bring warm clothing and food on these journeys.

**ROUTES** The road, in bad condition to Chachapoyas, follows a winding course through the N Andes, crossing the wide and deep canyon of the Río Marañón at Balsas. The road climbs steeply with superb views of the mountains and the valleys below. The fauna and flora are spectacular as the journey alternates between high mountains and low rainforest. After rain, landslides can be quite a problem.

## LEIMEBAMBA

This pleasant town derives its name from a visit in late June, 1480 by the Inca Túpac Yupanqui, who stayed to celebrate the Fiesta de Inti-Raymi. From that moment, the town came to be known as the Field of the Festival of The Sun, or Raymi-Pampa, which in turn became Leimebamba. There are plenty of ruins around this pleasant town, many of them covered in vegetation. Among them are: La Congona, La Joya, Torre Puco and Tim Bamba. Find a local to explain the area and show the way to the ruins as it is easy to get lost.

Of the ruins in the area **La Congona**, a Chachapoyan site, is easily reached without a guide. It is a brisk 2½ hrs walk along a clearly-marked trail which starts at the end of the street with the hotels. Follow the path up the far side of the small valley before turning left up a shoulder which leads to the cloud forest and the ruins. La Congona is a system of three hills: on the easterly, conical hill, the ruins are clustered in a small area, impossible to see until you are right above them. They are covered in brambles and thick undergrowth, so a machete would be useful (also a big stick to fend off fierce dogs). The views are stupendous and the ruins worth the effort. This is the best preserved of three sites, with 30 decorated round stone houses (some with evidence of three storeys) and a watch tower. The other hills have been levelled. There are two other sites, El Molinete and Pumahuanyuna, nearby. All three can be visited in a day but a guide (US$5) is essential.

- **Accommodation** Two hotels, the better of which is **G** ***Escobedo***, very basic, water in mornings and evenings, electricity in evenings only.

- **Places to eat** Several restaurants, inc ***El Sabor Tropical***, good chicken and chips, friendly; breakfast at restaurant a few doors down. ***Oasis***, just off Plaza de Armas, and ***El Caribe*** on the Plaza, basic meals.

- **Transport** Two buses leave Chachapoyas for Celendín on Tues and arrive in Leimebamba around 1400-1500; US$5.20; no guarantee of a seat. There are also kombis, minibuses and trucks.

## NORTH FROM LEIMEBAMBA

The road to Chachapoyas crosses the Utcubamba river then passes through **Palmira** and heads North. Before Puente Santo Tomás there is a turn-off which heads E beyond **Duraznopampa** to the small town of **Montevideo**.

An hour's walk SE of Montevideo is the ruined complex of **Rumichaco/Monja**, spread along a ridge above the town. The upper Rumichaco sector consists of massive undecorated platforms while the lower Monja sector is better preserved with some intricate fretwork on the platforms. Local guides can be hired; ask for Tito Rojas Calla in Montevideo. There are no hotels in the town but ask the owner of the only restaurant if you can sleep there.

Another Chachapoyan site is **Cerro Olán**, reached by colectivo to San Pedro de Utac, a small village beyond Montevideo, then a 30 mins walk. From the Plaza a clear trail rises directly into the hills E of town to the ruins, which can be seen from the village. Here are the remains of towers which some archaeologists claim had roofs like mediaeval European castles.

According to Morgan Davis this was essentially a military installation and once a small city of considerable luxury, similar in construction to La Congona (see above) but on a grander scale. Morgan Davis considers the latter and Cerro Olán the most impressive archaeological sites in the Chachapoyas region, after Kuelap (see below). (Morgan Davis, *The Cloud People, an Anthropological Survey*, 1988). Ask the alcalde for accommodation.

## PUENTE SANTO TOMAS

Further N are the towns of Yerbabuena and Puente Santo Tomás, which is at the turn-off for the burial *Chullpas* of **Revash**, belonging to the Revash culture (AD 1350-1538). In Yerbabuena there is one unnamed basic *hospedaje*, **G**, running water but no electricity. There is also *Restaurant Karina*, which is cheap.

The ruins are roughly 3 hrs walk from Puente Santo Tomás. Follow the dirt road towards Santo Tomás, then cross the wooden bridge on the right and take the dirt track towards the mountains; it is a steep climb up. Eventually small adobe houses can be seen in the cliff face, covered by an overhang. The houses are buff coloured with red roofs and resemble tiny Swiss cottages with crosses in the form of bricked-up windows; they are, in fact, small tombs. There are lots of human bones lying around and cave paintings. The tombs have long since been looted. To get close, climb up a small goat track and walk along a ledge. It is about an hour's walk back downhill from Santo Tomás to Puente Santo Tomás, from where there is transport N towards Chachapoyas.

## JALCA GRANDE

The attractive town of Jalca Grande (or La Jalka as it is known locally), at 2,600m, lies between Montevideo and Tingo, up on the E side of the main valley. In the town itself, one block W of the Plaza de Armas, is the interesting and well-preserved Chachapoyan habitation of **Choza Redonda**, which was inhabited until 1964. Half an hour W of the town are the ruins of **Ollape**, a series of platforms with intricate fretwork designs and wide balconies. A much larger site, though more primitive, is **Moyuk Viejo**, a 2½ hrs walk to the North. (Morgan Davis, 1988.)

• **Accommodation** There are no hotels but you can find a room at the alcalde. Don't expect too much privacy, however, as it is used until 2200, after which time there is no electricity. So bring a torch (and a pack of cards; there isn't much in the way of nightlife).

• **Transport** The town is accessed from Ubilon, on the main road N to Tingo, but transport is scarce. One kombi daily, or a strenuous 3 hr walk uphill.

There is not much in **Ubilon** itself, save for a few shops selling next to nothing. Cheap, basic accommodation is available at *Bodega Irmita*; several rooms with cold water. A kombi passes through on the way to Leimebamba around 1430, 1 hr journey, US$1.10.

## TINGO

Tingo (*Alt* 1,800m) is about 25 km from Leimebamba, 37 km S of Chachapoyas, up the Utcubamba valley. Much of the village was washed away in the floods of 1993. High up on mountains above Tingo is Tingo Nuevo. There is no running water or electricity in Tingo. Note that the police will ask to see documents as they register all foreigners going up the hill to Kuelap.

• **Accommodation & places to eat F** pp *Albergue León*, basic, friendly, built since the 1993 floods. *Miss Tony*, is by the police station, after the bridge coming from the Leimebamba direction, good food but a bit expensive; *Kuelap*, almost opposite, clean, okay. Also reasonable is *El Edén*, at Jr Kuelap 120.

• **Transport** There are several buses (from 0500) and pick-ups daily to Chachapoyas, 2 hrs, US$1.50, last back about 1400-1500. For Celendín, see **Transport** under that town. Several camionetas daily to Kuelap, US$2.20. There are occasional kombis to Puente Santo Tomás, US$1.35; or walk part of the way and board a passing kombi.

## KUELAP

A 4 hrs steep walk uphill (take waterproof, food and drink, and start early am), leads to **Kuelap** (3,000m) – or Cuelap as it is locally known – a spectacular pre-Inca walled city which was re-discovered in 1843.

Morgan Davis writes that though successive explorers have attempted to do justice to the sheer scale of this site even their most exaggerated descriptions have fallen short. Kuelap was built over a period of 200 years, from AD 1100 to 1300 and contained 3 times more stone than the Great Pyramid at Giza in Egypt.

The site lies sprawled along the summit of a mountain crest, more than a kilometre in length. It is divided into 3 parts: at the NW end is a small outpost; at the SE end of the ridge is a spread out village in total ruin; and the cigar-shaped fortress lies between the two. The massive stone walls, 700m long by 175m wide at their widest, are as formidable as those of any precolumbian city. The walls varied in height between 8 and 17m and were constructed in 40 courses of stone block, each one weighing between 100 and 200kg. It has been estimated that 100,000 such blocks went into the completion of this massive structure. Some reconstruction has taken place, mostly of small houses and walls, but the majority of the main walls on both levels are original, as is the cone-shaped dungeon. There are a number of defensive walls and passageways, many houses, but virtually no carvings of any type. An interesting feature is that all the buildings are circular.

Entrance fee is US$4.50 (including US$1 for use of camera), opening hours 0800-1700. The ruins are locked; the guardian, Gabriel Portocarrero, has the keys and accompanies visitors, he's very informative and friendly and provides dormitory accommodation, G pp; his wife will cook for you and sells soft drinks.

## The Cloud People

Theories about the cloud people indicate that the Chachapoyan empire was more spectacular than the Inca's. Cities, highways, terracing, irrigation, massive stonework and metalcraft were all fully developed. In addition, since the culture had longer to develop than the Inca Empire, the extent of metropolitan life in this period was far greater. There are ten times more ruins from the Middle Horizon than from the late (Inca) Horizon.

Mark Babington and Morgan Davis write: "This is surely a region which overwhelms even Machu-Picchu in grandeur and mystery. It contains no less than five lost, and uncharted cities, the most impressive of which is Pueblo Alto, near the village of Pueblo Nuevo (25 km from Kuelap).

"By far the majority of these cities, fortresses and villages were never discovered by the Spanish. In fact many had already returned to the jungle by the time they arrived in 1532. Many of the sites are to be found on or near the trails which today still provide the only medium of transport in this heavily populated and agricultural region. On a recent map of the area, with which we were provided in Chachapoyas, no less than 38 sites can be counted; but Ojilcho and Pueblo Alto, for example, are not charted on this 1977 map in spite of their enormous dimensions.

"The local farmers are conversant with the ruins, whether charted or not. It is among these people that one must look for information, provision and hospitality and, most important of all, guides and mules. The area, though well populated, provides virtually no facilities for the traveller. Hiking gear is essential: sleeping bags, tents and canned goods (and a machete – Ed). Small gifts are also much appreciated by the local people in return for their hospitality. (Take money in small notes as villagers do not have change for larger.) Heavy rain is a problem during the rainy season (Nov-April). Travelling at this time is not advised as the mountain passes are shin-deep in mud."

Charles Motley adds that most of the Chachapoyan cities were built in *La Ceja*, or eyebrow, of the Amazon. This is a dense jungle in the misty clouds overlooking the Amazon basin. The temperature is always in the 70s during the day but the nights are cool up around 3,000m. Many ruins are overgrown with ferns, bromeliads and orchids and easily missed.

- **Access** To reach Kuelap from Chiclayo: approx 12 hrs to Chachapoyas. Best to leave Chachapoyas early am to get to Kuelap, then spend the night near the ruins before returning to Chachapoyas the following morning; from there take bus back to Chiclayo. The roads are bad in the wet season and delays likely. The new road from Tingo to Kuelap is very circuitous ($1\frac{1}{2}$ hrs by car from Tingo; very few vehicles make it up to the ruins). A private truck may be hired in Chachapoyas, US$50 for 4 hrs; also donkeys can be hired for US$5-7/day. If walking from Tingo, follow the path upstream on the right-hand side of the river and take the path to the right before the bridge, after half an hour there is a sign to Kuelap, the track is steep. In the rainy season it is advisable to wear boots; at other times it is hot and dry (take all your water with you as there is nothing on the way up). After another hour you reach a cluster of houses; red arrows mark the path. Soon the walls of Kuelap become visible at the top of the hill.

- **Accommodation** The last house to the right of the track (*El Bebedero*) offers accommodation (bed, breakfast and evening meal US$6, good meals, friendly, helpful); a bit further on the left is an area of flat land outside Sr Portacerro's house (former Project Kuelap office). There is also a camping area.

- **Further accommodation and services** Oscar Arce Cáceres based at 'El Chillo' near the Río Utcubamba, $4\frac{1}{2}$ km outside Tingo, who owns a farm and knows the area very well, will help the traveller. He has accommodation with bath (US$10pp), good meals at US$5, stores luggage. The trek into this area, like the walk up to Kuelap, starts from Tingo; the way is all mule track. The walk from El Chillo to Kuelap is shorter than from Tingo; the return to El Chillo can be made via the village of Nogalcucho (ask for directions). In Magdalena (a 30 mins walk from Tingo), Abram Torres will be happy to provide one with his services as guide, and his mule, for the first leg of the journey as far as Choctamal, about 4 hrs away.

A lodge is being built at Choctamal by *Los Tambos Chachapoyanos*; the first floor and six bathrooms are complete. Choctamal is the mid-point on the 36-km tortuous road from Tingo to Kuelap. It is also three quarters of the way up the Abra Yumal pass, which crosses the cordillera to Gran Vilaya (see below). Staying at Choctamal thus makes it much easier to hike to Gran Vilaya; the lodge fee of US$10 includes food and guide for expeditions.

## GRAN VILAYA REGION

According to Morgan Davis, Gran Vilaya is something of a misnomer, created by US explorer, Gene Savoy who discovered this extensive set of ruined complexes in 1985. The region was divided into three *curacazgos* politically independent ethnic groups that made up the Chachapoyas confederation: Pausamarca, Rongia and Sesuya. These names can be traced back to late Incaic sources and old colonial records. There are about 30 sites spread over this vast area, 15 of which are considered important by Davis. Among the sites are Pueblo Alto, Pueblo Nuevo, Paxamarca and Machu Llacta. It is recommended to take a letter of introduction from Dr Carlos Torres Mas in Chachapoyas. Ask the alcalde for accommodation, meals and assistance in finding a guide, which is essential.

● **Access** The whole area stretches W from the Río Utcubamba to the Río Marañon. Head N from Tingo or S from Chachapoyas as far as the Huinchuco bridge across the Río Utcubamba. On the W bank of the river a road leads to the left, if heading N, to the town of Colcamar, which is the starting point for exploring this area.

## CHACHAPOYAS

**Chachapoyas** (*Pop* 15,000; *Alt* 2,234m), is the capital of the Department of Amazonas. PNP (Amazonas-police) are based on block 11 of C Amazonas. Archaeological and anthropological information can be sought from the local anthropologist, Carlos Torres Mas, who is the head of the Instituto Nacional de Cultura, Jr Junín 817; he also advises about walks in the area. The Instituto has a map of local ruins. César Torres Rojas, who also works here, is very helpful.

### Excursions

**Huancas**, which produces unique pottery, can be reached by a 2-hr walk on the airport road. There are also Inca and pre-Inca ruins.

### Local information

#### ● Accommodation

**A3** *Gran Vilaya*, Jr Ayacucho 700 block, T/F 757208, due to open early 1996. This hotel is being built as part of *Los Tambos Chachapoyanos*, a plan to build lodges to facilitate visits to this region (for information contact Charles Motley, 1805 Swann Ave, Orlando, Florida, USA 32809). Besides the above hotel and the INC lodge at Kuelap, projects are under way at Choctamal (see above) and Levanto (see below).

**E** *El Dorado*, Ayacucho 1062, T 757047, with bath, hot water, clean, helpful; **E** *Hostal Kuelap*, Amazonas 1057, T 757136, shared bath, hot water extra, rec; **E** *Johumaji*, Jr Ayacucho 711, T 757138, with bath, cold water.

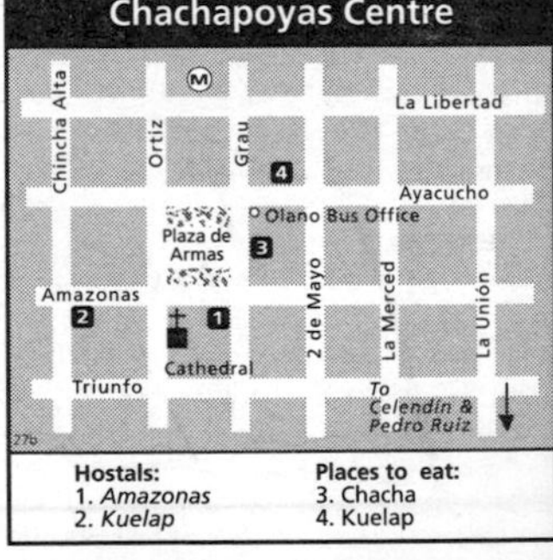

**F** *Continental*, Jr Ortiz Arrieta 441, T 751705, hot water, not great; **F** *Hostal Amazonas*, Plaza de Armas, T 757199, hot water, nice, patio, friendly, rec.

**● Places to eat**

*Chacha*, on Plaza de Armas, clean, good, huge portions, friendly, rec; *Burguer Mass*, Plaza de Armas, excellent juices, cakes, fruit salads; *Las Vegas*, Amazonas 1091; *Oh Qué Bueno*, Ayacucho 1033, limited menu; *Patisserie*, Jr 2 de Mayo 558, good pastries; *Kuelap*, on Ayacucho, good, large portions, friendly, rec; *Chifa El Turista*, Amazonas 575 nr post office, is reasonable, friendly and helpful; *Las Chozas de Marlissa*, Ayacucho 1133, friendly, good for typical food, pub-type place at night, serves the strangest *pisco sour* you'll ever taste; *Cuyería, Pollería y Panadería Virgen Asunto*, Puno 401, order *cuy* in advance; *La Estancia*, Amazonas 861, just off Plaza, video pub, cheapish and good place for a night out. Good bakery at Ayacucho 816.

**● Banks & money changers**

**Banco de Crédito**, on plaza, gives cash on Visa card, changes TCs. Street changers for cash near market.

**● Post & telecommunications**

**Post Office**: Dos de Mayo 438.

**● Tour companies & travel agents**

**Guide**: Martín Chumbe, Jr Piura 909, or via Comercial Zegarra on Plaza de Armas, or via *Gran Vilaya Hotel*, T/F (074) 757208. He is an official guide to most of the sites described above, charges US$25/day, and speaks some English at a push. He can store luggage. He has a copy of Gene Savoy's video on the Gran Vilaya expedition.

**● Transport**

**Air** A new airport has been built; Expreso Aéreo flies Lima-Cajamarca-Chachapoyas Thur and Sun, US$94. Grupo Ocho (army) flies every Sat, US$53: also every other Tues, Lima-Saposa-Mendoza-Chachapoyas-Chiclayo; on Wed, Chiclayo-Chachapoyas-Mendoza-Saposa-Lima. It may also be possible to fly with Transportes Aéreas Andahuaylas (TAA); usually only in dry season. Truck from Plaza de Armas to airport up to 2 hrs before flights leave, US$1; taxi US$3. Flights are not reliable and are often cancelled.

**Buses** To **Lima**, Civa from Plaza de Armas direct, Mon, Wed, Fri, US$28.50; on all other days there are buses to **Chiclayo** 230 km, 10-12 hrs (longer in the rainy season, Nov-April, when landslides are common), US$12 with Civa (comfortable, arrives 0600, departs for Chiclayo 1700); if blocked, take a colectivo to Pedro Ruiz and try to book for 1600 departure from there; also trucks daily. The route is via Bagua (see below) and Jaén (40 km from Bagua). The road is in bad condition and can be very difficult in the wet; but it is still an easier route than via Celendín. To **Bagua** (141 km) 4 hrs, US$5.20, trucks daily; easy to find a bus or truck on to Chiclayo. To **Celendín**, 227 km, for details see under Celendín (bus on Wed only, 0200). To **Mendoza**, 86 km, 4 hrs, US$4.35, one or two pick-ups daily, the road isn't too bad in dry season. To **Pedro Ruiz**, 54 km, 2 hrs, US$2.15, several trucks daily; on to **Rioja** 198 km, 7 hrs, can be longer in the rainy season, US$8.70. Trucks to Rioja now stop at **Nueva Cajamarca** (see page 189). The road is in poor condition, but spectacular as you drop from the high Andes to the high jungle. From Rioja to **Moyobamba** is a further 21 km, 1 hr, US$1.30; frequent pick-ups all day. It is advised to travel by day on buses in the Chachapoyas area.

## LEVANTO

The Spaniards built this, their first capital of the area, directly on top of the previous Chachapoyan structures. Although the capital was moved to Chachapoyas a few years later, Levanto, or Llauntu as it was originally named,

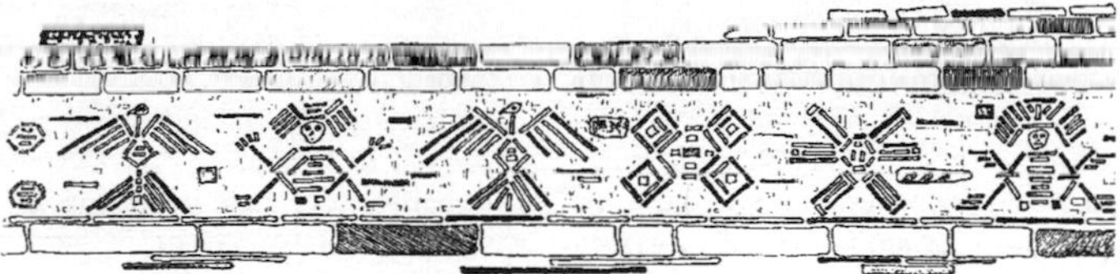

Condor frieze at Gran Pajatén

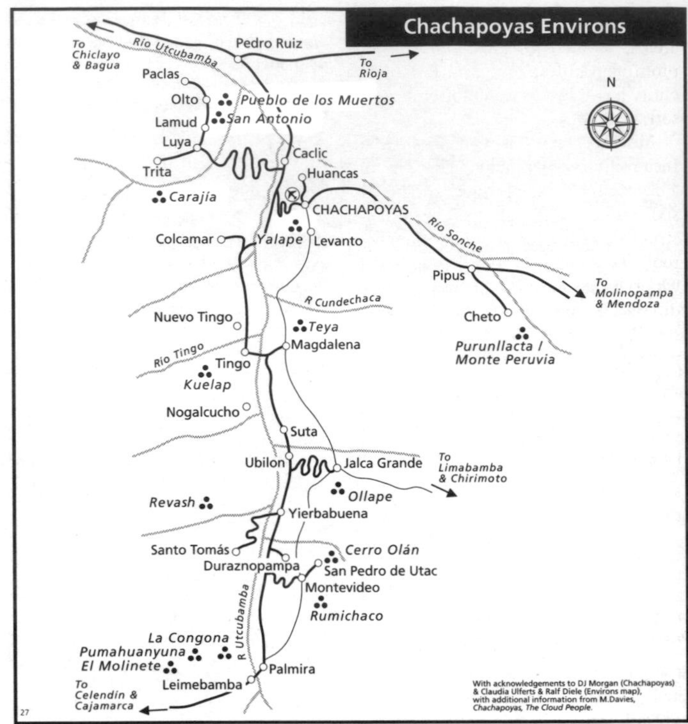


still retained its importance, at least for a while, as it had been one of the seven great cities of the Chachapoyans as described by Cieza de León and Garcilaso de la Vega. It was one of the largest and most important *curacazgos*.

The Kuelap East-West Highway starts at Levanto and links with the Inca military highway at Jalca Grande (see above). Levanto was about mid-way on the N/S route from Colombia to the Huari, then Inca hub, at Huánuco. This stone road crosses the modern vehicle road at La Molina, about 5 km from Chachapoyas. A 16 km walk downhill on this road from Levanto is worthwhile. Nowadays Levanto is a small, unspoilt, and very beautiful colonial village set on flat ground overlooking the massive canyon of the Utcubamba river. Kuelap can, on a clear day, be seen on the other side of the rift. Levanto is a good centre for exploring the many ruins around, being the centre of a network of ancient ruins, fortified redoubts, residential areas and many others.

**Excursions** Very close to Levanto are the ruins of **Yalape**, now almost completely overgrown. The local people are helpful and will guide you to the ruins. Yalape seems to have been a massive residential complex extending over many hectares and including many well-preserved examples of typical Chachapoyan architecture and masonry with quite elaborate and beautiful friezes, a pleasant walk uphill (30 mins). Its scale, like that of Kuelap, can be only described as titanic. In fact the whole area is covered in ruins, almost every prominent hilltop in the immediate vicinity has at least a watchtower of some sort.

Morgan Davis has reconstructed an Inca military garrison at Colla Cruz; on a classic Inca stone terrace, a regional-style round building has been constructed, with a 3-storey high thatched roof. This garrison guarded the road which ran past Colcamar, over the Cordillera Oriental on a 1.5 km staircase, through Gran Vilaya, to Cajamarca's central N/S road and on to the coastal highway.

Using Levanto as a staging point, many beautiful and interesting walks can be done in the area.

- **Accommodation & services** As yet there is no official accommodation in Levanto, although the village council and *Los Tambos Chachapoyanos* are planning to restore a colonial house on the square as a lodge. However, small groups of travellers are very welcome and beds and bedding are provided in the mayor's office and village meeting hall. There is one small shop and bar in the village (selling coffee and Pepsi, but little food).

- **Transport** Levanto is 2 hrs by truck or 6 hrs walk from Chachapoyas by new road. Trucks leave from the market in Chachapoyas most days at 0600, US$0.90, also from outside *Bodega El Amigo* on Jr Hermosura at 1400, 1½-2 hrs depending on the number of stops; or 3½ hrs by mule track, ask in Chachapoyas market if anyone returning to Levanto will guide you for a small fee. Taxi from Cachapoyas to Levanto and back, including driver waiting while you look around, US$25.

- **To walk from Tingo to Levanto** Head up to Magdalena (30 mins). From here it is about 30 mins by a short cut (uphill then downhill) to the bridge at Cundechaca. From the stone bridge walk 30 mins on the main road to Maino until you reach a wooden bridge; near here, 100m before a bend in the road look for the path which leads down into a small gorge, crosses the river (after 30 mins) and passes the little farm which is visible from the main road. From there it's a steep, 1-hr walk to a waterfall, from where you continue on the well-defined Inca road on a ridge between two gorges into Levanto. (You can add 2-2½ hrs to this walk by starting at Kuelap downhill to Tingo.)

## MONTE PERUVIA

40 km E from Chachapoyas, on the road to Mendoza, are the pre-Inca ruins of **Monte Peruvia** (known locally as Purunllacta), hundreds of white stone houses with staircases, temples and palaces. The ruins have been cleared by local farmers and some houses have been destroyed. A guide is not necessary.

- **Access & accommodation** There is no direct transport from Chachapoyas. Take a kombi at 0930 and 1500 from Jr Salamanca, 4th block down from market, to Pipus, which stands at the turn-off to Cheto; 1½ hrs, US$1.35. You may have a long wait in Pipus for transport to Cheto; a camioneta departs early am, US$0.90; or a 2-hr walk on a rough road. If stuck in Pipus, ask to sleep at restaurant *Huaracina* or police station next door. There are no hotels in Cheto but a house high up on the hill above the town with a balcony has cheap bed and board. The same family also has a house on the Plaza. There are 2 small shops selling very little and a small house with one room serves basic but good meals. The ruins are 2-hr walk from Cheto.

## EAST TO MENDOZA

The road E from Chachapoyas continues through Pipus to **Molinopampa**, 2 hrs drive from Chachapoyas. The town is the starting point of an adventurous five day hike to Rioja (see below). Katrina Farrar and Andy Thornton write: "Only experienced hikers should attempt this journey, which is very difficult. Food supplies for the whole journey should be purchased at Chachapoyas and a guide, absolutely essential, hired at Molinopampa. The steep trail leads through waist high unbridged rivers, over the cold, high sierra and then for three days one follows the muddy trail down to the dense and humid jungle. We were accompanied by exotic butterflies, and never a quiet moment with the chattering of birds and monkeys. The whole magic of the jungle

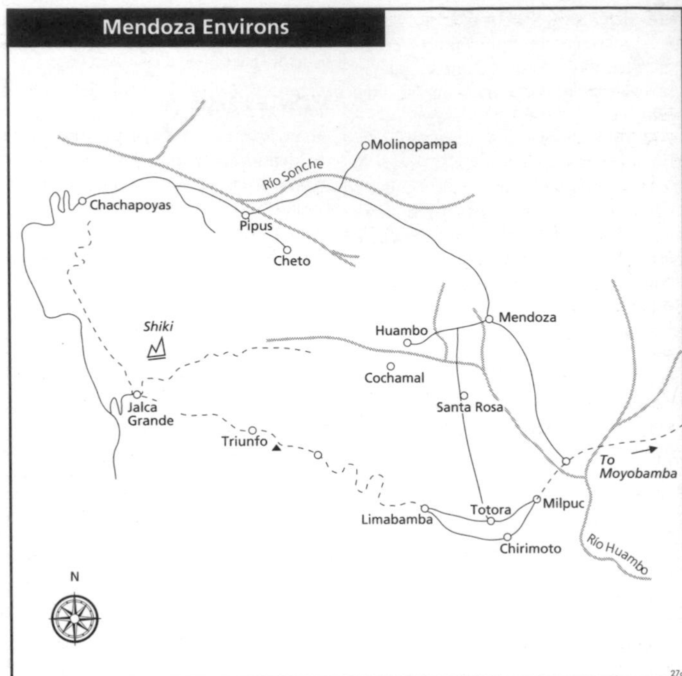


– trees, birds, animals and insects – can be seen untouched in their natural surroundings."

## MENDOZA

The road carries on to **Mendoza**, the starting point for an ethnologically interesting area in the Guayabamba Valley where there is a high incidence of very fair people.

The region is in the *selva*, very remote, and can be reached on foot from Mendoza or Limabamba (2 hrs by camioneta from Mendoza, or bus from Chachapoyas), but a road is under construction. Seek all advice locally. Ask for Padre Juan Castelli, an English priest who has been living in Limabamba since World War II, he is very knowledgeable. A number of tourist bungalows are being built in this region. For information, contact Charles Motley (address above). We are grateful to Helmut Zettl of Ebergassing, Austria, for this information.

- **Transport** 4 hrs from Chachapoyas to Mendoza by truck, daily at 1000, US$4.35 (return 0200, sometimes 0700).

## LAMUD

37 km NW of Chachapoyas, on a turn-off on the road N to Pedro Ruiz, is Lamud, which is a convenient base for several interesting sites.

At **San Antonio**, 1/2hr from Lamud, is a sandstone cliff face with several groups of burial tombs high on a ledge. They are difficult to see unless you know what you're looking for (they are basically small piles of stones). The ruins, set on the hill above, are a residential complex, thought to form part of a group of people belonging to the Chipuric. The

## The village of the whites

Chirimoto, lying east of Limabamba and south of Mendoza, in the Guayabamba valley, could be any other sleepy, sub-tropical settlement. A collection of wooden houses on a fertile plain where oranges, bananas, guava and yucca grow, where colourful butterflies and mesmerizing birdsong fills the warm, humid air. But the people of this tiny, remote hamlet are very different from your average jungle dweller. They are blond-haired, blue-eyed and fair-skinned and could easily have just stepped off the five o'clock flight from Stockholm.

The population of Chirimoto themselves don't know where they came from and opinions among experts vary. Some posit the theory that they originate from warring conquistador factions in the early 16th century. However, this doesn't explain the rarity of this phenomenon or the fact that the Spanish chronicler Garcilaso de la Vega describes them resisting the Incas before the conquest.

Professor Kaufmann-Doig of Lima and Dr Jacques de Mahieu of Buenos Aires believe the whites of Chirimoto to be descendants of the Vikings, who came to Peru in the 11th century. Such a theory is supported by the discovery on Easter Island, west of Chile, of drawings showing Viking longships, as well as linguistic parallels between the Quechua language and Scandinavian tongues.

Whatever the explanation, the incongruous presence of these fair-skinned people in such a remote part of the country will continue to attract the attention of ethnologists and the more curious and hardier of travellers.

main nucleus is almost completely ruined. A guide is not necessary; ask for directions.

3 hrs from Lamud (10 km on a very poor mule track), are the ruins of **Pueblo de los Muertos**, circular stone houses overlooking the valley. The view is spectacular but it is easy to lose your way and the ruins are very difficult to find as they are overgrown. Since being brought to public attention by Gene Savoy in the mid 1960s, the site has been largely destroyed by local grave robbers. Ask directions before setting out and be patient.

• **Accommodation & places to eat**
F *Hostal Kuelap*, Jr Garcilaso de la Vega, on Plaza, clean, basic, friendly, cold water only between 0700-0900. A few doors down is Restaurant ***María***, which is cheap, friendly and obliging, steak and chips is recommended, ask for *pension* which is 3 meals for US$1.80, excellent value, popular.

• **Transport** Buses and kombis to Lamud, and Luya, leave between 1000 and 1230 when full from near market by Plaza, US$1.50, 1 hr 20 mins. The road is unpaved but in reasonable condition.

### LUYA

A 20 mins drive S of Lamud, on the same road, is the village of Luya.

3 km or 1 1/2hrs walk from Luya is **Chipuric**, a residential complex belonging to the Chachapoyas culture. The site consists of burial tombs set in a cliff face on a high ledge with circular stone buildings on the hill above. The tombs, which are one metre high and look like beehives, have all been looted. Continue along the dirt road from Luya until it forks; take the higher road with the irrigation canal. At Pueblo Molino (a small cluster of houses and one shop), the cliff face and the burial tombs are visible. On the lower road which passes below the cliff on the other side of the river, is Chipuric town. The cliff is steep but it's possible to climb up to the tombs with some difficulty and quite a few scratches from the thorn bushes. Great views from the top.

**Carajía**, also known as Solmol, is 2½ hrs walk from Luya but more accessible from Trita. A short walk from Trita, in the valley behind the village, are the stone burial figures set into an impressive cliff face. Just below the tombs are plenty of human bones, if you look carefully. Ask for directions in Luya (2 hotels, both G). Best to take a local guide (US$3.50-5 a day).

A good way to get to know the local people and appreciate fully the scenery of this region is a 3-4 day trek starting from Luya. Walk 2-2½ hrs to **Shipata** and from there to the 'Sarcófagos' (30-40 mins). Ask around for directions. You cannot get to the Sarcófagos, but can view them from the other side of the valley, with binoculars preferably. At Shipata you can stay with Sra Rosa Zota, who will cook you dinner and breakfast. A better option, however, is to continue 1-1½ hrs to **Cohechen**. To get there from the Sarcófagos, you have to go back to Shipata.

Continue to **Belén** (4-5 hrs) and **Vista Hermosa** (2½-3 hrs). In this area there are several Chachapoyan ruins. You can lodge with Sr Cruz. From Vista Hermosa to **Youmal** involves a tough climb of 1600-1700m but from there to **Choctamal** the trail thankfully descends. It is possible to stay with Wilson Jiménez in Choctamal. It is a further 2½-3 hrs to **Tingo**.

## CHACHAPOYAS TO THE AMAZON

From Chachapoyas the road heads N through the beautiful river canyon for 2-3 hrs to a small crossroads, **Pedro Ruiz**, where you continue on to Yurimaguas or return to the coast.

• **Accommodation & transport** There is basic accommodation in **G** *Hostal Marginal* with good, cheap restaurant, and one other, **F**. A pick-up truck leaves Chachapoyas about 0830, or when full. Plenty of trucks in Pedro Ruiz go to the Selva and to Chiclayo (via Bagua not Celendín). It is advisable to stay the night if you arrive late as most trucks to Rioja leave at 0500-0700. Pedro Ruiz to Rioja is about 14 hrs, US$8, on an appalling piece of road. In the rainy season, this and the continuation to Moyobamba and Tarapoto can be very bad.

Half an hour before Rioja on this road is the new town of **Nueva Cajamarca**, with a few thousand inhabitants. There is a large market for local produce.

• **Accommodation & transport** **F** *Puerto Rico*, on main road, and **F** *Perú*, off to the right towards Rioja. Hourly colectivo to Rioja, US$1.30, 45 mins; colectivo to Chachapoyas US$12, 11-12 hrs.

### RIOJA

From **Rioja** there is a road to Naranjillo and Aguas Verdes, with a 5-hr walk to Venceremos, a pleasant way to see the jungle in good weather, but don't attempt otherwise.

An easy excursion can made to the Cueva de los Huácharos, unexplored caves, take a torch. Take a truck to La Unión (45 mins), walk 40 mins to Palestina then 50 mins more to the caves, ask locals for directions.

• **Accommodation & places to eat** There are three hotels: *Hostal San Martín*, Gran 540, *San Ramón*, Jr Faustino Maldonado 840 and *Carranza*, Jr Huallanga, all basic. *Restaurante Los Olivos* is recommended.

• **Transport Air** To **Lima** from Rioja, 2 hrs, US$75 one way, 3 times a week with Aero Continente, twice a week with Faucett (US$97) and once a week with Americana (US$75). To **Chiclayo**, 45 mins, twice a week with Faucett, US$63, and to Tarapoto, US$49 (Americana US$23, 4 a week). Continente also flies to Yurimaguas, US$24, and Iquitos US$48, twice a week; Americana to Trujillo, US$42. **Road** There is a mini-bus to Tarapoto at 1400, US$5.

## MOYOBAMBA

A road with plenty of transport (about 30 mins) runs to **Moyobamba** (*Pop* 14,000; *Alt* 915m; *Phone code* 094), capital of San Martín district. Tourists must register with the PNP. Moyobamba is a pleasant town, in an attractive valley. It was hit by an earthquake in April 1991. Mosquito nets can be bought cheaply. This area has to cope with lots of rain in the wet season; in some years the whole area is flooded. The ruins of Pueblo de los Muertos are nearby. **NB** There have been guerrilla and drug activities in this region so take good care.

### Excursions

**Puerto Tahuiso** is the town's harbour, where locals sell their produce at weekends. From **Morro de Calzada**, there is a good view of the area; take a truck to Calzada, 30 mins, then walk up, 20 mins. There are Baños Termales, 4 km from Moyobamba on the Rioja road, which are worth a visit.

The more adventurous can hike to the **Jera waterfalls**, 21 km from Moyobamba in the jungle. Take a truck in the direction of Tarapoto and get off at the restaurant at Km 218. Take a good path through a well-populated valley, crossing two bridges on the way, then head along the river through dense jungle. There are three more river crossings but no bridges, so potentially dangerous.

### Local information

#### ● Accommodation

**A3** *Turistas*, Puerto Mirador, Jr Sucre, T 562594/848, F 562050, with breakfast, 1 km from centre, fine situation, pool, good restaurant (in Lima T 442-3090, F 442-4180, Av R Rivera Navarrete 889, of 208, San Isidro).

**E** *Hostal Inca*, with bath, clean, good but noisy.

**F** *Hostal Country Club*, clean, comfortable, friendly, nice garden, rec; **F** *Hostal Cobos*, with bath, good; **F** *Hostal Los Andes*, clean.

*Monterrey* and *Mesía*, both basic and cheap.

#### ● Banks & money changers

Viajes Turismo Río Mayo, Jr San Martin 401.

#### ● Tourist information & guides

Information on excursions and hikes is available from the Instituto Nacional de Cultura, Jr Benavides, 3rd block. Guides: Emigdio Soto, an expert on trips to native communities in the Alto Mayo area, contact him at the Proyecto Especial Alto Mayo; Orlando Peigot Daza, for jungle trips (no English), at Yurayacu village.

#### ● Transport

**Air** To Lima, US$71 one way: 1 flight a week with Expreso Aéreo.

**Bus** To Yurimaguas, Guadalupe (Jr Callao block 5), US$8.75.

## TARAPOTO

The road is paved for a short way out of Moyobamba, then deteriorates to **Tarapoto** (*Phone code* 094), a busy town with several hotels. Good local market 1½ blocks from Plaza de Armas on Av Raimondi. Rioja, Moyobamba and Tarapoto are growing centres of population, with much small-scale forest clearance beside the road after Balsapata. The road is heavily used by trucks, with fuel and meals available. When/if the road is improved, the area will surely boom. Until then, food and accommodation will remain expensive.

### Excursions

**La Mina de Sal** is a salt mine outside the city. **Laguna Sauce** is 3 hrs by truck. **Laguna Venecia** can also be visited. **Laguna Azul** is a big lake with *cabañas* for rent on the shore, US$80/night (4 beds and shower), very simple, no fresh water or food available; colectivo from Tarapoto, 10 km, 2½ hrs, US$2.50. River rafting on the Río Mayo US$10 pp.

Between Tarapoto and Moyobamba a road leads off to **Lamas** where there is a small museum, with exhibits on local Indian community (Lamistas), ask at the café opposite if museum shut. Market in the early morning. Colectivo from Tarapoto, 30 mins, US$0.70, 35 km

About 14 km from Tarapoto on the spectacular road to Yurimaguas are the 50m falls of **Ahuashiyacu**, which can be visited by tour from Tarapoto (US$18 including lunch) or by hiring a motorcycle from *Grand Prix*, Shapajo y Raimondi, US$3.50 an hour. A restaurant nearby serves reasonable food and has 2 rooms to rent (G pp, basic but OK). The road continues for 10 km through lush vegetation to a small village (with restaurant).

### Local information

#### ● Accommodation

**A3** *Río Shilcayo*, Pasaje Las Flores 224, T 522225, F 524236 (in Lima T 447-9359), with bath, excellent meals, 1 km out of town, non-residents can use the swimming pool for a fee.

**D** *Edinson*, Av Raimondi, 1 block from Plaza de Armas, T 522723, with bath (less without), cold water, clean and comfortable; **D** *Hostal San Antonio*, Jr Jiménez Pimentel 126, T 522226, private bath and TV, courtyard, rec.

**E** *Tarapoto*, T 522150, with fan, clean.

**F** *Hostal Americano*, fan and private bath with each room; **F** *Juan Alfonso*, with shower, noisy, Jr Pedro de Urzúa; **F** *Las Palmeras*, just off Plaza, pokey, lacks water, not rec.

**G** *Los Angeles*, nr plaza, good value, laundry facilities, restaurant.

### ● Places to eat

Best are *Real* and *El Camarón*. *Las Terrazas*, typical food, rec. Many others; try also *El Mesón*.

### ● Banks & money changers

**Banco de Crédito**, Maynas 134, efficient, no commission on TCs. Many street changers around Plaza de Armas.

### ● Transport

**Air** US$1.75/taxi airport to town (no bus service, but no problem to walk). To **Lima**, 1 hr, US$76, Faucett, also Aero Continente. To **Rioja**, 20 mins, US$43 Faucett. **Yurimaguas**, 20 mins, US$23, 4 a week with Aero Continente, continuing to **Iquitos**, also Faucett direct 3 times a week, US$53. To **Pucallpa**, Aero Continente 2 a week, US$46; also to Juanjui, US$25, Tocache, US$38 and Tingo María, US$48, daily. Expreso Aéreo has flights to/from Tarapoto. Book in advance, particularly in rainy season. Those visiting Tarapoto and Iquitos would be advised to visit Tarapoto first, as aircraft leaving Iquitos tend to overfly Tarapoto; possible to be stuck there for days. Many smaller airlines operate flights to Yurimaguas, eg Aerotaxi Ibérico (US$40): turn up at airport at 0700-0800, wait for it to open, wait for people to turn up, wait for a list for your destination to be drawn up and you should get away later in the morning, 50 mins flight.

**Buses** The journey from Rioja to Tarapoto costs about US$7 and it is best to carry food and water because of road problems. To/from **Moyobamba**, 116 km, 3½ hrs, US$7 by colectivo, US$3.50 by colectivo, 5 hrs, several daily. There is a direct connection by bus (Chinchaysuyo) or truck from Tarapoto to **Chiclayo** via Moyobamba, Rioja, Bagua and Olmos, 690 km, 35-40 hrs, US$20. The same bus company also runs to Trujillo, at least 36 hrs. To **Yurimaguas**, US$5-10, trucks and pick-ups daily (see below for road conditions). Truck/pick-up leaves for Yurimaguas (usually 0800-0900, and in pm) from Jorge Chávez 175, down Av Raimondi 2 blocks, then left 5 blocks along Av Pedro de Uruaz (pick-ups from this street to other destinations).

## TARAPOTO TO YURIMAGUAS

The journey from Tarapoto to Tingo María (see page 391) is not advisable. In the rainy season the roads are impossible and it is a drugs-growing area. From Tarapoto to Yurimaguas on the Río Huallaga (136 km – see page 392), the spectacular road can be very bad in the wet season, taking 6-8 hrs for trucks (schedules above). Once the plains are reached, the road improves and there is more habitation. **Shapaja** is the port for Tarapoto, 14 km from town, served by colectivos. At Shapaja cargo boats can be caught to Yurimaguas; plenty of birdlife and river traffic to be seen. From Yurimaguas on the Río Huallaga, launches ply to Iquitos.

## CHACHAPOYAS TO THE COAST

**ROUTES** The road from Pedro Ruiz (see page 194) goes W to Bagua Grande(see page 189) and then follows the Río Chamaya. It climbs to the Abra de Porculla (2,150m) before descending to join the old Pan-American Highway at Olmos (see page 210). From here you can go SW to Chiclayo, or NW to Piura.

**Bagua Grande** is the first town of note heading W and a busy, dusty place with many hotels on the main street. If arriving late, ask to sleep on the bus until daybreak. *Restaurant Central* at Av Chachapoyas 1553 is good. Cars and camionetas depart from Av Chachapoyas when full to Pedro Ruiz, 1½ hrs, agree on the price but should be around US$2.70; return from Pedro Ruiz when full, from main street, US$2.25, 2 hrs.

## NORTH EAST TO SAMERIZA

From Bagua Grande the road continues NW, then forks; SW to **Chamaya** and NE to **Sameriza**. The NE branch passes through Aramango and **Nazareth** and continues to another fork, N to **Oracuza** and NE to Sameriza and **Puerto Delfus**, both on the Río Marañon. To reach Sameriza, pick-ups run twice daily from Bagua Grande to Imasa. Get out at Campamento Mesones Muro, 15 mins before Imasa (US$4, 7 hrs), where you must register with the police. This can be a time-consuming procedure. For 150 km from Mesones Muro to Sameriza, you have to wait for a pick-up – which can take anything up to 6 days – and then be prepared for a 2-3 day journey because of poor roads and missing bridges.

The m/n *Fernández* makes the journey from Sameriza to Iquitos every second week, 4 days downriver, 6 days upriver, take a hammock as there are only a few cabins available. **NB** We have received reports of violent attacks on tourists by local Aguarana Indians on this route.

### JAEN

47 km W of Bagua Grande, a road branches NW at Chamaya to **Jaén**, an old settlement, which has recently been revived as a rice-growing centre. The annual festival of the patron saint, Nuestro Señor de Huamantanga, is on 14 September.

• **Accommodation** **E** *Panamá*, Mcal Castilla 697, T 33, clean, secure, helpful, bath, rec; **F** *Santa Barbarita*, Av Villinueva Pinillos 360, not rec; *Hostal Lima*, not rec.

• **Transport** Bus to Chiclayo, Civa twice a day, US$4.35.

A road has been built N from Jaén to **San Ignacio** (114 km), near the frontier of Ecuador. It crosses the valley of the Chinchipe, renowned for its lost Inca gold. San Ignacio has a *fiesta* on 31 August.

## PACIFIC COAST NORTH OF TRUJILLO

When Spanish conquistadores first encountered the broad, northern Peruvian coastal valley oases, they marvelled at the creativity and sophistication of these desert farmers and fishermen. Early 16th century accounts describe enormous precolumbian settlements and sacred places. Recent archaeological discoveries near Chiclayo, the centre for today's rural population and capital of Lambayeque department, now attract scientists and tourists to the area.

Today's rural peasantry are inheritors of many of the customs and technologies of their Moche forebears, who were master craftsmen in many fields. Artisan markets, primitive ocean going vessels, folk curing sessions and colourful religious 'fiestas' enliven any visitor's stay. In addition, the N, with a rain free climate all year, sports Peru's finest beaches for bathing and surfing.

Sandwiched between the Pacific Ocean and the Andes, Lambayeque is one of Peru's principal agricultural regions, and its chief producer of rice and sugar cane. Even so, archaeological studies indicate that prehispanic people here cultivated some 25% more land than farmers today. The extensive irrigation canals and reservoirs of northern Peru constitute one of the major technological achievements of ancient America. Disused aqueducts and ridged fields can easily be explored.

## CHICLAYO

**Chiclayo** (*Pop* 280,000; *Phone code* 074), founded in the 1560s as a rural Indian village by Spanish priests, has long since outgrown other towns of the Lambayeque Department. A major commercial hub, Chiclayo also boasts distinctive cuisine and musical tradition (*Marinera*, *Tondero* and afro-indian rhythms), and an unparalleled archaeological and ethnographic heritage (see **Excursions**). A walking tour in the centre reveals the mixture of creole, Spanish and Indian architecture along curving, narrow streets, once precolumbian canals now filled and paved with cobble stones.

Chiclayo is dubbed 'The Capital of Friendship', and while that tag could

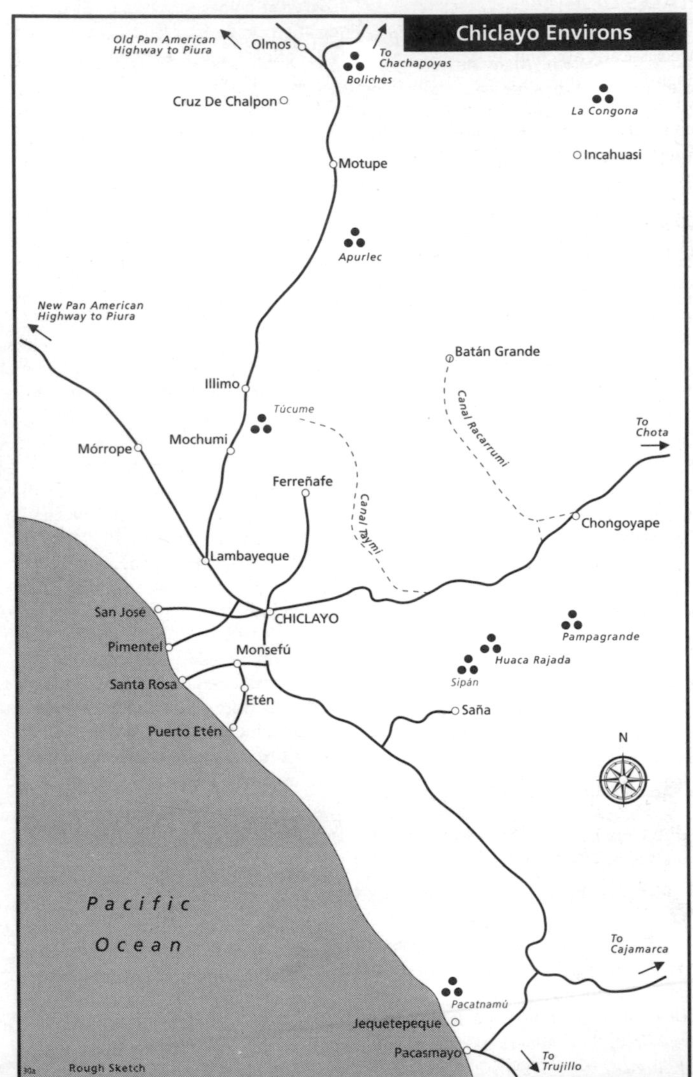

equally apply to most of the N coast of Peru, there is an earthiness and vivacity about its citizens that definitely sets it apart. It can be a difficult place to leave.

## PLACES OF INTEREST

On the Plaza de Armas is the 19th century neoclassical **Cathedral**, designed by the English architect Andrew Townsend, whose descendants can still be identified among the town's principals. The **Palacio Municipal** and private **Club de la Unión** are on C Balta, the major avenue.

Continue five blocks N on Balta to the **Mercado Modelo**, one of northern Peru's liveliest and largest daily markets. Don't miss the colourful fruits, handicrafts stalls (see *Monsefú*) and the well-organized section (off C Arica on the S side) of ritual paraphernalia used by traditional curers and diviners (*curanderos*). James Vreeland, a North American anthropologist, considers the Chiclayo *mercado de brujos* (witch doctors' market) to be one of the most comprehensive in South America, filled with herbal medicines, folk charms, curing potions, and exotic objects used by *curanderos* and *brujos* to cure all manner of real and imagined illnesses. The stallholders are generally very friendly and will explain the uses of such items as monkey claws, dried foetuses and dragon's blood! Sra Carmen Quispe Bios of Casa La Cabalonga, stand 44, near the corner of Av Arica and Héroes Cíviles, has been recommended as particularly helpful and informative. **NB** As in all markets, take good care of your belongings.

Drawing of the decoration of a Moche pot, depicting a warrior holding a naked prisoner

## EXCURSIONS

### Lambayeque

12 km NW from Chiclayo is the quiet town of Lambayeque (*Pop* 20,700). Its narrow streets are lined by colonial and republican houses, many retaining their distinctive wooden balconies and wrought iron grillwork over the windows. For some fine examples, head along Calle 8 de Octubre: at No 410 is the opulent **Casona Iturregui Aguilarte** and, at No 328, **Casona Cúneo** is the only decorated facade in the town; opposite is **Casona Descalzi**, perhaps the best preserved of all Lambayeque's colonial houses. Calle 2 de Mayo is also a good source of colonial and republican architecture, especially **Casa de la Logia o Montjoy,** whose 64 metre long balcony is said to be the longest in the colonial Americas.

Also of interest is the 16th century **Complejo Religioso Monumental de San Pedro** and the baroque church of the same name which stands on the **Plaza de Armas 27 de Diciembre.** The French neo-baroque **Palacio Municipal** is also on the plaza.

The town's most interesting feature, and the reason most people come to visit, is the well-known, highly recommended **Brüning Archaeological Museum**, located in an impressive modern building. It specializes in Mochica, Lambayeque, Sicán and Chimú cultures, and has a fine collection of Sipán and Lambayeque gold. The magnificent treasure from the tomb of a Moche warrior priest, found at Sipán in 1987, has also been displayed here (see below), open 0900-1800 daily; entry US$1.50, guided tour extra US$2.

• **Places to eat & transport** There are no hotels in the town but several good restaurants. *El Cántaro*, on the 1st block of 2 de Mayo, serves excellent traditional local dishes

## The legend of Naymlap

Like much else along this stretch of the Peruvian coast, the exact origin of the people's forebears is something of a mystery. The Spaniard, Cabello de Balboa, in 1578, is said to be the first outsider to hear of a local folk legend referring to a person named Naymlap who arrived on the coast of Lambayeque along with his court, his servants and his many concubines in numerous balsa rafts.

He then built residential buildings near the coast and a temple called Chota, where he placed an idol called Yampallec, from which Lambayeque is supposed to derive its name.

The name Naymlap came to occupy an important place in the religious imagery of later civilizations through the designs of *tumis*, or ceremonial knives, funerary masks and countless other objects. In the ancient Muchik language spoken by the Moche, ñam means bird and lá means water, and the figures on Moche ceramics, jewellery and temple walls often have bird-like features.

Naymlap had many children but only three are known of; Cium, Nor and Cala, who founded the present site of Túcume. This dynasty is said to have ended with the death of the last governor as a result of his illicit relationship with a demon in the shape of a beautiful woman.

cooked by Juanita; ***La Huaca***, on the 3rd block of Calle Junín, and ***La Cabaña***, on the 4th block of Calle Libertad, are both good for *cebiche*. Colectivos from Chiclayo US$0.50, 20 mins, leave from Elías Aguirre nr Plazuela Aguirre; also Brüning Express from Vicente de la Vega y San Martín, every 15 mins, US$0.20.

### Colonial and traditional towns

The colonial town of **Ferreñafe**, NE of Chiclayo, is worth a visit, as is the traditional town of **Monsefú**, SW, also known for handicrafts has a good market, 4 blocks from Plaza, open 0930-1700 but don't rush to get there early as most stallholders don't arrive until around 1000 or 1100 (see also **Local festivals** below).

**Mórrope**, on the Pan-American Highway N of Chiclayo, is worth a visit. The craftsmen of Mórrope still produce pottery for the towns of N Peru using prehispanic techniques. Step inside the beautifully-restored 16th century **Capilla de la Ramada** on the Plaza and you'll know how Jonah felt inside the whale. The pillars and rafters were hewed from the local *algarrobo* tree, giving the church interior the appearance of the skeleton of some enormous beast.

51 km S of Chiclayo is the ruined Spanish town of **Saña**, destroyed by floods in 1726, and sacked by English pirates on more than one occasion. The ruins of five colonial churches and the convents of San Agustín, La Merced and San Francisco bear witness to the former splendour of this town which, at one time, was destined to become the country's capital.

Further S, on the Pan-American Highway to Trujillo, lies **Chepén**. The town itself is not particularly fascinating but **Cerro Chepén**, towering over it, is the site of an ancient fortress, 1,000 years older than Machu Picchu. The Moche fortress contains the ruins of what may be a palace, surrounded by other buildings. The as yet unexcavated site could have been the main station in a chain of lookout posts along the N coast. Take any Trujillo bus, US$1.10.

### Coastal towns

North from Trujillo are three ports serving the Chiclayo area. The more southerly is **Puerto Etén**, a quaint port 24 km by road from Chiclayo. In the adjacent roadstead, Villa de Etén, panama hats are the local industry.

**Pimentel**, N of Etén, is a chic and expensive beach resort which gets very

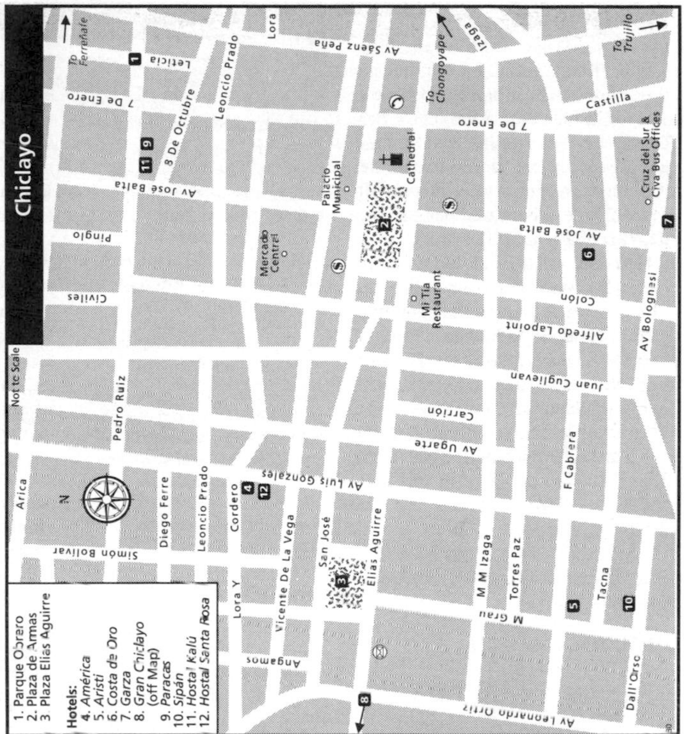


crowded on Sun. Holiday apartments of the Chiclayo wealthy line the seafront. There are no hotels, though you may be able to rent an apartment. The surfing between Pimentel and the Bayovar Peninsula is excellent, reached from Chiclayo (14½ km) by road branching off from the Pan-American Highway. Sea-going reed boats (*caballitos de totora*) are used by fishermen and may be seen returning in the late afternoon.

A more traditional and authentic fishing village is nearby **Santa Rosa**, where fishermen use two groups of boats *caballitos* and *bolicheros* – pastel-painted craft which line the shore after the day's fishing. Santa Rosa is a pleasant, 1-hr walk from Pimentel, though it's a better idea to walk from Santa Rosa to Pimentel to have the wind at your back.

• **Accommodation & places to eat** There is a small hostal, ***Puerto Magnolia***, basic, and restaurant ***Bello Horizonte***. The seafood is superb: two specialities are *tortilla de rayo* (manta ray) and *chingurito*, a ceviche of little strips of dried guitar fish which is chewy, but good.

• **Transport** The three ports may be visited on a pleasant half day trip. Aspcarpl kombis from Vicente de la Vega 400, 20 mins, US$0.25 to Pimentel. Colectivos run frequently from Pimentel to Santa Rosa, and on to Etén and back to Chiclayo (10 mins from Santa Rosa, 15 mins from Pimentel). To avoid paying excess luggage charges for weight above 15 kg, buy ticket in advance, and catch bus outside terminal (no scales!)

## LOCAL FESTIVALS

6 Jan, Reyes Magos in **Mórrope**, **Illimo** and other towns, a recreation of a medieval pageant in which precolumbian deities become the Wise Men. On 4 Feb, **Túcume** devil dances (see below). During Holy Week are traditional Easter celebrations and processions in many villages. 2-7 June, Divine Child of the Miracle, **Villa de Etén**. 27-31 July, Fexticum in **Monsefú**, traditional foods, drink, handicrafts, music and dance. On 5 Aug is the pilgrimage from the mountain shrine of **Chalpón** to **Motupe**, 90 km N of Chiclayo; the cross is brought down from a cave and carried in procession through the village. 24 Sept, Virgen de las Mercedes in **Incahuasi**, 12 hrs by truck E of Chiclay. Indians still sing in the ancient Mochica language in this post-harvest festival. At Christmas and New Year, processions and children dancers (*pastorcitos* and *seranitas*) can be seen in many villages, eg **Ferreñafe**, **Mochumi**, **Mórrope**.

## LOCAL INFORMATION

**Hotel prices**

| | | | |
|---|---|---|---|
| **L1** | over US$200 | **L2** | US$151-200 |
| **L3** | US$101-150 | **A1** | US$81-100 |
| **A2** | US$61-80 | **A3** | US$46-60 |
| **B** | US$31-45 | **C** | US$21-30 |
| **D** | US$12-20 | **E** | US$7-11 |
| **F** | US$4-6 | **G** | up to US$3 |

### ● Accommodation

**A1** *Costa de Oro*, Balta 399, T/F 233280, inc continental breakfast, parking nearby, good services but a bit pricey, good restaurant, casino, TV in room, cable TV in lobby; **A1-2** *Gran Hotel Chiclayo*, Villareal 115, T 234911/224031, ex-Turistas, refurbished 1995/96 to high standard, price includes taxes and breakfast, pool, safe car park, changes dollars, still undergoing improvements but rec; **A3** *Garza*, Bolognesi 756, nr Balta, T 228172, F 228171, excellent bar and restaurant, pool, car park, tourist office in lobby provides maps, information in English, Land Rovers, jeeps and minibuses for hire, highly rec; **A3** *Sipán*, Virgilio Dall'Orso 150, T 242564, F 242408, a/c, **B** without a/c, cable TV, restaurant, parking, rec.

**B-C** *América*, L González 943, T 229305, F 241627, inc continental breakfast, comfortable, friendly, restaurant, good value, has Travel Agency in reception, rec; **B-C** *Inca*, Av L González 622, T 235931, with TV and fan, restaurant, garage, comfortable.

**C** *Aristi*, Francisco Cabrera 102, T 231074, F 228673, with TV, fan, parking US$1/day extra, clean, comfortable, reasonable value; **C-D** *El Sol*, Elías Aguirre 119, T/F 231070, price inc taxes, with bath, hot water, restaurant, pool, TV lounge, clean, comfortable, free parking, good value; **C** *Hostal Santa Victoria*, La Florida 586, Urb Santa Victoria, T/F 241944, with bath and TV, hot water, restaurant, free parking, cash dollars exchanged, quiet, 15-20 mins' walk from the centre.

**D-E** *Europa*, Elías Aguirre 466, T 237919, with bath, cheaper without, some hot water, restaurant, a bit dingy and rundown but otherwise OK; **D** *Hostal Kalú*, Pedro Ruiz 1038, T 228767, F 229293, cable TV, taxi service, will reserve bus and air tickets, laundry, friendly and helpful, excellent value, rec; **D-C** *Hostal Santa Rosa*, L González 925, T 224411, F 236242, with bath, clean, friendly, laundry service, international phone service, good breakfast downstairs in snack bar, rec; **D** *Paraíso*, Pedro Ruiz 1064, T 228161, T/F 240190, nr market, with bath, hot water, cafeteria, TV US$2 extra, good value; **D** *Paracas*, Pedro Ruiz 1046, T 221611, T/F 236433, with bath, TV, good value, rec; **D** *Royal*, San José 787, T 233421, with bath, a big, rambling old building, a bit seedy and rundown, rooms on street have balcony but are noisy.

**E-F** *Aries II*, Av Pedro Ruiz 937, T 235235, shared bath, cheap, cold water; **E** *Hostal Colonial*, Lora y Lora 344, T 237871, with bath, hot water, basic but clean, noisy, convenient for buses; **E** *Hostal San Ramón*, Héroes Civiles 169, T 233931, with bath, cold water, friendly, clean, noisy, restaurant, reasonable value; **E** *Lido*, Elías Aguirre 412A, T 237642, with bath, fairly clean, safe, rooms near reception are noisy; **E** *Sol Radiante*, Izaga 392, T 237858, hot water, comfortable, friendly owner will provide breakfast; **E** *Tumi de Oro*, L Prado 1145, T 227108, shared bath, **D** with bath, hot water, simple but clean, good value; **F** *Hostal San José*, Juan Cuglievan, opp *Res Chavín*, basic, clean, acceptable, cold water.

There are several cheap hotels on Av Balta, near bus offices, which range from basic to hygienically-challenged. Most have only cold water:

## Is there a Witchdoctor in the house?

Forget courses of antibiotics or the psychiatrsts's couch, many Peruvians prefer to employ the services of a *curandero*, or curer, a person skilled in the use of herbs and potions to heal bodily ailments and fend off those potentially troublesome evil spirits.

Such curers performed similar functions in Moche times and methods have remained virtually unchanged since then.

The place where it all takes place bears little resemblance to your average doctor's surgery. Take the human skull sitting proudly centre stage. Human skulls are ever-present at these consultations as participants believe the spirit of the skull will protect them, as well as the curer, from sorcery or even from the evil spells of rival curers.

The session usually starts just before midnight and lasts most of the night. It all happens in total darkness. In order to get around this slight inconvenience, the curer, in his one concession to modern technology, will use a flashlight to identify the various potions, herbs and charms that cover his table. Potions are often made out of perfume mixed with such items as lime juice, sugar and holy water. They also use a hallucinogenic brew made from the San Pedro cactus.

As this ancient practice proceeds into the night the Maestro (curer) will even take a sword and fence with harmful spirits to keep them away from the sufferer. How many doctors would be prepared to do that on behalf of their patients these days?

**F** pp *Adriático*, No 1009, the best of a bad bunch, fairly clean. It is difficult to find decent cheap accommodation in Chiclayo

### ● Places to eat

***Fiesta***, Av Salaverry 1820 in Ocho de Octubre suburb, T 228441, local specialities, first class, very expensive; ***Le París***, MM Izaga 716, T 235485, excellent but expensive, international and creole food. First-class and very reasonable food (usually good breakfast) at ***Romana***, Balta 512, T 238601, popular with locals. Many cheap *pollerías* on Balta and Pedro Ruiz near market, eg ***Carbón Dorado***, Av Balta 1212. ***Che Claudio***, Bolognesi 334, T 237426, *parrillada* with reasonable *empanadas* and house wine; ***Mi Tía***, Aguirre 650, just off Plaza, cheap, huge portions, great value *menú*, very popular at lunchtime, rec; ***Govinda***, Balta 1029, good vegetarian, cheap, open daily 0800-2000; ***Men Wha***, Pedro Ruiz 1059, expensive Chinese but delicious, huge portions; ***Las Tinajas***, Elías Aguirre 957, excellent seafood at reasonable prices; ***Kafé D'Kaly***, San José 728, good *menú*, friendly; ***The Atrium***, M Izaga 220, good, friendly; ***24 Horas***, E Aguirre 884, good food, cheap, open 24 hrs; ***Las Américas***, Aguirre 824, open 0700-0200, good service, rec; ***El Algorrobo***, Av Saenz Peña 1220, good set lunch for US$1.10; ***Flippy***, San José 710, good fried chicken and salad for US$1.50, also juices, sandwiches etc.

***Lo Más Natural***, Arica 755, nr market, sells good natural/organic yoghurt, also dried fruits and granola; ***La Panadería***, Aguirre 610, for good bread, *pan integral*, etc, small cafetería.

**Local food and drink**: *Ceviche* and *chingurito* (see above); *cabrito*, spiced stew of kid goat; *arroz con pato*, paella-like duck casserole; *humitas*, *tamale*-like fritters of green corn; *King Kong*, baked pastry layered with candied fruit and milk caramel; *chicha*, fermented maize drink with delicious fruit variations.

### ● Airline offices

**Faucett**, MM Izaga 711, T 237932; **Americana**, San José 773, T 227402; **AeroPerú**, Elías Aguirre 712, T 242865; **Aero Continente**, A Ugarte 687, T 241202; **Expresso Aéreo**, San José 490, T 224802.

### ● Banks & money changers

**Banco de Crédito**, Balta 630, no commission on TCs for US$100 or more (US$11 commission if less), cash on Visa; **Interbanc**, on Plaza de Armas, no commission on TCs, OK rate, good rates for cash, Visa cash advance; **Banco Wiese**, on Plaza, cash on Mastercard. Be prepared to wait. Beware of counterfeit bills, especially among street changers on 6th block of Balta, on Plaza de Armas and 7th block of MM Izaga.

### ● Cultural centres

**Instituto Peruano Británico**, Av 7 de Enero 296; **Instituto Nacional de la Cultura**, Av L González 375, occasional poetry readings, information on local archaeological sites, lectures, etc; **Instituto de Cultura Peruano-Norteamericana**, Av Izaga 807.

### ● Entertainment

**Folklore**: *Los Hermanos Balcázar*, Lora y Cordero 1150, T 227922; *El Embrujo*, Vicente de la Vega, T 233984; *Recreo Parrillada El Gaucho*, Fco Cabrera 1291, T 234441. On Dall'Orso is *Oasis* peña; *Casona* disco and pub; and *Baku's* karaoke disco; all popular at weekends. Also *Crocos*, opposite Aristi Hotel on Grau, good at weekends.

### ● Hospitals & medical services

**Doctors**: *Juan Aita*, Clínica Chiclayo, Av Santa Victoria, T 239024, rec as good general medical practitioner; *José Gálvez Jaime*, eye specialist, English spoken, Elías Aguirre 011, T 238234.

### ● Post & telecommunications

**Post Office**: on 1 block of Aguirre, 6 blocks from Plaza.

**Telecommunications**: Telefónica del Perú on 7 de Enero 724, open 0700-2300, international phone and fax; also on 8th block of Aguirre.

### ● Shopping

***Paseo de Artesanías***, at 18 de Abril near Balta, stalls sell woodwork, basketwork and other handicrafts in a quiet, peaceful, custom-built open-air arcade. ***Mercado Moshoqueque***, Ricardo Palma y Calle Ancha, is a busy street teeming with people and good for buying food in bulk from merchants

### ● Tour companies & travel agents

***Indiana Tours***, Colón 556, T 242287, F 240833, daily tours to Sipán (US$15), Thor Heyerdahl's Kon Tiki museum, archaeological excavations in Túcume, Brüning Museum in Lambayeque, Batán Grande and a variety of other daily and extended excursions with 4WD vehicles; English and Italian spoken, Handbook users welcome. ***Sipán Tours***, Av Luis González 741, T/F 237413, good for tours locally, English-speaking manager, helpful, can arrange tailor-made tours. ***Lambayeque Tours***, Av Santa Victoria 300, T 244327, F 274452. ***Kaly Tours***, San José 728, T 238830, friendly, helpful, English spoken. The Brüning Museum, Sipán and Tucumé can easily be done by public transport. Expect to pay US$18-25 pp for a 3 hr tour to Sipán; US$25-35 pp for Túcume and Bruning Museum (5 hrs); Batán Grande is US$45-55 pp for a full-day tour inc Ferreñafe and Pomac; to Saña and coastal towns, US$35-55 pp. These prices are based on 2 people; discount for larger groups.

### ● Tourist offices

San José 733 y Plaza de Armas, very helpful and may store luggage and take you to the sites themselves; regional tourist board plans to open an office in the same building, T 233132, current office at Sáenz Peña 838. Brochure *Guía de Lambayeque 1996* available for US$5.

### ● Transport

**Local** Mototaxis are a cheap way to get around; US$0.50 anywhere in city.

**Air** José Abelardo Quiñones González airport 1 km from town; taxi from centre US$1. Daily flights to/from Lima daily, US$82, with all major airlines; to Piura and Tumbes, daily, US$15; to Tarapoto, US$48 with Expresso Aéreo, who also fly to Tingo María, Juanjui and Huánuco. AeroPerú to Iquitos 4 times a week, US$81.

**Buses** No *terminal terrestre*; most buses stop outside their offices on Bolognesi. To **Lima**, 770 km, US$8-9; Chiclayo Express, Mcal Nieto 119, T 237356; Civa, Av Bolognesi 757, T 242488; Cruz del Sur, Bolognesi 751, T 242164 (also Roggero, T 223216); Ormeño, Bolognesi 954A; Turismo Las Dunas, L González 291, T 229328, luxury service with a/c, toilet, meals, US$17.50, at 2000; Ortursa, Balta 598, *cama* service; most companies leave from 1600 onwards. To **Trujillo**, 209 km, with Emtrafesa, Av Balta 110, T 234291; and Vulkano, Av Bolognesi 638, T 234291; hourly 0530-2000, US$3.50, 3-4 hrs. Bus to **Piura**, US$3.50, hourly 0630-1930; **Sullana**, US$4.35; and **Tumbes**, US$6.50, 9-10 hrs, with Transportes Chiclayo, Av L Ortiz 010, T 233632l; Ortursa has night service 2015, arriving 0530 (a good bus to take for crossing to Ecuador next day, seats can be reserved, unlike other companies which tend to arrive full from Lima late at night).

Many buses go on to the Ecuadorean border at **Aguas Verdes**. Go to *Salida* on Elías Aguirre, mototaxi drivers know where it is, be there by 1900. All buses stop here after leaving their terminals to try and fill empty seats, so it's possible to get a substantial discount on the fare to the border. **NB** Bear in mind that the cheapest buses may not be the most secure.

Direct bus to **Cajamarca**, 260 km; with Vulkano, El Cumbe (Av Quiñones 425), Sud Americano (Colón 272, T 238566) and Turismo Arberia (Av Bolognesi 638, T 236981), US$6, 7 hrs, 3 a day at 1300, 2130 and 2200. To **Chachapoyas**, 230 km, Civa direct at 1700, US$6.50, 12 hrs. To **Tarapoto**, Chinchay-Suyo, Av Balta 179, T 231731, via Moyobamba, at 1030 and 1400, 24 hrs, US$17.50. Bus to **Huancabamba**, with Etipthsa, Mon, Wed and Fri from Tepsa terminal at Av Bolognesi 536, T 229217, at 1700, 12 hrs, US$9. Trucks going in all directions leave from C Pedro Ruiz 948 and from the market.

# ARCHAEOLOGICAL SITES NEAR CHICLAYO

## SIPAN

At this imposing twin pyramid complex a short distance E of Chiclayo, excavations since 1987 have brought to light a cache of funerary objects considered to rank among the finest examples of precolumbian art. Peruvian archaeologist Walter Alva, leader of the dig, continues to probe the immense mound that has revealed no less than five royal tombs filled with 1,800-year-old offerings worked in precious metals, stone, pottery and textiles of the Moche culture (ca AD 1-750). In the most extravagant Moche tomb discovered, El Señor de Sipán, a priest was found clad in gold (ear ornaments, breast plate, etc), with turquoise and

### The old Lord of Sipán

The excavations at Sipán by the archaeologist Walter Alva have already revealed a huge amount of riches in the shape of 'El Señor de Sipán'. This well-documented discovery was followed by an equally astounding find dating from AD 100. The tomb of the 'Old Lord of Sipán', as it has come to be known, predates the original Lord of Sipán by some 200 years, and could well be an ancestor of his.

Some of the finest examples of Moche craftsmanship have been found in the tomb of the Old Lord. One object in particular is remarkable; a crab deity with a human head and legs and the carapace, legs and claws of a crab. The gilded piece is over 2 ft tall – unprecedented for a Moche figurine. This crab-like figure has been called Ulluchu Man, because the banner on which it was mounted yielded some of the first samples yet found of this ancient fruit.

The ulluchu fruit usually appears in scenes relating to war and the ritual drinking of a prisoner's blood. One theory is that the ulluchu is part of the papaya family and has anticoagulant properties which are useful to prevent clotting before a man's blood is consumed.

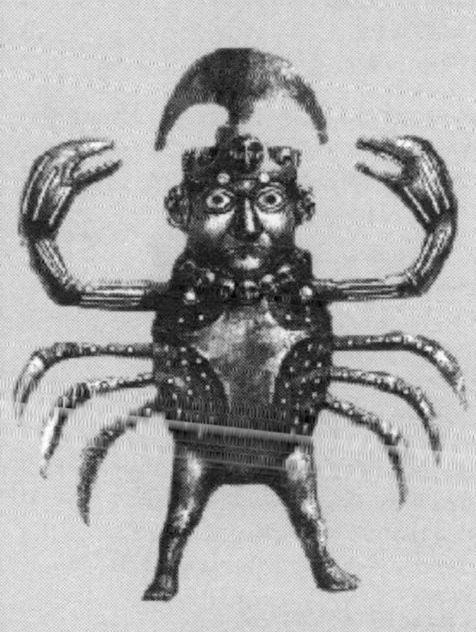

Crab deity

other valuables. A fine site museum was opened in 1992 featuring photos and maps of excavations, technical displays and replicas of some finds.

Following the 4-year restoration of the principle treasures in Germany, the Lord of Sipán's physical remains and extraordinary funerary paraphernalia were recently returned to the Brüning Museum in Lambayeque, which was remodelled in 1994 to accommodate over 600 new objects. In another tomb were found the remnants of what is thought to have been a priest, sacrificed llama and a dog, together with copper decorations. In 1989 another richly-appointed, unlooted tomb contained even older metal and ceramic artefacts associated with what was probably a high-ranking shaman or spiritual leader, called 'The Old Lord of Sipán'.

Tomb contents are being restored in the Brüning Museum by specialists trained in Europe. At the time of writing, yet another unlooted tomb is currently being excavated, which will take several years. You can wander around the previously excavated areas to get an idea of the construction of the burial mound and adjacent pyramids. For a good view, climb the large pyramid across from the Sipán excavation.

• **Accommodation** At nearby **Huaca Rajada** is a **F** *Parador Turística*, 2 rooms available, meals possible, camping and use of facilities for US$1 pp.

• **Entry & access** The site museum is open 0800-1800. Entrance for tombs and museum is US$1. To Sipán, colectivos leave from 7 de Enero y Leticia (take a taxi there), US$1, 1 hr.

## PAMPAGRANDE

25 km from Sipán is Pampagrande, a Mochica settlement interpreted by Canadian archaeologists in the 1970s as the first true N coast city, ca AD 550.

### Rise and downfall

This was the largest Moche complex 1,400 years ago, at which time as many as 10,000 people may have lived here. Pampagrande existed to enact ceremonies and rituals such as the drinking of prisoners' blood. These were presided over by a lord who also directed the production and distribution of precious materials to the artisans. Some experts believe that a prolonged drought around AD 550 displaced large groups of Moche people living to the S who moved to Pampagrande, which become the centre of a state holding sway over the Lambayeque and Jequetepeque valleys.

The precise reason for the downfall of this once-powerful city remains a mystery. The structures associated with the rich and powerful ruling class appear to have been selectively burned and then abandoned leading some to conclude that a peasant revolution may have been the cause.

A minor road runs to **Chongoyape**, a quaint old town 60 km to the E (3 km W are the Chavín petroglyphs of Cerro Mulato). Nearby are the vast Taymi precolumbian and modern irrigation systems. Also near Chongoyape are the aqueduct of Racarrumi, the hill fort of Mal Paso and the ruins of Maguín.

• **Accommodation & places to eat** Hotel, **F**, nr Plaza de Armas, without restaurant; ***Restaurant Cascada***, main street, limited menu.

• **Transport** Bus from Chiclayo, US$1, 1½ hrs, leaves from Leoncio Prado block and Saenz Peña.

## BATAN GRANDE

50 km from Chiclayo, has revealed several sumptuous tombs dating to the middle Sicán period, AD 900-1100. The ruins comprise some fifty adobe pyramids, where some of the best examples of precolumbian gold artefacts, notably the 915-gram Tumi, were found.

### The Mid-Sicán Culture

In the ancient Muchik language, Sicán means 'house or temple of the moon' and Batán Grande, or Poma, as it was also known, was the centre of this culture which shares many stylistic similarities with the later Chimú culture.

Professor Izumi Shimada has worked here for more than 15 years researching a culture which has, to a large extent, been forgotten. He has excavated **Huaca Loro**, one of five monument temples that make up the vast rectangle known as the Great Plaza. Research points to the existence of a well-structured theocracy led by a small class of priest-lords. Political, economic and religious dominance of the Sicán theocracy stretched over most of the N coast, from Sullana in the N to Trujillo in the S. Their dominion ended in the 14th century with the Chimú conquest.

The site, in 300 ha of desert-thorn forest of mezquite (*Prosopis pallida*), known locally as Pomac forest, is now a national sanctuary and is protected by police.

- **Access** Colectivos, US$1.20, leave from 7 de Enero block 15 and J Fanning to the main square of the sugar cane cooperative (in which the ruins are set). You must get permission to visit the site from the cooperative (need to speak Spanish and to pay), and go with site archaeologist; Mon-Fri only; private car (taxi) from cooperative to site, US$8.50. Need full day to visit; impossible in wet season, Jan-March. Seek sound advice before you go.

## TUCUME

About 35 km N of Chiclayo, beside the old Panamericana to Piura, lie the ruins of this vast city built over a thousand years ago. A short climb to the *mirador* atop **Cerro La Raya**, or **El Purgatorio**, as it is also known, offers the visitor an unparallelled panoramic vista of 26 major pyramids, platform mounds, walled citadels and residential compounds flanking a ceremonial centre and ancient cemeteries.

The entire complex covers 240 ha and measures 1.7 km from E to W and 2 km from N to S. One of the pyramids, Huaca Larga, where excavations are currently going on, is the largest adobe structure in the world, measuring 700m long, 280m wide and over 30m high.

There is no evidence of occupation of Túcume previous to the Lambayeque people who developed the site between AD 1000 and 1400 until the Chimú came, saw and conquered the region, establishing a short reign until the arrival of the Incas around 1470. The Incas built on top of the existing structure of **Huaca Larga** using stone from Cerro La Raya. Among the tombs excavated so far is one dating from the Inca period. It is thought to be that of a warrior, judging by the many battle scars. The body is heavily adorned and was interred along with 2 male compatriots and no less than 19 females aged between 10 and 30.

Among the other pyramids which make up this huge complex are: **Huaca El Mirador, Huaca Las Estacas, Huaca Pintada** and **Huaca de las Balsas** which is thought to have housed people of elevated status such as priests.

Excavations at the site, led by Norwegian explorer-archaeologist, Thor Heyerdahl of *Kon-Tiki* fame, are quickly challenging many conventional views of ancient Peruvian culture. Some suspect that it will prove to be a civilization centre greater than Chan Chán. There is also evidence, including art and remains of navigation gear, that the people of Túcume were intrepid seafarers. A 10-year excavation project led by Thor Heyerdahl is under way.

**A site museum** was opened in 1992, constructed of adobe and mezquite logs in prehispanic style, entrance US$1. Fatima Huaman Vera is a good English-speaking guide US$2.50. The collections show architectural reconstructions, photographs and drawings, highlighting recent finds, which include weaving paraphernalia, a ceremonial oar and a fabulous bas relief and mural depicting maritime scenes suggesting former sea trade and interregional contact. It was expanded in 1994. Meals and drinks are available on request.

## A tale of demons and fish

Just one of the many legends that abound in this part of Northern Peru pertains to the hill which dominates the pyramids at Túcume and the precise origin of its name. The hill is known locally as 'El Purgatorio' (purgatory), or more commonly, Cerro La Raya.

The former name derives from the conquering Spaniards' attempts to convert the indigenous people to the Christian faith. The Spanish invaders encountered fierce local resistance to their new religion and came up with the idea of convincing the people of Túcume that the hill was, in fact, purgatory. They told the locals that there lived on the hill a demon who would punish anyone not accepting the Roman Catholic faith.

In order to lend some credence to this tale, a group of Spaniards set out one dark, moonless night and built a huge bonfire at the foot of 'El Purgatorio', giving it the appearance of an erupting volcano and frightening the townsfolk half to death. Thus they came to accept the Spaniards' assertion that any unbelievers or sinners would be thrown alive into the flames of this diabolical fire.

As if that wasn't enough to terrify the local populace, the Spanish also concocted the fiendish tale of 'El Carretón', or waggon. This was an enormous waggon pulled by four great horses which supposedly would speed forth from the bowels of 'El Purgatorio' on the darkest of nights. Driven by a dandily-dressed demon boss, and carrying his equally dandy demon buddies, this hellish vehicle careered round the town of Túcume making a fearsome racket. Any poor unbelievers or sinners unfortunate enough to be found wandering the streets would immediately be carted off and thrown into the flames of purgatory.

The alternative name of Cerro La Raya refers to the local legend of a Manta Ray that lived in a nearby lake. The local children constantly tormented the fish by throwing stones at it, so, to escape this torment, the poor creature decided to move to the hill and become part of it. The lake then disappeared and ever since, the hill has been enchanted.

### The town of Túcume

This typical N coast town is a 10-15 mins walk from the site. On the Plaza is the interesting **San Pedro Church**, a mixture of baroque, churrigueresque and neo-classical styles. There are no hotels in town but *Casa Kon-Tiki*, a refuge built by Thor Heyedahl on Calle Augusto B Leguía, was due to open in 1996. The surrounding countryside is pleasant for walks and swimming in the river.

The present site of the town is not the original one but dates from 1720. Local legend has it that the town was moved following an apparition of the Virgin. The icon of the Virgin mysteriously disappeared but was later seen on top of Cerro Cueto, having her long hair combed by a native girl while gazing over pasture lands below. This was taken as a sign to relocate the church and the rest of the town with it.

Túcume celebrates the **Fiesta de la Purísima Concepción**, the town's Patron Saint, 8 days prior to Carnival in Feb, and also in September. This is the most important festival, with music, dancing, fireworks, cockfights, sports events and, of course, much eating and drinking. During the Dance of the Devils. The participants wear horned masks, forked tails and long capes and are said to represent the diabolical drunken Spanish priests from colonial times. It also features a song and dance dedicated to the native girl who was seen combing the Virgin's hair.

• **Transport** Kombi buses go from Chiclayo, Manuel Pardo block 6, US$1.50 pp, 1 hr; 30 mins walk from the town to the ruins. Kombi Tucumé-Brüning Museum, US$0.50, 30 mins.

## APURLEC

60 km N of Chiclayo, beside the old Panamericana, is a stone wall surrounding a hill and pyramids dating from the Tiahuanaco period, as well as irrigation canals and reservoirs. The system was enlarged during Mochica, Chimú and Inca occupation of the site.

• **Access** To get there from Chiclayo, take bus from Pedro Ruiz block 5 (bus continues to Motupe).

## CHICLAYO TO CAJAMARCA

The Chiclayo–Chota bus passes through Chongoyape to Cochabamba (no hotels, not a friendly place, police searches for drugs), 34 km before Chota, from where you can hitch in a truck to Cutervo.

## CUTERVO

(*Pop* 6,000; *Alt* 2,800m); a very friendly town which tourists rarely visit – don't be surprised if the local TV or radio station wants an interview. Cattle and vegetables are raised here in green meadows. There is a local market on Thur and Sun.

• **Accommodation** **G** pp *Hospedaje Marlen Central*, Jr 22 de Octubre, just off Plaza, clean, friendly, cold water in mornings; *San Juan* on plaza, cheap but has bugs; nicer one by Cine San Juan, several more.

• **Places to eat** *Salón Azul*, very good; *La Casita*, Jr Lima 717, near the Plaza, good, friendly, helpful with local information.

• **Transport** Many trucks to Cutervo, Tues-Sat, return Mon-Fri, bus from Chiclayo Sat, returns Sun 2000.

## CHOTA

This attractive town has a fine Sun market where weavings are cheaper than in Cajamarca. Cheap, friendly shops at 27 de Noviembre 144 and 246.

• **Accommodation & places to eat** There are several hotels. **F** *Plaza*, is the best, clean; also *Continental*, which is poor. *Restaurant San Juan* is good.

• **Transport** Daily bus to Chiclayo am, 12-14 hrs; bus to Cajamarca daily 1500 and 2000.

## BAMBAMARCA

Occasionally buses, and many trucks, run on to Bambamarca, which has an attractive Sun morning market.

• **Accommodation & places to eat** *Hotel Bolívar*, is the best; **G** *Hotel Velásquez*; *Hotel Perú*, has bugs. *Restaurant Pollos a la Brasa* is very good.

• **Transport** Truck from Chota US$1. Empresa Díaz bus to Cajamarca daily at 0600, 9 hrs, frequent stops, US$4; there is a 2 hrs stop in Bambamarca for the market; some days also with Peregrino.

**ROUTES** The road continues to **Hualgayoc**, a beautifully situated, quaint old mining town, and Cajamarca. It is a very interesting and beautiful journey, but few buses. The stretch from Bambamarca, about 90 km, to Cajamarca is exhilarating. The road climbs to about 4,000m through the Andean highlands with beautiful scenery of a *puna* landscape, nearly uninhabited, no fuel supply; it takes about 6 hrs in a 4WD car. The whole trip between Chongoyape and Cajamarca takes about 2 days in a car, the road is particularly bad between Chongoyape and Chota.

## NORTH OF CHICLAYO

### OLMOS

On the old Pan-American Highway 885 km from Lima, Olmos is a tranquil place. During the last week of June the Festival de Limón is celebrated here.

• **Accommodation** G *Hospedaje San Martín*, very dirty, bargain hard; *Hotel Remanso*, is in a restored farmstead, good food, friendly, but not cheap.

**ROUTES** At Olmos, a poor road (being improved) runs E over the Porculla Pass for Jaén and Bagua. The old Pan-American Highway continues from Olmos to Cruz de Caña and Piura. At Lambayeque the new Pan-American Highway, which is in good condition, branches off the old road and drives 190 km straight across the Sechura Desert to Piura. There are several restaurants between Km 845 and 848, one at the junction to Bayovar, where you can sleep, and another midway between Mórrope and Piura. There is also a coast road, narrow and scenic, between Lambayeque and Sechura via Bayovar.

## THE SECHURA DESERT

This large area of shifting sands separates the oases of Chiclayo and Piura. Water for irrigation comes from the Chira and Piura rivers, and from the Olmos and Tinajones irrigation projects which bring water from the Amazon watershed by means of tunnels (one over 16 km long) through the Andes to the Pacific coast. They will eventually water some 400,000 ha of desert land.

The northern river – the Chira – has usually a superabundance of water: along its irrigated banks large crops of Tangüis cotton are grown. A dam has been built at Poechos on the Chira to divert water to the Piura valley. In its upper course the Piura – whose flow is far less dependable – is mostly used to grow subsistence food crops, but around Piura, when there is enough water, the hardy long-staple Pima cotton is planted.

Cotton has been grown mainly on medium-sized properties, which have changed hands frequently in recent years and which now form communal or co-operative farms, sponsored by the agrarian reform programme. Worth seeing as an example of a fine old plantation is the former Hacienda Sojo (near Sullana) in the lower Chira valley. In 1983 the Niño current brought heavy rains and turned the Sechura desert into an inland sea. Damage to crops and infrastructure was around US$1bn.

**NB** Solo cyclists should not cross the Sechura Desert as muggings have been known to occur. Take the safer, inland route. In the desert, restaurants are every 30-40 km, but no hotels. Do not camp out if possible. Heading S, strong headwinds may make camping unavoidable. Do not attempt this alone.

## PIURA

A proud and historic city, 264 km from Chiclayo (*Pop* 324,500; *Phone code* 074) was founded in 1532, 3 years before Lima, by the *conquistadores* left behind by Pizarro. There are two well kept parks, Cortés and Pizarro (with a statue of the *conquistador*), and public gardens. Old buildings are kept in repair and new buildings blend with the Spanish style of the old city. Four bridges cross the Río Piura to Castilla, the oldest from C Huancavelica, for pedestrians, others from C Sánchez Cerro, from C Bolognesi, and the newest from Av Panamericana Norte, at N end of town.

The winter climate, May-Sept, is very pleasant although nights can be cold and the wind piercing; Dec to Mar is very hot.

### PLACES OF INTEREST

Standing on the **Plaza de Armas** is the **cathedral**, with gold covered altar and paintings by Ignacio Merino. A few blocks away is the **San Francisco** church, where the city's independence from Spain was declared on 4 January 1821,

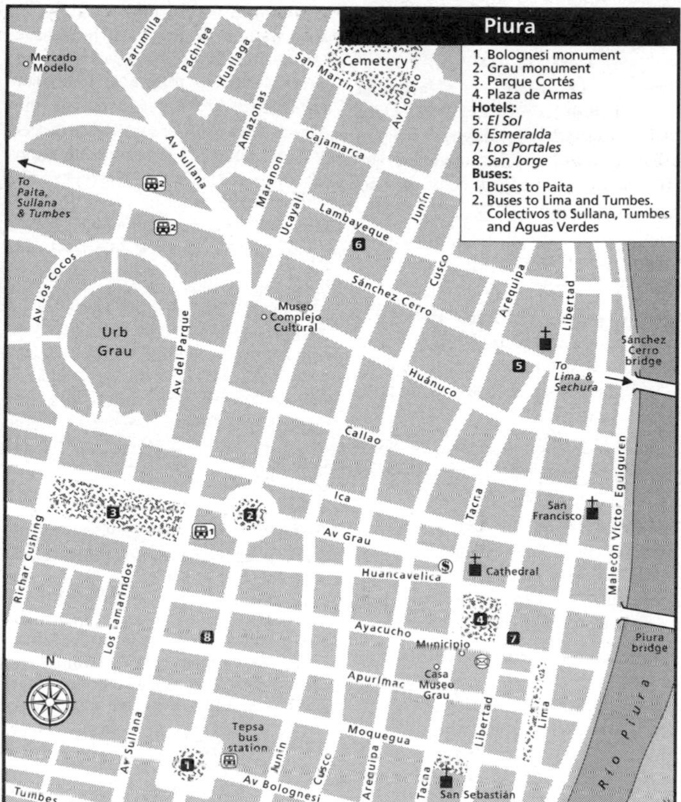


nearly 8 months before Lima.

The colonial church of **Las Mercedes** has ornately carved balconies, 3-tiered archway, hand-hewn supports and massive furnishings. **San Sebastián,** on Tacna y Moquegua, is also worth seeing. The birthplace of Admiral Miguel Grau, hero of the War of the Pacific with Chile, is **Casa Museo Grau**, on Jr Tacna 662, opposite the Centro Cívico. It has been opened as a museum and contains a model of the *Huáscar*, the largest Peruvian warship in the War of the Pacific, which was built in Britain.

Interesting local craftwork is sold at the **Mercado Modelo**. **Museo Complejo Cultural**, with archaeological and art sections, is open on Sullana, near Huánuco, and though small it is very interesting.

## EXCURSIONS

### Catacaos

12 km to the SW of Piura, the village is famous for its *chicha* (maize beer, be careful, quality not always reliable), *picanterías* (local restaurants, some with music, *La Casa de Tales*, recommended), tooled leather, gold and silver filigree jewellery, wooden articles, straw hats (pricey) and

splendid celebrations in Holy Week. Bargain when shopping for crafts as prices are known to be very inflated.

Two km S of Catacaos is the **Narihualá** archaeological site. It includes a large adobe pyramid, 40m high, from the Tallán culture which populated the Chira and Piura valleys before it was conquered by the Chimús.

• **Transport** Colectivos leave from Plaza Pizarro, US$0.50, bus US$0.35.

Also from Piura, one can visit the coastal town of **Sechura**. The fine 17th-century cathedral has a splendid W front which has been under renovation for a long time and is normally closed to the public.

• **Accommodation** *Hospedaje de Dios* is usually full of workmen from the oil terminal at Bayovar – forbidden to visitors.

## Coastal villages

**San Pedro** has a huge lagoon with edible crabs, flamingoes and a superb beach and a fierce sun. Best visited in the week. There are no hotels or facilities whatsoever.

• **Transport** Take bus or colectivo to the right fork past Vice, about 10 km from Sechura then hitch.

**Yacila** is a picturesque fishing village with a few fish restaurants and a church on the beach. Nearby are La Tortuga, Parachique, Matacaballo (which is the best beach of these four places), Chullachay (the nearest beach to Sechura), Los Puertos and Angostura. Balsa boats are common on the coast.

• **Accommodation & transport** At Los Cangrejos beach nearby you can rent an apartment from Sr Belcázar, but there is little food available. A motel opens in summer, but no facilities in winter. Yacila is reached also by camioneta for Paita.

## LOCAL INFORMATION

### ● Accommodation

**A1** *Los Portales*, Libertad 875, Plaza de Armas, T 322952, F 325920, ex-government hotel being refurbished, a/c, some rooms with hot water, pleasant terrace and patio, nice pool, the city's social centre.

**A3** *El Angolo*, Fortunato Chirichigno 661, Urb San Eduardo, T/F 326461, suites and bungalows, hot water, a/c, pool, cable TV, restaurant, airport pickup service.

**B** *Perú*, Arequipa 476, T 333421, F 331530, with bath, a/c, **C** with fan, clean, safe, friendly, laundry service, cold water, modern small rooms, restaurant.

**C** *El Sol*, Sánchez Cerro 411, T 324461, F 326307, bath, hot water, small pool, snack bar, parking, accepts dollars cash or TCs but won't change them; **C** *Esmeralda*, Loreto 235, T/F 327109, with bath, hot water, fan, clean, comfortable, good, restaurant; **C** *Miraflores*, Cayetano Heredia 503 y Av Guardia Civil, Castilla, T 327236, a/c, hot water, **E** with fan, comfortable, family run; **C** *Tangarará*, Arequipa 691, esq Ica, T 326450, F 328322, central location, with bath, hot water, fan, clean but expensive; **C** *Vicus*, Av Guardia Civil B-3, in Castilla across river on Sánchez Cerro bridge, T 322541, F 325687, with bath, hot water, fan, clean, quiet, parking.

**D** *Bolognesi*, Bolognesi 427, T 324072, with bath, no fan, OK but ageing; **D** *Cocos Inn*, José Olaya 197, Castilla, T 329004, inc breakfast, with bath, cheaper with cold water, converted colonial home in quiet residential area, terrace, clean, friendly; **D** *El Almirante*, Ica 860, T/F 335239, with bath, fan, clean, modern, owner is knowledgeable about the Ayabaca area (see page 215); **D** *San Jorge*, Jr Loreto 960, T 327514, F 322928, with bath and fan, hot water, clean; **D** *Turismo*, Huánuco 526, T 325950, with bath, fan, pleasant, front rooms noisy.

**E** *Hostal Aruba*, on Junín esq Huancavelica, opposite *Hotel Lalo*, small rooms but clean and comfortable, fan on request, very friendly, rec; **E** *California*, Jr Junín 835, T 328789, shared bath, own water-tank, mosquito netting on windows, roof terrace, clean, pleasant, rec; **E** *Continental*, Jr Junín 924, T 334531, some rooms with bath, clean, comfortable; **E** *Lalo*, Junín 838, T 325798, shared bath, cold water, very basic, **F** with double bed, washing facilities, friendly; **E** *Oriental*, Callao 446, T 328891, cheaper without bath and fan, clean, good value but very noisy, TV in reception; **E** *Terraza*, Av Loreto 530, 2 blocks from Grau monument, with bath, cheaper without, small rooms, basic, shabby, poor beds.

**F** *Hostal Ica*, Ica cuadra 7, dirty, very basic,

cheap. It is extremely difficult to find a room in the last week of July because of Independence festivities. The city suffers from water shortages.

**● Places to eat**

***Carburmer***, Apurimac 343 in Centro Comercial, very good but not cheap; ***El Puente Viejo***, Huancavélica 167, half a block from the rebuilt bridge, very good seafood (from owners' private beds offshore at Paita), rec; ***Gran Prix***, Loreto 395, good food, reasonable prices. Several good restaurants on Ayacucho between Cuzco and Arequipa, all popular, some are discos at night: ***Las Tradiciones***, No 579, regional specialities, nice atmosphere, also an art gallery; ***Bar Román***, No 580, excellent set meal for US$1.75, highly rec; ***La Cabaña***, No 598, esq Cuzco, serves pizzas and other good Italian food, not cheap; ***Ferny's***, next to *Hotel San Jorge*, good food, clean. ***Café Concierto***, Cuzco 933, pleasant, popular, not cheap; ***Chifa Canton***, Libertad 377, excellent, especially won ton soup and special rice, US$2.50 per dish, always busy; ***Chifa Oriental***, on Huancavelica, 1 block W of Plaza, cheap and good; ***Snack Bar***, Callao 536, good fruit juices; ***Chispita***, Sánchez Cerro 210, nr bridge, good set meal, à la carte, fruit juices. Good little cheap restaurants on Jr Junín: ***Chalán del Norte*** at 722, ***Bianca*** at 732, ***El Capri*** at 715. A good vegetarian restaurant is ***Ganímedes***, Sánchez Cerro y Lima, very popular set lunch, à la carte is slow but well worth it, try the excellent yoghurt and fruit. Two good places for sweets and ice-cream are: ***El Chalán***, Tacna 520 on Plaza de Armas; and ***D'Paull***, Lima 541.

**Local specialities**: Piura's special dishes include *Majado de Yuca*, manioc root with pork; *Seco de Chavelo*, beef and plantain stew; and *Carne Seca*, sun-dried meat. Its best- known sweet is the delicious *natilla*, made mostly of goats milk and molasses. Its local drink is *pipa fría*, chilled coconut juice drunk from the nut with a straw.

**● Airline offices**

**Americana**, Grau 116, T 328064, **Faucett**, Huancavélica 268, T 332165; **Aero Continente**, Grau 140, T 328223; **Aeroperú**, Libertad 951, T 328297.

**● Banks & money changers**

**Banco de Crédito**, Grau y Tacna, cash and TCs (no commission), TCs changed am only; **Banco Continental**, Plaza de Armas, changes TCs with commission. **Banco Latino**, cash only. *Casa de cambio* at Edif Plaza Fuerte, Arequipa cuadra 6; street changers on Grau and Arequipa.

**● Embassies & consulates**

**Honorary British Consul**, Casilla 193, T 325693, Mr Henry Stewart. **Honorary German Consul**, Jutta Moritz de Irazola, Las Amapolas K6, Urb Miraflores, Casilla 76, T 332920, F 320310.

**● Entertainment**

Many of the nightspots are concentrated on Ayacucho. In addition to those which are also restaurants (see above) are: *Bohemio's*, at 588; *Bloom Moon*, at 522; and *Café R & B Zelada*, at 562. *Discoteca La Cascada* is at *Hotel El Angolo*.

**● Post & telecommunications**

**Post Office**: on the corner of Libertad and Ayacucho on Plaza de Armas is not too helpful, perhaps better going to *Hotel Los Portales*.

**Telecommunications**: Loreto 259, national and international phone and fax; also at Ovalo Grau 483.

**● Shopping**

Fuji film at Grau 202; Kodak at Huancavélica 199 and 258. Good delicatessens around Plaza de Armas, selling local sweets. The *natilla* factory on Sánchez Cerro, Miraflores, 4 blocks from bridge, sells *natilla* and *algarrobina* syrup. Market on Sánchez Cerro, good for fruit. Chulucanas pottery can be bought at two shops on Libertad and from Milagros García de Linares, who lives in Urbanización Santa Inés, T 327322.

**● Laundry**

***Lavandería Liz-to***, Tacna 785, charges by weight.

**● Tour companies & travel agents**

There are several travel agents around the Plaza. Particularly helpful is ***Piura Tours***, C Ayacucho 585, T 328873, the manager Mario speaks very good English. He will arrange transport to Tumbes with the driver delivering *El Tiempo* newspapers who picks you up from your hotel around 0300 and drops you off where the colectivos leave for the border; costs only slightly more than the bus (US$9 instead of US$5) but safe and easy. Also helpful is ***Amauta Tours***, Apurimac 580, T 322976, F 322277.

**● Tourist offices**

Information at the Ministerio de Industria y

Turismo, Gobierno Regional, Urb San Eduardo, at N end of town, helpful when there are problems. Touring y Automóvil Club del Perú, Sánchez Cerro 1237, have only outdated maps.

### ● Transport

**Local Car rental** Daily rates range between US$40 for a small car and US$75 for a 4WD; book ahead as availability is limited. **Piura Rent-a-car**, Sánchez Cerro 425, T 325510, F 324658; **Sun Rent-a-car**, Arequipa 504, T/F 325456; **S y S Rent-a-car**, Libertad 777, T/F 326773. **Taxis** Radio Taxis, T 324509/324630.

**Air** To Lima daily with Faucett, AeroPerú, Aero Continente and Americana, 1½ hrs, US$94. To Chiclayo with Faucett and Aero Continente, US$15, 30 mins. To Trujillo, US$35 with Americana, US$30 with Faucett and AeroPerú, 30 mins. To Talara, daily flights with Faucett, 30 mins, US$15. To Guayaquil, Mon and Thur, with AeroPerú, US$100. Taxi to airport, US$1.50. For local private flights, contact pilot Félix Pérez, Corpac 212, Castilla Piura, T 324979, or through Aerotour SA, Lima, T 441-5884.

**Buses** Most companies are on Av Sánchez Cerro, blocks 11 and 12 (unless stated otherwise those listed below are found here). To **Lima**, 1,038 km, 14-16 hrs, US$13, on the Panamericana Norte; most buses stop at the major cities on route (see Lima, **Bus Companies** with routes to the N). In Piura, Civa is at Bolognesi y Av Sullana, T 328093. To **Chiclayo**, 190 km, 3 hrs, US$3.50, several buses daily; similarly to **Trujillo**, 7 hrs, 487 km, US$6. To **Tumbes**, 282 km, 5 hrs, US$5.25, several buses daily, eg Cruz del Sur (on Bolognesi)and El Dorado; colectivos, US$8. Bus to **Aguas Verdes** US$5.50 leaving 2300 arriving 0500. To **Sullana**, 38 km, 30 mins, frequent buses, US$0.50, and colectivos, US$1, from Roma y Sánchez Cerro and Loreto y Sánchez Cerro; to **La Tina** for Ecuadorean frontier, a further 122 km, 2-3 hrs, US$3; best to take an early bus to Sullana (start at 0630, every 20 mins), then a colectivo. To **Talara**, US$1.75, 2 hrs, with Talara Express and EPPO. To Máncora, US$3.50, 3 hrs, with EPPO and El Dorado. There are no direct buses to Bagua, Jaén or Chachapoyas; only from Chiclayo.

## EAST FROM PIURA

**Chulucanas**, 50 km NE of Piura and 10 km off the old Pan-American Highway (minibus US$1.50), is the centre of the lemon and orange growing area and of

### The potters of Chulucanas

In the small town of Chulucanas an ancient pottery technique has been discovered and revived in the last 30 years. The local potters formerly produced only large, utilitarian terracotta pots, until the 1960s when graverobbers brought to light examples of pottery from the Vicus and Tallane cultures dating from the second half of the first millenium BC.

A group of Quechua pottery specialists calling themselves *Sañoc Cayamoc* researched and experimented with forms and techniques based on the precolumbian finds. In particular they experimented with the 'negative painting' technique used by the Vicus potters.

In this process two firings are required, the first one after painting with an oxide. The fired pot is painted in parts with a solution of clay and water, then fired a second time, using mango leaves to blacken it with smoke. The painted areas are finally wiped clear, exposing the oxide colour which contrasts with the black of the rest of the pot. This produces a very subtle and unusual effect.

At first, the potters imitated the forms of the Vicus pieces but gradually they began to develop a freer expression using stylized figures from their own environment. The most popular form is the *Chichera*, a fat lady who makes and sells chicha.

The most creative potters now produce unique and highly-prized pieces, which are signed and then sold in galleries and shops in Lima and abroad. What began as a practical manufacturing industry has thus been transformed into an art form.

local pottery production. Excellent ceramics can be bought at a shop on the Plaza and three others are within one block. A pottery school is 5 km away, but inaccessible in the rainy season.

• **Accommodation & places to eat** **F** *Hotel Ica*, Ica 636; *Restaurant Cajamarquino*, Ayacucho 530, good.

The paved road continues from Chulucanas SE to Morropán from where a dirt road goes to **Canchaque**, a delightfully-situated small centre for coffee, sugar-cane and fruit production.

• **Accommodation** **F** *Hostal Don Félix*, central plaza, just tolerable; otherwise simple clean accommodation for about US$2 on right hand side of church.

• **Transport** Buses from Piura on Sánchez Cerro at 1200, 6 hrs, US$3; often cancelled during rainy season.

## HUANCABAMBA

The difficult and tiring road, impossible for ordinary vehicles in the wet season, continues over a pass in the Andes of more than 3,000m for 69 km to Huancabamba.

This very pretty town in a wonderful setting has three claims to fame. First, the predominance of European features, due to the fact that it was an important Spanish settlement in colonial times. Second, it is called 'the walking town, *la ciudad que camina*', as it is built on irregularly slipping strata which cause much subsidence. Evidence for this includes the fall of the bridge over the Río Huancabamba. Third, and by far the most remarkable element, it is the base for reaching **Las Guaringas**, a series of lakes at about 4,000m. Around here live the most famous witchdoctors of Peru, to whom sick people flock from all over the country and abroad.

Buses to the lakes leave at 0400 from the main Plaza. Horses to the lakes can be hired, US$5. Also trips to the village of San Antonio below Lago Carmen, and the village of Salalá below Lago Shumbe (**G** *Hotel San José*, very basic, take own food). Ignacio León, who owns a *bodega* opposite *El Dorado* runs an early pick-up service to outlying villages and takes trips at negotiable prices.

Local specialities include *rompope*, a rich and strong drink made of egg, spices and *cañazo* (sugar-cane spirit), roast *cuy* (guinea-pig) and local cheeses.

• **Accommodation** **F** *Hotel El Dorado*, good, clean, informative owner, with restaurant, on the main Plaza. There are also a couple of others on the Plaza.

• **Transport** A bus from Piura to Canchaque and Huancabamba leaves daily at 0900 and 1000, at least 10 hrs (and returns from Huancabamba 0700 and 1000), US$9, from the Civa office, Av Ramón Castilla 196 (buy ticket early on day before travelling). Truck US$11.50. If driving, take the Pan-American Highway S of Piura for 66 km where there is a signpost to Huancabamba.

• **Warning** In Nov 1995 Huancabamba remained a focus of terrorist activity; make local enquiries before travelling to the area.

## AYABACA

225 km NE of Piura in the highlands is the pleasant town of Ayabaca at 2,850m. This is the access point for the **Aypate** archaeological site and the **Samanga** hieroglyphics. It is also the home of **El Señor Cautivo de Aybaca**. Many devotees make pilgrimages to his shrine, especially on Oct 12.

• **Accommodation & transport** There are several *hostales* in town. Buses from Piura in am, starting at 0800, from Mercado Modelo, 6 hrs, US$7.

## PAITA

The port for the area, 50 km from Piura, **Paita** (*Pop* 51,500) exports cotton, cotton seed, wool and flax. Built on a small beach, flanked on three sides by a towering, sandy bluff, it is connected with Piura and Sullana by paved highways.

It is a very old fishing port. Several colonial buildings survive, but they are in poor condition. Bolívar's mistress,

Manuela Sáenz, lived the last 24 years of her life in Paita, after being exiled from Quito. She supported herself until her death in 1856 by weaving and embroidering and making candy after refusing the fortune left her by her husband. The house may be visited if you ask the people living in it, but there's not much to see. Fishing, fishmeal and whaling (at Tierra Colorada, 6½ km S of Paita) are prosperous industries.

### Excursions

On a bluff looming over Paita is a small colonial fortress built to repel pirates. Paita was a port of call for Spanish shipping en route from Lima to Panama and Mexico. It was a frequent target for attack, from Drake (1579) to Anson (1741). 25 km up the coast is **Colán**, reached by driving down a large, sandy bluff (no public transport). Near the base is a striking and lonely church over 300 years old, but in very poor condition. There is a good beach, but Colán is rather derelict since the agrarian reform. It used to be the favourite resort of the estate-owners.

### Local information

#### ● Accommodation

**D** *Miramar*, Malecón J Chávez 418, opposite Credicoop Paita, T 611083, a filthy old wooden mansion on seafront. The best is **E** *Las Brisas*, Av Ugarte, with bath but scant cold water, safe. Also *El Mundo*, on 300 block of Bolívar, not bad but short-stay; *Pacífico*, Plaza de Armas 140, T 611013. There are others but none is recommendable and mostly full anyway.

#### ● Places to eat

*El Mundo*, Jr Junín, quite good; much better is the restaurant on 2nd floor of Club Liberal building, Jorge Chávez 161, good fish, seafood and crêpes, good value; others on Plaza de Armas.

#### ● Banks & money changers

**Credicoop Paita**, Jr Junín 380 for dollars cash; helpful guard.

#### ● Transport

From Piura, colectivos and buses; TUPPSA, Sullana 527, Parque Cortez, every hour, 45 mins, US$0.90.

## SULLANA

**Sullana** (*Pop* 154,800), 39 km N of Piura, is built on a bluff over the fertile Chira valley and is a busy, modern place. Av José de Lama, once a dusty, linear market, has a green, shady park with benches along the centre. Many of the bus companies have their offices along this avenue. San Martín is the main commercial street. Parks and monuments were added in 1994/5, which have greatly improved the city's appearance. At the entrance, on the Pan-American Highway is an interesting mosaic statue of an iguana. There are lookouts over the Chira valley at Plaza Bolognesi and by the arches near the Plaza de Armas. The local fiesta and agricultural fair is *Reyes*, held on 5-29 January.

**NB** Although the city is safer than it once was, caution should still be exercised by the market and where colectivos leave for the Ecuadorean border.

### Local information

#### ● Accommodation

**A3** *Hostal La Siesta*, Av Panamericana 400, T/F 502264, at entrance to town, hot water, fan, cable TV, B with cold water, pool, restaurant, laundry.

**D** *Hostal Aypate*, Av José de Lama 112, T 502013, with bath, hot water, fan, clean, comfortable; **D** *Hostal Turicarami*, San Martín 814, T 502899, with bath, fan, some rooms have hot water, clean, **E** without bath or fan.

**E** *Hostal Fernando*, Grau 703, T 500727, with bath, fan, TV, clean, friendly; **E** *Hostal Lion's Palace*, Grau 1030, T 502587, with bath, fan, patio, pleasant , quiet; **E** *Hostal San Miguel*, C J Farfán 204, T 500679, cheaper without bath, basic, helpful, good showers, staff will spray rooms against mosquitoes, cafeteria.

**F** *Hostal Príncipe*, Espinal 588, clean and friendly.

**G** pp *Buenos Aires*, Av Buenos Aires, 15 mins SE from city centre in an unsafe neighbourhood, friendly, dirty bathrooms.

#### ● Places to eat

*El Parque*, E Palacios 173, corner San Martín,

good value set meal, expensive à la carte, good quality and service, rec; ***Chifa Canton***, Farfán 248, good cheap food, open evenings only; ***Due Torri***, E Palacios 122, Italian and regional, popular with locals; ***Pollería Ibañez***, J de Lama 350, grilled meats and chicken. There are several other restaurants nearby.

## ● Banks & money changers

**Banco de Crédito**, San Martín 685, will change cash and TCs. *Casas de cambio* and street changers on San Martín by Tarapacá.

## ● Post & telecommunications

**Post Office**: at Farfán 326.

**Telecommunications**: telephone and fax at Miró Quesada 213.

## ● Useful addresses

**Immigration**: Grau 939.

## ● Travel agents

**Pesa Tours**, Espinar 301 y Tarapacá, T/F 502237, for airline tickets (flights from Piura) and information, helpful and friendly.

## ● Transport

**Taxis** Radio Taxis, T 502210/504354.

**Buses** To **Tumbes**, 244 km, 4-5 hrs US$5, several buses daily. **Piura**, 38 km, 30 mins, US$0.50, frequent buses, colectivos, US$1, taxi US$2 (if you have time, it is worth continuing to Piura rather than staying in Sullana); **Chiclayo** and **Trujillo** see under Piura. To **Lima**, 1,076 km, 14-16 hrs, US$9-18, several buses daily, most coming from Tumbes or Talara, luxury overnight US$18, Cruz del Sur, Ugarte 1019; Continental (Ormeño), Tarapacá 1007. Colectivos to Paita, Colán and Esmeralda leave from the main road parallel to the market; buses to Máncora and Talara (Empresa EPPO) from market area.

## NORTH TO ECUADOR

At Sullana the Pan-American Highway forks. To the E it crosses the Peru-Ecuador frontier at La Tina and continues via Macará to Loja and Cuenca. The road is very scenic and is paved for 120 km as far as Suyo. Work on the remaining 16 km to the border was expected to be finished in 1996. The more frequently used route to the border is the coastal road which goes from Sullana NW towards the Talara oilfields and then follows the coastline to Máncora and Tumbes.

### FRONTIER AT LA TINA-MACARA

**● Peruvian immigration**

At the border the officials may try to get extra payments from those entering Peru, stand your ground if possible. The Peruvian immigration officer can be found at the nearby *cevichería* if not at his desk. The border is reported open 0800-1800 but it may close for lunch, so it is better to cross in the morning.

**● Accommodation**

There is one basic hotel in Suyo and two in Las Lomas (75 km from Sullana).

**● Transport to border**

Minivans leave from Sullana to the international bridge from Mercadillo Bellavista, Av Buenos Aires y Calle 4, which is a crowded market area. They leave between 0400 and 1300 when full, US$3 pp, 2 hrs. The Buenos Aires area is not safe, so it's best to take a taxi or moto-taxi to and from here. To get to Macará, walk over the bridge and take one of the pick-ups which run from the border. A bus leaves the Ecuadorean side at 1300 for Loja, so you can go from Sullana to Loja in 1 day.

**● Into Ecuador**

It is a 2½ km taxi ride or walk from the border to **Macará**, a dusty town in a rice-growing area (*Pop* 14,296; *Alt* 600m). There are hotels and restaurants in town and money can be changed on the street or in the market (not at the bank). The fare in a pick-up from the bridge to Macará is US$0.50-2, beware of overcharging. From Macará there are frequent buses to Loja, 6-8 hrs, US$3.50.

## TALARA

135 km from Piura and 1,177 km from Lima, is Talara (*Pop* 44,500), the main centre of the coastal oil area, with a State-owned 60,000 barrel-a-day oil refinery and a fertilizer plant. Set in a desert oasis, the city is a triumph over formidable natural difficulties, but was badly damaged in the 1983 floods and has many shanty districts. Water is piped 40 km from the Río Chira. Talara is reached via a 5 km side road E off the Pan-American Highway. La Peña beach, 2 km away, is still unspoilt.

### Excursions

Paved highways connect the town with the Negritos, Lagunitos, La Brea and other oilfields. Of historical interest are the old tarpits at La Brea, 21 km inland from Punta Pariñas, S of Talara, and near the foot of the Amotape mountains. Here the Spaniards boiled the tar to get pitch for caulking their ships. Punta Pariñas itself is the westernmost point of South America.

### Local information

**● Accommodation**

**NB** All hotels in Talara have problems with water supply.

**A3** ***Pacífico***, Av Aviación y Arica, T/F (074) 381719, most luxurious, suites, hot water, pool, restaurant, bar, parking, pay in dollars. Other top grade hotels are: ***Suites Punta Esmeralda***, Av Aviación s/n, bungalows, swimming pool; ***Hostal Charito***, Av B 143, T 381600.

**D** ***Hostal César***, Av Salaverry 9, T 382364, T/F 381591, with bath, clean, rather shabby carpets, fan, safe, snack bar; **D** ***Residencial Grau***, Av Grau 77, T 382841, nr main plaza, clean, friendly, possible to park one motor bike, owner changes dollars.

**E** ***Hostal Talara***, Av del Ejército 217, T 382186, clean and comfortable.

Other cheap hotels include: ***Hostal El Sol***, Av G 89, T 380823; ***Hostal Modelo***, Centro Comercial La Florida, T 381934; ***Hostal JJ***, El Parque 33, T 382784.

**● Places to eat**

There are many cheap restaurants on the main plaza. The better restaurants can be found in the main hotels. ***Bar Peña Cinthia***, Parque 14-10; ***Rinconcito Chimbotano***,

Parque 78-12; ***Pierre***, Parque 5-17; ***La Paquita***, Av B 89; ***Pichicho's***, Centro Cívico 131, grilled food; ***Centro Bar***, at the market; ***Snack Larco***, Esplanada Cine Grau 3.

● **Transport**

**Air** Airport with daily flights by Faucett to Lima, 1½ hrs, US$79; to Piura, daily with Faucett US$15; Tumbes twice a week.

**Buses** To **Tumbes**, 171 km, 3 hrs, US$3.50, most coming from Piura and most stop at major towns going N; several daily. To **El Alto** (Cabo Blanco), 32 km, 30 mins, US$0.75, continuing to Máncora, 28 km, 30 mins, US$0.75 to **Piura**, 111 km, 2 hrs, US$1.75. To **Lima**, US$15.

## BEACHES NORTH OF TALARA

### CABO BLANCO

32 km N of Talara, is the small port of Cabo Blanco, famous for its excellent sea-fishing and surfing. The scenery has, unfortunately, been spoilt by numerous oil installations. The turn-off from the Pan-American Highway is at the town of **El Alto**, where many oil workers are housed. There are several basic hotels here. Camping is permitted free of charge at Cabo Blanco, on the beach or by the Fishing Club overlooking the sea, at least in the off-season, June-Dec. The film of Hemingway's *The Old Man and the Sea* was shot here.

**The Marlin** grew scarce in the late 1960s due to commercial fishing and to climatologic and maritime factors but in the last few years the Marlin have returned. The old Fishing Club, built in the 1950s, has been remodelled in the shape of the *Fishing Club Lodge Hotel*. A launch also provides all the necessary facilities for deep-sea fishing. Now, would-be Ernest Hemingways can return to Cabo Blanco in search of their dream catch.

● **Accommodation B** *Fishing Club Lodge*, clean, attractive, rec, restaurant, pool, watersports, likely to be full in New Year period; cheaper is **D** pp *El Merlín*, good value, huge rooms, situated right on the beach, good restaurant.

**Los Organos**, another oil workers' town, is 15 km N of El Alto, at Km 1152 on the Pan-American Highway.

● **Accommodation** *Hotel Club Náutilus*, at the N end of town.

Past **Las Arenas** resort, 4 km S of Máncora, the road is impassable due to the damage wreaked by the 1983 floods. The beach is virgin, with armies of small crabs and abundant bird life, including frigates and masked and brown pelicans.

### MANCORA

13 km further N is Máncora , a small, attractive resort with good beaches. The water here is warm enough for bathing. This stretch of coast is famous for surfing (best Nov-Mar) and for its excellent *mero* (grouper). The Pan-American Highway runs through the centre of town and is the main street, called Avenida Piura. At the N end of town the beach is inaccessible and dirty, this is not a safe area. South of Máncora along the coastal road (old Pan-American Highway) are some excellent beaches which are being developed. There are 2 fine hotels (see below) and many beach homes of well-to-do Limeños. Fresh water is piped into the area, producing the incongruous but welcome sight of green lawns and lush gardens between the sea and desert cliffs. There is a line of rocks parallel to the beach, which form interesting bathing pools at low tide, though these can be dangerous at high tide.

● **Accommodation** Prices can increase by up to 100% in high season (Dec-Mar). From S to N: **D** ***Punta Ballenas***, S of Cabo Blanco bridge at the S entrance to town, T 447-0437 (Lima), **B** in high season, with bath, clean, lovely setting on beach, friendly, garden with small pool, expensive restaurant, rec; **D** ***La Posada***, by Cabo Blanco bridge, follow the dry river bed away from the beach, **C** in high season, in private home, nice garden, hammocks, rooms for larger groups, meals on request, parking, camping possible, good local knowledge, friendly, owner sometimes does tours in the hinterland; **E** ***Sol y Mar***, Piura cuadra 2, on beach, with bath, basic, clean, restaurant, popular with surfers, rec; **E** pp ***El Angolo***, Piura 262, on the beach, with bath, basic, nice terrace, friendly, restaurant, camping permitted in garden, rec. Due to open in 1996 is ***Sausalito***, at Piura 454, new hotel and restaurant. **E** ***Hostal Samara***, Piura 336, inc breakfast, shared bath, 3 rooms in private house; **E/F** ***Bambú***, Piura 636, basic, shared bath, clean, friendly; **E/F** ***Hospedaje Crillon/Tía Yola***, Paita 168, 1 block E of Piura, behind Tepsa office, shared bath, plenty of water, clean, friendly, rec; **F** ***Máncora***, Piura 641, shared bath, very basic, cheapest in town. Along the old Pan-American S of town are: **A2** *Las Pocitas*, 2 km S of Máncora, T/F 472-2065 (Lima), 13 rooms, attractive, nice pool and garden by the beach, very comfortable, friendly, arrange fishing and harpooning trips, balsa rafts, excellent food at US$9 for main meal, **A2** pp full board, during high season only full board available at **A1** pp, the pocitas (rock pools at low tide) are just S of the hotel; **L3** *Las Arenas*, 3.5 km S of Máncora, T/F 441-1542 (Lima), full board, 8 luxury bungalows, pool, lush gardens, trampoline, playground, kayaks for use, free transport from Tumbes airport, **L2** with full board during high season.

• **Places to eat** You can find excellent seafood, inc lobster and grouper, on Av Piura by the centre of town. ***César***, rec, also hires out bicycles for $2.50 per day; ***El Arpón***, good value, rec; ***Kiosko Betty***, close to *Sol y Mar*, friendly, good value meals; ***Regina's***, for fruit salad; also good are ***San Pedro*** and ***Espada***.

• **Banks & money changers Exchange**: Tienda Marlón, Piura 613, changes US$ cash at poor rates.

• **Post & telecommunications Telephone**: at Piura 509, opp the church, national and international calls, also collect. This is the only telephone in town. For hotel reservations leave message at (074) 320212.

• **Sports Horse riding**: German Heidi Ritter hires horses at her ranch, US$4.50 pp for 2-hr guided tour through beautiful countryside, rec. Take moto-taxi or bicycle to El Angolo, then take main road N and turn right after the bridge. After about 1 km, just before the corrals on the right, turn right and you'll see a doorway which leads to Heidi's corrals.

• **Transport** To Piura with EPPO, US$3.50, 3 hrs; to Tumbes (and points in between), minivans leave when full, US$1.55, 2 hrs.

5 km E of Máncora are hot mud baths (*baños del barro*), reported to be medicinal. The access is N of town, at Km 1168, from where it is about 2 km to the baths. Continuing along this road to Quebrada Fernández you can reach the **El Angolo game reserve**, which extends as far S as the Río Chira. Ask at *Hostal La Posada* for tours to this area.

## PLAYA PUNTA SAL

16 km N of Máncora is the *Carpitas* customs checkpoint, a large modern complex, where southbound vehicles are checked. 6 km further N, at Km 1187, is the turn-off for **Punta Sal Grande**, a resort town at the S end of beautiful Playa Punta Sal, a 3 km long sandy beach, with calm surf. A few restaurants operate in high season only and the town is very quiet in the low season. Water is trucked in so it is important to conserve it. Camping is reported to be safe along the beach between Talara and Punta Sal (Punta Negra rec).

• **Accommodation** For reservations in any of the hotels in the area, leave a message at Cancas public telephone, T/F (074) 320251. In town, from N to S are: **C** ***Los Delfines***, near beach, shared bath, clean, nice rooms, restaurant in high season, meals on request in low season, vegetarian available, Canadian-run, very friendly, full board **A2**, during high season **A1** full board, **A3** room only; **C** ***Hua***, on beach, T 448-5667 (Lima), with bath, pleasant terrace overlooking ocean, discount for IYHF card holders, meals available (US$15 for 3 meals), **B** in high season; **D** ***Estancia***, Calle Carrosable, back from beach, 4 rooms, 1 with bath, ask José Devescovi at first house at entrance to town, **B** in high season; **D** ***Las Terrazas***, at S end of bay, T/F 433-7711 (Lima), on a terraced hill overlooking the ocean, a few cheaper rooms without bath, nice views, pleasant, comfortable, friendly, meals available, British-run, **A1** full board in high season; **D** ***Caballito de Mar***, at S end of bay, T 442-6229 (Lima), new in 1996, some rooms with bath, nice location overlooking the ocean, comfortable, friendly, **B** full board, **A2** full board in high season. The N end of the beach is known as Punta Sal Chica: **A3** *Puerto Azul Beach Resort*, access road from Panamericana Km 1190, T/F 444-4131 (Lima), nice spacious bungalows on the beach, pool, tours to mangroves and Tumbes, Tumbes airport pick-up US$20, **A2** full board, **L3** full board in high season; **L3** *Punta Sal Club Hotel*, access road at Km 1192, T (074) 521386 (radio-phone via Tumbes), T/F 442-5961 (Lima), 18 bungalows, 12 rooms, solar heated water, attractive, comfortable, relaxing, good beach, watersports, pool, horse riding, deep-sea fishing, transport to Tumbes airport US$10 pp, **L2** with full board in high season, rec.

## PUNTA SAL TO LOS PINOS

The fishing village of **Cancas** is just N of Punta Sal Chica (Km 1193). It has a few shops, restaurants, a gas station and a police checkpoint where vehicles must stop and southbound foreigners may be required to register. From Punta Mero (Km 1204) N, the beach is used by *larveros*, extracting shrimp larvae from the ocean for use in the shrimp industry, and is no longer considered safe for camping.

• **Accommodation** Several new resorts are being built between Punta Mero and Tumbes: **A1** *Hotel Playa Florida*, at Km 1222, full board, resort/casino/condominium complex due to open in 1996, T/F (074) 320251, T 428-9110 (Lima); *Hotel Punta Camarón*, at Km 1236, with swimming pool. Between Bocapán and Los Pinos, 30 km from Tumbes, is **E** pp *Casa Grillo Centro Ecoturistico Naturista*, Los Pinos 563, Youth Hostel, take colectivo from Tumbes market to Los Pinos, or get

### The old man and the marlin

Though Ernest Hemingway's famous novel, *The Old Man and the Sea*, was set in a Cuban fishing village, the people of Cabo Blanco, on the N coast of Peru, claim that the great writer was inspired by their own fishing waters.

The protagonist of the book, the old fisherman, Santiago, was perhaps the product of Hemingway's own obsession with the idea of catching a marlin weighing more than 1,500 pounds. One of the very few places where such a feat is possible is off the coast of Cabo Blanco. Here, in the 1950s, the marlin were abundant and reached extraordinary sizes. Indeed, during that decade Cabo Blanco became a sort of world sport fishing capital and fishermen the world over congregated there to chase the great black marlin, the largest of its kind and the most difficult to catch owing to its tremendous strength.

So it was that when Hollywood producers decided to make a film based on Hemingway's novel they realized that the only place they could find a suitably large fish was in the waters off Cabo Blanco. In April 1955, the shooting team arrived with the writer, who was there to help them locate the fish that would appear in the movie.

Hemingway wasn't too interested in the movie, he was along for the fishing and quickly struck up a rapport with the down-to-earth local fisherfolk. In one particularly poignant anecdote they made him a gift of a bottle of pisco, a popular grape brandy, with a note saying "As long as the grapevines cry, I will drink their tears". The following morning, before going out to fish, the writer met those who had given him the pisco, smiled and said to them in Spanish, "I have drunk the tears".

Hemingway did not realize his dream of the 1,500 pound marlin during almost 2 months on the Peruvian coast, though he did manage to catch one weighing a little over 900 pounds. It was one of the largest black marlin he had ever caught and probably the last one of that size he would catch during the few remaining years of his life.

off bus on Pan-American Highway at Km 1236.5, T/F (074) 525207, T/F 446-2233 (Lima), excellent restaurant inc vegetarian, very friendly, great place to relax, variety of rooms, shared bath, hot water, laundry, also surfing, scuba diving, fishing, cycling, trekking, camping available, rec.

## ZORRITOS

**Zorritos**, 27 km S of Tumbes, is an important fishing centre, heavily damaged by the 1983 flooding but with a good beach (the water is not oily). The first South American oil well was sunk here in 1863.

• **Accommodation & places to eat** **D** *Hostal Turístico Zorritos*, former Hotel de Turistas. Several new hotels and resorts have recently been built: ***Punta Sal Chica***; ***Puerto Loco Beach***, under construction in 1995/96. The better of the 2 restaurants is ***Arriba Perú***.

This is the only part of the Peruvian coast where the sea is warm all year. There are two good beaches near Tumbes, one is at **Caleta La Cruz** 16 km SW, where Pizarro landed in 1532. The original Cruz de Conquista was taken to Lima. Regular colectivos run back and forth, US$0.80 each way.

• **Accommodation** **E** *Motel*.

## PUERTO PIZARRO

**Puerto Pizarro** is a small fishing beach 13 km NE of Tumbes; colectivo No 6 from Tumbes, US$0.50. Take a motor or sailing boat to visit the mangroves from Puerto Pizarro pier (fixed tariffs), or across the lagoon to reach a good clean sandy beach (about 10 mins' journey, bargain hard). The Festival of San Pedro y San Pablo takes place 29-30 June. Plenty of fishing and swimming and the beach is ideal for windsurfing and water-skiing but there are few facilities.

• **Accommodation & places to eat** *Puerto Pizarro Motel*, bungalows 10 km from beach, no hot water, restaurant expensive and slow but food good, swimming pool (which is usually empty), watersports; ***Restaurant Venecia***, seafood cheap, beware shellfish which may cause stomach upsets.

# TUMBES

**Tumbes** (*Pop* 34,000; *Phone code* 074), about 141 km N of Talara, and 265 km N of Piura, is the most N of Peruvian towns. It is a garrison town: do not photograph the military or their installations – they will destroy your film and probably detain you. There is a long promenade, the Malecón Benavides, decorated with arches,beside the high banks of the Río Tumbes, views of the river are good from here.

## PLACES OF INTEREST

There are some old houses in **Calle Grau**, and a colonial public library in the **Plaza de Armas** with a small museum. The **cathedral** is 17th century but restored in 1985. There are two pedestrian malls, arranged with benches and plants, Paseo de Los Libertadores on Bolívar and Paseo de la Concordia on San Martín, both leading N from the Plaza de Armas. There is a sports stadium and cockfights in the Coliseo de Gallos, Av Mcal Castilla, 9th block, Sun at 1500, special fights 28 July and 8 Dec. The main products are bananas and rice. The water supply is poor.

## LOCAL INFORMATION

### • Accommodation

**NB** Av Tumbes is still sometimes referred to by its old name of Teniente Vásquez.

**A3** *Sol de la Costa*, San Martín 275, Plazuela Bolognesi, T 523991, F 523298, ex-state run hotel, clean, hot water, minibar, fan, restaurant, good food and service, parking extra, has nice garden with swimming pool, racketball court, provides some tourist information.

**D** *Asturias*, Mcal Castilla, T 522569, with bath, fan, cafeteria, clean, comfortable, friendly, rec; **D** *César*, Huáscar 333, T/F 522883, with bath, fan, TV; **D** *Chicho*, Tumbes 327, T/F 523696, with bath, fan, mosquito net, TV, clean; **D** *Continental*, Huáscar 111, T 523510, with bath, fan, pool; **D** *Florián*, Piura 400 nr El Dorado bus company, T 522464, F 524725, clean, private bath, fan, rec; **D** *Lourdes*, Mayor Bodero 118, one block from main plaza, T/F 522758, with bath, fan, clean, friendly, roof restaurant, slow service, rec; **D** *Roma*, Bolognesi 425 Plaza de Armas, T 524137, with bath, fan, basic.

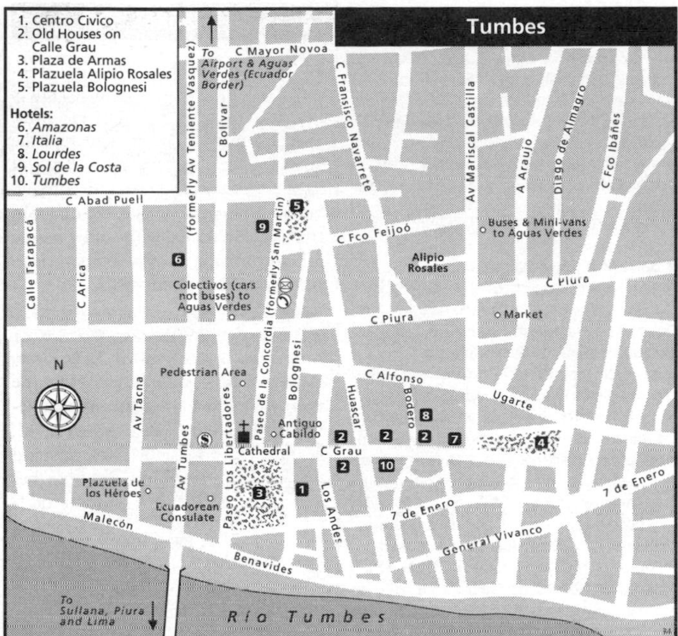


**E** *Amazonas*, Av Tumbes 317, T 520629, with bath, fan, clean, friendly, water in mornings unreliable; **E** *Córdova*, J R Abad Puell 777, with bath, no hot water, safe, friendly, safe for motorcycle parking; **E** *Elica*, Tacna 319, T 523870, with bath, clean, fan, quiet, good; **E** *Estoril*, Huáscar 317, 2 blocks from main plaza, T 524906, with bath, good, clean, friendly, discount for long stay; **E** *Franco*, San Martín, Paseo de la Concordia, T 525295, with bath, fan; **E** *Gandolfo*, Bolognesi 420, T 522868, with bath, **F** without, fan, OK; **E** *Hostal Premier*, Tumbes 227, T 522037, with bath, basic, dirty; **E** *Hostal Tumbes*, Grau 614, T 522203, with bath, cold water, fan, friendly, clean, good value, rec; **E** *Internacional*, Feijoó, T 525976, with bath, basic, dirty; **E** *Italia*, Grau 733, T 520677, cold showers, friendly, noisy, good; **E** *Joalsy*, Mcal Castilla 539, T 522199, by market and where minivans leave for border, basic, with bath, **F** without; **E** *Judgem*, Bolívar 344, T 523530, with bath, basic, OK; **E** *Kikos*, Bolívar 462, T 523777, with bath, basic; **E** *Kalulo*, Piura 1035, T 524995, with bath, **F** without, basic, OK, poor water supply; **E** *Los Once*, Piura 417, next to El Dorado bus office, with bath, basic; **E** *Toloa 1*, Av Tumbes 430, T 523771, with bath, fan, clean, safe, helpful; **E** *Toloa 2*, Bolívar 458, T 524135, with bath, fan, OK.

**F** *Cristina*, Mcal Castilla 758, nr market, T 521617, with bath, basic, cheap; **F** *Hostal Bolívar*, Bolívar 115, on Plaza de Armas, T 523007, shared bath, mosquito net; **F** *Sudamericano*, San Martín 110, Paseo de la Concordia, shared bath, very basic. Many other cheap hotels by the market. At holiday times it can be very difficult to find a vacant room.

## ● Places to eat

*Curich*, Bolívar, on the Plaza de Armas, good for fish, friendly, rec; *Europa*, off Plaza de Armas, rec, particularly for omelettes, expensive; *Latino*, Bolívar 163, on Plaza de Armas, good set meals, à la carte expensive, also *peña* most evenings; *Chifa Wakay*, Huáscar 417, smart, good, US$5-8, rec; *Río Tumbes*, Malecón Benavides s/n, at E end of seafront, excellent views of river, pleasant atmosphere, seafood specialities, not cheap; *Hawaii*, Av Bolívar 235, near Plaza de Armas, good, big portions; *Juliban*, Grau 704, good, generous set meal; ***El Algarrobo***, Huáscar across from Club Social, good; ***El Cautivo***, on road to airport, speciality on Sun is *Kupus*, a meat and vegetable dish cooked underground. There are other inexpensive restaurants on the Plaza de Armas and near the markets. ***Heladería La Suprema***, Paseo Libertadores 298, good ice cream, sweets and cold drinks; next door at 296 is ***Bam Bam***, for breakfast and snacks. Try *bolas de plátano*, soup with banana balls, meat, olives and raisins, and *sudado*, a local stew.

### ● Banks & money changers

**Banco de Crédito**, Paseo de los Libertadores 261, cash only, poor rates; **Banco de Comercio**, 5% commission; **Interbanc**, Bolívar 129, Plaza de Armas, cash and TCs at same fair rate, cash advance on Visa; **Banco Continental**, Bolívar 121, cash and Amex TCs only, US$5 commission. All banks close for lunch. Bad rates at the airport. In general better rates at Trujillo and Piura. **Cambios Ocoña**, Galería San Carlos, Piura near Paseo de la Concordia, US$ cash at good rates; **Cambios Internacionales**, Av Tumbes 245, cash only, good rates. Money changers on the street (on Bolívar, left of the Cathedral), some of whom are unscrupulous, give a much better rate than banks or *cambios*, but don't accept the first offer you are given. None changes TCs. If you are travelling on to Ecuador, it is better to change your Soles at the border as the rate is higher.

### ● Embassies & consulates

**Ecuadorean Consulate**, Bolívar 155, Plaza de Armas, T 523022, 0900-1300 and 1400-1630, Mon-Fri.

### ● Post & telecommunications

**Post Office**: San Martín 208; Entel **Telephone** office, San Martín 210; both on Paseo de la Concordia.

### ● Shopping

Well-stocked supermarket **Anilu**, Bolívar.

### ● Laundry

Lavandería at Piura 1002, by weight.

### ● Tour companies & travel agents

***Rosillo Tours***, Tumbes 293, T/F 523892, information, tickets, Western Union agents; ***Tumbes Tours***, Tumbes 351-A, tickets and information.

### ● Tourist offices

**Centro Cívico**, Bolognesi 194, p 2, helpful, provides map and leaflets. **Federación Peruana para la Conservación de la Naturaleza** (FPCN), Av Tarapacá 4-16, Urb Fonavi, T 523412.

### ● Transport

**Air** To Lima, daily flights with Faucett and Americana; US$65 one-way for foreigners at time of writing (1996); buy tickets outside Peru to avoid paying sales tax. It is essential to reconfirm flights 24 hrs before departure. It is better to buy tickets in Tumbes rather than at the airport. To Chiclayo, 45 mins, 5 days a week with Faucett and Americana. To Talara, Fri and Sun, US$15 with Faucett. Taxi to airport, US$4, 20 mins; minivans charge US$1.50; taxis meet flights to take passengers to border, US$7-9; no minivans from airport to border, beware of overcharging.

**Buses** Daily to and from **Lima**, 1,320 km, 12-20 hrs, depending on stopovers, US$15 (normal service), US$22 (luxury service), long trip on an excellent Panamericana Norte. Several buses daily (see Lima **Bus Companies** with routes to the N). All on Av Tumbes: Expreso Continental (Ormeño group), 314; Cruz del Sur, 319; Oltursa, 324 and 359, daily 1330, rec; Tepsa, 199, old buses, unsafe, often full, not rec. For other companies, ask around; cheaper ones usually leave 1600-2100, more expensive ones 1200-1400. Except for luxury service, most buses to Lima stop at major cities en route, although you may be told otherwise. You can get tickets to anywhere between Tumbes and Lima quite easily, although buses are often booked well in advance, so if arriving from Ecuador you may have to stay overnight. Piura is a good place for connections. To **Talara**, 171 km, US$3.50, 3 hrs. To **Sullana**, 244 km, 3-4 hrs, US$4.50, several buses daily. To **Piura**, 4-5 hrs, 282 km, US$5.25 with Empresa Chiclayo, Cruz del Sur, El Dorado (Piura 459) 6 a day, Dorado Express (Tumbes 297); Colectivo (Tumbes 302), US$7. To **Chiclayo**, 552 km, 6 hrs, US$7, several each day with Cruz del Sur, El Dorado, Dorado Express, Oltursa. To **Trujillo**, 769 km, 10-11 hrs, US$9, Continental, Cruz del Sur, El Dorado, Dorado Express. To **Chimbote**, 889 km, 13-14 hrs, US$10. Transport to the border, see **Frontier with Ecuador**, below.

**NB** Travellers who hold a Tumbes-Huaquillas-Guayaquil ticket with Panamericana Internacional (bought outside Peru as an onward ticket) should note that Panamericana does not have an office in Tumbes. However, this ticket can be used for a colectivo (but not a taxi) to the border, caught at corner of Piura and Bolívar. If the colectivo is full, you will be transferred to another company. Connection with bus at the border.

## EXCURSIONS FROM TUMBES

The Río Tumbes is navigable by small boat to the mouth of the river, an interesting 2 hr trip with fantastic birdlife and mangrove swamps.

The **Santuario Nacional los Manglares de Tumbes** is a national reserve, created to protect the mangrove ecosystem in the northernmost part of the Peruvian coast. It extends between the border with Ecuador in the N and Puerto Pizarro in the S. The mangrove swamps are full of pelicans; best to visit them at high tide. A few tame birds beg for fish on the beaches. Three islands, Isla Hueso de Ballena, Isla del Amor and Isla de los Pájaros may be visited by boat; bargain hard, good for swimming and picnics, take food and water. The remains of the Cabeza de Vaca cult centre of the Tumpis Indians can be found at Corrales, 5 km S of Tumbes. They were heavily damaged by 1983 rains; Museo de Sitio nearby. Another access to the mangrove reserve is via the Pan-American Highway N as far as Zarumilla, take the turn-off E, 9 km to El Algarrobo ranger station.

The **Parque Nacional Cerros de Amotape** was created to protect an area representative of the equatorial forest. It extends SE from the S bank of the Tumbes river, towards the El Angolo game preserve NE of Máncora. Some of the endemic species are the Tumbes crocodile, the river otter and white-winged turkeys. Access is via the road which goes SE from the Pan-American Highway at Bocapán (Km 1233) to Casitas and Huásimo, it takes about 2 hrs by car from Tumbes, best in the dry season (July-Nov); also access via Quebrada Fernández from Máncora and via Querecotillo and Los Encuentros from Sullana.

The **Zona Reservada de Tumbes**, formerly **Bosque Nacional de Tumbes** (75,000 ha), lies to the NE of Tumbes, between the Ecuadorean border and Cerros de Amotape National Park. It was created to protect dry equatorial forest and tropical rainforest. The wildlife includes monkeys, otters, wild boars, small cats and crocodiles. Access from Tumbes is via Cabuyal, Pampas de Hospital and El Caucho to the Quebrada Faical research station or via Zarumilla and Matapalo.

- Mosquito repellent is a must for Tumbes area.

## FRONTIER WITH ECUADOR

### ● Peruvian Immigration

Immigration for those leaving Peru is at an office 3 km before the border; for those entering Peru, immigration is at the end of the international bridge, W side, at Aguas Verdes. PNP is on the E side. All offices are open Mon-Sat 0800-1300 and 1400-1800, Sun 0800-1300 and 1400-1600. Best to arrive well in advance of closing times on either side. Latest reports are that on leaving Peru you have to stop at the large complex 3 km S of the bridge for an exit stamp.

**NB** Peruvian immigration formalities were reported greatly improved in 1995, with no hassles. Police officers on the Peruvian side of the international bridge continued to ask regularly for bribes, however. Try to avoid them if possible but if approached be courteous but firm. Porters on either side of the border charge exorbitant prices; don't be bullied. Also note that relations between Peru and Ecuador are not good; Ecuadorean customs may confiscate guidebooks and maps of Peru which show areas claimed by Ecuador as belonging to Peru

### ● Entering Ecuador

Having obtained your exit stamp, proceed across the bridge into Huaquillas; 100m up is Ecuadorean immigration on the left. You may have to buy two photocopied embarkation cards, which touts will try to sell for US$0.50, but which can be bought at the photocopy shop behind immigration for US$0.01. With a pass from the authorities at the border you can spend the day in Huaquillas, as long as you are back by 1800. There is nothing much to see there, but Peruvians go to hunt for bargains.

### ● Peruvian Customs

There are virtually no customs formalities at the border for passengers crossing on foot, but spot-checks sometimes take place. There is a large, modern and well-organized customs checkpoint S on the Pan-American Highway between Cancas and Máncora.

### ● Crossing by Private Vehicle

When driving into Peru vehicle fumigation is not required, but there is one outfit who will attempt to fumigate your vehicle with water and charge US$10. Beware of officials claiming that you need a carnet to obtain your 90-day transit permit; this is not so, cite Decreto Supremo 015-87-ICTI/TUR (but check that rules have not changed). Frequent road tolls between Tumbes and Lima, approx US$1.

### ● Accommodation

If stuck overnight in the border area there is a hotel in **Aguas Verdes**: **E** *Hostal El Bosque*, at S end of town on Av República de Perú 402, shared bath, clean, friendly, basic, mosquito nets. Aguas Verdes also has phone booths and airline ticket offices.

There are 4 hotels in **Zarumilla**, at Km 1290 on the Pan-American Highway, 5 km S of Aguas Verdes. There is a signpost on the highway and the main plaza is only a few blocks away from the turn-off: **E** *Imperial*, on the plaza, small, modern, very basic, cold water turned off at night, very clean, mosquito nets, very friendly, rec; **E/D** *El Rosedal*; **D** *Caribe*, newest and nicest; and *Yovica*.

### ● Exchange

The money changers on the Ecuadorean side sometimes give a better rate. Beware sharp practices by money changers using fixed calculators. If you are going to change TCs into Ecuadorean sucres in Huaquillas, make sure you cross the border in morning because the bank is closed after lunch. Do not change money on the minibus to Aguas Verdes, very poor rates.

### ● Transport

**From Tumbes to border**: colectivos leave from Calle Piura near corner of Bolívar, US$1 pp or US$6 to hire car, and wait at the immigration office before continuing to the border, 30-40 mins. **Make sure the driver takes you all the way to the border and not just as far as the complex 3 km S of the bridge**. Minivans leave from the market area along Mcal Castilla across from Calle Alipio Rosales, US$0.50, luggage on roof. They leave passengers at the immigration office. Run down city buses ply the same route as minivans, US$0.40, slower. Ortursa bus from Chiclayo also leaves passengers at the immigration complex. From the border complex to the bridge take colectivo, minibus (US$0.25) or moto-taxi (US$0.50). All vehicles only leave when full. They pass the turn-off for the airport from which it is a 500m walk to the terminal; colectivos to the airport charge US$1.50 pp, but often ask for much more. From the border to Zarumilla by moto-taxi costs US$0.50 pp.

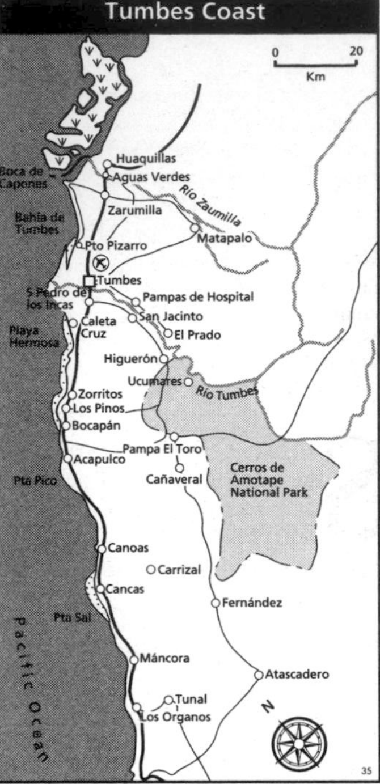


**Entering Peru**, it is easier to take a colectivo to Tumbes and then a bus S, rather than trying to get on a bus from the border to a southern destination.

### ● Into Ecuador

**Huaquillas** is a small city with a reasonable selection of hotels and other services. There is a tourist information centre just by the international bridge, staffed by tourism students who are friendly, helpful, but have limited information. Transport links to other parts of Ecuador (Quito, Guayaquil, Cuenca, Loja) are good; Transit Police, Customs and the Military have checkpoints on the road N so keep your passport to hand.

# The South Coast



SOME OF Peru's most remarkable precolumbian sites and its wine and pisco-producing oases punctuate the desert South of the capital. This is an area famous for its grapes and graves. The southerly valleys specialize in vines – Ica in particular is well known for this and its port, Pisco, shares its name with that well-known brandy. Further North, on the Paracas peninsula, is the home of the ancient Paracas Necropolis culture, famed for its elaborate burial techniques. The vines of Ica give way further South to the lines of Nasca. These mysterious configurations etched in the desert sand stretch across the vast Ingenio plain between Nasca and Palpa and continue to provoke scientific speculation as to their origin. The Panamericana Sur runs from Lima, through all the places now to be described, to Tacna and on to Chile. A very good paved highway runs all the way to the border, with battery chicken houses along the beach. The group of oases South from Lima grow Pima cotton, sugar-cane and vegetables. The grey blanket of fog, the *garúa*, which hangs over Lima for much of the year, finally lifts at Km 200, near Chincha.

Southern Peru
To Trujillo & Ecuador
To Cerro de Pasco
La Junin
Callao
LIMA
Chorrillos
Lurin
Chosica
Matucana
Junín
Acobamba
Palca
La Oroya
S Mateo
Morococha
Pucusana
Chilca
R Mala
Cerro Azul
Cañete
Jauja
Concepción
0
120
km
Lunahuaná
R Cañete
Huancayo
Tambo de Mora
Chincha
La Mejorada
R Mantaro
Pisco
R Chincha
R Pisco
Paracas
Huancavelica
Pámpano
Castrovirreyna
Huanta
Santa Inés
La Quinua
San Francisco
Ica
Huacachina
Apacheta
Ayacucho
Ocros
Pto Pajanal
R Apurimac
R Ica
Chincheros
Palpa
R Grande
Pacucha
Andahuaylas
Machu Picchu
Quillabamba
San Juan
Nazca
Pampachiri
Puquío
Abancay
Lomas
R Acari
R Yauca
Huachujasa 4,367m
Chalhuanca
Anta
Cuzco
Pisac
R de Chala
Huambutio
To Puerto Maldonado
Chala
Urcos
R Atico
Atico
Tinta
Atico Pte
Cailloma
Salamanca
R Ocoña
Sicuani
Andagua
Marangani
Aplao
R Colca
La Raya
Ocoña
Chivay
To Macusani
R Majes
Cabanaconde
Sta Rosa
Camaná
Pacific Ocean
R Siguas
Ayaviri
Imata
La Joya
Vitor
Tirapata
Pucara
Matarani
R Chili
Sta Lucía
Lampa
Azángaro
Arequipa
Mollendo
Pati
Juliaca
Vilque
R Tambo
Huancané
Puno
Chucuito
Torata
Loripongo
Ilave
BOLIVIA
Ilo
Moquegua
Toquepala
Juli
Lake Titicaca
R Locumba
Pomata
Yunguyo
Tiquina
R Sama
Desaguadero
Tarata
Tacna
Concordia
To La Paz
Arica
CHILE
To Santiago

## SOUTH FROM LIMA

The first 60 km from Lima are dotted with a series of seaside resort towns and clubs. First is **El Silencio**, at 30 km, which is good, then **Punta Hermosa** at 35 km, and **Punta Negra** at 40 km.

**San Bartolo** is 43 km S from Lima. Accommodation is available at *Posada del Mirador*, Malecón San Martín 105, T 290388, **C** in bungalows or **A3** full board, *Handbook* users are welcome.

**Santa María**, 45 km from Lima, has the beautiful **A3** *Santa María Hotel*, meals included.

### PUCUSANA

This charming fishing village is 60 km from Lima. There are excellent panoramas from the cliffs above the village. You can hire a boat for an hour, but fix the price beforehand and stick to it. Don't sail in the direction of the smelly factory, but to the rocks where you can see seabirds close at hand. There is a compulsory police checkpoint before the turning to Pucusana. The *Hotel Bahía* has good seafood.

### SOUTH FROM PUCUSANA

**Chilca** is a small beach resort 14 km S of Pucusana, 30 mins by colectivo from the market place. There isn't much to see, but a long, deserted beach does present camping possibilities. You can walk along the beach from Chilca to Salinas (5 km), which has mineral baths. There are a few restaurants and *pensiones*. In summer (Dec-Feb), these places fill up with holidaymakers from Lima.

At **Mala**, 24 km S of Pucusana, 2 km inland from Pan American highway, are 3 hotels, including **E** *Hostal Weekend*, with private bath, very clean and modern.

**NB** Most beaches have very strong currents and can be dangerous for swimming; if unsure, ask locals.

### SAN VICENTE DE CAÑETE

About 150 km S of Lima, on the Río Cañete, this prosperous market centre is set amid desert scenery. It is commonly called Cañete. The town hosts a festival during the last week in August. At Cerro Azul, 13 km N of Cañete, is a unique Inca sea fort known as **Huarco**, which is now badly damaged.

• **Accommodation & places to eat D** *Hostal San Francisco*, Santa Rosa 317, 2 blocks N of plaza, T 912409, with bath, **E** without, new, clean, friendly, quiet, rec; *Hostal Casablanca*, reasonable. A recommended restaurant is *Cevichería Muelle 56*, Bolognesi 156.

• **Transport Buses** The main bus stop is on the highway; wait for the service you want going N or S and hope there are free seats. To **Pisco**, US$1.30. To **Lunahuaná**: unless you are on a Lima-Cañete-Imperial bus, take a kombi from the highway to Imperial, then a bus to Lunahuaná.

## LUNAHUANA

A paved road runs inland, mostly beside the Río Cañete, through **Imperial**, which has a market on Sat, Sun and Mon (good for every type of household item), and **Nuevo Imperial** to the Quebrada de Lunahuaná. After the town of **Lunahuaná** (40 km from Cañete), the road continues unpaved to Huancayo up in the sierra; bus US$9 (see page 356).

Lunahuaná consists of the town of the same name and several *anexos* – Paullo, San Gerónimo, Langla, Jita, Condoray, Uchupampa and Catapalla. The whole valley is totally dependent on the Río Cañete, for irrigation and for its chief tourist attraction of rafting and kayaking. Beyond the reach of the water, the surrounding countryside is completely barren, but not without its own appeal. In early morning and at dusk the hills are painted in infinite shades of grey and brown, framed by the clear blue sky, fertile green valley and rushing water.

8 km before Lunahuaná is **Incawasi**, the ruins of an Inca city. A new road cuts

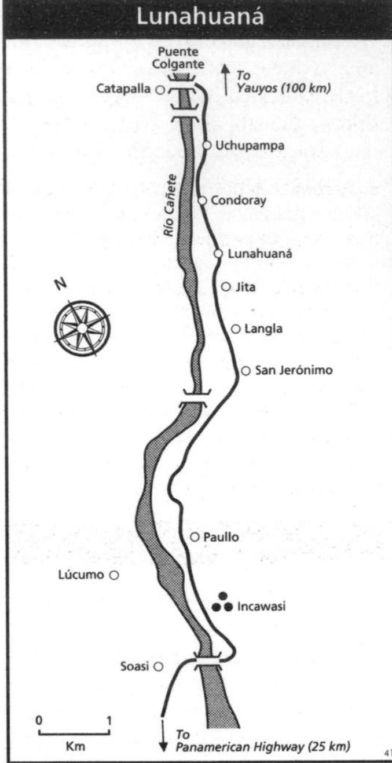


right through the middle of the site which dominates the valley and *quebradas* that run down into it. Incawasi is said to have been a replica of Cusco, with its divided trapezoidal plaza. The site was built outside the fertile zone of the valley and its rough walls blend in perfectly with the barren hills.

**Paullo** is the first of the *anexos* reached after Incawasi. Here stand the ruins of the first church of Lunahuaná. In summer, when the river is high, rafting trips start from just below the plaza. In the low river season a temporary footbridge crosses the river to **Lúcumo**.

2 km further on is **San Jerónimo**, the area's white-water rafting centre; there are several agencies to choose from (see below). Other adventure tourism activities include parapenting and there is an artificial wall for climbing.

**Lunahuaná** town is beyond **Langla** and **Jita**. The 18th century church on the plaza has a pleasant interior. Opposite the W door, at the top of the plaza, are the Banco de la Nación and Municipalidad. There is no phone in Lunahuaná.

Beyond Lunahuaná are **Condoray** and **Uchupampa**. Past Uchupampa the road paving ends before the road crosses the Río Cañete to **Catapalla**. A little further on is a *puente colgante* (suspension bridge). Across the road bridge turn right to the village or left to the pre-Inca remains of **Cantagallo**. The site is not signposted, ask directions. Miguel Casas Sánchez in Catapalla can guide to these ruins and others in the area.

## Bodegas

It is interesting to visit the *bodegas* (wine cellars) in the valley and try the wine. The best-known is *Los Reyes* (T 437-3187/ 434-0872), in the *anexo* of **Condoray** (see above), where you can try their pisco, wine, *manzanilla* and *arope* (a grape juice concentrate). A good time to visit is during Feb/Mar when you can see the traditional methods of treading the grapes by foot to the beat of the drum.

Other *Bodegas* in the area are: *El Olimpo*, in Uchupampa, beside the *Hotel Embassy*, T 460-7698 (see below); *Viña Santa María*, in Condoray, beside *Hostal Río Alto*, T 437-8892. Also in Condoray are *Del Valle*, by *La Laguna* restaurant; and *Viñas del Sur*, T 437-3187. There are also *Bodegas* in Catapalla, Socsi, Langla and Jita.

## Rafting and kayaking

Several places offer rafting and kayaking, eg *Camping San Jerónimo*, *Aldea*, *Aventura Perú* all in San Jerónimo and Paullo. From Nov-April the river is high (highest from Dec) and during those months the white-water rafting is at levels 4-5. May-Oct is the low water season when only boat trips are possible (levels 1-2). Excellent kayaking is 2½ hrs upriver. Rafting costs US$15 pp for 1½ hrs. Annual championships are held every February.

## Local festivals

Fiesta de la Vendimia, the grape harvest festival, is held in first weekend in Mar. At the end of Sept/beginning Oct is the lively Fiesta del Níspero (medlar festival).

## Local information

### ● Accommodation

**A3-B** *Embassy* and *Embassy Río*, in Uchupampa, 3 km, T 472-3525, all facilities, restaurants, disco, gardens, rafting, large property, good, popular with families.

**B** *Río Alto*, T 463-5490, in Condoray, just outside Lunahuaná, rooms, bungalows for 7, pool, with bath, hot water, restaurant, disco, rafting, very nice.

**C** *Del Valle*, in Condoray, T 449-9995, with swimming pool, restaurant and TV room. Nearby is **C** *Las Viñas*, in Condoray, just before Uchupampa, T 437-3187, bungalows, also camping, **F** pp, rafting. Also in Condoray are; **D** *Hospedaje Juan Paulino*, T 437-2624, restaurant does barbecues and *pachamanca* (stewed meat cooked underground), camping **F**; **E** pp *La Cabañita*, T 448-8515, and **E** pp *La Fogata*, T 473-8379; **E** pp *Hostal San Jerónimo*, in San Jerónimo, T 497-1601, with restaurant and disco; **E** pp *Hostal El Paso*, in Lita, T 424-0624, restaurant, garage. Also camping at *Camping Henry's*, at Langla, **F** pp.

**In Lunuhuaná**: **D** *Los Casuarinos*, Grau 295, T Cañete 034-912627; **D** *Hostal Lunahuaná*, T 424-0624, restaurant, disco; **D-E** *Grau*, Grau 205, shared bath, clean, all meals available. Camping at *Camping Win Wan*, **F-G** pp, with restaurant and disco.

### ● Places to eat

**In Lunahuaná are**: *Lester*, on block 3 of Grau, good; *Sol y Río*, Malecón Araoz, arranges rafting. There are several other restaurants in town and in the surrounding *anexos*.

## CHINCHA ALTA

35 km N of Pisco, near Chincha Baja, is **Tambo de Mora**, with nearby archaeological sites at Huaca de Tambo de Mora, La Centinela, Chinchaycama and Huaca Alvarado. **Chincha** itself is a fast-growing town where the negro/criollo culture is still alive.

The famous festival, Verano Negro, or Black Summer, is at the end of February. During this time the black culture of the area, repressed for so many centuries, is freely expressed in the dancing competitions, though black participation in the festival is still somewhat limited.

● **Accommodation B** *Hacienda San José*, is a 17th century ranch-house, just outside town, price is for full board, great lunch stop, the buffet is recommended, with pool, garden, small church, colonial crafts, underground runs a labyrinth of tunnels believed to link up with other ranches in order to facilitate the contraband trade in black slaves from Africa; the catacombs, where many of those slaves are interred, can be visited, US$15 pp. In the town of Chincha is **F** *Hostal La Rueda*, near the plaza, breakfast extra, hot showers, swimming pool, lounge. There are several other hotels.

# PISCO

(*Pop* 82,250; *Phone code* 034) Despite being christened as San Clemente de Macera by the Spanish in 1640, the town had already been unofficially named after the famous local brandy and always would be known as Pisco. Now the largest port between Callao and Matarani, 237 km S of Lima, it serves a large agricultural hinterland. It is a short distance to the W of the Panamerican Highway. The town was divided into two: Pisco Pueblo with its colonial-style homes with patios and gardens; and Pisco Puerto, which, apart from fisheries, has been replaced as a port by the deep-water Puerto Gen San Martín, beyond Paracas. The two towns have expanded into one, partly as a result of an influx of refugees from the Ayacucho region.

## PLACES OF INTEREST

In Pisco Pueblo, half a block W of the quiet Plaza de Armas, with its equestrian statue of San Martín, is the **Club Social Pisco**, at Av San Martín 132, the HQ of San Martín after he had landed at Paracas Bay. There is an old Jesuit church on San Francisco, 1 block from the plaza, separated from the Municipalidad by a nar-

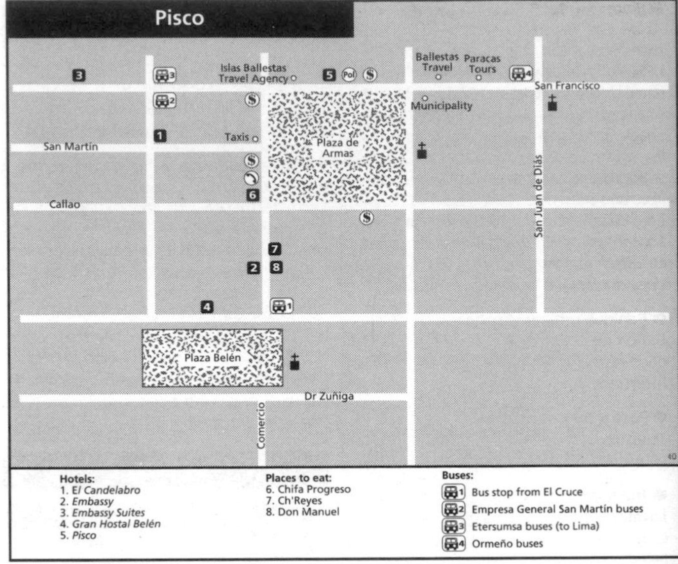


row park. The newer **Cathedral** is on the main plaza. Avenida San Martín runs from the Plaza de Armas to the sea. The pleasant cemetery at the end of C San Francisco was the centre of a female vampire craze in 1993, apparently connected with the grave of an English woman, Sarah Ellen, who died in 1913.

## LOCAL INFORMATION

### ● Accommodation

The town is full at weekends with visitors from Lima.

**A3** *El Candelabro*, Av San Martín, 1 block from plaza, F 534620, midweek rates available, TV, fridge, fax service, hot water, café, bar on roof, laundry, safe.

**C** *Embassy Suites* on San Francisco, TV, fax, *comedor*, 1 block from plaza; **C** *Hostal Candelabro*, Av San Martín 1148, T 534616, TV, fridge, restaurant, clean.

**D** *Embassy Boulevard*, Jr Comercio just off Plaza de Armas, with bath, clean, noisy, nice bar on roof, has disco, trips to Ballestas Islands, under same ownership as *Embassy Suites*; **D** *Hostal Belén*, Plaza Belén, with bath, clean, comfortable, electric showers, rec (on same plaza, *Hostal Perú*); **D** *Pisco*, on Plaza de Armas, T 532018, with bath, F without, hot water, clean, rooms without windows, good tour company adjoining hotel, parking for motorcycles; **D** *Posada Hispana Hostal*, Bolognesi 236, T 536363, F 461-4907 (Lima), 5 rooms each with loft, bath, hot water, can accommodate groups, comfortable, clean, new, information service, English, French, Italian and Catalonian spoken.

**E** *Hostal San Jorge*, Juan Osores 267, sometimes hot water, friendly, very clean, rec; **E-F** *Colonial*, Comercio, pedestrianized part, shared bath, large rooms with balcony overlooking plaza, very clean.

**F** *Hostal Progreso*, Progreso 254, communal bathrooms, clean, water shortages. Mosquitoes are a problem at night in the summer.

**At Pisco Puerto**: **E** *Portofino*, basic, friendly, clean, in slum area on sea front, good seafood at restaurant, expensive breakfast, arrange day excursion to Paracas, but avoid the nearby *peña* which is poor and can be dangerous.

**F** pp *Hostal Pisco Playa* (Youth Hostel), Jr José Balta 639, Pisco Playa, T 532492, clean, kitchen and washing facilities, quite nice, breakfast US$1.50.

● **Places to eat**
*As de Oro*, San Martín 472, good, reasonable prices, closed Mon; ***Don Manuel***, Comercio 187, US$2-4 for main dish; ***Ch'Reyes***, Jr Comercio (same block), good, set meal US$1; also on pedestrianized block of Comercio, ***El Boulevard***, ***Snack Pizza Catamarán***; ***Chifa Progreso***, Callao at Plaza de Armas, good lunches. There are seafood restaurants along the shore between Pisco and San Andrés, and in San Andrés (buses from Plaza Belén, near *Hostal Perú*) there are: ***La Fontana***, Lima 355, good food and pisco sours; ***La Estrellita***; ***Olimpia***, Grecia 200; and ***Mendoza***, for fish and local dishes, all are rec.

● **Banks & money changers**
**Banco de Crédito** on Plaza de Armas gives good rates, for Amex and cash; also on Plaza, **Interbanc**.

● **Post & telecommunications**
**Telephone**: telephone and fax office on Plaza de Armas between Av San Martín y Callao.

● **Transport**
**Local** Taxis on Plaza de Armas. Kombis from Cruce (see below), stop at Comercio by Plaza Belén.

**Buses** If arriving by bus, make sure it is going into town and will not leave you at the Cruce which is a 10-min kombi ride, US$0.30, from the centre. To **Lima**, 242 km, 3-4 hrs, US$3.50, buses and colectivos every hour, see under Lima, **Bus Companies** with routes to the S. Company offices in Pisco are: Ormeño, San Francisco, 1 block from plaza, and San Martín at San Martín 199. To **Ayacucho**, 13 hrs, US$8, few buses or trucks daily, not a well-travelled route; make sure to take warm clothing as it gets cold at night. To **Huancavélica**, 269 km, 14 hrs, US$8, only 1 bus a day (Oropesa, Conde de la Monclova 637) and a few trucks, the road condition is as for Ayacucho. To **Ica** US$2 by colectivo; US$1 by bus, 1 hr, 70 km, 11 daily; with Ormeño, also Saavedra (Callao 181). To **Nasca**, 210 km, by bus, US$3, 3 hrs, go via Ica, only direct bus at 1600 (Ormeño). To **Arequipa**, US$11, 10-12 hrs, 3 daily.

## PARACAS NATIONAL RESERVE

15 km down the coast from Pisco Puerto is the bay of **Paracas**, sheltered by the Paracas peninsula. It is named after the Paracas winds – sandstorms that can last for 3 days, especially in August. The wind gets up every afternoon, peaking at around 1500.

### Flora and fauna

The whole peninsula, a large area of coast to the S and the Ballestas Islands are all part of a National Reserve, created in 1975, which covers a total of 335,000 ha, on land and sea. It is one of the most important marine reserves in the world, with the highest concentration of marine birds. For this reason the region became economically important as a major producer of guano.

The fauna on view also includes a wide variety of sea mammals and rare and exotic birds. Condors can even be seen in Feb/Mar from the rough road between Paracas and Laguna Grande. These massive vultures feed on the

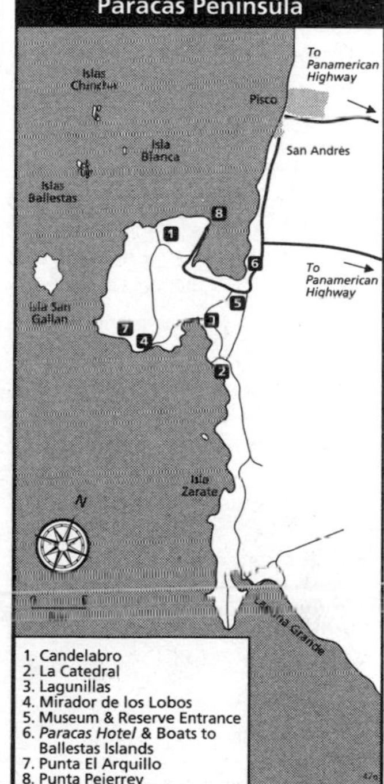

ready supply of sea lion carcasses.

Rather more delicate are the flamingos which feed in Paracas bay, a short walk from the museum (see below). Note that boat trips do not go to see the flamingos and that from Jan to Mar they head for the sierra (the flamingos, not the boats). It is said that these graceful red and white birds inspired General San Martín to design Peru's red and white flag of independence.

## Places of interest

The tiny fishing village of **Lagunillas** is 5 km from the museum across the neck of the peninsula. It has clean, safe beaches free from sting rays and good eating places, eg *Rancho de la Tía Fela*. A network of firm dirt roads, reasonably well signed, crosses the peninsula. For walking, details are available from the Park Office or ask for 'Hoja 28-K' map at Instituto Geográfico Nacional in Lima for US$5. Note that it is not safe to walk if alone and that it is easy to get lost in the hot, wide desert area.

The Candelabro

Other sites on the peninsula include **Mirador de los Lobos** at **Punta El Arquillo**, 6 km from Lagunillas, which looks down on a raucous mob of sea lions. **La Catedral** is a rock formation in the cliffs, 6 km from Lagunillas in the opposite direction. Some guides may tell you that this was the site for the filming of *Planet of the Apes*. Unfortunately, Charlton Heston isn't around to verify this claim.

Nearby, is a monument which marks the spot where San Martín landed in Peru, on 8 September 1820, after liberating Argentina. Soon after, a shipload of British troops, led by Lord Cochrane, arrived to help the General plan his strategy to break the Spanish stranglehold in the region.

About 14 km from the entrance to the Reserve is the precolumbian **Candelabro** (or Candelabra) traced in the hillside. At least 50m long, it is best seen from the sea, but still impressive from the land. There are differing theories as to its exact purpose. Some believe it to be linked to the Nasca lines (see page 248), 200 km to the S; others that it is related to the Southern Cross constellation and was used to help guide ancient sailors. Others still contend that it represents the cactus used by the ancient high priests for its hallucinogenic powers.

To reach the Candelabro, hitch along the paved road which leads to Punta Pejerrey, then get off at the left fork and you will see a trail. It is a 1½-hr walk under a blazing sun; take water and sunscreen.

## Museums

The **Julio Tello site museum** is at the entrance to the Reserve. The exhibits are from the burial sites discovered by the Peruvian archaeologist, Julio C Tello, under the Paracas desert in 1925. The best examples of textiles and funerary bundles can be found in the Museo de la

Nación and archaeological museum, Pueblo Libre, in Lima.

The Paracas Necropolis culture inhabited this region between 1300 BC and AD 200 and is renowned for its finely woven textiles, in particular their *mantos* (large decorated cloth) embroidered with anthropomorphic, zoomorphic and geometric designs. These *mantos* were used to wrap the mummified bodies in their funerary bundles whose discovery gave anthropologists and archaeologists vital clues into this civilization. The bodies were often found to have trepanned skulls. Trepanation was a form of brain surgery performed by the Paracas people in which metal plates were inserted to replace broken sections of skull – a common injury among warring factions at that time. The Paracas culture also practised the intentional deformation of infants' skulls for aesthetic reasons.

The museum is open daily 0900-1700, with a shop which sells guide books, film and drinks; entry US$0.65.

### Access to Paracas

The Reserve can be reached by the coast road from San Andrés, passing the fishing port and a large proportion of Peru's fishmeal industry. Alternatively, go down the Pan-American Highway to 14.5 km past the Pisco turning and take the road to Paracas across the desert. After 11 km turn left along the coast road and 1 km further on fork right to Paracas village.

Return to the main road for the entrance to the Reserve, where you can ask for a map. Here is the archaeological museum and a natural history museum. Entrance to the reserve is US$1 pp.

### Local information

#### ● Accommodation

**A3** *Paracas*, good hotel, bungalows on beach (T Pisco 532220 or Lima 472-3850, F 447-5073) good food, not cheap, good buffet lunch on Sun, fine grounds facing the bay, it is a good centre for excursions to the Peninsula and flights over Nasca; it has tennis courts and an open-air swimming pool (US$2 for non-residents); it also houses the Masson ceramics collection which is worth seeing.

**C** *Hostal Santa Elena*, a few kilometres from the Paracas National Park, reservations in Lima T 718222; very clean, with restaurant 'the cook is legendary', the beach is safe for swimming as there are no manta rays – dangerous

### An economic mess

The islands lying off the coast of Peru are the breeding grounds for millions of sea birds, whose droppings have accumulated over the centuries. These piles of mineral-rich excrement were turned into piles of cash during the last century.

Though the ancient Peruvians knew of the benefits of guano – the name given to the natural fertilizer – and used it on their crops, it wasn't until 1840 that the vast deposits of the stuff were exploited for commercial purposes. It was at this time that Peru first began to trade abroad, particularly with France and England. Almost simultaneously, guano began to replace rare metals as the country's main export.

However, with the economy heavily based on the sales of bird droppings, Peru was caught in a vicious circle of borrowing money on future sales, then having to repay loans at vastly-inflated rates. This unhealthy state of affairs was exacerbated in 1864 when Spain, in a petulant show of aggression towards her ex-colony, decided to occupy the guano islands of Chincha, to the south of Lima, thereby leaving the Peruvian government really up to its neck in it.

The main producers of guano are the Guanay Cormorant and the Peruvian Booby. They gather in colonies on the islands, attracted by the huge shoals of anchovy which feed on the plankton in the cold water of the Humboldt current.

fish with a sharp dorsal fin which hide in sand, local trips can be organized, the hotel is now sandwiched between two fishmeal factories; **C *El Mirador***, at the turn-off to El Chaco, hot water, no phone, good service, boat trips arranged, meals available, sometimes full board only, reservations in Lima, T 445-8496, ask for Sra Rosa. Camping is possible on the beach near the *Hotel Paracas* at a spot called La Muelle, no facilities, sea polluted. Ask for permission to camp in the reserve, but note that there is no water. Do not camp alone as robberies occur.

**● Places to eat**

Excellent fried fish at open-sided restaurants at El Chaco (see below), eg ***Jhonny y Jennifer***, friendly; ***El Chorito***, close to *Hotel Paracas*.

**● Transport**

**Local** Taxi from Pisco to Paracas about US$3-4; kombis to/from El Chaco beach (marked 'Chaco-Paracas-Museo') when full, US$0.50, 25 mins; several buses, US$0.30, leave from the market in Pisco. Make sure you catch the last bus back at about 1600. By private transport it takes about 50 mins to Lagunilla, 45 mins to La Mina and 1 hr to Mirador de los Lobos. Make sure your car is in good condition, never leave it unattended, and travel in a group as robbery has been a problem in the past. There is no public transport on the peninsula.

## BALLESTAS ISLANDS

Trips to the **Islas Ballestas** leave from the jetty at El Chaco, the beach and fishing port by Paracas village. The islands, dubbed the "poor man's Galápagos" by many, are nonetheless spectacular in their own right and well worth visiting. They are eroded into numerous arches and caves, hence their name; *ballesta* means bow, as in archery. These arches provide shelter for thousands of seabirds, some of which are very rare, and countless sea lions. A former guano factory can be seen on one of the islands and several others have installations. The book *Las Aves del Departamento de Lima* by Maria Koepcke is useful.

### Tours

For trips to Islas Ballestas: *Blue Sea Tours*, C Chosica 320, San Andrés, Pisco, T 034-533469, anexo 35, also at El Chaco, guides Jorge Espejo and Hubert Van Lomoen (speaks Dutch) are frequently rec; there is no time limit on tours. On C San Francisco, Pisco: *Paseo Turístico Islas Ballestas*, No 109, rec; *Ballestas Travel Service*, No 249, T 533095, rec; *Paracas Tours*, No 257. *The Zarcillo Connection*, Arequipa 164, T 262795, also good for Paracas National Reserve. The main hotels in Pisco and Paracas will also arrange tours, eg *Hotel Paracas*, US$30 in their own speed boat, 0900-1700.

Short trips last 3 hrs; it's better to go in the morning when the sea is not so rough. The full trip includes Isla San Gallán, where there are thousands of sea lions, and is rec. All boats are speedboats with life jackets, some are very crowded; wear warm clothing. You will see, close up, thousands of inquisitive sea lions, guano birds, pelicans, penguins and, if you're lucky, dolphins swimming in the bay. The boats pass Puerto San Martín and the Candelabra en route to the islands. Tours to the islands cost US$11 pp; to the peninsula US$20 pp; out of season tours are a lot cheaper.

## INLAND FROM PISCO

From the Pan-American Highway near Pisco, a road runs 317 km up to **Ayacucho** in the sierra, with a branch to **Huancavelica**. It is paved as far as **Huaytará** and is being paved thereafter. At **Castrovirreyna** it reaches 4,600m. The scenery on this journey is superb.

### TAMBO COLORADO

This is one of the best-preserved Inca ruins in coastal Peru. The site lies up the Pisco valley, 48 km from Pisco and includes buildings where the Inca and his retinue would have stayed. Many of the walls retain their original colours. On the other side of the road is the public plaza and the garrison and messengers' quarters. The caretaker will act as a guide, he has a small collection of items found on the site. Entrance is US$1.50.

From Humay, go to Hacienda Montesarpe, and 500m above the hacienda is the line of holes known as 'La avenida misteriosa de las picaduras de viruelas' (the mysterious avenue of smallpox spots) which stretches along the Andes for many kilometres. Its purpose is still unknown.

• **Transport** Buses from Pisco, 0800, Oropesa US$0.80 (3 hrs). Alight 20 mins after the stop at Humay; the road passes right through the site. Return by bus to Pisco in the afternoon. For the bus or truck back to Pisco wait at Sr Mendoza, the caretaker's house. Taxi from Pisco US$30.

## HUAYTARA

4 hrs by bus from Pisco. The whole side of the church is a perfectly preserved Inca wall with niches and trapezoidal doorways. 20 mins from town are the ruins of **Incahuasí** with thermal baths. On 24 June is the Fiesta of San Juan Bautista, which involves a week of processions, fireworks, bullfights and dancing day and night (and probably the occasional drink).

• **Accommodation & transport** **D** *Hotel de Turistas*, lodging, food and tours; **E** *Municipal*, no restaurant, warm water. Bus from Pisco US$2.25 (US$5.50 for festival); also Molina from Lima, 6 hrs.

# ICA

From Pisco the Pan-American Highway runs 60 km S to **Guadalupe**, where *Restaurant Sol de Mayo*, 1 block N of main plaza, does a good *menú* for US$1.50.

It then continues a further 10 km to **Ica** (*Pop* 152,300; *Phone code* 034), on the Río Ica. The San Jerónimo church at Cajamarca [illegible] has a fine mural behind the altar. Ica is famous for its *tejas*, a local sweet of *manjarblanco*, which is sold behind the Luren church. The waters of the Choclacocha and Orococha lakes from the eastern side of the Andes are tunnelled into the Ica valley and irrigate 30,000 ha of land. The lakes are at 4,570m. The tunnel is over 9 km long.

## WINE AND PISCO

Ica is Peru's chief wine centre. The **Bodega El Carmen** is on the right-hand side when arriving from Lima. This pisco distillery has an ancient grape press made from a huge tree trunk and is worth a visit.

The **Vista Alegre** wine and pisco distillery can be also be visited (though a good grasp of Spanish is essential) and its shop is recommended. They give official tours on Fri and Sat 0830-1130. A local bus drops you at the entrance, or it's a 10-15 mins' walk on the other side of the river.

10 km outside Ica, in the district of Subtanjalla, is José Carrasco González, **Bodega El Catador**, a shop selling home-made wines and pisco, and traditional handicrafts associated with winemaking. In the evening it is a restaurant-bar with dancing and music. The best time to visit is during harvest, late Feb to early April, when wine and pisco tasting is usually possible. It is open daily 0800-1800; take a bus from the 2nd block of Moquegua, every 30 mins, US$0.10.

*Cachina*, a very young white wine 'with a strong yeasty taste', is drunk about 2 weeks after the grape harvest.

Near Bodega El Catador is **Bodega Alvarez**. The owner, Umberto Alvarez, is very hospitable and won the gold medal for the best pisco in Peru in 1995. Ask about their *pisco de mosto verde* and the rarer, more expensive, *pisco de limón*, which will set you back US$40 per bottle.

A very good, strong *[illegible]* is made by Sr Luis Chipana and sold in unlabelled bottles. He is always short of bottles so best to take your own. A visit is recommended, but you'll need good Spanish. Sr Chipana lives on the main plaza beside his bodega; ask for him in the bar on the plaza.

## Pisco: a history in the making

A visit to Peru would not be complete without savouring a *pisco sour*, quite simply the finest beverage the country has to offer. Peruvians are mighty proud of their national tipple, which has turned out to be one of the few positive results of conquest.

Although the vines which produce the grapes for pisco were brought from Spain by the conquistadors, the role of the master coastal desert potters who crafted the first vessels for the Peruvian brandy was crucial. In the Pisco river valley an indigenous group, known as Piscos and descendants of the Paracas people, excelled in the art of making fired clay pots lined with beeswax for storing *chicha* and other spirits. When the Spanish arrived with their vines, they entrusted the Piscos with making the vessels to preserve and transport wine and, not long after, the brandy they distilled. Pisco, the name given to the vessel, was soon used to refer to the drink.

Peru was the first conquered territory in Spanish America to produce wines and brandies. The cultivation of grapes began with the import of vinestalks from the Canary Islands by Francisco de Caravantes and planted on the outskirts of Lima. The crop later reached as far as Cusco and Ayacucho in the Andes, but it was in Ica that the enterprise really took off, owing mainly to the region's exceptional climate.

Starting in the second half of the 16th century, the foundations of a wine and brandy industry were laid as grape juice became increasingly available with the resulting expansion in trade. The first significant mention of pisco is from a note in 1630 by López de Caravantes, who wrote that, "the valley of Pisco is where one can find more wines of excellent quality than anywhere in Peru. And a wine is grown there that rivals [our] sherry, that goes by the name of pisco, for it is made with the smallest of grapes, and it is one of the most exquisite spirits that can be consumed in the world".

A hundred years after the conquest, the wine and pisco trade had grown

### MUSEUMS

**Museo Regional** houses mummies, ceramics, textiles and trepanned skulls from the Paracas, Nasca and Inca cultures. There's a good, well-displayed collection of Inca counting strings (*quipus*) and clothes made of feathers. Also good and informative displays with maps of all sites in the Department. Behind the building there is a scale model of the Nasca lines with an observation tower; a useful orientation before visiting the lines. The attendant paints copies of motifs from the ceramics and textiles in the original pigments (US$1), and sells his own good maps of Nasca for US$1.65. To get there, take bus 17 from the Plaza de Armas (US$0.50). Museum open 0745-1900, Mon-Sat: Sun 0900-1300 (US$1.15, students US$0.65).

### EXCURSIONS

5 km from Ica, round a palm-fringed lake and amid impressive sand dunes, is the attractive oasis and summer resort of **Huacachina**. Its green sulphur waters are said to possess curative properties and attract thousands of visitors who come to swim and relax in this peaceful setting. Sleeping in the open is pleasant here, and swimming in the lake is beautiful, but watch out for soft sand (and, as elsewhere, watch your belongings). Sandboarding on the dunes has become a major pastime here, attracting fans from Europe and

considerably. Ica sent its wine to Huamanga, Cusco, Lima and Callao. And from Pisco ships left for other important ports like Guayaquil, Santa Fe, Panamá, Realejo and Sonsonate (in Central America), as well as Valparaíso and Buenos Aires. Reports of maritime trade in the 16th and 17th centuries reveal the growing prestige of grape brandy as pisco exports eventually displaced those of wine.

Pisco trade surged in spite of royal bans to halt the vineyard explosion that endangered the Spanish wine industry. In 1629, the prohibition included the transport of Peruvian wines aboard Atlantic-bound ships. But despite the restrictions, the industry continued to expand during most of the 18th century.

Nowadays, pisco is still mostly made by small, independent producers using mainly traditional techniques, though a few firms utilize modern procedures to manufacture and market larger quantities. The Ica valley still ranks as Peru's foremost producer of pisco, followed by the nearby valleys of Pisco, Chincha and Lunahuaná and Moquegua further south. Other production centres include Vitor in Arequipa, Locumba in Tacna and Surco in Lima.

Although modern mechanical crushers and presses are widely in use, the traditional method of crushing the grapes by foot can still be found. The extracted juices flow along pipes into the *puntaya*, tar-lined vessels which are then placed under the hot sun to ferment. Modern pisco makers now use concrete tanks inside wine cellars. Once fermentation is complete, the fermented grape juice is emptied into stills, or *falcas*, as traditional Peruvian stills are called. These are crucial to the process of true pisco production. In modern distilleries, large boilers are heated by oil or gas, but more conventional wineries still rely on wood from the *carob* tree. This slow-burning fuel is said to provide a constant source of heat that makes for a finer flavour, rather like food cooked over a charcoal fire.

Another important factor in pisco production is the type of grape. The unscented *quebranta* grape, brought to the Americas by the Spaniards, lends its unique characteristics to the making of the renowned "pure pisco". There are also fragrant piscos from Moscatel and Albilla varieties, "creole piscos" made with prime fragrant grapes and green piscos made with partially fermented grape juice.

elsewhere. Board hire US$0.50, from Manuel's restaurant, where you can also pitch a tent.

• **Accommodation** **C** *Hotel Mossone* (4 hrs' drive from Lima), or **A3**, full board, is at the eastern end of the lake, T 231651, F 236137. Another good hotel is the **F** ***Salvatierra***, with private bath. Both are great places to relax.

• **Transport** Bus from plaza in Ica to Huacachina, US$0.50, 10-15 mins; taxi US$1.50.

## LOCAL FESTIVALS

The wine harvest festival is held in early March. The image of El Señor de Luren, in a fine church in Parque Luren, draws pilgrims from all Peru to the twice-yearly festivals in Mar and Oct (15-21), when there are all-night processions.

## LOCAL INFORMATION

### ● Accommodation

Hotels are fully booked during the harvest festival and prices rise greatly.

**A2** *Las Dunas*, Av La Angostura 400, T 231031, F 231007, plus 18% tax and service, about 20% cheaper on weekdays, highly rec, in a complete resort with restaurant, swimming pool, horse riding and other activities, it has its own airstrip for flights over Nasca, 50 mins. Lima offices: Ricardo Rivera Navarrete 889, Oficina 208, San Isidro, Casilla 4410, Lima 100, T/F 442-4180.

**C-D** *Hostal Siesta I*, Independencia 160, T 233249, with bath, hot water, friendly owner; ***Siesta II***, T 234633, similar; **C** ***Hostal Silmar***, Castrovirreyna 110, T 235089, hot water, TV, carpets.

**E** *Tucaranda*, Lambayeque, next to Ormeño bus terminal, private bathrooms; **E** ***Colón***,

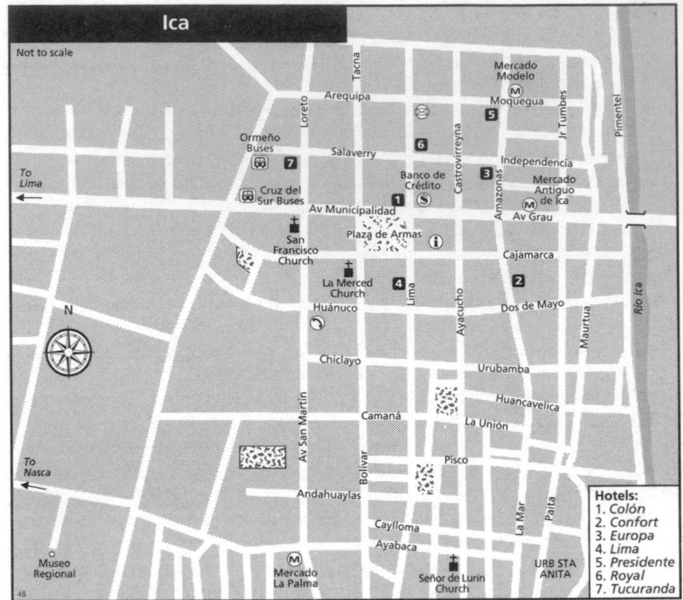


Plaza de Armas, with bath, F without, basic, dirty, old, noisy, restaurant; **E** ***Confort***, La Mar 251, 4 blocks from plaza, clean, possible to park motorcycle; **E** ***Hostal El Aleph***, Independencia 152, good.

**F** ***Lima***, Lima 262, basic but quiet; **F** ***Europa***, Independencia 258, clean, cold water, good.

### ● Places to eat

***Macondo***, Jr Bolívar 300, fish good, rec; ***El Otro Peñoncito***, Bolívar 255, lunch US$6, friendly, clean, good toilets; ***El Fogón***, Municipalidad 276, good and cheap. Good one at Ormeño bus terminal. ***El Edén, Casa Naturista***, vegetarian at Andahuaylas 204. ***Pastelería La Spiga***, Lima 243, rec; ***Pastelería Velazco***, on Plaza de Armas, clean, good service, rec.

### ● Banks & money changers

Avoid changing TCs if possible as commission is high. If you need to, though, **Banco de Crédito** is reasonable.

### ● Tourist offices

Some information at travel agencies. **Touring y Automóvil Club del Perú**, Manzanilla 523.

### ● Transport

**Buses** To **Pisco**, 70 km, 1 hr, US$1 by bus, several daily; colectivos from opp Ormeño. To **Lima**, 302 km, 4 hrs, US$5, several daily inc Soyuz and Flores (see also Lima, **Bus Companies**); in Ica Ormeño is at Lambayeque 180. All bus offices are on Lambayeque blocks 1 and 2 and Salaverry block 3. To **Nasca**, 140 km, 2 hrs, US$2, several buses and colectivos daily, inc Ormeño, last bus 2100. To **Arequipa** the route goes via Nasca, see under Nasca.

**Warning** Beware of thieves in the market, at the bus station and around the Plaza de Armas, even in daylight.

## SOUTH TO NASCA

The southern oases, S of Ica to the Chilean frontier, produce enough to support themselves, but little more. The highlands grow increasingly arid and the coast more rugged. There are only thin ribbons of cultivable lands along valley bottoms, and most of these can be irrigated only in their upper reaches. However, the cotton plantations between Ica and Nasca and the orange-growing centre at Palpa are exceptions. In several places the Highway is not protected against drifting sand and calls for cautious driving.

## PALPA

Known as the 'Capital de la Naranja' (the Orange Capital), **Palpa** (*Pop* 15,000) is a hospitable town 90 km S of Ica. The Plaza de Armas, on which the Municipalidad and church stand, is bordered by arches. Some colonial-style buildings survive. The climate is hot and dry (average annual temperature 21.4°C) and the main crops, besides oranges, are other fruits (eg plums, bananas) and cotton. There is also fishing for shrimp in the river.

### Excursions

Archaeological studies indicate that the Nasca culture, characterized by lines drawn on the desert and representations of animals and plants, began on the banks of the Río Grande, near present-day Palpa. There are several sites, of different periods, not far from the town. The **Ciudad Perdida de Hualluri**, on the W side of the Panamericana Sur, 16 km from Palpa, 5 km from the Highway (Distrito Santa Cruz), is a large pre-Inca city. At the entrance to the site is a huarango tree which is over 1,000 years old. In Sector Sacramento, 2 km from the Highway, is the **Puente Colgante del Inca**, built during the reign of Pachacútec, and mentioned by Felipe Guaman Poma in his chronicles. 15 km from Palpa, on the road to Laluta, are the **Petroglifos de Chichictara**, more than 360 drawings on 65 large rocks depicting human and anthropomorphic figures, felines, llamas, dogs, condors, snakes and other creatures. They are said to date from the Chavín period. Other drawings can be found at **Llipata** and at the **Reloj Solar**, N of the city, ½ km E of the Panamericana (the main design here is said to be a calendar marking the seasons of the year). The **Ciudadela de Santa Rosa** (5 km from Distrito Río Grande) and other ruins can also be visited.

### Local festivals

The main *fiesta* is on 15 August. The *ciruela* (plum) harvest is in March.

### Local information

**● Accommodation**

Hotels include the *Palpa* and the *San Francisco*. There are several *pensiones*, inc ***El Sol***, which is not recommended.

**● Guides and information**

Seek information from the Consejo Municipal. There are no travel agencies in town. Otherwise ask for information and guides in Nasca; recommended is César Barrios Castañeda at ***Alegría Tours*** (see below), who will take visitors at the cost of transport.

## NASCA

(*Pop* 30,000; *Alt* 619m; *Phone code* 034); Nasca lies 141 km S of Ica by the Pan-American Highway, set in a green valley amid a perimeter of mountains, 444 km from Lima. Its altitude puts it just above any fog which may drift in from the sea. The sun blazes the year round by day and the nights are crisp. Overlooking the town is Cerro Blanco (2,078m), the highest sand dune in the world, which is popular for sandboarding and parapenting.

### THE NASCA CULTURE

The Nascas had a highly developed civilization which reached its peak about AD 800. Their polychrome ceramics are world-renowned for their outstanding beauty and examples of these, along with wood carvings and adornments of gold, are on display in many of Lima's museums.

The economic, political and social system of the Nasca culture revolved around agriculture, which may account for the immense drawings known as the Nasca lines on the pampa between Nasca and Palpa (see after **Local information** for the Nasca Lines). As well as their remarkable ceramics and mysterious lines, the Nascas also left behind textiles of technical brilliance.

## MUSEUMS

The Nasca municipality's museum, on the main plaza, has a small but fine collection, though some of the glass cabinets could do with a wash. Entry, US$1, open Mon-Sat 0900-1200, 1600-1700.

## EXCURSIONS

The Nasca area is dotted with over 100 cemeteries and the dry, humidity-free climate has preserved perfectly invaluable tapestries, cloth and mummies.

At the cemetery of **Chauchilla**, 30 km S of Nasca, grave robbing *huaqueros* ransacked the tombs and left remains all over the place. Bones, skulls, mummies and pottery shards used to litter the desert, but latest reports suggest that practically nothing is left. A tour takes about 2 hrs and should cost about US$7 pp with a minimum of 3 people. On the Panamericana Sur, heading S from Nasca, Chauchilla is on the left, unsigned, 10 km from the highway.

20 km from Nasca, **Poroma** cemetery is on the right, signed (poorly). Cemetery tours usually include a visit to a gold shop. Gold mining is one of the main local industries and a tour usually includes a visit to a small family processing shop where the techniques used are still very old-fashioned.

Some tours also include a visit to a local potter's studio. That of Sr Andrés Calle Benavides, who makes Nasca reproductions, is particularly recommended. He is very friendly and takes time to explain the techniques he uses. He has a small gallery but prices can be a bit on the expensive side. Anyone interested in precolumbian ceramics is welcome to make an appointment to visit him independently. He is very knowledgeable on the coastal desert cultures.

**To the Paredones ruins and aqueduct**: the ruins, also called Cacsamarca, are Inca on a pre-Inca base. They are not well-preserved. The underground aqueducts, built 300 BC-700 AD, are still in working order and worth seeing. 33 aqueducts irrigate 20 ha each; they are cleaned end Oct/early Nov. By taxi it is about US$10 round trip, or go with a tour.

**Cantalloc** is a ½-1 hr walk through Buena Fe, to see markings in the valley floor. These consist of a triangle pointing to a hill and a *tela* (cloth) with a spiral depicting the threads. Climb the mountain to see better examples. This is best done with a guide, or by car.

**Cahuachi**, to the W of the Nasca Lines, comprises several pyramids and a site called **El Estaquería**. The latter is thought to have been a series of astronomical sighting posts, but more recent research suggests the wooden pillars were used to dry dead bodies and therefore it may have been a place of mummification. Tours cost about US$5 pp with a minimum of 3 people.

**Sacaco**, 30 km S of Nasca, has a museum built over the fossilized remains of a whale excavated in the desert. The keeper lives in a house nearby and is helpful. Take a bus from Nasca, C Bolognesi, in the morning (check times in advance) towards Puerto de Lomas, ask the driver where to get off and be ready for a 30 mins' (2 km) walk in the sun. Return to the Pan-American Highway no later than 1800 for a bus back. Do not go 2-3 days after a new moon as a vicious wind blows at this time.

**Puerto de Lomas** is a fishing village to the S of Nasca, with safe beaches which

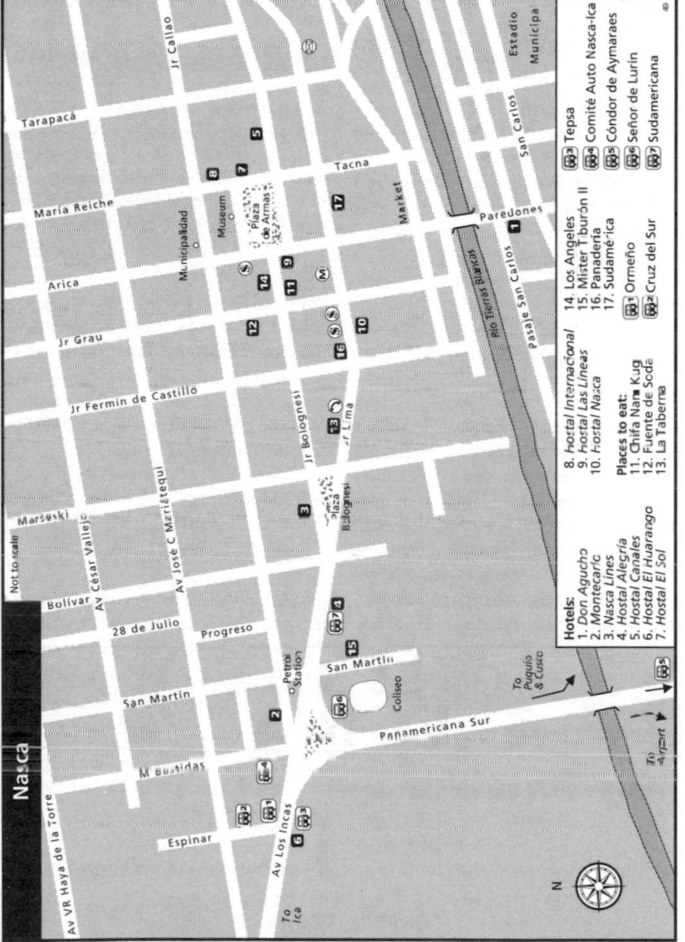

are popular in Feb-Mar. It is 1½ hrs by bus, US$1.75 (1 hr by car).

• **Accommodation & places to eat** C *Hostal Capricho de Verano*, T 210282, beautifully-situated on the cliffs, bungalows with bath, clean, same owner as *Hostal Don Agucho* in Nasca, run by very friendly elderly couple, special rates for young travellers, rec. 100m beyond is *Restaurant Alojamiento Melchorita*; also several fish restaurants.

## TOURS

*Algería Tours*, run by Efraín Alegría at *Hotel Alegría* offer inclusive tours (see Hotels below) which have been repeatedly rec. Guides with radio contact and maps can be provided for hikes to nearby sites. Juan Valdivia is very knowledgeable on the Nasca and Paracas cultures and speaks English. They are planning to run a specialized tour to the San Fernando Reserve to see the marine wildlife, as well as tours to Puerto Inca and the Inca ruins at Atiquipa.

The Fernández family, who run the *Hotel Nasca*, also run local tours. Ask for the hotel owners and speak to them direct. Also ask Efraín Alegría or the Fernández family to arrange a taxi for you to one of the sites outside Nasca (eg US$50 to Sacaco, 30 mins at site). It is not recommended to take just any taxi on the Plaza as they are unreliable and can lead to robbery. It is not dangerous to visit the sites if you go with a trustworthy person. Also rec is Juan Tohalino Vera of *Nasca Trails*, at Ignacio Morsesky 122, T 522858, he speaks English, French, German and Italian. Taxi drivers usually act as guides, but most speak only Spanish. All guides must be approved by the Ministry of Tourism: ask to see an identity card. Tour and hotel touts try to overcharge or mislead those who arrive by bus: do not conduct any business at the bus station.

## LOCAL FESTIVALS

Virgen de la Guadelupe 29 Aug-10 Sept.

## LOCAL INFORMATION

● **Accommodation**

**A3** *Nasca Lines*, Jr Bolognesi, T 522293, F 522293, a/c, comfortable, rooms with private patio, hot water, peaceful, restaurant, good but expensive meals, safe car park, pool (US$2.50 for non-guests, or free if having lunch), they can arrange package tours which include 2-3 nights at the hotel plus flight over the lines and a desert trip for around US$250, rec; **A3** *De La Borda*, T 522576, old hacienda, lovely gardens, pool, excellent restaurant, quiet, helpful, rec, at Majoro about 5 km from town past airstrip, English-speaking manageress.

**B** *Maison Suisse*, opp the airport, T/F 522434, nice, comfortable, safe car park, restaurant, pool, new rooms with jacuzzi, accepts Amex.

**C** *Hostal Don Agucho*, Paredones y San Carlos, T 522048, very clean, nice, friendly, pool, garage; **C** *Albergue Villa Verde*, Pasaje Angela s/n, T 523373, smallcountry-style lodge in quiet gardens, pursues environmental improvements, pool, bar, parking; **C-D** *Hostal Las Líneas*, Jr Arica 299, T 522488, clean, spacious, restaurant, rec; **C-E** *Hotel Alegría*, Jr Lima 168, T/F 522444, F 222150, nr bus station, new rooms with bath and continental breakfast, inc tax, or rooms with communal bath, clean, basic, hot water, cafeteria, garden, manager (Efraín Alegría) speaks English and Hebrew, rec, tours with English, French and German speaking guides, laundry facilities, safe luggage deposit (inc for bus passengers not needing a hotel), book exchange, very popular, flights and bus tickets arranged, those arriving by bus should beware being told that *Alegría* is closed, or full, and no longer runs tours, if you call the hotel they will pick you up at the bus station free of charge day or night.

**D** ***El Huarango***, Av Los Incas 117, opp Ormeño bus terminal, T 522497, with bath, E without, hot water, clean, good facilities, TV; **D** ***Hostal Canales***, Bolognesi 673, T 522099, F 522688, with bath, includes breakfast, cheaper without, tours arranged; **D** ***Internacional***, Av Maria Reiche, T 522166, with bath, clean, quiet, hot water, garage, café, new bungalows; **D** ***Montecarlo***, Jr Callao, T 522577, hot water (ask for it), with bath, quite old, small pool, offers flights over the Lines plus 1 night's lodging in bungalow but not all year round, mixed reports; **D** ***Via Morburg***, JM Mejía 108, T 522566, new, with bath, fan, hot water, quiet, pleasant, the hotel is associated with ***Restaurant El Huarango***, good food and prices, bar, live entertainment.

**E** ***Hostal El Sol***, Jr Tacna, on Plaza de Armas, T 522064, with bath, basic but friendly, hot showers, small; **E** see *Hotel Alegría* above.

**F** ***Nasca***, C Lima 438, T/F 522085, hot water, noisy, clothes washing facilities, luggage store, hard sell on tours and flights, bargain hard for better price, mixed reports, safe motorcycle parking, dirty bathrooms; **F** ***San Martín***, Arica 116, basic, electric showers.

**Camping**: in the grounds of *Restaurant Nido del Cóndor* opposite the airport.

### ● Places to eat

***Nido del Cóndor***, opp airport, also has shop, videos, swimming pool; ***Aviance***, Arica 213, rec for *menú*; ***Cañada***, Lima 160, cheap, good *menú*, excellent pisco sours, rec; ***Los Angeles***, ½-block from Plaza de Armas, good, cheap, try *sopa criolla*, and chocolate cake; similar is ***Concordia***, Lima 594, which rents bikes at US$1/hr; ***Chifa Nam Kug***, on Bolognesi near Plaza, rec; ***La Púa***, Jr Lima, next to *Hotel Alegría*, good; ***La Taberna***, Jr Lima 326, excellent food, live music, friendly, popular with gringos, worth a look just for the graffiti; ***Mister Tiburón II***, C San Martín, clean, good food; ***Sudamérica***, Lima 668, good local food, especially meat; ***Fuente de Soda Jumbory***, near cinema, good *almuerzo*; ***Panadería Pin-Pan***, Lima y F de Castillo. The pisco sours are recommended as the best in Peru.

### ● Banks & money changers

**Banco de Crédito**, Lima y Grau, changes cash and TCs, cash advance on visa, decent rates. **Banco de la Nación** exchanges at poor rate. **Interbanc**, on the Plaza de Armas, changes cash and will advance on Visa. Some street changers will change TCs, but at a poor rate.

### ● Post & telecommunications

At Lima 816, post office also at *Hotel Alegría*.

**Telephone**: Telefónica del Perú for international calls with coins on Plaza Bolognesi; also on Plaza de Armas and at Lima 359 where you can send or receive fax messages and make international collect calls.

### ● Shopping

Markets at Lima y Grau, small, and Mercado Central entre Arica y Tacna.

● **Useful addresses**
**Police**: at Av Los Incas.

● **Transport**
**Buses** To **Lima**, 446 km, US$5-8, 7 hrs, several buses and colectivos daily, luxury buses US$12.50 (see Lima, **Bus Companies**), Ormeño, on Av Los Incas near the *Montecarlo* hotel, rec; Cruz del Sur and Tepsa also on Los Incas; Señor de Luren, Lima y Panamericana at the Ovalo; Cóndor de Aymaraes and Wari Tours on Panamericana at the junction for Puquío; Sudamericana office in *Hotel Alegría*. To **Ica**, 140 km, 3 hrs, US$2 and to **Pisco** 210 km, 3 hrs, US$3, several buses and colectivos daily. Buses to **Camaná**, 390 km, 6 hrs, US$6, several daily; continuing to **Moquegua**, 244 km, 4 hrs, US$4. To **Tacna**, 793 km, 12 hrs, US$12, several buses daily. To **Arequipa**, 623 km, 9 hrs, US$9; several buses daily, inc Ormeño, at 1900 and 2100, Sudamericano, 0300 and 2030, and Cruz del Sur at 2000 and 2230, delays possible out of Nasca because of drifting sand across the road or because of mudslides in the rainy season. Travel in daylight

## The mystery of the lines

60 years ago Nasca was just a small Peruvian desert town of no particular note. Its anonymity was to end, however, in 1939 with the arrival of Dr Paul Kosok,a North American scientist who had come to Nasca to study what was believed to be the remains of an ancient irrigation system. On June 21st of that year, Kosok was flying over the pampa, or plain, north of the town when he noticed a series of strange lines which appeared to form some kind of design. Following one of these lines, Kosok discovered that it represented the outline of a bird. He quickly concluded that the lines had nothing to do with irrigation systems.

His curiosity aroused, Kosok made a return pass over the area where many of the lines converged. This time he noticed that the setting sun coincided exactly with the direction of one of the lines. By chance, Kosok's discovery took place on the winter solstice, leading him to believe that there must be some relation between the configuration of the lines and certain astronomical phenomena. So impressed was he, that he described the Nasca pampa as "the biggest astronomy book in the world".

Kosok may have been the first to "discover" these drawings etched in the Peruvian desert, but it was a young German mathematician who brought them to public prominence and put Nasca on the map. Maria Reiche had arrived in Peru eight years earlier to teach the German consul's children in Cusco. She got to know Dr Kosok while working as his translator at a seminar on the lines. Following his speech, Reiche spoke to the scientist and he encouraged her to study the lines. She would dedicate the rest of her life to the task.

Maria Reiche's years of meticulous measurement and study of the lines led her to the conclusion that they represented a huge astronomical calendar. She also used her mathematical knowledge to determine how the many drawings and symbols could have been created with such precise symmetry. She suggested that those responsible for the lines used long cords attached to stakes in the ground. The figures were drawn by means of a series of circular arcs of different radius. Reiche also contends that they used a standard unit of measurement of 1.30m, or the distance between the fingertips of a person's extended arms.

As well as the anthropomorphic and zoomorphic drawings, there are a great many geometric figures. Reiche believes these to be a symbolic form of writing associated with the movements of the stars. In this way, the lines could have been

if possible – buses that leave around 0300, 0330 do most of the journey in daylight. Book ticket on previous day. Watch out for bus companies charging the full fare from Lima to Arequipa and for overbooking.

Cóndor de Aymaraes and Wari run buses to **Cusco**, 659 km, 25 hrs, US$18; the route goes through **Reserva Nacional Pampas Galeras**, which has a vicuña reserve. There is a military base and park guard here. The road is paved as far as the Reserve; from there to Puquio, at 155 km, it is in poor condition, but slowly being upgraded. From Puquío, via Chalhuanca (where gasoline is sold from the drum) to Abancay (309 km), the road is poor but also being upgraded. From Abancay to Cusco the road is paved. There are now 2 bus companieswhichtraveltheLima-Nasca-Abancay-Cusco route – Cóndor de Aymaraes and Wari Tours. Their offices are at the exit from Nasca on the road to Puquío. Note that safety is not assured (terrorists or bandits) and most major bus lines have not resumed services on thisroute.

used as a kind of calendar that not only recorded celestial events but also had a practical day-to-day function such as indicating the times for harvest, fishing and festivals.

There are those who disagree with the German mathematician's hypothesis. The International Explorers Society, for example, were convinced that the desert artists would not have drawn something they themselves could not see. They set out to prove that the ancient Peruvians could fly, based on the fact that the lines are best seen from the air, and that there are pieces of ancient local pottery and tapestry showing balloonists as well as local legends of flying men. In 1975, they made a hot-air balloon of cloth and reed, called it *Condor I* and attempted to fly it for 15 minutes over the pampa. Unfortunately for them, the flight lasted only 60 seconds, thereby leaving the issue unresolved. An account of the flight is in *Nasca, the flight of Condor 1*, by Jim Woodman, Murray, 1980 (Pocket Books, NY 1977).

Some of the competing theories as to the function of the Nasca lines are rather far-fetched. Erich Von Daniken, in his book *Chariots of the Gods*, posited that the pampa was an extraterrestrial landing strip. This idea, however, only succeeded in drawing to the site thousands of visitors who proceeded to tear across the lines on motorbikes, 4-wheel drives, horses and whatever else they could get their hands on, leaving their indelible mark. It is now an offence to walk or drive on the pampa, punishable by heavy fine or imprisonment.

In 1980, George A Von Breunig claimed that the lines were part of a giant running track – presumably designed for an ancient Peruvian version of the Olympic Games. A similar theory was proposed by the English astronomer Alan Sawyer.

Other theories are that the Nasca designs represent weaving patterns and yarns (Henri Stirlin) and that the plain is a map demonstrating the Tiahuanaco Empire (Zsoltan Zelko). *The Nasca Lines – a new perspective on their origin and meaning* (Editorial Los Pinos, Lima 18), by Dr Johan Reinhard, brings together ethnographic, historical and archaeological data, including the current use of straight lines in Chile and Bolivia, to suggest that the Lines conform to fertility practices throughout the Andes. Another good book is *Pathways to the Gods: the mystery of the Nasca Lines*, by Tony Morrison (Michael Russell, 1978), obtainable in Lima.

Whatever the real purpose of the Nasca lines, one fact remains indisputable: that their status as one of the country's major tourist attractions is largely due to the selfless work of Maria Reiche, the unofficial guardian of the lines.

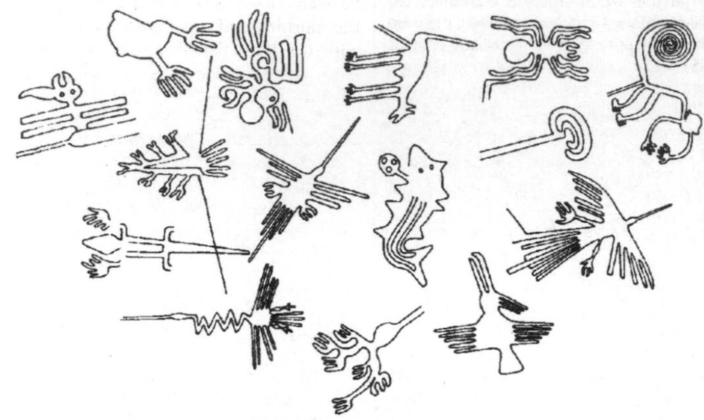

Sketches of some geogliphs from the Nasca and Palpa pampas
(Drawing: Hamilton Arce O)

## NASCA LINES

About 22 km N of Nasca, in the Ingenio valley, along the Pan-American Highway, are the famous Nasca Lines. Cut into the stony desert are large numbers of lines, not only parallels and geometrical figures, but also designs such as a dog, an enormous monkey, birds (one with a wing span of over 100m), a spider and a tree. The lines, which can best be appreciated from the air, are thought to have been etched on the Pampa Colorada sands by three different groups – the Paracas people 900-200 BC, Nascas 200 BC-AD 600 and the settlers from Ayacucho at about AD 630.

### Maria Reiche

The German expert, Dr Maria Reiche, who studied the lines for over 40 years, mostly from a step ladder, is now over 90 years old. She hasn't walked on the pampa since 1987 and was recently robbed of her sight through glaucoma. Her sister, Renate, who used to present a free lecture based on Dr Reiche's theories in the *Hotel Nasca Lines* every evening, died at the beginning of 1996. In mid 1996 there were plans to restart the talks with an archaeologist from the Maria Reiche Association, though no date had yet been fixed.

In 1976 Maria Reiche had a platform called the mirador put up at her own expense, from which three of the huge designs can be seen – the Hands, the Lizard and the Tree. Her book, *Mystery on the Desert*, is on sale for US$10 (proceeds to conservation work) at the hotel. In Jan 1994 Maria Reiche opened a small museum (entry US$0.50), 5 km from town at the Km 416 marker.

**● Tours on land**

Taxi-guides to the mirador, 0800-1200, cost US$7 pp, or you can hitch, but there is not always much traffic. Travellers suggest the view from the hill 500m back to Nasca is better. Ormeño bus leaves for the lines at 0900 (US$1.75); hitch back, but have patience. Go by an early bus as the site gets very hot. Better still, take a taxi and arrive at 0745 before the buses.

**● Tours by air**

Small planes take 3-5 passengers to see the Nasca Lines. Reservations can be made at the airport for flights with Aerocóndor; their office is opposite *Hotel Nasca Lines*. Flights can also be booked at *Hotel Nasca*, Aero Montecarlo (from hotel of that name), or Aerolca in Jr Lima and at the airport. These 3 companies are well-established and recommended; there are others. The price for a flight is US$50 pp, plus US$1.50 airport tax. It is best to organize a flight with Efraín Alegría at the *Hotel Alegría*, with Familia Fernández at *Hotel Nasca*, or direct with the airlines. Flights should last from 30 to 45 mins, but are sometimes cut to 20, and are bumpy with many tight turns – many people are airsick. Best times to fly are 0800-1000 and 1500-1630 when there is less turbulence and better light.

Aerocóndor in Lima (T 442-5663, or at the *Sheraton Hotel*, T 433-3320) and Aerolca (T 441-8614/8608) both offer flights over the lines from Lima in a 1-day tour (lunch in Nasca) for US$260 pp; or flights from Ica for US$130 pp. Aerolca also offers a night in *Maison Suisse* plus flight for US$65, but book 48 hrs in advance. Taxi to airport, US$1.35, bus, US$0.10. Make sure you clarify everything before getting on the plane and ask for a receipt. Also let them know in advance if you have any special requests.

## SOUTH OF NASCA

From a point 40 km beyond Nasca along the Pan-American Highway a branch road (39 km) runs to the ports of San Juan and San Nicolás, built to ship iron ore from the Marcona field, 29 km inland, and Acarí, 53 km E again, where a copper deposit is also being worked.

**San Juan**, 553 km S of Lima, has a beautiful deep-water bay. There is accommodation in **E** *Hotel Pacífico*, clean, rec. A tea room near the central market serves excellent cakes. A bus leaves from Lima to San Juan at 0600 via Nasca, US$7 from Lima.

After Nasca the Highway returns through impressive desert scenery to the coast at Puerto de Lomas and passes by Chala, **Atico** and Ocoña, to Camaná (392 km from Nasca). Cyclists warn that the headwinds between Nasca and Atico can be very severe.

### CHALA

173 km from Nasca, is a friendly fishing village with beaches where condors may be seen. Good fresh fish is available in the morning and possibilities of fishing with the local fishermen. There is no electricity after midnight. Many of the locals work in gold-panning.

• **Accommodation** **C** *Turistas*, in renovated building, with bath, D without, large rooms, good beds, friendly, hot water, restaurant, great sea view, rec; **F** *Hostal Grau*, very clean, has rooms facing the ocean; next door is ***Hostal Evelyn***, which is reported as similar. There are dozens of restaurants, mostly catering for passing buses.

### PUERTO INCA

10 km N of Chala are the large precolumbian ruins of **Puerto Inca** on the coast. On their discovery in the 1950s, the ruins were misunderstood and thus neglected. It is now recognized that this was the port for Cusco. The site is in excellent condition. The drying and store houses can be seen as holes in the ground (be careful where you walk). On the right side of the bay is a cemetery, on the hill a temple of reincarnation, and the Inca road from the coast to Cusco is clearly visible. The road was 240 km long, with a staging post every 7 km so that, with a change of runner at every post, messages could be sent in 24 hrs.

• **Accommodation & access** **C** *Beach Resort Puerto Inka*, Km 603 Panamericana Sur (for reservations; Central Telefónica Chala (054) 210260, or Arequipa T 254827, T/F 237122), with bath, D without, the water is brackish, excellent food, by the beautiful beach, great place to relax, boat hire, diving equipment rental, free camping (or tent hire, US$2), discount for longer stay, highly rec. Taxi from Chala US$6.75; 1-day tour from Nasca, US$10 pp. From Chala, at Km 603 on the Panamericana, follow an unpaved road on the left for a few kilometres to the hotel and ruins.

There is a good 4-hr walk from Puerto Inca to Chala following the coastline on the cliffs. Try to arrive in Chala by sunset, which leaves time to have dinner and catch the bus for Nasca or Arequipa which passes at around 2000.

# Arequipa and South to Chile



THE SOUTH-WESTERN corner of Peru is well-established on the tourist itinerary. The distinctive colonial architecture of Arequipa is only one of the attractions in a region of smoking volcanoes, deep canyons and terraced valleys. One of these canyons, the Cotahuasi, is the deepest in the world. Another, the Colca, is home to ancient peoples whose lives, until very recently, were completely untouched by the hand of tourism. It is also happens to be the best place in the whole country to get a close up view of the majestic condor.

There's a unique feeling to this part of Peru which, in part, stems from the stubborn pride of its people who have continuously attempted to gain independence from Lima. Fellow Peruvians will jokingly refer to this region as the "Independent Republic of Arequipa", but don't believe them when they kindly inform you of the need for a visa.

## Arequipa Environs

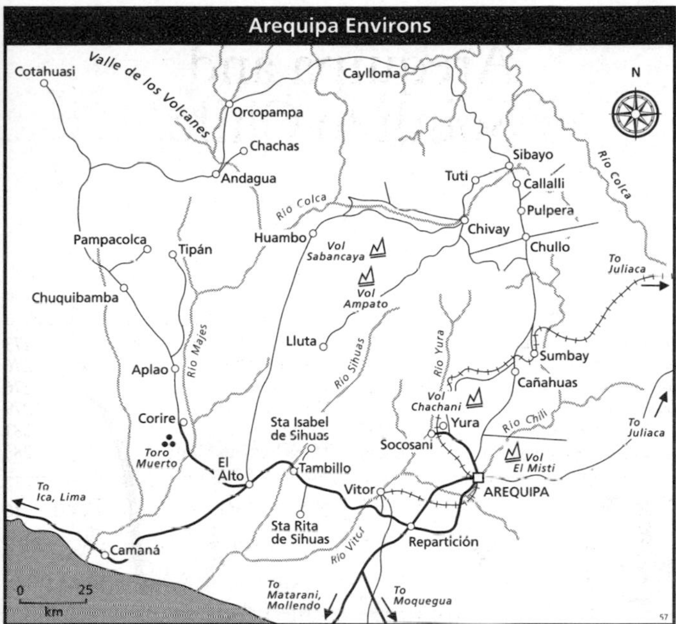


## THE COAST TO AREQUIPA

### CAMANA

Rice is the principal crop of this picturesque little coastal town, 222 km S from Chala, with a good food market. There is a small swimming pool on Av Mcal Castilla (new Pan-American Highway), US$1.

#### Excursions

5 km away is **La Punta**, the most popular of Camaná's beaches, especially during summer weekends when it is packed with young Arequipeños who come to party in the many bars and discos lining the beach road. One of these is *El Cangrejo*, one of the most popular discos in southern Peru; very busy and exclusive, US$8 cover charge. There are many cheap restaurants lining the beach road, though most don't look too clean.

The beach is pleasant but has little shade and is dangerous for swimming owing to the strong undertow. Parasols can be hired for US$1.50. Colectivos leave frequently day and night from Camaná, US$0.25.

32 km S of Camaná is the tiny, pleasant village of **Quilca** on the Río Quilca. Camaná sends its products to the small port here. In colonial times it was the unloading point for goods imported via Arequipa to Potosí. It is now a seedy harbour. The village of Quilca is further along, perched on a cliff overlooking the Río Siguas.

A bus leaves daily at 0900 and returns from Quilca at 1330; US$1.40, 2 hrs. The journey is spectacular and offers the chance of seeing large birds of prey and desert foxes. There is nothing much at the port so it's better to stay on until the village itself. The bus stops outside the only restaurant in town (which has a good set lunch), then continues to the fertile valley below before turning round for the return trip.

The coastal village of **Chira**, 12 km N of Camaná is worth a visit for its impressive sea cliffs, sea birds and quiet beaches. Catch a colectivo to **Atico** and ask to get off at Chira; US$0.70, 30 mins.

## Local information

### ● Accommodation

**C** *Plaza*, on the plaza; **C** *Turistas*, Av Lima, with bath, restaurant downstairs.

**D** *Camaná*, 9 de Septiembre, 1 block from plaza, with bath and hot shower; **D** *Lider 2*, Av Mcal Castilla 678 (new Pan-American Highway), T 571365, with bath, hot water, clean, comfortable, front rooms noisy; **D** *Residencial Selva*, Prolongación 2 de Mayo 225, Urb Granada, T 572063, with bath, cold water, modern, spacious, clean, very friendly, laundry facilities, cafeteria, patios and gardens, not very central but the owner will collect you if you call him on arrival in Camaná, discount for longer stays, highly rec.

**E** *Lider 1*, Av Lima 268 (old Pan-American Highway), with bath, clean, good restaurant, safe motorcycle parking for US$3. **NB** Hotels tend to be full in Jan, Feb and Mar.

### ● Places to eat

*Chifa Hong Kong*, Plaza de Armas, excellent food at reasonable prices, popular; *Turístico*, Av Pizarro 304, T 210280, seafood and *peña*; *Snack Barucci*, Jr 28 de Julio, corner of Plaza, modern and classy but overpriced, popular; *Willy Pollería*, Av Lima 137, good, cheap chicken and chips; *Savory Club*, Jr 28 de Julio 218, good food, overpriced but not over friendly. The best place breakfast is the food market, where you can enjoy excellent, cheap fruit juices, spinach pies and *empanadas*. The freshwater shrimps are delicious.

**Bars and discos**: *La Barra*, Av Mcal Castilla 600, good, loud music, popular; *Barucci*, Jr 28 de Julio, corner of Plaza, beneath snack bar of the same name, impressive sound and light system, US$2.50 cover charge; *Encuentros Video Pub*, Av Mcal Castilla, good videos, cheap beer, poor sound.

### ● Transport

Buses to **Lima**, many buses daily (eg Ormeño), US$12, 12 hrs. To **Arequipa**, many daily (eg Transportes Turismo), US$4, 3½ hrs. To **Pisco** Flores Hnos, Sudamericano, US$7, 8 hrs. Many companies have their offices on Av Lima.

**ROUTES** The Pan-American Highway swings inland from Camaná and runs along the top of a plateau with strange crescent-shaped dunes (see page 276). The sudden descents into the canyons of the Siguas and Vitor rivers are interesting, as is the pink stone valley at Km 945. The same colour is found on the 10 km road out of the valley S which, once surmounted, gives good views of the snowcapped mountains behind Arequipa. W of Arequipa, 74 km before Repartición, a dirt road branches left off the Pan-American Highway leading to Corire, Aplao and the valley of the Río Majes.

## TORO MUERTO

The world's largest field of petroglyphs at **Toro Muerto** is near **Corire**. There's a turn-off on the right heading back out of Corire. It's about a 1 hr walk. Ask directions en route. Just before the site is a tiny settlement of very basic wattle and daub huts. There are two signposts on the track leading up from here into the desert valley.

The higher you go, the more interesting the petroglyphs, though many have been ruined by graffiti. The sheer scale of the site is awe-inspiring and the view back down the arid desert valley against the backdrop of the distant lush, green irrigated fields is wonderful. Allow several hours to appreciate fully the place and take plenty of water and protection against the fierce sun, including sunglasses.

● **Accommodation** **F** *Hostal Willys*, Plaza de Armas, clean, helpful; *Hostal Manuelito*, 3 blocks from the plaza, good, friendly. Another *Hostal*, 1 block from plaza, is OK, hot water. There are several restaurants around the plaza and a *Banco de Crédito*.

● **Transport** Buses to Corire leave from Arequipa main terminal hourly from 0500, 3 hrs. One company has its office on Independencia 1634.

## COTAHUASI CANYON

Beyond **Aplao** the road heads N through **Chuquibamba**, traversing the western slopes of Nevado Coropuna, Peru's third highest peak at 6,425m, before winding down into **Cotahuasi**.

**The canyon**, situated in the NW of the Department of Arequipa, has been cut by the Río Cotahuasi, whose waters are formed by the Río Huayllapaña flowing from the N, above Pampamarca, and the Río Huarcaya from the W, above Tomepampa. The river cuts its way westwards and then southwards through the deepest parts of the canyon, below Quechualla. It flows into the Pacific as the Río Ocuña, having joined with the Río Marán along the way.

At its deepest, at Ninochaca (just below the village of Quechualla), the canyon is 3,354m deep, 163m deeper than the Colca Canyon and the deepest in the world. From this point the only way down the canyon is by kayak and it is through kayakers' reports since 1994 that the area has come to the notice of tourists. It was declared a Zona de Reserva Turística in 1988.

The vertiginous gradient of the canyon walls and the aridity of its climate allow little agriculture but there are several charming citrus-growing villages downstream, among them **Chaupa**, **Velinga** and **Quechualla**.

In Inca times the road linking Puerto Inca on the Pacific coast and Cusco ran along much of the canyon's course. It was used for taking fish to the ancient Inca capital. Parts of the road are still intact and there are numerous remains of *Andenes*, or terraces, which supported settlement along the route. There are also Huari and other pre-Inca ruins.

### Rafting in the canyon

It is possible to raft or kayak from a point on the Upper Cotahuasi, just past the town, almost to the Pacific (boats are usually taken out of the water at the village of Iquipi), a descent of 2,300m. The season is May-Aug; rapids class 3 to 5; some portaging is unavoidable. See the **Bibliography** under **Rafting and Kayaking** in the **Adventure Tourism** section.

### COTAHUASI

Cotahuasi town (*Pop* 4,000; *Alt* 2,600m) nestles in a sheltered hanging valley beneath Cerro Huinao, several km away from the erosive action of the Río Cotahuasi. Though above the citrus zone itself, it has fertile, irrigated environs. The name Cotahuasi derives from the Quechua words 'Cota' (union) and

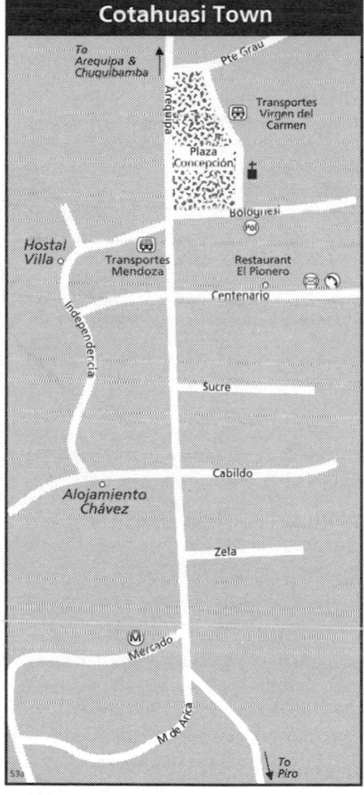

'Huasi' (house), literally translating as united house or close-knit community.

It is a peaceful, colonial town of narrow streets and whitewashed houses with gently subsiding balconies. The main street, Jirón Arequipa becomes a part of the plaza on busy Sun mornings. The only traffic seen is the occasional glimpse of the mayor's car, the odd tractor and the infrequent comings and goings of the 2 buses (see below).

• **Accommodation & places to eat** **F** *Hostal Villa*, just off plaza; **G** *Alojamiento Chávez*, Jr Cabildo 125, T 210222, rooms around pleasant courtyard, friendly, rec, Sr José Chávez is helpful on places to visit, if a little vague on timings. ***Restaurant El Pionero***, Jr Centenario, clean, good *menú*. Three small restaurants/bars on Jr Arequipa offer basic fare. There are many well-stocked *tiendas*, particularly with fruit and vegetables.

• **Useful services** There is no place to change money. **PNP**, on plaza; it is advisable to register with them on arrival and before leaving. **Maps** Some survey maps are available in the Municipalidad and PNP; they may let you make photocopies at the shop on the corner of the plaza and Arequipa. Sr Chávez has photocopies of the sheets covering Cotahuasi and surroundings.

• **Transport Buses** Two companies daily from Arequipa bus terminal, 13-14 hrs, US$9: Empresa Mendoza, 1400, returning from Cotahuasi plaza 1600; Empresa Virgen del Carmen 1430, returning 1500 from plaza. On arrival in Cotahuasi you may sleep on the bus till dawn. Both companies stop for refreshments in Chuquibamba, about halfway.

## TREKKING IN THE COTAHUASI CANYON

One of the main treks in the region follows the Inca trade road from **Cotahuasi to Quechualla**. The path starts next to the football pitch beside the airstrip. It heads downhill to **Piro**, which is almost a satellite of Cotahuasi and the gateway to the canyon (the path heads round to the right of the village, just above it). The path then crosses the river twice as it follows its course to **Sipia** (3 hrs), near which are the tremendously powerful, 150m high **Cataratas de Sipia**. Climb to the bluff just beyond the mouth of the black hole and you'll have a superb view downriver. Take care near the falls if it is windy. Water is a problem further down the canyon, if continuing, fill up your water bottles near the falls.

The next 3-hr stretch to **Chaupo** is not for those of a nervous disposition as the path is barely etched into the canyon wall, 400m above the river in places. The towering cliffs are magnificent reds and browns and dissected by near vertical water channels.

The first opportunity to camp comes at Chaupo, which lies on the pampa, 100m above the river. Water is available here. Ask permission to camp in the citrus groves and do not pick the fruit – it's cultivated as a cash crop. Llamas and other camelids are herded on the pampa.

Next is **Velinga**, a village which was almost wiped out by Chagas disease. Now only 6 families remain. Take the path down to the river before the village and cross over the concrete bridge to the right bank. Half a kilometre further on you may need to wade for about 15m at the foot of a cliff to regain the path. Stay on the same side of the river.

Before Quechualla are the extensive ruins of **Huña**. They are dilapidated but the remains of terraces and houses give a good idea of the importance of this route in precolumbian times. There is an almost intact 100m stretch of Inca road above a bend in the river on the approach to **Quechualla**. It can be a bit scary in parts but the alternative is to wade waist deep through the river.

Quechualla is a charming village and administrative capital of the district. It sits up on a cliff above the river. The church and school overlook the wooden bridge and the short climb up to the citrus groves. Trellised vines provide some welcome shade in the street. Though the village is populated by only

8 families, you may be able to sleep in the schoolhouse. Ask Sr Carmelo Velásquez Gálvez for permission. Below the village, on the opposite side of the river are the ruined terraces of **Maucullachta**.

A 16 km hike continues to the ruins of **Marpa**, which are in better condition than Maucullachta. The canyon walls, however, are too steep to continue along the river. You need to climb 8 km, on a path at right angles to the river, to Huachuy, then descend a further 8 km to the ruins near the river. There is no water en route; allow 4 more days.

**NB** If it rains, Quechualla can be cut off for days as sections where the river has to be waded become too deep and treacherous (eg just past Velinga).

### Other treks from Cotahuasi

It is a 3-hr walk to the ruins of **Pampamarca**, N of Cotahuasi. The ruins are impressive, as is the high waterfall. The village is well-known for rugmaking.

The thermal baths of **Luicho** lie between Tomepampa and Alca. Take a bus to Tomepampa; the first leaves at 0600, there are several more. A days' walk beyond Tomepampa is the spectacular rock forest of **Santo Santo**. Start the trek from Huaynacotas, near Luicho.

## TOWARDS THE VALLEY OF THE VOLCANOES

A road goes to the E from the Cotahuasi road to **Andagua**, a village lying at the head of the valley of the volcanoes.

A bus leaves from Arequipa, Sun, Wed, Fri, 1530, with Empresa Delgado; there are also trucks on this route. Basic accommodation is available at the mayor's house in Andagua.

The Arequipa-Andagua bus goes on to **Orcopampa**, from which the thermal springs of Huancarama can be visited. A mining lorry leaves Orcopampa for Cailloma on the 12th and the last day of each month; this enables one to make a round trip from Arequipa.

From Andagua there is a road to **Chachas**, a picturesque little village on the edge of a lake. Trucks sometimes run between the two villages. It has no restaurants, but there is a *hostal* on the plaza. The area is heavily cultivated and there are perfect views of the valley of the volcanoes from the top of the hill above Chachas. It is possible to hike from Chachas to Choco and on to Cabanaconde via the Río Colca in 4 days (see page 275).

## AREQUIPA

The city of **Arequipa**, 1,011 km from Lima by road, stands in a beautiful valley at the foot of El Misti volcano, a snow-capped, perfect cone, 5,822m high, guarded on either side by the mountains Chachani (6,057m), and Pichu-Pichu (5,669m). The city has fine Spanish buildings and many old and interesting churches built of *sillar*, a pearly white volcanic material almost exclusively used in the construction of Arequipa.

The city was re-founded on 15 August 1540 by an emissary of Pizarro, but it had previously been occupied by Aymara Indians and the Incas. It has since grown into a magnificent city – arguably the most strikingly beautiful in the country – exuding an air of intellectual rigour and political passion. Among its famous sons and daughters are former President Fernando Belaunde Terry and novelist and failed presidential candidate, Mario Vargas Llosa. Now, Arequipa is the main commercial centre for the S, and its fiercely proud people resent the general tendency to believe that everything is run from Lima.

**BASICS** *Pop* 1 million; *Alt* 2,380m; *Phone code* 054. The *climate* is delightful, with a

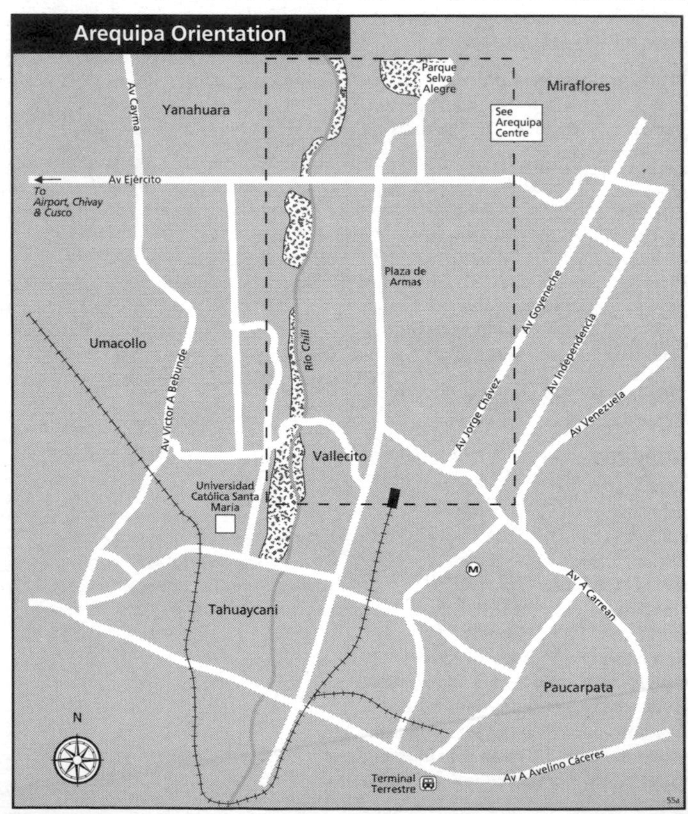

mean temperature before sundown of 23°C, and after sundown of 14½°C. The sun shines on 360 days of the year. Annual rainfall is less than 150 mm.

## PLACES OF INTEREST

The elegant **Plaza de Armas**, beautifully laid-out with palm trees, gardens and fountain, is faced on three sides by colonial arcaded buildings with many restaurants, and on the fourth by the Cathedral. Behind the cathedral there is a very attractive alley with handicraft shops.

The central **San Camilo market**, between Perú, San Camilo, Piérola and Alto de la Luna, is worth visiting, as is the Siglo XX market, to the E of the rail station. At **Selva Alegre** there is a shady park in front of the *Hotel Libertador* (ex-*de Turistas*), which is within easy walking distance of all the famous churches and main plaza.

Arequipa is said to have the best-preserved colonial architecture in Peru, apart from Cusco. The oldest district is **San Lázaro**, a collection of tiny climbing streets and houses quite close to the *Hotel Libertador*, where you can find the ancient **Capilla de San Lázaro**.

**A cheap tour** of the city can be made in a Vallecito bus, 1½ hrs for US$0.30. It is a circular tour which goes down Calles Jerusalén and San Juan de Dios.

## CHURCHES

Because of the ever-present danger of earthquakes churches in the city were built low. They are usually open 0700-0900 and 1800-2000. The massive, twin-towered **Cathedral** on the Plaza de Armas was founded in 1612 and largely rebuilt in the 19th century. It is remarkable for having its façade along the whole length of the church and takes up one full side of the Plaza. Inside is the fine Belgian organ and elaborately-carved wooden pulpit. The entrance to the Cathedral is on Santa Catalina and San Francisco.

A vist to the church of **La Compañía**, on General Morán and Ejercicios, is recommended. The main façade (1698) and side portal (1654) are striking examples of the florid Andean *mestizo* style. Also of note is the **Capilla Real** (Royal Chapel) to the left of the sanctuary, and its San Ignacio chapel with a beautiful polychrome cupola. The stark, impressive cloister is at Morán 118 y Palacio Viejo 115. Admission, US$0.50, open 0900-1200, 1500-1800 daily.

Also well worth seeing are the churches of **San Francisco** (Zela 103), **San Agustín** (corner of San Agustín y Sucre), the early 17th century **La Merced** (La Merced 303), and **Santo Domingo** (Santo Domingo y Piérola). Opposite San Francisco is a handicraft centre, housed in a beautiful former prison.

**La Recoleta**, a Franciscan monastery built in 1647, stands on the other side of the river, on Recoleta. It contains several cloisters, a religious art museum, a precolumbian museum, an Amazon museum, a library with many rarities, and is well worth visiting. Open Mon-Fri 0900-1200, 1500-1700, Sat 0900-1200; entry US$1.75. The church itself is open only 0900-1200, 1500-1800.

The **Santa Rosa Convent** is at San Pedro y Santa Rosa. It was founded on 12 July 1747, by nuns from the much larger Santa Catalina Convent.

### Santa Catalina Convent

By far the most interesting visit is to Santa Catalina Convent, opened in 1970 after four centuries of mysterious seclusion. This is the most remarkable sight in Arequipa and a complete contrast to what you would expect from nuns who had taken vows of poverty. The convent has been beautifully refurbished, with period furniture, pictures of the Arequipa and Cusco schools and fully-equiped kitchens. It is a complete miniature walled colonial town of over 2 ha in the middle of the city, where about 450 nuns lived in total seclusion, except

Santa Catalina Convent

for their women servants.

The few remaining nuns have retreated to one section of the convent, allowing visitors to see a maze of cobbled streets, flower-decked cloisters and buttressed houses. These have been finely restored and painted in traditional white, browns and blues.

The Convent is at Santa Catalina 301, T 229798; open 0900-1600 daily, admission US$3.90. The tour they offer you at the entrance is worthwhile; $1\frac{1}{2}$ hrs, no set price, many of the guides speak English. There is a small café, which sells cakes made by the nuns and a special blend of tea.

## Colonial houses

Arequipa has several fine seignorial houses with large carved tympanums over the entrances. Thanks to their being one-storey structures, they have mostly withstood the earthquakes which regularly pound this city. They are distinguished by their small patios with no galleries, flat roofs and small windows, disguised by superimposed lintels or heavy grilles.

One of the best examples is the 18th century **Casa Tristan del Pozo**, better known as the **Gibbs-Ricketts house** with its fine portal and puma-head waterspouts. It is now the main office of

Banco Continental, at San Francisco 108 y San José. Open to the public 1700-2000.

Other good examples are: the **Casa del Moral**, or Williams house, which also has a museum, in the Banco Industrial, on Calle Moral 318 y Bolívar; and the **Casa Goyeneche**, La Merced 201 y Palacio Viejo, which is now an office of the Banco Central de la Reserva, ask the guards who will let you view the courtyard and fine period rooms. Also worth seeing are: **Casa de la Moneda**, at Ugarte y Villalba; **Casa de los Pastor**, at Bolívar 206, now regional administration offices; **La Casona Chávez de la Rosa**, at San Agustín 104, now part of the Universidad San Agustín; and **Casa Irriberry** (1793), at Santa Catalina y San Agustín.

## MUSEUMS

Opposite the San Francisco church is the interesting **Museo Histórico Municipal** with much war memorabilia. It is open Mon-Fri 0800-1800; entry, US$0.50.

The **archaeological museum** at the Universidad de San Agustín, Av Independencia between La Salle and Santa Rosa, has a good collection of ceramics and mummies. Open Mon-Fri 0800-1400, entry US$1. Apply to Dr E Linares, the Director, T 229719.

## EXCURSIONS

In the hillside suburb of **Cayma** is the delightful 18th century church (open only until 1600), and many old buildings associated with Bolívar and Garcilaso de la Vega. Many local buses go to Cayma. There is a new luxury *Hotel Cayma*.

Another suburb is **Yanahuara**, where there is a 1750 *mestizo*-style church (opens 1500), with a magnificent churrigueresque façade, all in *sillar*. The thermal baths of Jesús are 30 mins by car, on the slopes of Pichu-Pichu; open 0500-1230. To get there cross the Gran Puente bridge and turn right up Lima. Accommodation is available at **B** *Hostal Kolping*, León Velarde 406, T 253748, F 253744, safe; and live music at *Peña El Moro*, on Parque Principal.

**Yura**, is a pleasant town, 29 km from Arequipa in a small, interesting valley on the W slopes of Chachani. It is popular with Arequipeños for its thermal baths and verdant riverside picnic spots. To reach the baths, walk down to the river from the main road by the *Yura Tourist Hotel* (sse below). The first set of baths contains 4 small pools which are not suitable for swimming. Follow the river to the next one, which is bigger. Further still is a large swimming pool (which was out of service in early 1996). They baths are open Tues-Sat, until 1500; entry US$1.50. Note that the water is not very hot. To return to Arequipa, catch a colectivo on the main road by the hotel.

- **Accommodation D** *Yura Tourist Hotel*, with bath, meals available; and an unsigned hotel opp, **F**, good.

- **Transport** A bus leaves every 3 hrs from San Juan de Dios, US$0.40.

**Tingo**, which has a very small lake and three swimming pools, should be visited on Sun for local food; *anticuchos* and *buñuelos*. To get there take bus 7, US$0.20.

3 km past Tingo, beside the Sabandía river on the Huasacanche road, and near the **Mirador Sachaca** with fine panoramic views, is **La Mansión del Fundador**. Originally owned by the founder of Arequipa, Don Garcí Manuel de Carbajal, in 1540, it has been open to the public since 1897 and restored as a museum with original furnishings and paintings. Entrance fee US$2.50, with cafeteria and bar.

4 km from Arequipa, in the district of Sachaca, is the **Palacio Goyeneche**.

8 km N of Arequipa is the **Molino de Sabandía**, the first stone mill in the area, built in 1621. There is a swimming bath and the surrounding countryside is pleasant; a worthwhile trip. Entrance fee US$1.50; round trip by taxi US$4.

Nearby is *Restaurante El Lago*, with swimming pool and horseriding.

Adjoining Sabandía is **Yumina**, with many Inca terraces which are still in use.

## FESTIVALS IN THE DEPARTMENT OF AREQUIPA

**2 Jan**: is the anniversary of the district of San Juan de Siguas. **6 Jan**: *El Día del Reyes* in the district of Tiabaya, traditionally celebrated by shaking the fruit from pear trees. Anniversary of the district of Mollendo, with festivities to herald the beginning of summer. **10 Jan**: *Sor Ana de Los Angeles y Monteagudo*, is a festival for the patron saint of Santa Catalina monastery. **20 Jan**: anniversary of the district of Chiguata. *Fiesta del Señor de la Sentencia*, in Chuquibamba and Siguas, with mass and procession in the main church. *El Día de San Sebastián* is celebrated over 5 days in Pinchollo.

**2-3 Feb**: *Fiesta de la Virgen de la Candelaria*, celebrated in the churches of Cayma, Characato, Chiguata and Chapi with masses, processions of the Virgin through the streets, and fireworks. It is also celebrated in the towns of Chivay and Cabanaconde, in the Colca Canyon (see page 270), with dancing in the plaza, and over 5 days in Maca and Tapay, also in the Colca Canyon. *Fiesta de la Virgen de Copacabana* involves pilgrimages to the village of Chuquibamba.

**3 Mar**: *Fiesta de La Amargura* is a moveable feast in Paucarpata, during which the Passion Play is enacted in the main plaza. *Domingo de Cuaresma*, in the district of Tiabaya, is also dedicated to Jesus Christ. Residents gather in the plaza and carry the cross from there up to a nearby hilltop, crossing the Río Chili.

**Mar-April**: the Semana Santa celebrations in Arequipa are carried out *Sevillano* style, with the townsfolk turned out in traditional mourning dress. There are huge processions every night, culminating in the burning of an effigy of Judas on Easter Sunday in the main plazas of Cayma and Yanahuara, and the reading of his 'will', containing criticisms of the city authorities. Afterwards, people retire to the *picanterías* to partake of a little *Adobo a la Antaño* with some *pan de tres puntas*. Semana Santa is celebrated with particular gusto in the villages of the Colca Canyon.

**27 April**: the celebration of the apostle Santiago. **April-May**: during these months many festivals are held in the Colca and Cotahuasi canyons.

**1 May**: *Fiesta de la Virgen de Chapi* is a great pilgrimage to the sanctuary of Chapi and one of the most important religious ceremonies in the region. **May** is known as the 'Month of the Crosses', with ceremonies on hilltops throughout the city. **3 May**: *Fiesta de la Tomilla* in Cayma. *La Cruz de Piedra* celebrated over 5 days in the main plaza in Tuti, near Chivay. **4 May**: the anniversary of Cotahuasi. **15 May**: the popular fiesta of *San Isidro Labrador* takes place in Sachaca, Chuquibamba and other towns and villages in the valley, and lasts for 7 days. **25-27 May**: anniversaries of the districts of Socabaya, Polobaya and Mollebaya.

**13 June**: a remembrance of San Antonio de Padua, patron of hopeless cases, is held in the churches of Tingo Grande and San Francisco, among others. San Antonio is also celebrated in the Colca Canyon, in the villages of Maca, Callalli and Yanque. **14 June**: in Sibayo and Ichupampa the *Fiesta de San Juan* is held over 5 days. **21 June**: the anniversary of the district of Chivay in Caylloma. **29 June**: in the district of Yanahuara the *Fiesta de San Juan*, the local patron saint, is held with a mass and fireworks. The fiesta of *San Pedro y San Pablo* is held in Sibayo, with music, dancing and processions.

**14-17 July**: *Fiesta de la Virgen del Carmen* is held in Cabanaconde and Pampacolca, when folk dancing takes place in the streets. Of particular interest is the dance of *Los Turcos*, which represents the indigenous peoples' struggle against the conquistadors. This fiesta is also held in the churches of Yura, Carmen Alto, Congata, Tingo Grande and the Convent of Santa Teresa. **25 July**: In Coporaque and Madrigal, in the Colca canyon, is the *Fiesta de Santiago Apostol*. **26 July-2 Aug**: various religious ceremonies, accompanied by dancing, are held in honour of the *Virgen Santa Ana* in Maca.

**3 Aug**: a procession through the city bearing the images of Santo Domingo and San Francisco. **6-31 Aug**: *Fiesta Artesanal del fundo El Fierro* is a sale and exhibition of artesanía from all parts of Peru, taking place beside Plaza San Francisco. **6-17 Aug**: during this period is the celebration of the city's anniversary; various events are held, including music, dancing and exhibitions. On the eve of the actual day, the 15th, there is a splendid firework display in the Plaza de Armas and a decorated float parade. There is also a mass ascent of El Misti from the Plaza de Armas. It is virtually impossible to find a hotel room during the celebrations. **15 Aug**: in Chivay is the fiesta of the *Virgen de la Asunta*, the town's patron saint, which lasts 8 days. **30 Aug**: *El Día de Santa Rosa* is celebrated in the churches of Tomilla, Cayma and Huancarqui in the Majes Valley.

**Sept**: in Tisco, in the Colca canyon, the *Virgen de la Natividad* is held over 5 days. **20 Oct**: *Santa Ursula*, also known as *La Virgen del Sombrero*, is held in Viraco, with the usual dancing, fireworks, bullfights and cockfights, all soaked in alcohol.

**2 Nov**: the Day of the Dead is celebrated. Go to the municipal cemetery, where Indians sing, dance, eat and drink with their dead. On Sun at about 1030 there is a civic and military parade on the Plaza de Armas. In Arequipa Nov is also the month of the traditional *guaguas*, which are *bizcochos* filled with *manjar*.

**8 Dec**: *Inmaculada Concepción* in Chivay and Yanque, groups of musicians and dancers present the traditional dance, the *Witite*, lasting 5 days. **25 Dec**: once again in Yanque, just in case you haven't had enough, the *Witite* is held over 6 days.

## LOCAL INFORMATION

**Hotel prices**

| | | | |
|---|---|---|---|
| L1 | over US$200 | L2 | US$151-200 |
| L3 | US$101-150 | A1 | US$81-100 |
| A2 | US$61-80 | A3 | US$46-60 |
| B | US$31-45 | C | US$21-30 |
| D | US$12-20 | E | US$7-11 |
| F | US$4-6 | G | up to US$3 |

### ● Accommodation

**A1** ***Presidente***, C Piérola 201, T 213641, F 239431, modern, bar, restaurant; **A2** ***Portal***, Portal de Flores 116, T 215530, F 234374, excellent, wonderful views, expensive, rooftop swimming pool, *El Gaucho* restaurant; **A2** ***Posada del Puente***, Av Bolognesi 101, T 253132, F 253576, beside Puente Grau, alongside Río Chili, attractive, small, friendly, good, restaurant, rec; **A2/3** ***Libertador***, Plaza Simón Bolívar, Selva Alegre, T 215110, F 241933, safe, swimming pool (cold), gardens, good meals, pub-style bar, cocktail lounge, tennis court; **A3** ***El Conquistador***, Mercaderes 409, T 212916, F 218987, clean, safe, lovely colonial atmosphere, owner speaks English, thin walls; **A3** ***Hostal Casa Grande***, Luna Pizarro 202, Vallecito, T 214000, F 214021, inc taxes, small, cosy, well-furnished, quiet, friendly, good services, rec; **A3** ***La Condesa***, C Piérola 207, T/F 213040, modern luxury hotel; **A3** ***Maison Plaza***, Portal San Agustín 143, T 218929, F 212114, with breakfast, bathroom and TV, clean, friendly, good value; **A3** ***Viza***, Perú 202, T 232301, inc tax and continental breakfast, TV, phone, garage, restaurant.

**B** ***Arequipa Inn***, Rivero 412, T 241711, modern hotel, with bath (US$4.60 for extra bed in room), garage, slow service, area not safe; **B** ***Casa de Mi Abuela***, Jerusalén 606, T 241206, F 242761, very clean, friendly, safe, hot water, laundry, self-catering if desired, English spoken, tours and transport organized in own agency, which has good information (T 226414), small library of European books, breakfast or evening snacks on patio or in beautiful garden, apartment for 5 US$40, highly rec; **B** ***Crismar***, Moral 107, T 215290, F 239431, opp the main Post Office, with shower, modern, safe, noisy, central, food good; **B-C** ***Jerusalén***, C Jerusalén 601, T 244441/81, F 243472, hot water, comfortable, modern, good restaurant, safe, carparking.

**C** ***Casa de Melgar***, Melgar 108-A, T 222459, 2 rooms, with bath, hot water all day (solar-panel), safe, clean; **C** ***Hostal Las Mercedes***,

Av La Marina 1001, end of C Consuelo, T/F 213601, includes breakfast, they will provide sandwiches and a soft drink instead if you're going on an early morning tour, clean, safe (but its surroundings are not too secure), snacks available, highly rec (but do not confuse with ***Hostal La Merced***, in C La Merced, which is not rec); **C** ***Hostal Latino***, Carlos Llosa 135, T 244770, with bath, cafeteria, garden, parking; **C** ***Hostal Premier***, Av Quiroz 100, T/F 241091, 50 rooms, 2-star, with bath, will store luggage, restaurant, garage, area not too safe; **C** ***Maison d'Elise***, Av Bolognesi 104, T/F 253343, Sra Elsa Podigo is very helpful; **C** ***Villa Baden Baden*** (Sra Bluemel de Castro), Manuel Ugarteche 401, Selva Alegre, T 222416, 6 rooms, breakfast included, German, French, English spoken, very informative

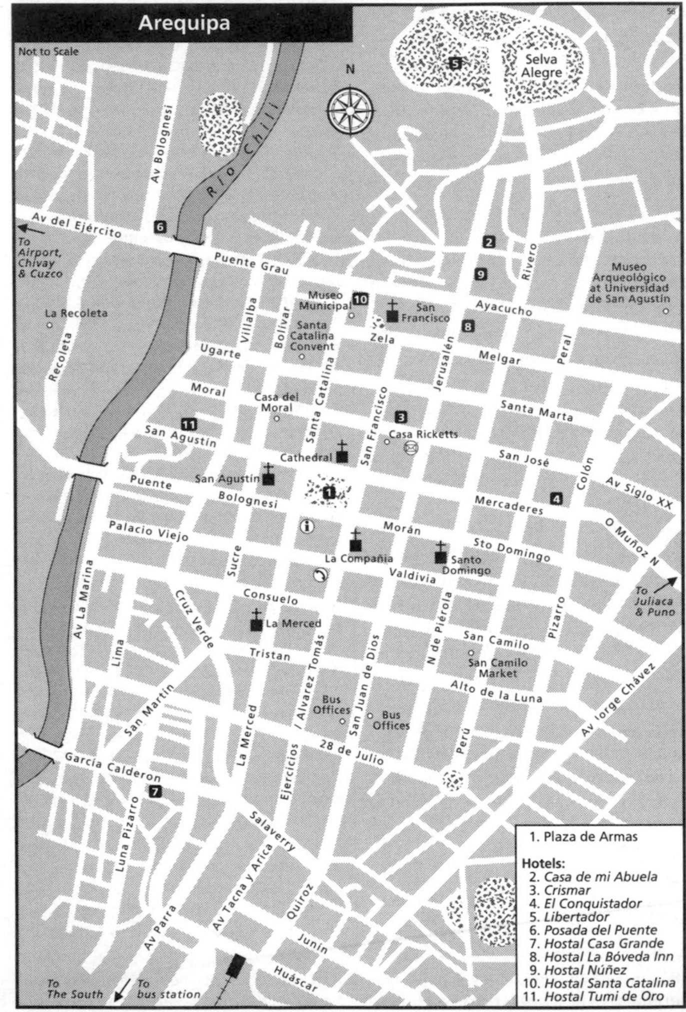

about city's environs and climbing, safe, rec.

**D** *El Gobernador*, Rivero 303, T 244433, with bath, E without, hot water, safe motorcycle parking, good beds, luggage store, rec; **D** *Posada de Sancho*, Santa Catalina 213 A, nr convent, T 287797, hot showers 24 hrs, clean, safe, nice patio and terrace with a view of El Misti, good breakfast, very friendly owners, English and German spoken, good travel information, offer cheap tours, very good value.

**E** ***Americano***, C Alvarez Tomás 435, T 211752, unsafe area, hot shower at any time, clean, safe hotel, friendly, doors close at 2130; **E** ***Crillón Serrano***, C Perú 109, T 212392, with bath, hot water am, friendly to Germans, unsafe area; **E** ***Hostal El Cóndor***, San Juan de Dios 525, T 213323, clean, new, good; **E** ***Hostal Fernández***, Quesada 106, Yanahuara, T 254152, 10 mins from centre, good for a longer stay, beautiful garden with parrot, views of El Misti, family affair, safe, breakfasts, hot water, clean, rec; **E** ***Hostal La Portada del Mirador***, Portal de Flores 102, Plaza de Armas, T 211539, basic, clean, safe, friendly, will store luggage, great views from the roof; **E** ***Hostal Núñez***, Jerusalén 528, T 233268, with bath, cheaper without, hot water, laundry, safe, friendly, comfortable, clean, small rooms, breakfast on roof terrace overlooking the city, rec; **E** ***Hostal Regis***, Ugarte 202, T 226111, colonial house, French-style interior, clean, hot water all day, cooking and laundry facilities, sun terrace with good views, safe, luggage store, new rooms being built, rec; **E** ***Hostal Santa Catalina***, Santa Catalina 500, T 233705, clean, hot water, friendly, noisy, safe, luggage stored, rec; **E** ***Hostal Tumi de Oro***, San Agustín 311A, 2½ blocks from Plaza de Armas, T 281319, F 231633, with bath, cheaper without, French and English spoken, hot water, roof terrace, cooking and laundry facilities, safe, rec; **E** ***La Bóveda Inn***, Jerusalén 402, above *Lashmivan* restaurant, T 281685, clean, safe, good showers, friendly, rec; **E** ***Lluvia de Oro***, Jerusalén 308, F 235730, English-speaking, breakfast US$1.40, restaurant open to non-residents, pisco sours rec; **E** ***Residencial Rivero***, Rivero 420, T 229266, with bath, clean, friendly, helpful, washing facilities, rec but not a very safe area.

**F** pp ***Rooms for tourists (Hostal La Reyna)***, Zela 209, T 286578, shared bath, hot showers, new, clean, very friendly, the daughter speaks a little English, great breakfast, will store luggage, excellent value, highly rec; **F** pp ***Tambo Viejo***, Av Mcal Cáceres 107, IV Centenario, unsigned, 6 blocks S of Plaza nr rail station, family home, quiet, very friendly, nice garden, hot water early am, laundry, cable TV, breakfast available (inc vegetarian), excellent, very highly rec; **F** pp ***Tito***, C Perú 105-B, T 234424, shared bath, good value, friendly.

## ● Places to eat

***Central Garden***, San Francisco 127, good food but expensive; ***Anushka***, Santa Catalina 204, open 1800-2300, or later if busy, live music, Fri and Sat, only place to get a hot meal after 2200, German specialities, friendly, handicrafts are sold on the same premises; ***Monza***, Santo Domingo 1½ blocks from Plaza, good set meal and breakfast; ***Bacuch***, Melgar 413, new, good Swiss food; ***Balcón Arequipa***, Merced y Bolognesi, good view over Plaza, popular with locals, good breakfasts and fruit juice, slow service; ***El Dólar***, San Juan de Dios 106, clean, cheap, friendly, all meals available, rec; ***El Fogón***, Santa Marta 112, good; ***La Casa del Pino***, Jerusalén 308, set in a small pleasant courtyard, good set lunch; ***Bonanza***, Jerusalén 114-116, for meat and pasta dishes, very good, US$5; ***Pizzería San Antonio***, Jerusalén y Santa Marta, popular with locals and tourists; also ***Pizzería Los Leños***, Jerusalén 407, near San Francisco, excellent, good atmosphere, evenings only; ***Pizza Presto***, Gen Morán 108, good and cheap; ***La Rueda***, Mercaderes 206, excellent *parrilladas* but expensive; ***Las Quenas***, San Francisco 215, opposite Santa Catalina convent, excellent *menú* for US$1.50, but expensive for dinner, also a *peña* in the evening; ***Mister Pollo***, Av Estados Unidos, Urb 13 de Enero, good, cheap chicken and chips; on the same street is ***El Good Fish***, good, cheap set meals. There are many good, cheap restaurants on Av Estados Unidos. ***André de París***, better known as *El Emperador*, Santa Catalina 207, excellent cheap set lunches; ***Tradición Arequipa***, Av Dolores 111, Paucarpata, T 242385, high quality restaurant serving excellent, moderately priced food, popular with tourists and locals alike.

**Vegetarian**: ***Govinda***, Jerusalén 505, excellent set meal US$1.25, good yoghurt and muesli (also called *Madre Natura*, which has a branch at Grau 310), rec; ***Lashmivan***, Jerusalén 402, good set lunch US$1.25, pleasant courtyard; ***Come y Vive Mejor***, C Nueva 410A, cheap and good; ***Mathesis***, Jerusalén 224, a bit more expensive than others; ***La***

***Avellana***, Santa Marta 317-B, good, cheap lunch *menú*.

**Cafés**: ***Café Manolo***, Mercaderes 113, great cakes and coffee; ***Pastelería Salón de Té***, Mercaderes 325, very clean, open early, good breakfasts; ***Café Suri***, on the Plaza, for sandwiches and pastries; ***Harumi*** snack bar, San José 216, Chinese, good value; ***El Café***, San Francisco 125, new, popular meeting place; ***Dairy Room***, Plaza de Armas, cakes and pastries, expensive ice cream.

There are several good cheap places down San Juan de Dios, eg ***El Chuquibambino***, No 625, or ***La Empanadita***, No 205, excellent *empanadas* and snacks. ***La Canasta***, Jerusalén 115, bakes authentic-tasting baguettes twice daily, excellent.

A score of *picanterías* specialize in piquant foods: *rocoto relleno* (hot stuffed peppers), *cuy chactado* (seared guinea-pig), *papas con ocopa* (boiled potatoes with a hot yellow sauce) and *adobo* (pork stew). Try them at lunchtime in Yanahuara suburb such as the ***Chalet de la Nova***, off Av Ejército, family run, excellent food in taverna style. Arequipeño food is also available at the San Camilo market. A good local speciality is Mejía cheese. You should also try the *queso helado*, which is frozen fresh milk mixed with sugar and a sprinkling of cinnamon. The local chocolate is excellent; *La Ibérica* – the factory on Jerusalén, NE of Plaza de Armas, gives tours on weekdays only; as is the toffee (eg at ***San Antonio Pizzería***); and the fruit drinks called *papayada* and *tumbada*, which are local specialities in the market and restaurants.

## ● Airline offices

All airline offices are on the Plaza de Armas: **Americana**, Portal San Agustín 119, T 284739/284740; **AeroPerú**, Portal San Agustín 145, T 211616; **Faucett**, Portal San Agustín 143-A, T 212352; **Aero Continente**, Portal San Agustín 113, T 219914/219788. Servicios Aéreos AQP, T 242030/216767, for private hire and tourist flights to the Colca Canyon. Most tour agencies sell air tickets; prices are quoted in dollars but payment is in soles so check exchange rate carefully.

## ● Banks & money changers

**Banco Internacional**, Mercaderes 217, exchanges Citicorp dollar cheques. **Banco de Crédito**, Santo Domingo y Jerusalén, accepts Visa Card and gives good rates, no commission, rec. **Banco Continental**, La Uruguaya Department Store, Mercaderes 133, Mon-Fri 0900-1200, 1600-1830. Others include: **Banco Popular**; and **Banco del Sur del Perú**, C Jerusalén, close to Post Office, will change TCs, low rates, accepts Mastercard, has ATM for withdrawals with Visa; **Arequipa Inversiones**, Jerusalén 190-C, T 238033; **Sergio A del Carpio D**, Jerusalén 126, T 242987, good rates for dollars; **Ideal Travel**, Zela 212; **Lima Tours**, Santa Catalina 120; **Via Tours**, Santo Domingo 114, good rates; **Diners Club**, San Francisco 112. It is almost impossible to change TCs on Sat pm or Sun; try to find a sympathetic street changer. Hotels will not help. Better rates for cash dollars in banks and *casas de cambio*.

## ● Cultural centres

**Instituto Cultural Peruano-Norte Americano**, in the Casa de los Mendiburo, Melgar 109, T 243201, has an **English Library**. **Instituto Cultural Peruano Alemán**, Ugarte 207, T 218567. **Instituto Regional de Cultura**, Gen Morán 118 (altos), T 213171; **Instituto Nacional de Cultura**, Alameda San Lázaro 120, T 213171; **Alianza Francesa**, Santa Catalina 208, T 218406/215579.

## ● Embassies & consulates

**British Consulate**, Mr Roberts, Tacna y Arica 145, T 241340, Mon-Fri 0830-1230, 1430-1800, reported as very friendly and helpful; **French Consulate**, Estadio Oeste 201-A, IV Centenario, T 232119 (Sun T 224915), Mon-Fri 1530-1900; **German Consulate**, in Colegio Max Uhle, Av Fernandini s/n, Sachaca, Mon-Fri 0900-1300, Casilla 743; **Dutch Consulate**, Mercaderes 410 (Banco Wiese), Sr Herbert Ricketts, T 219567, F 215437, Casilla 1, open Mon-Fri 0900-1300, 1630-1830; **Swedish Consulate**, Av Villa Hermosa 803, Cerro Colorado, T 259847/270616, open Mon-Fri 0830-1300, 1500-1730; **Swiss Consulate**, Av Miguel Forga 348, Parque Industrial, T 232723; **Italian Consulate**, La Salle D-5, T 221444, open 1130-1300, in the afternoon T 254686 (home); **Spanish Consulate**, Ugarte 218, p 2, T 214977 (home T 224915), open Mon-Fri 1100-1300, Sat 0900-1300; **Chilean Consulate**, Mercaderes 212, p 4, Of 401-402, Galerías Gameza, T/F 233556, entrance to lift 30m down passageway down Mercaderes on left, open Mon-Fri 0900-1300, present passport 0900-1100 if you need a visa; **Bolivian Consulate**, Piérola 209, p 3, Of 321, T 213391, open Mon-Fri 0900-1400, 24 hrs for visa, go early.

● **Entertainment**

***Romie***, Zela 202, T 234465, bar with *peña*, Tues-Sat; ***El Sillar***, Santa Catalina 215, T 215468, 'salón concierto', typical folk music, rec, Mon-Sat from 2000; ***Bohemios***, Santa Catalina 223, T 226887; ***Blues Bar***, San Francisco 319-A, T 233796, large but intimate disco, plays classic blues and often has live rock, US$5 cover if live band is playing, includes a drink, drinks US$1.50, very popular; ***Video Bar***, on Jerusalén, traditional disco, ***El Barril***, Moral y Jerusalén, snacks, good pisco sour; ***Peña Waykopac***, Jerusalén 204, good atmosphere, Fri and Sat; ***Peña Chunenea***, Pasaje la Catedral 4; ***Discoteca Casablanca***, Av Sucre, Puente Bolognesi, garage entrance, clean, well-run and safe; downstairs pool room; ***Disco Fragavoss***, Santa Catalina 109-A, T 232651, young crowd, rec. There are many good discos on Av Ejército in the suburb of Yanahuara. Watch out for the local folk-music group Chachani, said to be one of Peru's best.

● **Hospitals & medical services**

**Hospitals**: *Regional Honorio Delgado*, Av A Carrión s/n, T 238465/231818. *General Base Goyeneche*, Av Goyeneche s/n, T 211313. *Nacional del Sur*, Filtro y Peral s/n, T 214430 in emergency.

**Dentist**: *Dr José Corrales*, San Juan de Dios 216.

**Doctors**: *Dr Julio Postigo*, Independencia 225; *Dr Jorge A del Carpio Alvarez*, Santo Domingo 123, of 303, T 215483, rec, only Spanish spoken.

**Clinics**: *Clínica Arequipa SA*, esq Puente Grau y Av Bolognesi, T 253424, fast and efficient with English- speaking doctors and all hospital facilities, consultation costs US$18, plus US$4 for sample analysis and around US$7 for a course of antibiotics. *San Juan de Dios*, Av Ejército 1020, Cayma, T 252256/255544. *Monte Carmelo*, Gómez de la Torre 119, T 231444, T/F 287048. *Clínica de Urgencias Meza*, Urb Aurora J-11, cercado, T 234883.

**Pharmacy**: ***Farmacia Libertad***, Piérola 108, owner speaks English.

● **Language courses**

Silvana Cornejo, 7 de Junio 118, Cerrito Los Alvarez, Cerro Colorado, T 254985, US$6/hr, negotiable for group, rec, she speaks German fluently; her sister Roxanna charges US$3/hr. Fidelia and Charo Sánchez, T 224238, highly rec, Fidelia speaks French, Charo English. Also at Instituto Peruano-Norte Americano and Instituto Cultural Peruano Alemán.

● **Post & telecommunications**

The central Post Office is at Moral 118, opp *Hotel Crismar*. Letters can only be posted at the Post Office during opening hours, Mon-Sat, 0800-2000, Sun 0800-1400. Telephone and fax at Alvarez Thomas y Palacio Viejo.

● **Security**

Though theft can be a problem in the market area, especially after dark, and at the bus offices in San Juan de Dios, the police are friendly, courteous and efficient. (See **Security** in the **Introduction and Hints**).

● **Shopping**

***Casa Secchi***, Av Víctor Andrés Belaunde 124, in Umacollo (near the aeroplane statue), sells good arts, crafts and clothing; also ***Artesanías Peruanas***, Puente Bolognesi 147. ***Empresa Peruana de Promoción Artesanal (EPPA)***, Gen Morán 120. ***Alpaca 111***, Jerusalén 115, Of 208, T 212347, rec for high-quality alpaca and wool products. The covered market opposite the Teatro Municipal in C Mercaderes is rec for knitted goods, bags, etc. Also worth a try is the market around Valdivia and N de Piérola. Arequipa is noted for its leather work; the main street of saddlers and leather workers is Pte Bolognesi. The handicraft shop in the old prison opposite San Francisco is particularly good for bags. At ***Fundo del Fierro*** shop 14, on Plaza San Francisco, alpaca-wool handicrafts from Callalli in the Colca canyon are sold. ***Lanificio***, La Pampilla s/n, T 225305, the factory for high-quality alpaca cloth at better prices than Lima outlets. ***Sombrería El Triunfino***, N de Piérola 329-331, good selection of hats, but expensive. ***El Zaguán***, Santa Catalina 105, good for handicrafts. There are three antique shops in C Santa Catalina.

**Bookshops**: There are good bookshops near the Post Office. For international magazines, look along C San Francisco, between Mercaderes and San José. Old books and magazines are bought and sold at *Compra y Venta de Libros y Revistas*, on C Puente Grau.

**Laundry**: ***Magic laundry***, Av Cayma 617, coin-operated, open daily; ***Lavendería del Pueblo***, Ejercícios 558; ***Don Marcelo***, T 421411 (am), T 229245 (pm), delivery service.

**Photography**: Sr Fernando Delange, N-10 Urbanización Adepa, T 233120, repairs all kinds of electrical equipment as well as cameras. ***Foto Esparza***, Mercaderes 132-2, English spoken, cameras mended; ***Foto Mundo Color***, San Francisco 218-A, will develop good quality prints in 1 hr, US$3.50 for 24.

**Hairdressing**: *Peluquería Adán y Eva*, Piérola 108, haircut for US$2.70; *Peluquería La Favorita*, Mercaderes 130.

**Watch repairs**: *Cáceres e Hijos*, San Francisco 123.

### ● Tour companies & travel agents

*Ideal Travels*, Zela 212, on plaza San Francisco, T 244439, F 242088, Mon-Fri 0800-1900, Sat 0830-1300, tours to Colca Canyon (2 days, 1 night, US$60, all meals, rafting US$33), Cotahuasi Canyon, Andagua Volcanic valley, Majes River, Cotahuasi River, Toro Muerto, Callalli alpaca and vicuña ranch; jeep and microbus rentals, excellent bilingual guides, international ticket reservations, accepts credit cards.

Also rec are: ***Conresa Tours***, Jerusalén 409, Casilla 563, T 211847/ 223073/215820, specializes in trips to the Colca Canyon, and to the Toro Muerto petroglyphs, Las Salinas and Mejía lakes, and city tours; ***Santa Catalina Tours***, Santa Catalina 204, T 216994, F 217352, well-organized, good guides, rec; ***Colonial Tours***, Santa Catalina 205, of 1, T 285980, daily tours to Colca; ***Wasi Tours***, Jerusalén 613 and Santa Catalina 207, friendly, helpful advice; ***Illary Tours***, Jerusalén 204-B, T 220844, friendly, English-speaking guides; ***Expeandes***, La Merced 408, of 1, T 212888, F 228814, PO Box 1403, owner Ricardo Córdoba Mercado, adventure trips, well-organized, reliable, rents equipment, rec. A recommended guide for climbing, trekking, mountain biking and river rafting in the Colca Canyon is Vlado Soto, he can be contacted at La Merced 125, CC Unicentro, of 139, PO Box 1988, T 234818/225494, F 226610; he is knowledgeable and helpful and also rents equipment.

Many agencies on Jerusalén, Santa Catalina and around Plaza de Armas sell air, train and bus tickets and offer tours of Colca, Cotahuasi, Toro Muerto, Campiña and city; prices vary so shop around.

**Climbing**: Sr Carlos Zárate of the Mountaineering Club of Peru, has good information and advice, acts as a guide and rents some equipment, highly rec; contact him through Alianza Francesa, T 215579.

**NB** Don't pay for a tour in advance; always settle the details before starting the tour and check that there are enough people for the tour to run. Quite often travel agents work together to fill buses and use lots of touts. If a travel agency puts you in touch with a guide, make sure he/she is official. It is not advisable to book tours to Machu Picchu here. Make these arrangements in Cusco.

### ● Tourist offices

Office on Plaza de Armas, opposite the Cathedral, T 211021, ext 113, open 0800-1900, helpful, friendly, free street plans. **Oficina de Protección al Turista**, T 0800-42579, 24 hrs, toll-free, or T 212054, during office hours. Tourist Police, Jerusalén 317, T 251270/239888, very helpful with complaints or giving directions. **Ministry of Tourism**, La Merced 117, T 213116, will handle complaints. **Touring y**

**Automóvil Club del Perú**, Av Goyeneche 313, T 215631, mechanical assistance T 215640.

## ● Transport

**Local Car hire**: **National**, Bolívar 25, US$70/day inc tax, insurance and 200 km; **Avis**, Puente Bolognesi near plaza. **Car repairs**: *Automec*, Av Tahuaycani cuadra 2, Tahuaycani. **Bicycle repairs and equipment**: *Hoz Trek Bicicletas*, Villalba 428, T 223221. **Taxi**: US$4-5 airport to city (can be shared). US$1.75 bus terminal to Plaza de Armas; US$1.75 railway station to centre. Nova Taxi, T 252511; Fono Car, T 212121; Telemóvil, T 221515; Taxitur, T 422323.

**Air** Rodríguez Ballón airport is 7 km from town, T 443464. To and from **Lima**, 1 hr 10 mins, US$70-85 inc tax; several daily with Faucett, AeroPerú, Americana, Aero Continente. A special tourist fare may be available from as low as US$65, shop around. To **Tacna**, 30 mins, US$21, daily flights with all major airlines. To **Cusco**, 40 mins, US$46, daily flights. To **Juliaca** 30 mins, daily flights, US$41; to **Puerto Maldonado**, US$80 with Americana, daily.

A reliable means of transport to and from the airport to the hotel of your choice is with **King Tours**, T 243357/283037, US$1.30 pp; you need to give 24 hrs notice for the return pick-up from your hotel; journey takes 30-40 mins depending on traffic. Transport to the airport may be arranged when buying a ticket at a travel agency, US$1 pp, but not always reliable. Local buses go to about ½ km from the airport.

**Trains** The railway system goes from Arequipa to Juliaca, where it divides, one line going N to Cusco, the other S to Puno.

To Juliaca-Puno: the train leaves Tues, Wed, Fri and Sun at 2100. It arrives in Juliaca at 0645, and in Puno at 0830. The train returns from Puno at 1945; arrives in Juliaca at 2045; and arrives in Arequipa at 0600. To Cusco: the train leaves Puno at 0735, arrives 1800. Trains are subject to delays and cancellation in the rainy season, always check.

There are four different classes: 2nd class, no seat reservations, not recommended; 1st class, reserved seats, but anyone is allowed into the carriage (inc thieves), it's a good local experience if you do not mind watching your belongings all the time; pullman (*turismo ejecutivo*) class, with closed doors, only ticket holders are allowed in the carriage, safe, heating, recommended for the night journey which can be extremely cold; and Inca class, with reclining seats and video, only ticket holders are allowed in the carriage. You can travel all the way through if you stay in the same class; you only need change trains in Juliaca when changing classes. Fares: Arequipa-Puno, 2nd class US$9, 1st class US$11, pullman US$19, Inca US$23. Arequipa-Cusco, 2nd class US$16, 1st class US$20, pullman US$30, Inca US$46.

Tickets are now sold the day before departure. If you wish to reserve a seat in advance, you must pay a deposit (if the ticket seller doesn't mention a deposit, remind him of it). It is wise to reserve tickets at least 48 hrs before the day of departure, especially if you're travelling on weekends or public holidays. The ticket office is at Av Tacna y Arica 201; for reservations T 223600, information T 233928/229012; open 0630-1030, 1400-1800 Mon-Fri; 0800-1200, 1500-1800 Sat/Sun. You can buy tickets through travel agencies (check date and seat number). Try to board the train as early as possible as there isn't much room for luggage.

**Warning** Theft is a major problem on 1st and 2nd class. Thieves are very well-organized and work in groups, using all the tricks to distract you while someone else steals your bags. The best way is to lock your luggage on the rack and watch it (it is easier if you have only one bag). Pay attention at all times and do not leave the train. Sit with a group if possible to help each other. Always have a torch/flashlight to hand. The pullman class from Arequipa to Juliaca is recommended because it is safest at night. Take a taxi to and from the train station and do not hang around the station area.

If you feel bad on the train ask for the oxygen mask at once.

**Buses** The bus terminal is at Av Andrés A Cáceres s/n, Parque Industrial, opposite *Inca Tops* factory, S of the train station; 15 mins from the centre by colectivo US$0.20, or taxi US$1.75 (10 mins). A terminal tax of US$0.35 must be paid on entry. All the bus companies have their offices in the terminal, though a few also have offices on and around C San Juan de Dios (5-6 blocks from Plaza de Armas). Note that buses are only allowed to pick up and drop off passengers in this area early in the morning and late evening (eg the bus to the Colca Canyon).

Companies which also have offices on and

around San Juan de Dios includes: Ormeño, San Juan de Dios 657, T 218885/227852; Transportes Zevallos, San Juan de Dios 621, T 216325; Flores Hermanos, 28 de Julio 106-108, T 244988; Cruz del Sur, Av Salaverry 121, T 213905/238447.

**Warning** Theft is a serious problem in the bus station area and the surrounding restaurants. Thieves work in groups and are very organized. Take a taxi to and from the bus station and do not wander around with your belongings. Similarly, be careful on San Juan de Dios early and late.

To **Lima**, 1,011 km, 16-18 hrs, 'normal' service US$9, 'Imperial' US$22 (video, toilet, meals, comfortable seats, blankets) several daily, Ormeño (T 219126, or San Juan de Dios 657, T 218885) and Cruz del Sur (T 232014, or Av Salaverry 121, T 213905) rec; see Lima **Bus Companies** with routes to the S. The road is paved but drifting sand and breakdowns may prolong the trip. Buses will stop at the major cities en route, but not always Pisco. The desert scenery is spectacular.

To **Nasca**, 566 km, 9 hrs, US$9, several buses daily, mostly at night and most buses continue to Lima. Beware, some bus companies to Nasca charge the Lima fare. To **Moquegua**, 213 km, 3 hrs, US$4, several buses and colectivos daily. To **Tacna**, 320 km, 4 hrs, US$5, several buses daily; colectivo, Expreso Tacna, San Juan de Dios 537, T 213281, will collect you from your hotel, US$7.

To **Cusco**, 521 km, 13-17 hrs (longer in the rainy season), US$10-13; several daily, Cruz del Sur at 1600. The road was in good shape in 1995; the views are superb. In the rainy season the journey is not recommended because of mudslides. To **Juliaca**, 279 km, 9 hrs (also longer in the wet), US$8; colectivos charge US$12 and take 8 hrs in the dry season, leaving from C Salaverry, only when full. Most buses and colectivos, of which a few go daily, continue to Puno, another 44 km, 30 mins. Mudslides are a problem in the rainy season and the road is in poor condition, it also gets bitterly cold at night. To **Puno**, 297 km, 8-10 hrs, US$7.50, a few buses and trucks daily, 1600 and 1700; colectivo US$12, 9 hrs (all services take longer in the wet). Although the route does not go via Juliaca, the road conditions are identical. **NB** Check on the security situation before travelling Arequipa-Cusco by overnight bus.

## CLIMBING EL MISTI

At 5,822m, **El Misti** volcano offers a relatively straightforward opportunity to scale a high peak. Start from the hydroelectric plant, after first registering with the police there, then you need 1 day to the Monte Blanco shelter, at 4,800m. Start early for the 4-6 hrs to the top, to get there by 1100 before the mists obscure the view. If you start back at 1200 you will reach the hydroelectric plant by 1800. Alternatively, buses leave Arequipa for Baños Jesús, then on to Chiguata, where one can walk to the base of El Misti. Be sure to take plenty of food and water; it takes 2 days to reach the crater. Guides may be available at Cachamarca. Further information is available from Carlos Zárate (address above, **Climbing**). Also some travel agencies have information.

## Camelid fibre

4,000 years before the Spanish conquistadors set foot on Peruvian soil, the indigenous peoples excelled at the textile arts. This age-old weaving tradition would not have been possible, however, without the necessary raw materials.

While cotton was cultivated for this purpose on the arid coast, up on the high Andean plain there was a ready supply of weaving fibre in the shape of the native camelids – llamas, alpacas, vicuñas and guanacos – which are distant cousins to the camel. The alpacas and llamas are thought to have been domesticated as early as 4,000 BC.

The fibres and skins of the wild camelids – guanacos and vicuñas – were used prior to domestication of their cousins. In fact, guanaco skins were used as clothing by the early hunters who roamed the bleak, high Andean plateau, or altiplano, before 4,000 BC.

By 1,500-1,000 BC there is evidence of domesticated camelids on the coast while llamas were being used for ritual burial offerings, indicating their increasing prestige. Thus, the importance of camelids to Andean man, both in practical and ideological terms, was probably a long-established tradition by this time.

Because camelid fibre is so easy to spin and dye, the ancient weavers developed extraordinarily fine spinning techniques. The precolumbian peoples prized the silky-soft fibre of the alpaca, in particular. Living at altitudes of 4,000m, where temperatures can drop to -15°C, these animals have adapted to the extreme conditions and developed a coat that not only has thermal properties but is also soft and resistant.

It is these qualities that have led to worldwide demand. Production of alpaca fibre, however, remains low owing to the fact that more than 75% of Peru's alpacas are in the hands of small breeders and peasant communities who still herd and manage their animals in much the same way as their ancestors.

Alpacas

## COLCA CANYON

The Colca Canyon is twice as deep as the Grand Canyon. The Río Colca snakes its way through the length of this massive gorge, 3,500m above sea level at Chivay falling to 2,200m at Cabanaconde. The roads on either side of the canyon are at around 4,000m and Nevado Ampato, a short distance to the S, rises to 6,288m.

The name Colca derives from the Inca practice of storing harvested crops in sealed vaults which they called *colcas*, carved into the canyon walls. Now, though, the name is synonymous with a rather large bird. Would-be David Attenboroughs flock here for a rare glimpse of condors in the wild at the aptly-named *Cruz del Condor*.

There's much more to the Colca than vultures and stored food, however. This is an area of astounding scenic beauty. Giant amphitheatres of pre-Inca terracing become narrow, precipitous gorges, and in the background looms the grey, smoking mass of Sabancaya, one of the most active volcanoes in the Americas, and its more docile neighbour, Ampato. Unspoiled Andean villages lie on both sides of the canyon, inhabited by the Cabana and Collagua peoples. This is also a region of wild and frequent festivals (see **Local festivals** above for details).

Despite its history, this part of southern Peru was practically unknown to the outside world until the late 1970s when a Polish team made the first descent by raft and canoe. The canyon appears on 19th century maps and the first aerial reconnaissance was made in 1929 by US Navy Lt George R Johnson (published as *Peru from the Air* by the American Geographical Society, 1930). In 1931 Johnson returned by land with Robert Shippee and the account of their Shippee-Johnson Peruvian Expedition was reported in the *Geographical Review* of

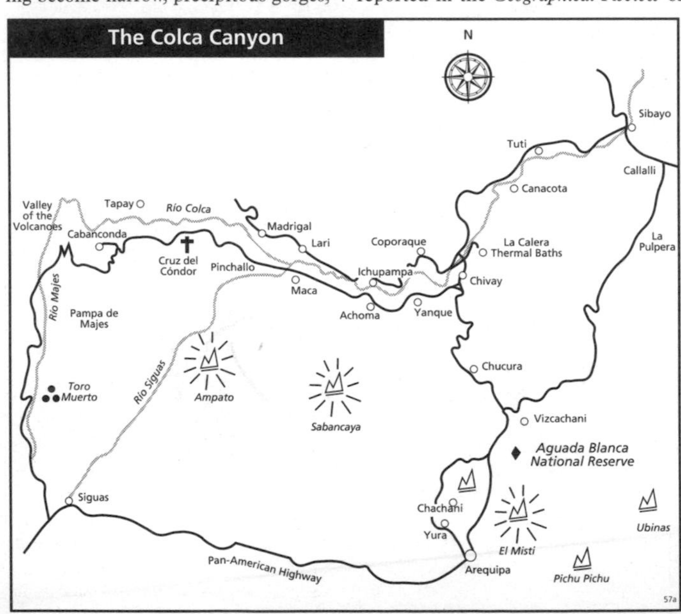

## Appeasing the Gods

To the Incas, Nevado Ampato, in the Colca region, was a sacred god who brought life-giving water and good harvests and, as a god claimed the highest tribute, the sacrifice of one of their own.

In Sept 1995, anthropologist, Johan Reinhard, of Chicago's Field Museum of Natural History, accompanied by Peruvian climber, Miguel Zárate, whose brother, Carlos is a well-known Arequipa mountain guide, were climbing Ampato when they made a startling discovery, at about 6,000m. They found the perfectly-preserved mummified body of an Inca girl. Wrapped tightly in textiles, this girl in her early teens must have been ritually sacrificed and buried on the summit.

Mummies of Inca human sacrifices have been found before on Andean summits, but never so close to Cusco, the heart of the Inca empire. Furthermore, the girl from Ampato, nicknamed Juanita, is the first frozen Inca female to be unearthed and her body may be the best preserved of any found in the Americas from precolumbian times. The discovery is considered of worldwide importance, as the body is better preserved even than the famous Tyrolean "Iceman" of Austria. The intact body tissues and organs of naturally mummified, frozen bodies are a storehouse of biological information. Studies will reveal how she died, where she came from, who her living relatives are and even yield valuable insights about the Inca diet.

Juanita's clothes are no less remarkable. The richly-patterned, dazzling textiles will serve as the model for future depictions of the way noble Inca women dressed. Her *lliclla* – a bright red and white shawl beneath the outer wrappings – has been declared "the finest Inca woman's textile in the world". This fits in with the Spanish chronicler, Pedro de Cieza de León, who wrote in 1553: "The dress of the ladies of Cusco is the most graceful and rich that has been seen up to this time in all the Indies [sic]."

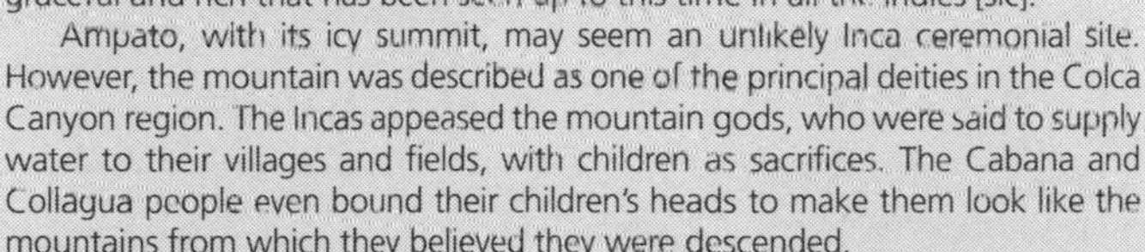

Ampato, with its icy summit, may seem an unlikely Inca ceremonial site. However, the mountain was described as one of the principal deities in the Colca Canyon region. The Incas appeased the mountain gods, who were said to supply water to their villages and fields, with children as sacrifices. The Cabana and Collagua people even bound their children's heads to make them look like the mountains from which they believed they were descended.

A subsequent ascent of Ampato revealed a further two mummies at the summit. One is a young girl and the other, though badly charred by lightning, is believed to be a boy. If so, it may mean that these children were ritually sacrificed together in a symbolic marriage. This would appear to lend credence to the contention by Spanish soldier, Juan de Betanzos, who married an Inca princess and wrote in 1551: "Many boys and girls were sacrificed in pairs, being buried alive and well dressed and adorned."

Nowadays, villages in the Colca continue to make offerings to the mountain gods for water and good harvests, but thankfully the gods' have modified their tastes, now preferring chicha to children.

(From *National Geographic*, Vol 189, June 1996.)

the American Geographical Society in Oct 1932 ('Lost Valleys of Peru') and the *National Geographic* of Jan 1934. The Colca Canyon was 're-discovered' from the air again in 1954 by Gonzalo de Reparaz. Two good studies of the region are *El Valle del Colca. Cinco Siglos de Arquitectura y Urbanismo*, by Ramón Gutiérrez (Buenos Aires, 1986) and *Discovering the Colca Valley*, by Mauricio de Romaña, with photographs by Jaume Blassi and Jordi Blassi (Barcelona, 1987). (With thanks to Daniel Buck, Washington DC.)

### Tours

Travel agencies in Arequipa arrange a '1-day' tour to the Mirador for US$18-20. They depart Arequipa at 0400, arriving at the Mirador at 0800-0900, followed by an expensive lunch stop at Chivay and back to Arequipa by 2100. It is not recommended, especially for those with altitude problems, as it is too much to fit into 1 day. 2 day tours cost US$20-26 pp with an overnight stop in Chivay. It is recommended to take at least 2-3 days when visiting the Colca Canyon.

## AREQUIPA TO CHIVAY

A poor dirt road runs N from Arequipa, over the altiplano, to Chivay, the first village on the edge of the Canyon. The road affords fine views of the volcanoes Misti, Chachani, Ampato and the active Sabancaya.

About an hour out of Arequipa, on the road to Chivay, is the **National Vicuña Reserve** (see map). If you're lucky, you can see herds of these rare and timid cameloids near the road. If taking a bus to the reserve to vicuña-watch, there should be enough traffic on the road to be able to hitch a ride back to Arequipa in the evening.

Chivay is the linking point between the two sides of the canyon, as it has the only bridge over the river. The road continues NE to **Tuti**, where there is a small handicrafts shop, and **Sibayo**, with a *pensión* and grocery store. A long circuit back to Arequipa heads S from Sibayo, passing through **Callalli**, **Chullo** and **Sumbay**. This is a little-travelled road, but the views of fine landscapes with vicuña, llamas, alpacas and Andean duck are superb.

Another road from Sibayo goes W, following the northern side of the Colca mountain range to **Cailloma**, **Orcopampa** and **Andagua** (see page 255). Water from the Colca river has been diverted through a series of tunnels and canals to the desert between Repartición and Camaná, to irrigate the Majes pampa.

Crossing the river at Chivay going W to follow the canyon on the far side, you pass the villages of **Coporaque**, **Ichupampa** (where a foot bridge crosses the river), **Lari**, **Madrigal** (which is connected to Maca) and **Tapay** (connected by road to Cabanaconde).

### CHIVAY

Chivay is the gateway to the canyon and the overnight stopping point for 2-day tours run by agencies in Arequipa. At 3,600m, the nights can be bitterly cold.

The hot springs of **La Calera** are 4-5 km away. To get there take one of the regular colectivos (US$0.25) or a 45-mins' walk from town, entrance US$0.70. There are several large pools and hot showers; highly recommended after a hard day's trekking.

• **Accommodation** **D** *El Posada del Inca*, with bath, hot water, carpeted rooms, safe, clean, restaurant next door is reported as overpriced with small helpings; **E** *Inca*, on Salaverry, very clean, spacious rooms, good restaurant; **F** *Hostal Municipal*, on W side of plaza, with bath, cold water, clean, friendly, rec; **F** *Hostal Plaza*, on the plaza, clean, friendly; **F** *Hostal Colca*, Salaverry 307, 2 blocks from plaza, dormitory rooms and some with private bath, good restaurant, friendly, water infrequent.

• **Places to eat** Good food can be found at the unnamed restaurant at C Siglo XX 107, just off the plaza. *El Volante*, on W side of plaza, excellent cheap set meals, popular.

There are other basic restaurants and a small market.

• **Entertainment** There is a video bar on the NW corner of the plaza and a basic disco behind the S side.

• **Transport** From Arequipa there are two routes to Chivay: the old route, via Cayma, called 'Cabreritas'; the new route, through Yura, following the railway, longer but quicker. The latter is being developed as a new route to Cusco from Arequipa. Several buses daily, some very old, from Arequipa to Chivay, 4 hrs (longer if it rains), US$3.50; they leave from the bus offices in C San Juan de Dios at 0330/0400 and from the terminal at 1230-1330. The Cristo Rey company has been recommended. Get your ticket the previous day and be there early to claim your seat. It is a rough route and cold in the morning, reaching 4,825m in the Pata Pampa pass, but the views are worth it. From Chivay to Sibayo, 35 km, 1 hr, US$0.75, several pick-ups daily. From Sibayo to Arequipa, via Callalli, 147 km. From Sibayo to Andagua, via Cailloma and Orcopampa, 194 km, and a further 290 km back to Arequipa; about 12 hrs, US$7.

## TREKS FROM CHIVAY

From Chivay you can hike to Coporaque and Ichupampa, cross the river by the footbridge and climb up to Achoma, a 1-day hike. It's better to follow the road, which seems longer, or you'll end up lost in a maze of terraced fields. The footbridge to Yanque (see below) is between Coporaque and Ichupampa. If you feel too tired to walk back to Chivay, why not catch a colectivo from the plaza in Yanque for US$0.25. It takes 2 days to walk from Chivay to Cabanaconde, you can camp along the route

## CHIVAY TO CABANACONDE

### Yanque

From Chivay, the main road goes W along the Colca Canyon. The first village encountered, after 8 km, is Yanque, a 4 hrs' walk with excellent views. There's an interesting church and a footbridge to the villages on the other side of the canyon. Two nuns, Sisters Antonia and Sara, will allow you to climb the old bell tower of the church. They also run a food help programme for poor families in the area; donations are much appreciated. **A3** *Colca Lodge*, reservations at Zela 212, Arequipa, T 245199, F 242088, with bath, hot water, swimming pool, restaurant, hiking, riding, cycling tours.

Across the river, near the thermal baths, is a *refugio*, **G** pp, food extra, with its own thermal bath and horse included, beautifully situated beside the river. Ask directions in the village. Nearby, on the road to Coporaque, is a ruined Inca settlement.

Next is **Achoma**, 30 mins from Chivay along the Cabanaconde road. **E** *Aldea Turística de Colca*, is a luxury bungalow complex, bungalows for 6 are **C**, all meals are provided, it has the only electricity, heating and hot water in the valley; book through Receptur in Lima or Arequipa, or Ricketts Turismo, Mercaderes 407, Arequipa, T 225382, open April-Nov only. There is also an old settlement for road workers where you can camp.

The road continues to **Maca**, which barely survived an earthquake in Nov 1991. People are still living in tents that were provided at the time. Then comes the tiny village of **Pinchollo**, with a basic *hospedaje*. You can walk from here to the Sabancaya geyser; approximately 7 hrs. For information, ask for Eduardo, who acts as a guide. He lives next to the plaza.

### Cruz del Cóndor

From Pinchollo the road winds its way on to the Mirador, or **Cruz del Cóndor** at the deepest point of the canyon. The view from here is wonderful but people don't come for the view. This is where the immense Andean vulture, the condor, can be seen rising on the morning thermals.

The reason this particular spot is so unique is that the condors swoop by in startling close up, so close, in fact, that you feel you can reach out and touch them. It is a breathtaking and very humbling experience. The best time to arrive

A condor

in the morning is a matter of some dispute, though the consensus is around 0900. If you get there by 0730, you won't miss them, but you may be faced with a long, chilly wait. The condors can also be seen returning from a hard day's food searching at around 1600-1800. Just below the Mirador is a rocky outcrop, which allows a more peaceful viewing. It is possible to camp at the mirador. The bus from Chivay usually stops here for about 10 mins, but ask in advance to make sure.

To get to the Mirador from Cabanaconde, take one of the return buses which set off at around 0330 and 0400, and ask to be dropped off at the Mirador to wait for sunrise and condors. You can walk, 3 hrs back along the road, or by a mule-track cut into the canyon wall, which will save you 30 mins. This latter route is not for vertigo sufferers as the track has been swept away in places by rockfalls, leaving a precarious, loose scree. Horses can be hired to save you the walk; arrange the night before in Cabanaconde.

## CABANACONDE

From the Mirador it is a 20-min bus ride to this friendly, typical village at 3,287m, the last in the Colca Canyon. New arrivals stagger off the bus, dazed and crumpled, into blinding sunlight, and a plaza brimming with life. Women squat on their haunches, selling bruised fruit and a few knobbly root crops. Their bright, flower-patterned hats, voluminous skirts and intricately embroidered blouses bring a splash of colour to the uniform brown adobe buildings. Children tend sheep, goats and llamas; old men lead burdened mules while pigs laze in the sun and chickens peck at the ground. Note that local women are very camera-shy; if you really must intrude, then at least ask permission first and be considerate if they say no.

The views into the canyon are excellent and condors can be seen from the hill just W of the village, a 10 mins' walk from the plaza. A path winds down into the canyon and up to the village of Tapay. A dirt road goes back from Cabanaconde to Arequipa via Huambo and El Alto. This is not a well-used route and there are no services between Cabanaconde and the Panamericana.

• **Accommodation & places to eat** Electricity in Cabanaconde lasts from 2000-2200, so a torch/flashlight is a good idea. There are several hotels, ranging from basic to hygienically-challenged: **G** pp ***Cruz del Cóndor***, on the plaza, nice, clean; **G** ***Solarex***, C Tingo 105, 1 block from plaza, very basic, ask for the sheets to be changed if they're too dirty; these two may not have either water or enough blankets (take sleeping bag), **G** ***Hostal Valle del Fuego***, 1 block from the plaza, basic but clean, friendly, good meals available for around US$3 at their restaurant ***Rancho del Sol***, the friendly owner, Pablo Junco, is a wealth of information, he usually meets the incoming buses but otherwise turn left facing the church on the plaza and it's 1 block along on the right. There are several basic restaurants around the plaza, inc ***Rancho del Colca***, which is mainly vegetarian.

• **Entertainment** Entertainment consists largely of reading other tourists' comments in the restaurant log-book, drinking and then trying to find your way back to your hotel in the dark.

• **Transport** Some buses from Arequipa to Chivay go on to Cabanaconde; a further 75 km, 6 hrs, US$4.35. The road can be very bad in the wet. Transandino buses leave Cabanaconde for Arequipa at 0930; all buses leave Chivay at 1300 from the market. To and from Cabanaconde via El Alto and Huambo, 255 km, the road is in poor condition but the views are magnificent.

## TREKKING IN THE COLCA CANYON

There are many hiking possibilities in the area. Make sure to take enough water as it gets very hot and there is not a lot of water available. Moreover, sun protection is a must. Some treks are impossible if it rains heavily in the wet season, but most of the time the rainy season is dry. Check beforehand. Ask locals for directions as there are hundreds of confusing paths going into the canyon. Buy food for longer hikes in Arequipa. Topographical maps are available at the Instituto Geográfico Militar in Lima, and good information at the South American Explorers Club.

2 hrs below Cabanaconde is an 'oasis' of palm trees and swimming areas which is worth visiting. It's 4½ hrs back up, ask for the best route.

The hike from Cabanaconde to Tapay takes 4 hrs on a good trail with great views. It's possible to stay overnight in Tapay, or camp at the houses just before the bridge. There is running water in a supply channel in the morning and evening; ask the locals. You can continue to Madrigal on foot, through a red-walled valley, which takes about 4 days. An hour before Madrigal is a working mine. The miners are friendly and helpful and will provide meals, accommodation and good, local information.

A longer hike from Cabanaconde goes to Chachas (4-5 days): follow a small path to the W, descending slowly into the canyon (ask locals for directions to Choco); then cross the Inca Bridge (Puente Colgado, 1,800m) and go up to Choco (2,473m), on to the pass at 5,000m and then down to Chachas (3,100m). Sometimes there is transport from Chachas to Andagua in the valley of the volcanoes; otherwise it is a day's hike. This is a superb walk through untouched areas and villages. You need all camping equipment, food and plenty of water.

## SOUTH TO CHILE

ROUTES At **Repartición**, 42 km SW of Arequipa, 134 km from Camaná, a branch of the Panamericana Sur leads S to the Chilean border. From this latter road a branch leads off from La Joya W to Mollendo and Matarani.

### MOLLENDO

130 km S of Arequipa, **Mollendo** (*Pop* 14,650; *Phone code* 054) has now been replaced as a port by Matarani (see below), though port workers still live mostly in Mollendo, where the main customs agencies are. Three beautiful sandy beaches stretch down the coast. The small beach nearest town is the safest for swimming; the swimming pool on the beach is open Jan-Mar.

Mollendo now depends partly upon the summer attraction of the beaches, during which time hotels can be full, and partly upon the 15,000 ha of irrigated land in the nearby Tambo valley. On the coast, a few kilometres SE by road, is the summer resort of Mejía. The small national reserve at the lagoons has 72 resident species of birds and 62 visiting species.

**Local festivals 6 Jan**: anniversary of the district and start of the summer season.

• **Accommodation** C *Hostal Cabaña*, Comercio 240, clean, good, but just a bit on the expensive side; **D** *Hostal Willy*, Deán Valdivia 437-443, with bath, hot water, TV, modern, clean and spacious, though some rooms may be noisy because of the nearby disco, rec; **E** *El Mueble*, on Arica, without bath, basic and not very clean. There are several other cheap options in the **E-F** range on Arica, also: *Aller*, Arequipa 681; **F** *Moderno*, Tacna 179; *Verana*, Arequipa 337, cheap. *Royal*, Tacna 155, basic, clean. Note that many hotels increase their rates over the weekend in the summer season.

• **Places to eat** *La Cabaña*, Comercio 208, excellent, cheap set meals; *Tambo*, Comercio, excellent food at moderate prices; *Sea Room*, Pasaje San Francisco, with ocean views; *Venezia*, Comercio 188. Avoid *Kentucky*, on Plaza Bolognesi, which serves greasy, uncooked food.

• **Entertainment** *Video Bar*, on Comercio, good music and videos, and big jugs of beer for US$2.50; *El Observatorio*, Comercio y Deán Valdivia, a massive, booming, semi-open-air disco, "has to be seen to be believed", no cover charge.

• **Transport** Buses to **Arequipa**, 129 km, buses and colectivos daily, 3 hrs, US$3, many companies on Comercio opp the church (the Comfort company is not recommended). To **Moquegua**, 156 km, 2 hrs, US$2-3, several buses and colectivos daily. To **Tacna**, 315 km, direct transport Thur only; otherwise take colectivo (ask where) at 0600 to connect with Arequipa-Tacna bus 0800-0900.

### MATARANI

14½ km to the NW of Mollendo, the port of Matarani is worth a visit if you get bored of lying on the beach all day. The town is small, pleasant and quiet. There is a good tourist restaurant near the main plaza. It can be reached by colectivo on a good road, US$0.50. Stay on the colectivo until you reach the port gates, where the port captain will be happy to show you around (take passport). You can walk back to the town, which is recommended for the views, or catch a colectivo from the gates.

ROUTES The Pan-American Highway runs S from La Joya through Moquegua to Tacna and Arica (Chile). Cyclists warn that the road to Moquegua is very hilly. About 100 km before Moquegua is a valley at El Fiscal (restaurant). The ash-grey sand dunes near La Joya, on the Pan-American Highway and almost half way from the coast to Arequipa, are unique in appearance and formation. All are crescent shaped and of varying sizes, from 6 to 30m across and from 2 to 5m high, with the points of the crescent on the leeward side. The sand is slowly blown up the convex side, drifts down into the concave side, and the dunes move about 15m a year.

## MOQUEGUA

**Moquegua** (213 km from Arequipa; *Pop* 110,000; *Alt* 1,412m), is a peaceful town in the narrow valley of the Moquegua river and enjoys a sub-tropical climate. The town was formerly known as Santa

Catalina de Guadalcazar, but thankfully reverted to its original name, which means 'silent place' in Quechua. This could be due to the rather taciturn nature of its inhabitants.

Moquegua is not a pretty sight from the Pan-American Highway, but the old centre, a few blocks above the road, is well worth a look for its quiet, winding, cobbled streets and 19th century buildings. The Plaza de Armas, with its mix of ruined and well-maintained churches, colonial and republican facades and llama-shaped hedges, is one of the most interesting small-town plazas in the country. The fountain is said to have been designed by Eiffel, though there is some debate on the matter. The decadent statuary of the fountain in front of the Santo Domingo church is seen by some as a challenge to the traditional Catholic religious iconography within the church. The roofs of many of the old houses are built with sugar-cane thatch and clay and their sculpted door surrounds are particularly notable.

The Inca Emperor, Mayta Capac, sent his captains to carry out a pacifying occupation of the fertile valleys around Moquegua. They founded two settlements, Moquegua and Cuchuna, which is thought to be the site of present-day Torata. Today, most of the valley below the city grows grapes and the upper part grows avocados (*paltas*), wheat, maize, potatoes, some cotton, and fruits. 23 km NE from Moquegua is Cuajone, one of the most important copper mines in Peru.

## Places of interest

There are several interesting colonial houses which make a good, short walking tour. **Casa de Regidor Perpetuo de La Ciudad** or **Casa Conde de Alastaya**, is an 18th century house at Jr Moquegua 404-414. **Casa de Fernández de Córdova** is at Jr Ayacucho 540, on the plaza. At Jr Lima 849 is **Casa de Samuel Ordónez**, which is now the PNP radio control HQ. **Casa de Doctor Martínez**, at Jr Ayacucho 828, has a collapsed interior but baroque elements can be seen in the ornate facade. **Casa de Jiménez de la Flor**, at Ayacucho 550-570, on Plaza de Armas, is notable for its high-relief carved retablo figures. Also worth seeing are: **Casa de Don Pacífico Barrios**, Jr

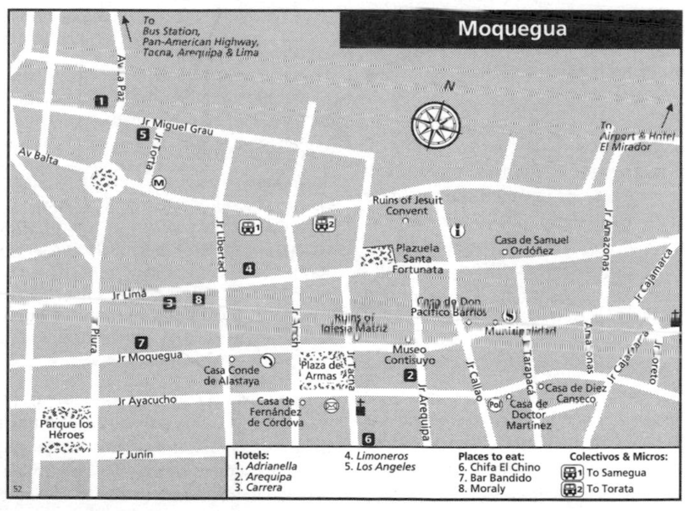

Moquegua 818-822; **Casa de Diez Canseco**, esq Tarapacá y Ayacucho. Some of these houses are private, but the owners may allow entry.

Near *Hotel El Mirador* (see below) are some interesting *bodegas*.

## Museums

**Museo Contisuyo** on the Plaza de Armas, is within the ruins of the Iglesia Matriz, which was rebuilt after many earthquakes over the centuries, but finally left as a ruin in 1868. It covers the Pucara, Huari, Tiahuanaco, Colla, Lupaca and Inca cultures and displays artefacts from around the area. Open Tues 1700-2000, Wed-Sun 1000-1300, 1500-1700.

## Excursions

24 km NE from Moquegua is **Torata**, a quiet, small town with nice, shaded plaza. Above the town, on a hill above the right of the 2 crosses which overlook the town, are the Huari ruins of Torata Alta, a 30-min walk away. The ruins are in a poor state but you can still get a good idea of their extent and the shape and size of the houses from the low surviving walls. The site enjoys good views over to Cerro Baúl.

• **Access** Take a micro or colectivo from Av Balta, between Jr Ancash y Tacna. From the cross on the Moquegua-Cuajone road the last few kms to Torata is not paved.

A highly recommended trip is to **Cerro Baúl**, 2,590m. This can be combined with the ruins at Torata to make a full day's excursion. The mountain is like a tepuy, with sheer sides and flat top, hence its name, which means trunk. There are excellent views for miles around from the summit. The mountain became famous in legend as the place of refuge for the Chuchunas, who resisted the peaceful invasion of the Incas. Eventually the Chuchunas were starved off the mountain, but the refuge had lasted for a considerable time as their children regularly made nocturnal food raids into the Inca camps below.

• **Access** Take a micro for Torata, or for Cuajone, and get off at the crossroads for Torata, at the top of the pass beneath the northern end of the mountain. The path leads up the gradual slope from the road. There is a steep section for the last 200m with some scrambling involved, but it's not too difficult or vertiginous. It takes 45 minutes from the road to the top. The path leads to a Christian shrine (2 crosses), where offerings are made for good crops and to allay sickness. At the near end are extensive Huari ruins. Covering the entire flat summit, which is 1½km long and 200m wide, are hundreds of modern arrangements of stones and miniature shrines, a mixture of pagan and Christian.

4½ km from Moquegua is **Samegua**, known as avocado town, with many restaurants. To get there take a micro from Av Balta, between Libertad and Ancash; 10 minutes.

**Omate** (*Alt* 2,160m; *Pop* 3,000), is a small town, 146 km to the N of Moquegua on an unpaved road, and 129 km to the S of Arequipa (5 hrs). The town is important for its famed Semana Santa processions. Nearby are the thermal baths at Ulucán.

## Local festivals

The main celebration is *Día de Santa Catalina* on 25 Nov, which is the anniversary of the founding of the colonial city.

## Local information

The main street is Av Balta. On Saturday nights Jr Moquegua, from the Plaza de Armas to Jr Piura, becomes the centre of activity.

### ● Accommodation

**C** *El Mirador*, 1 km from town on the road to the airport, pool, clean, friendly, hot water, disco; **C** *Limoneros*, Jr Lima 441, T 761649, with bath, hot water, **D** without bath, car park, discount for groups of more than 10, pool (usually empty), old house with basic rooms, nice garden; **D** *Los Angeles*, Jr Torata 100-A, T 762629, hot water, TV, friendly, may be able to negotiate discount for groups, special rates for children, rec; **D** *Hostal Adrianella*, Miguel Grau 239, T 763469, all rooms with bath, clean, new, modern, hot water, TV; **E** *Arequipa*, Jr Arequipa, clean, hot water sometimes; **F** *Hostal Carrera*, Jr Lima 320, T 762113, clean, friendly, rec.

● **Places to eat**

*Moraly*, esq Lima y Libertad, good sized portions, moderate prices, "best in town", rec; *Chifa El Chino*, Jr Tacna, just off the plaza, beside Santo Domingo church; *Bar Bandido*, Jr Moquegua 333, European-style bar, serves pizzas.

● **Banks & money changers**

**Banco de Crédito**, esq Moquegua y Tarapacá, is the only bank that changes TCs, will also advance money on Visa, open 0915-1315, 1630-1830.

● **Post & telecommunications**

**Post office**: on Plaza de Armas in a colonial house. **Telefónica del Perú**: is at Jr Moquegua 434.

● **Tourist offices**

Jr Callao 121, is more administrative than service oriented, closes 1600.

● **Transport**

Bus from **Lima**, US$16. **Moquegua-Ilo**, 95 km, 1½ hrs, US$1, a few buses daily. To **Tacna**, 159 km, 2 hrs, US$2, several buses and colectivos daily; to **Puno**, 262 km, 10 hrs, San Martín and others daily, US$7. To **Arequipa**, 3½ hrs, US$4, several buses daily.

## ILO

Moquegua's exports – avocados and wine – go by an excellent 96-km road to the fast developing industrial city and important port of **Ilo** (*Pop* 95,000; *Phone code* 054). Its main industries are copper refining, fishing, fish oil products and, more recently, tourism. In 1992, Bolivia was given part of the beach S of Ilo, now called Bolivia Mar, and Bolivia also got half of the Zona Franca, a tax free industrial zone, for the import and export of Bolivia's goods.

There are three Ilos: Ilo Viejo; Ilo Nuevo; and the present town. Ilo Viejo was founded by the French as a port for their ships. In precolumbian times, between 900 and 1300 AD, it was the centre of the Chiribaya culture. The old part has pleasant seafront gardens, an amphitheatre for theatre productions, a gazebo (La Glorieta) at the end of a short pier (not recommended for long walks), an old fishing pier (Muelle Fiscal), old port buildings and a sheltered fishing harbour. The present town is pretty ugly, with a fishmeal factory, oil tanks, and dusty cobbled streets and 'half-door' saloons. Uglier still is Ilo Nuevo, a breeze-block town built by the Southern Peru Copper Corporation for its engineers and their families on a plateau out of sight of Ilo Viejo.

### Places of interest

**Plaza Grau** is the smallest and the most attractive of the 3 main plazas and has a ship and mast in its centre. **Templo San Gerónimo**, on Plaza de Armas, was constructed in 1871; its clock tower was made in Germany. **La Glorieta**, the Mirador at the end of the pier, was built in 1915. It is a symbol of the prosperity of the old fishing port. Beside it is the old fishing quay, the Muelle Fiscal, which dates from 1870.

One of the more notable older civic buildings is known as the **Casa Antigua** and is opposite the Capitanía del Puerto. It now houses the Ilo Social Club. The **Casa de Cultura**, on Av Grau s/n on the seafront, doubles up as a source of tourist information, with leaflets on precolumbian culture. It is a very distinctive, red and white building, with very friendly and helpful staff.

### Museums

**Museo Eduardo Jiménez Lazo**, on Plaza de Armas, shows Chiribaya and more recent exhibits. **Museo Naval** is in the Capitanía building at the harbour, it is good on local nautical history and has navigational relics, diving gear, some of Admiral Grau's manuscripts and a good explanation of the War of the Pacific.

### Excursions

**Valle de los Olivares**, also known as Valle Ilo, lies 10 km to the N. The main attraction is the **Museo de Sitio El Algarrobal** which is dedicated to the local Chiribaya culture and displays mummies, ceramics and some textiles; open 0800-1200.

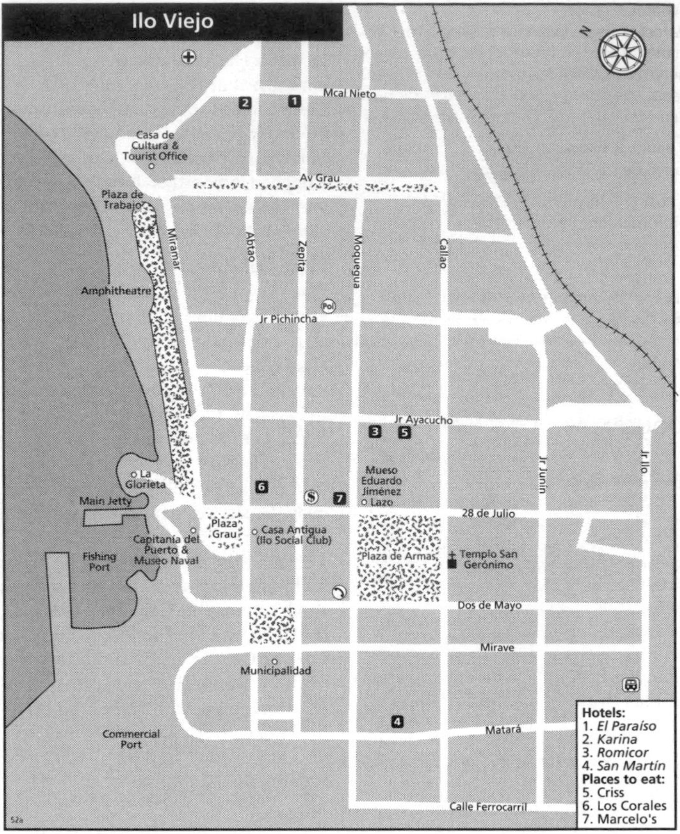

**Ilo Viejo**

**Hotels:**
1. *El Paraíso*
2. *Karina*
3. *Romicor*
4. *San Martín*

**Places to eat:**
5. Criss
6. Los Corales
7. Marcelo's

6 km S of Ilo lies **Punta Coles**, a Nature Reserve similar to the Ballestas Islands, further N near Pisco, where sea lions and guano birds can be seen. You need permission from the Capitanía del Puerto, which may or may not be given, then need to charter a boat.

There are many beaches nearby, eg **Playa de Lizas**, 6 km to the S of Ilo. It becomes very crowded with Peruvian tourists during the summer.

## Local information

### ● Accommodation

**C** *Gran Hotel*, Av Boca del Río s/n, a long way from the centre, T 782411, with bath, restaurant; **C** *Karina*, esq Abtao 780 y Mcal Nieto, T 781531, breakfast included, hot water, all rooms with bath, modern and very clean, very friendly, telephone, TV US$2 extra, car parking US$2 extra per day; **C** *Romicor*, esq Moquegua y Ayacucho, T 781195, with bath, hot water; **D** *El Paraiso*, esq Zepita 751 y Mcal Nieto, T 781432, all rooms with bath, hot water, dig the groovy 70s psychedelic interior; **D** *San Martín*, C Matara 325, with bath, cheaper without, hot water, car parking US$1.50 per night. There are many other hotels in town, some of which are almost certainly cheaper than those above, especially around the bus station.

**● Places to eat**

*Marcelo's*, esq Moquegua y 28 de Julio 335, on the corner of Plaza de Armas, good, basic, cheap *menú*; *Criss*, Ayacucho 416, good value *menú*; *Los Corales*, Jr Abtao 412, good but expensive.

**● Banks & money changers**

**Banco de Crédito**, esq Zepita y 28 de Julio.

**● Post & Telecommunications**

**Telefónica del Perú**: esq Moquegua y 2 de Mayo, corner of plaza.

**● Transport**

Buses to **Moquegua**, US$1.50 with Flores de Hnos. Many of the large bus companies which run buses between Moquegua and Lima start in Ilo, but they are not very full when they arrive in Moquegua.

## TOQUEPALA

70 km S of Moquegua a sign points to the **Minas de Toquepala**, which are 64 km further on a good road; a bus service runs from Tacna. There is a good view of the valley which is full of cacti. Toquepala village, lying in a hollow, has a guest house with swimming pool, a church, clubhouse and an American School, and is a pleasant place. However, it is a private mining community and permission from the management must be obtained in advance to visit the village.

A nearby cave contains paintings believed to date from 8,000 BC, but it is very hard to find. Helio Courier planes reach it from Moquegua in 12 minutes and from Ilo in 26 minutes. You can also take a taxi from Tacna.

The Southern Peru Copper Corporation is exploiting its copper property at Toquepala, E of Moquegua, at an altitude of 3,050m. All exports are through Ilo, along the 183 km railway and road from Toquepala. The SPCC smelter is on the coast, 18 km from the port of Ilo.

## TACNA

Backed by the snow-capped peak of Tacora, **Tacna** (*Pop* 150,200; *Alt* 550m; *Phone code* 054) is 156 km S of Moquegua by the Pan-American Highway, 42 km from the Chilean frontier, and 64 km from the international port of Arica, to which there is a railway. It is 1,292 km from Lima by road.

Tacna was in Chilean hands from 1880 to 1929, when its people voted by plebiscite to return to Peru. There are good schools, housing estates, a stadium to seat 10,000 people, an airport, many military posts and one of the best hospitals in Peru.

Around the city the desert is gradually being irrigated. The local economy includes olive groves, vineyards and fishing. The waters of Laguna Aricota, 80 km N, are now being tapped for further irrigation and hydroelectric power for industry.

### Places of interest

Above the city, on the heights, is the **Campo de la Alianza**, scene of a battle between Peru and Chile in 1880. The cathedral, designed by Eiffel, faces the main square, Plaza de Armas, which contains huge bronze statues of Admiral Grau and Colonel Bolognesi. The interior is austere but the round stained glass windows, each with a different motif, accentuate the fine, clean lines. The bronze fountain is said to be the duplicate of the one in the Place de la Concorde (Paris) and was also designed by Eiffel.

The **Parque de la Locomotora**, near the city centre, has a British-built locomotive, which was used in the War of the Pacific. There is a very good railway museum at the station; open 0800-1300, entry US$0.45. The museum in the **Casa de la Cultura** has precolumbian pottery and war relics, it is very good and entry is free.

### Local information

**NB** Everything closes 1300-1600.

**● Accommodation**

Accommodation is hard to find in the centre, especially at Christmas-time, because of Chileans on shopping sprees.

**A2** *Gran Hotel Tacna*, Av Bolognesi 300, T 724193, F 722015 (ex Hotel Turistas), gardens,

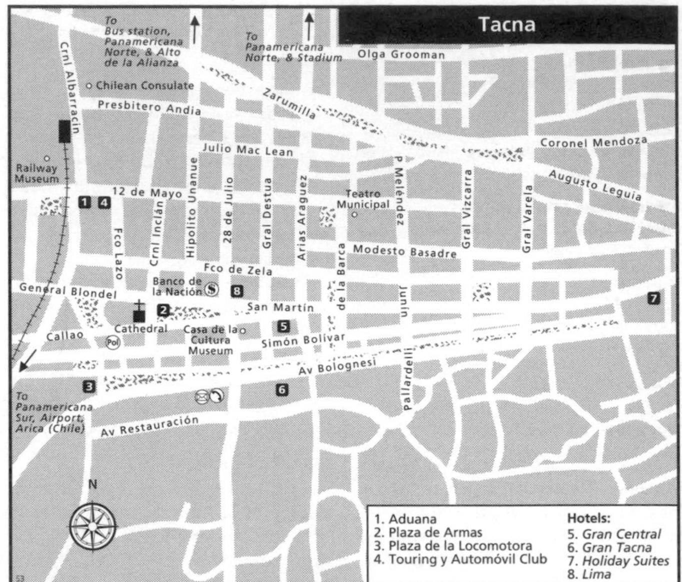


2 swimming pools, safe car park, good breakfast for US$4, English spoken, disco, casino, gym, friendly; **A3** ***Holiday Suites***, Alto de Lima, T 715371, F 711764, 10 mins' walk from centre, follow Av Bolognesi to the University, from where it's 1 block to the left, pool and car park.

**B** ***Gran Hotel Central***, San Martín 561, T 712281, F 726031, central, friendly, secure, English spoken rec; **B-C** ***El Mesón***, Unánue 175, T 725841, F 721832, modern, nice, phone and TV, friendly.

**D** ***Lima***, San Martín 442, T 711912, on Plaza de Armas, sporadic hot water, with bath, bar, good restaurant, friendly, stores luggage, smelly; **D** ***San Diego***, Ayacucho 86-A, T 712398, shared bath, clean, friendly, basic.

**E** ***Hostal HC***, Zela 734, T 712391, hot water, discounts available, cafeteria next door, laundry service, videos, very friendly, rec; **E** ***Lido***, C San Martín 876, near Plaza de Armas, with hot showers, rec.

**F** ***Hostal Buen Amigo***, 2 de Mayo 445, clean, secure, no water at night; **F** ***Hostal Arica***, Pasaje Bacigalupo, Av Leguía, T 715818, good value, friendly, hot water.

### ● Places to eat

***Sur Perú***, Ayacucho 80, rec; ***Los Tenedores***, San Martín 888, good, clean, expensive; ***Hostal Lido***, San Martín 876 A, good value; ***Pizzeria Puco***, Libertad pedestrianized street, ½ block from San Martin, good; ***El Sameño***, Arias Aráguez, entre Zarumilla y Olga Grooman, good value fish restaurant; ***Delfín Azul***, Zela 747, good; ***Helados Piamonte***, 1 block from *Hotel Tacna*, good ice cream. Hot food from supermarket ***Caneda y Cía***, San Martín 770.

### ● Airline offices

**Americana**, Av San Martín 408, Plaza de Armas, T 723870; **Aero Continente**, Apurímac 265; **Faucett**, Apurímac 205; **AeroPerú**, Ayacucho 96.

### ● Banks & money changers

**Banco de Crédito**, San Martín 574, no commission for TCs (Amex, Citicorp, City Bank) into soles; similarly at **Banco Wiese**, San Martín 476; **Banco de Perú**, C Gral Blondel, between Gral Deustua y Arias Aráguez, changes TCs into soles at reasonable rate, open Sat 0930-1200. Best rates are at the *cambio* on Junín, between *Hotel Junín* and Av Bolognesi.

● **Post & telecommunications**

**Telefónica del Perú**: Zela 727.

● **Tourist offices**

Some travel agencies will provide information (not very reliable, though). **Secretaría de Estado de Turismo**, Av Bolognesi 2088, T 3778. **Touring y Automóvil Club del Perú**, Av 2 de Mayo 55.

● **Transport**

**Air** To **Lima**, 2 hrs, US$93 one way; daily flights with AeroPerú, Americana, Aero Continente and Faucett. To **Arequipa**, 35 mins, US$21, all airlines; with connecting flight to **Juliaca**, US$41. Taxi to town and bus terminal US$5. There is no transport direct to the border; cheapest way is to take a taxi to town first, then take a colectivo.

**Buses** Bus station on Hipólito Unánue, 1 km from plaza (colectivo US$0.25); well-organized, local tax US$0.40, baggage store, easy to make connections to the border, Arequipa or Lima. To **Moquegua**, 159 km, 2 hrs, US$2, several buses and colectivos daily. There are no direct buses to **Mollendo**, so catch one of the frequent buses to El Fiscal (US$4, 4 hrs), then a colectivo to Mollendo for US$1.50. To **Arequipa**, 4 hrs, US$5, several buses daily, 0800-1000, 1900-2200 (eg Ormeño, Aráguez 698 y Grooman). To **Nasca**, 793 km, 12 hrs, US$9, several buses daily, most en route for Lima. Several buses daily to **Lima**, 1,239 km, 21-26 hrs, US$27 with Cruz del Sur and Ormeño, rec (see Lima **Bus Companies** with routes to the S).

Tickets can be purchased several days before departure and buses fill up quickly. At the Tacna/Moquegua departmental border there are checkpoints at which all buses stop for inspection of imported goods from Chile (there are loads!). This can take time as negotiation with the officials is required and they can be impossible. Do not carry anything for a Peruvian, only your own belongings.

Buses leave from the Zona Franca near the airport and market area, **not** the bus terminal, to Ilave on the Puno-La Paz highway, 320 km, 16 hrs (can be longer in the rainy season), US$6; Gironda, Rio Blanco and Ponce companies. The road, via Tarata (where Inca terraces are still in use) and Challapalca, is in fair condition, but it is a bumpy and cold journey and can be hard in the wet, though the views are spectacular. Luggage packed on the roof racks has been known to disappear. It might be better to fly to Juliaca and then take a bus. Plenty of local buses and colectivos leave all day from Ilave to **Puno**, a further 55 km, 1 hr, US$1. To **La Paz**, either go from Puno to Yunguyo, or take the direct Litoral bus, T 724761, Wed 0700, US$17.50, 13-16 hrs (but it can be much longer in the rainy season).

**NB** Soon after buses leave Tacna, passengers' passports and luggage are checked, whether you have been out of the country or not.

## FRONTIER WITH CHILE

● **Peruvian immigration**

There is a checkpoint before the border, which is open 0900-2200. Peruvian immigration is closed on public holidays. You need to obtain a Peruvian exit stamp (quick) and then a Chilean entrance stamp, which can take a while, but formalities are straightforward. Drivers will help, or do it all for you. If you need a Chilean visa, you have to get it in Tacna (open only during office hours, closed weekends and holidays). Note that no fruit or vegetables are allowed into Chile.

● **Crossing by private vehicle**

For those leaving Peru by car buy *relaciones de pasajeros* (official forms, US$0.45) from the kiosk at the border or from a bookshop; you will need 4 copies. Next, return your tourist card, visit the PNP office, return the vehicle permit and finally depart through the checkpoints.

● **Exchange**

Coming into Peru from Chile, you can only change pesos into soles with street money changers in Tacna at a poor rate. Banco de la Nación will not change money. Money changers line Av Bolognesi, they are also at one end of the new bus terminal where the rates are described as 'not too bad' (see also **Banks & money changers** above).

● **Transport**

**Road** 46 km, 1-2 hrs, depending on waiting time at the frontier. Buses to Arica charge about US$2 and colectivo taxis about US$4 pp. All leave from the bus terminal in Tacna throughout the day. If you're in a hurry, make sure that the colectivo you choose is full (most of the time 6 passengers) because it will not leave before. You can change your remaining soles at the bus terminal. A Chilean driver is perhaps more likely to take you to any address in Arica. 'Agents' operate on behalf of taxi drivers at the bus terminal; you may not see the colectivo until you have negotiated the price and filled in the paperwork.

**Trains** Mon, Wed and Fri at 0530 and 0700 (check times) from Tacna to Arica, US$1.25, 2 hrs. The station opens 1 hr before departure to prevent smugglers from entering as the trains are normally used by smugglers. There are customs, but no immigration facilities for those arriving by train from Chile.

**NB** Between Oct and Mar Peruvian time is 1 hr earlier than Chilean time, 2 hrs earlier Oct to Feb or Mar, varies annually.

### ● Into Chile

**Arica**, Chile's most northerly city, is 19 km S of the border (*Pop* 174,064). It has road and rail links with La Paz, Bolivia, road links with the rest of Chile and is a good starting place for visits to Andean national parks, such as Lauca. It has a wide selection of hotels, restaurants and services.

# Lake Titicaca



TRAVELLERS crossing the bleak altiplano South to Bolivia or North to Peru will experience the deep, azure waters of mystical Lake Titicaca. This, the highest navigable lake in the world, at 3,856m above sea level, covers a massive 8,000 sq km, not including its 30-plus islands. The chilly town of Puno is the starting off point for a trip to the lake's islands and an insight into a traditional way of life.

## AREQUIPA TO JULIACA

### By rail

The railway from Arequipa winds its way up the valley towards Juliaca. Skirting El Misti and Chachani the train climbs steadily past Yura, Socosani and Pampa de Arrieros. After another 80 km it reaches Crucero Alto, the highest point on the line, at 4,500m. The beautiful lakes Lagunillas and Saracocha lie on opposite sides of the railway, which flirts with their shores for nearly an hour.

As the descent continues streams become more plentiful. The scenery changes over the next few hours from desolate mountain peaks to a fertile pampa with a fairly populous agricultural community.

**NB** since there is no day train, much of this stunning scenery is, unfortunately, not visible en route. The train, however, is more comfortable than travelling by bus.

### By road

The rough road from Arequipa to Juliaca climbs steeply for the first 50 km, before reaching a plateau. Its highest point is at Alto de Toroya, 4,693m. The scenery is beautiful as the road passes lakes, salt flats and small villages. If driving, a 4WD is strongly recommended. Even in the dry season, there are rivers to cross and sand stretches. After heavy rain it is impassable.

This takes 3 days by bicycle. If heading for Puno it is better to go via Juliaca than taking the direct branch to Puno. Restaurants along the way sell mostly basic foodstuffs and drinks: at **Chiguata**, Km 30; **Salinas**, Km 82; at Km 113, S from **Pati**; **Alto de Toroya**, Km 176; **Tincopalca**, Km 176, where it is also possible to sleep; **Santa Lucía**, Km 218, also *alojamiento*; and at **Deustua**, Km 252. The route covers 282 km in total.

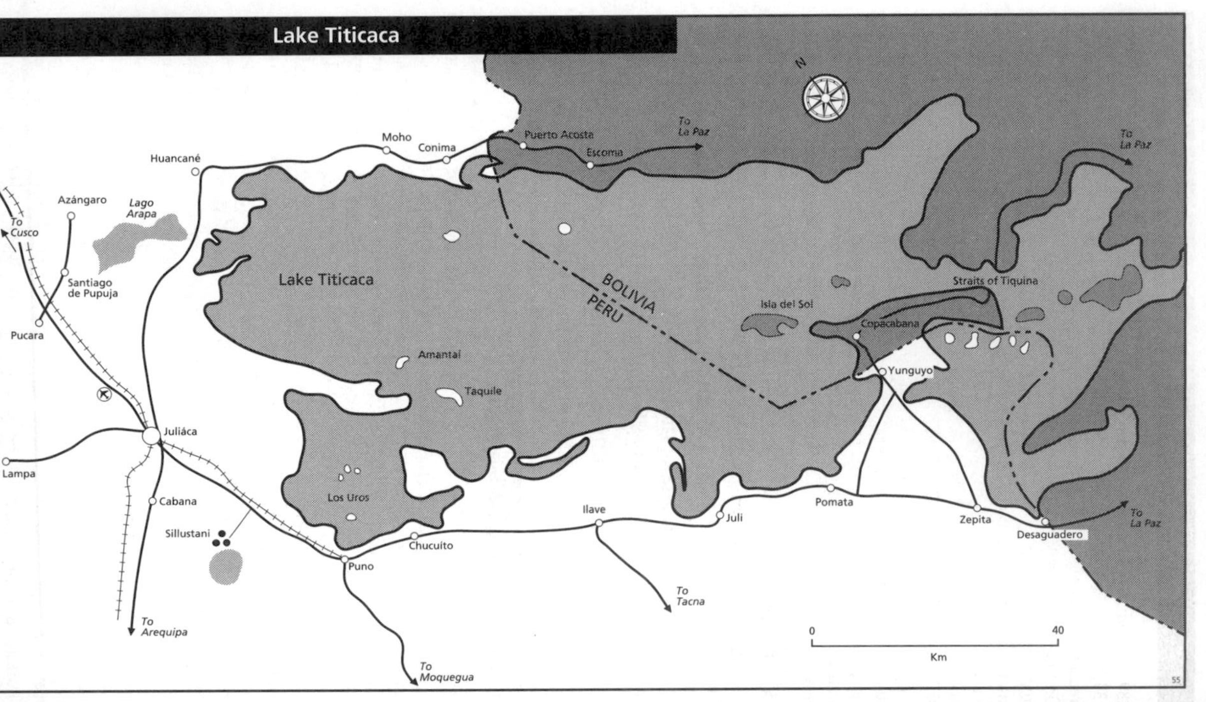
Lake Titicaca
N
Moho
Conima
Puerto Acosta
Escoma
To La Paz
To La Paz
Huancané
Azángaro
Lago Arapa
To Cusco
Santiago de Pupuja
Pucara
Lake Titicaca
BOLIVIA
PERU
Isla del Sol
Straits of Tiquina
Copacabana
Yunguyo
Amantaí
Taquile
Juliáca
Lampa
Cabana
Los Uros
Sillustani
Chucuito
Puno
Ilave
Juli
Pomata
Zepita
Desaguadero
To La Paz
To Tacna
To Arequipa
To Moquegua
0
40
Km

## JULIACA

289 km NE of Arequipa, **Juliaca** (*Pop* 134,700; *Alt* 3,825m; *Phone code* 054), is freezing cold at night, poor and run down. On the huge Plaza Melgar, several blocks from the main part of the town, is an interesting colonial church. At the large market in the plaza on Mon, you can buy wool and alpaca goods. There is another daily market in the plaza outside the railway station, which is more tourist oriented. Tupac Amarú market, on Moquegua 7 blocks E of railway line, is a cheap black market. A first class hospital is run by the Seventh Day Adventists.

### EXCURSIONS

There are good thermal springs at village of **Putina**, 84 km NE of Juliaca, 5½ hrs by bus or truck, US$2.50. 71 km NE of Juliaca is the old town of **Azángaro** with a famous church, La Asunción, filled with *retablos* and paintings of the Cusco school.

The town of **Pucara** lies 63 km to the N, with pre-Inca ruins and its famed pottery (see page 290). The sheep farm of San Antonio, between Ayaviri and Chiquibambilla, owned by the Prime family, who are descendants of British emigrants, can be visited.

23 km NW of Juliaca is the unspoiled little colonial town of **Lampa**, known as the 'Pink City', with a splendid church, La Inmaculada, containing a copy of Michelangelo's 'Pietà'. Also of interest is the Kampac Museo, Ugarte 462, a museum with sculptures and ceramics from the Lampa and Juli areas; the owner lives next door. It also has a good Sun market. There is a basic *hostal*, G pp. Buses and trucks daily, 1 hr, US$0.60

### LOCAL INFORMATION

#### ● Accommodation

**B** *Turistas*, Av Arequipa 1381, T 71524, on the outskirts of town, good, but the water is turned off at 2300, meals US$3-5.

**C** *Hostal Samari*, Noriega, T 321870, F 321852, clean, modern, with restaurant.

**D** *Karlo's Hostal*, Unión 317, T 322568, clean, comfortable, hot water; **D** *Royal Inn*, San Román 158, T 321561, F 321572, clean, decent accommodation, private bath and TV, rec, restaurant good.

**E** *Hostal Perú*, Bracesco 409, railway plaza, T 321510, with bath, cheaper without, clean, comfortable, hot water sometimes, rec, has a basic restaurant; **E** *Yasur*, Jr M Núñez 414, with bath, F without, clean, safe, friendly, a small bar and restaurant are open in the evening.

**G** *Hostal Ferrocarril*, San Martín 249, clean, friendly, water until 1900. There are water problems in town, especially in the dry season.

#### ● Places to eat

*Trujillo*, on San Martín, basic, typical food, good value, US$3-4 for a meal.

#### ● Security

Beware of pickpockets and thieves, especially at the station, where they get on the train to join those already on board. Also beware of overcharging by taxi drivers at the railway station.

#### ● Transport

**Air** Airport refurbished 1995, small but well-organized. To Lima, 1 hr, 45 mins, daily with AeroPerú, Faucett, Americana and Aero Continente, US$77; check if the US$65 'tourist coupon' is in effect. To Arequipa, 30 mins, US$40, daily with all main airlines. To Cusco, 35 mins, US$40, Faucett 3 a week, Americana daily. Americana has its office at Jr Noriega 325, T 321844. Taxi to airport 15 mins, US$2.10. Alternatively, walk 200m to airport entrance and catch a city bus, US$0.15. A colectivo runs direct from the airport to Puno, US$1.70 pp, 1 hr.

**Trains** See information under Arequipa (including **Warning**), Puno or Cusco. The station at Juliaca is the junction for services between Arequipa, Puno and Cusco. Carriages are put onto the right rails for their next destination, a process which can take several hours and can prove too much for tired passengers. It is advisable to get off the train and continue to Puno by bus or colectivo (US$0.50, 1 hr), which is much quicker, safer and more comfortable. You do not have to change trains in Juliaca if you buy a through ticket from one terminus to the other using the same class all the way. Stay in your carriage at Juliaca and watch your possessions closely.

You have the opportunity to buy alpaca goods through the carriage window, but bargain hard. The ticket office opens when the train comes in. Trains for Puno arrive about 0645; for Arequipa at about 2045. Prices to

Cusco and Arequipa are the same as from Puno.

**Buses** To **Cusco**, 344 km, 12 hrs (longer in the rainy season), US$8; buses and trucks daily. The road is in very poor condition as the train is used more. When the train does not run in the rainy season, the bus has to be taken, unless conditions are so bad that buses are not running either. It is not advisable to take a night bus to or from Cusco, as robberies, or worse, can occur; at least take the more expensive tourist bus. To **Puno**, 44 km, 1 hr, US$0.45, US$1, leaving from Calle Nicolás de Piérola, past the railway; combis to Puno leave from Plaza Bolognesi, also US$0.45. Taxi to Puno is about US$15. From Puno transport goes to the Bolivian border and on to La Paz. To **Huancané** (on the N side of Lake Titicaca), 51 km, 3½ hrs, US$1.75, several buses and trucks daily; it is a bumpy ride on a poor road, but the views are wonderful. It is a further 50 km, US$1.75, to the Bolivian border; there are several checkpoints and the trip can take a few hours. Buses and trucks leave daily, but not very frequently, on this route.

## PUNO

On the NW shore of Lake Titicaca, **Puno** is Capital of its Department and Peru's folklore centre with a vast array of handicrafts, festivals and costumes and a rich tradition of music and dance.

Puno isn't the most attractive of cities and being so high up leaves you feeling like a badly barbecued sausage – charred on the outside by day and frozen solid inside by night. But with its surly seediness comes a certain vitality. The main plaza is worth a look and the lakeside quarter, largely flooded since the rise in the lake's water level, is interesting, but dirty.

The impressive baroque exterior of the **Cathedral**, completed in 1657, belies an austere interior. Beside the Cathedral is the famous **Balcony of the Conde de**

### Aymara culture and religion

The Aymaras, who populate the Titicaca region, are a deeply religious people whose culture is permeated with the idea of the sacred. They believe that God, the Supreme Being, gives them security in their daily lives and this God of Life manifests him/herself through the deities, such as those of the mountains, the water, the wind, the sun, the moon and the *wa'qas* (sacred places).

As a sign of gratitude, the Aymara give *wax'ta* (offerings), *wilancha* (llama sacrifices) and *ch'alla* (sprinkling alcohol on the ground) to the *achachilas* (the protecting spirits of the family and community), the *Pachamama* (Mother Earth), *Kuntur Mamani* and *Uywiri* (protecting spirits of the home).

The remote mountains of the bleak altiplano are of particular importance for the Aymara. The most sacred places are these high mountains, far from human problems. It is here that the people have built their altars to offer worship, to communicate with their God and ask forgiveness. The community is also held important in the lives of the Aymara. The *achachila* is the great-great grandfather of the family as well as the protector of the community, and as such is God's representative on earth.

The offerings to the sacred mountains take place for the most part in August and are community celebrations. Many different rituals are celebrated: there are those within the family; in the mountains; for the planting and the harvest; rites to ask for rain or to ask for protection against hailstorms and frosts; and ceremonies for Mother Earth.

All such rituals are led by Aymara *Yatiris*, who are male or female priests. The *Yatiri* is a wise person – someone who knows – and the community's spiritual and moral guide. Through a method of divination that involves the reading of coca leaves, they guide individuals in their personal decision-making.

**Lemos**, on the corner of Deustua and Conde de Lemos, where Peru's Viceroy stayed when he first arrived in the city. A short walk up Independencia leads to the **Arco Deustua**, a monument honouring those killed in the battles of Junín and Ayacucho. Nearby, is a mirador giving fine views over the town, the port and the lake beyond. The walk from Jr Cornejo following the Stations of the Cross up a nearby hill, with fine views of Lake Titicaca, has been recommended, but be careful and don't go alone.

**BASICS** *Pop* 80,000, with 8,000 students; *Alt* 3,855m. *Climate* Puno gets bitterly cold at night: in June-Aug the temperature at night can fall to -25°C, but generally not below -5°C.

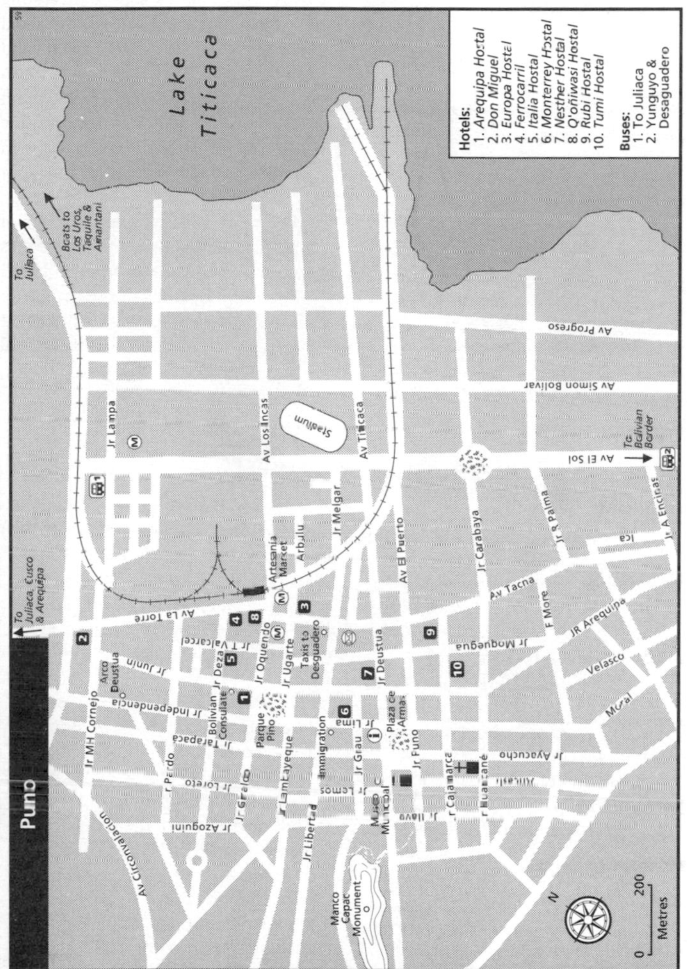

## A load of bulls

The village of Pucara, north of Juliaca, is famous for its distinctive pottery, a detailed style dubbed grotesque because the figures' features are wildly exaggerated. The figures are usually left unpainted and unglazed, and the earth colour and rough surface play a part in the overall effect. Among the figures produced, the best known is the Pucara bull.

The llama was a votive symbol for the Incas, often carved out of stone and used for burning incense and other sacred purposes, until the bull, introduced to the Americas by the invading Spanish, took its place as a symbol of strength and virility. In some fiestas in the surrounding area, bulls are cut on the neck and their blood offered to *Pachamama*, the mother earth. Flowers are then thrown at the animal and coca leaves placed on its wounds to cure the pain.

Coca leaves are even painted on the ceramic versions of the popular Pucara bull, which gained fame with the introduction of the Puno-Cusco railway. The train stops frequently and the bulls can be sold easily to passing travellers. (Extracted from *Arts and Crafts of South America*, by Lucy Davies & Mo Fini, Tumi).

### MUSEUMS

The **Museo Municipal** has been combined with the private collection of precolumbian artefacts bequeathed to the city by their owner, Sr Carlos Dreyer. It is at Conde de Lemos 289; open Mon to Fri 0730-1330, entrance US$1.

The historic ship, *Yavari*, which is the oldest ship on Lake Titicaca, is berthed in the port of Puno and is now open to visitors as a Museum and Bar.

The iron-hulled ship, *Yavari*, recently painted in her original livery of black, white and red, is moored alongside the jetty from which the launches to Los Uros Island leave. The ship was built in England in 1862 and, together with her twin, the *Yapura* (now the Peruvian Navy's Hospital ship and called the *BAP Puno*), was shipped in kit form to Arica. From Arica, the two ships went by rail to Tacna from where the 2,766 pieces were carried by mule to Lake Titicaca. The journey took 6 years. The *Yavari* was eventually launched on Christmas Day 1870 and on 14 June 1871 sailed on her maiden voyage. The *Yapura* followed in 1873.

The Bolinder 4-cylinder hot bulb semi-diesel engine on view today replaced the original dried llama dung steam engine in 1913.

Since after the War of the Pacific until the nationalization of the Railways and Lake Fleet in 1975, the *Yavari* was operated as a passenger/cargo vessel by the London-based Peruvian Corporation. The ship was bought in 1987 and is being restored by an Anglo-Peruvian Association.

Visitors are very welcome on board the *Yavari* and will be shown over the ship and its exhibition of archival documentation and memorabilia on the Lake Fleet by the Captain, Carlos Saavedra. The entrance charge of US$2 is to help with maintenance costs.

• **Project addresses** England: 61 Mexfield Road, London, SW15 2RG, T/F (44) 181 874 0583; Peru/Lima: c/o *Invertur*, Av Las Magnolias 889, Of 208, San Isidro, Lima 27, T (00511) 442-3090, F (00511) 442-4180; Puno: c/o *Solmartours*, Jr Arequipa 140, Puno, T (005154) 352901, F (005154) 351654.

## EXCURSIONS

Anybody interested in religious architecture should go from Puno to visit the villages along the western shore of Lake Titicaca.

### Chucuíto

An Inca sundial can be seen near the village of Chucuíto, which has an interesting church, La Asunción, and houses with carved stone doorways. Nearby, are cave paintings at Chichiflope

• **Accommodation** D *Las Cabañas*, per night in 4-bedded bungalow, nice, quiet location, T 352108, leave message for Alfredo Sánchez.

### Juli

The best examples of religious architecture are at Juli, which has four churches.

**San Pedro**, designated as the Cathedral, has been extensively restored. It contains a series of superb screens, some in ungilded mahogany and others taken from other churches, as well as some fine paintings, and a collection of coloured objects in the sacristy.

**San Juan Bautista** has two sets of 17th century paintings of the lives of St John the Baptist and of St Teresa, contained in sumptuous gilded frames. San Juan is now a state museum, open in the morning only (US$0.15); it also has intricate *mestizo* carving in pink stone.

**Santa Cruz** is another fine Jesuit church, partly roofless, so that it is easy to photograph the carvings of monkeys, papayas and grapes. The keys to Santa Cruz and San Juan Bautista are kept by the couple who look after San Juan Bautista.

The fourth church, **La Asunción**, now abandoned and its fine bell tower damaged by earthquake or lightning, has an archway and atrium which date from the early 17th century. A school of picture restoration is working on its mass of paintings.

Beautiful needlework can be bought at the plaza in Juli. There is a nice walk from Juli to the red rock formations known as Caballo Cansado. Near Juli is a small colony of flamingos. Many other birds can be seen from the road.

• **Accommodation** G *Alojamiento El Rosal*, Puno 128, just off the Plaza, basic but OK.

### Pomata

The church at **Pomata**, which is being restored, is spectacular, with beautiful carvings, in Andean *mestizo* baroque, of vases full of tropical plants, flowers and animals in the window frames, lintels and cornices, and a frieze of dancing figures inside the dome – which is unusual in Peru – and alabaster windows (John Hemming). The church at **Zepita** is also worth visiting.

• **Accommodation in Pomata**: ask for Sra Rosa Pizano, on the plaza, No 30.

### Ilave

On the road to Juli is Ilave, where the road for Tacna branches off. It is typical of a gaunt *altiplano* town, with a good Sun market where you can buy woven goods – beware bag slashers.

• **Transport** Many buses and colectivos go there from Puno (US$1.40). Ilave-Tacna, 320 km, US$6, 16 hrs, at 1400 and 1700 with Transportes Ponce (the best), and Gironda.

### Sillustani

Near Puno, are the *chullpas* (precolumbian funeral towers) of Sillustani in a beautiful setting on a peninsula in Lake Ayumara, 32 km from Puno on an excellent road. A trip there is highly recommended.

"Most of the towers date from the period of Inca occupation in the 15th century, but they are burial towers of the Aymara-speaking Colla tribe. The engineering involved in their construction is more complex than anything the Incas built – it is defeating archaeologists' attempts to rebuild the tallest 'lizard' *chullpa*. Two are unfinished: one with a ramp still in place to raise blocks; the other with cut stones ready to go onto a very ambitious corbelled false dome. A series of stone circles to the east of the site are now thought to be the bases of domed thatch or peat living huts, rather than having any religious meaning. The quarry near the towers is also worth seeing." (John Hemming).

There are local people at the site, in traditional costume. Camera fans will find the afternoon light best, though this is when the wind is at its strongest and can kick up a mini-sandstorm; best not to wear contact lenses. The scenery is barren desert, but nonetheless impressive. On the lake before the ruins there are flamingos and ducks. Take warm clothing, water and sun protection. The site has a restaurant, but no electricity; admission, US$2.25.

There are Inca ruins at Tancatanca and Caluxo.

• **Transport** Take an organized tour; about 3-4 hrs, leave 1430. Some include transport and entrance fee, about US$7-8; some offer only transport US$3, meaning it is cheaper to pay the entrance fee at the site. Bus, including site entrance, from C Tacna, 1430, US$5. Alternatively, take a Juliaca bus to the Sillustani turnoff (US$0.35); from here a 15-km paved road runs across the altiplano to the ruins. Moto-taxis and some kombis run to Atuncolla (10 km, lovely colonial church): moto-taxi US$0.40, or US$0.85 to Sillustani. Go early to avoid tour groups at the site. A taxi from Puno costs about US$25.

## LOCAL FESTIVALS

The very colourful **Fiesta de la Virgen de la Candelaria** takes place during the first 2 weeks in February. Bands and dancers from all the local towns compete in this *Diablada*, or Devil Dance, with the climax coming on Sun. The festival is famous for its elaborate and grotesque masks, which depict characters in local legends as well as caricatures of former landowners and mine bosses. The festivities are better at night on the streets than the official functions in the stadium. Check in advance on the actual date because Candelaria may be moved if pre-Lentern carnival coincides with it. This festival is great fun and shouldn't be missed if you're in the vicinity around this time.

Other festivals include a candlelight procession through darkened streets, which takes place on Good Friday, with bands, dignatories and statues of Jesus. On 3 May is Invención de la Cruz, an exhibition of local art. On 29 June is the colourful festival of San Pedro, with a procession at Zepita (see page 291). Another takes place on 20 July. In fact, it is difficult to find a month in Puno without some sort of celebration.

On 4-5 Nov is an impressive pageant dedicated to the founding of Puno and the emergence of Manco Capac from the waters of Lake Titicaca. The procession from the lake winds its way to the stadium where a ceremony takes place with dancers from local towns and villages. This is not the best time to visit Taquile and Amantaní since many of their inhabitants are at the festival.

## LOCAL INFORMATION

**Hotel prices**

| | | | |
|---|---|---|---|
| **L1** | over US$200 | **L2** | US$151-200 |
| **L3** | US$101-150 | **A1** | US$81-100 |
| **A2** | US$61-80 | **A3** | US$46-60 |
| **B** | US$31-45 | **C** | US$21-30 |
| **D** | US$12-20 | **E** | US$7-11 |
| **F** | US$4-6 | **G** | up to US$3 |

● **Accommodation**

Hotel rooms are difficult to find after the trains arrive as everyone else is also looking, but hotel touts besiege arriving train passengers. If you're taking a room with a bathroom, check first if it has hot or cold water. Check on the early morning water supply, as some only have water after 0730, too late if you are going out by train or on an island tour. There are clean public showers nr the football stadium. Note that Puno suffers from power and water shortages.

**A3** *Isla Esteves* (ex Tourist Hotel), T 353870, spacious, good views, on an island linked by a causeway 5 km NE of Puno (taxi US$1.75), built on a Tiahuanaco-period site, phone, bar, good restaurant, disco, good service, electricity and hot water all day, camping allowed in car park.

**B *Hostal Hacienda*, Jr Deustua 297, T/F 356109, refurbished colonial house, with bath, hot water, TV, inc breakfast, café, comfortable, friendly, rec; B *Sillustani***, Jr Lambayeque 195, T 351431, includes breakfast, good service, clean, friendly, cold rooms, ask for an electric heater, hot water.

**C *Don Miguel***, Av Torre 545, T 351371, with shower, with restaurant, clean; **C *El Buho***, Lambayeque 142, T 351409, clean, hot water, nice rooms, friendly, ask for a room with a radiator, rec; **C *Ferrocarril***, Av La Torre 185, T 351752, opp station, with bath and hot water, E without bath and with cold water in the old part of the building, modern, good rooms, but noisy, poor service, central heating adequate, accepts many credit cards and changes Bolivian currency; **C *Hostal Colón Inn***, Tacna 290, T 351432, recently renovated, colonial style, good rooms with private bathroom and hot shower, clean, good service, restaurant and pizzería, the Belgian manager Christian Nonis is well known, especially for his work on behalf of the people on Taquile island; **C *Hostal Italia***, Teodoro Valcarcel 122, T 352521, 2 blocks from the station, with bath, good, safe, hot water, good food, clean, staff helpful, rec; **C *Hostal La Rosa Lacustre***, Jr Arequipa 386, T 355173, with bath, hot water, café.

**D *Hostal Arequipa***, Arequipa 153, T 352071, clean, friendly, cold water, will change TCs at good rates, stores luggage, secure, adequate; **D *Hostal Imperial***, Teodoro Valcarcel 145, T 352086, with bath, hot water, friendly, helpful, stores luggage, clean, comfortable, safe; **D *Hostal Rubi***, Jr Cajamarca 152-154, T 356058, T/F 353384, friendly, safe, breakfast US$2, good; **D *Hostal Tumi***, Cajamarca 237, T 353270, clean, friendly, safe, plenty of hot water, breakfast available, friendly and helpful, highly rec; **D *Internacional***, Libertad 161, T 352109, with shower, an extra bed costs US$1.50, hot water morning and evening, secure, central.

**E *Europa***, Alfonso Ugarte 112, nr the station, T 353023, 'gringo hotel', luggage may be stored, but don't leave your valuables in the room, shared bathrooms, hot water sometimes, garage space for motorcyles; **E *Hostal Monterrey***, Lima 447A, T 351691, 'gringo hotel', reasonable, some rooms with bath, better than those without, communal bathrooms are reported dirty, hot water 0630-0900 but unreliable, restaurant poor, secure for luggage, motorcycle parking US$0.50, has colectivo service to La Paz, US$12; **E *Hostal Nesther***, Deustua 268, T 351631, also 3-bedded rooms, with bath, hot water, 0730-0900, clean, rec; **E *Los Uros***, Teodoro Valcarcel 135, T 352141, cheaper without bath, hot water 1900-2100, plenty of blankets, clean, breakfast available downstairs, quiet, good value, small charge to leave luggage, laundry service, friendly, often full, changes TCs at a reasonable rate.

**F *Hostal Los Incas***, Los Incas 105, basic, hot showers US$1; **F** pp ***Hostal Q'oñiwasi***, Av La Torre 135, T 353912, opp rail station, clean, warm rooms, friendly, luggage store, breakfast available, safe, rec; **F *Hostal Roma***, Libertad 115, T 351501, basic; **F *Hostal Virreynal***, Arequipa 342, friendly, clean, no hot water.

**G** pp ***Hostal Inti***, Av La Torre, opp station, noisy, basic, hot shower US$1 extra, small.

**Youth Hostel**: **G** pp ***Albergue Juvenil***, Ilave 236, no sign, huge rooms, well-furnished, hot water, "awesome bathroom", good location, quiet, friendly and helpful owners, will wash your clothes for a reasonable fee, full breakfast for US$1.30, a real bargain, highly rec.

### ● Places to eat

***Don Piero***, Lima 360, huge meals, live music, try 'pollo coca-cola', chicken in a sweet and sour sauce, slow service, popular, tax extra; not to be confused with the restaurant next door, also called ***Don Piero***, where you can get decent chicken, salad, fries and a soft drink for US$1.50; ***Café Internacional***, Libertad 161, 2 blocks from Plaza, 'gringo', excellent trout, not cheap and service variable; ***Pizzería del Buho***, Jr Libertad 386, good pizza, cosy atmosphere, open 1800 onwards; ***Al Paso Antojitos***, Lima 373, rec snack bar for cake, pies and coffee; ***Peña Hostería***, Lima 501, good music, rec; ***Pascana***, Lima 339, specializes in *parrilladas*, vegetarian dishes available, folk shows;

## Pot luck

One of the most intriguing items for sale in Andean markets is *Ekeko*, the god of good fortune and plenty and one of the most enduring and endearing of the Aymara gods and folk legends.

He is a cheery, avuncular little chap, with a happy face to make children laugh, a pot belly due to his predilection for food and short legs so he can't run away. His image, usually in plaster of paris, is laden with sacks of grain, sweets, household tools, baskets, utensils, suitcases, confetti and streamers, rice, noodles and other essentials. Dangling from his lower lip is the ubiquitous lit cigarette. Believers say that these little statues only bring luck if they are received as gifts, and not purchased.

***Hilda's House***, Moquegua 189, excellent food, reasonable prices; ***Samaná***, Puno 334, inconsistent service, sometimes has live folk music from 2100, open fire and snacks and drinks; ***Chez Maggy***, Grau 138, delicious pizza and pasta, great atmosphere, friendly staff, evening meal US$2.50, great value; ***Ricardos***, Jr Lambayeque 117, clean, good breakfasts, serves sandwiches, friendly, rec; ***Monterrey***, behind hotel of same name, good fish, good value lunches, otherwise expensive. There is a nameless café on the corner of Libertad and Tacna, which serves good breakfasts and pastries. Also an excellent patisserie at Lima 430, for croissants, fresh bread and cakes. ***Café Delissa***, Libertad 215, open 0600, espresso coffee, good vegetarian food, excellent set lunch US$1.50; ***Rico Pan***, Arequipa 459, café and bakery, great cakes, excellent capuccino, espresso and Irish coffee, good juices and pastries, good breakfasts and other dishes, reasonable prices, great place to relax, open 0600-2300, closed Sun; ***Mi Perú***, on the corner of Arequipa and Jr Deza, popular with locals, cheap, huge portions, friendly; ***Goodmann***, Pardo, vegetarian, popular, and ***Adventista***, Jr Deza 349, good. Above the city is a quinta called ***Kantuta***, Arequipa 1086, good local dishes, open until 1700, rec.

### ● Banks & money changers

**Banco de Crédito**, Lima y Grau, before 1300 for TCs, US$1 commission, cash advance on Visa. For cash go to the *cambios*, the travel agencies or the better hotels. The best rates are with the money changers at the market but check your Peruvian soles carefully. The rates for soles to Bolivianos is poor; it's better to wait till Yunguyo at the border.

### ● Embassies & consulates

**Bolivian Consulate**, Jr Arequipa between Parque Pino y Jr Deza, visa on the spot, US$10, open 0830-1330 Mon to Fri.

### ● Laundry

***Lavandería América***, Jr Moquegua 169, very expensive; ***Lavandería Lava Clin***, Deustua 252, El Sol 431 and Teodoro Valcarcel 132, also very expensive. In general, Puno laundries charge per item and are very expensive places to wash your clothes. It's better to wait until Cusco, where they charge by the kilo.

### ● Post & telecommunications

**Post Office**: Jr Moquegua 267.

**Telephone**: Telefónica at Arequipa y Moquegua.

### ● Shopping

In the covered part of the market mostly fruit and vegetables are sold, but there are also model reed boats, attractive carved stone amulets and Ekekos (see above). The ***Market*** on the railway between Av Los Incas and Lampa is one of the best places in Peru (or Bolivia) for llama and alpaca wool articles, but bargain hard, especially in the afternoon. Many of the jumpers, hats and gloves are still hand-made. You will be hassled on the street, and outside restaurants to buy woollen goods, so take care! There is also a food and clothing market next to the stadium. **NB** We have received reports of robbery in the market.

### ● Tour companies & travel agents

Agencies organize trips to the Uros floating islands and the islands of Taquile and Amantaní (which is usually included in the Taquile trip), as well as to Sillustani, and other places. Make sure that you settle all details before embarking on the tour. Alternatively, you can easily go down to the lake and make your own arrangements with the boatmen.

We have received good reports about the

following: ***Puno Travel Service***, Tacna 254; ***Kinjyo Travel Service***, C Arequipa 401; ***Kontiki Tours***, Melgar 188 for 'mystical tours'; ***Cusi Tours***, Valcarcel 103, T 352591; ***Kolla Tour***, Jr Moquegua 679, T 352961, F 354762, airline tickets, own boat for tours on the lake, friendly; ***Feiser Tours***, Teodoro Valcarcel 155, T 353112, guide Edgar is rec for Sillustani; ***Ecoturismo Aventura***, Jr Lima 458, T 355785, friendly and very helpful; ***Allways Travel***, Jr Puno 318, T 352823, very helpful, speak German, French, English and Italian, ask for Eliana if you have any problems in general; ***Air Travel Services SRL***, Oquendo 250 (Sr Jorge Oliart García), rec for travel arrangements; ***Imperio Tours***, Valcarcel 191, T 367690, good for travel to La Paz. Note that agencies don't sell train tickets, they go and buy them for you at 25% commission.

### ● Tourist offices

**InfoTur**, C Lima y C Deustua, helpful with general information, friendly, **Ministry of Tourism**, Jr Deustua 351, T 352811, helpful with complaints; **Touring Automóvil Club del Perú**, C Arequipa 457.

### ● Useful addresses

**Immigration**: Libertad 403, T 352801, for renewing entry stamps, etc. The process is very slow and you must fill in 2 application forms at a bank, but there's nothing else to pay.

### ● Transport

**Trains** The railway runs from Puno to Juliaca (44 km), where it divides, to Cusco (281 km) and Arequipa (279 km). There are 2 trains daily: to **Cusco** Mon, Wed, Thur, Sat at 1925, arriving about 0600 (try to sit on the right hand side) and to **Arequipa** Mon, Wed, Fri, Sun at 1945, arriving about 0600. In the wet season the services may be cut to 2-3 times a week, or even be cancelled for short periods. Always check.

Fares: Puno-Cusco, 2nd class, US$11; 1st class, US$19; pullman, US$24; Inca class, US$26. Puno-Arequipa, 2nd class, US$9; 1st class, US$11; pullman (*turismo ejecutivo*), US$19; Inca US$23. The ticket office is open from 0630-1030, 1600-1900 Mon-Sat, Sun pm only and tickets can be bought 1 day in advance, or 1 hr before departure if there are any left. Travel agencies are sometimes the only option, but they can be unreliable; do not pay in full before receiving the tickets and always check the date and seat number. Hotels can help with getting tickets as well. See under Arequipa **Trains** for the standards and safety of the three classes. See also under Arequipa and Juliaca on safety. Take the pullman carriage if you do not want to worry about theft (reportedly less of a problem recently), but take 1st class for a real local experience. There is a *menú* available in the pullman carriage (US$6.50 for lunch or dinner); take your own food as a standby.

A good idea in Puno, Juliaca and other Andean towns, when moving about with heavy baggage, is to hire a 3-wheel cycle cart, 'Trici-Taxi', which costs about US$0.20/km.

**Buses** Most companies have offices on Av Sol, eg Cruz del Sur. To **Arequipa**, 297 km, 8-10 hrs (longer in the rainy season), US$7-8. A few buses and trucks go daily, the route does not go through Juliaca. Colectivos charge US$12, 9 hrs, minimum. The road is in poor condition and mudslides cause problems in the rain. All buses seem to go at night; a very cold journey. Continuing to **Lima**, 1,011 km, US$18, all buses go through Arequipa, sometimes with a change of bus. See under Arequipa. To **Juliaca**, 44 km, 1 hr, US$0.50, colectivos run all day. Taxi to Juliaca about US$15. To **Cusco**, 388 km, 12 hrs, US$8, buses (only at night) and trucks daily, but the train is more commonly used. **NB** There is a serious danger of robbery on this route; not advised. To **Moquegua**, 262 km, 10 hrs, US$7, a few buses daily, poor road, bumpy and cold. To **Tacna**, via Ilave, 375 km unpaved, 17 hrs (can be longer in the wet season), US$7. The road is not too bad but it is rough and cold and can be difficult in the rainy season. The views are spectacular.

**Boats on Lake Titicaca** The boat terminal is being rebuilt and boats to the islands currently leave from Av Floral at the NE of town; minibus or *trici-taxi*, US$2.

## The sacred lake

Lake Titicaca has played a dominant role in Andean beliefs for over 2 millenium. This, the highest navigable body of water in the world, is the most sacred lake in the Andes.

Near Titicaca arose the population and ceremonial centre of Tiahuanaco, capital of one of the most important civilizations of South America. Tiahuanaco ceremonial sites were built along its shores, indicating that the lake was considered sacred at least 2,000 years ago.

At the time of the Spanish conquest, one of the most important religious sites of the Inca empire was located on the Island of the Sun, on the Bolivian side of the lake. From its profound, icy depths emerged the Inca creator deity, Viracocha. Legend has it that the sun god had his children, Manco Capac and his sister, Mama Ocllo, spring from the lake's azure waters to found Cusco and the Inca dynasty.

Legends about the lake abound. Among them are several which describe underwater cities, roads and treasures. One such treasure is said to be Inca Huáscar's gold chain weighing 2,000 kilos and kept in the Temple of the Sun, in Cusco, until it was thrown into the lake to prevent it from falling into greedy Spanish hands.

Titicaca was perceived by its ancient cultures to be an inland sea connected to the ocean, mother of all waters. Today, people still believe that the lake is involved in bringing rain and that, closely associated with mountain deities, it distributes the water sent by them. The people who utilize the lake's resources make offerings to her, to ensure sufficient totora reeds for the boats, which are still made, for successful fishing, for safe passage across its waters and for a mild climate.

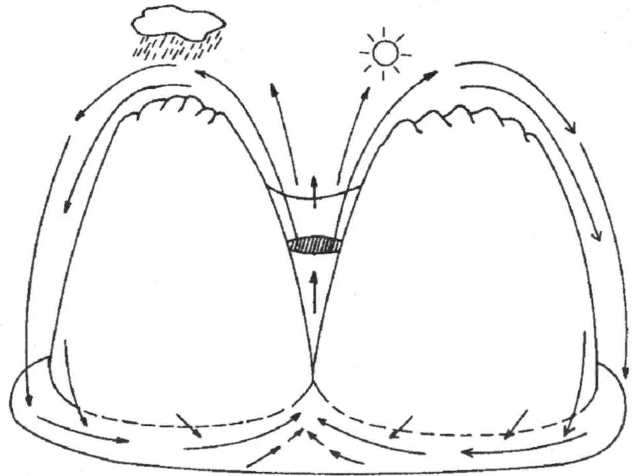

The origin and circulation of the waters of Lake Titicaca as perceived by the Incas

# LAKE TITICACA

## UROS

The Uros 'floating islands' are made of piles of reeds. Though the Uros on the islands have intermarried with the Aymara and no pure Uros exist, the present Puno Bay people still practise some Uro traditions. Aymara influence, however, predominates. The islanders fish, hunt birds and live off the lake plants, most important of which are the reeds they use for their boats, houses and the very foundations of their 5 islands.

Though tourism has eased the flow of islanders to the mainland to escape the grinding poverty, its effects have been criticised. Tourism has not only opened their simple, private lives to the glare of cameras and camcorders, but has also helped to erode much of their proud culture as the Uros people have modified their traditional ways to cater for tourists' tastes.

Many tourists report that though the people are friendly, they are very poor and consequently visitors are subjected to a hard-sell approach for handicrafts as well as constantly being asked for "tips", though this is less persistent out of season. Rather than giving the children money or gifts, you could buy their little reed boats or give fruit. There is no drinking water on the floating islands and you need to be careful where you walk, as the surface can be very unsteady underfoot. Those furthest from Puno are most worth seeing but travellers should note that the more sensitive among them may find this "peep show" a rather uncomfortable and unsettling experience.

• **Transport** Motorboats charging upwards of US$3.50 pp take tourists to the islands; prices should not be over US$5-6 (which is what agencies charge in season). Pay half before you leave and half on your return. Boats go about every 30 mins from about 0630 till 1000, or whenever there are 10 or more people to fill the boat, and take 3-5 hrs. Local boats may also be hired. The earlier you go the better, to beat the crowds of tourists. Out of season there are no regular boats, so either get a group together and pay US$10 for the boat, rent a boat at US$1-2 pp, or pay an agency US$15-20.

## TAQUILE

A much less depressing and more interesting island to visit is **Taquile**, some 45 km from Puno, on which there are numerous pre-Inca and Inca ruins, and Inca terracing. The island is quiet and hospitable, except at the height of the season, though it has variously been described as "touristy" and spoiled.

The island is narrow, only about 1 km wide, but 6-7 km long. On the N side of the island is the warmest part of Lake Titicaca. Ask for the (unmarked) museum of traditional costumes and also where you can see and photograph local weaving. There is a cooperative shop on the plaza that sells exceptional woollen goods which are not cheap but of very fine quality. They are cheaper in the market at Puno. Travellers report that you need to spend a night on Taquile to really appreciate its stark beauty and, therefore, it may be better to travel independently and go at your own pace.

Numerous festivals take place on the island: at Easter; from the 2 to 7 June; the *Fiesta de Santiago* over 2 weeks in mid-July; 1 and 2 Aug are the principal festival days with many dances in between.

**The influx of tourists** unfortunately prompts persistent requests for sweets and money which irritates many travellers. Above all, stay good-humoured. You will have to listen to at least one hastily-formed *peña* band and pay for the privilege, and don't be surprised if some familiar faces show up later under the guise of a different band. Gifts of fruit, torches (there is no electricity), moisturizer or sun block (the children suffer sore cheeks), pens, pencils or notebooks are appreciated. Buy their

## A lasting tradition

One of the most enduring textile traditions in Peru is found among the Aymara people of Taquile. Each family possesses at least 4 different types of costume: for work; leisure; weddings and festivals.

For weddings, which all take place on 3 May, when the planet Venus – *Hatun Chaska* – is visible, the bridegroom wears a red poncho provided by the best man. As a single man he wore a half red, half white cap, but to signify his married status he wears a long red hat and a wide red wedding belt, or *chumpi*. His bag for coca leaves, *ch'uspa*, is also filled.

The bride wears a wide red hat (*montera*) and her hands are covered with a ritual cloth (*katana-oncoma*). A *quincha*, a small white cloth symbolizing purity, is hidden in her skirt. With her red wedding blouse, or *gonna*, she wears a gathered skirt or *pollera*, made from 20 different layers of brightly-coloured cloth. She also wears a belt (*faja*) and black cloak known as a *chukoo*.

The wool used for weaving is usually spun by the women, but on Taquile men spin wool, as well as knitting their conical hats (*chullos*). In fact, only the men on Taquile know how to knit. By the age of 10, a boy can knit his own *Chullo Santa María*, which is white-tipped to show single status. When he marries, or moves in with a woman, he adopts the red-tipped *chullo*, which is exclusive to the island. Today, much of the wool for knitting is bought ready-spun from factories in Arequipa.

Traditionally, every piece of textile of a particular community had identical symbols and colours, which were a source of identity. Each piece also carried specific symbols and told a story. In the Andean world the planet Venus played an important part in mythology and agriculture. The Sun also predominated in textile decoration and both were universal to *ayllus*, the self-sufficient and self-governing Inca communities.

On Taquile, they use *Inti* and *Chaska* (Venus) symbols, as well as motifs such as fish and birds, unique to the islands. Another symbol, which is shown on the *chumpis*, is the *suyos*, a circle divided into 6 segments, signifying the 6 *ayllus* which traditionally own the island between them and hold a piece of land in common.

Extracted from *Arts and Crafts of South America*, by Lucy Davies & Mo Fini, Tumi.

handicrafts instead of handing out sweets indiscriminately, eg friendship bracelets. The same applies to Amantaní (see below).

• **Accommodation** Plentiful accommodation can be found in private houses but it is best to take warm clothes and a sleeping bag. Apparently the islanders refused to allow any hotels to be built on the island to help preserve their way of life. No previous arrangements can be made; on arrival you walk up a steep path for 30 mins (remember you are at 3,800m), are greeted by the locals, pay a US$0.10 fee, sign the guest book and, if wishing to stay, are 'assigned' a family to stay with G pp, or F pp including all meals.

• **Places to eat** There are several small restaurants on the island; eg *El Inca* on the main plaza. Fish is plentiful and the island has a trout farm, but meat is rarely available and drinks often run out. Meals are a little more expensive than on the mainland. You are advised to take with you some food, particularly fruit, bread and vegetables, water, plenty of small-value notes, candles and a torch. Take precautions against sunburn.

• **Transport** Boats leave Puno daily at 0800-0900; 4 hrs, return 1400/1430, arriving 1830, US$4.50 one way. This doesn't leave enough time to appreciate the island fully in 1 day.

## Mother earth

Ecotourism is the current trendy buzzword on the lips of all self-respecting travellers and tour operators. But though ecology may be a relatively new concept in the travel business, to the people of the bleak southern Peruvian altiplano, this idea is absolutely fundamental to their very culture and almost as old as the land itself.

Pachamama, or Mother Earth, occupies a very privileged place in Aymara culture because she is the generative source of life. The Aymara believe that Man was created from the land, and thus he is fraternally tied to all the living beings that share the earth. According to them, the earth is our mother, and it is on the basis of this understanding that all of human society is organized, always maintaining the cosmic norms and laws.

Women's and men's relationship with nature is what the Aymara call ecology, harmony and equilibrium.

The Aymara furthermore believe that private land ownership is a social sin because the land is for everyone. It is meant to be shared and not only used for the benefit of a few.

Vicenta Mamani Bernabé of the Andean Regional Superior Institute of Theological Studies states: "Land is life because it produces all that we need to live. Water emanates from the land as if from the veins of a human body, there is also the natural wealth of minerals, and pasture grows from it to feed the animals. Therefore, for the Aymaras, the Pachamama is sacred and since we are her children, we are also sacred. No one can replace the earth, she is not meant to be exploited, or to be converted into merchandise. Our duty is to respect and care for the earth. This is what white people today are just beginning to realize, and it is called ecology. Respect for the Pachamama is respect for ourselves as she is life. Today, she is threatened with death and must be liberated for the sake of her children's liberation."

Wise words Indeed. It is a great pity that the Spanish conquistadors did not leave with these thoughts instead of vast quantities of precious metals.

Organized tours can be arranged for about US$16 pp, but only give you about 2 hrs on the island. Boats sometimes call at Uros on the outward or return journey. Make sure you and the boatman know exactly what you are paying for.

## AMANTANI

Another island well worth visiting, is **Amantaní**. It is very beautiful and peaceful, and many say is less spoiled, more genuine and friendlier than Taquile. There are six villages and ruins on both of the island's peaks, Pacha Tata and Pacha Mama, from which there are excellent views. There are also temples and on the shore there is a throne carved out of stone.

On both hills, a fiesta is celebrated on 15 Jan (or thereabouts). The festivities in Jan have been reported as spectacular, very colourful, musical and hard-drinking. There is also a festival the first Sun in Mar with brass bands and colourful dancers. Another fiesta is the Aniversario del Consejo (of the local council).

The residents make beautiful textiles and sell them quite cheaply at the Artesanía Cooperativa. The people are Quechua speakers, but understand Spanish.

• **Accommodation & places to eat** There are no hotels but you are assigned to stay with local families on a rota basis; or ask your boat owner where you can stay. Accommodation, inc 3 meals, is in our F range. There is one restaurant, *Samariy*.

● **Transport** Boats from the harbour in Puno at 0800 daily, return 1430, US$9 round trip. The journey takes 4-5 hrs, take water. A 1 day trip is not possible as the boats do not always return on the same day. Several tour operators in Puno offer 2-3 day excursions to Amantaní, Taquile and a visit to the floating islands, US$16-30 pp, inc meals, depending on the season and size of group; 1 night on Amantaní and 3-4 hrs on Taquile. It may be better to visit the islands independently and go at your own pace. If you wish to visit both Taquile and Amantaní, it is better to go to Amantaní first; from there a boat goes to Taquile around 0800, US$2.50 pp. There is no regular service; the boat leaves if there are enough passengers.

## FRONTIER WITH BOLIVIA

There are four different routes across the border. The first three described are the least travelled.

### ● Along the east side of Lake Titicaca

This is the most remote route, via **Huancané**, **Moho** and **Puerto Acosta** (Bolivia). There is accommodation in Moho, G; one bus leaves on weekdays to Juliaca, 7 hrs, but it is often cancelled. This route is recommended only on weekends when there is more traffic. After Puerto Acosta, the road is very bad. Make sure you get an exit stamp in Puno.

### ● Puno-Desaguadero

This is the most direct route road (150 km paved), passing through **Chucuíto, Ilave, Juli** and **Pomata. Desaguadero** is a miserable place, with dubious accommodation at **F** *Alojamiento Internacional*. Colectivos and buses run Puno-Desaguadero, 2 hrs, US$1.50 by bus. Get your exit stamp on the Peruvian side, cross the border and get an entrance stamp on the Bolivian side. Border offices are open 0800-1200 and 1400-1700. There are a few buses to La Paz (105 km from Desaguadero), 4 hrs, US$2-3. It is easy to change money on the Peruvian side. The road to La Paz is in poor condition. This particular border crossing allows you to stop at Tiahuanaco en route.

### ● To La Paz by hydrofoil or catamaran

There are luxury services from Puno/Juli to La Paz by *Crillon Tours*' hydrofoil, with connections to tours, from La Paz, to Cusco and Machu Picchu. All Puno travel agents have details, or Av Camacho 1223, PO Box 4785, La Paz, T 374566/7, F 391039 (in USA: 1450 South Bayshore Drive, Suite 815, Miami, FL 33131, T 305-358-5353, F 372-0054). The itinerary is: Puno-Copacabana by bus; Copacabana-Isla del Sol-Huatajata (Bolivia) by hydrofoil; Huatajata-La Paz by bus; 13 hrs US$173 pp. At Huatajata *Crillon* has the **A1** *Inca Utama Hotel and Spa*, 5-star accommodation, health facilities based on natural remedies, together with the Andean Roots cultural complex (4 different museums representing 7 cultures) and an observatory. *Crillon* also has *La Posada del Inca*, a hotel in a restored colonial hacienda on the Isla del Sol. Visits to these establishments can be incorporated into *Crillon's* tours.

Similar services, by catamaran, are run by *Transturin*, whose dock is at Chúa, Bolivia; bookings through Transturin: offices in Puno at Libertad 176, ask for Esther de Quiñones, T 352771; Cusco, Portal de Panes 109, of 1, Plaza de Armas, T 222332; La Paz, Av Mcal Santa Cruz 1295, 3rd Floor, T 373881/342164.

## PUNO-LA PAZ VIA YUNGUYO AND COPACABANA

### ● Peruvian immigration

Is located 5 mins' drive from **Yunguyo** (shared taxi from plaza US$0.25 pp); open 0700-2100 (Bolivian immigration is open 24 hrs a day, knock on the door). When leaving you must get an exit stamp before crossing the border and a tourist visa on the other side. 90 days is normally given when entering Peru (30 days for Bolivia). Be aware of corruption at customs and look out for official or unofficial people trying to charge you a departure fee (say that you know it is illegal and ask why only gringos are approached to pay the 'embarkation tax').

**NB** Peruvian time is 1 hr behind Bolivian time.

### ● Bolivian Consulate

Near the main plaza in Yunguyo, open Mon-Fri 0830-1500, for those who need a visa; some nationalities have to pay, eg US$12 for French, US$20 for Canadians. There is no consulate in Puno, you must get a visa here.

### ● Accommodation

Is available in **Yunguyo**: **E** *Hostal Isabel*, San Francisco 110, at Plaza de Armas, T 350233 ext 19, shared bath, hot water, basic, clean, pleasant; **G** *Hostal Amazonas*, basic, restaurant; **G** *Hostal Yunguyo*, clean, but often no water or electricity.

● **Exchange**
Good rates are available in the main plaza, Yunguyo, better than at the border, and good for changing bolivianos, cash only. TCs can be exchanged in the cambio here, though rates are poor.

● **Transport**
The road is paved from Puno to Yunguyo and the scenery is interesting. The views are also good on the Bolivian side. Several agencies in Puno sell bus tickets for the direct route from Puno to La Paz, taking 6-8 hrs, US$7.50; check in advance that your ticket includes the Tiquina ferry crossing and other charges. They leave Puno at 0800 and stop at the borders and for lunch in Copacabana, arriving in La Paz at 1700. You only need to change money into Bolivianos for lunch on this route. Bus fare Puno-Copacabana, US$3.50 with Panamericana. There are local buses and colectivos all day between Puno and Yunguyo, 2-3 hrs, US$1.50; they leave from Mercado Laytoka in Puno. From Yunguyo to the border (Kasani), kombis charge US$0.20. From the border it is a 20-min drive to Copacabana; colectivos and minibuses leave from just outside Bolivian immigration, US$0.50. Taxi from Yunguyo to Copacabana costs about US$1.50 pp.

● **Into Bolivia**
The Bolivian border town of **Copacabana** is famous for its miracle-working Dark Virgin of the Lake, La Virgen de Candelaria, housed in a fine basilica. From the town, excursions can be made to Isla del Sol and Isla de la Luna in Lake Titicaca. There is a variety of hotels, restaurants and other services. All road transport from Copacabana to La Paz has to take the ferry across the lovely Straits of Tiquina.

## PUNO TO CUSCO

### By rail
On the way from Puno to Cusco there is much to see from the train, which runs at an average altitude of 3,500m. At the stations on the way, people sell food; roast lamb at Ayaviri and stuffed peppers at Sicuani; local specialities such as pottery bulls at Pucara, where rooms are available at the station; woollen caps, wool and rugs at Sicuani; knitted alpaca ponchos and pullovers and miniature llamas at Santa Rosa, where rooms are also available.

There are three hotels in **Ayaviri**, including **G** *Hostal Ayaviri*, Grau 180, basic, unfriendly.

The railway crosses the altiplano, climbing to **La Raya**, the highest pass on the line; 210 km from Puno, at 4,321m. Up on the heights breathing may be a little difficult, but the descent along the Río Vilcanota is rapid. To the right of **Aguas Calientes**, the next station, 4 km from La Raya, are steaming pools of hot water in the middle of the green grass; a startling sight. The temperature of the springs is 40°C, and they show beautiful deposits of red ferro-oxide. The springs are not developed, but bathing is possible to the left, where the hot spring water joins the cold creek. At **Maranganí**, the river is wider and the fields greener, with groves of eucalyptus trees.

### By road
The road Puno-Cusco is in very poor condition and may be impassable in the rainy season as there are many rivers to cross. There are reports that it is to be paved. Most people take the train but, as said above, in the wet season, trains may be cancelled.

The paved road ends at Juliaca, from where there is a very rough gravel track over La Raya pass up to **Tinta**, 69 km S of **Urcos**, and paved from Tinta all the way to Cusco.

## SICUANI

38 km beyond La Raya pass **Sicuani** (*Alt* 3,960m) is an important agricultural centre and an excellent place for items of llama and alpaca wool and skins. They are sold on the railway station and at the excellent Sun morning market. Around Plaza Libertad there are several hat shops selling local hats. There are mineral baths at Uyurmiri. Sicuani lies 250 km from Puno and 137 km from Cusco (bus, US$1.25). (For more information about places between Sicuani and Cusco, see page 324.)

● **Accommodation D** *Centro Vacacional,*

best in town, some way from centre, rec; **F** *Manzanaral*, Av 28 de Julio, cold shower, basic, friendly, noisy, parking in *taller*, about 2 blocks away on a parallel street; **G** *Obada*, communal shower, basic; **G** *Quispe*, basic, no shower, friendly.

• **Places to eat** *Viracocha* on main plaza, OK.

ROUTES Branch roads both S and N of Sicuani lead to a road past the Tintaya mines which forms an alternative route Cusco-Arequipa. The surface is OK to the mines, and bad thereafter, but it is a spectacular journey. Only 1 bus a day (Chasqui) passes and it is usually full. From Sicuani, the road passes the pretty lake, Laguna Langui Layo, then climbs to a radio-transmission antenna. At El Descanso is a checkpoint. A few kilometres from the road is **Yauri**, isolated on a plateau by a canyon; accommodation at **G** *Hostal El Tigre*, nice rooms, water shortages. A road SW from Yauri, requiring high clearance vehicles, leads on to Sibayo, Chivay and Arequipa. Alternatively, to the SE, the road skirts **Laguna Condorama**, one of the highest lakes in South America (4,700m), past more mining operations, the Majes irrigation scheme and on to the Arequipa-Juliaca road. Sicuani to Arequipa is about 400 km. If driving this route, check directions with the police.

The Vilcanota plunges into a gorge, but the train winds above it and round the side of the mountain. At **Huambutío** the railway turns left to follow the Río Huatanay on the final stretch to Cusco. The Vilcanota here widens into the great Urubamba canyon, flanked on both sides by high cliffs, on its way to join the Ucayali, a tributary of the Amazon.

# Cusco and the Sacred Valley



ACCORDING to the central Inca creation myth, the sun god sent his son, Manco Capac and the Moon her daughter, Mama Ocllo, to spread culture and enlightenment throughout the dark, barbaric lands. They emerged from the waters of Lake Titicaca and began their journey in search of the place where they would found their kingdom. When they reached the site of present-day Cusco, Manco plunged his golden staff into the ground in order to test its suitability, and it duly sank deep into the fertile soil. This was the sign they were looking for to choose where to found the capital of their empire. They named the spot Cusco – meaning "navel of the earth". Thus was the significance of Cusco and the Sacred Urubamba Valley established for many hundreds of years to come. Today, this is the prime destination for the vast majority of Peru's visitors.

## CUSCO

The ancient Inca capital is said to have been founded around 1100 AD, and since then has developed into a major, commercial centre of 275,000 inhabitants, most of whom are Quechua. The city council has designated the Quechua, Qosqo, as the official spelling.

Just as Cusco's architectural beauty cannot be overstated, neither can its historical importance. As Peter Frost states in his *Exporing Cusco*: "Cusco was more than just a capital city to the Incas and the millions of subjects in their realm. It was a Holy City, a place of pilgrimage with as much importance to the Quechuas as Mecca has to the Moslems. Every ranking citizen of the empire tried to visit Cusco once in his lifetime; to have done so increased his stature wherever he might travel."

Cusco's roots are still buried deep in its proud past. Today, the city is a fascinating mix of Inca and colonial Spanish architecture: colonial churches, monasteries and convents and extensive preco lumbian ruins are interspersed with countless hotels, bars and restaurants that have sprung up to cater for the hundreds of thousands of tourists who flock here to savour its unique atmosphere. Almost every central street has remains of Inca walls, arches and doorways. Many streets are lined with perfect Inca stonework, now serving as the foundations for more modern dwellings. This stonework is tapered upwards (battered); every wall has a perfect line of inclination towards the centre, from bottom to top. The stones have each edge and corner rounded. The curved stonework of the Temple of the Sun, for example, is probably unequalled in the world.

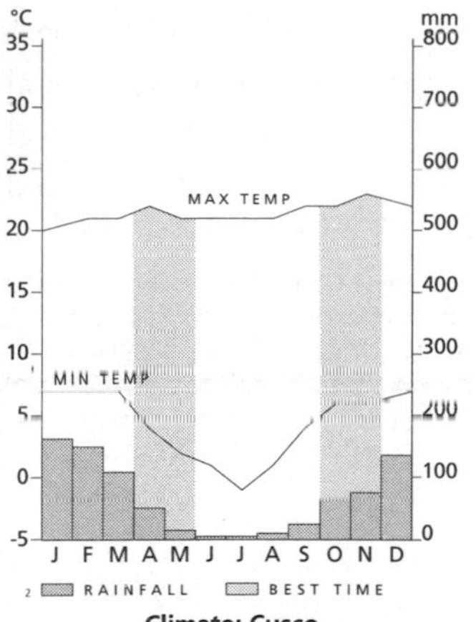


Climate: Cusco

Despite its growth, Cusco is still laid out much as it was in Inca times. The Incas conceived their capital in the shape of a puma and this can be seen from above, with the river Tullumayo forming the spine, Sacsayhuamán the head and the main city centre the body. The best place for an overall view of the Cusco valley is from the puma's head; the top of the hill of Sacsayhuamán.

**Information and advice** (*Phone code* 084). Cusco stands at 3,310m, a little lower than Puno, so you should respect the altitude: 2 or 3 hrs' rest after arriving makes a great difference; avoid meat and smoking, eat lots of carbohydrates and drink plenty of clear, non-alcoholic liquid; remember to walk slowly. To see Cusco and the surrounding area properly – including Pisac, Ollantaytambo, Chinchero and Machu Picchu – you need 5 days to a week, allowing for slowing down because of altitude. Those on a tight itinerary should note that this a difficult city to leave and many a carefully-planned travelling schedule has been revised in the face of its overwhelming attraction. Anyone interested in seeing more than the inside of a pizzería is advised to purchase Peter Frost's excellent guide, *Exploring Cusco*, which is available throughout the city.

### PLACES OF INTEREST

**Visitors' Tickets** It is possible to purchase individual entrance tickets to the churches and ruins in and around Cusco: each site costs up to US$2. The best value,

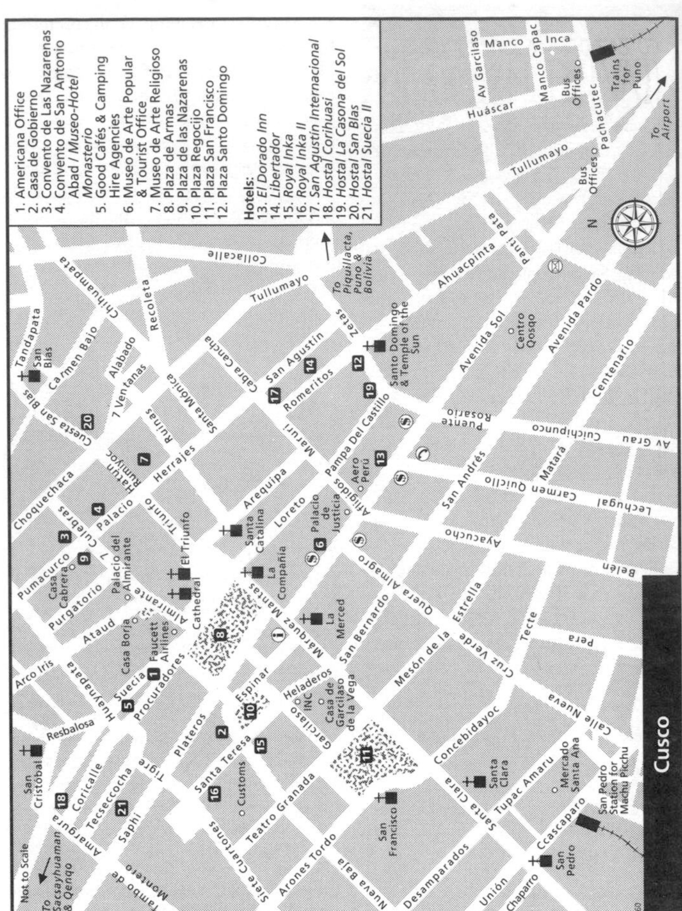


though, is to buy a combined ticket (Boleto Turístico Unico, or "BTU") from: a) the OFEC office, Av Sol 103, on the ground floor of Galerías Turísticas, just before the Banco de Crédito; or b) any of the sites included on the ticket, which are listed below, though the best of these is Santo Domingo-Qoricancha, where many of the tours begin. The ticket costs US$10 and is valid for 5 or 10 days. There is a 50% discount with a green ISIC card, which is only available at the OFEC office on Av Sol.

The combined ticket allows entry to: the Cathedral, San Blas, Santa Catalina, Santo Domingo-Qoricancha, Museo de Arte Religioso, Museo de Historia Regional, the Piquillacta ruins, Pisac, Chincheros, Ollantaytambo, Sacsayhuamán, Qenqo, Puku Pukara and Tambo Machay (the last four are US$5 if separate). Note that all sites are very crowded

Drawing of a 'Quipo Camayoc' (quipu reader) by the Inca Chronicler Guaman Poma de Ayala

on Sun. No photographs are allowed in any museums. Many churches are closed to visitors on Sun, and the 'official' opening times are unreliable.

Machu Picchu, the Museo Arqueológico and the church of La Merced are not included on the ticket. Tickets for Machu Picchu and the Inca Trail can be bought at the INC office, on Garcilaso y Heladeros.

## Plaza de Armas

The heart of the city, as in Inca days, is the Plaza de Armas. It was originally, however, more than twice its present size. The part that remains today was once called the *Aucaypata*, or Square of War. This was the great civic square of the Incas, flanked by their palaces, and was a place of solemn parades and great assemblies. Each territory conquered by the Incas had some of its soil taken to Cusco to be mingled symbolically with the soil of the Aucaypata, as a token of its incorporation into the empire.

As well as the many great ceremonies, the Plaza has also seen its share of executions, among them Túpac Amaru, the last Inca, the rebel conquistador Diego de Almagro the Younger, and Túpac Amaru II, the 18th century indigenous leader. (Peter Frost, *Exploring Cusco*).

Around the present-day Plaza are colonial arcades and four churches. To the NE is the early 17th century baroque **Cathedral,** built on the site of the Palace of Viracocha. The high altar is solid silver and the original altar *retablo* behind it is a masterpiece of native wood carving. In the sacristy are paintings of all the bishops of Cusco and a painting of Christ attributed to Van Dyck. The choir stalls, by a 17th-century Spanish priest, are a magnificent example of colonial baroque art. The elaborate pulpit and the sacristy are also notable. Much venerated is the crucifix of El Señor de los Temblores, the object of many pilgrimages and viewed all over Peru as a guardian against earthquakes.

The Cathedral is open until 1000 for genuine worshippers – Quechua mass is held 0500-0600. Those of a more secular inclination can visit Mon-Sat 1400-1730. The doors from the Cathedral open into the church of **Jesús María** (1733), which stands to its left as you face it.

The tourist entrance to the Cathedral is through **El Triunfo** (1536), on its right. Built on the site of *Suntur Huasi* (the Roundhouse), El Triunfo was the first Christian church in Cusco. It has a fine granite altar and a statue of the Virgin of the Descent, reputed to have helped the Spaniards repel Manco Inca when he besieged the city in 1536. It also has a painting of Cusco during the 1650 earthquake – the earliest surviving painting of the city – in a side chapel. In the far right hand end of the church is an interesting local painting of the Last Supper. But this is the Last Supper with a difference, for Jesus is about to tuck into a plate of *cuy*, washed down with a glass of *chicha*, instead of the standard Cusco fare of a slice of pizza and bottle of Cusqueña.

On the SE side of the plaza is the beautiful **La Compañía de Jesús**, built on the site of the Palace of the Serpents (*Amarucancha*) in the late 17th century. Its twin-towered exterior is extremely graceful, and the interior rich in fine murals, paintings and carved altars. The cloister is also noteworthy, though it has been closed since 1990 for restoration.

Much **Inca stonework** can be seen in the streets and most particularly in the Callejón Loreto, running SE past La Compañía de Jesús from the main plaza. The walls of the *Acllahuasi* (House of the Chosen Women) are on one side, and of the *Amarucancha* on the other. There are also Inca remains in Calle San Agustín, to the E of the plaza. The famous stone of 12 angles is in Calle Hatun Rumiyoc halfway along its 2nd block, on the right-hand side going away from the Plaza.

## Churches

**La Merced**, on Calle Márquez, was first built 1534, and rebuilt in the late 17th century. Attached is a very fine monastery with an exquisite cloister. Inside the church are buried Gonzalo Pizarro, half-brother of Francisco, and the two Almagros, father and son. Their tombs were discovered in 1946. The church is most famous for its jewelled monstrance, on view in the monastery's museum during visiting hours. The superb choir stalls, reached from the upper floor of the cloister, can be seen by men only, but you must persuade a Mercedarian friar to let you see them.

The church and monastery are open 0830-1200, 1430-1730; admission US$0.50, students US$0.35. The church was closed for restoration, late 1995.

**San Francisco**, on Plaza San Francisco, 3 blocks SW of the Plaza de Armas, is an austere church reflecting many indigenous influences. Its monastery is being rebuilt and was still closed in 1996. The church is open 0600-0800, 1800-2000.

The magnificent **Santa Catalina** church, convent and museum are on Arequipa, opposite C Santa Catalina; open Mon-Thur and Sat 0800-1800, Fri 0800-1900. There are guided tours by English-speaking students; tip expected.

Delicious marzipan is sold next to the museum by the nuns through a revolving wooden door, US$1 for 200 grams.

**San Pedro**, in front of the Santa Ana market, was built in 1688. Its two towers were made from stones brought from an Inca ruin. It is open Mon-Sat 1000-1200, 1400-1700.

The nuns' church of **Santa Clara** is on Santa Clara, through an arch from Plaza San Francisco. It is unique in South America for its decoration, which covers the whole of the interior, but is virtually impossible to visit.

The smaller and less well-known church of **San Blas**, on Carmen Bajo, has a beautiful carved *mestizo* cedar pulpit, which is well worth seeing; open Mon-Sat 1400-1730.

Above Cusco, on the road up to Sacsayhuamán, is **San Cristóbal**, built to his patron saint by Cristóbal Paullu Inca. North of it, you can see the 11 doorway-sized niches of the great Inca wall of the Palacio de Colcampata.

**Belén de los Reyes**, in the southern outskirts of the city, was built by an *indígena* in the 17th century. It has a striking main altar, with silver embellishments at the centre and goldwashed *retablos* at the sides. The church is open 1000-1200, 1500-1700 except Thur and Sun.

**Santo Domingo**, SE of the main Plaza, was built in the 17th century on the walls of the Qoricancha Temple of the Sun and from its stones. Current excavation is revealing more of the five chambers of the Temple of the Sun, which shows the best Inca stonework to be seen in Cusco. The Temple of the Sun was awarded to Juan Pizarro, the younger brother of Francisco, who willed it to the Dominicans after he had been fatally wounded in the Sacsayhuamán siege.

The baroque cloister has been gutted to reveal four of the original chambers of the great Inca temple – two on the W have been partly reconstructed in a good imitation of Inca masonry. The finest stonework is in the celebrated curved wall beneath the W end of Santo Domingo. This was rebuilt after the 1950 earthquake, at which time a niche that once contained a shrine was found at the inner top of the wall. Below the curved wall was a garden of gold and silver replicas of animals, maize and other plants. Excavations have revealed Inca baths below here, and more Inca retaining walls. The other superb stretch of late Inca stonework is in C Ahuacpinta outside the temple, to the E or left as you enter (John Hemming).

A visit to Santo Domingo is recommended: open 0900-1700; entry US$0.85; English-speaking guides, tip expected.

## Colonial buildings

The **Palacio del Almirante**, just N of the Plaza de Armas on Ataud, is impressive. It houses the Museo de Arqueología (see below). Note the pillar on the balcony over the door, showing a bearded man and a naked woman.

Nearby, in a small square on Cuesta del Almirante, is the colonial house of **San Borja**, where Bolívar stayed after the Battle of Ayacucho. **The Casona del Marqués de Valleumbroso,** on San Bernardo y Márquez, 3 blocks SW of the Plaza de Armas, was gutted by fire in 1973 and is being restored.

The **Palacio Arzobispal** stands on Hatun Rumiyoc y Herrajes, 2 blocks NE of Plaza de Armas. It was built on the site of the palace occupied in 1400 by the Inca Roca and was formerly the home of the Marqueses de Buena Vista. It contains the Museo de Arte Religioso (see below).

Above San Cristóbal church, to the left, is a private colonial mansion, once the home of the infamous explorer and murderer, Lope de Aguirre. Also worth a visit is the palace called **Casa de los Cuatro Bustos** at San Agustín 400, which is now the *Libertador-Marriott Hotel*. The **Convento de las Nazarenas**, on Plaza de las Nazarenas, now houses the offices of Copesco. You can see the Inca-colonial doorway with a mermaid motif, but ask permission to view the lovely 18th century frescos inside. Also on Plaza Nazarenas is **Casa Cabrera**, which is now a gallery and used by Banco Continental.

## Other sites

On the way to the airport on Av del Sol, 20 mins' walk from the Plaza de Armas, there is a statue of the Inca Pachacútec placed on top of a lookout tower, from which there are excellent views of Cusco. Open 1000-2000; entrance free; small galleries and restaurant. The tourist police have an office here.

The **Astronomical Observatory** is at Km 3 on the road W to Cachimayo and affords fine views of Cusco and the Sacred Valley. It has a pleasant restaurant where you can enjoy the views while you are dining. Observations are 1830-2300.

## MUSEUMS

**Museo Arqueológico** is housed in the Palacio del Almirante (see above). It contains a first-rate precolumbian collection, Spanish paintings of imitation Inca royalty dating from the 18th century, as well as an excellent collection of textiles. Visitors should ask to see the forty miniature pre-Inca turquoise figures found at Piquillacta and the golden treasures, all kept under lock and key but on display.

Open Mon-Fri 0800-1730, Sat/Sun 0800-1400, but check in advance as the museum is frequently closed, US$1 entry; the staff will give a guided tour but please give a tip.

**Museo de Arte Religioso**, in the Palacio Arzobispal (see above), has a fine collection of colonial paintings and furniture. The collection includes the paintings by

Motifs commonly found on Inca pottery, where geometric and symmetrical designs predominate

the Indigenous master, Diego Quispe Tito, of a 17th century Corpus Christi procession that used to hang in the church of Santa Ana, and you should insist on seeing them. The museum is open Mon-Sat, 0830-1200, 1500-1730.

**Museo de Historia Regional**, in the Casa Garcilaso, Jr Garcilaso y Heladeros, tries to show the evolution of the Cuzqueño school of painting. It also contains Inca agricultural implements, colonial furniture and paintings, a small photographic exhibition and mementos of more recent times. It is open 0800-1800.

**Museo de Arte Contemporáneo** is in the Casa de Gobierno, on Plaza Recogijo.

## EXCURSIONS

### Sacsayhuamán

There are some magnificent Inca walls in the ruined ceremonial centre of Sacsayhuamán, on a hill in the northern outskirts. The Incaic stones are hugely impressive. The massive rocks weighing up to 130 tons are fitted together with absolute perfection. Three walls run parallel for over 360m and there are 21 bastions.

Sacsayhuamán was thought for centuries to be a fortress, but the layout and architecture suggest a great sanctuary and temple to the Sun, which rises exactly opposite the place previously believed to be the Inca's throne – which was probably an altar, carved out of the solid rock. Broad steps lead to the altar from either side. Zig-zags in the boulders round the 'throne' are apparently '*chicha* grooves', channels down which maize beer flowed during festivals. Up the hill is an ancient quarry, the Rodadero, which is now used by children as a rock slide. Near it are many seats cut perfectly into the smooth rock.

The hieratic, rather than the military, hypothesis was supported by the discovery in 1982 of the graves of priests, who would have been unlikely to be buried in a fortress. The precise functions of the site, however, will probably continue to be a matter of dispute as very few clues remain, due to its steady destruction.

The site survived the first years of the conquest. Pizarro's troops had entered Cusco unopposed in 1533 and lived safely at Sacsayhuamán, until the rebellion of Manco Inca, in 1536, caught them off guard. The bitter struggle which ensued became the decisive military action of the conquest, for Manco's failure to hold Sacsayhuamán cost him the war, and the empire. The destruction of the hilltop site began after the defeat of Manco's rebellion. The outer walls still stand, but the complex of towers and buildings was razed to the ground. From then, until the 1930s, Sacsayhuamán served as a kind of unofficial quarry of pre-cut stone for the inhabitants of Cusco. (Peter Frost).

The site is about a 30-min walk from the town centre; walk up Pumacurco from Plaza de las Nazarenas.

It is open daily 0700-1730; free student guides, but you should give them a tip. The gates open daily from 0700-1730, but you can get in earlier if you wish and definitely try to get there before midday when the tour groups arrive.

## Other sites near Cusco

Along the road from Sacsayhuamán to Pisac, past a radio station, is the temple and amphitheatre of **Qenqo**. These are not exactly ruins, but rather one of the finest examples of Inca stone carving *in situ*, especially inside the large hollowed-out stone that houses an altar. The rock is criss-crossed by zig-zag channels that give the place its name and which served to course *chicha*, or perhaps sacrificial blood, for purposes of divination.

On the same road is **Cusillyuioc** (K'usilluyuq), a series of caves and Inca tunnels in a hillside. It's best to take a torch/flashlight to find your way around.

The Inca fortress of **Puka Pukara** (Red Fort), was actually more likely to have been a *tambo*, a kind of post-house where travellers were lodged and goods and animals housed temporarily. The site is worth seeing for the views alone.

A few hundred metres up the road is the spring shrine of **Tambo Machay**, which is in excellent condition. Water still flows by a hidden channel out of the masonry wall, straight into a little rock pool traditionally known as the Inca's bath. It seems much more likely that the site was a centre of a water cult.

Taking a guide to the sites mentioned above is a good idea and you should visit in the morning for the best photographs. Carry your multi-site ticket, there are roving ticket inspectors. You can visit the sites on foot. It's a pleasant walk through the countryside requiring ½ a day or more, though remember to take water and sun protection, and watch out for dogs. An alternative is to take the Pisac bus up to Tambo Machay (US$0.35) and walk back. Another excellent way to see the ruins is on horseback, arranged at travel agencies (US$16 pp for 5 hrs). An organized tour (with guide) will go to all the sites for US$6 pp, not including entrance fees. A taxi will charge US$15-20 for 3-4 people.

**NB** It is safest to visit the ruins in a group, especially if you wish to see them under a full moon. Take as few belongings as possible, and hide your camera in a bag.

## LOCAL FESTIVALS

**6 Jan**: festival of the Magi in Ollantaytambo, with dancing and parades. **14 Jan**: festival and market in Pampamarca. **20 Jan**: procession of saints in the San Sebastián district of Cusco.

**Carnival** in Cusco is a messy affair with flour, water, cacti, bad fruit and animal manure thrown about in the streets. (The length of the Sacred Valley, Carnival is lively.) **Easter Monday** sees the procession of **El Señor de los Temblores** (Lord of the Earthquakes), starting at 1600 outside the Cathedral. A large crucifix is paraded through the streets, returning to the Plaza de Armas around 2000 to bless the tens of thousands of people who have assembled there. **2-3 May**: **Vigil of the Cross**, which takes place at all mountaintops with crosses on them, is a boisterous affair.

**June**: On **Corpus Christi** day, the Thur after Trinity Sunday, statues and silver are paraded through the streets. This is a colourful event. The Plaza de Armas is surrounded by tables with women selling *cuy* and a mixed grill called *chiriuchu* (*cuy*, chicken, *tortillas*, fish eggs, water weeds, maize, cheese and sausage). **Early June**: 2 weeks before Inti Raymi (see below) is the highly recommended Cusqueño beer festival, held near the rail station, which boasts a great variety of Latin American music. The whole event is well-organized and great fun; entry US$6.

**Mid June: Q'Olloriti**, the ice festival, is held at a 4,700m glacier. To get there involves a 2-hr walk up from the nearest road at Mawayani, beyond Ocongate, then it's a further exhausting climb up to the glacier. It's a good idea to take a tent, food and plenty of warm clothing. Note that it can be very confusing for those who don't understand the significance of this ancient ritual. Many trucks leave Cusco, from Limacpampa, in the days prior to the full moon in mid June; prices from US$2 upwards. This is a very rough and dusty overnight journey lasting 14 hrs, requiring warm clothing and coca leaves to fend off cold and exhaustion. Several agencies now offer tours.

**24 June**: the pageant of **Inti Raymi**, the Inca festival of the winter solstice, where locals outnumber tourists, is enacted at 1300 at the fortress of Sacsayhuamán. It lasts 2½ hrs, and is in Quechua.

Tickets for the stands can be bought a week in advance from the Municipali-

## The festival of Inti Raymi

The sun was the principal object of Inca worship. The Inca emperor claimed direct descent from it. Symbolically he shed light on his people, nourished them and made them grow. At their winter solstice, in June, the Incas honoured the solar deity with a great celebration known as Inti Raymi, the sun festival. The Spanish suppressed the Inca religion, and the last royal Inti Raymi was celebrated in 1535.

However, in 1944 a group of Cusco intellectuals, inspired by the contemporary "indigenist" movement, revived the old ceremony in the form of a pageant, putting it together from chronicles and historical documents. The event caught the public imagination, and it has been celebrated every year since then on June 24, now a Cusco public holiday.

Hundreds of local men and women play the parts of Inca priests, nobles, chosen women, soldiers (played by the local army garrison), runners, and the like. The coveted part of the Inca emperor Pachacuti is won by audition, and the event is organized by the municipal authorities. It begins around 1000 at the Qoricancha – the former sun temple of Cusco, with its adjacent new park attached – and winds its way up the main avenue into the Plaza de Armas, accompanied by songs, ringing declarations and the occasional drink of chicha. At the main plaza, Cusco's presiding mayor is whisked back to Inca times, to receive Pachacuti's blessing and a stern lecture on good government. Climbing through Plaza Nazarenas and up Pumacurcu, the procession reaches the ruins of Sacsayhuamán at about 1400, where scores of thousands of people are gathered on the ancient stones.

Those who pay their money and watch from the bleachers on the esplanade receive an official program, with a description of the proceedings in Spanish and English. For the rest, here is what happens: the master of ceremonies is the *Sinchi*, representing Pachauti's chief general. Before Pachacuti arrives the *Sinchi* ushers in contingents from the four *Suyus* (regions) of the Inca empire.

Much of the ceremony is based around alternating action between these four groups of players. A *Chaski* (messenger) enters to announce the imminent arrival of the Inca and his *Coya* (queen). Men sweep the ground before him, and women scatter flowers. The Inka takes the stage alone, and has a dialogue with the sun. Then he receives reports from the governors of the four *Suyus*. This is followed by a drink of the sacred chicha; the re-lighting of the sacred fire of the empire; the sacrifice (faked) of a llama; and the reading of auguries in its entrails. Finally the ritual eating of *sankhu* (corn paste mixed with the victim's blood) ends the ceremonies. The Inca gives a last message to his assembled children, and departs. The music and dancing continues until nightfall. (Peter Frost, 1996.)

dad, and cost US$25. Standing places on the ruins are free but get there at about 1030 as even reserved seats fill up quickly, and defend your space. Travel agents who try to persuade you to buy a ticket for the right to film or take photos are being dishonest. On the night before Inti Raymi, the Plaza de Armas is crowded with processions and food stalls. Try to arrive in Cusco 15 days before Inti Raymi; the atmosphere in the town during the build up is fantastic and something is always going on (festivals, parades etc).

**16-22 June:** the **Huiracocha** dance festival takes place in the village of Raqchi (see also page 327).

**16 July**: the festival of the **Virgen del Carmen** is held in Paucartambo, Huarocondo and Quillabamba. Masked dancers enact rituals and folk tales in the streets. **28 July**: Peruvian Independence Day. Prices shoot up during these celebrations. In Combapata is the **Yawar Fiesta** (Blood Festival), the famous ritual struggle between a condor and bull, which symbolizes the struggle between the natives and invaders. This is not a good place to be if you're an animal lover.

**Aug**: on the last Sun is the **Huarachicoy** festival at Sacsayhuamán, a spectacular reenactment of the Inca manhood rite, performed in dazzling costumes by boys of a local school.

**8 Sept**: **Day of the Virgin** is a colourful procession of masked dancers from the church of Almudena, at the SW edge of Cusco, near Belén, to the Plaza de San Francisco. There is also a splendid fair at Almudena, and a free bull fight on the following day. **14 Sept**: is the local festival of **El Señor de Huanca**, a religious pilgrimage to the shrine, set in a beautiful mountain landscape between Pisac and San Salvador. Tourists should be very discreet at these celebrations.

**1 Nov: All Saints Day**, celebrated everywhere with bread dolls and traditional cooking. **8 Dec**: is Cusco day, when churches and museums close at 1200. **24 Dec**: **Santuranticuy**, 'the buying of saints', a huge celebration of Christmas shopping, with a big crafts market in the plaza.

## LOCAL INFORMATION

**Hotel prices**

| | | | |
|---|---|---|---|
| **L1** | over US$200 | **L2** | US$151-200 |
| **L3** | US$101-150 | **A1** | US$81-100 |
| **A2** | US$61-80 | **A3** | US$46-60 |
| **B** | US$31-45 | **C** | US$21-30 |
| **D** | US$12-20 | **E** | US$7-11 |
| **F** | US$4-6 | **G** | up to US$3 |

### ● Accommodation

Book more expensive hotels well in advance through a good travel agency, particularly for the week or so around Inti Raymi, when prices are greatly increased. Prices given are for the high season in June-Aug. When there are fewer tourists hotels may drop their prices by as much as half. Always check for discounts. On the Puno-Cusco train there are many hotel agents for medium-priced hotels. Prices can often be negotiated down to F category, but it is best to pay the agent for 1 day only and then negotiate with the hotel. Rooms offered at Cusco station are usually cheaper than those offered on the train. Taxis and tourist minibuses meet the train and take you to the hotel of your choice for US$0.50, but be insistent. It is cold in Cusco, and many hotels do not have heating. It is worth asking for an 'estufa', a space heater which some places will provide for an extra charge. The whole city suffers from water shortages, and hotels usually only have supplies in the mornings, so plan your day accordingly.

The best are **L1** *Monasterio del Cusco*, Palacio 140, T 226871, F 237111 (in Lima T 440-8043, F 440-6197), price includes tax 5-star, beautifully restored Convent of San Antonio Abad, inc the chapel, wonderful rooms, courtyards and cloisters (the president has his own suite), good restaurant, friendly staff; **L3** *Libertador* (5-star), in the Casa de los Cuatro Bustos at C San Agustín 400, T 232601/231961, 28% tax, good, especially the service, but in July and Aug rooms in the older part of the hotel are cold and dark.

**A1** *Cusco*, Heladeros 150, T 224821, administered by Sociedad de Beneficencia Pública del Cusco, hot water, largest and best known, it

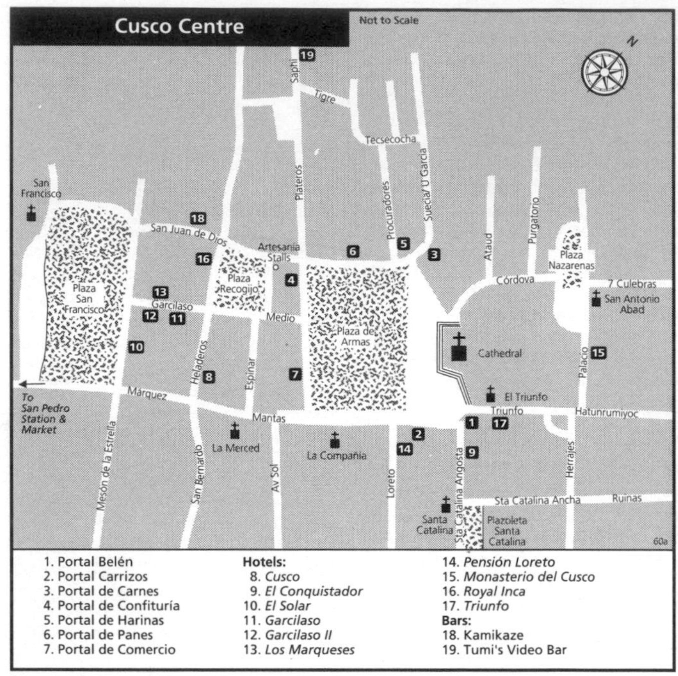


is described as 'old fashioned, not cheap and a little fusty', central location.

**A2** *El Dorado Inn*, Av Sol 395, T 233888, F 240993, good, can be noisy in the morning, food good but expensive; **A2** *Holiday Inn Court*, Av Sol 602, T 224457, F 233315, all rooms with safe, fridge, heating, TV, rooms with handicapped facilities from Jan 1996, stylish; **A2** *Royal Inka I*, Plaza Regocijo 299, T 231067, price includes taxes and breakfast, bar, dining room, good service, rec; **A2** *Royal Inka II* on the same street, larger and better, good sauna, US$7; **A2** *San Agustín Plaza*, Av Sol 594, T 238121, includes taxes and breakfast, shower, TV, phone, modern, very good, clean, safe, English spoken, very expensive to send fax; **A2** *San Agustín Internacional*, San Agustín y Maruri 390, T 231001, F 221174, includes taxes and breakfast, more expensive than *Plaza* but higher standard.

On Plazoleta Las Nazarenas, the colonial Casa de la Torre (No 211) is being converted into *Posada Las Nazarenas*, 13 rooms, 3-4 star, due open mid-late 1997, T 232829, Tierras Altas SA, or Los Pinos 584, San Isidro, Lima 27, T 440-5476.

**B** *Conquistador*, Santa Catalina Angosta 149, T 224461, price includes breakfast, clean, safe, phone, restaurant, parking, good; **B** *Hostal La Casona del Sol*, Plazoleta Santo Domingo 263, T/F 232704, TV, laundry, medical service, looks nice; **B** *Hostal Carlos V*, Tecseccocha 490, T 223091, includes tax and breakfast, has charm and character, restaurant, refurbished, pleasant; **B-C** *Raymi*, Av Pardo 950, T 225141, with bath, heater, includes breakfast, rec; **B** *Wiracocha*, Plaza de Armas, corner of Mantas, T 222351, PO Box 502, clean, hot water, restaurant opens at 0600, good breakfast.

**C** *Hostal Corihuasi*, C Suecia 561 (not a safe street at night), T/F 232233, includes breakfast, colonial house, laundry arranged, hot water, quiet, friendly, electric heaters, good views, rec; **C** *Hostal Garcilaso*, Garcilaso de la Vega 233, T 233031, with bath, safe for luggage, refurbished, clean, historic charm; **C** ***Hostal Garcilosa III***, Garcilosa de la Vega 237, quiet, clean, bath, helpful; **C** ***Hostal Qosqo***, Portal Mantas 115, near Plaza de Armas, with bath, hot water, clean, friendly, helpful, includes breakfast, heating on request at no extra charge, rec; **C** ***Los Portales***, Matará 322, T 223500, includes airport pickup, tastefully renovated hotel with modern facilities but plenty of character, very clean, very friendly and helpful, English spoken, safe deposit, luggage store, highly rec; **C** ***Loreto***, Pasaje Loreto 115, Plaza de Armas, clean, very friendly, rooms with Inca walls and electric heaters, a bit dark, cheap laundry service, great atmosphere, taxis and other travel can be arranged, Lucio here is a good guide, safe luggage deposit, rec; **C** ***Los Marqueses***, Garcilaso 256, T 232512, with bath, heaters extra, early colonial house, beautiful patio, comfortable, clean and convenient.

**D** ***El Inca***, Quera 251 (F in low season), clean, heating, hot water variable, luggage store, restaurant, includes breakfast, Wilbur speaks English, and is helpful, rec, noisy disco in basement till 0100; **D** ***Hostal Amaru***, Cuesta San Blas 541, T 225933, with bath, cheaper without, hot water 24 hrs, laundry, clean, friendly, safe, nice views, rec; **D** ***Hostal Amparito***, Av Regional 898, near train station, 15 minutes' walk from Plaza de Armas, T 224898, hot water, with bath, very clean, quiet, owner is a policeman who will help organize tours to Machu Picchu; **D** ***Hostal Apu Wasi***, Pumacurco y Concepción, T 237249, E downstairs, includes breakfast, colonial house, very clean, very friendly and helpful, hot showers, big rooms, good views, laundry facility; **D** ***Hostal Cahuide***, Saphi 845, T 222771, discount for long stay, hot water in en suite bathrooms, good rooms, quiet, clean, good laundry service, storage facilities, helpful, café serving good value breakfasts, but strong box is insecure; **D** ***Hostal Corregidor***, Portal de Panes, Plaza de Armas, T 232632, good; **D** ***Hostal El Arqueólogo*** (room or dormitory), Ladrillos 425 not far from Sacsayhuamán (T 232569, not a safe street at night), inc breakfast, hot water, helpful, French and English spoken, clean, will store luggage, garden, cafeteria and kitchen, rec; **D** ***Hostal El Solar***, San Francisco 162, T 232451, E during low season, clean, rec; **D** ***Hostal Imperial Palace***, Tecseccocha 492, T 223324, with breakfast, prices negotiable for longer stays, café, bar, restaurant, clean, a bit cold, but well furnished, English spoken, good, friendly, safe deposit open only 0700-1100; **D** ***Hostal Incawasi***, Portal de Panes 147, Plaza de Armas, T 238245, hot water 0800-0900, 2000-2200, clean, good beds, bargain for long stays, secure, helpful, good value; **D** ***Hostal San Blas***, Cuesta San Blas 526, T 225781, basic, friendly, secure for luggage, includes breakfast; **D** ***Huaynapata***, Huaynapata 369, T 228034, small rooms, quieter rooms at the back, clean, family-run, hot water, stores luggage, friendly, rec; **D** ***Inca World***, Tecseccocha 474 (opp *Suecia II*), with bath and hot water, small restaurant, huge rooms, safe, stores luggage; **D** ***Kristina***, Av Sol 341, T 227251, nice rooms, private bath, hot water, breakfast-restaurant, friendly, reliable, rec; **D** ***Suecia II***, Tecseccocha 465, T 239757, rooms with or without bath, good beds and blankets, clean, good security procedures, breakfast at 0500, US$1.50, beautiful building, good meeting place for trekkers doing the Inca Trail, best to book if arriving on same day as Puno train, rec; **D** ***Tambo***, Ayacucho 233, T 236788, clean, heating in rooms, laundry facilities, safe for luggage, central, hot water intermittent, restaurant fair, rec.

**E** ***Hostal Bellavista***, Av Santiago 100, with bath, F without, hot water, very friendly, safe, 10 minutes' walk from centre, not a safe area at night, breakfast available, will store luggage, rec; **E** ***Hostal Bosanova***, on Afligados entre Sol y Loreto, no sign, enter through *Café Canela* 2nd floor, hot showers, laundry service, small, clean, friendly; **E** ***Hostal El Puerto***, Fierro 571-577, nice, friendly, family-run, use of kitchen, garden; **E** ***Hostal Familiar***, Saphi 661, with bath, cheaper without, hot water 0700-0900, luggage store US$2/item, owner Cecilia speaks excellent English; **E** ***Hostal Pakcha Real***, Tandapata 300, San Blas, T 237484, no sign, brown house, friendly, family run, hot water, cooking and laundry facilities, TV and video lounge, use of kitchen, rec; **E** ***Hostal Quipu***, Fierro 495, T 236179, clean, very friendly, good value, colonial-style house, attractive courtyard, not a safe part of town; **E** ***Hostal Residencial Rojas***, Tigre 129, hot water, safe, family-run, clean; **E** ***Hostal Royal Qosqo***, Tecseccocha 2, basic, safe, luggage store, usually hot water; **E** ***Hostal Sapantiana***, Pumacurco 490, without bath, hot water on request but problems with supply, safe, pleasant; **E** ***Suecia***, C Suecia 332, shared rooms, uncomfortable beds, will store luggage, can use their bulletin board to arrange groups for the Inca trail.

**F** ***El Arcano***, Carmen Alto 288, San Blas district, T 232703, very clean, water 24 hrs, safe to leave luggage, 7 rooms for 1-4 people, very friendly owner, rec; **F** ***Hostal Cáceres***, Plateros 368, 1 block from Plaza de Armas, luggage store, clean, friendly, laundry service, can put motorcycle in patio; **F** ***Hostal Familiar Casa***, Pasaje España 844, T 224152, off Prado, shared bath, basic rooms, quiet, friendly, safe, hot water in mornings only, baggage stored for a small fee, laundry, rec; **F** pp ***Hostal Pumacurco***, Pumacurco 336, Interior 329, T 227739, 3 mins from Plaza de Armas, newly restored part of a very old colonial house, hot water, owner Betty is very friendly and helpful, some large rooms, clean, safe, washing facilities; **F** pp ***Hospedaje Sol Naciente***, Av Pardo 510, T 228602, hot water, comfortable, laundry facilities, luggage stored for a small fee, very clean, family-run; **F** ***Hostal Unión***, Unión 189, T 231580, 5 blocks from Plaza de Armas, ½ block from Santa Ana market, shared bath, hot water, safe, laundry facilities, kitchen/café, luggage store, knowledgeable, helpful, very noisy but rec; **F** pp ***Hospedaje Vírgen de los Remedios***, 156 Santa Catalina Angosto, 1 block from Plaza de Armas, no sign, follow the passage to the back to find the entrance, quiet, very nice owners, comfortable beds, water intermittent; **F** ***Imperio***, C Chaparro, run by Elena and family, nr San Pedro station, be careful at night in this part of town, hot water, friendly, clean, noisy, motorcycle parking, safe to leave luggage, highly rec; **F** pp ***Qorichaska***, Nueva Alta 458, T 228974, close to centre, clean, hot water, will store luggage, cafeteria open till 2100, safe, friendly, great value, rec.

**G** pp ***Hostal Chaski***, Portal Confituría 257, Plaza de Armas, T 236093, hot water, laundry service, cafeteria, safe deposit; **G** pp ***Hostal San Cristóbal***, Quiscapata 242, nr San Cristóbal, in dormitory, cooking and clothes-washing facilities, baggage deposit, friendly and reliable, if full, Sra Ema de Paredes will let you spread a sleeping bag on the floor, rec.

**Youth hostel**: *Albergue Municipal*, Quiscapata 240, San Cristóbal, T 252506, US$7 pp in dormitories, new, very clean, helpful staff, luggage store, great views, bar, cafeteria, laundry, safe deposit, discount for members; ***El Procurador***, Procuradores 366, T/F 221172, US$7 pp with bath, US$5 without, includes breakfast, hot water, laundry, motorcycle parking, friendly, rec.

**Camping**: is not safe anywhere in the Cusco area. For renting equipment, there are several places around the Plaza area. Check the equipment carefully as it is common for parts to be missing. An example of prices per day: tent US$3, sleeping bag US$2, stove US$3. A deposit of US$100 is asked, plus credit card, passport or plane ticket. ***Soqllaq'asa Camping Service***, owned by English-speaking Louis Aedo, at Plateros 354, T/F 222224, is recommended for equipment hire, but, as elsewhere, check the stoves carefully. Upstairs Sra Luzmila Bellota M has a workshop where she makes alpaca wool fleece jackets to order, US$60 upwards, but try bargaining. White gas (*bencina*), US$1.50/litre, can be bought at hardware stores, but check the purity; stove spirit (*alcoól para quemar*) is available at pharmacies; blue gas canisters, costing US$5, can be found at some hardware stores and at shops which rent gear. You can also rent equipment through travel agencies. A shop with useful, imported (so expensive) camping gear: *Camping Deportes*, Centro Comercial Ollanta, Av del Sol 346, shop no 118; it also sells insect repellent, Deet, US$10 for a small bottle.

## ● Places to eat

**International and local cuisine, expensive**: For a good meal and décor try ***Inti Raymi*** in the *Libertador*; ***Mesón de los Espaderos***, Espaderos y Plaza de Armas, *parrilladas*, good; ***Paititi***, Plaza de Armas, live music, good atmosphere, Inca masonry; next door is ***Taberna del Truco***, live music at dinner time.

**Medium class, local cuisine**: ***Trattoria Adriano***, C Mantas y Av Sol, just off SE corner of Plaza de Armas, open for breakfast at 0700, fairly good Italian cuisine and great desserts, friendly but not cheap; ***Peña Los Incas***, Plaza de Armas, good *menú* at lunchtime for US$3, *peñas* at night; ***Pucará***, Plateros 309, Japanese run, highly rec, good meals throughout the day, pleasant atmosphere, try the chocolate cake, pottery, silver jewellery and designer alpaca sweaters for sale.

**Pizzerías**: *Chez Maggy*, Plateros 339, open 1800, good atmosphere, popular with tourists, live music nightly, pasta, soups, pizzas freshly baked in wood-burning oven, service sometimes slow; ***Pizzería América***, at 316 and ***Americana***, at 369, both on Plateros, highly rec; ***Pizzería Wasi***, Procuradores 347, good pizzas, also meat dishes, helpful German owner; ***Los Balcones***, upstairs at Espaderos 125, also has vegetarian menu; at Espaderos 136 is ***Pizzería Espaderos***, good pizzas, smokey atmosphere; ***Tizziano Trattoria***, Tecesiccocha 418, good Italian food, homemade pasta, excellent value *menú* Mon-Sat 1200-1500 and 1800-2300, also vegetarian, rec.

**Cheaper restaurants, local cuisine**: ***Royal Qosco***, Plateros 345, cheap, 3-course set meals, good soups and fish, rec; ***Urpi***, Procuradores 332, good, popular with locals; ***Los Candiles***, Plateros 323, set lunch US$2.50; ***La Yunta***, Portal de Carnes, Plaza de Armas, vegetarian, good salads, pancakes and juices, popular with gringos, same owners as *Instinct Travel Agency*, rec; next door upstairs is ***Café Bagdad***, nice balcony with good views, cheap set lunch, friendly, good atmosphere, happy hour 1930-2130, German owner Florian Thurman speaks good English; ***El Solar***, San Francisco, good lunch menu, rec; ***Conde***, Plaza San Francisco 364, 24 hrs, rec; ***Víctor Victoria***, Tigre 130, Israeli and local dishes, highly recommended for breakfast, good value; ***El Cuate***, Procuradores 386, Mexican food, rec; ***La Retama***, Maruri 315, friendly, folk music most nights; ***Ama Lur***, Plaza de las Nazarenas 159, clean, cheap, varied menu, excellent food, vegetarian dishes available, foreign newspapers and magazines; ***Chez Víctor***, Ayacucho 217, good, popular; ***El Rey***, San Andrés y Almagro, trout and chicken, good and quiet; ***El Mariño***, Espinar y Mantas, good seafood; ***Tronquito***, Plateros 327, huge portions; ***La Tranquera***, Plaza Túpac Amaru 137, cheap local and international food; ***El Trujillo***, Matará, northern Peruvian specialities. For good, cheap local food ***Nikos***, on Pampa del Castillo, is recommended, always packed with locals. To try other local specialities, in the suburbs: ***Quintas Eulalia***, Choquechaca 384, closed on Mon.

**Vegetarian**: ***Govinda***, Espaderos 128, just off W corner of Plaza de Armas, sometimes good, try the yoghurt-muesli fruit bowl, always busy, slow service; ***El Tordo***, Tordo 238, vegetarian, good value, tiny place, very cheap 1-course lunch, also has rooms to let, rec; ***John Bore***, Tecseccocha 418, open daily 0600-2400, friendly, recommended for *menú* US$1.80 and à la carte; ***Acuarium***, Cuesta del Almirante 211, good vegetarian *menú*.

**Cafés and snackbars**: ***Café Hualliy***, Plateros 363, set lunch US$1.20, good for comments on guides, popular meeting place, especially for breakfast, has good snacks and 'copa Hually' – fruit, muesli, yoghurt, honey and chocolate cake, also good vegetarian *menú*; ***Ayllu***, Portal de Carnes 208, open at 0600, Italian, classical/folk music, good atmosphere, has a superb range of milk products and wonderful apple pastries, try *leche asada*, good breakfast, quick service, rec; ***Café Literario Varayoc***, Espaderos 142, good meeting place, excellent coffee, pizzas and chocolate cake; ***Oasis***, Av Sol 453, new, good set lunch; ***Misky Wasi***, Tigre 110, for breakfasts, snacks, excellent *pie de limón*; ***Tumi's Video Bar***, Saphi 478, good café, local and European dishes, open late, good value lunch, 4 movies daily, US$1.30, owner Maurice Drews has good local information (see also **Language classes** below); ***Café Plus***, Portal de Panes 151, p 2, same owners as *Hostal Apu Wasi*, delicious cakes, excellent coffee, friendly, good service; ***La Tertulia***, Procuradores 50, p 2, nice setting above courtyard, run by Johanna Berendse and her Peruvian husband, who also run the *Amauta* Language School (see below), excellent breakfast buffet is served 0700-1300, includes muesli, homemade bread, yoghurt, eggs, juice and coffee, eat as much as you like for around US$3, superb value, also book exchange, newspapers, classical music, vegetarian buffet served daily 1800-2200.

### ● Bars

***Cross Keys Pub***, Plaza de Armas, Portal Confiturías 233, p 1, open 1800-0130, run by Barry Walker, a Mancunian and bird expert, darts, great atmosphere, happy hour once or twice a night (1800 and 2000/2100), not for beer; ***Kamikaze***, Plaza Regocijo, *peña* at 2200, folk and rock music, candle-lit cavern atmosphere, many gringos, entry US$2.50 but usually you don't have to pay, T-shirts for sale, rec; ***Mama Africa***, Espaderos 135, p 2, live music at weekends, very popular with gringos, free entry with a pass which you can get on the plaza; ***Taberna Cusicusi***, E side of Plaza de Armas, nice atmosphere, reasonable prices, good music, sometimes live; ***Hocus Pocus Rock Café***, Plaza de Armas, good atmosphere, music and snacks; ***Puputi Pub***, on the corner of Procuradores and Plaza de Armas, café until 1800, good, cheap breakfast, cakes, juices, good view of plaza, bar afterwards with live music every night, happy hour 1900-2130 Sun-Thurs, great atmosphere; ***Ukuku's***, Plateros 316, US$1.35 entry, good, friendly atmosphere, happy hour 0730-0930. Also, ***Manu Pub***, Procuradores 351, p 2; ***El Manguare Jungle Bar***, Triunfo 393; ***Las Quenas*** in the basement of the *Hotel Savoy*, rec; ***Chichería El Fogón***, good atmosphere, on Pumacurco.

### ● Airline offices

**AeroPerú**, Av Sol 317; **Americana** at El Dorado Inn and Portal de Harinas, Plaza de Armas, T 231373; **Aero Continente**, Portal Comercio 179, Plaza de Armas, T 252635; **Faucett**, Portal Comercio 195, and Portal de Carnes, T 233151; **Imperial Air**, Garcilaso y Granada, Plaza San Francisco, T 238877.

### ● Banks & money changers

The best places are the banks along Av del Sol, although it can be time-consuming and, in some cases, only at certain hours (not at weekends): **Banco de Crédito**, is recommended for cash advances on Visa, TCs 1% commission to soles, 3% to dollars; **Interbanc**, Sol y Pulucha-pata, no commission on TCs, Visa; and next door **Banco Continental**, US$5 commission. For cash on Mastercard, **Banco del Sur**, Av Sol 459, also Amex and Thomas Cook TCs, Mastercard, reasonable rates. You can withdraw dollars or soles from the several ATMs at the banks along Av Sol. Many travel agencies and *casas de cambio* change dollars; some of them change TCs as well, but charge 4-5% commission. The street changers hang around Av del Sol, blocks 2-3, every day; they will also change TCs. In banks and on the street check the notes.

### ● Embassies & consulates

**US Agent**, Olga Villa García, Apdo 949, Cusco, T 222183 or 233541. **German**, Sra Maria-Sophia Júrgens de Hermoza, San Agustín 307, T 235459, Casilla Postal 1128, Correo Central, open Mon-Fri, 1000-1200, appointments may be made by phone, also book exchange. **French**, C Espinar (M Jean Pierre Sallat, *Farmacia Vallenas* – may let French people leave luggage if going to Machu Picchu). **British**, Dr Raul Delgado de la Flor, *Hotel San Agustín Internacional*, T 222322 or 231001, address above, the Austrian Consul is also there. **Finnish**, Emmel 109, Yanahuara, T 223708.

### ● Entertainment

**Folklore shows**: regular nightly folklore show at *Centro Qosqo*, Av del Sol 604 next to Holiday Inn, at 1900, entrance fee US$6; and at *Teatro Inti Raymi*, Saphi 605, nightly 1845, US$4.50 and well worth it. Local *peña* at *Inka's Restaurant Peña*, Portal de Panes 105, Plaza de Armas; at Portal de Panes 109, *Clave del Sol*, good fun. *Teatro Municipal*, C Mesón de la Estrella 149, T 227321 for information 0900-1300 and 1500-1900, a venue for plays, dancing, shows, mostly Thur-Sun; ask for their programmes.

### ● Hospitals & medical services

**Dentists**: *Tomás Flores*, T 222844; *Gilbert Espejo*, T 228074.

**Health**: *Hospital Regional*, Av de la Cultura, rec. If lab tests are needed, Lab Pasteur, Tullumayo 768 is rec. *Dr Oscar Tejada* (PO Box 425, Cusco, T 233836 or 240449 day or night) is a member of the International Association for Medical Assistance to Travellers and is prepared to help any visitor in an emergency, 24-hr attention; he charges according to that organization's scales, which are not expensive. *Dr Gustavo Garrido Juárez*, Matará 410, T 239761, English and French spoken. *Jaime Triveño*, T 225513, can be reached 24 hrs a day.

### ● Language classes

***Exel***, Cruz Verde 336, T 235298, Señorita Sori is highly rec, US$3-4/hr; the school can arrange accommodation with local families. ***Tumi's*** have a school at Awaqpinta 732, Spanish US$3/hr one-to-one; they also employ English teachers. ***Amauta***, Procuradores 50, p 2, T/F 241422, PO Box 1164, classes in Spanish and Quechua, workshops in Peruvian cuisine, dance and music, also apartments to rent for US$50/week, arrange excursions, can help find voluntary work, owners also have *La Tertulia* café (see above). Spanish classes are run by the ***ACUPARI***, the German-Peruvian Cultural Association, San Agustín 307.

### ● Laundry

Laundry service at ***Lavamatic***, Procuradores 341, US$1.20/kg, laundry brought early in the morning will be returned the same afternoon, rec; ***Lavanderías Superchick***, Saphi 635, US$1.25 for 2 kg. Cheap laundry service at Siete Cuartones 317, US$1/kilo. There are several cheap laundries on Procuradores, and also on Suecia and Tecseccocha. **NB** In damp or overcast weather, allow plenty of time for clothes to be dried properly.

### ● Post & telecommunications

**Post Office**: Principal one is on Av del Sol, block 5, Mon-Sat 0730-2000; 0800-1400 Sun and holidays. Stamps and postcards available. Sending packages from Cusco is not cheap, reliable or quick; it's much better to wait until Lima or La Paz. *Poste restante*, US$0.25/letter.

**Telecommunications**: Telefónica del Perú, Av del Sol 386, for telephone and fax, open Mon-Sat 0700-2300, 0700-1200 Sun and holidays. International calls by pay phone or go through the operator (long wait possible), deposit required, national call US$3, international US$12. Fax to Europe costs US$3.50/page; to receive a fax costs US$2/page, the number is (084) 241111.

**Radio messages**: Radio Tawantinsuyo, Av del Sol 806, open Mon-Sat 0600-1900, Sun 0600-1600, messages are sent out between 0500 and 2100 (you can choose the time), in Spanish or Quechua, price/message US$1; this is sometimes helpful if things are stolen and you want them back. Radio Comercial, Av del Sol 457, of 406, T 231381, open daily 0900-1200, 1600-1900, for making contact with other radio-users in Cusco and the jungle area. Helpful if you wish to contact people in Manu; price US$1.50 for 5 mins.

### ● Security

More police patrol the streets, trains and stations than in the past, which has led to an improvement in security, but one should still be vigilant. Look after your belongings, leaving valuables in safe keeping with hotel management, not in hotel rooms. Places in which to take care are: when changing money on the streets; in the railway and bus stations; the bus from the airport; the Santa Ana market (otherwise rec); the San Cristóbal area and at out-of-the-way ruins. Also take special care during Inti Raymi. Avoid walking around alone at night on narrow streets, between the stations and the centre, or in the market areas.

### ● Shopping

*Santa Ana Market*, opposite Estación San Pedro, is the best market for a variety of goods; best value is at closing time or in the rain. There's another market on the corner of San Andrés and Quera, which is good for local handicrafts. *Mercado Artesanal*, Av del Sol, block 4, is good for cheap crafts. *Coordinadora Sur Andina de Artesanía*, C del Medio 130, off Plaza de Armas, has a good assortment of crafts and is a non-profit organization. *La Pérez*, Urb Mateo Pumacahua 598, Huanchac, T 232186/222137, is a big cooperative with a good selection; they will arrange a free pick-up from your hotel.

Cusco is the weaving centre of Peru, and excellent textiles can be found at good value: ***Alpaca Llampu***, C Ruinas, genuine, 100% alpaca goods, but not cheap. ***Artesanía La Paloma***, Cuesta San Blas 552 and Plazuela Santa Catalina 211, good but expensive. ***Sr Aller***, Plaza Santo Domingo 261, sells interesting antiques. ***Josefina Olivera***, Santa Clara 501, sells old ponchos and antique mantas, without the usual haggling. ***Kaliran***, Cuesta San Blas 522, sells musical instruments and Andean music. Be very careful of buying gold and silver objects and jewellery in and around

The traditional arybola and plate used by the Incas to carry *chicha* (fermented corn beer)

Cusco; we have received many reports of sharp practices. Cusco market is said to be the cheapest for slide and print film, eg Fuji US$4.50.

Sacks to cover rucksacks are available in the market by Estación San Pedro for US$0.75. A good supermarket for buying supplies for the Inca trail is *Carrillo*, at C Plateros 348, near Plaza de Armas.

**Bookshops**: ***Librería Studium***, Marqués Mantas 239, stocks guidebooks. ***Los Andes***, Portal Comercio 125, Plaza de Armas, has a good range of books and large boxes of postcards.

**Local crafts**: in the Plaza San Blas and the surrounding area, authentic Cusco crafts still survive. Wood workers may be seen in almost any street. Leading artisans who welcome visitors include Hilario Mendivil, Plazoleta San Blas 634, who makes biblical figures from plaster, wheatflour and potatoes and Edilberta Mérida, Carmen Alto 133, who makes earthenware figures showing the physical and mental anguish of the Indian peasant. Víctor Vivero Holgado, at Tandapata 172, is a painter of pious subjects, while Antonio Olave Palomino, Siete Angelitos 752, makes reproductions of precolumbian ceramics and colonial sculptures. Maximiliano Palomino de la Sierra, Triunfo 393, produces festive dolls and wood carvings, and Santiago Rojas, near San Blas, statuettes. Luis Aguayo Revollar, *Galería de Arte Aguayo*, Cuesta del Almirante 211-256, y Av Sol 616, T 237992, makes fine wood carvings. Museo Inca Art Gallery of Amílcar Salomón Zorrilla, Huancaro M-B – L8, T 231232 (PO Box 690), telephone between 0900 and 2100, is good for contemporary art. Visit Nemesio Villasante, Av 24 de Junio 415, T 222915, for Paucartambo masks, and Miguel Chacón Ventura, Portal Confituría 265, Plaza de Armas, for watercolour paintings.

**● Tour companies & travel agents**

There are many travel agencies in Cusco. We divide them into two categories: a) the expensive, long-established, reliable, well-organized agencies, with English-speaking staff, and b) the cheaper, less reliable agencies which are always changing. Most tours have set prices, but the second category agencies will offer cheaper packages. Always check details before making arrangements, shop around and be aware that overcharging and failing to keep to arrangements are common, especially in the high season. Also beware agencies quoting prices in dollars then converting to soles at an unfavourable rate when paying. Do not deal with guides who claim to be employed by agencies listed below without verifying their credentials. It is better to deal direct with the agencies. Seek advice from visitors returning from trips for the latest information. Beware also of tours which stop for long lunches at expensive hotels. In Cusco, its environs and Machu Picchu, check the standard of your guide's English (or whichever language is required) as some have no more than a memorized spiel.

A day tour Pisac-Ollantaytambo-Chinchero costs US$10-15 pp; ½-day tour visiting the four ruins around Cusco, US$6 pp, not inc entrance fees; ½-day city tours cost US$3-3.50.

Category a) ***Lima Tours***, Portal de Harinos 177, Plaza de Armas, T 228431/223791, F 221266, Amex representative, gives TCs against Amex card, but no exchange; also DHL office, to receive a parcel you pay 35% of the marked value of customs tax; ***GaTur***, Puluchapata 140, T 223496, F 238645; ***Explorandes***, Av del Sol, block 5, T 238380, F 233784, good equipment for rent; ***Southern Cross Adventures***, Portal de Panes 123, of 301, on Plaza de Armas, T 237649, F 239447, manager Hugo Paullo, friendly, helpful, good for information, specializes in horseback trips; ***APU Expediciones***, Portal Comercio 157, Plaza de Armas, PO Box 24, T 235408/235061, F 241111, adventure tours and river trips, mountaineering expeditions with good equipment, nature tours and packages to Manu National Park, Tambopata and other jungle areas, transport facilities, guide Mariella Bernasconi Cilloniz is highly rec; ***Tambo Treks***, Atocsaycuchi 589, Plaza San Blas, T 237718, adventure trips; ***Peruvian Andean Treks***, Av Pardo 705, T 225701, manager Tom Hendrikson, adventure tours; ***Kinjyo Travel Service***, Portal de Panes 101, Plaza de Armas, T 231101, F 239044; ***Expediciones Manu***, Procuradores 50, T 226671, F 236706, PO Box 606, run by Barry Walker of Cross Keys Pub, recommended for jungle trips; ***El Aventurero***, Portal Confiturías 265, T/F 263278, run by Julio Vargas.

Category b) ***Kantu Tours***, Portal Belén 258, T 221381, F 232012, rec for local tours, competitive, offers good horse treks around Cusco (US$10 for 6 hrs), experience not necessary, but sun protection is, manager Gloria Hermosa Tapiá speaks good English; ***Snow Tours***, Portal de Panes 109, of 204, T 241313, managed by Edith Bellota Guzmán, local tours, Inca Trail, climbing, Manu, etc, camping equipment hired; ***Río Bravo***, Almagro 120 (off Av Sol), T 232301, white water rafting specialists; ***Instinct***, Procuradores 107, T 233451, Benjamín speaks good English and is recommended, also Juan Muñil, white water rafting trips, mountain bike hire, rec; ***Mach Tour***, Arequipa 275, T 234033, will arrange personalized tours, rec; ***Ecotours***, Heladeros 150, T 231288, reliable and competitively priced; ***Eco Amazonia Lodge***, Plateros 351, T 236159, Julio Vargas Vega, friendly, rec. The following are 1996 recommendations, all on Plaza de Armas: ***Naty's Travel***, Portal de Confitería 273, T/F 239437; ***United Mice***, Plateros 348, T 221139, F 238050, repeatedly recommended for the Inca Trail, especially Vicente Gómez, US$65 pp; ***Coopsetur***, Portal Comercio 141, T 231515, Humberto and Silverio are reliable guides, recommended for Sacred Valley and Machu Picchu; ***Luzma Tours***, Portal de Panes Los Ruiseñores, of 308, T 235370, F 236229, good for information, helpful, friendly, manager Luz-Marina, rec. River rafting trips cost on average US$20 pp.

**Recommended private guides**, divided into two groups: c) classic, standard tours, and d) adventure trips. All of those listed speak English. Set prices: city tour US$15/day; trekking, Machu Picchu and other ruins US$30/day. Private guides can be contacted through the tour companies.

Category c) **Amalia Escobar**, T 222258, also does trekking. **Juana Pancorbo**, Av Los Pinos D-2, T 227482. **Haydee Mogrovejo**, T 221907; **Marco Arragón**, T 233733; **Boris Carnas**, T 221482; **Wilbert Yáñez**, T 232511; **Elisha García**, T 237916; **Satoshi Shinoda**, T 227861 and **Michiko Nakazahua**, T 226185, both Japanese-speaking guides; **Victoria Morales Condori**, San Juan de Dios 229, T 235204; **David Quintana**, T 225757, or through SAS Travel, Plaza de Armas 109, Portal Belén, T 224247, he speaks English; **Rubén Huallapuma**, works out of *Hostal Garcilaso*, he is very knowledgeable about Inca civilization, and flexible; **Fredy Palacios Palva**, T 240281/239716, English-speaking; **Luís Guillén Pinelo**, T 224385.

Category d) **Aurelio Aguirre**, T 232797; **Darwin Camacho**, T 233884; **Manuel Luna**, T 226083; **Pieter Bohn**, T 234234, German; **Gunther Haue**, T 236916; **Marco Pérez**, T 227414; **Roger Valencia Espinoza**, T 251278; **Tino Aucca**, Urb Titio Q-1-13 Wanchaq, T 235850, a biologist studying the birds of the Polylepis forest. **Victor Estrada**, Parque España E-3, Urb Ucchullo Grande, T 224049, is a shaman and spiritual guide who is also very knowledgeable about local history, architecture, etc; US$75/day.

### ● Tourist offices

There is a new tourist office on Av del Sol 103, at the same entrance as Museo de Arte Popular. INC tourist office is at Garcilaso y Heladeros for buying tickets for Machu Picchu and the Inca Trail. Official tourist information and Servicio de Protección al Turista is at Mantas 188, opposite La Merced; 24-hr hotline 252974, open 0800-2000. **Ministry of Tourism**, Av Manco Capac 1020, p 4, Huanchac, T 233701/232347, Mon-Fri 0800-1300. The University is also a good source of information, especially on archaeological sites. They sell good videos of Cusco and surroundings.

**Automóvil Club del Perú**, Av del Sol 457, next to Banco del Sur, p 3, of 305, has some maps. Motorists beware; many streets end in flights of steps not marked as such. There are very few good maps of Cusco available.

## Maps and guidebooks

Maps of the city, the Inca Trail and the Urubamba Valley are available at tour companies. There are lots of information booklets on Machu Picchu and the other ruins at the bookshops. The best book on Cusco, the Sacred Valley, Inca Trail, Machu Picchu and other ruins is *Exploring Cusco*, by Peter Frost, which is available in Cusco bookshops. Also recommended for general information on Cusco is *Cusco Peru Tourist Guide*, published by Lima 2000. *The Sacred Center*, by Johan Reinhard, explains Machu Picchu in archaeological terms. *Apus and Incas*, by Charles Brod, describes cultural walks in and around Cusco, and treks in the Cordilleras Vilcabamba, Vilcanota and Urubamba, plus the Manu National Park (2nd edition, Inca Expeditions, 2323 SE 46th Ave, Portland, OR 97215, USA, US$10.95 plus US$1.50 postage, or from bookshops in N America, Europe and Peru).

Asociación de Conservación para la Selva Sur, ACSS, Comercial Los Ruiseñores, Portal de Panes 123, of 305, T/F 240911, for information and free video shows about Manu National Park and Tambopata-Candoma Reserve. They are friendly and helpful and also have information on programmes and research in the jungle area of Madre de Dios, as well as being distributors of the expensive (US$75), but beautiful book on the Manu National Park by Kim MacQuarrie and André Bartschi.

## Useful addresses

**Police**: Tourist police, in Av Sol, on the W side of the grounds of Santo Domingo-Qoricancha, T 221961, they are very helpful. If you need a *denuncia* (a report for insurance purposes), which is available from the Banco de la Nación, they will type it out. Always go to the police when robbed, even though it will cost you a bit of time. Stolen cameras often turn up in the local market and can be bought back cheaply; remember the person selling them is not the thief. If you can prove that the camera is yours, contact the police. National Police, C Saphi, block 4.

## Transport

**Local Motorcycle mechanics**: Eric and Oscar Antonio Aranzábal, Ejercicios 202, Tahuantinsuyo, T 223397, highly recommended for repairs; also Autocusa, Av de la Cultura 730 (Sr Marco Tomaycouza), T 240378/239054. **Taxis**: in Cusco are inexpensive and recommended when arriving by air, train or bus. They have fixed prices: in the centre US$1.10; to the suburbs US$1.25. Trips to Sacsayhuamán US$10; to the ruins of Tambo Machay US$15, 3 hrs; for a whole day trip US$40.

Recommended taxi drivers: José Cuba, Urb Santa Rosa, Pasaje R Gibaja 182, T 226179, who is a guide and can organize tours, accommodation as necessary, he speaks English, his daughter Alejandra is a multilingual tour guide (see Mach Tours above); he parks at the airport during flight hours and at the station to await train arrival. Angel Salazar, Saguán del Cielo B-11, T 224597 to leave messages, English speaking, highly rec, helpful, arranges good tours. José G Valdivia Díaz, T 222210, he is not an official guide but has been recommended as knowledgeable and helpful. Ferdinand Pinares Cuadros, Yuracpunco 155, Tahuantinsuyo, T 225914, English, French and German spoken, reasonable prices, rec. Taxis on call are reliable but expensive, in the centre US$1.25: Radio Car T 222222; El Dorado, T 221414.

**Tourist transport**: to rent a minibus for the day costs US$80 (US$40 for ½-day), inc guide (less without guide), maximum 10 people: ***Gardenias Tours***, José Castillo, T 222828, tours around Cusco; ***Orellana***, Edilberto Orellana, T 239167/225996, tours around Cusco; ***Explorers Transporte***, C Plateros 345, T 233498, to all places in Peru.

**Air** The airport is at Quispiquilla. To **Lima**, 1 hr, daily flights with Faucett, AeroPerú, Americana, Aero Continente and Imperial; there are often promotional offers, eg Aero Continente US$55, Imperial US$50. Grupo Ocho (military) flies every Wed, US$47. Flights are heavily booked on this route in the school holidays (Jan-Feb) and national holidays.

To **Arequipa**, 35 mins, 3 a week with Faucett, daily with Americana (US$53), AeroPerú, Aero Continente and Imperial. To **Juliaca**, US$41, Americana daily, Faucett 3 a week. To **Tacna**, Americana daily. To **Puerto Maldonado**, 45 mins, daily with Americana and AeroPerú, US$38, Imperial US$33. Grupo Ocho has 2 flights a month, US$15, via Iberia from which there is a dry season route to Brazil (see under Iñapari, page 419). As well as the above flights, Americana has daily connections from Cusco to Pucallpa, Iquitos, Trujillo, Chiclayo, Piura and Ayacucho. Special deals may be available if buying tickets for more than one person.

To **La Paz**, AeroPerú flies daily except Sun, US$114.

Airport information T 22611/222601.

Taxi to and from the airport costs US$2.50 (US$3.50 by radio taxi), extra US$0.50 if you enter the car park. Colectivos cost US$0.20 from Plaza San Francisco or outside the airport car park. You can book a hotel at the airport through a travel agency, but this is not really necessary. Many representatives of hotels and travel agencies operate at the airport, with transport to the hotel with which they are associated. Take your time to choose your hotel, at the price you can afford.

**Warning** on the Cusco-Lima route there is a high possibility of cancelled flights during the wet season; tourists are sometimes stranded for several days. It is possible for planes to leave early if the weather is bad. Sit on right side of the aircraft for the best view of the mountains when flying Cusco-Lima; it is worth checking in early to get these seats. Make sure you reconfirm 24 hrs before your flight departure.

**Trains** There are two stations in Cusco. To Juliaca, for the Arequipa and Puno services, trains leave from the Av Sol station. When arriving in Cusco, a tourist bus meets the train to take visitors to hotels whose touts offer rooms on the train. Machu Picchu trains leave from Estación San Pedro, opposite the Santa Ana market.

The train to **Juliaca** leaves at 0800, Mon, Wed, Fri and Sat, arriving at about 2100; sit on the left for the best views. If going to Puno, it is quicker to get off at Juliaca and take a bus or colectivo from there. See under Juliaca for details on the splitting of the train and services to **Arequipa** and **Puno**; also for a description of the three classes of travel. A popular choice is 1st class to Juliaca and then pullman to Arequipa; this will involve changing carriages in Juliaca. Always check on whether the train is running, especially in the rainy season, when services can be reduced or completely cancelled.

Fares: Cusco-Puno, 2nd class US$11, 1st class US$14, pullman US$19, Inca US$23; Cusco-Arequipa, 2nd class US$16, 1st class US$20, pullman US$30, Inca US$46; 23 hrs. Tickets are sold 1 day in advance, open Mon-Sat 0700-1230, 1430-2100, Sun 0900-1200. Tickets sell out quickly and there are queues from 0400 before holidays in the dry season. In the low season tickets to Puno can be bought on the day of departure. You can buy tickets through a travel agent, but check the date and seat number. Meals are served on the train; US$6.50 in pullman.

**Warning** See under Arequipa, but note that 1st class Cusco-Puno is much emptier than Puno-Cusco and therefore more liable to theft.

To Anta, Ollantaytambo, Machu Picchu and Quillabamba, see page 329, 342 and page 346.

**Buses** Most bus offices are in C Pachacútec. To **Juliaca**, 344 km, 12 hrs (longer in the rainy season), US$8, a few buses and trucks do this route daily. The route is in very poor condition since it is not as well-used as the railway. When the train is not running it is necessary to go by bus, but even buses do not run after heavy rain. Continuing to **Puno**, 44 km from Juliaca, 1 hr, US$0.50 (Cruz del Sur, C Pachacútec, Cusco-Puno); see under Puno for more details and routes to La Paz. A tourist bus to Puno in the daytime is worth paying the extra for the views. **NB** It is **not recommended** to take a night bus to Juliaca or Puno, robberies or worse occur on this route.

To **Arequipa**, 521 km, 13-17 hrs, US$10-13, the road is described under Arequipa. Buses travel mostly at night and it's a very cold journey, so take a blanket. See under Arequipa and the relevant sections for continuation to Nasca and Lima. Most buses to **Lima** go via Arequipa, 36-40 hrs, eg Cruz del Sur, 1600, US$17.50, others are cheaper.

To **Abancay**, 195 km, 7 hrs (longer in the rainy season), US$7, several buses and trucks leave daily from Av Arcopata, eg Transcusal 0600, 1000, 1300. The road continues to **Andahuaylas**, 135 km, 5½ hrs minimum, US$5, and on to **Ayacucho**, 252 km, 12 hrs (again longer in the wet), US$8-9. Note that the only direct bus to Andahuaylas leaves at 0300. Most companies will claim that they go direct, but you will have to change in Abancay and wait several hours for another. From Limatambo to Abancay the road is mostly paved and in fairly good condition, otherewise road conditions are poor, but the spectacular scenery compensates.

Continuing from Abancay to **Nasca** via Puquío is in bad shape; Expresso Cusco, Av Grau 820, 3 times a week, US$20, can be up to 2½ days. There are many military checkpoints, but some stunning scenery. Seek advice before taking this route to the coast. There are direct buses from Cusco to Lima.

**Buses to the Sacred Valley**: to Pisac, 32 km, 1 hr, US$0.50; to Calca, 18 km, 30 mins, US$0.10; to Urubamba a further 22 km, 45 mins, US$0.40. Colectivos, minibuses and

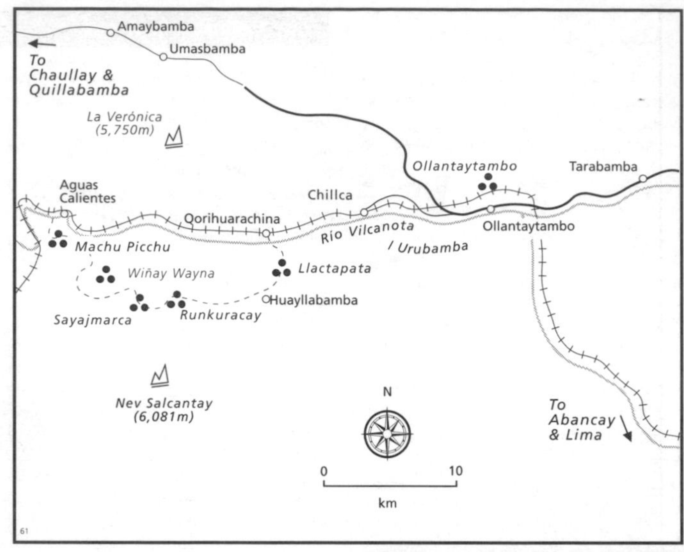


buses leave from bus station at Tullumayo 125 whenever they are full, between 0600 and 1600; also trucks and pick-ups. An organized tour can be fixed up anytime with a travel agent for US$5 pp. Taxis charge about US$25 for the round trip. To Chinchero, 23 km, 45 mins, US$0.45; to Urubamba a further 25 km, 45 mins, US$0.45 (or US$0.85 Cusco-Urubamba direct). Colectivos, minibuses and buses leave from C Arcopata when full, or from Intica-huarina 305, every 20 mins; also from the same place as buses from Cusco via Pisac. Again tours can be arranged to Chinchero, Urubamba and Ollantaytambo with a Cusco travel agency. To Chinchero, US$6 pp; taxi US$25 round trip. Usually only day tours are organized for visits to the valley; see under **Travel Agencies**. Using public transport and staying overnight in Urubamba, Ollantaytambo or Pisac will allow much more time to see the ruins and markets.

For US$50 a taxi can be hired for a whole day (ideally Sun) to take you to Cachimayo, Chinchero, Maras, Urubamba, Ollantaytambo, Calca, Lamay, Coya, Pisac, Tambo Machay, Qenqo and Sacsayhuamán. If you wish to explore this area on your own, Road Map (*Hoja de ruta*) No 10 from the Automóvil Club del Perú is an excellent guide.

## THE SACRED VALLEY

Cusco is at the W end of the gently sloping Cusco valley, which stretches 32 km E as far as Huambutío. This valley, and the partly isolated basin of Anta, NW of Cusco, are densely populated. Also densely populated is the Urubamba valley, stretching from Sicuani (on the railway to Puno) to the gorge of Torontoi, 600m lower, to the NW of Cusco.

The best time to visit is April-May or Oct-Nov. The high season is June-Sept, but the rainy season, from Dec to March, is cheaper and pleasant enough.

## SOUTHEAST FROM CUSCO

There are many interesting villages and ruins on this road. **Tipón** ruins, between the villages of Saylla and Oropesa, include baths, terraces, irrigation systems and a temple complex, accessible from a path leading from just above the last terrace, all in a fine setting.

**Oropesa** church contains a fine ornately carved pulpit. **Huacarpay**, the

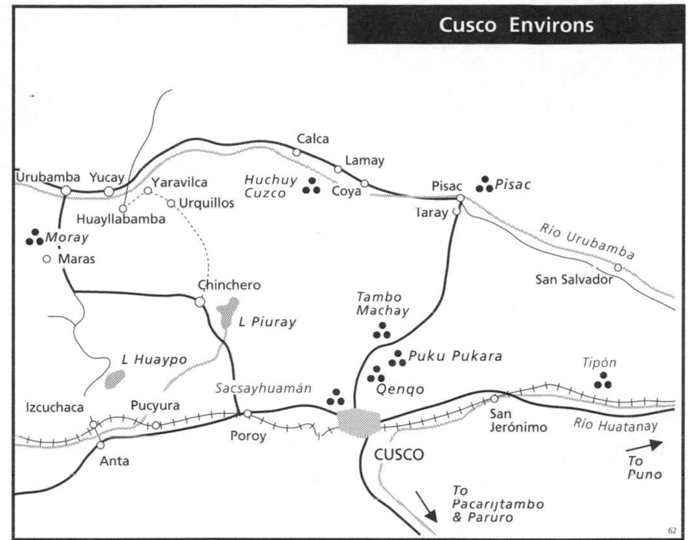


well-preserved ruins of the Inca town of Kañaracy, are nearby, reached from a path behind the Albergue. The site is on Lago Muina, with the *Albergue Urpicañcha* on the shore, offering accommodation and a restaurant. This is a popular place with locals at weekends.

At **Lucre**, 3 km from Huacarpay, there is an interesting textile mill, and many unexplored ruins. Ask the local history teacher, Sr Hernán Flores Yávar, for details. About 3 km from Huacarpay is **C** *El Dorado Inn*, in a converted monastery, some of the rooms are done in a remarkable style and the service is very good.

At **Huambutío**, N of Huacarpay, the road divides; NW to Pisac and N to Paucartambo, on the eastern slope of Andes.

## PAUCARTAMBO

This remote town has become a popular tourist destination. The *Fiesta del Carmen* is a major attraction and well worth seeing (see **Local festivals** page 313 for details). Note that the *Fiesta* dates change and should be checked in advance in Cusco.

- **Accommodation** **G** *Quinta Rosa Marina*, nr the bridge, basic; **G** *Albergue Municipal Carmen de la Virgen*, basic.

- **Transport** Private car hire for a round trip from Cusco on 16 July, US$30; travel agencies in Cusco arrange this. A minibus leaves for Paucartambo from Av Huáscar in Cusco, every other day, US$4.50, 3-4 hrs; alternate days Paucartambo-Cusco. Trucks and a private bus leave from the Coliseo, behind Hospital Segura in Cusco, 5 hrs, US$2.50.

From Paucartambo, in the dry season, you can go 44 km to **Tres Cruces**, along the Pilcopata road, turning left after 25 km. Sr Cáceres in Paucartambo will arrange this trip for you. Tres Cruces gives a wonderful view of the sunrise in June and July and private cars leave Paucartambo between 0100 and 0200 to see it; they may give you a lift.

You can walk from Paucartambo to the *chullpas* of **Machu Cruz** in about an hour, or to the *chullpas* of **Pijchu** (take a guide). You can also visit the Inca for-

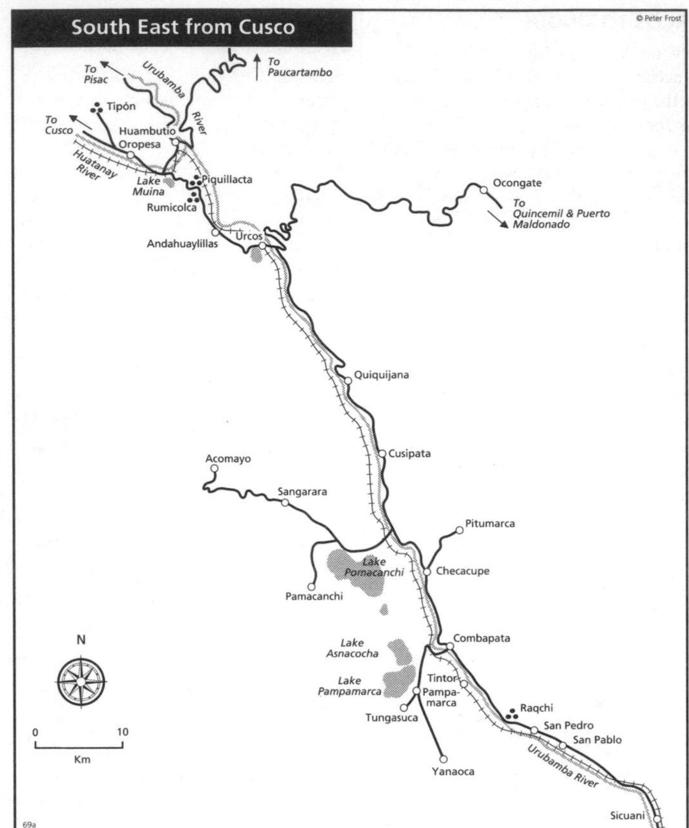


tress of **Huatojto**, which has admirable doorways and stonework. A car will take you as far as Ayre, from where the fortress is a 2-hr walk.

## TO ANDAHUAYLILLAS

Further on from Huacarpay are the Huari (pre-Inca) adobe wall ruins of **Piquillacta**, the monkey temple and the wall of Rumicolca. Piquillacta is quite large, with some reconstruction in progress. Buses to Urcos from Av Huáscar in Cusco will drop you at the entrance on the N side of the complex, though this is not the official entry. Walk through to the official entry and continue to Rumicolca on the other side of the highway. The site is open daily, 0700-1730.

**Andahuaylillas** is a village 32 km SE from Cusco. It boasts a particularly fine early 17th century church, with beautiful frescoes, a splendid doorway and a gilded main altar. Ask for Sr Eulogio; he is a good guide, but speaks Spanish only. Taxis go there, as does the Oropesa bus (from Av Huáscar in Cusco) via Tipón, Piquillacta and Rumicolca. There are other unexcavated ruins just beyond Andahuaylillas.

## URCOS TO TINQUI

Beyond Andahuaylillas is **Urcos**. There is accommodation in municipal rooms on the plaza, or better ones in the 'hotel'; ask for directions.

A spectacular road from Urcos crosses the Eastern Cordillera to Puerto Maldonado in the jungle (see page 413). 47 km after passing the snow-line Hualla-Hualla pass, at 4,820m, the super-hot thermal baths of Marcapata, 173 km from Urcos, provide a relaxing break (entry US$0.10).

82 km from Urcos, at the base of **Nevado Ausangate** (6,384m), is the town of **Ocongate**, which has two hotels on the Plaza de Armas. Beyond Ocongate is **Tinqui**, the starting point for hikes around Ausangate and in the Cordillera Vilcanota. On the flanks of the Nevado Ausangate is Q'Olloriti, where a church has been built close to the snout of a glacier. This place has become a place of pilgrimage (see Cusco **Local festivals**, page 311).

• **Hiking around Ausangate** *Arrieros* and mules can be hired in Tinqui for US$4/day. Make sure you sign a contract with full details. The hike around the mountain of Ausangate takes about 5 days. It is spectacular, but quite hard, with 3 passes over 5,000m, so you need to be acclimatized. It is recommended to take a guide or *arriero*. Buy all food supplies in Cusco. Maps are available at the IGM in Lima or the South American Explorers Club. Some tour companies in Cusco have details about the hike, or check with the Mountain Guide Club, T 226844.

• **Accommodation & transport G** *Hostal Tinqui Guide*, on the right-hand side as you enter the village, friendly, meals available, the owner can arrange guides and horses. From Cusco, take a truck to Tinqui, via Urcos and Ocongate; 172 km, 8 hrs, US$8.

## SOUTHEAST FROM URCOS

**Huaro** has a church whose interior is covered entirely with a colourful mural painting. **Cusipata**, with an Inca gate and wall, is where the ornate bands for the decoration of ponchos are woven. Close by is the Huari hilltop ruin of Llallanmarca.

Between Cusipata and Checacupe a road branches W to **Acomayo**, a pretty village which has a chapel with mural paintings of the 14 Incas. Accommodation is available in *Pensión Aguirre*.

From Acomayo, one can walk to Huáscar, which takes 1 hr, and from there to Pajlia; a climb which leads through very impressive scenery. The canyons of the upper Apurímac are vast beyond imagination. Great cliffs drop thousands of metres into dizzying chasms and huge rocks balance menacingly overhead. The ruins of Huajra Pucará lie near Pajlia. They are small, but in an astonishing position.

• **Transport** to Acomayo, take a Cusco-Sicuani bus or truck, US$1, 1½ hrs, then a truck or bus to Acomayo, 3 hrs, same price. Alternatively, alight at Checacupe and take a truck on to Acomayo.

The church at **Checacupe** is, according to John Hemming, very fine, with good paintings and a handsome carved altar rail.

**Tinta**, 23 km from Sicuani, has a church with brilliant gilded interior and an interesting choir vault.

• **Accommodation & transport F** *Casa Comunal*, dormitory accommodation, clean with good food. There are frequent buses and trucks to Cusco, or take the train from Cusco.

## RAQCHI

Continuing to Sicuani, Raqchi is the scene of the region's great folklore festival in mid-June, when dancers come to Raqchi from all over Peru. Through music and dance they illustrate everything from the ploughing of fields to bull fights.

**John Hemming adds**: "The Viracocha temple is just visible from the train, looking from the distance like a Roman aqueduct. What remains is the central wall, which is adobe above and Inca masonry below. This was probably the largest roofed building ever built by the

Incas. On either side of the high wall, great sloping roofs were supported by rows of unusual round pillars, also of masonry topped by adobe. Entrance to the site is US$2. Nearby is a complex of barracks-like buildings and round storehouses. This was the most holy shrine to the creator god Viracocha, being the site of a miracle in which he set fire to the land – hence the lava flow nearby. There are also small Inca baths in the corner of a field beyond the temple and a straight row of ruined houses by a square. The landscape is extraordinary, blighted by huge piles of black volcanic rocks."

• **Transport** To reach Raqchi, take a bus or truck from Cusco towards Sicuani, US$1.50.

### SOUTH FROM CUSCO

**Pacarijtambo** is a good starting point for the 3-4 hrs' walk to the ruins of **Maukallaqta**, which contain good examples of Inca stonework. From there, one can walk to **Pumaorca**, a high rock carved with steps, seats and a small puma in relief on top. Below this are more Inca ruins.

• **Accommodation & transport** From Cusco, buses and trucks to Pacarijtambo take 4 hrs, US$2. You can find lodging for the night in Pacarijtambo at the house of the Villacorta family and leave for Cusco by truck the next morning. On the way back, you'll pass the caves of Tambo Toco, where a legend says that the four original Inca brothers emerged into the world.

## NORTHWEST FROM CUSCO

### CHINCHERO

**Chinchero** (3,762m), is NW from Cusco on a direct road to Urubamba. It has an attractive church built on an Inca temple. The church is only open Sun for mass. Recent excavations there have revealed many Inca walls and terraces. The site is open daily, 0700-1730, and can be visited on the combined entrance ticket (see page 305). The food market and the handicraft market are separate. The former is held every day, on your left as you come into town. The latter, on Sun only, is up by the church, and though small, is attractive. Chinchero attracts few tourists, except on Sun. The town celebrates the day of the Virgin, on 8 Sept.

• **Accommodation** F *Hotel Inca*, with restaurant.

**Chinchero to Huayllabamba hike**: there is a scenic path from Chinchero to Huayllabamba, a village on the left bank of the Río Urubamba, or Vilcanota, between Yucay and Calca (see below). The hike is quite beautiful, with fine views of the peaks of the Urubamba range, and takes about 3-4 hrs. Follow the old Chinchero-Urubamba dirt road, to the left of the new paved road. Ask the locals when you are not sure. It runs over the pampa, with a good view of Chinchero, then drops down to the Urubamba valley. The end of the hike is about 10 kms before the town of Urubamba. You can either proceed to Urubamaba or back to Cusco.

An alternative hike from Chinchero could be by following the Maras-Moray-Pichingoto salt mines route. This brings you to the main Urubamba valley road, about 10-12 kms beyond the town of Urubamba. You could also take the more direct main road from Chinchero to Urubamba, with occasional shortcuts, but this route is a lot less interesting.

### MORAY

This remote but beautiful site is well worth a visit. There are three 'colosseums', used by the Incas as a sort of open-air crop laboratory, known locally as the greenhouses of the Incas. Peter Frost (*Exploring Cusco*) writes: "There are no great ruined structures here to impress visitors. Moray is more for the contemplative traveller with an affinity for such phenomena as the Nasca Lines, the stone rings of Avebury and the menhirs of Brittany."

• **Access** The easiest and most interesting way to get to Moray is from Urubamba via the Pichingoto bridge over the Río Urubamba. The climb up from the bridge is fairly steep but easy, with great views of Nevado Chicon. The path passes by the spectacular Maras salt pans, which are still in production after thousands of years. Moray is about 1½ hrs further on. The *Hotel Valle Sagrado de los Inkas* in Urubamba can arrange horses and guide and a pick-up truck for the return; US$30-40 pp (see page 334). Alternatively, wait for a pickup on the bridge on the Chinchero road. This will take you near to Maras. Walk to Maras (30 mins) and on through it, bearing left a little, and ask directions to Moray; 1½ hrs walk in total. Hitching back to Urubamba is quite easy, but there are no hotels at all in the area, so take care not to be stranded.

At **Tiobamba**, near Maras, a fascinating indigenous market-festival is held on 15 Aug, where Sacred Valley yellow maize is exchanged for pottery from Lake Titicaca.

## WEST FROM CUSCO

The Cusco-Machu Picchu train reaches the heights N of the city by a series of switchbacks and then descends to the floor of the Anta basin, with its herds of cattle. In **Anta** itself, felt trilby hats are on sale. *Restaurant Dos de Mayo* is good. Bus to Anta, US$0.30.

The railway goes through the Anta canyon for 10 km, and then, at a sharp angle, the Urubamba canyon, and descends along the river valley, flanked by high cliffs and peaks.

76 km from Cusco, beyond Anta, on the Abancay road, 2 km before Limatambo at the ruins of **Tarahuasi**, a few hundred metres from the road, is a very well-preserved **Inca temple platform**, with 28 tall niches, and a long stretch of fine polygonal masonry. The ruins are impressive, enhanced by the orange lichen which give the walls a beautiful honey colour.

Dr Ken Heffernan, Turner, ACT, Australia, writes: "The ruins at Tarahuasi were part of of the Inca *Tanpu* called 'Limatambo' in the 16th century, along the road to the famous Apurímac bridge. The lands immediately surrounding the *tanpu* were then claimed by a son of Huayna Capac, Cristóbal Paullu Inca and his wife, Doña Catalina Tocto Usica. The extent of Inca agricultural terraces in the valley of Limatambo and Mollepata exceeds 100 ha."

• **Accommodation & places to eat In Limatambo**: **F** *Albergue*; there is also a nice restaurant hidden from the road by trees.

100 km from Cusco along the Abancay road is the exciting descent into the Apurímac canyon, near the former Inca suspension bridge that inspired Thornton Wilder's *The Bridge of San Luis Rey*. Also, 153 km along the road to Abancay from Cusco, near Curahuasi, famous for its anise herb, is the stone of **Sahuite**, carved with animals, houses, etc, which appears to be a relief map of an Indian village. Unfortunately, 'treasure hunters' have defaced the stone. There are other interesting carvings in the area around the Sahuite stone.

• **Accommodation & places to eat In Curahuasi**: camping is possible on the football pitch, but ask the police for permission. There is a restaurant on the main road into town.

## THE URUBAMBA VALLEY

From Cusco a paved road climbs to the pass, continues over the pampa before descending into the Urubamba valley. It crosses the river by bridge at Pisac and follows the N bank of river to the end of the paved road at Ollantaytambo. It passes through Calca, Yucay and Urubamba (also reached from Cusco by the beautiful, direct road through Chinchero, described above). There is always transport, and it is always full. A word of advice for those arriving in Cusco by air: it makes a lot of sense to get down to the Valley, at 2,800m compared to Cusco's 3,400m, and make the most of your first couple of days. There are 3 good hotels in Urubamba and Yucay. At this relatively low altitude you will experience no headaches and you can eat and sleep comfortably.

## PISAC

30 km N of Cusco, high above the town, on the mountainside, is a superb Inca fortress. Pisac has a Sun morning market, described as touristy and expensive, which comes to life after the arrival of tourist buses around 1000, and is usually over by 1500. Pisac has other, somewhat less crowded, less expensive markets on Tues and Thurs morning. It's best to get there before 0900. On the plaza are the church and a small interesting Museo Folklórico. The town is worth strolling around, and while you're doing so, look for the fine façade at Grau 485. There are many souvenir shops on Bolognesi. Local fiesta: 15 July.

### Pisac ruins

There is transport up to the archaeological site on market days only so, at other times, you must walk, at least 1 hr uphill all the way. Horses are available for US$3 pp, but travellers with a couple of dollars to spare should get a taxi from near the bridge up to the ruins and walk back down. A van from the plaza to the ruins costs US$2.50 each way. The walk up to the ruins begins from the plaza, past the Centro de Salud and a new control post.

The path goes through working terraces, giving the ruins a context. The first group of buildings is Pisaqa, with a fine curving wall. Climb then to the central part of the ruins, the Intihuatana group of temples and rock outcrops in the most magnificent Inca masonry. Here are the Reloj Solar ('Hitching Post of the Sun') – now closed because thieves stole a piece from it, palaces of the moon and stars, solstice markers, baths and water channels. From Intihuatana, a path leads around the hillside through a tunnel to Q'Allaqasa, the 'military area'. Across the valley at this point, a large area of Inca tombs in holes in the hillside can be seen. The end of the site is Kanchiracay, where the agricultural workers were housed. Road transport approaches from this end. For full details, see Peter Frost's *Exploring Cusco*.

The descent takes 30 mins. At dusk you will hear, if not see, the *pisaca* (partridges), after which the place is named. If lucky you will also see deer. To appreciate the site fully, allow 5 hrs if going on foot. If you do not show your multi-site ticket, or pay US$2.25, on the way up, you will be asked to do so by the warden. The site is open 0700-1730; guides charge US$5.

### Tours

You can continue the Sun morning tour to Pisac along the Urubamba to Ollantaytambo, with lunch at Yucay or at the *Hotel Valle Sagrado de Los Inkas* (or elsewhere) in Urubamba. Tours from Cusco usually allow only 1½ hrs at Pisac. This is not enough time to take in the ruins and splendid scenery. Apart from Sun when Pisac is crowded, there are very few tourists. If you're not interested in the market, it would be a good idea to ask the driver to do the tour clockwise, Chinchero, Ollantaytambo, then Pisac, thereby missing the crowds.

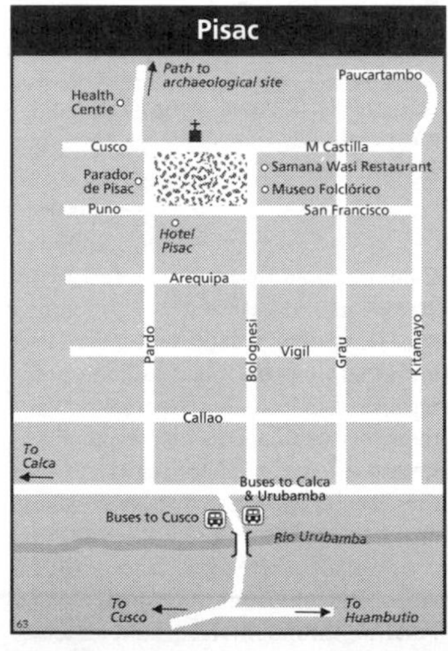

## A market for beads

A major feature of Pisac's popular market is the huge and varied collection of multi-coloured beads on sale. Though commonly called 'Inca beads', this is something of a misnomer. For although the Incas were highly talented potters and decorated their ware with detailed geometric motifs, they are not known to have made ceramic beads.

These attractive items have become popular relatively recently. They used to be rolled individually by hand and were very time-consuming to produce. Now, in a major concession to consumerism, they are machine-made and produced in quantity, then hand-painted and glazed.

Today, the clay beads are produced in countless, often family-run, workshops in Cusco and Pisac. Some are made into earrings, necklaces and bracelets, but many thousands are sold loose.

## Local information

**● Accommodation**

**D** pp *Pisaq*, Pardo y Arequipa, on the plaza in front of the church and marketplace, T (084) 203062, recently renovated, run by a young couple, Roman Vizcarra and his wife Fielding Wood from New Mexico, 15 rooms, 3 with private bath, price with shared bath is **E** pp, hot water, clean, pleasant decor, sauna, friendly, knowledgeable, meals available at the hotel's café on the plaza, good homemade pizza, rec. A new 5-star hotel, ***Royal Inca III***, opened mid-1996, 1 km out of town, a converted hacienda with 75 rooms, pool, sauna, Jacuzzi, phone the ***Royal Inca I*** or ***II*** in Cusco for further details.

**● Places to eat**

*Samana Wasi*, on the plaza, reasonable. Good, cheap trout is available in many restaurants. The bakery at Mcal Castilla 372 sells excellent cheese and onion *empanadas* for US$0.25, suitable for vegetarians, and good wholemeal bread.

## PISAC TO URUBAMBA

**Calca**, 2,900m, is 18 km beyond Pisac. The plaza is divided in two: Urubamba buses stop on one side; and Cusco and Pisac buses on the other side of the dividing strip. Look out for the *api* sellers with their bicycles loaded with steaming kettle and assortment of bottles, glasses and tubs. The *Fiesta de la Vírgen Asunta* is held on 15-16 Aug.

It is a 2-day hike from Cusco to Calca, via Sacsayhuamán, Qenqo, Puka Pukará, Tambo Machay and Huchuy Cusco with excellent views of the Eastern Cordilleras, past small villages and along beautifully built Inca paths. There are many places to camp, but take water. At **Coya**, between Calca and Pisac, there's a fiesta during 14-18 Aug.

**● Accommodation** There are a couple of very basic hotels. One is opposite the market place, 1 block from the plaza, **G** *Hostal Martín*, dirty, cold water only; also **E** *Hostal Pitusiray*, on the edge of town. There are some basic restaurants around the plaza.

**● Guides** Walter Góngora Arizábal, T 202124, is a kombi driver who does private trips; US$31 to Cusco, US$18 to Pisac, including wait.

There are mineral baths (cold) at **Minas Maco**, 30 mins' walk along the Urubamba, and at **Machacancha**, 8 km E of Calca. If you continue past Minas Maco, and bear right up a small footpath leading by a clump of trees, the first house you come to after crossing a small stream and climbing a hill is a precolumbian ruin. 3 km beyond Machacancha are the Inca ruins of **Arquasmarca**. The ruins of a small Inca town, **Huchuy Cusco**, are across the Río Urubamba, and up a stiff climb, 3 to 4 hrs. There is a 2-storey house, paved with flat stones, and a large stone reservoir at Huchuy Cusco.

Between Calca and Yucay a bridge crosses the river to the village of **Huayllabamba**. E along the bank of the river, near the community of Urquillos, on a working maize farm is **A1** *Posada-Hacienda Yarivilca*, due open in mid-late 1997. Due open earlier in 1997 is **Albergue Hacienda Urpi Wata**, on the headwaters of the Río Urquillos just below Chinchero; this is also a working farm, with maize and milk/cheese production. **Urpi Wata** will accommodate both backpackers and other guests; visitors to the farm are welcome at any time. Both hotels are run by Tierras Atlas SA (managing director Scotsman Ken Duncan); further information in Cusco, at Las Nazarenas 211, T 232829; or Lima: Los Pinos 584, San Isidro, Lima 27, T/F 440-5476.

## YUCAY

3 km E of Urubamba, Yucay has two grassy plazas divided by the restored colonial church of Santiago Apóstol, with its oil paintings and fine altars. On the opposite side from Plaza Manco II is the adobe palace built for Sayri Túpac (Manco's son) when he emerged from Vilcabamba in 1558.

• **Accommodation** On the same plaza as the adobe palace mentioned above is the **A2** *Posada del Inca*, a converted 300-year-old monastery, T 201107, price includes tax, it is like a little village with plazas, chapel, different types of room (all well-appointed), restaurant, conference centre and a museum with the owner's private collection of pre-Inca ceramics, gold and silver pieces and weavings. Also **B-C** *Hostal Y'Llary*, on Plaza Manco II, T 201112, with bath, inc breakfast.

In Yucay monks sell fresh milk, ham, eggs and other dairy produce from their farm on the hillside. Behind *Posada del Inca* a steep trail leads up a river valley to the "Black Lake", at the foot of Nevado San Juan. The circuit continues down to Huayllabamba. It is a day's hike in total.

## URUBAMBA

Like many places along the valley, Urubamba (*Alt* 2,863m) is in a fine setting with snow-capped peaks in view and enjoys a mild climate. The main plaza, with a fountain capped by a maize cob, is surrounded by buildings painted blue. Calle Berriozabal, on the W edge of town, is lined with pisonay trees. The large market square is 1 block W of the main plaza. The main road skirts the town and the bridge for the road to Chinchero is just to the E of town.

### Places of interest

A visit to the ceramics workshop of Pablo Seminario, who uses precolumbian techniques and designs, is highly recommended. He can be found at M Castilla cuadra 9 y Zavala, T 201002.

### Excursions

6 km W of Urubamba is the village of **Tarabamba**, where a bridge crosses the Río Urubamba. If you turn right after the bridge you'll come to Pichingoto, a tumbled-down village built under an overhanging cliff. Also, just over the bridge and before the town to the left of a small,

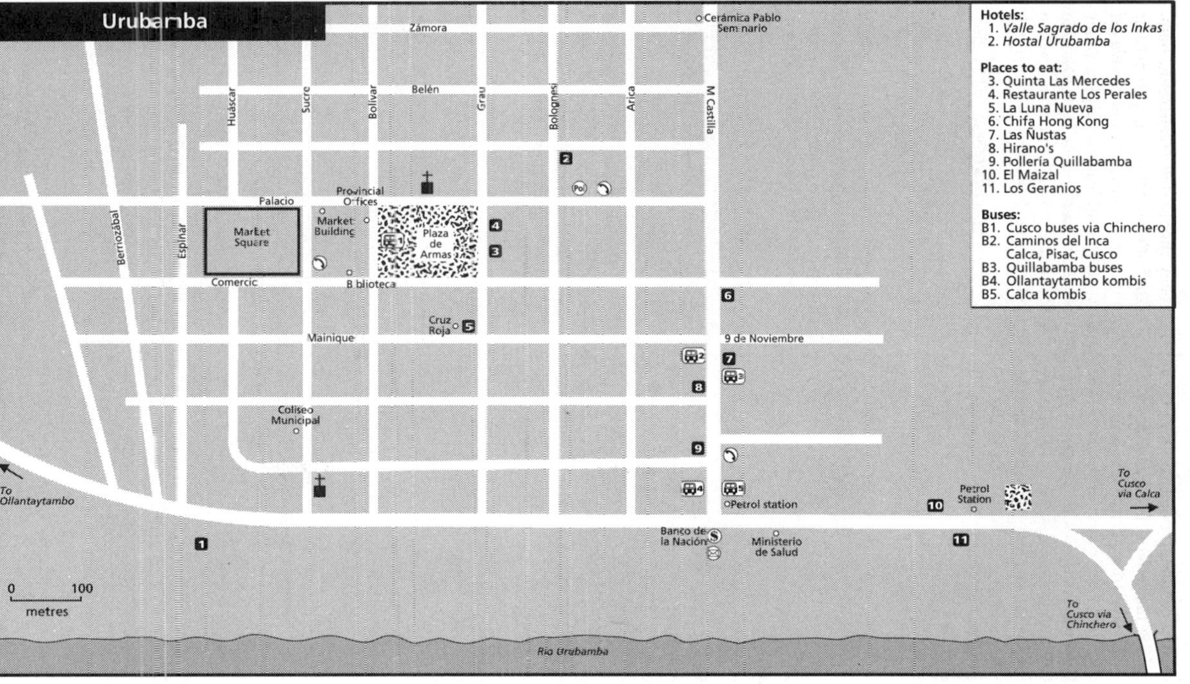
Urubamba
Hotels:
1. Valle Sagrado de los Inkas
2. Hostal Urubamba
Places to eat:
3. Quinta Las Mercedes
4. Restaurante Los Perales
5. La Luna Nueva
6. Chifa Hong Kong
7. Las Ñustas
8. Hirano's
9. Pollería Quillabamba
10. El Maizal
11. Los Geranios
Buses:
B1. Cusco buses via Chinchero
B2. Caminos del Inca Calca, Pisac, Cusco
B3. Quillabamba buses
B4. Ollantaytambo kombis
B5. Calca kombis
Cerámica Pablo Seminario
Zámora
Belén
Huáscar
Sucre
Bolivar
Grau
Bolognesi
Arica
M Castilla
Palacio
Provincial Offices
Market Building
Market Square
Plaza de Armas
Berriozábal
Espinar
Comercio
Biblioteca
Cruz Roja
Mainique
9 de Noviembre
Coliseo Municipal
Pol
Petrol station
Petrol Station
Banco de la Nación
Ministerio de Salud
To Ollantaytambo
To Cusco via Calca
To Cusco via Chinchero
0
100
metres
Río Urubamba

walled cemetery is a salt stream. Follow the footpath beside the stream and you'll come to Salinas, a small village below which are a mass of terraced Inca salt pans which are still in operation. It's a very spectacular sight as there are over 5,000. The walk to the salt pans takes about 30 minutes. Take water as this side of the valley can be very hot and dry.

## Local festivals

May and June are the harvest months, with many processions following mysterious ancient schedules. Urubamba's main festival, *El Señor de Torrechayoc*, takes place during the first week of June.

## Local information

### ● Accommodation

**A2** *Valle Sagrado de los Inkas* (ex-*Turistas*, being upgraded), 5 minutes' walk from the centre, special rates available, 67 comfortable bungalows with gardens, 15 suites and 50 rooms, English-owned, restaurant, bar, disco, 2 pools, T 201126/27, F 201071, there are plans for a rail shuttle to Machu Picchu (1996-97), also horse riding (eg to Moray), mountain biking, kayaking, rafting; **A2-3** ***Turquesa***, 20 mins' walk from town, towards Yucay, small pool, restaurant, buffet on Tues/Thur/Sun US$3.50, room service, comfortable, part of San Agustín chain, reservations at *San Agustín Internacional* in Cusco; **D** pp ***Hostal Urpihuasi***, without private bath, **C** pp with full board, pleasant modern rooms, clean, friendly, small outdoor pool, sauna, quiet and relaxing, recommended (manager Rae Pieraccini runs a project for street children, financed by the hotel's income); **E** pp ***Hostal Rumichaca***, 3 km W of Urubamba, back from the Rumichaca bus stop, full board, beautiful location, vegetarian food available, run by Martín and Ada, Martín is also a mountain guide, Ada is a great cook and "does a mean pisco sour", great place to relax.

In the town of Urubamba: **F** ***Hostal Urubamba***, Bolognesi, basic, pleasant, cold water.

### ● Places to eat

Several restaurants on M Castilla: *Hirano's*, good food; *Las Ñustas*, corner of Mainique. ***Luna Nueva***, Grau y Mainique, homemade pasta, good food and atmosphere, live music, rec. On the main road, before the bridge, are: ***Quinta los Geranios***, excellent lunch for US$3 with more than enough food; and ***El Maizal***, which is OK.

### ● Services

Banco de la Nación, with Correos behind it, is on the main road, opposite the petrol station at M Castilla.

### ● Transport

From Urubamba to Calca, Pisac (US$0.80, 1 hr) and Cusco, about 2 hrs, US$1, with Caminos del Inca, M Castilla y Mainique, from 0530; buses to Cusco via Chinchero leave from the W side of the plaza. El Señor de Huanca kombis run to Calca from the petrol station on M Castilla when full between 0700 and 1900; from the opposite side of the street kombis run to Ollantaytambo, 45 mins, US$0.30. Buses to Quillabamba from M Castilla outside *Hirano's*.

## OLLANTAYTAMBO

The Inca town, or Llacta, on which the present-day town is based (*Alt* 2,800m) is clearly seen in the fine example of Inca *canchas* (blocks), which are almost entirely intact and still occupied behind the main plaza.

Entering Ollantaytambo from Pisac, the road is built along the long wall of 100 niches. Note the inclination of the wall: it leans towards the road. Since it was the Incas' practice to build with the walls leaning towards the interiors of the buildings, it has been deduced that the road, much narrower then, was built inside a succession of buildings. The road out of the plaza leads across a bridge, down to the colonial church with its enclosed *recinto*. Beyond is a plaza (and car park) with entrances to the archaeological site, which is open 0700-1730.

The so-called **Baño de la Ñusta** (bath of the princess) is of grey granite, and is in a small area between the town and the temple fortress. Some 200m behind the Baño de la Ñusta along the face of the mountain are some small ruins known as Inca Misanca, believed to have been a small temple or observatory. A series of steps, seats and niches have been carved out of the cliff. There is a complete irrigation system, including a canal at shoulder level, some 6 inches deep, cut out of the sheer rock face (under renovation).

The flights of terraces leading up above the town are superb, and so are the curving terraces following the contours of the rocks overlooking the Urubamba. These terraces were successfully defended by Manco Inca's warriors against Hernando Pizarro in 1536. Manco Inca built the defensive wall above the site and another wall closing the Yucay valley against attack from Cusco. These are still visible on either side of the valley.

The temple itself was started by Pachacuti, using Colla Indians from Lake Titicaca – hence the similarities of the monoliths facing the central platform with the Tiahuanaco remains. The Colla are said to have deserted half-way through the work, which explains the many unfinished blocks lying about the site.

Admission is by combined entrance ticket, which can be bought at the site, otherwise US$2. If possible arrive very early, 0700, before the tourists. The guide book *Ollantaytambo* by Víctor Angles Vargas is available in Cusco bookshops, and Peter Frost's *Exploring Cusco* is also useful. Ask for Dr Hernán Amat Olazábal, a leading Inca-ologist, at the Parador for further explanation. The museum in the Parador was due to open in 1996.

Recently a "pyramid" has been identified on the W side of the main ruins of Ollantaytambo. Its discoverers, Fernando and Edgar Elorietta, claim it is the real Pacaritambo, from where the 4 original Inca brothers emerged to found their empire, contrary to the more popular legend (see page 328). Whether this is the case or not, it is still a first-class piece of engineering with great terraced fields and a fine 750m wall aligned with the rays of the winter solstice, on 21 June.

The mysterious "pyramid", which covers 50-60 hectares, can be seen properly from the other side of the river. This is a pleasant, easy 1-hr walk, W from the Puente Inca, just outside the town. You'll also be rewarded with great views of the Sacred Valley and the river, with the snowy peaks of the Verónica massif as a backdrop.

## Excursions

A major excavation project has been car-

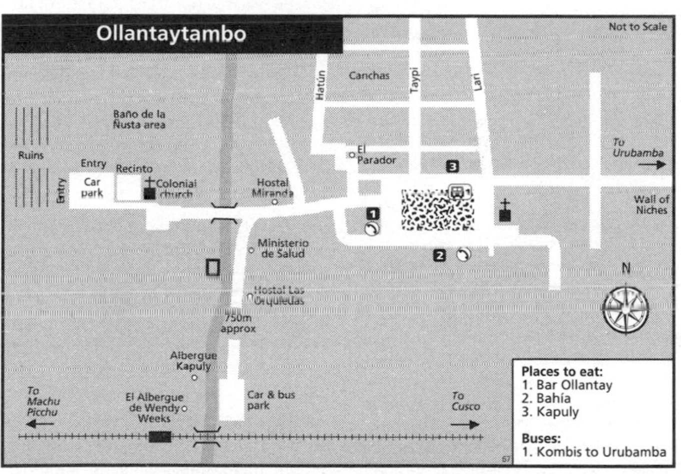

ried out since 1977 under the direction of Ann Kendall in the **Cusichaca** valley, 26 km from Ollantaytambo, at the intersection of the Inca routes. Only 9 km of this road is passable by ordinary car. The Inca fort, Huillca Raccay, was excavated in 1978-80, and work is now concentrated on Llactapata, a site of domestic buildings. Ann Kendall is now working in the Patacancha valley NE of Ollantaytambo. Excavations are being carried out in parallel with the restoration of Inca canals to bring fresh clean water to the settlements in the valley.

Pinculluna, the mountain above Ollantaytambo, can be climbed with no mountaineering experience, although there are some difficult stretches – allow 2-3 hrs going up. The path is difficult to make out; best not to go on your own. Walk up the valley to the left of the mountain, which is very beautiful and impressive, with Inca terraces after 4 km.

## Local festivals

The Sun following Inti Raymi, there is a colourful festival, the **Ollanta-Raymi**. On 6 Jan there is the festival of Reyes (the Three Wise Men), with music, dancing, processions. Around 26 Oct there is a 2-day, weekend festival with lots of dancing in traditional costume and many local delicacies for sale.

## Local information

### ● Accommodation

**D** pp *El Albergue*, next to, and access via, the railway station, T/F (084) 204014, or in Cusco at Expediciones Manu, T 226671, manager Wendy Weeks (American), 6 rooms, charming, homely, with sauna, meals available on request, convenient for Machu Piccu train, good place for information, highly rec. Next door is **D** *Albergue Kapuly*; **E** *Hostal Chuza*, 3 minutes below the main plaza, new, very clean, friendly, rec; **E-F** *Hostal Miranda*, between the main plaza and the ruins, with shower, basic, friendly, clean; **G** pp *Alojamiento Yavar*, 1½ blocks from the main plaza, if they're full, they'll let you sleep on the floor for free, basic, friendly, no water in the evening, they have information on horse riding in the area.

### ● Places to eat

There are several restaurants on the Plaza: *Bahía*, on the S side of Plaza, very friendly, vegetarian dishes on request.

### ● Sports

**Horse riding**: horses can be hired for US$5/day; a gentle day's ride or hike is to La Marca, along the beautiful river valley; ask Wendy Weeks for details. You can also visit the Inca quarry on the other side of the river.

### ● Transport

For those travelling by car and intending to go to Machu Picchu, it is recommended to leave the car at Ollantaytambo railway station, which costs US$1/day; ask Wendy Weeks at *El Albergue* for details. Check in advance the time trains pass through here. It's best to have your ticket in advance. The Ollantaytambo ticket office has to check if there's room on the train. Both the tourist and local trains stop on the way to and from Machu Picchu. The station is 10-15 minutes' walk from the plaza. There are colectivos at the plaza for the station when trains are due.

## THE INCA TRAIL TO MACHU PICCHU

The spectacular 3 to 5 day hike runs from Km 88, Qorihuayrachina (2,299m), a point immediately after the first tunnel 22 km beyond Ollantaytambo station. A sturdy suspension bridge has now been built over the Urubamba River. An entrance ticket for the trail must be bought at Km 88, which costs US$17. There is a 50% discount for students, but note that officials are very strict, only an ISIC card will be accepted as proof of status. It also gives entry to Machu Picchu if you get it stamped there. Guided tours often start at Km 83; check whether the price includes site entrance.

### ● Equipment

The trail is rugged and steep (beware of landslides), but the magnificent views compensate for any weariness which may be felt. It is cold at night, however, and weather conditions change rapidly, so it is important to take not only strong footwear, rain gear and warm clothing but also food, water, insect repellent,

### In the footsteps of the Incas

The wonder of Machu Picchu has been well documented over the years. Equally impressive is the centuries-old Inca Trail that winds its way from the Sacred Valley near Ollantaytambo. Thousands hike this trail each year, taking 3 to 4 days to cover the 43 km from Km 88 on the Cusco-Quillabamba railway, to Machu Picchu.

What makes this hike so special is the stunning combination of Inca ruins, unforgettable views, magnificent mountains, exotic vegetation and extraordinary ecological variety. The government acknowledged this uniqueness in 1981 by including the trail in a 325 sq km national park, the Machu Picchu Historical Sanctuary.

Machu Picchu itself cannot be understood without the Inca Trail. Its principal sites are ceremonial in character, apparently in ascending hierarchical order. This Inca province was a unique area of elite access. The trail is essentially a work of spiritual art, like a gothic cathedral, and walking it was formerly an act of devotion.

The long journey to the sacred site begins at Cusco's San Pedro rail station in the early hours to catch the first train. It's every man, woman and backpacker for themselves in the sheer chaos that greets the opening of the ticket window. If you can survive the suffocating crush and mad scramble for tickets and seats then you're probably well-equipped to cope with the rigours of the trail. A bumpy 3 hr ride later the train reaches **Qorihuayrachina** – or Km 88 – at 2,600m, which is the disembarkation point for the intrepid trekker.

The first ruin is **Llaqtapata**, near Km 88, the utilitarian centre of a large settlement of farming terraces which probably supplied the other Inca trail sites. From here, it is a relatively easy 3-hr walk to the village of **Huayllabamba**. A series of gentle climbs and descents leads along the Río Cusichaca, the ideal introduction to the trail. The village is a popular camping spot for tour groups, so it's a better idea to continue for about an hour up to the next site, **Llulluchayoc** – "three white stones" – which is a patch of green beside a fast-flowing stream. It's a steep climb but you're pretty much guaranteed a decent pitch for the night. If you're feeling really energetic, you can go on to the next camping spot, a perfectly flat meadow, called **Llulluchapampa.** This means a punishing 1½ hr ascent through cloud forest, but it does leave you with a much easier second day. There's also the advantage of relative isolation and a magnificent view back down the valley.

For most people the second day is by far the toughest, though horses can be hired en route to carry your backpack. It's a steep climb to the meadow, followed by an exhausting 2½ hr haul up to the first pass – aptly named **Warmiwañusqa**

a supply of plastic bags, coverings, a good sleeping bag, a torch/flashlight and a stove for preparing hot food and drink to ward off the cold at night. A stove using paraffin (kerosene) is preferable, as fuel can be bought in small quantities in markets. Camping gas (white gas) is available in hardware stores in Cusco, US$1.50/litre. A tent is essential, but if you're hiring one in Cusco, check carefully for leaks. Walkers who have not taken adequate equipment have died of exposure. Caves marked on some maps are little better than overhangs, and are not sufficient shelter to sleep in. You could also take a first-aid kit; if you don't need it the porters probably will, given their rather basic footwear.

All the necessary equipment can be rented; see page 320 under **Travel agencies**. Good maps of the Trail and area can be bought from the South American Explorers Club in Lima. If you have any doubts about carrying your own pack, reasonably-priced porters/guides are available, most reliably through Cusco agencies. You can also hire porters in Ollantaytambo; speak to the men in the plaza wearing red ponchos. Expect to pay US$7/day plus basic foodstuffs. Carry a day-pack nonetheless in case you walk faster than the porters

(Dead Woman) – at 4,200m. The feeling of relief on reaching the top is immense and there's the added, sadistic pleasure of watching your fellow sufferers struggling in your wake. After a well-earned break it's a sharp descent on a treacherous path down to the Pacamayo valley, where there are a few flat camping spots near a stream if you're too weary to continue.

Halfway to the second pass, comes the ruin of **Runkuracay**, which was probably an Inca tambo, or post-house. It is no longer permitted to camp here. A steep climb up an Inca staircase leads to the next pass, at 3,850m, with spectacular views of Pumasillo (6,246m) and the Vilcabamba range. The trail then desends to **Sayacmarca** (Inaccessible town), a spectacular site overlooking the Aobamba valley. Just below Sayacmarca lies **Conchamarca** (Shell town), a small group of buildings standing on rounded terraces – perhaps another tambo.

A blissfully gentle 2-hr climb on a fine stone highway, leads through an Inca tunnel and along the enchanted fringes of the cloud forest, to the third pass. This is the most rewarding part of the trail, with spectacular views of the entire Vilcabamba range, and it's worth taking the time to dwell on the wonders of nature. Then it's down to the extensive ruins of **Phuyupatamarca** (Cloud-level town), at 3,650m, where adjacent Inca observation platforms offer awesome views of nearby Salcantay (6,270m) and surrounding peaks. There is a 'tourist bathroom' here, where water can be collected, but purify it before drinking.

From here an Inca stairway of white granite plunges more than three thousand feet to the spectacularly-sited and impressive ruins of **Wiñay-Wayna** (Forever Young), offering views of newly uncovered agricultural terraces at **Intipata** (Sun place). A trail, not easily visible, goes from Wiñay-Wayna to the newly-discovered terracing. There is a "tourist complex" at Wiñay-Wayna, with bunk beds (F pp), showers and a small restaurant, but the place is in state of disrepair and facilities are appallingly run down. Should you forego the dubious privilege of using the sleeping facilities, there is enough space for a few tents. After Wiñay-Wayna there is no water, and no place to camp, until Machu Picchu.

From here it is a gentle hour's walk through another type of forest, with larger trees and giant ferns, to a steep Inca staircase which leads up to **Intipunku** (Sun gate), where you look down at last upon Machu Picchu, basking in all her reflective glory. Aching muscles are quickly forgotten and even the presence of the functional hotel building cannot detract from one of the most magical sights in all the Americas. (Peter Frost, 1996)

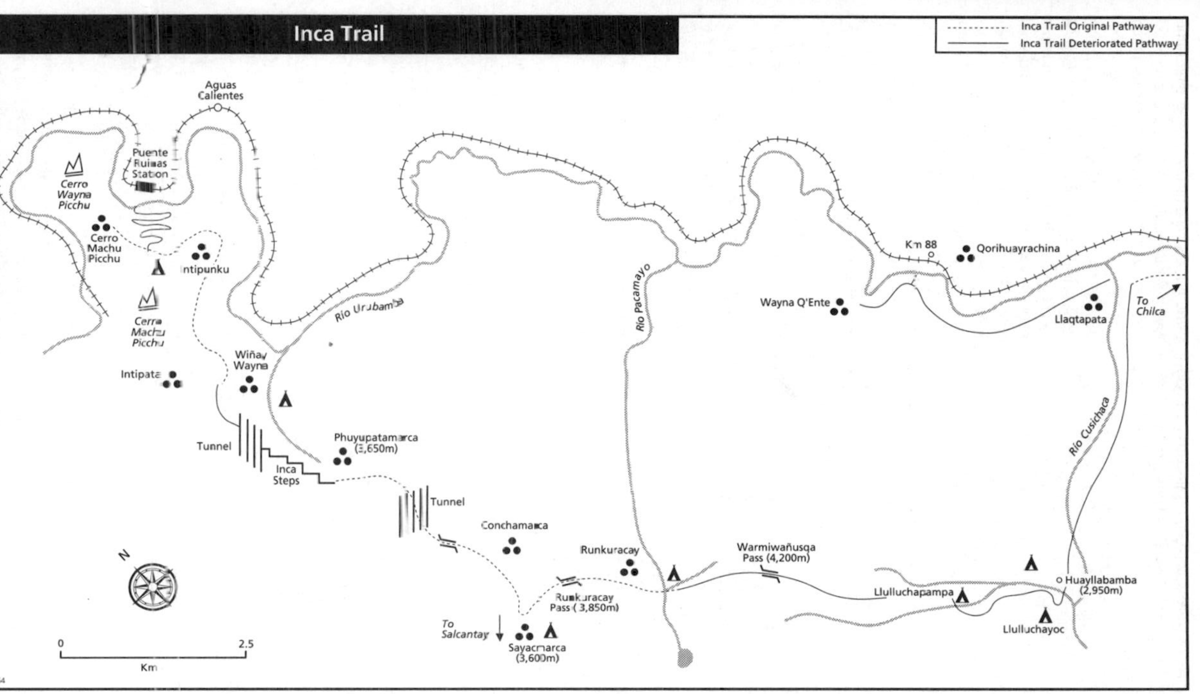
Inca Trail
Inca Trail Original Pathway
Inca Trail Deteriorated Pathway
Aguas Calientes
Puente Ruinas Station
Cerro Wayna Picchu
Cerro Machu Picchu
Intipunku
Cerro Machu Picchu
Intipata
Wiñay Wayna
Río Urubamba
Tunnel
Inca Steps
Phuyupatamarca (3,650m)
Tunnel
Conchamarca
Río Pacamayo
Runkuracay
Runkuracay Pass (3,850m)
To Salcantay
Sayacmarca (3,600m)
Warmiwañusqa Pass (4,200m)
Llulluchapampa
Huayllabamba (2,950m)
Llulluchayoc
Río Cusichaca
Km 88
Qorihuayrachina
Wayna Q'Ente
Llaqtapata
To Chilca
N
0
2.5
Km
64

and you have to wait for them to catch you up.

### ● Tours

You can do the Inca Trail independently or with a Travel Agency in Cusco who will arrange transport to the start, equipment, food, etc, for an all-in price, generally around US$60-70 pp. Agency treks range from the more expensive, with smaller groups, better equipment and transport arrangements, to cheaper, cost-cutting outfits with large groups and basic gear. Almost everyone reports that things do not go to plan. Most complaints are minor, but do check equipment carefully. Ask around for people who have done the trip and take supplemental food and water. Do not accept under-age porters or inexperienced guides.

### ● Transport

Only the local train stops at Km 88; about 3 hrs after leaving Cusco. The tourist train does not stop here. Be ready to get out at Km 88, at the village called Chamana, as it's easy to pass it; from Ollantaytambo US$0.80. If you do not wish to travel on the local train, the simplest method is to go to Ollantaytambo, or Chillca and start walking from there.

From Ollantaytambo it takes about 8 hrs to the start of the Inca Trail: follow the railway in the direction of Machu Picchu until you come to Chillca village where you can cross the river. Sometimes there is a truck going to Chillca. From Chillca to the start of the Trail takes 5 hrs: climb up to a path that runs parallel to the river. This is an original Inca trail (still in use) that leads to Llaqtapata on the Inca Trail. **Warning** It's best not to spend a night on this trail. Theft is possible because you have to sleep near the villages.

### ● General information & advice

Get to Machu Picchu as early as possible, preferably before 0830 for best views but in any case before the tourist train arrives at 1030. **NB** Camping is not allowed at Intipunku; guards may confiscate your tent. You can, however, go down through Machu Picchu (your ticket will be stamped but you can use it the next day) to a patch of grass 300-500m past the hotel, where you can camp free. There is water at a tap 100m further down and meals are available at the small house nearby.

4 days would make a comfortable trip (though much depends on the weather) and you would not find yourself too tired to enjoy what you see. **NB** You are not allowed to walk back along the trail, though you can pay US$4.50 at Intipunku to be allowed to walk back as far as Wiñay-Wayna. You cannot take backpacks into Machu Picchu; leave them at ticket office, US$0.50.

**NB** The first 2 days of the Trail involve the stiffest climbing, so do not attempt it if you're feeling unwell. Try to camp in groups at night, leave all your valuables in Cusco and keep everything inside your tent, even your shoes. Security has, however, improved in recent years. Avoid the July-Aug high season and the rainy season from Nov to April (note that this can change, check in advance). In the wet it is cloudy and the paths are very muddy and difficult. Also watch out for coral snakes in this area (black, red, yellow bands).

Due to regular clean-ups the trail is usually litter free. To keep it this way, please remove all your rubbish, including toilet paper, or use the pits provided. Do not light open fires as they can get out of control. The Earth Preservation Fund sponsors an annual clean-up July-Aug: volunteers should write to EPF, Inca Trail Project, Box 7545, Ann Arbor, Michigan 48107, USA. Preserving the Inca Trail: in Lima contact APTA, Percy Tapiá, T 478078, or Antonio Bouroncle, T 450532. In Cusco, different agencies organize the clean-up each year.

## A New Inca Trail

A short Inca trail has recently opened for those who don't want to endure the full hike. Get off the train at Km 104, where a footbridge gives access to the ruins of Chachabamba and the trail which ascends through the ruins of Choquesuysuy to connect with the main trail at Wiñay-Wayna. This first part is a brutal ascent (take water) and the trail is narrow and exposed in parts. It takes about 2½-3½ hrs to reach Wiñay-Wayna.

The regular train arrives around 0930-1030; arrange with conductor to make sure it stops. Entry to the trail is US$12. There is a good hike from Aguas Calientes (see page 345) to Km 104.

## MACHU PICCHU

42 km from Ollantaytambo by rail (2,380m), **Machu Picchu** is a complete city. For centuries it was buried in jungle, until Hiram Bingham stumbled upon it

in 1911. It was then explored by an archaeological expedition sent by Yale.

The ruins – staircases, terraces, temples, palaces, towers, fountains and the famous Intihuatana (the so-called 'Hitching Post of the Sun') – require at least a day. Take time to appreciate not only the masonry, but also the selection of large rocks for foundations, the use of water in the channels below the Temple of the Sun and the surrounding mountains.

**Huayna Picchu**, the mountain overlooking the site (on which there are also ruins), has steps to the top for a superlative view of the whole site, but it is not for those who are afraid of heights and you shouldn't leave the path. The climb takes up to 90 minutes but the steps are dangerous after bad weather. The path is open 0700-1300, with the latest return time being 1500; and you must register at a hut at the beginning of the trail.

The other trail to Huayna Picchu, down near the Urubamba, is via the Temple of the Moon, in two caves, one above the other, with superb Inca niches inside, which have sadly been blemished by graffiti. For the trail to the Temple of the Moon: from the path to Huayna Picchu, take the second trail to the left – both are marked 'Danger, do not enter'. The danger is in the first 10 minutes, after which it is reasonable, although it descends further than you think it should. After the Temple you may proceed to Huayna Picchu. The round trip takes about 4 hrs. Before doing any trekking around Machu Picchu, check with an official which paths may be used, or which are one way.

The famous Inca bridge is about 45 minutes along a well-marked trail S of the Royal Sector. The bridge – which is actually a couple of logs – is spectacularly sited, carved into a vertiginous cliff-face. East of the Royal Sector is the path leading up to **Intipunku** on the Inca Trail (45 minutes, fine views). The tombs at Chaskapata, near Machu Picchu, have recently been opened.

## Local information

### ● Access

The site is open from 0700 to 1700. You can deposit your luggage at the entrance for US$0.50, though theft has been reported; check for missing items and demand their return. Entrance fee is US$10; second day ticket half price. It may be possible to pay in dollars, but only clean, undamaged notes will

## The mystery of Machu Picchu

The mystery and intrigue that surrounds Machu Picchu is exceeded only by the hype. But in this case, it is entirely justified. There is a tremendous feeling of awe on first witnessing this incredible sight. The ancient citadel straddles the saddle of a high mountain with steep terraced slopes falling away to the fast-flowing Urubamba river snaking its hairpin course far below in the valley floor. Towering overhead is Huayna Picchu, and green jungle peaks provide the backdrop for the whole majestic scene.

'Rediscovered' by the American explorer Hiram Bingham in July, 1911, Machu Picchu was a stunning archaeological find. The only major Inca site to escape 400 years of looting and destruction, it was remarkably well preserved. And it was no ordinary Inca settlement. It sat in an inaccessible location above the Urubamba gorge, and contained so many fine buildings that people have puzzled over its meaning ever since.

Bingham claimed he had discovered the lost city of Vilcabamba, and for 50 years everyone believed him. But he was proved wrong, and the mystery deepened. Later discoveries have revealed that Machu Picchu was the centre of an extensive Inca province. Many finely preserved satellite sites and highways also survive. This is craggy terrain, and the value of a province with no mines and little agricultural land – it was not even self-sufficient – is hard to determine. Bingham postulated it was a defensive citadel on the fringes of the Amazon. But the architecture fails to convince us, and in any case, defense against whom?

The Incas were the first to build permanent structures in this region, which was unusual because they arrived at the tail end of 4,000 years of Andean

be accepted. Guides are available at the site, they are often very knowledgeable and worthwhile, US$15 for 2½ hrs. Permission to enter the ruins before 0630 to watch the sunrise over the Andes, which is a spectacular experience, can be obtained from the Instituto Nacional de Cultura in Cusco, but it is often possible if you talk to the guards at the gate. After 1530 the ruins are quieter, but note that the last bus down from the ruins leaves at 1700. Walking down to Aguas Calientes, if staying the night there, takes 1-1½ hrs.

Mon and Fri are bad days because there is usually a crowd of people on guided tours who are going or have been to Pisac market on Sun, and too many people all want lunch at the same time. The expensive hotel is located next to the entrance, with a self-service restaurant. Lunch costs US$15 pp, so it's best to take your own food and drink, and take plenty of drinking water. Note that food is not officially allowed into the site.

### ● Recommended reading

*Lost City of the Incas* by Hiram Bingham (available in Lima and Cusco); *A Walking Tour of Machu Picchu* by Pedro Sueldo Nava – in several languages, available in Cusco. See also *The Sacred Center*, by Johan Reinhard. *Exploring Cusco*, by Peter Frost has good information about the site. The Tourist Hotel sells guides, although at a rather inflated price. The South American Explorers Club in Lima has detailed information on walks here, and so have Hilary Bradt's and Charles Brod's books.

### ● Accommodation

**L3** *Machu Picchu Ruinas*, electricity and water 24 hrs a day, will accept American Express TCs at the official rate, restaurant for residents only; the hotel is usually fully booked well in advance, try Sun night as other tourists find Pisac market a greater attraction; for reservations T (511) 221-0826/440-8043, F 440-6197, San Isidro, Lima. The South American Explorers Club in Lima advise against trying to make your own reservation as this can be very frustrating; they will do it for you; call them several months in advance with details, inc credit card number; T 51-1-425-0142.

### ● Transport

**Trains** The railway runs from Cusco (San Pedro station), up the zig-zag route to the pass before

civilization. 16th-century land titles discovered in the 1980s revealed that Machu Picchu was built by the Inca Pachacuti, founding father of the Inca empire. But they do not tell us why he built it. One reasonable speculation is that this area provided access to coca plantations in the lower Urubamba valley. However, the fine architecture of Machu Picchu cannot be explained away simply as a coca-collecting station.

Recent studies have shown that the "torreón" was an observatory for the solstice sunrise, and that the "Intihuatana" stela is the centre-point between cardinal alignments of nearby sacred peaks. The Incas worshipped nature: the celestial bodies, mountains, lightning, rainbows, rocks – anything, in fact, that was imbued with "huaca", or spiritual power. And here Pachacuti found "huaca" in unusual abundance.

This spiritual component is the key to understanding Machu Picchu. The Bingham expedition identified 75% of the human remains as female, and a common belief is that Machu Picchu was a refuge of the Inca "Virgins of the Sun". However, the skeletons were re-examined in the 1980s using modern technology, and the latest conclusion is that the gender split was roughly 50/50.

Machu Picchu was deliberately abandoned by its inhabitants – when, we do not know. This may have happened even before the Spanish invasion, perhaps as a result of the Inca civil wars, or the epidemics of European diseases which ran like brushfires ahead of the Spanish in the New World. One theory proposes that the city ran dry in a period of drought, another suggests a devastating fire. Or the city may have been evacuated during the period of Inca resistance to the Spanish, which lasted nearly 40 years and was concentrated not far west of Machu Picchu. (Peter Frost, 1996)

descending all the way to Quillabamba, 130 km. It passes through Ollantaytambo, Km 88, Aguas Calientes (the official name of this station is 'Machu Picchu') and Machu Picchu (officially called 'Puente Ruinas'). There is a paved road between 'Machu Picchu' and 'Puente Ruinas'. There are two local trains, two *autovagones* and one tourist train a day.

The local train has 2nd and 1st class; US$4.50 and US$5.50 one way respectively. The train is really crowded and you should watch your possessions carefully as bag-slashing is common. Take as little as possible, and no valuables, on the train. When on your way to hike the Inca Trail, equipped with a big backpack, try to be in a group, watching each other's gear. The first train leaves Cusco Mon-Sat at 0645, stopping in Ollantaytambo at about 0900 and Puente Ruinas at 1025; it continues to Quillabamba, arriving about 1130; leaves Quillabamba at 1430, stopping at Puente Ruinas at 1600, Ollantaytambo 1730 and arrives in Cusco at 2100. Be at Puente Ruinas station by 1400 for a ticket; very few are available so jump on and pay on board; the train is always crowded. The second train leaves Cusco daily at 1310, stops in Ollantaytambo at 1545, Puente Ruinas 1730, arriving in Quillabamba at 1830. It leaves Quillabamba the next day at 0530, arriving at Puente Ruinas at 0700, Ollantaytambo 0815 and Cusco 1100.

The tourist train has one class, pullman, with closed doors (only ticket holders allowed on); US$27 return. It leaves Cusco daily at 0625, stopping at Ollantaytambo at 0830 and Puente Ruinas at 1000; it returns from Puente Ruinas at 1600, arrives in Ollantaytambo at 1740 and arrives in Cusco at 2000.

There are two *autovagones*; US$47 return, with toilets, video, snacks and drinks for sale. The first one leaves Cusco at 0600, stops in Ollantaytambo at 0745 and Puente Ruinas at 0930 ( it also stops at Km 88 to let the local train pass). It returns at 1500, reaches Ollantaytambo at 1630 and Cusco at 1830. The second one leaves Cusco at 0900; arrives in Ollantaytambo 1100; Puente Ruinas 1220. It returns at 1800; arrives in Ollantaytambo at 1950, and Cusco at 2150.

The *autovagón* and tourist train do not stop at Aguas Calientes. Travellers on inclusive tours

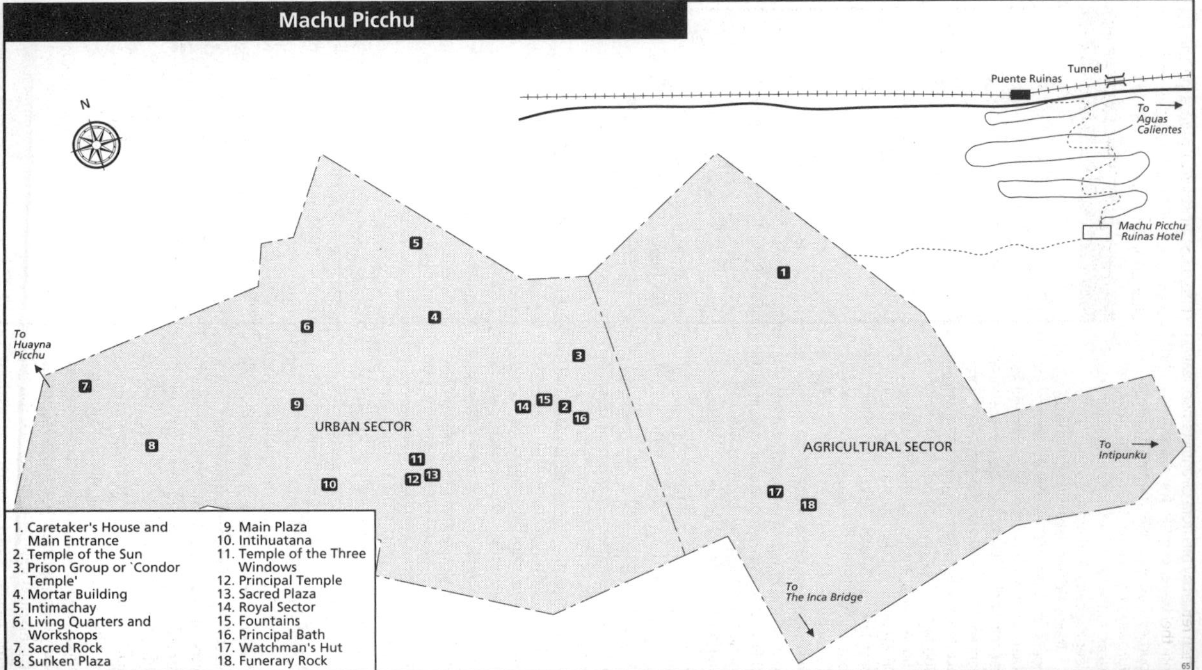
Machu Picchu
N
Puente Ruinas
Tunnel
To Aguas Calientes
Machu Picchu Ruinas Hotel
To Huayna Picchu
URBAN SECTOR
AGRICULTURAL SECTOR
To Intipunku
To The Inca Bridge
1. Caretaker's House and Main Entrance
2. Temple of the Sun
3. Prison Group or `Condor Temple'
4. Mortar Building
5. Intimachay
6. Living Quarters and Workshops
7. Sacred Rock
8. Sunken Plaza
9. Main Plaza
10. Intihuatana
11. Temple of the Three Windows
12. Principal Temple
13. Sacred Plaza
14. Royal Sector
15. Fountains
16. Principal Bath
17. Watchman's Hut
18. Funerary Rock

often return by bus from Ollantaytambo, leaving the trains emptier for the slower uphill journey to Cusco. **NB** The video sold on the *autovagón* is said not to work on any system. It can get very cold at night, so a blanket or sleeping bag could prove useful.

Train schedules are unreliable and delays of hours are common, especially on the local train. In the rainy season mudslides cause cancellations. Tickets can be bought in advance or on the day at the railway station or at a travel agency (always check date and seat number, and don't pay the agency in advance). Theoretically, the ticket office is open daily 0600-0830, 1000-1100 and 1500-1700. Expect long queues at Cusco for the morning local train in the high season and on holidays.

Tourist tickets: there are two types, 1) round trip in the *autovagón*, round trip in the bus up to the ruins, entrance fee, guide, for US$110. 2) Round trip on the local train, buffet class, round trip in the bus to the ruins, entrance fee and guide, US$60 (cheaper for Peruvian nationals). These tickets can be booked through any travel agency, who will pick you up at your hotel and take you to the train station. On the *autovagón* and tourist train try to get tickets with seat numbers. Independent travellers should try to buy their return leg to Cusco as soon as they arrive at Puente Ruinas.

Buses leave Puente Ruinas station for Machu Picchu from 0630 and 0730; 25 mins, US$5.80 return. The last buses up depart after the last morning train has arrived. From Aguas Calientes to the ruins, there is a bus service from 0730-1130, US$7 return. There is a bus from the ruins to Puente Ruinas and Aguas Calientes from 1230-1700. The walk up takes 2 hrs, and 1 hr down, following the zig-zag road.

## AGUAS CALIENTES

1½ km back along the railway from Puente Ruinas, this is a popular resting place for those recovering from the rigours of the Inca Trail. Most activity is centred around the railway station, on the plaza, or on Av Pachacútec, which leads from the plaza to the thermal baths.

The baths consist of a communal pool, 10 minutes' walk from the town. They were under repair in 1996, but are still open, 0500-2200, US$2.50. You can rent towels and bathing costumes (US$0.65) at several places on the road to the baths. There are basic toilets and changing facilities and showers for

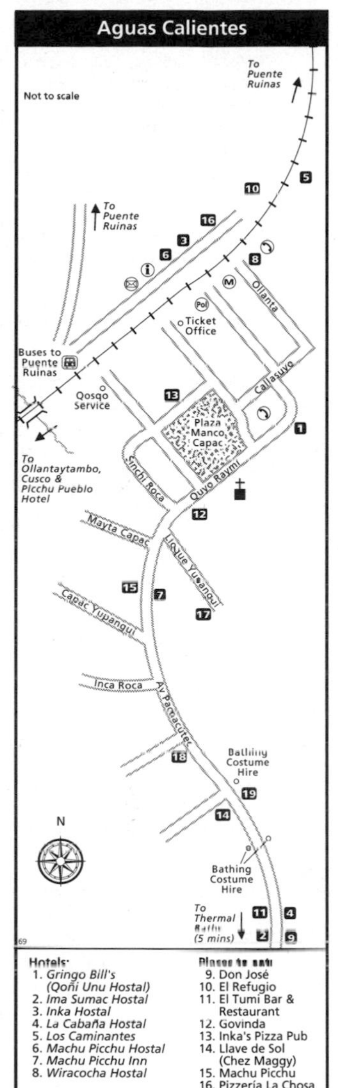

washing *before* entering the baths; take soap and shampoo.

• **Accommodation A1-2** ***Machu Picchu Pueblo Hotel***, Km 110, Aguas Calientes (Cusco 232161/223769, Procuradores 48; Lima 461915, F 455598, Andalucía 174, Lima 18), individual bungalows with bath, hot water, heating, meals extra in nice, expensive restaurant, pool, lovely gardens, rec, 5 minutes' walk along the railway from the town, the tourist train from Puente Ruinas stops here; **B** ***Hostal Inka***, at station, T 211084, includes breakfast, rec; **B** ***Hostal Machu Picchu Inn***, Av Pachacútec, with bath, **C** without, good, friendly; **C** ***Hostal Ima Sumac***, Av Pachacútec, 5 mins before the baths, T 211021, will exchange money; **D** ***Gringo Bill's*** (***Hostal Q'oñi Unu***), Qoya Raymi, third house to left of church, T 211046, shared bath, relaxed, hot water, laundry, money exchange, good but expensive meals served (usually slowly), they offer a US$2 packed lunch to take up to the ruins, luggage stored, good beds, don't stay in the rooms nearest the entrance as they flood during heavy rain; **D-E** ***Hostal Machu Picchu***, at the station, clean, basic, quiet, friendly, especially Wilber, the owner's son, with travel information, hot water, nice balcony over the Urubamba, grocery store, rec; **E** ***Hostal Inti Sumi***, at the top of the hill near the baths, hot water, clean; **E** pp ***Hostal Los Caminantes***, by the railway just beyond the station, with bath, **F** pp without, basic, but friendly and clean. **Camping**: the only official campsite is in a field by the river, just below Puente Ruinas station. Do not leave your tent and belongings unattended.

• **Places to eat** At the station: ***El Refugio***, expensive, good food, slow service; ***Aiko***, rec; ***El Chosa Pizzería***, pleasant atmosphere, good value; ***Wiñay-Wayna***; and many others. ***Clave de Sol***, Av Pachacútec 156, same owner as *Chez Maggy* in Cusco, good cheap Italian food US$3.70, changes money, has vegetarian menu, great atmosphere. Also on this street: ***Govinda***, just off the plaza, vegetarian; ***Machu Picchu***, good, friendly; ***Chifa Hong Kong***; and others. ***Inka's Pizza Pub***, on the plaza, good pizzas, changes money, accepts TCs, rec. On the road to the baths is ***Waisicha Pub***, good music and atmosphere.

• **Tourist information & Services** Travel agency, *Información Turística Rikuni*, is at the station, Nydia is very helpful; also *Qosqo Service*, by the railway. The Post Office at the station sells maps of Machu Picchu. The telephone office is on the plaza. There are lots of places to choose from for exchange. The town has electricity 24 hrs a day.

## QUILLABAMBA

The railway goes on 79 km through Chaullay to **Quillabamba** (*Pop* 24,000; *Alt* 1,054m) in the Urubamba Valley, where there is a Dominican mission.

The train follows the Río Urubamba much of the way from Machu Picchu, and the improvised station at Quillabamba is right on the river. Cross a footbridge put up by the Lions Club and then climb up a 100-odd flight of stairs to reach the town. There are not many attractions for the tourist, but this is a good place to bask in the sun or take a swim in the river, though ask the locals where the safe stretches are, as the current is quite rapid in places. There are also a clean market building and a football stadium. Unless you're here during the high season – June and July – you won't see many other gringos in these parts.

• **Accommodation D** ***Comercio***, Libertad, with bath; **D** ***Quillabamba***, Prolongación y M Grau 590, unmarked entrance next to Autoservicio behind market, roof terrace restaurant, laundry service, rec; ***Hostal Don Carlos***, clean, private shower, generally hot water; **F** ***Hostal Alto Urubamba***, on Dos de Mayo, clean, good, with or without bath, hot water, restaurant. There is other accommodation, **G** and upwards, near the market.

• **Places to eat** ***Pub Don Sebas***, Jr Espinar 235 on Plaza de Armas, good place to eat, great sandwiches, run by Karen Molero who is very friendly and always ready for a chat; ***El Gordito***, on Espinar, good place for chicken, US$3. There are many *heladerías*, which are much needed in the heat. The best of these is on the NW corner of the Plaza de Armas.

• **Banks & money changers** Banco de Crédito, good for TCs.

• **Transport Trains** See above for train information. **Road** A minibus leaves Cusco in the morning when full, from C Gen Buendía near Machu Picchu station; also trucks go in the daytime; 233 km, 6-11 hrs, US$4.50.

**ROUTES** The road between Ollantaytambo and Quillabamba passes through Peña, a place of great beauty with snowy peaks already appearing on either side of the valley. Once out of Peña, the climb to the pass begins in earnest – on the right is a huge glacier. Soon on the left, Verónica begins to appear in all its huge and snowy majesty. After endless zig-zags and breathtaking views, you reach the Abra Málaga pass. The descent to the valley shows hillsides covered in lichen and Spanish moss. At Chaullay, the road meets the railway to Quillabamba, Machu Picchu and Cusco. The road crosses the river at the historic Choquechaca bridge. You can drive from Chaullay to Santa Teresa, where there are hot springs, but ask the locals for directions. From here, the railway goes to Machu Picchu. Note that driving in this area is very demanding owing to the number of hairpin bends.

## VITCOS

From Chaullay you can drive to the village of **Huancacalle**, the best base for exploring the nearby Inca ruins of **Vitcos**, with the palace of the last four Inca rulers from 1536 to 1572, and Yurac Rumi, the impressive sacred white stone of the Incas.

Hans Ebensten of Key West, Florida, writes: "While a visit to the ruins of Vilcabamba Vieja, near Espíritu Pampa, is still a formidable undertaking, involving at least eight days of hiking over rough trails (others have done the trip in five days), taking all camping gear, food, etc, the ruins of Vitcos and the Yurac Rumi, the Inca sacred stone, are now easily accessible. Both are well worth the effort of a visit. Vitcos remains romantically overgrown by jungle, much as Dr Hiram Bingham found it (and Machu Picchu) in 1911, but unlike Machu Picchu it has all the documented historical associations which make a visit particularly interesting and rewarding. The Yurac Rumi, the most sacred site in South America, must be one of the most impressive religious sites in the world; far larger and more intricately and elaborately carved than any descriptions of it. Dr Hiram Bingham was chiefly concerned in stressing the importance of Machu Picchu, and thus in his books and reports dismissed Vitcos and the Yurac Rumi as almost insignificant."

Huancacalle can be reached from Quillabamba daily by truck and bus, the journey takes between 4 and 7 hrs. There is a small hotel at Huancacalle, or alternatively villagers will accept travellers in their very basic homes (take sleeping bag). The Cobo family permits travellers to put up their tents on their property. Allow plenty of time for hiking to, and visiting the ruins. It takes 1 hr to walk from Huancacalle to Vitcos, 45 minutes Vitcos-Yurac Rumi, 45 mins Yurac Rumi-Huancacalle. Horses can be hired if you wish.

You can also hike up to **Vilcabamba La Nueva** from Huancacalle; a 3-hr walk through beautiful countryside with Inca ruins dotted around. There is a missionary building run by Italians, with electricity and running water, where you may be able to spend the night.

## VILCABAMBA VIEJA

Travellers with ample time can hike from Huancacalle to **Espíritu Pampa**, the site of the **Vilcabamba Vieja** ruins, a vast pre-Inca ruin with a neo-Inca overlay set in deep jungle at 1,000m.

The site is reached on foot or horseback from Pampaconas. From Chaullay, take a truck to Yupanca, Lucma or Pucyura: there rent horses or mules and travel through superb country to Espíritu Pampa. You can then continue to Koshireni on the Río San Miguel. The jungle in the area of Vilcabamba Vieja is full of wildlife and worth the trip on its own. At Espíritu Pampa is a sister stone of the Yurac Rumi.

To visit this area you must register with the police in Pucyura. You are advised to seek full information before travelling. Distances are considerable – it is at least

100 km from Chaullay to Espíritu Pampa – the going is difficult and maps appear to be very poor. If you intend to attempt this trip, you should first read *Sixpac Manco: travels among the Incas*, by Vincent R Lee, which is available in Cusco. It contains accurate maps of all the archaeological sites in this area, and describes 2 expeditions into the region by the author and his party in 1982 and

## The last Incas of Vilcabamba

After Pizarro killed Atahualpa in 1532 the Inca empire disintegrated rapidly, and it is often thought that native resistance ended there. But in fact it continued for 40 more years, beginning with Manco, a teenage half-brother of Atahualpa.

The conquistadors at first used Manco as a tool for controlling their newly-conquered lands. But in 1536, their puppet escaped, and returned leading a massive army against them. He besieged Cusco and Lima simultaneously, and came close to dislodging the Spaniards from Peru.

Spanish reinforcements arrived and Manco fled to Vilcabamba, a mountainous forest region west of Cusco that was remote, but still fairly close to the Inca capital, which he always dreamed of recapturing. The Spanish chased Manco into Vilcabamba as far as the fortress of Vitcos. Failing to capture him, they invaded deep into Vilcabamba again in 1539, this time reaching the forest location of a new capital city Manco was building. Yet both times Manco escaped and lived to fight another day, and the costly Spanish expeditions achieved little, for while there was a living Inca, there was a resistance.

Manco continued his guerrilla war, raiding Spanish commerce on the Lima highway, and keeping alive the Inca flame. Then, in 1544, Spanish outlaws to whom he had given refuge murdered him, ending the most active period of Inca resistance.

The Inca line passed to his sons. The first, a child too young to rule named Sayri Túpac, eventually yielded to Spanish enticements and emerged from Vilcabamba, taking up residence in Yucay, near Urubamba in 1558. He died mysteriously – possibly poisoned – 3 years later.

His brother Titu Cusi, who was still in Vilcabamba, now took up the Inca mantle. Astute and determined, he resumed raiding and fomenting rebellion against the Spanish. Sensing their aversion to yet another wearisome invasion, Titu Cusi played a clever diplomatic game with them, tantalising them with hopes he would emerge, but also seeking permanent recognition for his native state. But in 1570, Titu Cusi fell ill and died suddenly. A Spanish priest was accused of murdering him. Anti-Spanish resentment erupted, and the priest and a Spanish viceregal envoy were killed. The Spanish Viceroy reacted immediately, and the Spanish invaded Vilcabamba for the third and last time in 1572.

A third brother, Túpac Amaru was now in charge. He lacked his brother's experience and acuity, and his destiny was to be the sacrificial last Inca. The Spanish overran the Inca's jungle capital, and dragged him back to Cusco in chains. There, Túpac Amaru, the last Inca, was publicly executed in Cusco's main plaza.

The location of the neo-Inca capital of Vilcabamba was forgotten over the centuries, and the search for it provoked Hiram Bingham's expeditions, and his discovery of Machu Picchu. Bingham did also discover Vilcabama the Old, without realizing it, but the true location at Espíritu Pampa was only pinpointed by Gene Savoy in the 1960s, and was not confirmed irrefutably until the work of Vincent Lee in the 1980s. (Peter Frost, 1996)

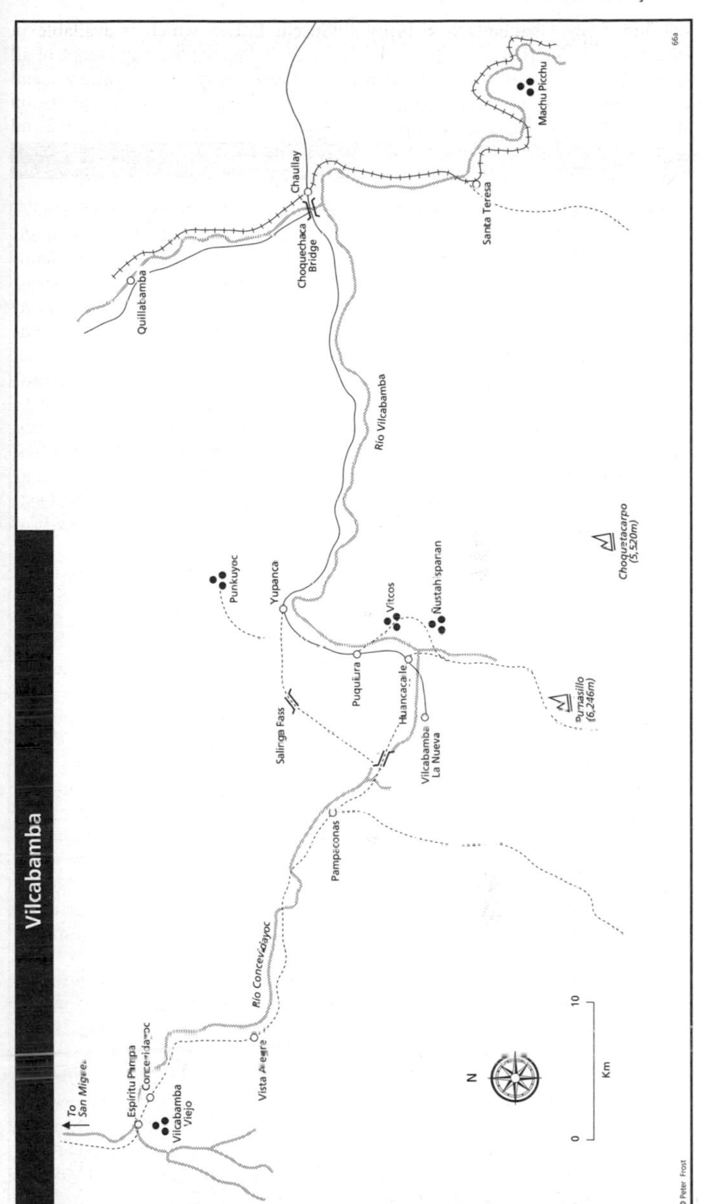
Vilcabamba
66a
To San Miguel
Espíritu Pampa
Concevidayoc
Vilcabamba Viejo
Vista Alegre
Río Concevidayoc
Pampaconas
Saliriga Pass
Vilcabamba La Nueva
Huancacalle
Puquiura
Yupanca
Punkuyoc
Vitcos
Ñustahispanan
Pumasillo (6,246m)
Choquetacarpo (5,520m)
Río Vilcabamba
Quillabamba
Choquechaca Bridge
Chaullay
Santa Teresa
Machu Picchu
N
0
10
Km
© Peter Frost

1984, following in the footsteps of Gene Savoy, who first identified the site in the 1960s. His book, *Antisuyo*, which describes his expeditions here and elsewhere in Peru, is also recommended reading.

Allow 5-8 days if going on foot. The best time of year is May-Oct. During the wet season it really does rain, so be prepared to get very wet and very muddy. Insect repellent is essential. Also take pain-killers and other basic medicines; these will be much appreciated by the local people should you need to take advantage of their hospitality.

Guides for Vilcabamba Vieja: Vidal Albertes, contact in Huancacalle; Paulo Quispe Cusi in Yupanca. Another local guide in Pucyura is Gilberto Quintanilla. Adriel Garay at *White River Tours*, Plateros, Cusco, or C Bayoneta 739, Cusco, T 234575.

## KITENI

You can also go by boat to Kiteni from Koshireni and then by truck to Quillabamba; 12-15 hrs, US$5. There is basic accommodation at **G** *Hotel Kiteni*, and several restaurants. At Kiteni you must register on arrival with the police. Take a torch/flashlight as there is no electricity.

Irregular boats go to the Pongo de Maynique, where the river goes through the mountain with a rock wall of several hundred metres on either side, before descending into the jungle, where you can see many varieties of animals, birds, butterflies, snakes etc. It is 2 days from Quillabamba to Pongo. Seek advice in advance on the river conditions; at certain times it is too high.

# The Central Highlands



THE CENTRAL Andes of Peru comprises the departments of Apurímac, Ayacucho, Huancavelica, Junín, Pasco and Huánuco. This a vast, relatively unexplored area of stunning mountain scenery, dotted with tiny, typical villages, and terrible roads. The road into the central Andes from Lima has been improved, however, and is paved throughout.

For those who appreciate traditional, good quality textiles and ceramics, or who enjoy a lively festival, this part of the country is not to be missed. Huancayo, the Mantaro valley, Ayacucho and the surrounding villages are the main production centres of textiles and ceramics.

Because of heavy terrorist disruption in the 1980s and early 1990s, large parts of the central highlands are only just opening up to tourism once more. People in these parts are relieved to see tourists return to their towns and cities and treat them with great friendship and hospitality.

Ayacucho was the home of the Maoist terrorist movement, Shining Path, and has suffered greatly over the past years. The region now seems to be under the control of the military, judging by its heavy presence. Consequently, there are many checkpoints and it is advisable to travel only during the day. Knowledge of Spanish is essential, as is informing yourself regularly of the current political situation.

Travellers should note that the northern part of the central Andes, N from Tingo María, in the Huallaga valley, is the main cocaine producing region and largely under the control of narco-traffickers. If travelling in this area, travel only by day and do not, under any circumstances, stray from the main routes, unless you wish to be mistaken for a US Drug Enforcement Agency employee and dealt with accordingly.

## LIMA TO HUANCAYO

On the Central Railway passenger trains have not run since 1991. All passenger traffic now goes by road until there is sufficient demand for the service to be restored. See under La Oroya, **Roads and Buses**, for transport details. The Central Highway between Lima and Huancayo more or less parallels the course of the railway.

The Lima to Huancayo railway is one of the great engineering feats of the 19th century. This masterpiece was the project of the great American railway engineer, Henry Meiggs, who supervised the construction from 1870 until his death in 1877. It was built by the Pole Ernesto Malinowski, with imported Chinese labour, between 1870 and 1893.

The ruling grade of the Central Railway is about 4½°. Along the whole of its length (335 km to Huancayo) it traverses 66 tunnels, 59 bridges, and 22 zig-zags where the steep mountainside permits no other way of negotiating it. During its years of operation, this was a tough journey, with altitude sickness an ever-present problem. This discomfort was more than compensated, though, by the spectacular views during the ascent which are beyond compare. Railway buffs may like to know that the last Andes type 2-8-0 steam locomotive, No 206, is still in working order, although usually locked in a shed at Huancayo. It was built specifically for this route in 1953 by Beyer Peacocks of Manchester.

### Bus travel in the Andes

Stepping onto a bus at the beginning of a journey in the Peruvian Andes can be an unnerving experience. Maybe it's the sight of those shiny, bald tyres which look as if they haven't seen tread since the driver was last in short trousers. Or maybe it's the comprehensive collection of religious imagery decorating the driver's cab, leaving one to contemplate prayer as the best means of ensuring a safe trip. On the other hand, it could simply be the fact that the bus is packed to suffocation point. For you can bet your last banana pancake that, on board, there will be enough passengers, luggage and livestock to fill a super-tanker. Overcrowded, it seems, is a word not included in the Andean vocabulary.

As the bus heads off and you settle down into your 10 sq centimetres of available space, thoughts may turn to the road. In the Andes roads tend to range from badly pot-holed dirt tracks, barely wide enough for two buses to pass, to badly pot-holed dirt tracks, barely wide enough for two anorexic llamas to stand shoulder-to-shoulder without one of them falling off the side.

The term pot hole comes from a time before roads began to be paved and refers to the common practice of digging holes in the roads in order to provide sufficient material for pot-making. This would explain the very large number of pots in these parts. Such a prevalence of pot holes does have its compensations, though. It makes for some amusing near head-on collisions as your driver veers back and forth across the carriageway in an attempt to avoid them. In places, the pot holes join up, so that the road becomes one giant pot hole with the driver veering wildly from one side to the other in a desperate attempt to avoid hitting the few remaining bits of original road that stick up like stalagmites, turning the road into a kind of obstacle course.

But pot holes are only a minor distraction. Rather more worrying are the crosses that all-too frequently appear by the side of the road. These are placed by the relatives of those who have perished in road accidents at the precise spot where the vehicle plunged over the side. This means that they can serve as some

## CHOSICA

The Central Highway between Lima and Chosica has several places to stay and eat. Some are given under Lima; there are others in the residential district of **Chaclacayo**, just before Chosica.

**Chosica** (*Pop* 31,200; *Alt* 860m) is the real starting place for the mountains, 40 km from Lima. It is a popular winter resort because it is above the cloudbank covering Lima in winter. Beyond the town looms a precipitous range of hills almost overhanging the streets.

• **Accommodation** There are four basic *hostales* in Chosica, two are off the main road nr the market, and the other two up the hill on the left. All have water problems and are in **E** range. The best is ***Residencial Chosica***, a big old building on the pedestrian street perpendicular to 28 de Julio, rec; unlike ***Hostal Chosica***, 28 de Julio, which is unwelcoming.

• **Transport** Colectivos for Chosica leave from the first block of Montevideo (around the corner from Ormeño), when full, between 0600 and 2100, US$0.60.

## MARCAHUASI

40 km beyond Chosica, up the picturesque Santa Eulalia valley, is **Marcahuasi**, a table mountain about 3 km by 3 km at 4,200m, near the village of **San Pedro de Casta**.

The *meseta* has been investigated by the late Daniel Ruzo. There are 3 lakes, a 40m high 'monumento a la humanidad', and other mysterious lines, gigantic figures, sculptures, astrological signs and megaliths which display non-American

macabre point-scoring system to indicate the degree of difficulty of any particular bend. On the most dangerous bends, there may be so many that they form a makeshift crash barrier, preventing others from suffering the same fate.

Guiding you along these thin strips of mountain roads which coil their way through the Andes are people you will come to fear and respect – the drivers. At times you may be convinced that many of these drivers are members of a strange religious cult whose sole aim is to wipe out the entire travelling public. What other explanation could there be for hurtling at breakneck speed along roads that would cause a tortoise to put the brakes on?

Some drivers manage to combine their formula one racing skills with a nice line in sadistic humour. There you'll be, crawling along behind an excruciatingly slow-moving farm vehicle on a road as straight as a pool cue. Then, as you approach the first bend for miles, the driver will suddenly pull out to overtake. Just as suddenly, he pulls back in, comfortably missing the onrushing ten-ton timber truck by, oh, at least two millimetres. You have to laugh.

Though you will often curse the driver's apparent disregard for your well-being, you'll also have occasion to sing his praises. For when the bus breaks down (as it invariably does), he can display his breathtaking mechanical genius. More often than not, this will happen in the middle of the night, several hundred kilometres from the nearest dwelling, with the temperature outside well below zero. The engine has blown up, the wheels fallen off and the driver disappears into a cloud of black smoke wielding nothing more than a metal pipe, an old cigarette packet and a length of string. Miraculously, an hour later, you're on your way once more. Uncanny.

But it's not all discomfort and near death experiences. The intimacy of bus travel makes for some interesting encounters and, if your Spanish is up to it, can prove the beginning of many a beautiful friendship. Buses can also be a unique insight into Andean life. And at dinner parties in years to come, it'll be these experiences that have your guests glancing anxiously at their wristwatches and reaching for their jackets.

symbolizm. Ruzo describes this pre-Incaic culture in his book, *La Culture Masma*, Extrait de l'Ethnographie, Paris, 1956. Others say that the formations are not man-made, but the result of wind erosion. The trail starts behind the village of San Pedro, and bends to the left. It's about 2 hrs to the *meseta*; guides cost about US$3 a day, and are advisable in misty weather.

• **Accommodation & transport** The bus to San Pedro de Casta leaves Chosica from Parque Echerique, opp the market, daily except Sun, at about 0800 (when full), 3 hrs, US$2. The road is in a reasonable condition until the Callahuanca hydroelectric station. The only accommodation in San Pedro is in a cold shelter, for less than US$1. Take all necessary camping equipment and buy food in Chosica as there is nothing beyond that point. Tours can be arranged with travel agencies in Lima.

Beyond Casta is **San Juan de Iris**, a tiny village, outside which impressive ruins have been discovered. A bus or truck leaves from *Restaurant 41* in Chosica at 0900, if you're lucky, 7 hrs.

There are the ancient ruins of a small town on the hill of San Pedro de Casta, which date from 1500 BC. Also a fortress on the hills of **Loma de los Papas** (daily bus from Chosica at 0800), the ruins of **Tambo Inca**, and an ancient cemetery to the south.

## CHOSICA TO LA OROYA

For a while, beyond Chosica (see page 353), each successive valley looks greener and lusher, with a greater variety of trees and flowers.

**San Bartolomé**, Km 57, at 1,513m, is the terminus of the only passenger service currently running; a Sun train from Lima, in the dry season only.

**Matucana**, Km 84, at 2,390m, is set in wild scenery, where there are beautiful walks. The road continues to climb, passing **San Mateo** (Km 107, 3,215m), where the San Mateo mineral water originates. From here a spectacular side-road branches off to the Germania mine.

Beyond San Mateo is **Infiernillo** (Little Hell) Canyon, at Km 100. Car excursions can be made from Lima.

• **Accommodation** **F** *Ritz*, fair; and *Grau*, cheap.

Between Río Blanco and **Chicla** (Km 127, 3,733m), Inca contour-terraces can be seen quite clearly. After climbing up from **Casapalca** (Km 139, 4,154m), there are glorious views of the highest peaks, and more mines, at the foot of a deep gorge. The road ascends to the Ticlio Pass, before the descent to **Morococha** and **La Oroya**. A large metal flag of Peru can be seen at the top of Mt Meiggs, not by any means the highest in the area, but through it runs Galera Tunnel, 1,175m long, in which the Central Railway reaches its greatest altitude, 4,782m.

**Ticlio**, at Km 157, is the highest passenger station in the world, at 4,758m. It lies at the mouth of the tunnel, on one side of a crater in which lies a dark, still lake. There are still higher points on the railway on the branch of the line that goes through Morococha – 4,818m at La Cima, and 4,829m on a siding. At Morococha is the Centromín golf course, which welcomes playing visitors. It stands at 4,400m and disputes the title of the world's highest with Mallasilla, near La Paz, in Bolivia.

## LA OROYA

This is the main smelting centre for the region's mining industry. It can seem a dreary place with its slag heaps, but is nevertheless full of vitality. It stands at the fork of the Yauli and Mantaro rivers, 187 km from Lima by a road (*Pop* 36,000; *Alt* 3,755m). (For places to the E and N of La Oroya, see page 377 and 380 respectively.)

• **Accommodation** **F** *Hostal Regional*, Lima 112, T 391017, with bath, basic, hot water in the morning; **F** *Hostal Inti*, Arequipa 117, T 391098, shared bath, hot water, clean; **F** *Hostal Chavín*, Tarma 281, shared bath, good, cheap restaurant; **F** *Mister*, Arequipa

113, T 391149, basic, front rooms are better, the back rooms are dingy.

• **Places to eat** *La Caracocha*, Lima 168, cheap, good menú; ***Punta Arenas***, Zeballos 323, good seafood, chifa; ***El Tambo***, 2 km outside town on the road to Lima, good trout and frogs, rec as the best restaurant. There are lots of *pollerías* in front of the train station in C Lima.

• **Transport** For buses see under Lima, **Bus Companies** with routes to the central area. To **Lima**, 4½ hrs, US$5.20; comité 3 hrs, US$7.85. To **Jauja**, 80 km, 1½ hrs, US$1; and on to **Huancayo**, a further 44 km, 1 hr, US$1. To **Tarma**, 1½ hrs, US$1.35. To **Cerro de Pasco**, 131 km, 3 hrs, US$2.20. To **Huánuco**, 236 km, 6 hrs, US$4.35; on to **Tingo María**, 118 km, 3-4 hrs, US$1.75, and on to **Pucallpa**, 284 km, 7-9 hrs, US$7.85. Buses leave from Zeballos, adjacent to the train station. Colectivos also run on all routes (see under Lima). They are quicker but only leave when full and prices are double that of the bus fares.

ROUTES At La Oroya, the central highway divides: S, following the valley of the polluted Río Mantaro, to Huancayo, and on to Huancavelica or Ayacucho; N to Cerro de Pasco and on to Huánuco, Tingo María and Pucallpa. 25 km N along this road is the fork E for Tarma and La Merced. The road is paved from Lima to Huancayo, but all the other roads are in poor condition, especially when wet.

## JAUJA

80 km SE of La Oroya is the old town of **Jauja** (*Alt* 3,330m), Pizarro's provisional capital until the founding of Lima. It has a very colourful Wed and Sun market. Jauja is a friendly, unspoilt town, in the middle of a good area for walking.

### Places of interest

There is an **archaelogical museum**, which is recommended for the Huari culture. A modernized church retains 3 fine 17th-century altars. The **Cristo Pobre** church is claimed to have been modelled after Notre Dame and is something of a curiosity.

### Excursions

On a hill above Jauja there is a fine line of Inca storehouses, and on hills nearby the ruins of hundreds of circular stone buildings from the Huanca culture (John Hemming). There are also ruins near the **Paca lake** 3½ km away.

18 km to the S, on the road to Huancayo, is **Concepción** (*Alt* 3,251m), with a market on Sun as well as a colourful bullfight later in the day during the season. From Concepción a branch road (6 km) leads to the **Convent of Santa Rosa de Ocopa**, a Franciscan monastery set in beautiful surroundings. It was established in 1725 for training missionaries for the jungle. It contains a fine library with over 20,000 volumes and a biological museum with animals and insects from the jungle. The monastery is open 0900-1200 and 1500-1800, and closed Tues.

8 km from Concepción is **Ingenio**, with a fish farm in lovely countryside and restaurants in which to try the trout.

### Local information

**• Accommodation**

**E** *Cabezon's Hostal*, Ayacucho 1027, T 362206, with bath, hot water, the best in town; **E** *Ganso de Oro*, R Palma 249, T 362165, shared bath, hot water, good restaurant, US$2-4/meal; **E** *Hostal Los Algarrobes*, Huancayo 264, T 362633, shared bath, hot water in morning, prices will rise; **E** *Hostal Francisco Pizarro*, Bolognesi 334, opp the market, T 362082, shared bath, hot water.

**• Places to eat**

*Marychris*, Jr Bolívar 1166, T 362386, for lunch only, *menú* US$1.55, excellent food; *Hatun Xauxa*, Jr Ricardo Palma 165, good, cheap food and hot rums; *Centro Naturista*, Huarancayo 138, fruit salad, yoghurt, granola, etc; *Fuente de Soda "Rossy's"*, Jr Bolognesi 561, great cakes, OK pizza and snacks.

**• Banks & money changers**

No TCs are accepted at the Banco de Crédito. **Dollar Exchange Huarancayo**, on Jr Huarancayo, gives a much better rate than Banco de Crédito.

### ● Post & telecommunications

**Telefónica**: at Bolognesi 546, T (064) 362020, T/F 361111; also at Ricardo Palma, opp *Hotel Ganso de Oro*, T/F 362395, better service and prices.

**Correo Central**: Jr Bolívar.

### ● Transport

**Local** Mototaxi to Laguna de Paca, US$0.90 minimum for 2 people, plus US$0.45 per additional person. *Combis* to Laguna de Paca, Paca, Acolla, etc, leave from Jr Tarma several times daily, US$0.45.

**Buses** To **Lima**, direct with Mcal Cáceres, from Plaza de Armas, daily at 1100 and 2230, US$5.35-6.65, service from Huancayo, highly rec; also with Sudamericano, Plaza de Armas, and Costa Sierra, R Palma 145, a subsidiary of Ormeño, rec. To **Cerro de Pasco**, with Oriental (28 de Julio 156) and Turismo Central (28 de Julio 150), 5 hrs, US$3.55. Oriental and Turismo Central also go to **Huánuco**, 7 hrs, US$5.35; **Tingo María**, 12 hrs, US$6.65; and **Pucallpa**, 24 hrs, US$12. To **Tarma**, US$2.25, hourly with ET San Juan from Jr Tarma; continues to **Chanchamayo**, US$4.50. To **Satipo**, with Turismo Central, 12 hrs, US$6.25.

ROUTES The road to Satipo branches off near the Convento de Santa Rosa de Ocopa. The scenery is spectacular, with snow-capped mountains in the Paso de la Tortuga, followed by a rapid drop to the Caja de Silva in Satipo (see page 379

## HUANCAYO

The city (*Pop* 359,000; *Alt* 3,271m; *Phone code* 064) is in the beautiful Mantaro Valley. It is the capital of Junín Department and the main commercial centre for inland Peru. All the villages in the valley produce their own original crafts and celebrate festivals the year round. At the important festivals in Huancayo, people flock in from far and wide with an incredible range of food, crafts, dancing and music. The Sun market gives a little taste of this every week even though it has been described as expensive and offering little choice. It gets going after 0900. It is better to go to the villages for local handicrafts. Jr Huancavelica, 3 km long and 4 stalls wide, still sells typical clothes, fruit, vegetables, hardware, handicrafts and, especially, traditional medicines and goods for witchcraft. There is also an impressive daily market behind the railway station.

### PLACES OF INTEREST

The museum at the Salesian school has over 5,000 pieces, including a large collection of jungle birds, animals and butterflies, insects, reptiles and fossils.

### A growing tradition

One of Peru's most popular and traditional handicrafts is gourd carving, or *mate burilado*. During the colonial period gourd carving decreased dramatically but limited carving continued and new European styles were developed. After independence a new style developed which incorporated traditional and narrative scenes. This made gourds more commonplace as objects and more meaningful to more people since the motifs had relevance to their own lives.

The gourds come from a creeping plant – *Lagenria Vulgaris* – which grows only in warm, dry regions, such as the coastal valleys. The decoration is produced by a combination of carving and burning. The outlines are carved freehand by skilled craftspeople and a red-hot stick is used to burn and blacken areas of the surface. It is a slow, laborious process and some carvers can take as long as 6 months to finish a large, finely-carved gourd.

Today, carving is centred around the small communities of Cochas Grande and Chico, near Huancayo, having spread there from the earlier centres of Huanta and Mayoc in Ayacucho. The carvers now sell their art in Huancayo as well as Lima, from where it is exported.

Extracted from *Arts and Crafts of South America*, by Lucy Davies and Mo Fini, Tumi.

For a rare insight into the world of Andean mysticism and magic, you can visit *Wali Wasi* ('sacred house' in Quechua), run by mystic, Pedro Marticorena Oroña Laya. He has paintings of Andean visions, masks made of cow dung and roots turned into gods and animals, and also offers Quechua lessons and cheap accommodation. A visit is described as "a truly memorable experience". Take a *micro* marked 'Umuto' and get off 1 block before the cemetery; the house is at Hualahoyo 2174.

## EXCURSIONS

**In the Mantaro Valley** The whole valley is rich in culture, music, typical food, dances and handicrafts. On the outskirts of town is **Torre-Torre**, impressive, eroded sandstone towers on the hillside. Take a bus to Cerrito de la Libertad and walk up. Not far from here is a large park with a depressing zoo, but with a good swimming pool; entry US$0.25.

### West of the Mantaro river

8 km from Huancayo, at **Sapallanga**, the *fiesta* of the Virgen de Cocharcas on 8 Sept is famous. **Viques** (19 km) is known for the production of belts and blankets. **Huayucachi** (7 km) organizes festivals with dancing and impressive costumes in Jan and Feb and also makes embroidery. At **Tres de Diciembre** is a fish farm, with some good restaurants and swimming pool. To get there, walk from Huamancaca.

The ruins of **Warivilca** (15 km) are near **Huari**, with the remains of a pre-Inca temple of the Huanca tribe. There is a museum in the plaza, with deformed skulls, and modelled and painted pottery of successive Huanca and Inca occupations of the shrine. The ruins and museum are under the supervision of a local archaeologist and are slowly being restored. The ruins are open 1000-1200, 1500-1700, US$0.15 admission; the museum is open in the morning only. To get there, take one of the *micros* for Chilca, which leave from Calle Real.

Between Pilcomayo and Huayo (15 km) is the **Geophysical Institute of Huayo**, on the 'Magnetic Equator' – 12½° S of the geographical equator. Here meteorological, seismic and cosmic-ray observa-

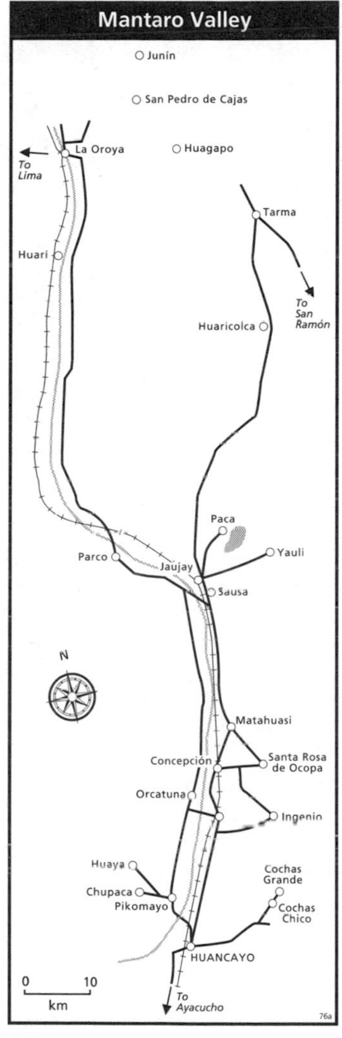

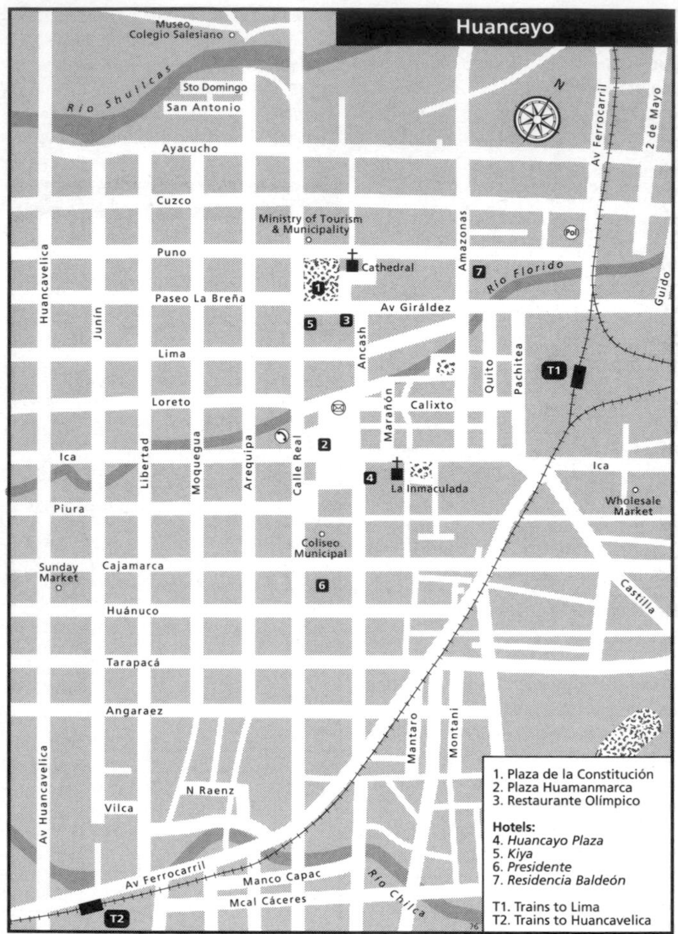


tions are made. A visit is recommended and the best time is in the morning, or when the sun is shining.

**Chupaca** is a picturesque village with a good Sat market. A colectivo leaves from the fruit and vegetable market. On the way to Chupaca is the village of **Ahuac**. One block down from the Plaza de Armas, in the Colegio Amauta, is a museum with items found at the nearby Huanca ruins of **Arwaturo**. Opposite the school is a shop where you can buy excellent chicha from the señora. There is a small restaurant on the plaza in Ahuac, which serves a set lunch for US$1.

Also W of the river, 17 km from Huancayo, is **Laguna Nahuinpuquio**, a nice lake with pleasant surrounding countryside. **Sicaya** (8 km), holds festivals in Aug and has an 18th century church.

The ruins of **Guaqui-Guaqui** are just outside the village of **Matahulo**. **Muquiyauyo** is famous for its Semana Santa celebrations.

### East of the Mantaro river

The villages of **Cochas Chico** and **Cochas Grande**, 11 km away, are both well worth visiting, for this is where the famous *mate burilado*, or gourd carving, is done. You can buy them cheaply direct from the manufacturers, but ask around. You can also enjoy beautiful views of the Valle de Mantaro and Huancayo. *Micros* leave from the corner of Amazonas y Giráldez, US$0.25.

**Hualahoyo** (11 km) has a little chapel with 21 colonial canvases. **San Agustín de Cajas** (8 km) makes fine hats, and **San Pedro** (10 km) makes wooden chairs. In the village of **Hualhuas** (12 km) you can find fine alpaca weavings. One particularly recommended place to buy them is *Tahuantisuyo*, run by Familia Faustino Maldonado y Agripina, on a side road on the way to the San Jerónimo junction.

The village of **San Jerónimo** is renowned for the making of silver filigree jewellery, on sale at the Wed market. The village holds its fiesta in August. There are ruins 2-3 hrs' walk above San Jerónimo, but seek advice before hiking to them.

## LOCAL FESTIVALS

There are so many festivals in the Mantaro Valley that it is impossible to list them all. Practically every day of the year there is a celebration of some sort in one of the villages.

We offer a selection. **Jan**: 1-6, New Year celebrations; 20, *San Sebastián y San Fabián*. **Feb**: there are carnival celebrations for the whole month, with highlights on 2, *Virgen de la Candelaria*, and 17-19 *Concurso de Carnaval*.

**Mar-April**: *Semana Santa*, with impressive Good Friday processions. **May**: *Fiesta de las Cruces* throughout the whole month. **June**: 15 *Virgen de las Mercedes*; 24, *San Juan Bautista*; 29, *Fiesta Patronal*. **July**: 16, *Virgen del Carmen;* 24-25, *Santiago*. **Aug**: 4, *San Juan de Dios*; 16, *San Roque*; 30, *Santa Rosa de Lima*.

**Sept**: 8, *Virgen de Cocharcas*; 15, *Virgen de la Natividad*; 23-24, *Virgen de las Mercedes*; 29, *San Miguel Arcángel*. **Oct**: 4, *San Francisco de Asís*; 18, *San Lucas*. **Nov**: 1, *Día de Todos los Santos*. **Dec**: 3-13, *Virgen de Guadalupe*; 8, *Inmaculada Concepción*; 25, *Navidad* (Christmas).

## LOCAL INFORMATION

| Hotel prices | | | |
|---|---|---|---|
| L1 | over US$200 | L2 | US$151-200 |
| L3 | US$101-150 | A1 | US$81-100 |
| A2 | US$61-80 | A3 | US$46-60 |
| B | US$31-45 | C | US$21-30 |
| D | US$12-20 | E | US$7-11 |
| F | US$4-6 | G | up to US$3 |

### ● Accommodation

**NB** Prices may be raised in Holy Week. Note that the Plaza de Armas is called Plaza Constitución.

**B** *Huancayo Plaza*, Ancash 729, T 231072, F 235211, ex Turistas, old building, with bath, some rooms small, quiet, good meals for US$3.50; **B** *Presidente*, C Real 1138, T 231736, F 231275, with bath, clean, friendly, helpful, safe, breakfast only, rec.

**C** *Hostal Alpaca*, Giráldez 494, T 223136, with bath, hot water, TV, carpets, friendly, snack bar downstairs; **C** *Kiya*, Giráldez 107, Plaza Constitución, T 231431, F 235619, with bath, hot water, restaurant does not serve breakfast, phone, avoid noisy rooms on Av Real; **C** *Santa Felicita*, Plaza Constitución, T 235476, F 235285, with bath, hot water, good.

**D** *El Dorado*, Piura 428, T 223947, with bath, hot water, friendly, clean, some rooms with TV in **C** category; **D** *Hostal La Breña*, Arequipa 510, T 223490, with bath, hot water all day, new, clean, carpets; **D** *Hostal Plaza*, Ancash 171, T 210509, clean, hot water, ask for rooms at front; **D** *Percy's*, Real 1399, T 231208, shared bath, hot water in morning, basic, clean; **D** *Roger*, Ancash 460, T 233488, with bath, hot water, basic, clean; **D** *Rey*, Jr Angaráes 327, T 226324, with bath, hot water in morning, OK.

**E** pp *Casa Alojamiento de Aldo y Soledad Bonilla*, Huánuco 332, ½ block from Mcal Cáceres bus station, T 232103 (Lima 463-1141), inc breakfast, **D** pp full board, beautiful colonial house, hot water all day, heaters, owners speak English, laundry, secure, relaxing, nice courtyard, can arrange tours, book ahead to gaurantee a reservation, highly rec; **E** *Confort*, Ancash 231, 1 block from the main Plaza, T 233601, all rooms with bath, those with hot water are nicer, but more expensive, very clean, ask for a room not facing the street for peace and quiet, car parking US$1; **E** *Hostal Palace*, Ancash 1127, T 238501, with bath, clean, hot water, restaurant; **E** *Pussy*, Giráldez 359, T 231565, with bath, **F** without, hot water all day, safe, friendly, luggage stored, comfortable beds.

**F** pp *Hostal Baldeón*, Amazonas 543, T 231634, friendly, kitchen and laundry facilities, hot shower; **F** pp *La Casa de Mi Abuela*, Av Giráldez, hot shower, inc breakfast, good value, clean, friendly, laundry facilities, meals available, run by Lucho Hurtado's mother (see page 361); **F** pp *Pensión Huanca*, Pasaje San Antonio 113, 3 blocks from Av Centenario, 10 mins' walk from the centre, T 223956, clean rooms with hot showers, several with private bath, safe area, cosy atmosphere, run by Sra Juana, friendly, rec.

The following *hostales* are all **F** with shared bath and cold water, unless stated otherwise: *Central*, Loreto 452, T 211948, large place, basic, hot water in the morning; *Hostal San Martín*, Ferrocarril 362, clean, charming place, nr the rail station; *Los Angeles*, Real 245, T 231753, hot water, basic, restaurant; *Prince*, Calixto 578, T 232331, large and basic, hot water in the morning; *Torre-Torre*, Real 873, T 231118, shared bath, hot water. Luis Hurtado has 2 rooms, **G** inc breakfast, with hot water, washing and cooking facilities at La Cabaña restaurant (see below).

### ● Places to eat

The following are a selection of the better class, more expensive restaurants, serving typical dishes for about US$4-5, plus 18% tax, drinks can be expensive: *El Inca*, Puno 530, good salads; *Inti Palacio*, Lima 354; *Olímpico*, Av Giráldez 199, rec as the best in town, but not cheap.

Recommended cheaper places for typical food, about US$2-3 a dish, or with a fixed price *menú*, inc: *Lalo's*, Giráldez 365; *El Pino*, Real 539; *Pinkys*, Giráldez 147; *Los Tres Sillares*, Lima 170, serves typical Arequipeña food; *Chifa El Centro*, Giráldez 238, Chinese, good service; *La Cabaña*, Av Giraldez 652, outstanding pizzas, ice-cream, *calentitos*, and other dishes, great atmosphere, repeatedly rec (owned by Beverly Stuart and Lucho Hurtado – see below); *Marco Antonio*, Av Giráldez 255, cheap, excellent set lunch, friendly, rec; *Los Maduros*, Puno 599, nr main plaza, good pizzas; *Nuevo Horizonte*, Jr Ica 578, excellent set meal for only US$1. There is an excellent vegetarian restaurant on Arequipa 700 block, between Loreto and Ica. Lots of cheap restaurants along Av Giráldez serving set *menú*. *Chez Viena*, Puno 125, good cakes. *Café Billar*, Paseo de Breña 133, open 0900-2400, serves beer and snacks, pool tables. Breakfast is served in Mercado Modelo from 0700.

### ● Banks & money changers

**Banco de Crédito**, Real 1039, changes TCs with no commission, cash advance on Visa. **Western Union Money Transfer**, Ancash 540, Of 302, T 224816/235655, open Mon-Fri 0900-1300 and 1600-2000; Sat 0900-1300. There are several *casas de cambio* on the 4th and 5th blocks of Real; street changers hang out there as well. Also travel agencies and banks will change dollars.

### ● Cultural centres

**Peruvian-North American Cultural Institute**: Jr Guido 740.

### ● Entertainment

**Cinemas**: *Ciné Pacífico*, Real, block 6, and *Ciné Mantaro*, Real 950, El Tambo. Tickets US$2.

**Discotheques**: *El Molino*, Huancas, by the river; *A1A*, Bolognesi 299. Most discos open around 2000 and close at 0200. Some charge an entrance fee of US$3-4.

**Peñas**: all the *peñas* have folklore shows with dancing, open normally Fri, Sat and Sun from 1300 to 2200. Entrance fee is about US$2 pp. *Taki Wasi*, Huancavelica y 13 de Noviembre; *Ollantaytambo*, Puno, block 2. *Restaurante La Cabaña*, see above, has folk music at weekends.

### ● Security

Huancayo had a bad reputation for robbery, especially in the market and at the train and bus stations, but recent reports suggest that things are safer now (1996). The military presence is greatly reduced. You should travel only by day, especially in the coca growing areas in the central jungle beyond Huancayo.

Mate Burilado

● **Shopping**

**Crafts**: all crafts are made outside Huancayo in the many villages of the Mantaro Valley, or in Huancavelica. The villages are worth a visit to learn how the items are made. ***Casa de Artesano***, on the corner of Real and Paseo La Breña, at Plaza Constitución, has a wide selection of good quality crafts. There is a large cooperative, ***Kamaq Maki***, Santa Isabel 1856, which exports alpaca goods, open Mon-Fri 0900-1400. It is well-organized and employs many artesans; its aim is to control the market and prices. It is very helpful and will be happy to take you to meet the manufacturers of the goods. The workshop has a small shop. Contact Arturo Durán, T 231206/233183. ***Artesanía Sumaq Ruray***, Jr Brasilia 132, San Carlos 5th block, T 237018, produces fine weaving, but it's not cheap.

● **Tourist offices**

**Ministry of Tourism**, is now housed in the *Casa de Artesano* (see above), has information about the area, helpful, open 0730-1330 Mon-Fri. **Lucho (Luis) Hurtado**, who is from Huancayo and speaks good English, and his wife, Beverly Stuart, from New Zealand, own *Pizzería La Cabaña* (see above); you are always welcome for a slice of pizza and a side order of information. They organize Spanish courses for beginners for US$150/week, inc accommodation with local families, rec, weaving, playing the pan flute, Peruvian cooking and lots of other things. They also have maps and a book exchange. Lucho is an excellent private guide who arranges adventurous, cultural trips in the mountains or jungle, giving a personal touch, and hires bikes for tours of rural communities. He has been highly and repeatedly rec as a guide. Contact him in Huancayo, or through the South American Explorers Club in Lima. **Turismo Huancayo**, C Real 517 Of 6, T 233351, organizes local tours, rec.

● **Transport**

**Trains** There are two unconnected railway stations. The Central station serves Lima, via La Oroya, 298 km, 10 hrs, when the service is running, which it hasn't been since 1991.

From the small station in Chilca suburb (15 mins by taxi, US$1), trains run to **Huancavelica**, 142 km, narrow gauge 3 ft. There are 2 trains: the *autovagón* (*expreso*) at 0630 Mon-Sat, at 1400 on Sun; US$2.20 normal, US$3.50 buffet class. The journey takes 4½ hrs, and is a spectacular one with fine views, passing through typical mountain villages. Meals, drinks and snacks are served on the train, and at the village stations vendors sell food and crafts. The local train leaves at 1230 Mon-Sat, and takes 6½ hrs; US$1.75 2nd class, US$2 1st class and US$3.50 buffet class. You can buy tickets 1 day in advance, or 1 hr before departure. Services can be suspended in the rainy season.

**Road** To **Lima**, 6-7 hrs on a good paved road, US$9-10. Travelling by day is rec for the fantastic views and, of course, for safety. If you must travel by night, take warm clothing. Recommended companies: Mcal Cáceres, Jr Huánuco 350, T 231232; Cruz del Sur, Ayacucho 287; Etucsa, Puno 220, several a day (*bus cama*, US$11). Many other companies ply this route, many are cheaper but also less comfortable and less safe. Small buses for Lima congregate 15 blocks N of Plaza Constitución on C Real; there is much competition for passengers. Comités 12 and 22, both on C Loreto, and Comité 30, C Giráldez, run to Lima in 6 hrs, when the car is full, which can mean waiting all day; US$12 pp.

To **Ayacucho**, 319 km, 11 hrs, US$7. Empresa Molina, C Angaraes 287, at 0700, 1700 and 1800 and TransFano at 1830, both rec; also Antezana, Arequipa 1301, at 2100. The road has improved but is still very difficult in the wet. Take warm clothing. The military seem to have established control over this route after years of terrorist disruption. Check the situation in advance, though, travel by day, and keep abreast of what is going on. After Izcuchaca, on the railway to Huancavelica, there is a good road to the Kichuas hydroelectric scheme, but thereafter it is narrow with hair-raising bends and spectacular bridges. The scenery is staggering, but sit on the right or you'll have 11 hrs of staring at a solid rock wall. From Huanta the road descends into Ayacucho.

To **Huancavelica**, 147 km, 5 hrs, US$3, several buses a day; Empresa Hidalgo, Loreto 350, San Pablo, Ancash 1248, at 1400. The road is in poor condition but being improved, and takes much longer in the wet. The scenery is spectacular. Most travellers use the train.

To **Cerro de Pasco**, 255 km, 5-6 hrs, US$3-4. There is quite a good paved road to La Oroya, but a dirt road from there to Cerro de Pasco. Transporte Salazar, Giráldez 245, Sun and Mon at 2100. Oriental, Ferrocarril 146, 3 a week; on to Huánuco, 105 km, 3 hrs, US$2; Tingo María, 118 km, 5 hrs; and Pucallpa, 11 hrs. Comité 12 does this route for US$15 pp when full.

To **Satipo**, 229 km, 12 hrs, on a very difficult road, which is impossible in the wet; San Juan, Quito 136, rec. The bus goes via Jauja, Tarma and La Merced; 5 hrs, US$4.50. San Juan and Los Canarios (Puno 725) go to Oxapampa, 12 hrs. To **Cañete**, 289 km, 10 hrs, US$4, some trucks and a few buses travel this route. It is a poor road, with beautiful mountain landscapes before dropping to the valley of Cañete. To **Jauja**, 44 km, 1 hr; colectivos leave from Huamaumarca y Amazonas; ones via San Jerónimo and Concepción have 'Izquierda' on the front. Most buses to the Mantaro Valley leave from several places around the market area. Buses to Hualhuas, Cajas and Huamancaca leave from block 3 of Pachitea. Buses to Cochas leave from Amazonas y Giráldez.

## IZCUCHACA

Between Huancayo and Huancavelica, Izcuchaca is the site of a bridge over the Río Mantaro. The name in Quechua means 'stone bridge'. The bridge was partly rebuilt in the 18th century. On the edge of town is a fascinating pottery workshop whose machinery is driven by a water turbine. There is also a small shop.

A nice hike is to the chapel on a hill overlooking the valley; 1-1½ hrs each way.

• **Accommodation & places to eat** There are 2 hotels: one is on the plaza, **G**, with no bathroom, you have to use the public bath by the river; the other is just off the plaza, a yellow 3-storey house, **G**, no shower, toilet suitable for men only, chamber pot supplied, only blankets on bed, cold. ***Restaurant El Parque*** on plaza, opens 0700, delicious food.

• **Transport** The 0630 train from Huancavelica arrives at 0800, then continues to Huancayo; US$1.15. The train tends to be very crowded. Sit on the left for the best views. The train from Huancayo passes at around 1700. Daily colectivo to Ayacucho at 1000-1100, 8 hrs.

ROUTES There is an alternative route to Ayacucho, little used by buses, but which involves not so much climbing for cyclists. Cross the pass into the Mantaro valley on a reopened road to **Quichuas**, which has no hotel, but there is a basic place, 3 km away by a dam. Then on to **Anco**, rebuilding after a flood in 1977, where there is a small, basic lodging with running water, and to **Mayocc** (lodging). At Mayocc a bridge is being repaired. From Mayocc go to **Huanta**, crossing a bridge after 10 km, 20 km from Huanta, then it's a paved road to Ayacucho.

## HUANCAVELICA

Capital of its Department, Huancavelica is a friendly and attractive town (*Pop* 37,500; *Alt* 3,680m), surrounded by huge, rocky mountains. It was founded in the 16th century by the Spanish to exploit rich deposits of mercury and silver. Very few of the mines remain open, and those that do are a few hours from town. It is predominantly an Indigenous town, and people still wear traditional costume. There are beautiful mountain walks in the neighbourhood.

### Places of interest

The cathedral, located on the Plaza de Armas, has an altar considered to be one of the finest examples of colonial art in Peru. Also very impressive are the five other churches in town. The church of San Francisco, for example, has no less than 11 altars. Sadly, though, most of the churches are closed to visitors.

Bisecting the town is the Río Huancavelica. S of the river is the main commercial centre. North of the river, on the hillside, are the thermal baths; US$0.15 for private rooms, but the water is not very hot, US$0.10 for the hot public pool, also hot showers, take a lock for the doors, open 0600-1500. There is a colourful daily market, which is smaller than in the past, and most handicrafts are transported directly to Lima, but you can still visit craftsmen in neighbouring villages. There is a daily food market at Muñoz y Barranca. The Potaqchiz hill, just outside the town, gives a fine view, about 1 hr walk up from San Cristóbal.

## Local festivals

The whole area is rich in culture. In Sept there is a tourist week with a huge crafts market, music and dancing. Typical festivals: 6 Jan, Niño Occe; 12 Jan, Fiesta de Negritos; carnival in Feb; Palm Sunday procession; Semana Santa; June, Fiesta de Torre-Torre; Nov, Todos los Santos; 25 Dec, Los Galos.

## Local information

**NB** The department of Huancavelica saw much terrorist activity in the past, but since 1992 the military has regained control and it is safer to visit. Always carry your documentation, travel by day and find out about latest conditions before travelling.

### ● Accommodation

**C** ***Presidente***, Plaza de Armas, T 952760, ex Tourist Hotel, cheaper without bath, lovely colonial building, overpriced.

**E** ***Mercurio***, Jr Torre Tagle 455, T 952773, unfriendly, basic, cold water.

**F** ***Camacho***, Jr Carabaya 481, best of the cheap hotels, hot shower in the morning only, clean and well maintained, excellent value; **F** ***Hostal Tahuantinsuyo***, Carabaya 399, T 952968, with bath, hot water in mornings, dirty and dingy; **F** ***Santo Domingo***, Av Barranca 366, T 953086; and **F** ***Savoy***, Av Muñoz 294, both cheap, very basic, shared bath, cold water; **F** ***Virrey***, Av Barranca 317, basic, cold water.

### ● Places to eat

There are lots of cheap, basic restaurants on C Muñoz and Jr Virrey Toledo. All serve typical food, mostly with set *menú*, US$1.50. Also cheap are: ***La Estrellita***, Av Sebastián Barranca 255; ***Olímpico***, Jr JM Chávez 124; ***Super Gordo***, Av Celestino Muñoz 488; ***Yananaco***, Av Cáceres 533. Better are: ***Paquirri***, Jr Arequipa 137, good, expensive; ***Mochica Sachún***, Av Virrey Toledo 303, great *menú* US$1.50, otherwise expensive, popular; ***Pollería Joy***, Toledo y Arequipa, good for chicken; ***La Casona***, Jr Virrey Toledo 230, cheap and good *menú*, also a *peña*; ***Las Magnolias***, Manuel Muñoz 1 block from the Plaza, OK.

### ● Banks & money changers

**Banco de Crédito**, Virrey Toledo 300 block.

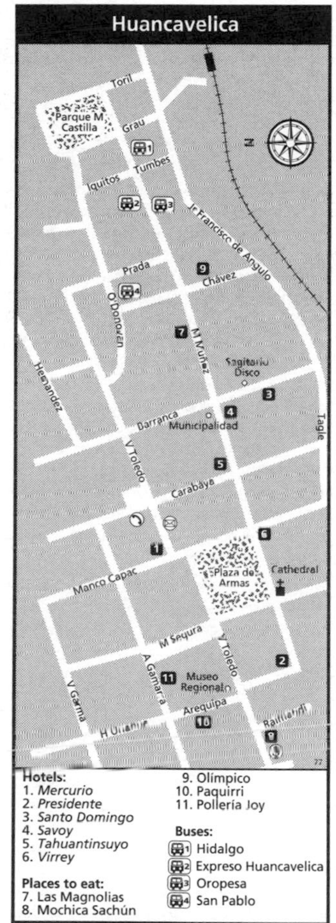

### ● Post & telecommunications

**Post Office**: on Toledo, 1 block from the Plaza de Armas.

**Telephones**: Carabaya y Virrey Toledo.

### ● Tourist offices

**Ministerio de Industria y Comercio, Turismo y Artesanías**, Jr Nicolás de Piérola 180, open Mon-Fri 0730-1400, very helpful. **Instituto Nacional de la Cultura**, Plaza San Juan de Dios, open Mon-Sat 1000-1300, 1500-1900, director Alfonso Zuasnabar, a good source of information on festivals, archaeological sites, history, etc. Gives courses on music and dancing, and lectures some evenings. There is also an interesting but small archaeology and anthropology museum.

### ● Transport

**Trains** See under Huancayo; the *autovagón/expreso* leaves for Huancayo daily at 0630, the local train at 1230, Mon-Sat.

**Road** All bus companies have their offices on and leave from C Muñoz. To **Huancayo**, 147 km, 5 hrs, US$3.50, it's a rough road but is being improved, several buses a day, eg Expreso Huancavelica and Empresa Hidalgo. To **Lima** there are two routes: one is via Huancayo, 445 km, 13 hrs minimum, US$8. Most buses to Huancayo go on to Lima, there are several a day. The other route is via **Pisco**, 269 km, 12 hrs, US$9. Only one bus a day at 0600, with Oropesa, buy your ticket 1 day in advance. Some trucks also travel this route. The road is in very poor condition, but the views are spectacular and worth the effort. Be prepared for sub-zero temperatures in the early morning as the bus passes snowfields, then for temperatures of 25-30°C as the bus descends to the coast in the afternoon.

Getting to **Ayacucho** (247 km) is a problem, as there are no buses. Either take the train to Izcuchaca, stay the night and take the colectivo (see above), or take the morning train to La Mejorada where you can catch the 1000 Expreso Molino bus from Huancayo to Ayacucho. Alternatively take a bus to Santa Inés, then a truck to Rumichaca, the junction where buses and trucks on the Lima-Ayacucho route pass. Buses go through Rumichaca at 0300-0400 only, but there are many trucks and police at the checkpoint who may help with lifts. Take an Oropesa bus from Huancavelica to Santa Inés at 0600, which allows plenty of time for a truck to Rumichaca and then another to Ayacucho. Rumichaca-Ayacucho is 7 hrs by truck and 4 hrs by bus. The road is in an appalling condition. The journey is a cold one but spectacular as it is the highest continuous road in the world, rarely dropping below 4,000m for 150 km.

## HUANCAVELICA-AYACUCHO VIA SANTA INES

Out of Huancavelica the road climbs steeply with switchbacks between herds of llamas and alpacas grazing on rocky perches. Around Pucapampa (Km 43) is one of the highest habitable *altiplanos* (4,500m), where the rare and highly prized ash-grey alpaca can be seen.

**Santa Inés**, 78 km, has one very friendly restaurant where you can sleep and several others. Nearby are two lakes (Laguna Choclacocha) which can be visited in 2½ hrs. 50 km beyond Santa Inés at the Abra de Apacheta (4,750m), 98 km from Ayacucho, the rocks are all colours of the rainbow, and running through this fabulous scenery is a violet river. These incredible colours are all caused by oxides. 11 km later is the Paso Chonta and the turnoff to Huachocolpa. By taking the turnoff and continuing for 3 km you'll reach the highest drivable pass in the world, at 5,059m.

Clay model of Quinua church near Ayacucho

## AYACUCHO

**Ayacucho** (*Pop* 101,600; *Alt* 2,740m; *Phone code* 064) is the capital of its Department. The city was founded by the invading Spanish on 9 January 1539, who named it San Juan de la Frontera. This was changed to San Juan de la Victoria after the Battle of Chupas, when the king's forces finally defeated the rival Almagrist power. Despite these Spanish titles, the city always kept its original name of Huamanga. It became an important base for the army of the Liberator Simón Bolívar in his triumphant sweep S from the Battle of Junín. It was here, on the Pampa de Quinua, on 9 December 1824, that the decisive Battle of Ayacucho was fought, bringing Spanish rule in Peru to an end. Huamanga was, therefore, the first city on the continent to celebrate its liberty. In the midst of the massive festivities, the Liberator decreed that the city be named Ayacucho – meaning 'City of Blood'.

For much of the 1980s and early 1990s, this title seemed appropriate as the Shining Path terrorized the local populace, severely punishing anyone they suspected of siding with the military. Now, though, peace has returned to this beautiful colonial Andean city. It is a warm, hospitable, tranquil place, where the inhabitants are eager to promote tourism. It also boasts a large, active student population. The University, founded in 1677, and closed in 1886, was reopened in 1958.

The city is built round Parque Sucre, the main plaza, with the Cathedral, Municipalidad and Palacio de Gobierno facing on to it. It is famous for its hugely impressive Semana Santa celebrations, its splendid market and, not least, a plethora of churches – 33 of them no less – giving the city its alternative name *La Ciudad de las Iglesias*. A week can easily be spent enjoying Ayacucho and its hinterland. The climate is lovely, with warm, sunny days and pleasant balmy evenings.

### PLACES OF INTEREST

For a fascinating insight into Quechua art and culture, a visit to **Barrio Santa Ana** is a must. The district is full of *artesanía* shops, galleries and workshops. *Galería Latina*, at Plazuela de Santa Ana 605, has been recommended. The owner, Alejandro Gallardo Llacctahuamán, is very friendly and has lots of information on weaving techniques.

Also recommended is the *Wari Art Gallery*, run by Gregorio Sulca and his

### A church on every roof

Many of the pre-Hispanic art forms and traditions, lost over the centuries following the conquest, have been resurrected in recent decades. One example of this is the folk art of the village of Quinua, outside Ayacucho.

Pottery has been produced here for many centuries, but over the past decade conflict between the Peruvian military and the Shining Path guerrillas has left Quinua almost deserted, as many of the artisans fled to the relative safety of Lima, where they had to adapt to different clay and working conditions. Today, the area is more peaceful and it is hoped they will return.

The pieces made in Quinua range from model churches and nativity figures to humorous groups of musicians and gossiping women. The rich red local clay is modelled mainly by hand and decorated with local mineral earth colours. Traditionally, the churches are set on the roofs of newly-occupied houses to ward off evil spirits. Virtually every roof in the village has a church on it – including the church itself.

Extracted from *Arts and Crafts of South America*, by Lucy Davies and Mo Fini, Tumi.

family, at Jr Mcal Cáceres 302, Santa Ana, T 912529. Gregorio, like his father before him, is one of the foremost Quechuan artisans and artists in all Peru and the gallery displays a selection of their works. He will gladly explain the Quechua legends, weaving and painting techniques, and anything else you care to know, including the problems the city encountered at the hands of Shining Path. A recurring theme in his work is the desire for peace during the years of terrorism. The technique he uses, learned from his father, is unique, and considering the quality and length of time involved, his textiles are reasonable priced. Gregorio also keeps a garden of Andean plants and will explain their various uses. A good grasp of Spanish is essential to appreciate fully this unique experience. Visitors to the gallery should climb to the roof of the Instituto de Cultura Quechua next door, which affords wonderful views of the city and surrounding hills.

Also worth a visit is the **Mirador Turístico**, on Cerro Acuchimay, which offers great views over the city. Take a *micro* from the corner of 28 de Julio and Plaza de Armas to Carmen Alto, then walk 2 blocks.

### Churches

The construction of Ayacucho's many colonial religious buildings is said to have been financed by wealthy Spanish mine-owners and governors. Unfortunatley many have fallen into disrepair and are closed to the public. Visitors are advised to see the 17th century **Cathedral**, built in 1612. Its 3 strong, solid naves are of simple architecture, in contrast to the elegant decoration of the interior, particularly the superb gold leaf altars. The Cathedral is open daily 1730-1845; it also has a Museo de Arte Religioso, but it is closed indefinitely.

**San Cristóbal** was the first church to be founded in the city, and is possibly the oldest in South America. Buried beneath its floor are the remains of some of the combatants from the Battle of Chupas. Another old church is **La Merced**, whose high choir is a good example of the simplicity of the churches of the early period of the Viceroyalty. In 1886 a flagstone was discovered with the sculpted image of a sleeping warrior, known popularly as the 'Chejo-Pacheco'. **La Compañía de Jesús** (1605), has one of the most important facades of Viceregal architecture. It is of baroque style and guarded by two impressive 18th century towers. It is open Sun 1200-1230 and 1730-1800. The church also has an adjacent chapel.

Also of note are the churches of **San Francisco de Asís** (open daily 1000-1200 and 1500-1700), and **Santa Teresa** (1683, open daily 0600-0700) with its monastery. Both have magnificent gold-leafed altars heavily brocaded and carved in the churrigueresque style. **Santa Clara** is renowned for its beautifully delicate coffered ceiling, and as the place where La Monja Alferez took refuge to avoid execution; open Wed-Sun 0630-1600. One of the city's most notable churches is **Santo Domingo** (1548). Its fine façade has triple Roman arches and Byzantine towers. Open daily 0700-0800.

### Colonial houses

Ayacucho is well-endowed with Seignorial houses. To the N of the Parque Sucre, on the corner of Portal de la Unión and Asamblea, are the **Casonas de los Marqueses de Mozobamba y del Pozo**, also called Velarde-Alvárez. On the same Portal is the house of Canon Manuel Frías, where the writer and caricaturist, Abraham Valdelomar (who also used the pseudonym El Conde de Lemos after 1915), tragically died. In the Portals to the W, where the family seats of Astete and Guevara were once found, is the Casona where the chief magistrate, Nicolás de Boza y Solís, lived and which served as a prison cell for the Independence heroine, María Parado de Bellido.

**Casa Jaúregui** is situated opposite

the church of La Merced, and **Casa Olano** is in C De la Compañía. On the 5th block of Jr Grau, before San Blas, is the house where Simón Bolívar and José Antonio de Sucre stayed. In 1824 the house was occupied by the Flores family and is perhaps the finest example of a typical Castillian house. On the 5th block of 28 de Julio is **Casona Vivanco** (see **Museums** below).

## MUSEUMS

**Museo Histórico Natural**, Jr Arequipa 175, in the University, open daily 0900-1300, US$0.35. The museum was reported as closed at the time of writing (mid-1996). **Museo Arqueológico Hipólito Unanua** is opposite the University Residences, on Av Independencia, at the N end of town, open 0800-1300, 1500-1700, Mon-Fri, 0900-1300 Sat, US$1.30. It has many Huari artefacts. **Museo Andrés A Cáceres**, is housed in the late 16th century Casona Vivanco, Jr 28 de Julio 508, open 0900-1230, 1400-1700, Mon-Sat, US$0.45. The museum displays prehispanic, colonial, republican and contemporary art.

## EXCURSIONS

### Vilcashuamán

These impressive Inca ruins are to the S,

### From Pagan ritual to folk art

*Retablos* – or St Mark's boxes, as they were originally known – were introduced to Latin America by the Spanish in the 16th century. These simple, portable altars containing religious images were intended to aid in the task of converting the native population to Catholicism. Early examples often contained images of St James, patron saint of the Spanish army.

The *retablos* were made from a variety of materials and 2 distinct styles evolved to suit different needs. Those of clay, leather and plaster were destined for the native rural population, while those for use by the colonial hierarchy were made of gold and silver, or the famous alabaster of Ayacucho, known as Huamanga stone.

Traditional *retablos* had 2 floors inside a box. On the top floor were the patron saints of animals: St Mark, patron saint of bulls; St Agnes, patron saint of goats; and St Anthony, patron saint of mules, among others. On the lower floor was a scene of a cattle thief being reprimanded by a landowner.

From the 17th century onwards, the native rural population used the *retablo* in ceremonies accompanying cattle branding. During Aug, a ritual believed to have its roots in pagan fertility festivals took place in which the *retablo* was placed on a table and surrounded by offerings of food and coca leaves. People danced round and sang in front of the box, asking for protection for their animals and celebrating their well-being.

In the 1940s the first *retablo* reached Lima, by which time the art of making them had virtually disappeared. However, with the new-found outside interest a revival began. The traditional elements began to be varied and the magical or ritualistic value was lost as they became a manifestation of folk art. The artist Joaquín López and his family created the early examples, but today they are made in many workshops.

The figures are made from a mixture of plaster and mashed potato, modelled or made in moulds, sealed with glue, then painted and positioned inside the brightly painted box. Some miniature versions are made in chiclet boxes or egg shells, while, at the other end of the scale, some have 5 floors and take months to complete.

Extracted from *Arts and Crafts of South America*, by Lucy Davies and Mo Fini, Tumi.

## The Huari influence

The city of Huari had a population of 50,000 and reached its apogee in AD 900. Its influence spread throughout much of Peru: N to Cajamarca; along the north coast to Lambayeque; south along the coast to Moquegua; and south across the sierra to Cusco. Before the Inca invasion the Huari formed a *chanca* – a confederation of ethnic groups – and populated the Pampas river and an area W of the Apurímac. This political agreement between the peoples of Ayacucho, Andahuaylas, Junín and Huancavelica was seen by the Incas in Cusco as a threat. The Incas fought back around 1440 with a bloody attack on the Huari on the Pampa de Ayacucho, and so began a period of Inca domination. The scene of this massacre is still known as *Rincón de los Muertos*.

beyond Cangallo. John Hemming writes: "There is a 5-tiered, stepped *usnu* platform faced in fine Inca masonry and topped by a monolithic 2-seat throne. The parish church is built in part of the Inca sun temple and rests on stretches of Inca terracing. Vilcashuamán was an important provincial capital, the crossroads where the road from Cusco to the Pacific met the empire's north-south highway."

Tours can be arranged with Travel Agencies in Ayacucho, US$55 pp for 2 people, full day tour, including Intihuatana; alternatively stay overnight. Market day is Wed.

• **Accommodation** There are 3 hotels in the village of Vilcashuamán, all **F**, and all basic but clean.

• **Transport** Buses and colectivos run from Av M Castilla, Tues, Thurs and Sat at 0600, returning Wed, Fri and Sun at 0600, 5-6 hrs, US$4.50.

Near Vilcashuamán is the village of **Vischongo**. About an hour's walk uphill from the village are the Inca baths of **Intihuatana**, which are worth seeing as much for their superb location on a beautiful lake as for the ruins themselves.

From Vilcashuamán to Vischongo takes 1 hr, US$0.45. Vischongo to Ayacucho, 5 hrs, US$2.70. It is possible to see both ruins in a day, though it's more relaxing to spend the night in Vilcashuamán, or better still, camp at the lake near Vischongo.

### Huari

A good road going N from Ayacucho leads to Huari (see page 357), dating from the 'Middle Horizon', when the Huari culture spread across most of Peru. This was the first urban walled centre in the Andes and was used for political, administrative, ceremonial, residential and productive purposes. The huge irregular stone walls are up to 12m high and rectangular houses and streets can be made out. There are large areas of flat stone which may have been for religious purposes and there are subterranean canals and tunnels. The most important activity here was artistic productivity. High temperature ovens were used to mass produce ceramics of many different colours. The Huari also worked with gold, silver, metal and alloys such as bronze, which was used for weapons and for decorative objects. Examples of pottery finds at the site can be seen in the archaeological museum in Ayacucho.

• **Transport** Buses leave from Ovalo in Barrio Magdalena. There are no specific times, they leave when full from 0700 onwards. Buses go on to La Quinua, US$1, and Huanta, US$1.35 (see below). Trips can be arranged to Huari, La Quinua village and the battlefield; US$16-17 pp for 2 people (see **Travel agents** below).

**La Quinua** village, 37 km NE of Ayacucho, has a charming cobbled main plaza and many of the buildings have been restored. There is a small market on Sun. Nearby, on the Pampa de Quinua, a huge obelisk commemorates

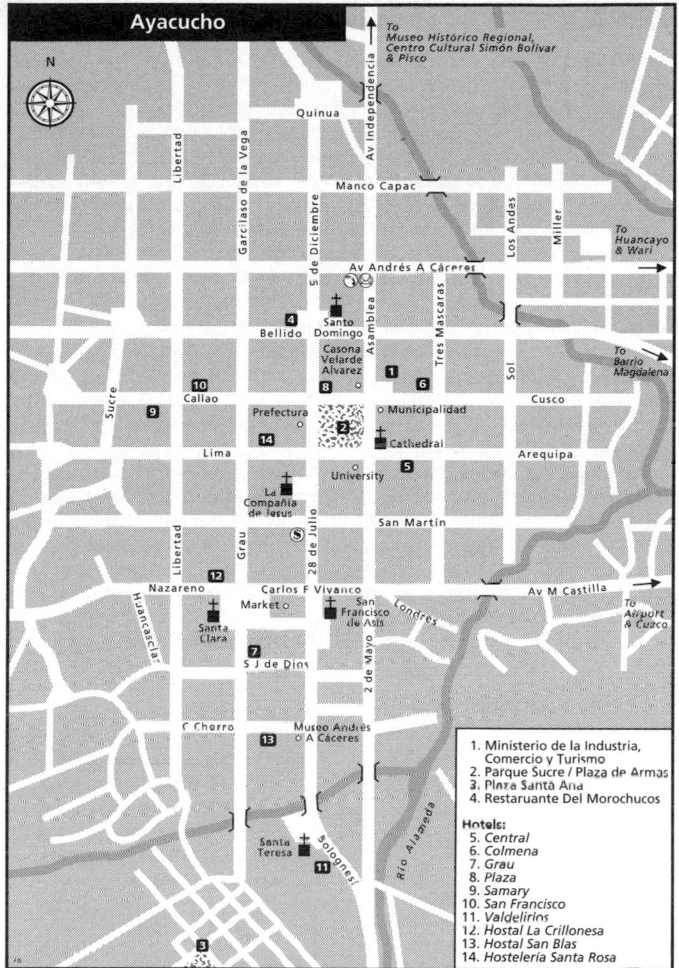


the battle of Ayacucho. The obelisk is 44m high, representing 44 years of struggle for independence. There is also a small, poorly displayed museum; US$1.40. The village's handicrafts are recommended, especially ceramics, though many potters have moved to Lima. Most of the houses have miniature ceramic churches on the roof. San Pedro Ceramics, at the foot of the hill leading to the monument, and Mamerto Sánchez, Jr Sucre, should be visited. The village's festival, *Fiesta de la Virgen de Cocharcas*, is celebrated around 7-8 Sept; 3 days of processions, dancing and bullfighting.

It is a beautiful 18 km walk downhill from La Quinua to Huari, where trucks

## Semana Santa

Ayacucho is renowned throughout Peru, and South America, for its celebration of Semana Santa, or Holy Week, when scores of thousands of devout Peruvians congregate on the city, occupying every hotel bed and spare inch of friends' and relatives' floor space. Like most religious festivals in the Quechua-speaking world, this is a union of the Catholic religion and native Andean elements. The build up to Holy Week begins on the Friday before, with a procession of Christ on the cross and the *Virgen Dolorosa*. This is very beautiful, but the suffering is 'symbolized' by the custom of flinging pebbles from slingshots. The following day is "Sábado de Víspera", when the image of *El Señor de la Parra* is carried through the town.

The festivities begin in earnest with a charming Palm Sunday procession, beginning at 1600. Palm-bearing women and children accompany a statue of Christ riding on a white donkey. On arrival at the Cathedral on the Plaza de Armas, the ceremony of *Primera Roseña* – which only takes place here and in Seville in Spain – begins. This is a representation of the struggle between light and darkness and is symbolized by a red cross and a black flag held by a priest dressed as a penitent. The congregation maintains a strict silence, until the moment when good triumphs over evil, when they burst into song.

On Monday, the image of *El Señor del Huerto* is carried from the Church of La Buena Muerte, laden with candles, wax adornments and olive branches, in commemoration of the death of Christ. This procession is notable for being exclusively for women, who are dressed in a variety of traditional and regional costume. Tuesday sees the procession of *El Señor de la Sentencia*, from the Church of La Amargura, symbolizing the capture and sentencing of Jesus. His image is paraded through the town, its bearers with bound hands and appearing to suffer, in a gesture of empathy.

One of the most emotional events takes place on Wednesday. Setting off from the Church of Santa Clara, the patron of Huamanga, Jesus of Nazareth, is lifted

leave for Ayacucho until about 1700. Tombs of the Huari nobles are being excavated along the road from Ayacucho to Quinua.

### The Huanta valley

This picturesque region, 48 km NE of Ayacucho, consists of the districts of Huanta, Luricocha, Santillana, Ayahuanco, Iguaín and Huamanaguilla. The town of Huanta is 1 hr from Ayacucho, on the road to Huancayo. It was here that the Pokras and Chancas warriors put up their last, brave fight against the Inca invasion. From Huanta, the lakes of Qarqarcocha, San Antonio, Chakacocha, Yanacocha and Pampacocha can be visited, also the valley of Luricocha, 5 km away, with its lovely, warm climate. Huanta celebrates the *Fiesta de las Cruces* during the first week of May, with much music and dancing. Its Sun market is large and interesting.

The area is notable as the site of perhaps the oldest known culture in South America, 20,000 years old, evidence of which was found in the cave of **Pikimachay**. The remains are now in Lima's museums. The cave is 24 km from Ayacucho, on the road to Huanta. It is a 30-min walk from the road.

## LOCAL FESTIVALS

The area is well-known for its festivals throughout the year. Almost every day there is a celebration in one of the surrounding villages. Check with the Ministry of Tourism.

**Semana Santa** begins on the Fri before Holy Week. There follows one of the world's finest Holy Week celebrations, with candle-lit nightly processions, floral

high amidst a sea of devotees. At the same time, from the other corners of the main Plaza appear the images of *La Dolorosa, San Juan* and *La Verónica*. The emotional drama of the whole passionate scene reaches its climax when the Virgin finally appears directly opposite her son and the masses break down in floods of tears. The night-time activities centre on Parque Sucre. The plaza is full of stalls selling food and *ponche*, which is only drunk during Holy Week.

Compared to the emotional drain of the previous day, Thursday is an altogether quieter, more solemn affair, being the eve of the crucifixion. This is followed on Good Friday by a collective mourning for the death of Jesus. The Sermon of the 3 hours is said in Quechua and Spanish and is an interpretation of the Christ's final pronouncement from the cross.

Saturday, or *Sábado de Gloria*, sees a return to celebratory mood, in anticipation of the Messiah's resurrection. Groups of musicians from all over the region gather early in the day in preparation for the grand finale. In the afternoon, a pilgrimage takes place to the cross atop Cerro Acochimay. This soon becomes a huge fair, covering the whole hill and is well worth a visit.

Then begin the real festivities of the week, which continue long into the night. In the main plaza stalls provide free beer, chicha and food, while bulls and horses are paraded around. The atmosphere grows ever livelier, reaching a kind of mass hysteria as dawn approaches. At around 0530, a huge float, adorned with thousands of wax images and candles, is borne by 300 men, from the atrium of the Cathedral to the Plaza, symbolizing the resurrection of Jesus Christ. Its arrival is greeted by a massive explosion of fireworks, ringing of church bells and an ecstatic crowd. The atmosphere can only be described as magical.

In the afternoon things are a bit more sedate, with horse racing in the Leoncio Prado stadium. And so ends Semana Santa in Ayacucho, one of the truly great festivals of Latin America.

'paintings' on the streets, daily fairs (the biggest on Easter Saturday), horse races and contests among peoples from all central Peru. All accommodation is fully booked for months in advance of Holy Week. Many people offer beds in their homes during the week. Look out for notices on the doors, especiually on Jr Libertad.

Carnival in Feb is reported as a wild affair. On 25 April is the anniversary of the founding of Huamanga province. 4-10 Dec is *Semana de la Libertad Americana*, to honour the Battle of Ayacucho.

## LOCAL INFORMATION

**NB** Ayacucho suffered the most from terrorist activity because it was where Sendero Luminoso started operating in 1980. Since 1992 the area has been under military control and even though there are lots of checkpoints, few travellers have encountered problems visiting the region in 1995/96. Tourist services are being quickly re-established, and many new hotels have opened in the past few years. Make sure you get the latest information before going, and travel by day

### ● Accommodation

Ayacucho suffers from water shortages. There is usually no water between 0900 and 1500. Many hotels have their own water tanks.

**A3** *Plaza*, 9 de Diciembre 184, T 912202, F 912314, beautiful colonial building but the rooms don't match up to the palatial splendour of the reception, comfortable, TV, some rooms overlook plaza.

**B** *Valdelirios*, Bolognesi 520, T 913908, F 914014, lovely colonial-style mansion, beautifully-furnished, pickup from airport US$1.30, restaurant, bar, disco at weekends, reserve at least 24 hrs in advance, rec; **B-C** *Yañez*, Mcal Cáceres 1210, T 912464, with bath, clean, cable TV, well furnished rooms, it's a former hospital so the decor is slightly clinical, a bit pricey.

**C** ***Hostal 3 Máscaras***, Jr 3 Máscaras 194, T 914107, with bath, **D** without, nice colonial building with patio, clean, basic rooms, hot water 0600-1100, overpriced; **C** ***Hostelería Santa Rosa***, Jr Lima 166, T/F 912083, lovely colonial courtyard, hot water mornings and evenings, friendly, car park, restaurant, rec; **C** ***San Francisco***, Jr Callao 290, T 912959, F 914501, inc breakfast, new, friendly, comfortable, nice patio, rec.

**D** ***Colmena***, Jr Cusco 140, T 912146, with bath, hot water 0700-0900, clean, small rooms, secure, pleasant courtyard; **D** ***Hostal El Mirador***, Jr Bellido 112, T 912338, new, clean, large rooms, washing facilities, great view from the roof terrace; **D** ***Hostal Las Orquídeas***, Jr Arequipa 287, T 914435, with bath, intermittent hot water, clean, basic, noisy from disco next door at weekends; **D** ***Hostal Plateros***, Jr Lima 206, with bath, hot water, clean, comfortable; **D** ***Residencial La Crillonesa***, Nazareno 165, T 912350, with bath, clean, friendly, hot water, washing facilities, discount for longer stay, great views from roof terrace; **D** ***Samary***, Jr Callao 335, T/F 912442, discount for foreigners, clean, safe, hot water in mornings, friendly, rec; **D** ***Hostal San Blas***, Jr Chorro 167, T 910552, with bath, hot water all day, new, clean, friendly, washing facilities, nice rooms, cheap meals available, discount for longer stay, Carlos will act as a local tour guide and knows everyone, rec.

**E** ***Central***, Jr Arequipa 188, T 912144, shared bath, clean, large rooms, good value, **F** in low season; **E** ***Grau***, Jr San Juan de Dios 192, T 912695, with bath, hot water, clean, washing facilities, good value; **E** pp ***Hostal El Sol***, Av Mcal Castilla 132, T 913069, hot water all day, new, clean, well-furnished large rooms, rec; **E** ***Hostal Luz Imperial***, Jr Libertad 591 (altos), with bath, cheaper without, hot water in mornings, basic, clean, friendly; **E** ***Hostal Wari***, Mcal Cáceres 836, T 913065, shared bath, hot water in morning, clean, basic, large rooms; **E** ***Huamanga***, Jr Bellido 535, T 912725, basic, clean, hot water US$1.30 extra; **E** ***Magdalena***, Mcal Cáceres 810, T 912910, with bath, cheaper without, basic but good.

**F** ***Hostal Ayacucho***, Jr Lima 165, T 912759, shared bath, cold water, basic; **F** ***Santiago***, Nazareno 177, T 912132, shared bath, hot water in mornings, clean, OK.

### ● Places to eat

***Tradición***, San Martín 406, popular, good cheap *menú*; ***San Agustín Café Turístico***, Jr Cusco 101, good food and lemon meringue pie, rec for snacks; ***La Casona***, Jr Bellido 463, regional specialites, try their *puca picante*, beef in a thick spicy sauce, rather like Indian curry, rec; ***Del Morochucos***, Jr 9 de Diciembre 205, opp Santo Domingo church, large selection, pizzas, *parrillada* etc, very popualr, live music, nice colonial-style building; ***Portales***, on Plaza, Portal Unión, popular; ***Urpicha***, Jr Londres 272, typical food, rec; ***La Buena Salud***, Jr Asamblea 206, vegetarian, cheap *menú*; ***Pollería Nino***, Jr Garcilaso de la Vega 240, friendly, rec for chicken, US$2.25; same owner as *Restaurant Nino*, Jr Salvador Cavero 124, which is rec for local dishes. Also good for chicken is ***Tivole***, Jr Bellido 492. ***Fuente de Soda La Compañía***, 28 de Julio 151, good for juices, cakes and snacks. Try *mondongo*, a soup made from meat, maize and mint, at the market nr Santa Clara on Jr Carlos Vivanco; Sra Gallardo has been rec. Those wishing to try *cuy* should do so in Ayacucho as it's a lot cheaper than Cusco.

### ● Airline offices

**Aero Continente**, Jr 9 de Diciembre 160, T 912816; **Faucett**, Grau y Lima; **Americana**, 28 de Julio 112, T 912356.

### ● Banks & money changers

**Banco de Crédito**, 28 de Julio y San Martín, no commission on TCs, cash advance on Visa. Many street changers at Portal Constitución on Plaza, good rate for cash. **Casa de Cambio DMJ**, at Portal Constitución 4, good rates for cash, TCs at 1% commission, open Mon-Sat 0800-1900. To change cash or TCs on a Sun, contact Andrés Harhuay Macoto or Carito Acevedo Vallejo at Portal Constitución, or T 913547.

### ● Entertainments

**Bars**: *Taberna Liverpool*, Mcal Cáceres 620, good for blues and rock music, owner Edwin is a great Beatles fan, he also plays Quechua rock music, also videos and pizzas; *Punto Caliente Video Pub*, Asamblea 131, open Tues-Sun, very popular, good atmosphere; *Crema Rica*, restaurant and video pub, very popular; *Peña Machi*, on Jr Grau, *peña* on Fri and Sat, the rest of the week it's a disco.

**Cinema**: on 9 de Diciembre, opp *Hotel Plaza*.

### ● Post & telecommunications

**Post Office** and **Telefónica**: Asamblea 293.

## Hats off to the Morochucos

Those who travel to Ayacucho will more than likely hear talk of the Morochucos, a near-legendary people who live in the Pampas de Cangallo, south-west of the city.

The Morochucos are said to be direct descendants of the Almagristas who lost the battle of Chupas against Pizarro and chose to hide in the Pampas. Their name is derived from 2 Quechua words: Moro meaning many coloured and Chuco which means cap. They were given this name by the Spanish, who came with these distinctive hats as protection against the cold.

As well as their distinctive dress, the Morochucos are different in other ways. They have pale skin, light hair and light coloured eyes, and are tall. They do share several characteristics with other Andean people, though, in being tough, brave, resilient, honest and loyal. They also like fiestas and are known for their heavy drinking.

Their famous hat is tied under the chin, and a red scarf tied under it. They wear long, dark coloured ponchos and ride with shoes called *Ojotas*, which are a kind of typical peasant sandal. On their legs they wear rough woollen tights of different bright colours, and on their belts the ubiquitous bag of coca leaves.

Unlike other *campesinos* in the Andes, the Morochucos' daily work is with livestock. They are renowned for their brilliant horsemanship, which is not surprising given that boys go to school by horse from 6 years old. These horse are descendants of Arab horses; agile, resilient, imposing and dominating. The long bridle, called a *cocobolo*, can also be used as a weapon. It consists of a piece of lead covered with a length of leather, which is like a kind of truncheon, with a ball on the end.

Such strength and equestrian prowess is not limited to the menfolk Women catch bulls, gallop on horses without saddles and run through the pampas with their child tied in a blanket on their backs.

These are quite obviously people to have on your side, as did the Liberator, Simón Bolívar during the Wars of Independence.

### ● Shopping

**Handicrafts**: Ayacucho is a good place to buy local crafts inc filigree silver, which often uses *mudéjar* patterns. Also look out for little painted altars which show the manger scene, carvings in local alabaster, harps, or the pre-Inca tradition of carving dried gourds. The most famous goods are carpets and *retablos*. In both weaving and *retablos*, scenes of recent political strife have been added to more traditional motifs.

Owing to the dramatic decline in tourism in recent years, many craftsmen left Ayacucho, but are now returning and re-establishing their businesses. For carpets, go to Barrio Santa Ana, ***Familia Sulca***, Jr Mcal Cáceres 302 (see under **Places of interest** above); or ***Familia Fernández***. In Barrio Belén, ***Familia Pizarro***, Jr San Cristóbal 215, works in textiles and *piedra huamanga* (local alabaster), good quality.

### ● Tour companies & travel agents

*Morochucos Travel Service*, Portal Constitución 14, T/F 912261, city tours, tours to Huari, Quinua, Huanta and Inca ruins at Vilcashuamán, also agent for AeroPerú. Also local tours with ***Wari Tours***, Portal Independencia 70, T 913115; and ***Quinua Tours***, Jr Asamblea 195, T 912191, manager Zumilda Canales de Pérez is very helpful.

### ● Tourist offices

**Ministerio de Turismo** (MICTI), Asamblea block 4, T 912548/913162, open Mon-Fri 0800-1300, friendly and helpful.

### ● Useful addresses

**Tourist Police**: at Dos de Mayo y Arequipa. For information on the recent and current political situation, journalist Ylpidio Enrique

Vargas Palomino, at Jr 3 Máscaras 171-A, T 912987, has been rec as friendly and helpful.

### ● Transport

**Air** To **Lima**, 40 mins, US$46 one way, Faucett, Aero Continente and Americana have daily flights, AeroPerú 5 a week; US$30 with Imperial. To **Cusco**, US$41, daily with Americana and Aero Continente; also with Imperial, US$38. A taxi to the airport costs US$1; buses or colectivos leave from the Plaza de Armas. At the airport walk ½ block down the street for a bus to the centre.

**Buses** To **Pisco**, 332 km, 10-12 hrs in the dry season, US$7-10, between 1500 and 1700. It is a poor road but with good views. Most buses go on to Lima, 14-15 hrs, US$9-11. Companies inc: Fano, Pasaje Cáceres 150, T 912813; TransMar, Av Mcal Cáceres 896; Trans Molina, Tres Máscaras 551. To Pisco you are dropped off at San Clemente, 5 km from town on the Panamericana. This area is dangerous at night, so take a taxi. To **Huancayo**, 319 km, 8-10 hrs, US$6-7; Trans Molina, Fano, Yazala (Av Mcal Cáceres 879, T 914422) and Antezana (Av Manco Cápac 467) daily at 1800-1900. The road is paved as far as Huanta, thereafter it is rough, especially in the wet season, but the views are breathtaking. For **Huancavelica**, take a Pisco bus to Pámpano, via the Abra de Apacheta (Apacheta-Pámpano, 5 hrs). In Pámpano wait in a restaurant till next day; there are no hotels. A bus runs to Santa Inés at 1100 or 1200, arriving at 1900. From Santa Inés take a truck to Huancavelica, or there is a bus between 1600-1700. It is 3 hrs Santa Inés-Huancavelica.

To **Andahuaylas**, 252 km, 12 hrs (more in the rainy season), US$8-9. Trans Fano, Mon, Wed, Fri, Sat at 0600; Ayacucho Tours, Av Mcal Cáceres 880, daily at 0630, continuing to **Abancay**, 135 km, 5½ hrs, US$5, and on to **Cusco**, a further 195 km, 7 hrs in the dry season, US$7. It takes 2 days to Cusco, with an overnight stop in Andahuaylas. There are no direct buses. Trucks to Abancay and Cusco leave from opp *Hostal El Sol*, 0500-0600. Road conditions are terrible, and landslides a common occurrence in the wet season. The scenery, though, is stunning and makes up for it. Terrorist activity has declined in recent years, but robberies are a problem and there are numerous military checkpoints. Buses sometimes even travel in convoy with a police escort. The route is reasonably safe.

## NORTH TO THE RIO APURIMAC

**San Francisco** is in the jungle on the Río Apurímac. There are 3 basic hotels: **E** *Suria*, the best but still dirty. The town can be reached by *micros* from Ayacucho, which leave from the Ovalo in Barrio Magdalena on Sat (return Mon), 10-12 hrs on a very bad road, often impassable in the wet season and very cold at night. Check on the political situation before travelling.

From San Francisco you can take a morning canoe to **Luisiana**, about 2 hrs upstream. There is an airstrip at Luisiana with daily connections to Ayacucho, for over five passengers. Details are available in the Ayacucho Tourist Office. From San Francisco you can make excursions to nearby villages on cargo canoes, but it is very difficult to

find transport all the way to Pucallpa unless you have a large group of people and are willing to pay handsomely.

## AYACUCHO TO CUSCO

### CHINCHEROS

The road towards Cusco goes through Chincheros, 158 km from Ayacucho and 3 hrs from Andahuaylas. It's a picturesque town and a nice place to stop and break up the Andahuaylas-Ayacucho trip. The townsfolk are very friendly. Ask for the bakery with its outdoor oven. 15 mins before Chicheros, on the road from Andahuaylas, is Uripa with a good Sun market. *Micros* regularly run between the two towns.

About 3 hrs to the N of Chincheros is the town of **Huaccana**. There are four little lakes on the way and a larger one near the town which can easily be visited. The valley is beautiful and practically free from other tourists. There is very basic dormitory on the plaza in Huaccana, and a basic, unmarked restaurant.

- **Accommodation In Chincheros**: **G** pp *Hostal Don José*, clean, friendly, pleasant courtyard, warm; **G** pp *Hostal Municipal*, on the plaza, clean, very quiet.

- **Transport** A bus leaves for Ayacucho at 0400 and 1300. You may be able to hitch a lift with one of the trucks, if you're up before daybreak.

### ANDAHUAYLAS

80 km further on from Chicheros, in a fertile, temperate valley of lush meadows, cornfields and groves of eucalyptus, alder and willow, stands Andahuaylas. The town offers few exotic crafts, no lighting except in the plaza, poor transport, but beautiful scenery. There is a good market on Sun.

**Excursions** The scenery is pleasant on the old road by the river to **Talavera**. **San Jerónimo** is another picturesque town nearby.

Most worth seeing is **Pacucha** (*pop*

#### An officer and a not-so-gentle nun

One of the most bizarre tales knocking around in the annals of Ayacucho's history relates to the mysterious case of the missing nun and the gender-bending soldier.

At the beginning of the 17th century, the courageous and audacious Army officer, Antonio de Frauzo, was finally captured and brought to justice, after putting several of his adversaries to the sword up and down the length and breadth of the country. He was condemned to death and duly asked a priest to hear his last confession and give him communion.

However, seconds before the priest could administer it, the soldier took the host in his hands and fled. No one dared stop him for fear of committing an act of sacrilege. He took refuge in a nearby church (not difficult given the profusion of them in this city) where he asked for Bishop Fray Agustín de Carbajal to hear his confession.

The townsfolk, who had been eagerly watching events unfold, soon learned the astonishing truth. The officer was, in fact, a woman called Catalina, who, on being chosen by her parents for the service of God, fled from a Spanish convent, assuming the disguise of a male person.

On putting an end to the mystery of her identity, Catalina mysteriously escaped once more, assumed a new identity and spent her last days in Mexico, dressed as a man and working as an *arriero*, or mule-herd. To the people of Ayacucho, however, Catalina would always be known as *La Monja Alferez*, the officer nun.

2,000), the largest of six villages on the shores of a large lake, with a view of the mountains to the NW. In the plaza, where the trucks stop, women sell bread, coffee and hot lunches, the only food for 16 km. There are dirt roads around the lake. Allow at least 3 hrs to walk round its circumference – more if you want to take it easy and have a chat with the locals, who are courteous and friendly – but be back in Pacucha before dark to ensure transport back to Andahuaylas. The wildlife includes many types of wild duck and other birds, sometimes including flocks of green parrots.

Opposite Pacucha, some 2 km past the lake, are the ruins of a Chanka fortress called **Sóndor**. Except for Andahuaylas itself, this is a mainly Quechua-speaking region. It is also one of the poorest parts of Peru. Mini-vans leave daily when full to Pacucha from the centre of Andahuaylas, about every 30 mins. It's a 40-min ride, US$0.65. Sun is market day.

• **Accommodation & places to eat** **C-D** *Turístico Andahuaylas*, Av Lazaro Carrillo 620, T (084) 721224; **E** *Las Américas*, nr *Delicias*, hot water in the morning and evening, clean, friendly, rec; **F** *Cusco*, Casafranca 520, hot shower; **F** *Delicias*, Ramos 525, hot showers, basic but rec, 7 rooms, ask for extra blankets, cold at night; **F** *Wari*, Ramos 427, hot shower; **G** *Bienvenidos*, Andahuaylas 364, cheap, adequate. Good, cheap food can be found at ***Corazón Ayacuchano***, Av Andahuaylas 145; ***Las Floridas***, serves a good set meal for US$0.80.

• **Transport** **Air** Daily flights to Lima, US$43, with Imperial Air and Transporte Andahuaylas; Grupo Ocho every Wed, US$34. **Buses** To **Ayacucho**, a minimum of 12 hrs, US$8-9, daily buses with Ayacucho Tours, also Fano, leave between 1300 and 1500. There are no direct buses early in the morning, so you will miss most of the stunning scenery. To **Abancay** with Señor de Huanca at 0600 and 1300 daily, 5½ hrs, US$5; to **Cusco**, same company at 0600, and Emp Andahuaylas at 1300, 12 hrs, US$9.

## ABANCAY

Nestled between mountains in the upper reaches of a glacial valley, this friendly town is first glimpsed when you are 62 km away. There is a petrol station.

• **Accommodation** **B** *Hotel de Turismo Abancay*, Av Díaz Barcenas 500, T (084) 321017 (Cusco, 223339), with bath, food good, US$3, comfortable, old-fashioned house, safe car park, camping permitted at US$3; **E** *Leonard I*, clean and safe; as is **F** *Leonard II*; **F** *Hostal Sawite*, on Nuñez, hot water 24 hrs, clean, friendly, ask them to turn off the TV in the main passage if you want to sleep; **G** *El Misti*, fair; **G** *Gran*, with bath.

• **Places to eat** *Elena*, is on the same street as the bus companies, and is good.

• **Transport** Several bus companies leave from Abancay to Cusco on Av Arenas nr the market, daily at 0600 and 1300, US$7, 6-7 hrs (in the dry season), also colectivos. The scenery is dramatic, especially as it descends into the Apurímac valley and climbs out again. There is a checkpoint at the Apurímac border. Coming from Cusco, after the pass it takes an hour to zig-zag down to Abancay. The 2000 bus from Cusco arrives around 0300, there is no guarantee of a seat to Andahuaylas, even with a through ticket. See page 329 for sites of interest between Abancay and Cusco. Services to Andahuaylas US$4, 6 hrs, 0300, 0500, 0600, 1300 and 2000 daily; change there for Ayacucho. Landslides are common on this route, as well as lots of checkpoints, which involve getting off the bus. To **Nasca** on the Panamericana Sur, 464 km, via Chalhuanca and Puquío, 20 hrs, US$14, bus or truck daily. **NB** The route from Cusco to Nasca is still considered unsafe and many bus companies are not yet travelling this road.

## EAST OF LA OROYA

ROUTES The 60-km surfaced road to Tarma follows the Cerro de Pasco road for 25 km, then branches off to rejoin the old road quite near Tarma, which is 600m lower than La Oroya.

## TARMA

This nice little flat-roofed town, founded in 1545, with plenty of trees, is now growing, with garish modern buildings (*Pop* 105,200; *Alt* 3,050m). It still has a lot of charm. The Semana Santa celebrations are spectacular, with a very colourful Easter Sunday morning procession in the main plaza. Accommodation is hard to find at this time but you can apply to the Municipalidad for rooms with local families. The town is also notable for its locally-made fine flower-carpets. The cathedral is dedicated to Santa Ana. The surrounding countryside is beautiful.

**NB** The immediate area is now free from terrorist activity but it's best to travel by day for safety and scenery.

### Excursions

8 km from Tarma, the small hillside town of **Acobamba** has the futuristic **Santuario de Muruhuay,** with a venerated picture painted on the rock behind the altar. It also has fine *tapices* made in San Pedro de Cajas which depict the Crucifixion. There are festivities during May.

• **Accommodation** There are two *alojamientos*, both **G**: Doña Norma's, nr the plaza, is basic but clean and friendly.

• **Transport** Daily buses leave Acobamba to Tarma (US$0.20, or a pleasant 2 hrs' walk), La Oroya (US$0.60) and Huancayo. 3 buses a week go direct to Lima (Coop San Pedro).

The **Grutas de Guagapo**, also known as *La gruta que llora* (the cave that weeps), is 4 km from the town of **Palcamayo**. The caves can be entered for about 300m. Even without a guide you can penetrate the cave for some way with a torch. A bus leaves twice daily from Tarma; US$1, 2 hrs.

Beyond Palcamayo, the road continues to **San Pedro de Cajas**, a large village which used to produce most of the coloured sheep-wool weavings for sale in Lima. Most of the weaving families have now moved to Lima. There are no buses, but you can walk it in 3 hrs. This road joins the one from La Oroya to Cerro de Pasco below Junín. There is accommodation in the village at **G** *Hotel Comercio*, in Calle Chanchamayo; also 2 restaurants, but no shops.

### Local information

● **Accommodation**

**B** *Los Portales*, Av Castilla 512, T 321411, out of town, with bath, hot water; **B-C** *La Florida*, 6 km from Tarma (for reservations T Lima 424-6969, F 432-4361), 18th century hacienda, 6 rooms with bath, hot water, inc breakfast, owned by German-Peruvian couple Inge and Pepe, excursions, highly rec, also camping US$3.

**D** *Hostal Galaxia*, on Plaza de Armas, T 321449, with bath, hot water, car park US$1; **D** *Hostal Internacional*, Dos de Mayo 307, T 321830, with bath, hot water 1800-0800, clean.

**E** *Hostal Bolívar*, Huaraz 389, T 321060, with bath, hot water, reasonable; **E** *Hostal Central*, Huánuco 614, shared bath, hot water, has an observatory, open Fri 2000; **E** *Hostal El Dorado*, Huánuco 488, T 321598, hot water, reasonable; **E** *Hostal Tuchu*, Dos de Mayo 561, shared bath, hot water in the morning; **E** *Vargas*, Dos de Mayo 627, T 321460, with bath, hot water in morning, OK.

**F** *Hostal Ideal*, Moquegua 389, basic.

● **Places to eat**

*Señorial*, Huánuco 138, good *menú*, 'best in town'; *Chavín Café*, beneath *Hostal Galaxia*, on Plaza de Armas, trout is rec; *Don Lucho*, Lima 175, good; *El Rosal*, on Callao nr Transportes Chanchamayo, reasonable and clean. There are also several places on Lima, inc a vegetarian. The *manjarblanco* of Tarma is famous, as well as *pachamanca*, *mondongo* and *picante de cuyes*.

● **Banks & money changers**

**Banco de Crédito**, Lima 407, changes Amex TCs.

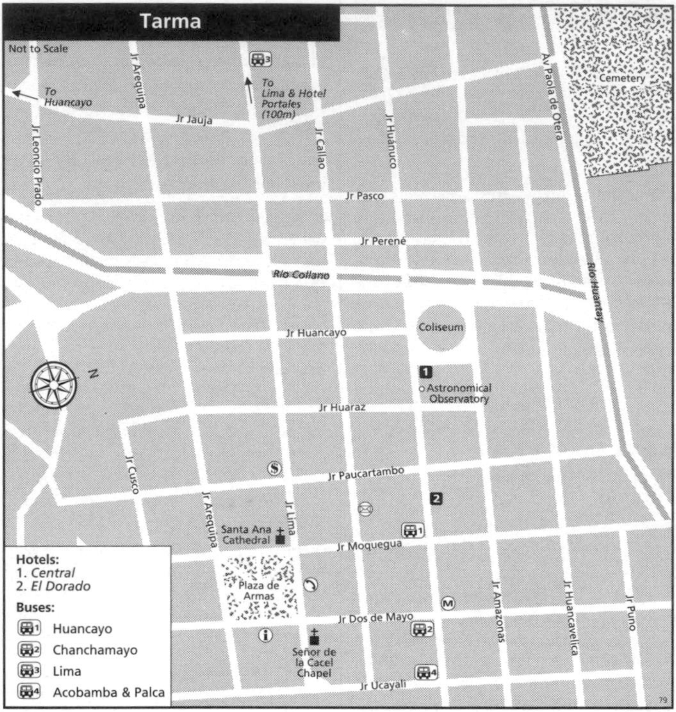

**Tarma**

Not to Scale

Hotels:
1. *Central*
2. *El Dorado*

Buses:
1 Huancayo
2 Chanchamayo
3 Lima
4 Acobamba & Palca

### ● Post & telecommunications

**Telefónica del Perú**: is on the Plaza de Armas.

### ● Tourist offices

*Club de Turismo de Tarma*, Moquegua 653, offer tours of the local area which cost around US$4.50-9, depending on the length of the tour: eg to San Pedro de Cajas, Grutas de Guagapo, Acobamba and El Señor de Muruhuay. They go on weekends and need a minimum of 15 people, which is easy during the dry season but can be difficult during the rainy season, except at peak holiday times. Alfonso Tapía E at *Hostal Central* will show people around. He is very friendly and likes to practise his English and German.

### ● Transport

Buses to **Lima**, 231 km, 6 hrs, US$5.25, direct buses daily; Transportes Chanchamayo, Callao 1002, T 321882, is rec as the best; also Expreso Satipo, Ucuyali 384. There is a good lunch stop at El Tambo before La Oroya, with superb fried trout. The road is paved throughout. To **Jauja**, US$1.80; and **Huancayo**, 3 hrs, US$2.50. Daily colectivos from Jr Huánuco 439 run almost hourly to Huancayo, US$4, 2½ hrs. Bus to **La Oroya**, US$2.40, colectivo, US$3. Bus to **La Merced**, US$2.65. Colectivos often leave for La Merced and San Ramón (collectively known as Chanchamayo – see below), from Dos de Mayo blocks 2 and 3, US$3.45.

ROUTES Beyond Tarma the road is steep and crooked but there are few places where cars cannot pass one another. In the 80 km between Tarma and La Merced the road, passing by great overhanging cliffs, drops 2,450m and the vegetation changes dramatically from temperate to tropical. This is a really beautiful run.

## CHANCHAMAYO

The towns of San Ramón and La Merced are collectively known as Chanchamayo.

**San Ramón** (*pop* 7,000) is 11 km before La Merced.

• **Accommodation & places to eat E** *Conquistador*, on the main street, shower, parking. *La Estancia*, Tarma 592, serves local specialities. There are other places on the main street.

• **Transport Air** Flights leave from San Ramón. There is an 'air-colectivo' service to **Puerto Bermúdez**, 10 kg baggage allowance, US$5/kg of excess luggage. The service continues to Atalaya, Satipo, Puerto Inca (see page 398) and Pucallpa. Air-colectivos go to Lima and to most places in the jungle region where there is an airstrip. Flights are cheap but irregular, and depend on technical factors, weather and goodwill. Aero-taxis can be chartered (*viaje especial*) to anywhere for a higher price; maximum 5 people, you have to pay for the pilot's return to base.

**La Merced** (*pop* 10,000), lies in the fertile Chanchamayo valley. Sometimes Campa Indians come to town selling bows and arrows. There is a festival in the last week of September.

• **Accommodation & places to eat E** *Cosmos*, opp the police station, with bath, best value; **F** *Romero*, Plaza de Armas, T 2106, good but noisy and water in evenings only.

The best restaurant is *Shambari-Campa*, on the Plaza de Armas.

• **Transport** Many buses go here from **Lima**: Transportes Chanchamayo, Av Luna Pizarro 453, La Victoria, Lima, is the best, also Expreso Satipo; 9 hrs, US$6.40. Also many buses from **Tarma**, US$2.65, 3 hrs. Bus to **Puerto Bermúdez**, 8 hrs, US$6.40, at 1000 with Túpac Amaru. To get to **Pucallpa**, take a launch from Puerto Bermúdez to Laurencia (which takes 8 hrs or more, be prepared for wet luggage), then a truck to Constitución (20 mins), and from there a colectivo to Zungaro, 1½ hrs. From Zungaro, colectivos take 4½ hrs to Pucallpa. Alternatively, you can take a truck from La Merced to Pucallpa. The journey takes 3 days, and between 0830 and 1400 each day expect to be drenched by rain.

## EAST OF LA MERCED

About 22 km N from La Merced is **San Luis de Shuaro**, 3 km before which a road runs E up the valley of the Perené river. There are large coffee plantations at an altitude of only 700m. Sat and Sun are market days.

### SATIPO

The jungle town of Satipo is the main centre of this region.

• **Accommodation D** *Hostal Majestic*, with bath, no clothes-washing facilities, electricity 1900-2300 only; **F** *La Residencial*, 4 rooms, clean, garden, swimming pool, rec. There are many smaller hotels, all very basic, the best being **E** *Palmero*, with bath, not very clean. For good food try *Dany's Restaurant*.

• **Transport** Buses to get to Satipo take a Lobato or Los Andes bus from La Merced, US$7.20, 0800. Daily buses run direct from Satipo to Huancayo and Lima at night, a very cold journey, US$9.50, 12 hrs, with Los Andes and Lobato. Check whether the tunnels are open before travelling.

• **Warning** Latest reports suggest that Oxapampa, the Perené region and Satipo are still dangerous due to narco-terrorist activity. Check on the situation before travelling into these areas.

## NORTH OF LA MERCED

The road has been extended from San Luis de Shuaro over an intervening mountain range. A turn off E leads to **Puerto Bermúdez** on the Río Neguachi. There is clean accommodation in **F** *Hostal Tania*, opposite the dock where motorized canoes tie up; and an eating house opposite the airstrip. Boat passages possible from passing traders.

### OXAPAMPA

56 km from La Merced is Oxapampa (*Pop* 5,140; *Alt* 1,794m), 390 km from Lima, in a fertile plain on the Río Huancabamba, a tributary of the Ucayali. A third of the inhabitants are descendants of a German-Austrian community of 70 families which settled in 1859 at **Pozuzo**, 80 km downstream, and spread later to Oxapampa. There is much livestock farming

and coffee is planted on land cleared by the timber trade.

• **Accommodation & places to eat In Oxapampa**: **E** *Rey*, with bath, clean, cold water, small beds; **F** *Arias*, cheaper without bath, clean, new, best value; **F** *José*, without bath, hot water, clean, pleasant; **F** *Hostal Jiménez*, Grau 421, refurbished, clean, cold water, shared bath; **F** *Hostal Liz*, Av Oxapampa 104, clean, small rooms, cold water. The following are in old buildings: **F** *Santo Domingo*, clean, no hot water; **G** *Hostal Santa Isolina*, Jr M Castilla 177, with bath, cold water; **G** *La Cabaña*, on plaza, smelly, cold water, a dump; worse is **G** *San Martín*, tiny rooms, smelly bathroom. *Oasis*, is a highly rec restaurant.

• **Transport** Colectivo La Merced-Oxapampa; taxis at 0600, US$2, 4 hrs.

## NORTH OF OXAPAMPA

25 km from Oxapampa is **Huancabamba**, from where it is 55 km to Pozuzo. The whole road between La Merced and Pozuzo is very rough, depending on the season. There are no less than 30 rivers to be crossed. Downstream 40 km from Pozuzo is Nuevo Pozuzo; there is no transport, it's a 2-day walk. There is an interesting museum opposite the church in the town centre.

• **Accommodation In Pozuzo**: **E** *Hostal Tirol*, full board, clean, rec; **F** *Hostal Prusia*, clean; **F-G** *Hostal Maldonado*, clean, rec.

• **Transport** Buses from Lima to Pozuzo with La Victoria, from 28 de Julio 2405, Mon, Thur, Sat, 0800, US$12, about 16 hrs.

# NORTH OF LA OROYA

A paved road runs 130 km N from La Oroya to Cerro de Pasco. It runs up the Mantaro valley through narrow canyons to the wet and mournful Junín pampa at over 4,250m, one of the world's largest high-altitude plains. An obelisk marks the battlefield where the Peruvians under Bolívar defeated the Spaniards in 1824. Blue peaks line the pampa in a distant wall. This windswept sheet of yellow grass is bitterly cold and the only signs of life are the youthful herders with their sheep and llamas. The rail line follows the E shores of the Lago de Junín. The town of **Junín**, with its picturesque red-tiled roofs, stands beside the lake.

Some 13 km E of the village of **Shelby**, served by the railway from La Oroya to Cerro de Pasco, a good section of Inca road may be seen. Its course is marked by the lonely ruins of Bonbón, an Inca community centre only recently identified, which in turn lies close to the modern dam holding back the Río Mantaro as it flows out of the northern end of Lago de Junín.

**NB** The central highlands have suffered from terrorist activity in recent years, but since 1992 the area seems to be under military control. Travellers have started to visit the region again, with good reports. Before going, though, check on the situation, only travel by day, and stay in contact with the locals.

## LIMA TO CERRO DE PASCO

An alternative to the La Oroya route from Lima to Cerro de Pasco is the road via **Canta**. From Canta you can visit the pre-Inca ruins of **Cantamarca** – many of the buildings still have roofs, supported by pillars. It is a 2-3 hrs' walk up to the ruins, from where there are extensive views.

• **Accommodation & transport** Accommodation is limited, but *Hostal Kalapacho* is friendly and good value. There is one good restaurant in town. There are 3 buses daily to and from Lima, US$3.60 – El Canteño company, San Román 151-153, Lima.

Continuing through the beautiful high pass of La Viuda (4,748m), the road goes to the mines of **Alpamarca**. A truck leaves from Canta at 0200, take warm clothes, a blanket, camping gear and food. From Alpamarca there are 2-3 buses per week to **Huallay**, near where are the Inca ruins of **Bon Bón Marca** and the thermal baths at **Calcra**.

## CERRO DE PASCO

The main line goes to this long-established mining centre (*Pop* 29,810; *Alt* 4,330m; *Phone code* 064), 130 km from La Oroya by road. The town is famous as the site of one of the battles of the War of Independence, on 6 December 1820, when local hero, Antonio Alverez de Arenales, defeated Diego de O'Reilly's royalist troops. The actual battlefield is 1 km away, on Cerro Uliachin.

Cerro de Pasco is not an attractive place but is nevertheless very friendly. For a long time, it was known as the first settlement in South America, when the Italian explorer, Antonio Raimondi, discovered 10,000-year-old remains here. It is also interesting as Peru's major mining community. Copper, zinc, lead, gold and silver are mined here, and coal comes from the deep canyon of Goyllarisquisga, the 'place where a star fell', the highest coal mine in the world, 42 km N of Cerro de Pasco.

The town seems to defy gravity as its buildings and streets cling precariously to the edge of a huge abyss. Not surprisingly for a place that claims to be the highest city in the world, nights are bitterly cold. Travellers should also note that the streets don't conform to the usual grid pattern, so it can be quite easy to get lost.

A new town – San Juan de Pampa – has been built 1½ km away. There is accommodation in the *Gran Hotel*, noisy, no hot water, poor service.

### Excursions

40 km SW of Cerro de Pasco, on the way to Lima, is **Huayllay**. Nearby is the **Santuario Bosque de Piedras**, unique weathered limestone formations in the shape of a tortoise, elephant, alpaca, etc. There is a small *campesino* settlement nearby.

- **Access** Take a bus from Cerro de Pasco and get off at the crossroads near Villa de Pasco. It is about 15 mins out of town, on the road to Lima. Camionetas pass by bound for Huayllay, which is about 1 hr away.

80 km SE of Cerro de Pasco is the **Valle de Huachón**. There are excellent hiking opportunities in the valley and around the *nevados* of Incatama (5,130m), Jancahuay (5,180), Ranrajanca (5,182m) and Carhuarajo (5,160m). The valley also gives access to Nevado Huaguruncho (5,730m), which is the snowy peak visible from the road on the way to Huánuco. To reach the valley, take a bus

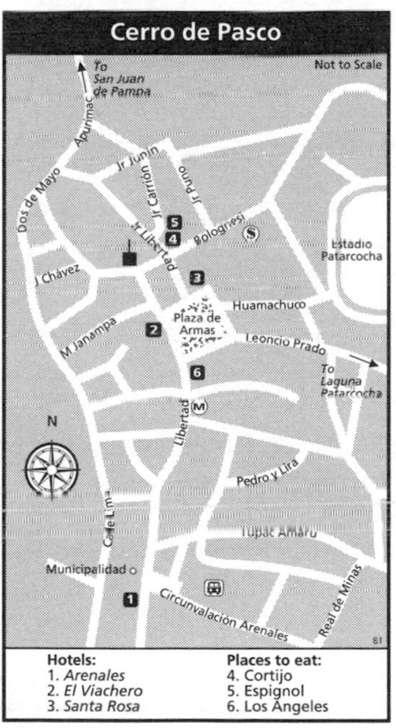

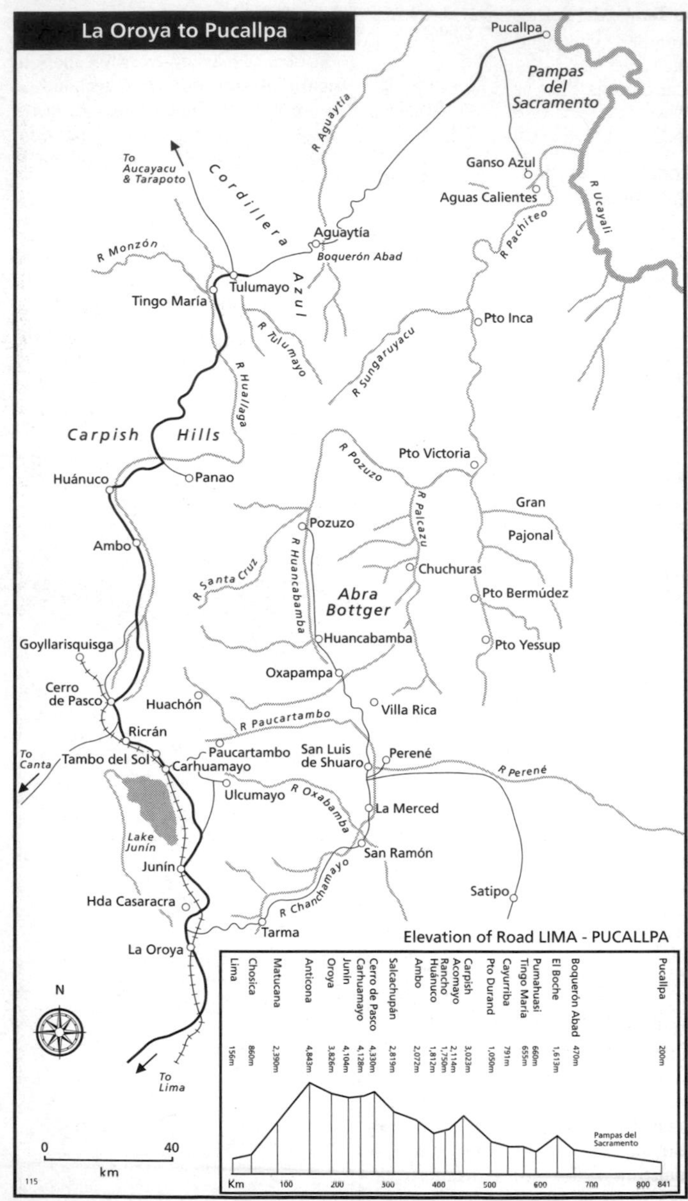
La Oroya to Pucallpa
Pucallpa
Pampas del Sacramento
R Aguaytia
To Aucayacu & Tarapoto
Cordillera Azul
Ganso Azul
Aguas Calientes
R Ucayali
R Pachitea
Aguaytía
Boquerón Abad
R Monzón
Tulumayo
Tingo María
R Tulumayo
Pto Inca
R Sungaruyacu
R Huallaga
Carpish Hills
Pto Victoria
R Pozuzo
Huánuco
Panao
R Palcazu
Gran Pajonal
Pozuzo
Ambo
R Huancabamba
Chuchuras
R Santa Cruz
Abra Bottger
Pto Bermúdez
Goyllarisquisga
Huancabamba
Pto Yessup
Oxapampa
Cerro de Pasco
Huachón
Villa Rica
R Paucartambo
Ricrán
To Canta
Tambo del Sol
Paucartambo
San Luis de Shuaro
Perené
Carhuamayo
R Perené
Ulcumayo
R Oxabamba
La Merced
Lake Junín
San Ramón
Junín
R Chanchamayo
Satipo
Hda Casaracra
Tarma
La Oroya
N
To Lima
0
40
km
115
Elevation of Road LIMA - PUCALLPA
Lima 156m
Chosica 860m
Matucana 2,390m
Anticona 4,843m
Oroya 3,826m
Junín 4,104m
Carhuamayo 4,128m
Cerro de Pasco 4,330m
Salcachupán 2,819m
Ambo 2,072m
Huánuco 1,812m
Rancho 1,750m
Acomayo 2,114m
Carpish 3,023m
Pto Durand 1,050m
Cayurriba 791m
Tingo María 655m
Pumahuasi 660m
El Boche 1,613m
Boquerón Abad 470m
Pucallpa 200m
Pampas del Sacramento
Km
100
200
300
400
500
600
700
800
841

to **Tambo del Sol**, on the road to Lima. Another recommended excursion is to the precolumbian funeral towers at **Cantamasia**, reached on muleback. West of Cerro de Pasco, off the Huayllay road, is the **Laguna de Pun Rún**.

## Local information

### ● Accommodation

**E** *Hostal Arenales*, Jr Arenales 162, nr the bus station, new, clean, friendly, hot water; **F** *El Viajero*, on the plaza, clean but no hot water; **F** *Santa Rosa*, also on the plaza, basic, very cold.

### ● Places to eat

*Los Angeles*, Jr Libertad, nr the market, rec; *El Espignol I*, Jr Libertad 195; *El Espignol II*, Jr Arenales 164, for fish, chicken, *menú* and other dishes. Local specialities are trout and fried frog.

### ● Banks & money changers

Banco de Crédito is on Jr Bolognesi.

### ● Transport

**Trains** Since 1991 the train service has been suspended.

**Buses** To **Lima**, depart at 0830 and 2000, 9 hrs, US$7, with Empresa de Transportes Carhuamayo, their office is nr the Av Montivideo entrance to the market (in Lima: Av Grau 525, T 433-0785, F 427-8605). To **La Oroya**, bus from Plaza Arenales, 0900 and later, 3 hrs, US$2.20; cars also travel this route, leaving when there are enough passengers, US$9.50. To **Huancayo**, 5-6 hrs, US$3-4. Colectivos to **Huánuco**, US$6.20, from Plaza de Armas. There are also buses between 0800 and 0900, 5 hrs, US$2. Cerro de Pasco has a central bus station, which is unusual in Peru.

## THE YANAHUANCA VALLEY

Some 65 km NW of Cerro de Pasco is **Yanahuanca**, in the beautiful valley of the same name. From the village one can reach one of the longest surviving stretches of Inca road. 2 km up the Yanahuanca Valley a lesser valley cuts northwards between the towering crags. The road, its paving uneven and disturbed by countless horse and donkey convoys, leads up the smaller valley, its course sometimes shared by a stream, to the village of **Huarautambo**, about 4 km distant. This village is surrounded by many pre-Inca remains. For more than 150 km the *Camino Incaico* is not only in almost continuous existence from the Yanahuanca Valley but is actually shown on the map issued by the Instituto Geográfico Militar. The clearest stretch ends at Huari in Ancash, having passed by such places as La Unión (see page 388) and San Marcos. After Huari its route may be followed, less distinctly, through Llamellín and in the hills behind San Luis, Piscobamba and Pomabamba (see page 146).

## Green leaves and white powder

After failing to eradicate coca chewing among the natives of South America in the 16th century, the Spanish decided to control the sale of the leaves, and made a fortune. Today fortunes are still made from the sale of this leaf, in the form of its chemically-processed derivative, cocaine. Though Peru produces most of the raw material – 60% of all coca leaf is grown in Peru – the profits are concentrated in Colombia, which dominates its production and smuggling to the markets of North America and Europe.

Coca leaves have long been used by the people of the Andes as a tonic. As casual as a coffee-break and as sacred as Communion, coca chewing is an ancient ritual. Chewing, however, is not strictly the right word. There isn't one in English, but there are special words in Spanish. *Coquear* – which roughly translates as 'to coca' – is the most frequently used. The correct technique is to move the wad of leaves in your cheek and suck from it, using also a piece of *cal*, or lime, which activates with the saliva. Some cocaine will be absorbed into the bloodstream through the mouth , providing a slight numbing of cheek and tongue; more will be absorbed in the stomach and intestinal tract. The desired effect is to numb the senses, which helps stave off hunger pangs and exhaustion, and to help people live at high altitude with no ill-effects.

As well as being a prerequisite for manual workers, such as miners, coca is also taken in a social context. The native population used to deny this because, in the eyes of the bosses and clergy, an increase in labour productivity was the only permissible reason for tolerating consumption of "the devil's leaf". But the only places where coca is not chewed is in church and in the marital bed. The masticated leaves are spat out at the bedside.

Coca is also used in various rites, such as in offerings to Pachamama, or Mother Earth, to feed her when she gets hungry. Various items such as flowers and sweets, along with the coca leaves, are put together in bundles called *pagos* and burned on the mountains at midnight. In Andean markets different *pagos* are sold for different purposes: to put into the foundation of a new house; for help in matters of health, business or love; or for magic, white or black. The leaves are also used for fortune-telling.

The coca shrub was first domesticated in Peru some 4,000 years ago. Awareness of coca in the First World is rather more recent, however. In 1862 German chemists had taken coca leaves brought by an Austrian scientific expedition from Peru and isolated an alkaloid, or nitrogen-based compound which they labelled cocain. By around 1880, it was being tried as a cure for opium addiction and alcoholism. The young Dr Sigmund Freud, reading of its effect on tired soldiers, took some himself and pronounced it a "magical substance", which was "wonderfully stimulating". Probably the most famous cocaine user of all was a fictional one. Arthur Conan Doyle's great detective, Sherlock Holmes, regularly injected it. Some believe that Holmes' obsession with the master criminal, Professor Moriarty, who he believed was persecuting him, could have been a portrayal of cocaine-induced paranoia.

Today, there is a huge demand for this drug from the millions of North Americans and Europeans who sniff, smoke or inject it. Supply on this scale is not a problem. Making cocaine hydrochloride is as easy as baking bread. The leaves go into a plastic pit with a solution of water and a little sulphuric acid where they are left to soak for a few days. Then follows a succession of mixing and stirring with more chemicals until the liquid turns milky-white and then curdles, leaving tiny, ivory-coloured granules. This cocaine base is then transported to Colombia, where it is refined into the familiar white powder, before being shipped abroad. The costs involved to produce a kilo of the stuff are around US$5,000. The return on this investment can be as much as US$50,000.

Cocaine also has its legal uses. Patent medicines containing cocaine were popular – for hay fever, sinusitis and as a general tonic. Today, it is still used in hospitals world-wide as a local anaesthetic. Another legal use of cocaine is in soft drinks. The most famous soft drink in the world doesn't actually contain cocaine, but has something from the coca plant in it. Coca leaves from Peru and Bolivia are shipped to the USA where cocaine is extracted for medical use. From what's left comes a flavouring agent which goes into Coca-Cola, enjoyed in practically every country around the globe.

The Huallaga valley, north from Tingo María, is the biggest illicit coca producer in the world. This area, known as *la ceja de la selva* (the eyebrow of the jungle), is where the mountains meet Peru's Amazon basin. The climate is good in these broad tropical valleys – warm and not too dry – and the altitude ideal at around 600-700 metres. For centuries, people from the sierra have traded with jungle farmers, taking potatoes, corn and *cuy* and bringing back coffee, cacao or bananas. In recent years, those jungle farms have turned to coca for the cocaine trade.

Easily grown at altitudes ranging from 300-2,000m, coca can be harvested 4 times a year and provides a relatively good return. This may strike some as unethical, but to the *campesinos* living in grinding poverty and desperate to provide a better future for their children, cocaine is just a business. It may cause addiction, misery, and even death at the end of the line, but how else can they make a decent living?

And getting rid of it isn't easy. The coca plant is tough. Plantings up to 2 years old can easily be pulled up, but after 5 years, when they're waist high, you need a winch or have to dig them out. Unless they're cut at ground level, they'll sprout again, producing more than ever. The ideal way to eradicate them would be with defoliant sprayed from aircraft, but this has been prevented, mainly because of protests from local and international conservationists worried about the effect that chemicals would have on the surrounding landscape. The painful truth is that cocaine means economic growth for entire regions in Peru, economic survival for many, and massive profits for some.

## THE HUALLAGA VALLEY

The Central Highway from Cerro de Pasco continues NE another 528 km to Pucallpa, the limit of navigation for large Amazon river boats. The western part of this road (Cerro de Pasco-Huánuco) has been rebuilt into an all-weather highway (see map, page 382, for its contour).

The sharp descent along the nascent **Río Huallaga** is a tonic to travellers suffering from *soroche*. The road drops 2,436m in the 100 km from Cerro de Pasco to Huánuco, and most of it is in the first 32 km. From the bleak vistas of the high ranges the road plunges below the tree line revealing views of great beauty. The only town of any size before Huánuco is **Ambo**.

**NB** The Huallaga valley is the country's main coca-growing area, with both drug-trafficking and guerrilla activity.

The main centre of activity is between Tingo María and Tarapoto, so it is best to avoid the region at present. It does appear to be safe to visit Huánuco, Tingo María and Pucallpa, but as the area is under military control there are many checkpoints. Travelling during the day is advised and seek full information before going.

## HUANUCO

An attractive Andean town (*Pop* 82,240; *Alt* 1,894m; *Phone code* 064) on the Upper Huallaga with an interesting market.

### Places of interest

The two churches of **San Cristóbal** and **San Francisco** have both been much restored. The latter has some 16th century paintings. There is a small but interesting natural history museum at Gen Prado 495, called **Museo de Ciencias;** many of the displays have multiple language signs; entry, US$0.50.

### Excursions

5 km away on road W to La Unión is **Kotosh** (*alt* 1,812m), the Temple of Crossed Hands, the earliest evidence of a complex society and of pottery in Peru, dating from 2000 BC. You must ford a stream to get there, and beware of the vicious black flies. The ruin has been sadly neglected since the original excavation in 1963.

A good area for camping is the **Five lakes of Pichgacocha**. Take a *camioneta* to La Libertad – 31 km from Huánuco; turn-off the main road to Lima near Santa Rosa – then walk 20 km.

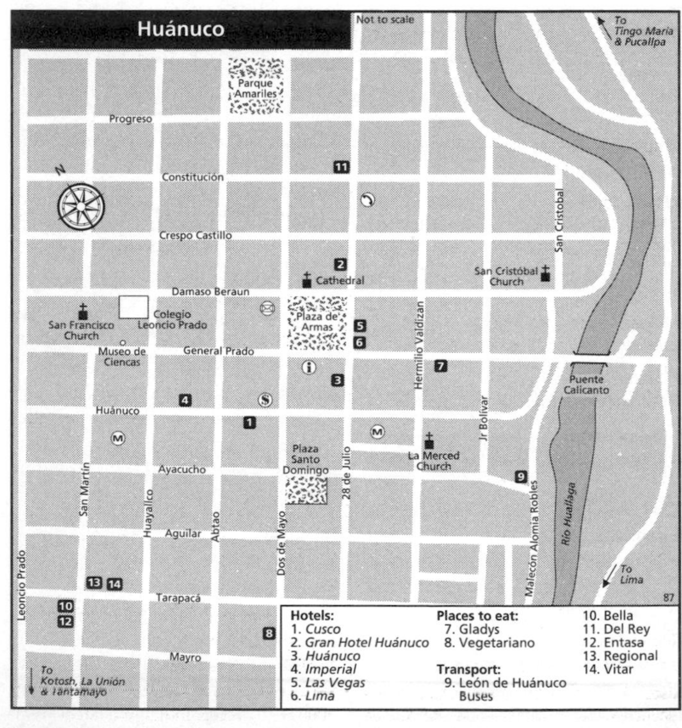

### Local festivals

**20-25 Jan**: is *Carnaval Huanuqueño*. **1 May**: festival of *El Señor de Chacos* in San Rafael, in the province of Ambo. **3 May**: *La Cruz de Mayo*, in Huánuco. **16 July**: *Fiesta de la Virgen del Carmen*. **12-18 Aug**: Tourist Week in Huánuco. **28-29 Oct**: *Fiesta del Rey y del Señor de Burgos*, the patron of Huánuco. **25 Dec**: *Fiesta de los Negritos*.

### Local information

**● Accommodation**

**C** *Gran Hotel Huánuco*, with bath, no hot water, restaurant.

**D** *Cusco*, Huánuco 616, 2 blocks from Plaza de Armas, with bath, cafeteria, OK.

**F** *Hostal Residencial Huánuco*, Jr Huánuco, nr Plaza de Armas, with bath, hot water, garden, use of kitchen, washing facilities, it's more expensive than others in this range but excellent value, highly rec; **F** *Imperial*, Huánuco 581, with cold shower (intermittent water), reasonable value, clean, quiet; *Las Vegas*, on Plaza de Armas, rec; **F** *Lima*, Plaza de Armas, 28 de Julio 9222, with bath. Hotels are often fully booked, so you should arrive early.

**Camping**: it's possible to camp by the river, nr the stadium.

**● Places to eat**

*La Casona de Gladys*, Gen Prado 908, good, cheap local food; *Vegeteriano*, Dos de Mayo 751. Also try the *chifas* on Damaso Beraun, 1 block W of the Plaza de Armas.

**● Banks & money changers**

**Banco de Crédito**, at Dos de Mayo 1005.

**● Telecommunications**

**Telefónica del Perú:** at 28 de Julio 1157.

**● Tourist offices**

Gen Prado 716, on the Plaza de Armas. A good contact for adventure tours is *César Antezana*, Jr Pedro Puelles 261, T 513622.

**● Transport**

**Air** To/from **Lima**, 1 hr, US$59, daily flights with Expreso Aéreo. There are connecting flights to Tingo María, Tocache, Juanjui, Pucallpa, Saposoa, Tarapoto, Yurimaguas, Moyobamba, Rioja, Trujillo and Chiclayo. Flights may be cancelled in the rains or if not full.

**Buses** To **Lima**, US$9, 9 hrs, with León de Huánuco, Malecón Alomía Robles 821 (28 de Julio 1520, La Victoria, Lima); 3 a day in the early evening. A colectivo to Lima, US$20, leaves at 0400, arrives 1400; book the night before at Gen Prado 607, 1 block from the Plaza, rec. Transportes del Rey, 28 de Julio 1201 (28 de Julio 1192, La Victoria, Lima), also have buses to Lima. Daily buses to **Cerro de Pasco**, 5 hrs, US$2. 'Mixto' Huánuco-Cerro de Pasco, half bus, half truck, departs at 0400, 3 hrs, US$3.60; also colectivo 1 or 12, US$6.20 at 0500. To **Huancayo**, 8-9 hrs, US$5-6. Buses to **Tingo María**, 3-4 hrs, US$1.75; colectivo, US$4.35, 2 hrs, many start from nr the river bridge, 2 blocks from the main plaza. Bus to **Pucallpa**, US$11, with La Perla del Oriente (Etposa), 0800 and 1600, 10-12 hrs, rec. Buses make stops for meals but some of them are few and far between, so it's a good idea to take your own food, especially given the frequency of breakdowns. This route has many checkpoints and robberies can occur. You are advised to travel by day and check on the current situation regarding safety.

## WEST OF HUANUCO

The road to La Unión and Tantamayo passes the 'Crown of the Inca', also known as Lacsahuarina, meaning 'Two Princesses' in Quechua. This distinctive rock formation is at the pass before the descent into the upper canyon of the Río Marañon.

### TANTAMAYO

Tantamayo (3,600m) is a farming village surrounded by precolumbian ruins from the **Yarowillca** culture.

**Japallan** is perhaps the most scenically sited, guarding the entrance to the valley leading from the spectacular Marañon canyon. To get there, cross the river from Tantamayo and walk W to San Pedro de Pariarca. At the start of the village take the path to the right to Pariash (Upper Pariarca), and head for the ruins silhouetted on a ridge.

The ruins of **Selinin** are just above Pariash. The most elaborate ruins are **Piruru** and **Susupillu**. Piruru was occupied continuously for 1,700 years, from 3000 BC as a ceremonial, and later ceramics, centre. Both sites have high-rise stone dwellings. To reach Susupillu head NE through the tiny village of La Florida. There are other ruins further afield.

All the above mentioned ruins are visible from Tantamayo and can be reached on foot in about 3-4 hrs; guides are available to visit the sites. The walks to the ruins are arduous; take warm clothing, a hat and suntan lotion. The scenery is stunning. Pictures and information on the sites are available from Huánaco Post Office.

• **Accommodation & places to eat** In Tanatamayo there are 4 basic hotels and one restaurant, *Ortega*, on the corner of the Plaza.

• **Transport** Buses from Huánuco: Transportes Balla, San Martín 575, US$6.50, 10 hrs, depart 0730 and 0800, return 1800 and 0100.

## LA UNION

From Huánuco, a road leads to La Unión, capital of Dos de Mayo district. It's a friendly town, but electricity can be a problem and it gets very cold at night.

On the pampa above La Unión are the Inca ruins of **Huánuco Viejo**, a 2½ hr walk from the town, a great temple-fortress with residential quarters. To get there, take the path starting behind the market and climb towards the cross, which is at the edge of a plateau. Continue straight through the village on the wide path. Note that, though the locals are friendly, some of their dogs are not always well disposed to strangers. The views of the pampa, surrounded on all sides by mountains, are beautiful. Seemingly at the foot of a mountain, in front and to your right, is a silvery metalic roof of a little chapel, behind which are the ruins – about a 20-min walk through herds of cattle. You should take warm clothing and be prepared for some violent thunderstorms. (Karen Kubitsch, Germany).

• **Accommodation G** ***Hostal Turista*** and **G** ***Hostal Dos de Mayo***, neither are safe for left luggage; ***Restaurant El Danubio***, nr the market, good home cooking.

• **Transport** From Huánuco, 2 buses daily at 0745, leave from Tarapacá, return 0600 and 0700, US$4.35, 8 hrs. A truck leaves in the late morning, 10½ hrs. La Unión-Tingo Chico, US$2.70. There is a daily bus to Lima which gets crowded.

ROUTES It is possible to get to the Callejón de Huaylas from here. La Unión-Huaraz direct is very difficult because most transport does the route La Unión-Chiquián-Lima: change buses in Chiquián (see page 133) or at the Conococha crossroads, but check times if you can to avoid being stranded in the dark. Alternatively ask for trucks going to Huallanca and from there to Pachacoto, 1 hr S of Huáraz. Check local political conditions before taking this route.

You can, if you're so inclined, hike to the Cordillera Raura (see page 158) from **Laguna Lauricocha**. To reach the lake from La Unión take a camioneta to **Baños**, then take another camioneta from there to **Antacolpa**. It's half a day's walk to the lake from here. In 1959, caves were discovered by the lake with 9,500 year-old human remains and some paintings. This is where the Río Marañon rises, eventually becoming the Ucayali and then Amazon rivers, before spilling into the Atlantic Ocean, 5,800 km away to the E.

# Amazon Basin



WHEN THE Spanish first arrived in Peru in the 16th century they heard fantastic stories of the riches of the Incas. One such tale told of the golden empire of El Dorado hidden deep in the heart of the tropical rainforest and it was this which inspired the conquistadors to head East in search of gold. All they found, however, was a hostile and mysterious world from which many of them never returned. Today, it is more likely to be tourists who flock to this vast, relatively unexplored region, not in search of gold but simply to experience its incredible biological diversity.

Cooled by winds sweeping down from the Andes but warmed by its jungle blanket, this region contains some of the most important tropical flora and fauna in the world. It would be wrong, however, to describe the Amazon jungle as a homogeneous landscape. It is very varied, with grasslands and tablelands of scrublike vegetation, inaccessible swamps, and forests up to 2,000m above sea level. This diverse landscape is also changeable. When the rivers are in spate they vary their course and appearance so that from one year to another any given place may become unrecognizable.

It is this great diversity which makes the Amazon basin a paradise for nature lovers, be they scientists or simply curious amateurs. This part of Peru contains some 10 million living species, including 2,000 species of fish and 300 mammals. Thanks mainly to its jungle zone, Peru has the second highest number of bird species in the world, the sixth highest number of mammals, the seventh in amphibians and butterflies, and the eighth in reptiles.

This incredible biological diversity, however, brings with it an acute ecological fragility. Ecologists consider the Amazon rainforest as the lungs of the earth and any fundamental change in its

## The origin of the Amazon

The legends of the Incas only served to fuel the greed and ambition of the Spanish invaders, who dreamed of untold riches buried deep in the Amazon jungle. The most famous and enduring of these was the legend of El Dorado which inspired a spate of ill-fated expeditions deep into this mysterious and inhospitable world.

Francisco Pizarro, conqueror of the Incas, sent his younger brother, Gonzalo, to seek out this fantastic empire of gold. In 1542, an expedition under the command of Gonzalo Pizarro left what is now Quito with 200 Spanish soldiers, 4,000 Indian slaves, horses, llamas and livestock. They headed across the Andes and down through the cloud forest until they reached the Coca river.

After following the Coca for some distance, the expedition began to run out of food. Rumours that they would find food once they reached the Napo river led one of the *conquistadores*, Francisco de Orellana, to set out with his men to look for this river and bring back provisions. But the jungle natives fled their small farms as soon as they saw the Spanish approach and Orellana and his party found nothing.

Without food and not being able to cross the river against the current, there was no point in returning. Orellana sent 3 messengers on foot to inform Gonzalo Pizarro of their decision to continue down river. After a few weeks they reached the Amazon river – so called by Orellana because he claimed to have been attacked by the legendary women warriors of the same name.

A few months later, Orellana arrived at the mouth of the Amazon and returned to Peru, via Panama. Eighteen months after first setting out, Francisco Orellana and a ragged band of 80 men staggered back into Quito, having become the first Europeans to travel the 3,500 km of the mighty Amazon river.

constitution, or indeed its disappearance, could have disastrous effects for our future on this planet.

## THE NORTHEASTERN JUNGLE

The principal means of communication in the jungle is by its many rivers, the most important of which is the Amazon. This mighty waterway was so named by the Spaniard Francisco de Orellana, during his epic voyage in 1542, owing to an encounter with a hostile, long-haired indigenous group which he took to be the fearsome women warriors of Greek legend.

The Amazon rises high up in the Andes as the Marañon, then joins the Ucayali to become the longest river in the world. In sections, where it is joined by its great tributaries, it is impossible to see its banks, giving the impression of being at sea. Standing on its banks is the city of Iquitos, made famous during the rubber boom of the late 19th century and now the main tourist attraction in this part of the Peruvian jungle. Iquitos stands in splendid isolation, accessible only by air or river, and still retains something of its frontier feel. Further S, the region's second city, Pucallpa, can be reached by road from the Central Andes.

ROUTES **The journey to Tingo María from Huánuco**, 135 km, is very dusty but gives a good view of the jungle. Some 25 km beyond Huánuco the road begins a sharp climb to the heights of Carpish (3,023m). A descent of 58 km brings it to the Huallaga river again; it then continues along the river to Tingo María. The road is paved from Huánuco to Tingo María, including a tunnel through the Carpish hills. Landslides along this section are frequent and construction work causes delays.

**NB** Although this route is reported to be relatively free from terrorism, robberies do occur and it is advisable to travel only by day. There are three police/army checkpoints where soldiers may demand money to pass through; it is not necessary to pay.

## TINGO MARIA

**Tingo María** (*Pop* 20,560; *Alt* 655m; *Phone code* 064; *Climate* tropical, annual rainfall 2,642mm) is on the middle Huallaga, in the Ceja de Montaña, or edge of the mountains, isolated for days in rainy season. The altitude prevents the climate from being oppressive. The Cordillera Azul, the front range of the Andes, covered with jungle-like vegetation to its top, separates it from the jungle lowlands to the E. The mountain which can be seen from all over the town is called La Bella Durmiente, the Sleeping Beauty.

The meeting here of Sierra and Selva makes the landscape extremely striking. Bananas, sugar cane, cocoa, rubber, tea and coffee are grown. The main crop of the area, though, is coca, grown on the *chacras* (smallholdings) in the countryside, and sold legitimately and otherwise in Tingo María.

Watch out for gangs of thieves around the buses and do not leave luggage on the bus if you get off. Note that this is a main narco-trafficking centre and although the town itself is generally safe, it is not safe to leave it at night. Also do not stray from the main routes, as some of the local population are suspicious of foreign visitors.

### Places of interest

A small university outside the town, beyond the *Hotel Turistas*, has a little museum-cum-zoo, with animals native to the area, and botanical gardens in the town. Entrance is free but a small tip would help to keep things in order.

### Excursions

6½ km from Tingo, on a rough road, is a fascinating cave, the **Cueva de las Lechuzas**. There are many nocturnal parrots in the cave and many small parakeets near the entrance. Take a motorcycle-taxi from town, US$1.75; US$0.45 for the ferry to cross the Río Monzón just

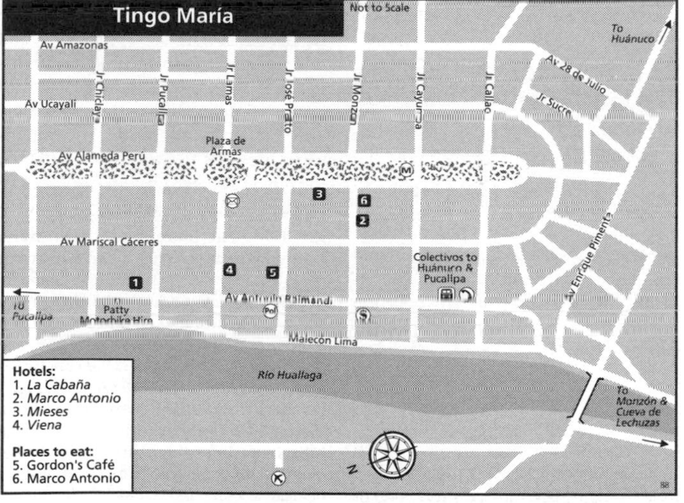

before the cave; entry to cave, US$0.90. Take a torch, and do not wear open shoes. The Cave can be reached by boat when the river is high.

13 km from Tingo is the small gorge known as **Cueva de las Pavas**, which is good for swimming.

## Local information

### ● Accommodation

**C** *Turistas*, on road to Huánuco nr University, with and without bath, restaurant, very good, swimming pool, some way out of town.

**E** *Hostal Marco Antonio*, Jr Monzón 364, T 562201, with restaurant next door.

**F** *Hostal Aro*, Av Ucayali 553; **F** *Hostal Mieses*, Av Alameda Perú 365, nr the plaza; **F** *La Cabaña*, Raimondi 6th block, fairly clean, good restaurant; **F** *Viena*, Jr Lamas, with bath, good value, clean. Hotels are often fully-booked.

### ● Places to eat

*Gordon's Café*, Jr José Pratto 229, clean, friendly, good food and service, cheap pisco sours.

### ● Transport

**Air** Expreso Aéreo fly daily to Lima, US$65. Also flights to: Huánuco, US$30; Chiclayo and Trujillo, US$80; Juanjui, US$60; Tarapoto, US$65; check the times. Their office is at Av Raimondi 218. Services are unreliable; there are cancellations in the rainy season or if the planes are not full.

**Buses** To **Huánuco**, 118 km, 3-4 hrs, US$1.75, several micros; colectivos US$4.35, 2 hrs. Direct buses continue to Lima (see Lima **Bus Companies**). To **Pucallpa**, 284 km, 12 hrs, US$5.50. Many of the big bus companies (eg: Leon de Huánuco, Transmar and Transportes del Rey) pass through Tingo María on their way to Pucallpa, from Lima, in the middle of the night. Ucayali Express colectivos leave from the corner of Raimondi and Callao; also other colectivos and taxis, which all leave in the early morning in convoy, with a police guard (Jan 96). To **Juanjui**, 340 km, 15-20 hrs, US$9, daily transport, not a rec journey because of narco-terrorist activity; continuing to **Tarapoto**, a further 145 km, 4 hrs, US$2.

## NORTH TO YURIMAGUAS

The Río Huallaga winds northwards for 930 km. The Upper Huallaga is a torrent, dropping 15.8m/km between its source and Tingo María. The Lower Huallaga moves through an enervation of flatness, with its main port, Yurimaguas, below the last rapids and only 150m above the Atlantic ocean, yet distant from that ocean by over a month's voyage. Between the Upper and Lower lies the Middle Huallaga: that third of the river which is downstream from Tingo María and upstream from Yurimaguas.

The valleys, ridges and plateaux have been compared with Kenya, but the area is so isolated that less than 100,000 people now live where a million might flourish. The southern part of the Middle Huallaga centres upon Tingo María. Down-river, beyond Bellavista, the orientation is towards **Yurimaguas**, which is connected by road with the Pacific coast, via Tarapoto and Moyobamba (see page 195).

At **Tulumayo**, soon after leaving Tingo María, a road runs N down the Huallaga past **La Morada**, successfully colonized by people from Lima's slums, to **Aucayacu** and **Tocache**, which has an airport. The road is paved to 20 km past Aucayacu, thereafter it is gravel.

● **Accommodation In Aucayacu**: **E** *Hotel Monte Carlo*, with bath, and one other hotel; both are poor. **In Tocache**: **F** *Hostal San Martín*; and **F** *Hostal Sucre*.

● **Transport Air** A small plane flies between Tocache and Juanjui; 25 mins. **Road** Colectivos run Tingo-Tocache US$13, 4½ hrs; or bus US$9.50, 6 hrs. The road has been pushed N to join another built S from Tarapoto and has now been joined at Tarapoto to the Olmos-Bagua-Yurimaguas transandine highway to the coast at Chiclayo. Tarapoto-Tocache, US$7.50 by colectivo. Colectivos and taxis run from Tocache to Yurimaguas on a serviceable unpaved road; daily camioneta Tarapoto-Yurimaguas, US$7-9, 6-8 hrs. The Juanjui-Tocache road has five bridges, but the last one across the Huallaga, just before Juanjui, was washed away in 1983 to be replaced by an efficient ferry; US$9.20/vehicle. Juanjui-Tarapoto by colectivo US$12.50. **River** For the river journey, start early in the morning if you do not wish to spend a night at the river village of Sión. There are no facilities, but the nights are not cold. The river runs through marvellous jungle with high cliffs. Boats sometimes run aground in the river nr Sión. Take food and water purifier. Balsa wood rafts also ply this stretch of river.

## YURIMAGUAS

The town (*Pop* 25,700) has a fine church of the Passionist Fathers, based on the Cathedral of Burgos, in Spain. A colourful market is held from 0600-0800, full of fruit and animals. Tourist information is available from the Consejo Regional building on the main plaza.

**Interesting excursions** in the area include the gorge of Shanusi and the lakes of Mushuyacu and Sanango. Mopeds can be hired for US$2.35 per hour, including fuel.

**Warning** There has been guerrilla activity in the Yurimaguas region; visitors can expect attention from the police. It is also a centre for anti-narcotics operations. A good contact is Lluis Dalman; The South American Explorer's Club in Lima has his address and telephone number.

• **Accommodation** **E** *Leo's Palace*, Plaza de Armas 104-6, good, friendly, reasonably-priced, restaurant; **F** *Camus*, Manco Capac 201, no sign, cheap.

• **Banks & money changers** Interbanc or travel agents; poor rates.

• **Transport Air** To Lima, 2 hrs, Aero Continente (4 a week), and Faucett (2 a week). To **Tarapoto**, 20 mins, same airlines, same frequency. To **Iquitos**, 45 mins, Aero Continente (4 a week). Flights are cancelled in the wet season or if they're not full. **Buses** To Moyobamba, with Guadalupe (Raymondi y Levean, T 3990), 0630, US$8.75. **River** By ferry to **Iquitos** takes 2 days and 2 nights (upstream takes longer), take a hammock, mosquito net, water-purification, fruit and drinks; there are police inspections at each end of the trip. Fares usually include meals, US$18, cabins cost more. To buy a hammock costs US$20-30 in Yurimaguas, mosquito nets are poor quality. Ask at the harbour for smaller boats, which can take up to 10 days.

## YURIMAGUAS TO IQUITOS

The river journey to Iquitos can be broken at **Lagunas**, 12 hrs from Yurimaguas. You can ask the local people to take you on a canoe trip into the jungle where you will see at very close range alligators, monkeys and a variety of birds, but only on trips of 4 days or so.

• **Accommodation** **G** *Hostal La Sombra*, Jr Vásquez 1121, shared bath, basic, friendly, good food; *Montalbán*, Plaza de Armas, no sign, 2 clean rooms, friendly owner, Sr Inga, 20-mins' walk from the jetty, also accommodation at the Farmacia.

• **Transport River** The *Constante* plies Yurimaguas to Lagunas 2-3 times a week (US$4.50); from there connections are difficult to Iquitos. Times of boats to Iquitos and Pucallpa are very vague; you should confirm departures the day before by radio. The boats pass by the villages of Castilla and Nauta, where the Huallaga joins the Ucayali and becomes the Amazon.

There are good jungle trips from Lagunas to the **Pacaya-Samiria Reserve**. When arranging a guide and boat from Lagunas, make sure you take enough fuel for the boat. Before entering the Reserve you pass through a village where you must pay US$4.50. Officially, you need a permit from INRENA in Lima.

Edinson and Klever Saldaña Gutiérrez, Sgto Flores 718, are good guides; also Job and Genaro (ask at *Hostal La Sombra*), who include basic food, with fishing and hunting; Juan Huaycama, at Jáuregui 689, is highly rec, mostly on the river, sleeping in hammocks, and fishing. The typical cost for a party of 5 for 12 days is US$200, with 2 guides and 2 boats. One person for 5 days with one guide is charged US$45. Take water purifier and mosquito repellent on excursions that involve living off the land.

## TINGO MARIA TO PUCALLPA

From Tingo María to the end of the road at Pucallpa is 288 km, with a climb over the watershed – the Cordillera Azul –

## Lope de Aguirre

One of the most famous expeditions into the mysterious, inhospitable world of the Amazon jungle in search of El Dorado was made by a Spanish noble from Navarra, Ursúa, along with his wife, Doña Inés and the adolescent daughter of his second-in-command, Lope de Aguirre. The rest of the party comprised over 300 Spaniards and 500 Indians.

Leaving Lima in 1560, his party crossed the Andean cordillera before penetrating the dense rainforest and navigating the Huallaga river. The journey, however, was cut short for Ursúa one night when he was murdered by the mutinous Lope de Aguirre, whose loyalty to the Spanish Crown was beginning to weaken. He felt that he had not been adequately compensated for his heroic exploits and hardship.

Lope de Aguirre took command of the group and resolved to punish any signs of loyalty to the Spanish Crown by death. During the rest of the journey he kept true to his threat, even killing Doña Inés, on the pretext that her bed could no longer be supported by the deteriorating ship.

Despite the decimation of the expedition group, Lope de Aguirre's lust for gold drove him on down the Amazon, turning off down the Río Negro and Orinoco, before reaching the Atlantic. It is an exciting, if infamous tale, well dramatized by German film director, Werner Herzog, in the film, "Aguirre, Wrath of God".

between the Huallaga and Ucayali rivers. The road is good for 60-70 km after Tingo María and 70 km before Pucallpa. In between it is affected by mud and landslides in the rainy season. There are eight army checkpoints.

When the road was being surveyed it was thought that the lowest pass over the Cordillera Azul was over 3,650m high, but an old document stating that a Father Abad had found a pass through these mountains in 1757 was rediscovered, and the road now goes through the pass of Father Abad, a gigantic gap 4 km long and 2,000m deep. At the top of the pass is a Peruvian Customs house; the jungle land to the E is a free zone. Coming down from the pass the road bed is along the floor of a magnificent canyon, the Boquerón Abad. It is a beautiful trip through luxuriant jungle and ferns and sheer walls of bare rock punctuated by occasional waterfalls plunging into the roaring torrent below.

East of the foot of the pass the all-weather road goes over the flat pampa, with few bends, to the village of **Aguaytía**. Here you'll find a narcotics police checkpoint, gasoline, accommodation in the *Hostal San Antonio* (**F**, clean), and 2 restaurants. From Aguaytía the road continues for 160 km to Pucallpa – 5 hrs by bus, US$4.35. There are no service stations on the last half of the journey.

## PUCALLPA

The capital of the Department of Ucayali is a rapidly expanding jungle town (*Pop* 400,000; *Phone code* 064) on the Río Ucayali, navigable by vessels of 3,000 tons from Iquitos, 533 nautical miles away. The town's newer sections have paved streets, sewers and lights, but much of the frontier atmosphere still exists. The central part is under development (early 1996) and there is a vacant lot covering an entire side of the Plaza de Armas. Pucallpa is notable for defying the rules of Spanish pronunciation – the double 'l' is pronounced as one.

The floating port of La Hoyada and Puerto Italia are about 5 km away and worth a visit to see the canoe traffic and open-air markets. Both are reached by

## A symbolic art form

Along the Ucayali river, near Pucallpa, the Shipibo-Conibo women practise a distinctive ceramic art believed to be unchanged for many generations.

Their pieces are unique in the Americas for their geometric decoration, but no one knows their true significance. One theory is that the lines represent a primitive map of the waterways of the region; others that they represent the constellations.

The same designs are stamped on cloth and were formerly painted on people's bodies during certain tribal rituals. Mud from the banks of local rivers is used to dye their ceramics and textiles. The mysterious geometric lines are painted on white cotton fabrics woven on their backstrap looms. When the mud dries and the fabric is washed, the design remains.

The Shipibo vessels are made with a specific purpose in mind and each one is regarded as imbued with deep spiritual meaning. Today, the Shipibo have organized themselves to market their products, though the forms and techniques of production remain unchanged.

Extracted from *Arts and Crafts of South America*, by Lucy Davies and Mo Fini, Tumi.

dirt roads. The economy of the area includes sawmills, plywood factories, a paper mill, oil refinery, fishing and boat building; timber is trucked out to the Highlands and the coast. Large discoveries of oil and gas are being explored, and gold mining is underway nearby. The Ganso Azul oilfield has a 75-km pipeline to the Pucallpa refinery.

The climate is tropical: the dry season is during July and Aug; the rainy seasons Oct-Nov and Feb-Mar. The town is hot and dusty between June and Nov and muddy from Dec to May. **NB** There is much military control because of narcotics activity, which is expanding. The city itself is safe enough to visit, but don't travel at night.

### Places of interest

**Parque Natural Pucallpa** is a zoo on the left on the road to the airport. You can see many jungle animals and most of the cages are OK, though some are inadequate. The zoo is set in parkland with a small lake; entry US$0.90.

**Museo Regional**, at Jr Inmaculada 999, has some good examples of Shibipo ceramics, as well as some delightful pickled snakes and other reptiles; open 0800-1200 and 1600-1800, US$0.90.

### Excursions

The Hospital Amazónico Albert Schweitzer, which serves the local Indians, and Summer School of Linguistics for the study of Indian languages (callers by appointment only) are on picturesque Lake **Yarinacocha**, the main tourist attraction of the area, especially with Peruvians. River dolphins can be seen in the lake. The Indian market of Moroti-Shobo ('The House of Selling and Buying') is a cooperative, organized by Shipibo-Conibo craftsmen. Fine handicrafts are sold in their shop and you can visit them in Yarinacocha; T 571551.

A good place to swim is at **San José**. Take the road out behind the power station round the lake beyond the Summer School of Linguistics.

**San Francisco** and **Santa Clara** can be visited at the far end of the lake on its western arm. Both are Shibipo villages still practising traditional ceramic and textile crafts. A canal near Santa Clara links Lake Yarinacocha with the Rio Ucayali. There are a few other villages nearby, such as Nuevo Destino and Santa Marta, which are within 1 hr's walk. The Shibipo people are very kind and friendly and a visit is recommended.

- **Accommodation** In San Francisco a nice

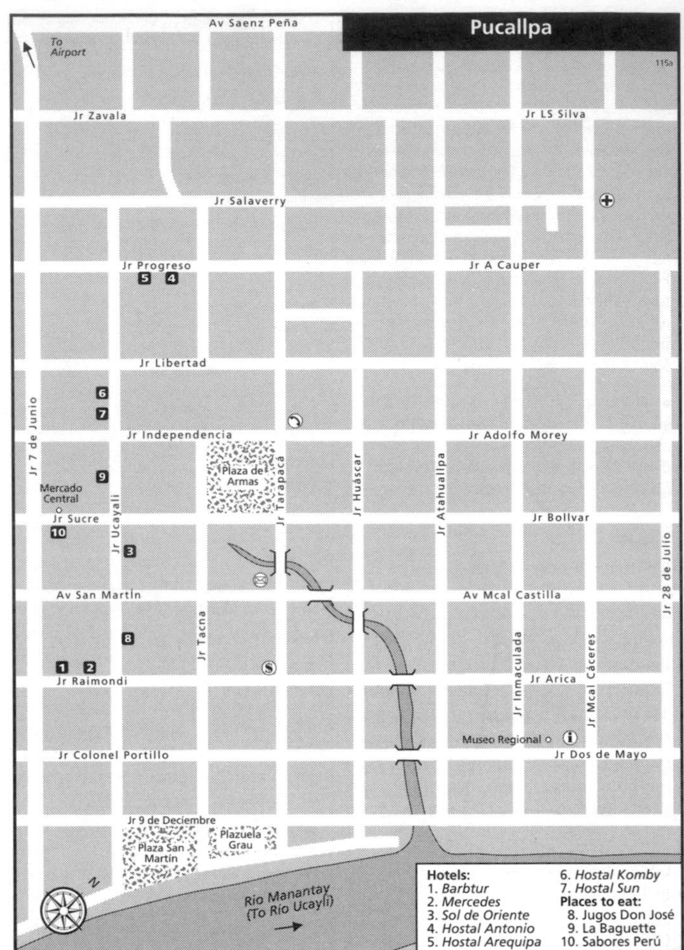


place to spend the night is in the house of Alberto Sánchez Ríos, *Casa Artesanal Shibipo*, which is very friendly and warmly rec.

• **Transport** To reach these villages take one of the motorized canoes, *peke-pekes*, which leave from Puerto Callao when full, US$0.90.

Certain sections of Lake Yarinacocha have been designated as a reserve. The beautifully-located **Jardín Botánico Chullachaqui** can be reached by boat from Puerto Callao to Pueblo Nueva Luz de Fátima. It's a 45-min trip, then 1 hr's walk to the garden, entry is free. For information about traditional medicine contact Mateo Arevalomayna, San Francisco de Yarinacocha, president of the group Ametra, an organization which is working to reestablish the use of traditional remedies; T 573152, or ask at Moroti-Shobo.

• **Accommodation In Yarinacocha**: **C** pp *La Cabaña*, by appointment only, price rises in high season, includes all meals and transport to and from Yarinacocha harbour, same Swiss owner as *Mercedes* in Pucallpa, good service and food, excellent guide, Isabel, for short expeditions, will organize plane excursions to Indian villages, or elsewhere; next door is **B-C** pp *La Perla*, includes all meals, German-Peruvian owned, English and German spoken, no electricity after 2100, good, jungle tours organized; **D-E** *Los Delfines*, new rooms with bath, fan, fridge, some with TV, clean; **F** *El Pescador*, in Puerto Callao, cheapest in town, friendly, restaurant, it was undergoing renovation early 1996, 20 new rooms were planned for July 1996 and an extension for 1997. Some small houses for rent on weekly basis.

• **Places to eat** There are many restaurants and bars on the waterfront and nr the Plaza, and also stalls which barbecue fresh fish and local dishes. Among the restaurants are: *El Cucharón*, good food; *Grande Paraíso*, good view, also has a *peña* at night, popular with young people; *Orlando's*, Jr Aguaytía, good local food.

• **Transport** Yarinacocha is 20 mins by colectivo or bus from the market in Pucallpa, US$0.30, or 15 mins by taxi, US$2.

Another recommended excursion in the Pucallpa area is 6-7 hrs by boat S to **Laguna Imitia** and **Laguna Chauya**. There are many indigenous villages on the shores and boats sometimes glide through the dense, overhanging vegetation around the lakes. To get there take a colectivo (US$9 pp), *peke-peke* or a hired boat from the port in Pucallpa.

## Local festivals

Feb, Carnival; 24 June, San Juan; 5-20 Oct, Pucallpa's *Aniversario Political* and the Ucayali regional fair.

## Local information

### ● Accommodation

**A3** *Sol del Oriente*, Av San Martín 552, T 575154, T/F 575510, with bath, pool, good restaurant; **A2** *Divina Montaña*, 14 km outside Pucallpa on the road to Tingo María, T 571276, bungalows for rent, restaurant, swimming pool, sports facilities.

**B** *Hostal Antonio*, Jr Progreso 547, T 573122, F 573128, has gym.

**D** *Arequipa*, Jr Progreso 573, with bath, good, clean; **D** *Mercedes*, good, but noisy with good bar and restaurant attached, swimming pool.

**E** *Barbtur*, Raymondi 670, T 572532, with bath, **F** without, friendly, clean, central, opp the bus stop, good beds; **E** *Komby*, Ucayali 300 block, comfortable, swimming pool, excellent value; **E** *Sun*, Ucayali 380, with bath, cheaper without, clean, good value, next to *Komby*; **E** *Tariri*, Raymondi, clean, good food.

**F** *Marinhor*, Raymondi 699, grubby but economical, helpful; **F** *Hostal Mori*, Jr Independencia 1114, basic.

### ● Places to eat

*El Alamo*, Carretera Yarinacocha 2650, good typical food; *El Sanguchón*, Jr Tarapacá 829, nr Banco de Crédito, clean, good sandwiches and coffee; *El Golf*, Jr Huáscar 545, *cevichería*; *Jugos Don José*, Jr Ucayali y Raimondi, one of the oldest in town; *Cafetería Antonio*, Cnel Portillo 307, 2 blocks from the *Museo Regional*, good coffee.

**Typical dishes**: *patarashca* is barbecued fish wrapped in *bijao* leaves; *zarapatera*, a spicy soup made with turtle meat served in its shell, but consider the ecological implications of this dish; *chonta salad*, made with palm shoots; *juanes*, rice with chicken or fish served during the San Juan festival; *tacutacu* is banana and sauces. The local beer 'San Juan' has been rec.

### ● Banks & money changers

It is easy to change dollars cash at the banks, travel agencies, the better hotels and bigger stores. There are also lots of street changers (watch them carefully). Banco de Crédito is the only place to change TCs. Cash on Visa at Banco de Crédito and Interbanco del Perú.

### ● Cultural centres

**Art school**: *Usko Ayar Amazonian School of Painting*, in the house of artist Pablo Amaringo, a former *vegetalista* (healer), Jr LM Sánchez, Cerro 465-467. The school provides art classes for local people, and is financially dependent upon selling their art. The internationally-renowned school welcomes overseas visitors for short or long stays to study painting and learn Spanish and/or teach English with Peruvian students. The painting is oriented around the Amazonian cultures, in particular the healing and hallucinogenic effects of *ayahuasca*. For more information see the book, *Wizard of the Upper Amazon*.

### ● Shopping

*Artesanías La Selva*, Jr Tarapacá 868, has a reasonable selection of indigenous craftwork.

For local wood carvings visit the workshop of sculptor, Agustín Rivas, at Jr Tarapacá 861. Many Shibipo women carry and sell their products around Pucallpa and Yarinacocha.

### ● Tour companies & travel agents

*Laser Viajes y Turismo*, Jr 7 de Junio 1043, T 571120, T/F 573776, helpful, rec for planning a jungle trip. **NB** Pucallpa is recovering from years of terrorist disruption and jungle tours are still in a disorganized state. It's best to negotiate a price for a group with the boatmen on the waterfront; expect to pay around US$30/day pp. Only use accredited guides.

### ● Tourist offices

**Ministerio de Industria y Turismo** (MICTI), Jr Dos de Mayo 999, T 571303, T/F 575110, helpful with tourist information. Ask for advice about visiting the Río Piski area, which has authentic Shibipo culture. There is no passenger traffic, so the trip may be expensive.

### ● Transport

**Local** Small **motorcycles** for hire from Karen Motorbikes, Av San Martín 634, US$3.50/hr, plus deposit.

**Air** To **Lima**, 1 hr, daily flights with Faucett, Americana, AeroPerú and Aero Continente; Grupo Ocho every Fri, US$45. To **Iquitos**, 40 mins, with Americana, AeroPerú and Aero Continente, daily. To **Tarapoto**, with Americana. TASA charter air taxis to jungle towns, US$300/hr, Jr Progreso 547, next to *Hostal Antonio*, T 575221, F 573128. Americana, Jr Ucayali 868, T 574208. Airport to town, bus US$0.25; *motos* US$1; taxi US$2-3.

**Buses** Much of the Pucallpa-Lima road is now paved, though there is a rough stretch between Tingo María and Pucallpa (see above) and there are regular bus services to Lima. To **Lima**, 812 km, 18-20 hrs (longer in the rainy season, Nov-Mar), US$11, see under Lima **Bus Companies**. To **Tingo María**, 284 km, 7-9 hrs, US$7.80, kombis leave at 0600, 0700 and 0800 with Ucayali Express, 7 de Junio y San Martín. All buses have police guard and go in convoy (Jan 96). Take blankets as the crossing of the Cordillera at night is bitterly cold. It's rec to cross the mountains by day as the views are wonderful.

**River** Buses and colectivos go to the port, La Hoyada. In the dry season boats dock 3 km from the bus stop, it's a dusty walk, or taxi US$3. To **Iquitos**, some are better than others; only 3 boats with cabins, don't count on getting one (hammocks are cooler): *Florico*, *Carolina* and *Manuel*, trip takes 3-4 days, US$22 pp, US$27 inc food.

**NB** Travellers to Iquitos may need confirmation from the PNP that their documents are in order, this must then be signed by the Capitanía otherwise no passenger can be accepted on a trip leaving Pucallpa. No such clearance is necessary when returning to Pucallpa. Passenger services are in decline owing to competition by air and priority for cargo traffic; it may be better to make journeys in short stages rather than Pucallpa-Iquitos direct. There's a risk of illness as the river water is used for cooking and drinking.

Tinned food, mosquito netting, hammock and fresh water are necessary purchases, and fishing line and hooks are advisable. Vegetarians must take their own supplies. Bottled drinking water is reportedly impossible to find in Pucallpa. 2 litre bottles of carbonated water are readily available but expensive at US$4-6 a bottle. Also take lots of insect repellent, water purifier and tummy pills.

The smaller boats call often at jungle villages if you want to see them, but otherwise the shores can only be seen at a distance. Boats leave very irregularly. When conditions are bad they leave in convoy and none may leave afterwards for 4 to 6 weeks. Avoid boats that will be loading en route, this can take up to 6 days. Further down the Río Ucayali are **Contamaná**, with a frontier-town atmosphere, and **Requena**, from which launches sail to Iquitos, taking 12 hrs. Unlike most other villages, which are *mestizo*, **Roroboya**, about 12 hrs downstream from Pucallpa, is Shipibo Indian.

You can go to Puerto La Hoyada and Puerto Italia to find a smaller boat going to Iquitos; the Capitanía on the waterfront may give you information about sailings, but this is seldom reliable. Do not pay for your trip before you board the vessel, and only pay the captain. Some boat captains may allow you to live on board a couple of days before sailing. Boats going upstream on the Amazon and its tributaries stay closer to the bank than boats going down, which stay in mid-stream.

You can take a colectivo from Pucallpa S to **Zungaro** (US$4.50), where a boat (30 mins) can be taken to **Puerto Inca** on the Río Pachitea, about 120 km N by air from Puerto Bermúdez (see page 379) and close to the Carretera Marginal (under construction). It is a gold-rush town, expanding quickly, with two hotels: *Don José's Alojamiento*, **G**, clean, safe, laundry, big rooms, rec.

## IQUITOS

Capital of the Department of Loreto and chief town of Peru's jungle region, **Iquitos** (*Pop* 350,000; *Phone code* 094) stands on the W bank of the Amazon. Some 800 km downstream from Pucallpa and 3,646 km from the mouth of the Amazon, the city is completely isolated except by air and river.

Founded in 1757 as San Pablo de los Napeanos by the Jesuits, this was the first port of note on the great river. Rapid growth followed the Rubber Boom of the late 19th century, though the city's new-found wealth was short lived. By the second decade of this century the rubber industry had packed its bags and left for the more competitive Oriental suppliers. Remnants of the extravagant opulence of the boom period can still be seen in the fine, 2-storey houses decorated with Portuguese tiles which lend an air of faded beauty to the river embankment.

Iquitos has recently taken on a new lease of life as the centre for oil exploration in Peruvian Amazonia. It is also the main starting point for tourists wishing to explore Peru's northern jungle, with direct flights to and from Miami. Though it may seem at times that the city is attempting a new world record for the highest concentration of motorcycles in a built-up area, it is nevertheless a friendly, relaxed place with an almost languorous pace of life.

### PLACES OF INTEREST

The incongruous **Iron House** stands on the Plaza de Armas, designed by Eiffel for the Paris exhibition of 1889. It is said that the house was transported from Paris by a local rubber baron and is constructed entirely of iron trusses and sheets, bolted together and painted silver. It now houses a snack bar.

**Belén**, the picturesque, friendly waterfront district, is lively, but not safe at night. Most of its huts are built on rafts to cope with the river's 10m change of level during floods, which are most likely Nov to April. *Pasaje Paquito* is a bar with typical local drinks, as is *La China*. The main plaza has a bandstand made by Eiffel. Canoes can be hired on the waterfront to visit Belén, US$3/hr, but don't try paddling yourself as the current is very strong. The market at the end of the Malecón is well worth visiting, though you should get there before 0900 to see it in full swing.

The **University of Amazonia of Loreto** (1962) specializes in engineering and agriculture. See also the old Hotel Palace, now the army barracks, on the corner of Malecón Tarapacá and Putumayo. Of special interest are the older buildings, faced with *azulejos* (glazed tiles). They date from the rubber boom of 1890 to 1912, when the rubber barons imported the tiles from Portugal and Italy and ironwork from England to embellish their homes. Werner Herzog's film *Fitzcarraldo* is a *cause célèbre* in the town and Fitzcarrald's house still stands on the Plaza de Armas.

### MUSEUMS

**Museo Municipal**, Távara 3rd block s/n, has a large, old collection of stuffed Amazonian fauna. The guide will explains the exhibits; open Mon-Sat 0800-1800, US$1.30.

### EXCURSIONS

There is a beautiful white, sandy beach at **Bellavista**, which is safe for swimming and very popular at weekends in summer. Boats can be hired from here to see the meeting of the Nanay and Amazon rivers, and to visit villages en route. There are lots of food stalls selling typical local dishes. Take a bus from Jr Próspero to Bellavista, 15 mins, US$0.40.

Launches leave Iquitos for the village of **Indiana**. Get off at the 'Varadero de Mazán' and walk through the banana plantations to the Río Mazán. A trail leads from the village of Mazán through the jungle to Indiana, where there is hotel; it's about a 2-hr walk. Catch the launch back to Iquitos at 1300.

### Lake Quistococha

13.5 km S of the city, is beautifully situated in lush jungle, with a fish hatchery at the lakeside. The Parque Zoológico de Quistococha on the lake gives an example of the local wildlife, though conditions are pretty squalid. At the entrance are pictures and texts of local legends, which are interesting. The ticket office will supply a map of the lake and environs. There's a good 2-hr walk through the surrounding jungle on a clearly marked trail. See particularly the *paiche*, a huge Amazonian fish whose steaks (*paiche a la loretana*) you can eat in Iquitos' restaurants. There are also bars and restaurants on the lakeside and a small beach. Boats are for hire on the lake and swimming is safe but the

## The rubber boom

The conquest and colonization of the vast Amazon basin was consolidated by the end of the 19th century with the invention of the process of vulcanizing rubber. Many and varied uses were found for this new product and demand was such that the jungle began to be populated by numerous European and North American immigrants who came to invest their money in rubber.

The rubber tree grew wild in the Amazon but the indigenous peoples were the only ones who knew the forests and could find this coveted tree. The exporting companies set up business in the rapidly-expanding cities along the Amazon, such as Iquitos. They sent their "slave-hunters" out into the surrounding jungle to find the native labour needed to collect the valuable rubber resin. These natives were completely enslaved, their living conditions were intolerable and they perished in their thousands. This led to the extinction of many indigenous groups.

One of the richest rubber barons of this period was Arana, who had been granted control of the entire Putumayo region by the Peruvian government. He treated his 12,000 slaves so harshly that none survived and today no ethnic groups exist in this region.

Another important figure from the rubber boom was Fitzcarrald, son of an immigrant Englishman who lived on the Peruvian coast. He was accused of spying during the 1879 war between Peru and Chile and fled to the Amazon where he lived for many years among the natives. He would go on to become one of the richest men in the region.

Thanks to Fitzcarrald, the isthmus between the basin of the Ucayali river and that of the Madre de Dios river was discovered. Before this, no natural form of communication was known between the two rivers. The first steamships to go up the Madre de Dios were carried by thousands of natives across the 8 km stretch of land which separated the two basins. Fitzcarrald died at the age of 36 when the ship on which he was travelling sank.

The Rubber Barons lived in the new Amazonian cities and travelled around in the luxurious boats which plied the great river. Every imaginable luxury was imported for their use: their women dressed in the latest Parisian fashions; the men enjoyed the finest foreign liqueurs; even the best musical shows were brought over from the Old World. There was no limit to their whims.

This period of economic boom came to a sudden end in 1912 when rubber grown in the French and British colonies in Asia and Africa began to compete on the world market.

sandflies are vicious, so take insect repellent. Entry is US$1.30, open daily 0900-1700.

● **Transport** Kombis leave every hour until 1500 from Plaza 28 de Julio; the last one back leaves at 1700. Alternatively take a *motocarro* there and back with a 1-hr wait, which costs US$13. Perhaps the best option is to hire a motorbike and spend the day there. The road is under repair at present (early 1996) and very difficult in parts, especially after rain.

On the road to Quistococha, is the turn-off to the village of **Santo Tomás**, about 20 km away, and a favourite weekend retreat of inhabitants of Iquitos. The village has a good restaurant and canoes may be hired. Trucks go there, taking passengers.

## LOCAL FESTIVALS

**5 Jan**: Anniversary of the founding of Iquitos. **Feb-Mar**: Carnival, when you can see the local dance 'La Pandilla'. **Third week in June**: Tourist week, with regional music, held in the *Mercado Artesanal de San Juan*. **24 June**: Festival of San Juan, patron saint of Loreto. **28-30 Aug**: Santa Rosa de Lima, celebrated in Rumococha. **22-25 Sept**: Santo Tomás, in the village of the same name. **8 Dec**: Immaculate Conception, celebrated in Punchana, near the docks.

## LOCAL INFORMATION

**Hotel prices**

| | | | |
|---|---|---|---|
| L1 | over US$200 | L2 | US$151-200 |
| L3 | US$101-150 | A1 | US$81-100 |
| A2 | US$61-80 | A3 | US$46-60 |
| B | US$31-45 | C | US$21-30 |
| D | US$12-20 | E | US$7-11 |
| F | US$4-6 | G | up to US$3 |

Iquitos generally seems more relaxed than the rest of Peru and theft is not normally a problem, but the normal advice applies nonetheless. If possible, avoid visiting Iquitos around Peruvian Independence Day (27 and 28 July) and Easter as it is very expensive and crowded and excursion facilities are overloaded. Hotels are generally more expensive than the rest of the country, but discounts of 20% or more can be negotiated in the low season (Jan-April).

● **Accommodation**
**A1** ***Real Hotel Iquitos***, Malecón Tarapacá, 1 block from Plaza de Armas, T 231011, F 236222, ex Tourist Hotel, recently upgraded, inc tax and breakfast, many good a/c rooms with bath.

**A2** ***El Dorado***, Napo 362, T 237326, F 232203, pool (open to restaurant users), cable TV, bar and restaurant, highly rec; **A2-3** ***Victoria Regia***, Ricardo Palma 252, T 231983, F 232499, hot showers, a/c, frige, free map of city, safe deposit boxes in rooms, good restaurant and pool, rec.

**A3** ***Hostal Acosta***, Calvo de Araujo y Huallaga, T 235974, similar to *Victoria Regia* minus the swimming pool; **A3** ***Jhuliana***, Putumayo 521, T/F 233154, inc tax and breakfast, friendly, nice pool, restaurant, rec.

**B** ***Amazonas***, Plaza de Armas, Arica 108, T 232015, modern, a/c, phone, frigo bar, TV; **B** ***Hostal Ambassador***, Pevas 260, T 233110, inc tax, shower, a/c, transport to and from airport, member of Peruvian Youth Hostel Association, cafeteria, owns Sinchicuy Lodge (see above), rec; **B** ***Europa***, Brasil 222, T 231123, F 235483, a/c, cable TV, phone and fridge in every room, pleasant café/bar, good views from 5th floor.

**C** ***Hostal Caravel***, Próspero 568, T 232176, new, clean, expensive; **C** ***Internacional***, Próspero 835, T/F 234684, a/c, with bath, cable TV, fridge, phone, friendly, secure, medium-priced restaurant, good value, rec.

**D** ***El Sitio***, Ricardo Palma 541, T 239878, with bath, spotlessly clean, fan, cafeteria, highly rec; **D** ***Hostal Bon Bini***, Pevas 386, T 238422, with bath, very clean, fridge, good value, rec; **D** ***Hostal La Pascana***, Pevas 133, T 231418, with cold shower, basic, fan, clean, breakfast available, luggage store, TV lounge, luxuriant garden, relaxed, popular, book exchange, highly rec.

**E** ***Hostal Don José Inn***, Fitzcarrald 456, T 234257, with bath, fan, TV, clean, good, breakfast and evening meal on request for US$2.25; **E** ***Hostal Rolando's Amazon River***, Esq Fitzcarrald y Nauta 307, T 233979, with bath and fan, restaurant, also own *Albergue Supay* (see **Jungle tours** below); **E** ***Hostal Vargas***, Av Quiñones, outside town on the road to the airport, clean, good value, rec; **E** ***Hostal Karina***, Putumayo 467, T 235367, water all day, fans; **E** ***Isabel***, Brasil 164, T 234901, with bath, very good, clean, but

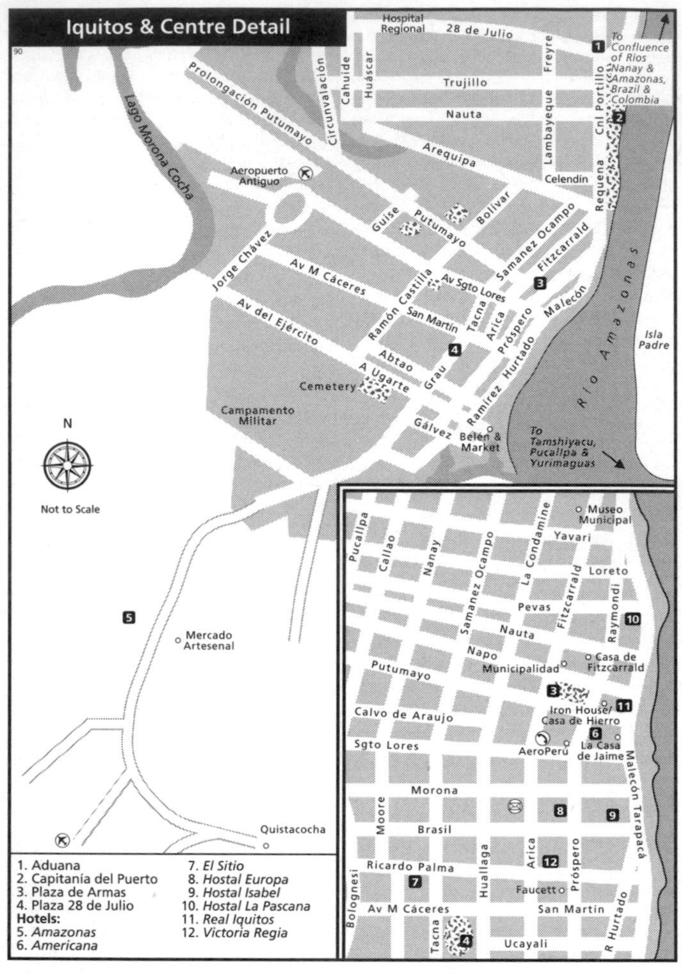


plug the holes in the walls, secure, often full; **E** *Loreto*, Próspero 311, T 234191, with bath, clean, basic, fan; *Hostal Lozano*, Ramírez Hurtado 772, T 232486, bath, friendly, quiet; *Lima*, Próspero 459, T 235152, bath, fan, cold water; **E** *Pensión Económico*, Moore 1164, T 265616, clean, large rooms, water all day, quiet, not central, no sign outside, friendly, breakfast on request, rec.

**F** pp *Hostal Aeropuerto*, Av Corpac block 100 y Malvinas, nr airport, clean, OK, fan in room, friendly, other 'services' available; **F** *Hostal Anita*, Ramírez Hurtado 742, T 235354, with bath, no fan, basic; **F** *Hostal Tacna*, Tacna 516, T 230714, fans, basic but clean, good value, rooms at front with balcony noisy.

## ● Places to eat

*El Dorado Inn*, C Huallaga 630, good value and good menu; *El Mesón*, Jr Napo 116, local specialities include venison stew and wild pig, the broiled alligator is rec, also try the delicious *paiche*; ***La Terraza***, Malecón Tarapacá y Napo, commanding views of river, good; ***La Casa de Jaime***, Malecón Tarapacá 137, excellent steaks, also vegetarian meals, owner Jaime Acevedo is charming, speaks perfect English, also German, and will give excellent advice about jungle trips, the wonderful mozzarella cheese is not to be missed, it comes from water buffaloes brought from Africa by Cubans and produced locally in a factory built by Italians, also book exchange, frequented by tour operators, consuls and ex-pats, interesting ambience, book exchange, very highly rec; ***La Pascana***, Ramírez Hurtado 735, good fish and *ceviche*, friendly, popular, try the *vientequatro raices*, 20% discount for Handbook users; ***Wai Ming***, San Martín at Plaza 28 de Julio, good, expensive; ***Hueng Teng***, esq Pucallpa y Nauta, Chinese, cheap, rec. The cheapest restaurants are to be found on and around Plaza 28 de Julio. ***Heladería La Favorita***, Próspero 415, good ice-cream (try local flavour *aguaje* – see below); ***Juguería Paladar***, Próspero 245, excellent juices; ***Casa de Hierro***, Plaza de Armas, Próspero y Putumayo, friendly snack bar inside Eiffel's iron house, good chocolate cake, try malta beer with egg and fresh milk, a useful pick-me-up; ***Ari's Burger***, Plaza de Armas, Próspero 127, medium-priced fast food, popular with gringos; ***Olla de Oro***, Calvo de Araujo 579, close to the main indoor market, excellent food, friendly service, rec.

**Bars**: the liveliest are along the riverside in the first couple of blocks of Malecón Tarapacá: ***Pipi Vela***, live music Fri; ***La Ribereña***, Raymondi 453, terraced seats on a newly-built plaza with jukebox; ***El Encanto del Amazonas***, Malecón Tarapacá block 4, palm-roofed bar with river view, sells *siete raices* (see below); ***Snack Bar Arandu***, beers, drinks, good views of the Amazon river; ***El Mirador***, Requena next to steps leading down to the wharf, cheap drink, fantastic view; ***Teatro Café Amauta***, Nauta 248, live music, open 2200-2400, good atmosphere, popular, small exhibition hall.

Pineapples are good and cheap. Try the local drink *chuchuhuasi*, made from the bark of a tree, which is supposed to have aphrodisiac properties but tastes like fortified cough tincture (for sale at Arica 1046), and *jugo de cocona*, and the alcoholic *cola de mono* and *siete raices* (aguardiente mixed with the bark of 7 trees and wild honey), sold at *Exquisita Amazónica*, Abtao 590. You can eat cheaply, especially fish and *ceviche*, at the three markets. Palm heart salad (*chonta*), or *a la Loretana* dish on menus is excellent; also try *inchicapi* (chicken, corn and peanut soup), *cecina* (fried dried pork), *tacacho* (fried green banana and pork, mashed into balls and eaten for breakfast or tea), *juanes* (chicken, rice, olive and egg, seasoned and wrapped in bijao leaves and sold in restaurants) and the *camu-camu* is an interesting but acquired taste, said to have one of the highest vitamin C concentrations in the world.

### ● Airline offices

**Aero Continente**, Próspero 331, T 233162, F 233990; **Americana**, Próspero 215, T 237062/237204, F 239873; **Faucett**, Próspero 632-40, T 239766, F 243198; **AeroPerú**, Próspero 248, T 232513; **SAA** (Servicios Aéreos Amazónicos), Arica 273, T 230776, F 243776.

### ● Banks & money changers

**Banco de Crédito**, Plaza de Armas, Visa, cash and TCs, good rates. **Banco Continental**, Sgto Lores 171, Visa, Mastercard, 1% commission on TCs. **Banco de la Nación**, Condamine 478, good rates, 0915-1530, changes Deutschmarks. **Banco Latino**, Próspero 310. **Banco Wiese**, Próspero 282, Visa, Mastercard, changes TCs with no commission, rates for cash not great. *Casas de Cambio* stay open late: Tacna 380 and Fitzcarrald 120. There are many money changers on Próspero in the 3 blocks S of Plaza de Armas. Their rates are good on weekdays but not at the weekend.

### ● Embassies & consulates

**Consulates**: **Brazil**, Sgto Lores 363, T 232081, Mon-Fri 0800-1200, 1500-1800, need photo and yellow fever certificate for visa; **Britain**, Mr Lewis Power, Arica 253, T 234110 or 234383; **Colombia**, Putumayo 247, T 231461; **Spain**, Av La Marina, T 232483; **France**, Napo 346, T 232353; **Germany**, Max Drusche, Yavari 660, T 232641, F 236364.

### ● Entertainment

**Cinemas**: *Bolognesi*, San Martín 390, on Plaza 28 de Julio.

**Discotheques**: *Bamboleo*, Malecón Tarapacá 328, very popular, open 2300 till late; ***La Pantera Rosa***, Moore 434, free entrance, Mon-Sat until 0300; ***La Estancia***, Napo 1 block, restaurant by day, dancing at night, popular; ***Francesco***, Pevas 1 block, good atmosphere; ***Yutopia Karaoke***, Napo 168;

***Dreams***, Samanez Ocampo 120; ***Calipso***, Putumayo 15 block. There are also discos on Av Quiñones; ***Latin Limits*** and ***Las Vegas***.

### Hospitals & medical services

**Medical services**: *Clínica Loreto*, Morona 471, T 233752, 24-hr attention, rec, but only Spanish spoken; *Hospital Iquitos*, Av Grau, emergency T 231721; *Hospital Regional de Loreto*, 28 de Julio, emergency T 235821; *Clínica Ana Stahl*, Av La Marina 3rd block.

### Post & telecommunications

**Post Office**: on the corner of C Arica with Morona, nr Plaza de Armas, open daily 0700-2000. **Telefónica del Perú**, at Arica 276.

### Shopping

***Artesanías del Perú***, Putumayo 128; ***Mercado Artesanal de Productores***, 4 km from the centre in the San Juan district, on the road to the airport, take a colectivo; ***Artesanías de la Selva***, R Palma 190; unnamed shop at Próspero 435. Camera accessories at ***Aspinwall***, Raimondi 138. There are pharmacies at Tacna 156 and at Próspero 361-3. Records and tapes at ***Discotiendas Hikari***, San Martín 324. Cheap haircuts at ***Barbería Jupiter***, Napo 323. A good local newspaper is *La Región*.

**NB** Locals sell necklaces made with red and black rosary peas (Abrus pecatorius), which are extremely poisonous. Do not give them to children. They are illegal in Canada, but not in the USA.

### Tour companies & travel agents

***Cumacebo Expediciones***, Putumayo 160, T/F 232229, 2 days/1 night, US$90 pp; ***Amazonia Expeditions***, Napo 156, T 222049, owned by Carlos Grández Pérez, camping, wildlife, jungle survival and trekking; tours from 2-15 days, US$50 pp/day; ***Amazon Experience***, Echenique 473, T 236224. Also see **Jungle tours** below. A rec, accredited guide is Hernán Silva Peixoto, Requena 142. Note that competition is fierce and there some unscrupulous operators. Also avoid the many hustlers at the airport on arrival. For good advice ask Jaime Acevedo at *Casa de Jaime*, see above, **Places to eat**.

### Tourist offices

At Napo 176, 0730-1330, for maps and general tourist literature, try the Gobierno Regional de Loreto, Ricardo Palma 113, T 233321. Useful town maps, maps of the Quistacocha zoo and literature are available from the main jungle tour operators. You can also get a town map from ***Librería Mosquera***, Jr Próspero.

PARD, Preservation of the Amazon River Dolphin, Pevas 253, T/F (51-94) 238585, Roxanne Kremer or Frank Aliaga for information.

### Useful addresses

**Immigration**: Malecón Tarapacá 382, quick service.

### Transport

**Local Motorcycle hire**: *Rider*, Pevas 219; *Park Motors*, Tacna 579, T/F 231688. Expect to pay: mopeds, US$2.60/hr, US$35/24 hrs; Honda 125, US$4.50/hr, US$44/24 hrs; Honda 125, US$4.50/hr; Yamaha DT175, US$5.20/hr, US$65/24 hrs.

**Air** Francisco Secada Vigneta airport handles national and international flights (to/from Miami), T 231501/233094. Taxi to the airport costs US$2.50 pp; *motocarro* (motorcycle with 2 seats), US$2.20. A bus from the airport, US$0.20, goes as far as the market area, about 12 blocks from the Plaza de Armas, a taxi from there is US$1.30.

To **Lima**, daily; Faucett, US$81; Americana, US$61; Aero Continente, US$61; AeroPerú, US$65 (some flights via Chiclayo). Aero Continente and Americana fly via **Pucallpa**, US$35; also AeroPerú 3 times a week, US$41, and Faucett 2 a week. To **Yurimaguas** and **Tarapoto** Aero Continente and Faucett, US$53, 3 a week. Iquitos-**Cusco** with Faucett direct on Sun; daily with Americana, US$106; Americana also to Arequipa, via Pucallpa and Lima. To **Miami**, with Faucett Sat, US$510 return. When entering Peru on this flight, a 90-day tourist visa is given on arrival. Iquitos flights are frequently delayed; be sure to reconfirm your flight in Iquitos, as they are often overbooked, especially over the Christmas period; check times in advance as itineraries frequently change. TANS office, Sgto Lores 127, T 234632; they have flights to Angamos, Requena, Orellana, Pampahermosa, Contamanda and Estrecho; they leave from Grupo 42 base at Moronacocha every fortnight. TANS hydroplane flies NNW along the river to Peneya, opp Leguizamo in Colombia, or Gueppi, the military frontier post from where you can get to Puerto Asís (Colombia) by boat. On this flight, locals take precedence. SAA fly to Caballococha (US$45, 45 mins) and Leticia, Colombia (US$50, 55 mins) 3 times a week, returning the same day; they also charter 34-seater jets for US$1500/hr to any destination.

**Aircraft for hire**: Expertour, Putumayo 124, T 238162; Cessna with bilingual US pilot, US$225/hr, minimum 3-4 people; 1-hr flight over Iquitos, US$37 pp.

**Shipping Upstream**: river boats to **Pucallpa**, leave every second day, usually at 1700, 6/7 days when river is high, 3/4 days when low; price depends on demand, eg US$22 pp in hammock, US$26 pp with bed and cabin. To **Yurimaguas**, 4/5 days, longer if cargo is being carried, which is usually the case, US$13-18 pp, more or less daily. Information on boats and tickets at Bellavista, Malecón Tarapacá 596; or Puerto Masusa district of Puchana, Av La Marina with Masusa, bus from centre, 10 mins. Cabins are 4 berth and you have to buy both a first class ticket, which entitles you to food (whether you want it or not) and deck space to sling your hammock, and a cabin ticket if you want the 'luxury' of a berth. Adequate washing and toilet facilities, but the food is rice, meat and beans (and whatever can be picked up en route) cooked in river water. There is a good cheap bar on board.

**Downstream**: a weekly luxury 54-passenger boat, *Río Amazonas*, plies between Iquitos and **Tabatinga** (Brazil), leaving Sun, operated by Amazon Tours and Cruises (see **Jungle tours** below), US$525 pp (US$445 for groups of 10 plus), return journey to Iquitos Wed; also M/V *Arca*, US$495 pp (US$420 groups of 10 plus), return journey Wed-Sat.

There are no boats direct to Manaus. Take a boat to **Islandia**, opp Tabatinga (Brazil); US$26 pp cabin plus food, US$22 pp hammock plus food. It takes 3 days to Islandia; 4/5 boats leave each week on Thurs and Sat, usually at 1700-1800. From Islandia take a small boat to Benjamín Constant and from there boats leave for Manaus. It is roughly 8 days from Islandia to Manaus. Boats for Manaus also leave from a little way down-river from Marco, the port for Tabatinga. Speedboats run between Iquitos and Islandia with Amazon Tours and Cruises, US$75, Tues, Fri and Sun, book ahead (2 days upstream, 11 hrs downstream). The *Ruiz* is highly rec for river journeys to the frontier; 3 days, US$20 with your own hammock, no food, or Pucallpa. *Ecograss* is also rec, US$25-30 pp inc food.

**NB** From May to July the river rises and the port in Iquitos moves. Boats leave from Puerto Nanay at Bellavista or from Puerto de Moronacocha.

**General hints for river travel** A hammock is essential, but they are expensive in Iquitos. A double, of material (not string), provides one person with a blanket. Board the boat many hours in advance to guarantee hammock space. If going on the top deck, try to be first down the front; take rope for hanging your hammock, plus string and sarongs for privacy. On all boats, hang your hammock away from lightbulbs (they aren't switched off at night and attract all sorts of strange insects) and away from the engines, which usually emit noxious fumes. Another useful tip is not to sling your hammock near the bottom of the stairwell on double decked river boats, as this is where the cook slaughters the livestock every morning.

Guard your belongings from the moment you board. There is very little privacy; women travellers can expect a lot of attention. Stock up on drinking water, fruit and tinned food in Iquitos. Take plenty of prophylactic enteritis tablets; many contract dysentery on the trip. Also take insect repellent.

If you plan to stop off along the way at small villages on the river in Peru, you can usually get a passing boat to make an unscheduled stop and pick you up. The best way to do this is to flag it down with a white sheet. This is what the villagers do if they want a passing boat to stop at their village. Note that this method doesn't work on the Brazilian part of the river, where boats don't make unscheduled stops. The only way to board a Brazilian boat between stops is to hire a canoe to take you out to meet it in mid-river then flag it down.

Public river transport can be extremely uncomfortable, but with patience, perseverance and a strong stomach it is still far from impossible.

### ● Crossing the Frontier

Details on exit and entry formalities seem to change frequently, so when leaving Peru, check in Iquitos first at Immigration (see above) or with the Capitanía at the port. Latest reports are that the boat to Islandia stops in Santa Rosa for Peruvian exit/Brazilian entry formalities.

Note that the Brazilian immigration office in Tabatinga is open during the weekend and late into the night. Do not listen to any taxi drivers who may tell you otherwise. Immigration officials are reported as relaxed and extremely helpful. They may even help you find a berth for your onward journey to Manaus.

### The debonnaire dolphin

One of the most bizarre examples of the wide diversity of flora and fauna in the Peruvian Amazon is a strange, prehistoric-looking mammal which can transform itself into a suave gentleman in a white linen suit.

Or so local legend would have it. But the Amazonian river dolphin is a strange creature indeed. Part myth, part real, this beast can change its skin colour from a pale grey to a bright, luminescent pink. The indigenous people of the Amazon rainforest have long revered what they call the *bufeo*, and even today, unwanted pregnancies within Indian communities are sometimes blamed on this magical animal with an impressive line in seduction techniques.

The Jaguar tribes of North-eastern Peru have passed down stories from generation to generation about the *bufeo*. One such tale is of an underwater city where the *bufeo* walk on pavements made from turtle shells and lie in hammocks strung from anacondas. While the more formal and elegant white suit is donned when in human form, underwater they prefer the casual look and lounge around in catfish shorts and stingray hats. The site of this animal Atlantis is said to be Lake Caballococha, downriver from Iquitos, near the Peru-Colombia border.

Another common belief serves to protect the dolphins from being hunted by local fishermen. This stems from the analogy between dolphins and witchdoctors. The *bufeo* can be a malevolent creature, if hunted, and will avenge the death of one of their own. To kill a dolphin, then, is the same as killing a powerful witchdoctor, with the same inevitable consequences.

These pink river dolphins were, until recently, a forgotten species, considered extinct. All that remained was the skeleton of one in Paris, brought back from South America as a gift to Napoleon, and a few vague scientific papers dating from the 19th century in the Natural History Museum in London. The *bufeo* was re-discovered by a British expedition in 1956, but then forgotten again. Until 1987, when Jacques Cousteau astounded TV viewers around the world with the first ever pictures of pink dolphins frolicking in the waters of the Amazon.

Now the adventurous traveller can see the *bufeo* in the flesh – be it grey or pink, or even dressed in a white suit. But women travellers should beware any charming, smartly-dressed gentlemen in these parts.

## JUNGLE TOURS FROM IQUITOS

All agencies are under the control of the local office of the Ministry of Tourism. They arrange 1 day or longer trips to places of interest with guides speaking some English. Package tours booked in Lima are much more expensive than those booked in Iquitos. Some agencies are reported as too easy going about their responsibilities on an organized trip. Take your time before making a decision, shop around, and don't be bullied by the hustlers at the airport. Find out all the details of the trip and food arrangements before paying; expect to pay about US$40-50/day. Launches for river trips can be hired by the hour or day; prices are negotiable, but usually about US$20-30/hr.

### ● Tour operators

*Explorama Tours*, are rec as the most efficient and, after 32 years in existence, certainly the biggest and most established. Their offices are by the riverside docks on Av La Marina 340, PO Box 446, T 51-94-252526/252530, F 51-94-252533; in USA, Selective Hotel Reservations, Toll Free, T 800-223-6764; MA (617) 581-0844, F 581-3714. They have three sites: *Explorama Inn*, 40 km (1½ hrs) from Iquitos, hot water, comfortable bungalows in a jungle setting, good food, attractive walks, a rec jungle experience for those who want their creature comforts, US$175 pp for 1 night/2 days, US$75 for each additional night (1-2 people); *Explorama Lodge* at Yanamono, 80 km from Iquitos, 2½ hrs from Iquitos, palm-thatched accommodation with separate bath and shower facilities connected by covered walkways, US$250 for 3 days/2 nights and US$75 for each additional day (1-2 people); ***Explornapo Camp*** at Llachapa, 160 km (4 hrs) from Iquitos, is more primitive, but better for seeing fauna, with an impressive new canopy walkway some 35m above the forest floor and 500m long, set in 105,000 ha of primary rainforest, "a magnificent experience and not to be missed". It is also possible to stay in the ACEER laboratory, a scientific research station, only 10 mins from the canopy walkway; the basic programme costs US$1,000 for 5 days/4 nights (2 people), the first and last nights spent at Explorama Lodge. A US$25 donation to the Foundation for Conservation of Peruvian Amazon Biosphere (Conapac) is included if visiting the walkway; to spend a night at the ACEER lab is US$55; each extra night to the basic programme costs US$90. Prices include transfers, advance reservations, etc; local rates are much lower. Flight inclusive packages are available from Miami with Faucett, US$835 for 7 days.

*Paseos Amazónicos Ambassador*, Pevas 246, T/F 233110, operates the *Amazonas Sinchicuy Lodge*, US$70 pp/night; the lodge is 1 hr 15 mins from Iquitos on the Sinchicuy river, 10 mins by boat from the Amazon river. The lodge consists of several wooden buildings with thatched roofs on stilts, cabins with bath, no electricity but parrafin lamps are provided, good food, plenty activities, visits to local villages, rec. They also organize visits to Lake Quistacocha.

***Lima Tours*** offers 3 days/2 night tours to Iquitos and the Amazon from Lima for US$510 pp, flight included (US$900 for 2 passengers).

***Amazon Tourist Services***, Requena 336, T (51-94) 233931, F 231265; in USA, 8700 W Flagler St, suite 190, Miami, FL 33174, T 305-227-2266, toll free 800-423-2791, F 305-227-1880, American owned company: Lodge itineraries to 42-room *Amazon Camp*, 1 night/2 days US$105, extra night US$55. Various cruises available: on M/V *Arca* Iquitos-Leticia-Iquitos, US$500 pp; nature cruises on M/V *Delfín*. They also organize rugged expeditions to various jungle *tambos* (thatched shelters), rec as conscientious and efficient.

***Anaconda Lara Lodge***, Pevas 210, T 239147, F 232978, 40 km from Iquitos, full day tours US$50, also offers adventure expeditions to Río Yarapa, 180 km away.

***Las Colinas de Zungarococha Amazon Resort***, operated by Paucar Tours, Próspero 648-Altos, T 235188/232131, or through *Hostal Acosta*, or Ricardo Rivera Navarrete 645E, San Isidro, Lima, T/F 442-4515, comfortable lakeside bungalows, swimming pool, watersports, mini-zoo, full day US$40, 1 night/2 days US$70.

***Amazon Lodge***, Raymondi 382, T 237142; Av Alvarez Calderón 155, Of 302, San Isidro, Lima, T (51-1) 221-3341, F 221-0974, 48 km downriver from Iquitos, rec as friendly and comfortable; 3 days/2 nights, US$200 pp, 2-4 people, US$50 pp for each additional night.

***Albergue Supay*** is a floating hotel on Supay lake close to the Río Nanay, 2 hrs by boat from Iquitos, or taxi and canoe, 1 to 5 day tours from US$60 to US$290 pp, run by Austrian Roland Röggl and Peruvian Luz Elena Montoya; contact Apdo 532, Correo Central, Iquitos, or Jr Próspero 635, T 234785; they also have *hostal* at Fitzcarrald y Nauta 307 (see above).

***Amazonia Expeditions***, Napo 150, T 222049, owned by Carlos Grandez Pérez, camping, wildlife, jungle survival and trekking tours from 2-15 days, US$50/day; ***Amazon Experience***, Echenique 473, T/F 236229.

***Yacumama Lodge***, Jr Arica 513-A, T/F 241022; Av Benavides 212, Of 1203, Miraflores, Lima; 4 days/3 nights, US$389, 6 days/5 nights, US$559 (minimum 2 people); part of the fee is invested in local conservation.

## ● General information & advice

It is advisable to take a waterproof coat and shoes or light boots on such trips, and a good torch, as well as *espirales* to ward off the mosquitoes at night – they can be bought from drugstores in Iquitos. *Premier* is the most effective local insect repellent. The dry season is from July to Sept; Sept is the best month to see flowers and butterflies.

Note that the area within a 50 km radius of Iquitos is too inhabited to support much large wildlife and there is probably no primary rainforest within 100 km of Iquitos. The Napo or Ucayali rivers have more to offer and excursions from Lagunas (see page 393) are more rewarding than those from Iquitos. Similarly with the area around the jungle lodges, however, there is plenty of scope for seeing small fauna and learning about the flora. Trips to visit Yagua Indians are reported to offer little in the way of an authentic cultural experience.

## THE SOUTHEASTERN JUNGLE

The southern selva is made up of the Madre de Dios department, a region once inhabited by the Mojos tribe who put up fierce resistance to the Inca conquest. Created in 1902, the department contains the Manu National Park (1,881,000 ha), the Tambopata-Candamo Wildlife Reserve (1,500,000 ha) and the Heath National Sanctuary.

The forest of this lowland region (*Alt* 260m) is technically called Sub-tropical Moist Forest, which means that it receives less rainfall than tropical forest and is dominated by the floodplains of its meandering rivers. The most striking features are the former river channels that have become isolated as ox-bow lakes. These are home to black caiman and giant otter. Other rare species living in the forest are jaguar, puma, ocelot and tapir. There are also howler monkeys, macaws, guans, currasows and the giant harpy eagle.

As well as containing some of the most important flora and fauna on Earth, however, the region also harbours gold-diggers, loggers, hunters, drug smugglers and oil-men. For years, logging, gold prospecting and the search for oil and gas have endangered the unique rainforest, though fortunately, the destructive effect of such groups has been limited by the various conservation groups working to protect it.

The frontier town of Puerto Maldonado is the starting point for expeditions to one of the national parks and is only a 30-min flight from Cusco. The best time to visit is during the dry season when there are fewer mosquitoes and the rivers are low, exposing the beaches. This is also a good time to see nesting and to view the animals at close range, as they stay close to the rivers and are easily seen. Note that this is also the hottest time. A pair of binoculars is essential and insect repellent is a must.

The climate is warm and humid, with a rainy season from Nov to Mar and a dry season from April to October. Cold fronts from the South Atlantic, called *freajes*, are characteristic of the dry season, when temperatures drop to 15-16°C during the day, and 13° at night. Always bring a sweater at this time.

- **Recommended reading** *Birds of Venezuela* (Princeton University) and *South American Birds*, by John Dunning, give the best coverage of birds of Peru; also *Neotropical Rainforest Mammals, A field guide*, by Louise H Emmons. *Tropical Nature*, by Adrian Forsyth and Ken Miyata, gives an explanation of the rainforest. *Manu National Park*, by Kim MacQuarrie and André and Cornelia Bartschi, is a large, expensive and excellent book, with beautiful photographs. *The Ecology of Tropical Rainforests*, by 'Trees', is a booklet with an introduction for ecotourists. *Madre de Dios Packet*, by the South American Explorers Club, gives practical travel advice for the area.

## MANU BIOSPHERE RESERVE

The Manu Biosphere Reserve covers an area of 2,233,693 ha and is one of the largest conservation units on Earth, encompassing the complete drainage of the Manu river. No other reserve can compare with Manu for the diversity of life forms. The reserve holds over 850 species of birds and covers an altitudinal range from 200 to 4,100m above sea-level. Giant otters, jaguars, ocelots and 13 species of primates abound in this pristine tropical wilderness, and uncontacted indigenous tribes are present in the more remote areas, as are indigenous groups with limited access. Protection of this unique part of rainforest is not strictly controlled but Manu remains one of the worlds great wilderness experiences. The best time to visit is in the dry season from April to mid Nov, but trips can be planned during the rainy season too.

**NB** In 1996 the Reserve was closed from 1 Jan to 1 May, and only Manu Nature Tours, which has a lodge in the Reserve Zone, could run trips to the

## The miracle plant

The indigenous tribes of the Peruvian Amazon basin have many thousands of plants at their disposal to heal their bodies and souls. One of these plant species is the so-called *Uña de Gato* (Cat's Claw), a gigantic vine that grows to a height of 25m and looks like it belongs in a Tarzan movie set.

The fame of this remarkable plant in modern medical circles has very recently spread across the globe but its application in traditional medicine goes back a long way. The precolumbian peoples considered it magical and healthy. Today it is drunk by Peruvians in the form of a tea brewed from the bark that covers the vines to cure rheumatoid diseases and tumours.

The discovery of the plant's curative properties and its recent development as a "miracle drug" was thanks to a German pioneer, Arthur Brell, who lived for half a century in the jungle region of Chanchamayo, side by side with the Campa and Amuesha Indians until his death in 1978. He noted that the locals were untroubled by cancer, despite constant exposure to the smoke of charcoal fires which produce the carcinogenic elements found in tar. Years of painstaking research led him to the conclusion that this was due to a powerful immune system and he had the chance to put his theory to the test when a friend suffering terminal lung cancer came to Brell for help. After a couple of years of dosing him with preparations made from the miraculous plant, the sick man made a full recovery, much to the amazement of the doctors who had been treating him.

Research into *Uña de Gato* after Brell's death in Lima practically ceased, until 1990 when a large agro-industrial firm picked up where he had left off and began sponsoring further research. The most recent studies carried out have shown that its amazing therapeutic powers come from its acid and alkaloid components. Scientists claim that it can suppress cancerous cells and is a powerful immunological stimulant, possibly even a new weapon against the scourge of AIDS.

Nowadays, the plant extract is produced in highly-concentrated pill form in pharmacies and drugstores throughout Europe and North America and its export is increasing. It is also used to treat arthritis, rheumatism, diabetes, benign and malignant tumours.

No other Peruvian medicinal plant since quinine, which first came on the scene as a fever cure in the 17th century, has caused such a stir internationally.

reserve in the wet season. The Culture Zone remained open and could be visited by those who survived the road trip in.

**The reserve is split into 4 zones**: the **Manu National Park** (1,532,000 ha), where only government sponsored biologist and anthropologists may visit with permits from the Ministry of Agriculture in Lima, the **Reserved Zone** of the Manu Biosphere reserve (257,000 ha), which is set aside for applied scientific research and ecotourism, the **Multiple Use Zone** which contains aculturated native groups and colonists, and the **Nahua-Kugapakori Reserved Zone** (92,000 ha), set aside for these two Nomadic Native groups, where the locals still employ their traditional way of life.

The multiple zone is accessible to anyone and several lodges exist in the area (see **Accommodation** below). The reserved zone of the Manu Biosphere Reserve is accessable by permit only. Entry is strictly controlled and visitors must visit the area under the auspices of an authorized operator with an authorized guide. Permits are limited and reservations should be made well in advance. In the reserved zone of the Manu Biosphere Reserve the only accommodation is in the comfortable Manu Lodge or in Safari-style camps.

## Park information

**In Lima**: **Asociación Peruana para la Conservación de la Naturaleza** (Apeco), Parque José Acosta 187, p 2, Magdalena del Mar, T 616316. **Fundación Peruana para la Conservación de la Naturaleza** (FPCN), Av de los Rosales 255, San Isidro, T 426706/426616. **Asociación de Ecología y Conservación** (Ecco), Dos de Mayo 527, Miraflores, T 472369.

**In Cusco**: **Asociación para la Conservación de la Selva Sur** (ACSS), is a local NGO that can help with information, at Of 305, Centro Comercial Ruiseñores, Plaza de Armas, T 226392, open 1000-1300, 1500-1900. Further information can be obtained from the Manu National Park Office, Of 1, Av El Sol, Edif San Jorge, Pasaje Grace, Cusco, T 224683, F 221020. Their office is next door to *Manu Nature Tours*, open 0800-1400. They issue a permit for the Reserve Zone which costs US$10. The two tour companies given below will answer any question on the park. *Manu Nature Tours* has a good video on the area.

### ● Tours

The following companies organize trips into the Culture and Reserve Zones. Contact them for more details. ***Manu Nature Tours EIRL***, Av Pardo 1046, Cusco, T 252721, F 234793, e-mail: postmaster@mnt.com.pe, owned by Boris Gómez, they run lodge-based trips and are owners of Manu Lodge, and part owners of Manu Cloudforest Lodge, highly rec; or Centro Plaza Conquistadores, 396-S-101, San Isidro, Lima, T/F 428990. They own the only lodge in the Reserve Zone (*Manu Lodge*) open all year, situated on an ox-bow lake, providing access to the forest, US$75 a night inc meals. Guides are available. Activities include river-rafting and canopy-climbing. It is highly rec for experiencing the jungle in comfort. An 8-day trip with flights both ways costs US$1,493, with road/boat transport there, plane back, US$1,695; 4-day trip US$998, plane both ways. At the same address is Eco-tour Manu, a non-profit making organization made up of tour operators which assures quality of service and actively supports conservation projects in the area. When you travel with an Eco-tour member you are assuring you support tropical rainforest conservation projects. Eco-tour Manu comprises Expediciones Manu, Manu Nature Tours, Amazonia Lodge, Pantiacolla Lodge and Blanquillo Lodge; contact Boris Gómez Luna.

***Expediciones Manu***, Av Sol 582, Cusco, T 226671, F 236706, owned by ornthologist, Barry Walker. They operate 4-9 day trips in Safari camps and lodges and specialize in birdwatching trips. They are part owners of the Parrot Inn, which is highly rec.

Also rec are ***Pantiacolla Tours***, Calle Plateros 360, Cusco, T 238323, F 233727, owners of Pantiacolla Lodge, they also run camping trips in the Manu area.

Beware of pirate operators on the streets of Cusco who offer trips to the Reserved Zone of Manu and end up halfway through the trip changing the route "due to emergencies", which, in reality means they have no permits to operate in the area.

### ● Accommodation

**In the Cultural Zone**, where no permit is needed, are four lodges. ***Amazonia Lodge***, on the Río Alto Madre de Dios just across the river from the small town of Atalaya, on the road to Shintuya, US$40 a night, is a pleasant family run converted Hacienda, a great place to relax. In Cusco T/F 231370, Sr Santiago. ***Erika Lodge***, on the Río Alto Madre de Dios, 25 mins from Atalaya, is a biological station used by the FPCN, it is not prepared for tourism.

***Pantiacolla Lodge***, located in Itahuania, 30 mins downriver from the road's end at Shintuya. owned by Marianne (Dutch) and Gustavo Moscoso. Book through Pantiacolla Tours (see above). US$25pp/night (US$40 pp inc meals). They organize trips into the Reserve at US$110 pp for 5 or more for boat and boatman and US$55/day for guide, 8-day camping trip into the Reserve, US$450. Also 9-day trips from Cusco, inc transport, guide, food, boat, gear for US$950 (minimum 6, maximum 19 people). Contact them through ***Pantiacolla Tours***, C Plateros, Cusco.

***Blanquillo Lodge***, 1½ hrs down the Río Madre de Dios from Boca Manu, situated on an ox-bow lake nr a *collpa* (macaw lick), US$25 pp/night, owned by Abraham Huamán and Carol Mitchell (American); run by ***Expediciones Manu*** (address above). They run similar 8-day trips from Cusco as *Pantiacolla*; both rec as good value. 30 mins downriver from *Blanquillo Lodge* is the Blanquillo Macaw lick, where a lodge project (Parrot Inn) is underway. The wildlife at Blanquillo is similar to that found in the reserved zone of the Manu Biosphere Reserve, but the bio-diversity is greater due to a greater incidence of forest types. The Macaw Lick is where large numbers of Macaws and Parrots congregate to eat clay, essential to their digestion, surely one of the worlds great wildlife spectacles. Permits are not required to visit this area, just reservations for Parrot Inn which can be made at the Manu Expeditions office.

A rec guide is Percy Núñez, biologist, Umanch'ata 136, Cusco. *Manu Cloud Forest Lodge* is situated at 1,800m above sea level in the cloud forest, only basic camping facilities are available at present but plans to construct bungalows are under way.

**Individual trips** may only enter the Reserve Zone with a recognized guide who is affiliated to a recognized tour company. This makes it difficult to go by yourself. There are only 2 places to camp and these are used constantly by tour groups. Buy all supplies in Cusco: camping gear, fishing tackle, food (for the boatmen and guide as well) and gasoline (it is twice as expensive in Shintuya); take finely woven, long-sleeved and long-legged clothing and effective insect repellent. Note that for individual travellers, only the multiple use zone is an option. Lodge reservations should be made at the relevant offices in Cusco as these lodges are often not set up to receive visitors without prior notice.

## CUSCO-PUERTO MALDONADO VIA MAZUKO

From Cusco take a bus to Urcos; 1 hr, US$2.25. Trucks leave from here for **Mazuko** around 1500-1600, arriving around 2400 the next day; 33 hrs, US$6.65. Catch a truck early in the morning from here for Puerto Maldonado, US$4.50, 13-14 hrs. It's a painfully slow journey on an appalling road; trucks frequently get stuck or break down. **Quincemil**, 240 km from Urcos on the road to Mazuko, is a centre for alluvial gold-mining with many banks. Accommodation is available in **F** *Hotel Toni*, friendly, clean, cold shower, good meals. Ask the food-carriers to take you to visit the miners washing for gold in the nearby rivers. Quincemil marks the half-way point and the start of the all-weather road. Gasoline is scarce in Quincemil because most road vehicles continue on 70 km to Mazuko, which is another mining centre, where they fill up with the cheaper gasoline of the jungle region.

The journey takes up to 50-55 hrs in total. The road is 99% unpaved and the journey is very rough, but the changing scenery is magnificent and worth the hardship and discomfort. The road is impassable in the rainy season. The trucks only stop 4 times each day, for meals and a short sleeping period for the driver. You should take a mosquito net, repellent, sunglasses, sunscreen, a plastic sheet, a blanket, food and water.

## TO PUERTO MALDONADO VIA PILCOPATA AND SHINTUYA

The arduous 255 km trip over the Andes from Cusco to Pilcopata takes about 12-15 hrs by local truck (20-40 hrs in the wet season). It is long and uncomfortable, but, throughout, the scenery is magnificent. From Cusco you climb up to the pass before Paucartambo (very cold at night), before dropping down to this mountain village at the border between the departments of Cusco and Madre de Dios. The road then ascends to the second pass (also cold at night), after which it goes down to the cloud forest and then the rainforest, reaching **Pilcopata** at 650m. At Pilcopata you can stay at a little hostal (the only one) of Sra Robella for US$2.50 pp, very basic.

Trucks leave from Cusco from behind the Coliseo Cerrado at about 1000, on Mon, Wed and Fri; US$10. Be there by 0800 and make sure your driver is not inebriated! They return the following day, but there is no service on Sun. Recommended are: Príncipe, Armando Cana, Carrasco and Tigre. There is also a local bus owned by Angel Valencia; T 224458 for reservation. Private transport can be arranged through Explorers Transportes, T 237518, or ask at the tour companies. Only basic supplies are available after leaving Cusco, so take all your camping and food essentials, including insect repellent. Transport can be disrupted in the wet season because the road is in poor condition (tour companies have latest details). You may be able to rent a seat on a more comfortable tour bus by asking at the agencies.

**Pilcopata to Shintuya** After Pilcopata, the route is hair-raising and breath-taking, passing through **Atalaya**, the first village on the Alto Madre de Dios river, which consists of a few houses. Meals are available at the family of Rosa and Juan (very friendly people), where you can camp. To get river transport from here, however, you have to be very lucky. The route continues to Salvador, where the Park Office and the Park Entrance are situated. If you did not get a permit in Cusco, this is your last chance. There are basic hostals and restaurants. From Pilcopata, truck traffic is infrequent to Atalaya (1 hr, US$5) and Shintuya (4-6 hrs, US$8). Trucks leave in the morning between 0600 and 0900. Make sure you go with a recommended truck driver. Basic restaurants can be found in Pilcopata and Atalaya.

The end of the road is **Shintuya**, at 485m, the starting point for river transport. The inhabitants are Masheos Indians. It is a commercial and social centre, as wood from the jungle is transported from here to Cusco. There are a few basic restaurants and you can camp (beware of thieves). The priest will let you stay in the dormitory rooms at the mission. Supplies are expensive. It is hard to find guides or boats in Shintuya; the ones that are willing to take you have no permits and little knowledge of the rainforest.

**Shintuya to Puerto Maldonado** Cargo boats leave for the gold mining centre of Boca Colorado on the Río Madre de Dios, via Boca Manu, but only when the boat is fully laden; about 6 to 8 a week, 9 hrs, US$15. Very basic accommodation can be found here, but it is not recommended for lone women travellers. To Boca Manu is 3-4 hrs, US$12. From Colorado you can catch a boat to Laberinto, 6-7 hrs, US$20, from where regular colectivos run to Puerto Maldonado, 1½ hrs.

**NB** It is not possible to arrange trips to the Reserved Zone of the Biosphere Reserve from Shintuya, owing to park regulations. All arrangements must be made in Cusco.

**Boca Manu** is the connecting point between the rivers Alto Madre de Dios, Manu and Madre de Dios. It has a few houses, an air strip and some food supplies. It is also the entance to the Manu Reserve. The Park Office is located in Romero, 1 hr by boat from Boca Manu. You need to show your permit here. There are huts available for accommodation and it is possible to camp. At Boca Manu there is an airstrip and semi-regular flights are available 3 times a week during the dry season (check with the tour operators in Cusco). Aero Sur flies to Boca Manu from Cusco, T (084) 224638.

**To the Reserve Zone** Upstream on the Río Manu you pass the *Manu Lodge* (see Manu Nature Tours), on the Cocha Juárez, 1 hr by boat; visitors are charged an entrance fee of US$5 (taken care of by tour companies). You can continue to Cocha Otorongo, 2½ hrs and Cocha Salvador, 30 mins, the biggest lake with plenty of wildlife. From here it is 2 hrs to Pakitza, the entrance to the Park Zone. This is only for biologists with a special permit.

Between Boca Manu and Colorado is **Blanquillo**, a private reserve (10,000 ha), where jungle trips can be arranged. Bring a good tent with you and all food. Guides are available for US$6 pp; Walter and Rolando are recommended. Wildlife is abundant and costs work out cheaper than Manu National Park. There are good views of macaws and parrots at the macaw lick near *Blanquillo Lodge* (see above). There are occasional boats to Blanquillo from Shintuya, US$10, 6-8 hrs.

## PUERTO MALDONADO

**Puerto Maldonado** (*Pop* 17,000; *Alt* 250m; *Phone code* 084) is the capital of the Department of Madre de Dios. Overlooking the confluence of the rivers Tambopata and Madre de Dios, it is an important starting point for visiting the rainforest, or for departing to Bolivia. Nothing much happens here, it's a hot, humid and sleepy place, disturbed only by the fleeting visit of tourists heading to or from the jungle lodges.

Its isolation makes Puerto Maldonado an expensive town and because of the gold mining and timber industries, the surrounding jungle (including most of the mahogany trees) has been destroyed and cultivated.

### Excursions

The beautiful and tranquil **Lago Sandoval** is a 1-hr boat ride along the Río Madre de Dios, and then a muddy 5-km walk into the jungle (take boots). There is a newly built **G** *Sandoval Lodge*. Boats may be hired at the port for about US$30 a day to go to Lago Sandoval, bargain hard, and don't pay the full cost in advance. (See **Tour companies** below).

Upstream from Lago Sandoval, towards the Amazon Cusco Lodge, is the wreck of the *Fitzcarraldo*. A flood swept the steamer from the Madre de Dios to the next river bed, which is said to have inspired German director, Werner Herzog, to make his famous film of the same name. The steamer was formerly owned by a Spanish doctor who turned it into

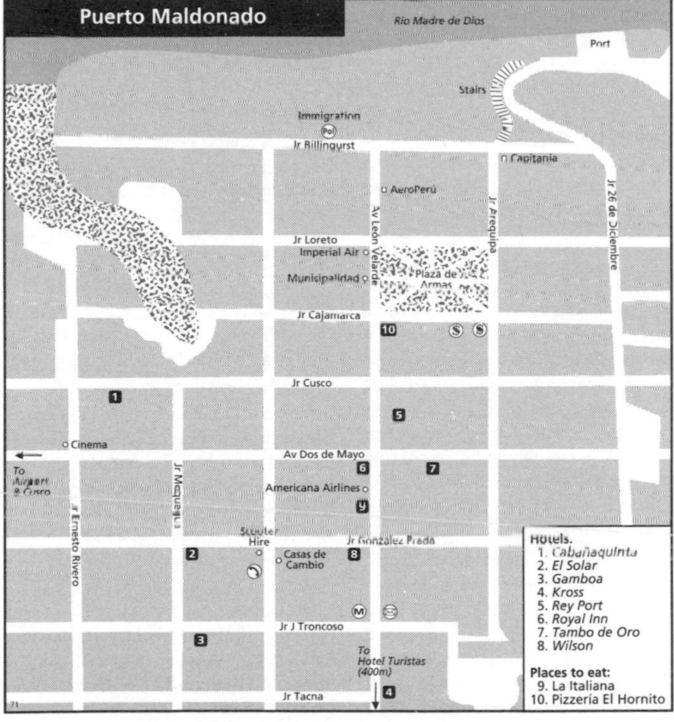

a hospital and gave medical treatment to the indigenous people in return for food.

For those interested in seeing a gold rush, a trip to the town of **Laberinto** is suggested. There is one hotel, several poor restaurants. Kombis and trucks leave from Puerto Maldonado, 1½ hrs, US$2.50, and returns in the afternoon daily. Boats leave from here to Manu.

## Local information

### ● Accommodation

**C** *Turistas*, Av León Velarde s/n, T 571029, T/F 571323, nice view over Río Tambopata, a/c, restaurant, TV, phone, good.

**D** *Cabañaquinta*, Cusco 535, T 571863, F 571890, with bath, fan, good restaurant, friendly, lovely garden, very comfortable, airport transfer, rec.

**E** *Hostal El Astro*, Velarde 617, T 572128, with bath, basic, cheap; **E** *Hostal El Solar*, González Prada 445, T 571571, basic but clean, fan; **E** *Hostal Gamboa*, Jaime Troncoso 293, T 571388, with bath, a bit run down, large rooms, fan; **E** pp *Hostal Iñapari*, 4 km from centre, 5 mins from the airport, run by a Spanish couple Isabel and Javier, price includes breakfast and dinner, excellent food, very relaxing, friendly, clean, rec; **E** *Hostal Kross*, Velarde 721, with bath, basic, fairly clean, cheap, fans but no nets; **E** *Rey Port*, Av León Velarde 457, T 571177, with bath, clean, fan, good value, friendly, insecure; **E** *Wilson*, Jr González Prada 355, T 571086, with bath, clean, basic, good value, popular, the best of the lower range hotels, rec.

**F** *Tambo de Oro*, Av Dos de Mayo 277, T 572057, cheap, basic, clean, water 24 hrs.

The following hotels are all **G** pp, popular with gold miners, and range from very, very basic down to barely inhabitable: *Hostal Central*, Velarde 657; *Hostal Moderno*, Billinghurst 359; *Chávez*, L Velarde 440; *Oriental*, Jr Loreto. As there are many miners in Maldonado, rooms can be scarce in these cheaper hotels.

### ● Places to eat

There are several good restaurants in town. *La Cusqueñita 2*, Av Ernesto Rivero 607, good, cheap; *Kalifa*, Piura, some regional specialities, closed in evening, rec; *El Hornito*, on Plaza, good pizzas; *Chifa Wa Seng*, Dos de Mayo 353. Cheap set lunch at *Club Madre de Dios*, Carrión esq Plaza.

### ● Airline offices

**Americana**, Velarde 506, T 572119; **Imperial Air**, on Plaza, T 571765; **Aero Pua**, González Prada 360, T 571656.

### ● Banks & money changers

**Banco de Crédito**, cash advances with Visa, no commission on TCs. **Banco de la Nación**, cash on Mastercard, quite good rates for TCs. The best rates for cash are at the *casas de cambio* on Puno 6th block, eg *Cárdenas Hnos*, Puno 605.

### ● Embassies & consulates

**Bolivian Consulate**: latest reports are that it has closed (mid 1996).

**Peruvian immigration**: is on Billinghurst, get your exit stamp here.

### ● Post & telecommunications

**Serpost**: at Velarde 6th block.

**Telefónica**: on Puno.

### ● Tour companies & travel agents

*Turismo de los Angeles*, Jr Puno 657, T 571070, run trips to Lago Sandoval (US$25pp/day) and Lago Valencia. *Luly Tours*, Av Velarde 620, T 572133, friendly, informative. Reputable guides are: Hernán Llave Cortez, who can be contacted through *Hotel Wilson*; Willy Wither, Av Leon Velarde 391, T/F 571183; Edwin Latorre, T 571340, or through *Hotel Cabañaquinta*. Insist on a detailed explanation of the tour offered, if necessary sign a contract and make sure that, once you have paid, the programme is not scaled down.

### ● Transport

**Motorcycle hire**: scooters and mopeds can de hired from *Ocoñita*, on the corner of Puno and G Prado for US$1.35. This is the standard rate in town.

**Air** To **Lima**, daily with Americana, US$93; Imperial Air, US$87. To **Cusco**, daily with Americana, US$44; and Imperial Air US$66. Grupo Ocho (military flight) have flights to Iberia and then Iñapari once a week. Their office is at the airport. To **Rio Branco** (Brazil), with Aero Pua, once a week, US$100. A mototaxi from town to the airport is US$1.35.

**Road** To **Cusco**, 525 km, 50-55 hrs (longer in the rainy season), US$13; only trucks do this route, several a day. It is a hard but spectacular route, from low jungle up to the highest pass at Hualla-Hualla (4,820m). The road passes through Quincemil (see page 411), 241 km, 15-20 hrs; Marcapata, where there are hot thermal springs, a further 69 km, 5 hrs; Ocongate, a further 92 km, 7 hrs (see page 327) and Urcos (see page 327), a further 82 km, 6 hrs. This road is impossible in the wet season. Make sure you have warm clothing for travelling through the Sierra.

**River** To **Boca Manu and Shintuya**, via Colorado. You can get a daily cargo boat from Puerto Maldonado to Colorado, 8 hrs, US$12, and from there to Boca Manu and Shintuya, 9-10 hrs, US$15. From Shintuya trucks go to Pilcopata and Cusco (see above under **Manu Biosphere Reserve**). To **Puerto Heath** (Bolivian border), it can take several days to find a boat going all the way to the Bolivian border. Motorized dugout canoes go to Puerto Pardo on Peruvian side, 5 hrs, US$4.50 pp (no hotels or shops); wait here for a canoe to Puerto Heath. It is fairly hard to get a boat from the border to Riberalta (a wait of up to 3 days is not uncommon), 3 days, US$15-20; alternatively, travel to the naval base at América, then fly.

## JUNGLE TOURS FROM PUERTO MALDONADO

Trips can be made to **Lago Valencia**, 60 km away near the Bolivian border, 4 hrs there, 8 hrs back. It is an ox-bow lake with lots of wildlife. Many excellent beaches and islands are located within an hour's boat ride. The Indians living nearer Puerto Maldonado, like those near Iquitos and Manaus, are strictly tourist Indians. Mosquitoes are voracious. If camping, take food and water.

### Tambopata-Candamo Wildlife Reserve

It is quite easy to arrange a boat and guide from Puerto Maldonado (see **Tour companies** below) to this Reserve, located between the rivers Madre de Dios, Tambopata and Heath. The area was declared a reserve in Jan 1990 by the Peruvian government. The Tambopata reserve makes up part of the area and has been under protection since 1977, assigned to Peruvian Safaris. Some superb ox-bow lakes can be visited and the birdwatching is wonderful.

Some of the lodges along the Tambopata river offer guiding and research placements to biology and environmental science graduates. For more details send an SAE to TReeS: UK – J Forrest, 64 Belsize Park, London, NW3 4EH. USA – W Widdowson, 5455 Agostino Court, Concord, CA 94521.

### Santuario Pampas del Heath

For a trip up the Río Heath, you need all camping gear, food, etc. Also, a guide is essential. Boats leave sporadically and the cost depends on the number of passengers. Organized tours are available in Puerto Maldonado, see below. From Puerto Maldonado the trip goes to Puerto Pardo, on the Peruvian-Bolivian border, up the Río Heath for about 2 hrs, before reaching the **Santuario Pampas del Heath**. Jungle hikes can be made from there. If you want a longer experience of the jungle, ask Fernando Rubio, C Daniel A Carrión 310, Puerto Maldonado, T/F (0051 84) 571638, a month in advance, to use you as a volunteer worker in the Santuario Pampas del Heath, usually Jan-Mar or Aug-Oct; also tours available, US$35 pp/day.

**● Jungle Lodges**

*Cusco Amazonico Lodge* (*Albergue Cusco Amazónico*), 45 mins by boat down the Río Madre de Dios, jungle tours and accommodation, US$80 pp/day (inc meals and guides), a naturalists programme is also provided, negotiable out of season, about 30 bungalows with private bathrooms, friendly staff but mixed reports; avoid in Feb when everyone goes on holiday inc the mechanic. Book at Andalucía 174, Lima 18, T 462775, F 455598, or Procuradores 48, Cusco, T 232161/223769.

*Explorers Inn*, book through Peruvian Safaris, Garcilaso de la Vega 1334, Casilla 10088, T 313047 Lima, or Plateros 365, T 235342 Cusco. The lodge is located in the Tambopata-Candamo wildlife reserve, in the part where most research work has been done, 58 km from Puerto Maldonado. It's a 3-hr ride on the Río Tambopata (2 hrs return, in the early morning, so take warm clothes and rain gear), one of the best places in Peru for seeing jungle birds (547 species have been recorded here), butterflies (1,100-plus

## The future for Tambopata

Research along the Tambopata (Bahauja – in the local Ese'eja language) river over the last 20 years has shown the enormous biodiversity of this area. To prove the point, the local town council in Puerto Maldonado has recently adopted the slogan of 'bio-diversity capital of the world'. All this is a far cry from the wild, inhospitable environment described by Colonel Faucett 90 years ago when he travelled down the river while determining the Peru/Bolivia border.

Much of the scientific investigation has been undertaken in the forest surrounding the Explorer's Inn tourist lodge. In 1977 the Tambopata Reserved zone (TRZ), 5,500 ha adjoining the lodge, was designated to offer some protection to world record numbers of species – 592 birds; 1,230 butterflies; 600 leaf beetles; and many others. The variety of tree species per hectare is also one of the highest recorded on Earth and many UN Red Data species have been sighted there, including the giant river otter, jaguar, giant anteater and harpy eagle.

Reserved Zone status in Peruvian law signifies the temporary protection of an area while further studies are undertaken to decide the long-term designation of the area. In the case of the TRZ, it was not large enough to offer long-term protection to many of the mammal species found there which roam over far larger territories.

In 1990 the Tambopata-Candamo Reserved Zone (TCRZ), at 1,479 million ha a much more viable potential conservation unit, was declared. It covers the whole of the Tambopata drainage basin and was designated after lobbying by the UK-based Tambopata Reserve Society (TReeS) and the US based Asociación de la Selva Sur (ACSS). The area now encompasses tropical savanna and cloudforest ecosystems as well as the luxuriant sub-tropical moist forest, swamp forest and bamboo thickets of the lower Tambopata.

Reserved Zones, along with all other protected areas in Peru, are managed by the Instituto Nacional de Recursos Nacionales (INRENA), a sub-division of the Ministry of Agriculture. INRENA supports a local office concerned with the TCRZ in Puerto Maldonado, staffed by one junior official with very limited resources. As a result it was the international conservation organisations which submitted proposals for the zonification and conservation management of the TRZ. These included the establishment of the Bahuaja-Sonene National Park, in the upper part of the region and buffer zones in the lower inhabited area. In the latter a variety of sustainable development projects would be created to try to manage effectively the existing forest.

The proposals were submitted in 1993 but were placed on hold once it became apparent that large oil and gas reserves might lie below the upper Tambopata region. The Ministry of Energy has traditionally carried more influence in central government than the Ministry of Agriculture within which INRENA is an underfunded division. In 1996 Mobil Oil signed a contract to undertake 7 years of exploration in the area as well as elsewhere across the department of Madre de Dios.

Many local organisations immediately expressed serious concerns given the social and environmental devastation that has occurred in certain areas of the northern Peruvian Amazon and, especially, in the Ecuadorean Oriente. The Conservation Committee of Madre de Dios was formed linking the above-mentioned groups plus the Federation for Native Communities (FENAMAD) and the Federation of Local Farmers (FADEMAD) and other local conservation and development non-governmental organisations (NGO's). With funding principally channelled via TReeS,

FENAMAD and FADEMAD embarked on a series of workshops in May/June 1996 in their respective communities to establish a community response to these developments. A Forum bringing together representatives from all communities who had participated in the workshops was due to be held in Madre de Dios in Aug 1996, to formulate a collective response from local people to the Peruvian government and Mobil.

Against this background, it came as a surprise when the Peruvian government suddenly designated part of the proposed Bahuaja-Sonene National Park in July 1996. The National Park covers about 325,000 ha in the mid-Tambopata region and includes the previously protected Rio Heath National Santuary (102,000 ha), adjoining the Bolivian border. The Upper Tambopata region, arguably the most biodiverse part of the Tambopata drainage basin and containing the largest 'collpa' (macaw salt-lick) in the world, was excluded for the present. This area lies within the Mobil oil and gas exploration lot but the declaration provides for the area to be included within the National Park at a later date depending on the outcome of Mobil's investigations. It must be hoped that this occurs sooner rather than later as it is arguable whether the territory of the new National Park, though a step in the right direction, constitutes a viable conservation unit. The area outside the new National Park remains a Reserved Zone.

Unfortunately, the lack of a management plan for the whole TCRZ leaves a vacuum in the remaining Reserved Zone areas with timber extraction along the Puerto Maldonado/Cusco road and gold-mining on the western side of the TCRZ continuing unchecked. Under Reserved Zone status no new concessions are granted for mineral and timber extraction and various other activities, but this does not prevent such activities from taking place. INRENA is due to set up a basic guard post on the Tambopata river at the entrance to the new National Park. Such posts already exist along the river Heath. The non-native 'guards', however, are unlikely to receive more than basic funding and training, and will have few powers other than to monitor activities along the river.

It now seems likely that one of the richest areas on Earth, of the most biodiverse ecosystem, will be held in limbo for several years until the oil companies have completed their studies. The Andes mountains no longer limit 'development' as they once did and, after many decades of neglect, central government is taking a closer interest in the region. The threat of long-term degradation now hangs over much of the area until it is known whether exploitable oil and gas deposits are located there.

(J Forrest, Trees, London).

species), dragonflies (over 150 species) as well as tree species and mammals (inc a giant otter), but you probably need more than a 2-day tour to benefit fully from the location. The guides are biologists and naturalists from around the world who study in the reserve in return for acting as guides. They provide interesting wild-life-treks, inc to the Collpa macaw lick. US$160 for 3 days, 2 nights, at the lodge; 5 days/4 nights at the Collpa lick US$450 pp, discounts are available in the low season Jan-Mar, and for larger groups, mixed reports on the food.

***Tambo Lodge***, bungalows 15 km out on the opp bank of the Río Madre de Dios, 2, 3 and 4-day Jungle programmes available, from US$40 pp In low season, perhaps too close to Puerto Maldonado, good food, basic, guide Víctor is knowledgeable and speaks good English, book through Cusco-Maldonado Tour, Plateros 351 (T 222332), Cusco. ***Tambopata Jungle Lodge***, on the Río Tambopata, make reservations at Peruvian Andean Treks, Av Pardo 705, Cusco, T 225701, F 238911; from US$65 pp/night (children half price), all inclu-

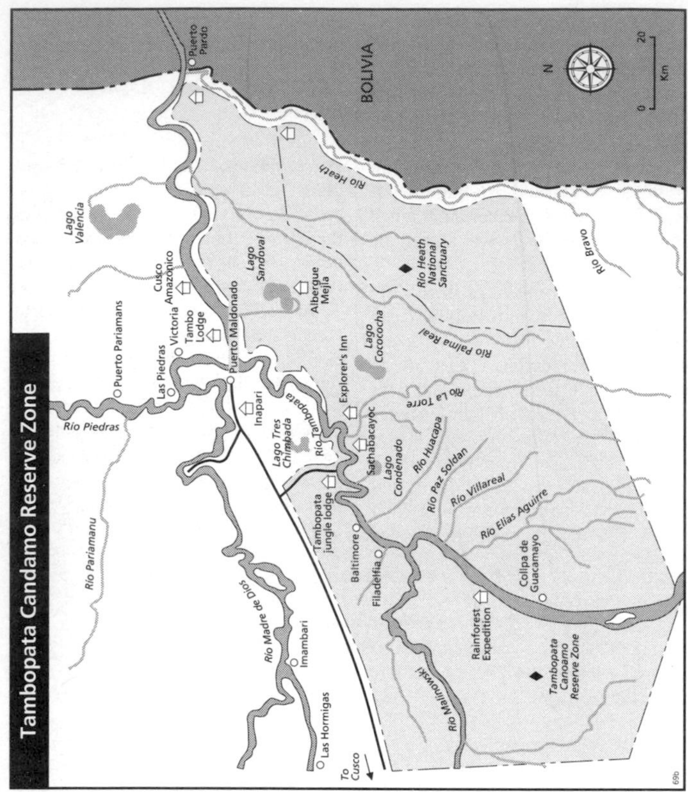


sive, naturalists programme provided, rec; US$160 for 3 nights 4 days.

## TO IBERIA AND IÑAPARI

A very worthwhile 1 or 2-day excursion by motorcycle (see hire rates above) is by boat across the Río Madre de Dios and follow the road towards **Iberia** and **Iñapari** on the border with Brazil. This can only be done in the dry season. Along the road are picturesque *caserios* (settlements) that serve as collecting and processing centres for the Brazil nut. Approximately 70% of the inhabitants in the Madre de Dios are involved in the collection of this prized nut. Many trucks, of varying vintage, take this road and will offer lifts for US$10-20.

At **Planchón**, 40 km up the road, there is a hotel, **G**, which is clean, but has no mosquito nets, and 2 bar/restaurants. **Alegría** at Km 60 has a hotel/restaurant and Mavilla, at Km 80, a bar.

The hotel at **Alerta**, Km 115, is a room with 4 beds, **G**. The river is safe to swim in. If there is a boat here, it is the quickest route to Brasiléia (Brazil), apart from the plane, US$10-20 pp in cargo canoe, or *peque-peque*, to Porvenir and then by road to Cobija (Bolivia), across the border from Brasiléia.

At **San Lorenzo**, Km 145, is the *Bolpebra* bar, which serves cheap food and drink and is generally merry.

**Iberia**, Km 168, has two hotels, the best is **F** *Hostal Aquino*, basic, cold shower, rooms serviced daily.

**Iñapari**, at the end of the road, Km 235, has one hotel and a restaurant, but **Assis Brasil** across the border is much more attractive. Just wade across the river to get there.

There is a road from Assis Brasil into Brazil and connections to Bolivia. It can be cold travelling this road, so take a blanket or sleeping bag. There are no exchange facilities en route and poor exchange rates for Brazilian currency at Iñapari. From time to time it is possible to get a boat from Puerto Maldonado all the way to Iñapari. Note that taking shorter trips may mean getting stuck for days, or even weeks. Try Ricardo, an ex-student from Lima, but avoid a character known as El Chino.

## CROSSING TO BOLIVIA AND BRAZIL

Ensure that you get an exit stamp in Puerto Maldonado at the Peruvian immigration office or at the PNP. You cannot get an exit stamp in Iberia or Iñapari at the border. Also check that you do not need a consular visa for Brazil or Bolivia; they are not issued at the border.

**To Bolivia**: take the boat to Puerto Heath (see above) and get a tourist visa at the Bolivian immigration office (though it was closed at the time of writing).

**To Brazil**: by truck to Iñapari or flight to Iberia and truck from there. Get a tourist visa at the Brazilian immigration in Iñapari.

# Information for travellers



## BEFORE TRAVELLING

### ENTRY REQUIREMENTS

● **Documents**

**Tourist cards** No visa is necessary for citizens of Western European and Scandinavian countries, Canada, the USA, Japan, all Latin American and Caribbean countries (except Cuba), South Africa and South Korea. Australians and New Zealanders must have visas. A Tourist Card (*Cédula C*, obligatory) is obtained free from the immigration authorities on arrival in Peru for visits up to 90 days, 60 days in the case of Bolivia, Chile, Colombia, Dominican Republic (insist on getting the full 90 days, at some borders cards valid for 60, or even only 30 days have been given). It is in duplicate, the original given up on arrival and the copy on departure, and may be renewed (see below). A new tourist card must be obtained for each re entry or when an extension is given. If your tourist card is stolen or lost, apply for a new one at Migraciones, Paseo de la República 585, Lima, 0900-1300; very helpful. If you try to leave Peru without your tourist card, the fine is US$40.

**Tourist visas**, for citizens of countries not listed above, cost £8.40 or equivalent, for which you require a valid passport, a departure ticket from Peru, two colour passport photos, one application form and proof of economic solvency. All foreigners should be able to produce on demand some recognizable means of identification, preferably a passport. You must present your passport when reserving tickets for internal, as well as, international travel. An alternative is to photocopy the important pages of your passport – including the immigration stamp, and legalize it by a 'Notario público' (US$1.50). This way you can avoid showing your passport. We have received no reports of travellers being asked for an onward ticket at Tacna, Aguas Verdes, Yunguyo or Desaguadero. If you do not have one on arrival at the border, you may be forced to pay US$15 minimum for an out-going bus ticket. The best bet is to buy a bus ticket, Tacna-Arica if travelling to Chile, and Puno-La Paz if going to Bolivia, at the Ecuadorean border, eg Machala. Alternatively, a Tumbes-Guayaquil ticket will do. Travellers arriving by air report no onward flight checks at Lima airport.

Remember that it is your responsibility to ensure that your passport is stamped in and out when you cross frontiers. The absence of entry and exit stamps can cause serious difficulties: seek out the proper migration offices if the stamping process is not carried out as you cross. Also, do not lose your entry card; replacing one causes a lot of trouble, and possibly expense.

You should always carry your passport in a safe place about your person, or if not going far, leave it in the hotel safe. If staying in Peru for several weeks, it is worth while registering at your Embassy or Consulate. Then, if your passport is stolen, the process of replacing it is simplified and speeded up.

**Renewals and extensions** Tourist visas and entry permits may be renewed for 60 days at Migraciones in Lima, address above (also in major towns like Cusco, Iquitos or Arequipa). You must present your passport, a valid return ticket to a destination outside Peru, a *solicitud* (written request for an extension) and payment of US$40 or the equivalent in soles. If you wish to extend your entry permit after 90 days have already elapsed since your entry into Peru this is possible at the discretion of the authorities, but on payment of a fine of US$20. The maximum stay in such a case would be 150 days from the first entry. If you are in the Puno area when your visa expires, it is sometimes quicker and easier to cross the border to Bolivia for a day and return with a new visa, often for 90 days, which you would not get in Lima or Cusco.

**Business visas** If a visitor is going to receive money from Peruvian sources, he/she must have a business visa: requirements are a valid passport, two colour passport photos, return ticket and a letter from an employer or Chamber of Commerce stating the nature of business, length of stay and guarantee that any Peruvian taxes will be paid. The visa costs £18.90 (or equivalent). On arrival business visitors must register with the Dirección General de Contribuciones for tax purposes.

**Student visas** To obtain a 1 year student visa one must have: proof of adequate funds, affiliation to a Peruvian body, a letter of recommendation from your own and a Peruvian Consul, a letter of moral and economic guarantee from a Peruvian citizen and 4 photographs (frontal and profile). One must also have a health check certificate which takes 4 weeks to get and costs US$10. Also, to obtain a student visa, if applying within Peru, you have to leave the country and collect it in La Paz, Arica or Guayaquil from Peruvian immigration (it costs US$20).

If you are in full-time education you will be entitled to an International Student Identity Card, which is distributed by student travel offices and travel agencies in 77 countries. The ISIC gives you special prices on all forms of transport (air, sea, rail etc), and access to a variety of other concessions and services. If you need to find the location of your nearest ISIC office contact: The ISIC Association, Box 9048, 1000 Copenhagen, Denmark T (+45) 33 93 93 03.

Students can obtain very few reductions in Peru with an international student's card, except in and around Cusco. To be any use in Peru, it must bear the owner's photograph. An ISIC card can be obtained in Lima from San Martín 240, Barranco, T 774105, for US$20.

### ● Tourist information

The Fondo de Promoción Turística (Foptur) closed its national and international offices in 1992. Tourism was placed under the Ministerio de Industria, Comercio, Turismo e Integración, which has an office in each major town. Staff are helpful with advice. Some former Foptur offices in large cities have been taken over by former employees within a private organization called Infotur.

Outside Peru, tourist information may be obtained from Peruvian Embassies and Consulates.

## MONEY

### ● Currency

The new sol (s/) is divided into 100 céntimos. In 1991 the new sol replaced the inti at the rate of S/1 = 1 million intis. Notes in circulation are: S/100, S/50, S/20 and S/10. Coins: S/5, S/2, S/1, S/0.50, S/0.20 and S/0.10. The last remaining inti note in circulation, 5,000,000, is being replaced by the 5 sol coin. Some prices are quoted in dollars in more expensive establishments, to avoid changes in the value of the sol. You can pay in soles, however. Try to break down large notes whenever you can. In Oct 1996 the exchange rate was S/2.52 = US$1.

**Warning** A large number of forged notes (especially US$20 and larger bills) are in circulation; check the numbers if possible, and hold notes up to the light to inspect the line which can be seen on the lefthand side of the bill spelling out the bill's amount. There should also be tiny pieces of thread in the paper (not glued on). Always check every bill when changing money. There is a shortage of change in museums, post offices, railway stations and even shops, while taxi drivers are notorious in this regard – one is simply told "no change". Do not accept this excuse.

## ● Credit cards

Visa (most common), Diners Club, and Mastercard (Access/Eurocard) are accepted. An 8% commission is charged on their use. Visa is accepted at Banco de Crédito, at better rates than for TCs and cash can be withdrawn – local currency only – at no commission, in most cities. Mastercard is not as widely accepted as shop signs indicate. Cash against Mastercard can be obtained, with commission, at Banco del Sur and Banco Wiese. ATMs of the Mastercard/Cirrus network can be found at all branches of Banco Regional del Norte. Credit cards cannot be used in smaller towns, only in the main cities. Credit card loss can be reported in Lima, T 444-1891/1896; card number required.

## ● Exchange

There are no restrictions on foreign exchange. Banks are the best place to change TCs into new soles; most charge no commission. They will also change cheques into dollars cash at 2-3% commission. The services of the Banco de Crédito have been repeatedly rec. *Casas de cambio* are good for changing dollars cash into soles. There is no difference in the exchange rate given by banks and *casas de cambio*. Always count your money in the presence of the cashier. It is possible to have US$ or DM sent from your home country. Take the cheque to the banks and ask for a *liquidación por canje de moneda extranjera*. You will be charged 1% commission in US$ or soles. US dollars are the most useful currency (take some small bills), but Deutsche marks can be negotiated in all large towns; other currencies carry high commission fees. For changing into or out of small amounts of dollars cash, the street changers give the best rates avoiding paperwork and queuing, but they also employ many ruses to give you a bad deal (check your soles before handing over your dollars, check their calculators, etc, and don't change money in crowded areas). If using their services think about taking a taxi after changing, to avoid being followed. Street changers usually congregate near an office where the exchange 'wholesaler' operates; he will probably be offering better rates than on the street.

Soles can be exchanged into dollars at the banks at Lima airport, and one can change soles for dollars at any border. Dollars can also be bought at the various frontiers.

**NB** No one, not even banks, will accept dollar bills that look 'old', or are in any way damaged or torn.

American Express state that they will sell TCs and give out emergency money, but only in Lima. Travel agents are allowed to accept foreign currencies in payment for their services, and to exchange small amounts. Try to avoid changing TCs outside the main cities: commission is high and it is often a difficult process. Travellers have reported great difficulty in cashing TCs in the jungle area, even Iquitos, and other remote areas. Always sign TCs in blue or black ink or ballpen. Thomas Cook/Mastercard refund assistance point: Viajes Laser, C Espinar, 331, Lima, T 449-0134/137. For Western Union, T Lima 440-7934.

## ● Cost of living

Living costs in the provinces are from 20 to 50% below those of Lima. Since Aug 1990, when prices were increased steeply by the government, Peru has become expensive for the tourist, especially for those on a tight budget. For low and middle-income Peruvians, prices of many items are beyond their reach. In 1996 the South American Explorers Club estimated a budget of US$25-30 pp a day for living comfortably, inc transport, or US$12-15 a day for low budget travel. Hotel prices range from US$6 pp to US$50. For meal prices, see Food below.

## ● General tips

Low-value US dollar bills should be carried for changing into local currency if arriving in a country when banks or *casas de cambio* are closed. They are also useful for shopping. If you are travelling on the cheap it is essential to keep in funds; watch weekends and public holidays carefully and never run out of local currency. Take plenty of local currency, in small denominations, when making trips into the interior.

It is a good idea to take two kinds of TCs: if large numbers of one kind have recently been forged or stolen, making people suspicious, it is unlikely to have happened simultaneously with the other kind.

There are two international **ATM** (automatic telling machine) acceptance systems, Plus and Cirrus. Many issuers of debit and credit cards are linked to one, or both (eg Visa is Plus, Mastercard is Cirrus). Look for the relevant symbol on an ATM and draw cash using your PIN. Frequently, the rates of exchange on ATM withdrawals are the best available. Find out before you leave what ATM coverage there is in the countries you will visit and what international 'functionality' your card has. Check if your bank or credit card company imposes handling charges. Obviously you must ensure that the account to which your debit card refers contains sufficient funds. With a credit card, obtain a credit limit sufficient for your needs, or pay money in to put the account in credit. If travelling for a long time, consider a direct debit to clear your account regularly. Do not rely on one card, in case of loss. If you do lose a card, immediately contact the 24-hr helpline of the issuer in your home country (keep this number in a safe place).

Money can be transferred between banks. A recommended method is, before leaving, to find out which local bank is correspondent to your bank at home, then when you need funds, telex your own bank and ask them to telex the money to the local bank (confirming by fax). Give exact information to your bank of the routing number of the receiving bank. Cash in dollars, local currency depending on the country can be received within 48 banking hours.

## GETTING THERE

### BY AIR

#### ● From Europe

Direct flights Amsterdam (KLM), Frankfurt (Lufthansa), Paris (AOM), Rome (Alitalia) and Madrid (Iberia). Cheap flights from London: one way is to go via Madrid with Iberia, or standby to Miami, then fly the airlines shown below. Aeroflot fly to Peru from Moscow via Shannon and Havana; the flight can be joined either in Moscow, or in Shannon, but it is *vital* to check that these services are in operation when you want to travel. To avoid paying Peru's 18% tax on international air tickets, take your used outward ticket with you when buying return passage.

#### ● From Latin America

Regular flights to all South American countries and most Central American; in most cases, daily. Lloyd Aéreo Boliviano (LAB) is usually the cheapest airline for flights out of Lima but tickets bought in Peru are more expensive.

#### ● From USA and Canada

Miami is the main gateway to Peru with flights every day with American, United, also AeroPerú, daily, and Faucett, 5 a week (Faucett also flies Miami-Iquitos-Lima once a week). Other direct flights from New York (Lan Chile; American and United via Miami, Lacsa with change in San José; Avianca in Bogotá) and Los Angeles (Lacsa, AeroPerú, Aerolíneas Argentinas, Varig, Lan Chile). Regular connections can be made from many other North American cities. AeroPerú and Faucett offer discounts on internal flights when you buy a Miami-Lima return ticket, eg US$250 for unlimited flights (check in advance for restrictions).

**Air passes** AeroPerú operates Sudameripass, a 60-day return ticket which is one of the cheapest ways of flying around the continent. If starting a journey in Miami, Mexico City or Cancún, it costs US$1,099 for up to 6 coupons on AeroPerú's network; if starting in Buenos Aires or Los Angeles it costs US$1,299. Extra coupons can be bought for US$100 each. There are seasonal permutations. Check with JLA for up-to-date details. Iberia and its partners, Viasa and Aerolíneas Argentinas, offer Latin American Circular Fares: available from the UK only, the fares are for circular routes (no back-tracking) in North, Central and South America. There are two zones, mid-Atlantic and South Atlantic, and a flat fare applies to each: mid-Atlantic £847 high season, £680 low; South Atlantic £968 high, £793 low. Two free stopovers are allowed, plus Caracas on mid-Atlantic routes, or Buenos Aires on South Atlantic routes. Additional stops are £35 each. Fares are valid for 3 months (extensions and business class available).

## ● General tips

Airlines will only allow a certain weight of luggage without a surcharge; this is normally 30 kg for first class and 20 kg for business and economy classes, but these limits are often not strictly enforced when it is known that the plane is not going to be full. On some flights from the UK via Paris special outbound concessions are offered (by Iberia, Viasa, Air France, Avianca) of a 2-piece allowance up to 32 kg, but you may need to request this. Passengers seeking a larger baggage allowance can route via USA, but with certain exceptions, the fares are slightly higher using this route. On the other hand, weight limits for internal flights are often lower; best to enquire beforehand.

## ● Prices and discounts

**1.** It is generally cheaper to fly from London rather than a point in Europe to Latin American destinations; fares vary from airline to airline, destination to destination and according to time of year. Check with an agency for the best deal for when you wish to travel.

**2.** Most airlines offer discounted fares of one sort or another on scheduled flights. These are not offered by the airlines direct to the public, but through agencies who specialize in this type of fare. In UK, these include Journey Latin America, 16 Devonshire Road, Chiswick, London W4 2HD (T 0181-747 3108); Trailfinders, 48 Earl's Court Road, London W8 6EJ (T 0171-938 3366); South American Experience, Fovant Mews, 12 Nonya Road, London SW17 7PH (T 0181-767 8989); Last Frontiers, Swan House, High Street, Long Crendon, Buckinghamshire, HP18 9AF (T 01844 208405); Passage to South America, 113 Shepherds Bush Road, London, W6 7LP (T 0171-602 9889); STA Travel, Priory House, 6 Wrights Lane, London W8 6TA (T 0171-938 4711), Cox & Kings Travel, St James Court, 45 Buckingham Gate, London (T 0171-873 5001).

The very busy seasons are 7 Dec – 15 Jan and 10 July – 10 Sept. If you intend travelling during those times, book as far ahead as possible. Between Feb-May and Sept-Nov special offers may be available.

**3.** Other fares fall into three groups, and are all on scheduled services:

**Excursion (return) fares** with restricted validity eg 5-90 days. Carriers are introducing flexibility into these tickets, permitting a change of dates on payment of a fee.

**Yearly fares**: these may be bought on a one-way or return basis. Some airlines require a specified return date, changeable upon payment of a fee. To leave the return completely open is possible for an extra fee. You must, fix the route (some of the cheapest flexible fares now have 6 months validity).

**Student (or Under 26) fares** (Do not assume that student tickets are the cheapest; though they are often very flexible, they are usually more expensive than A or B above). Some airlines are flexible on the age limit, others strict. One way and returns available, or "Open Jaws" (see below). **NB** If you foresee returning home at a busy time (eg Christmas, Aug), a booking is advisable on any type of open-return ticket.

**4.** For people intending to travel a linear route and return from a different point from that which they entered, there are "Open Jaws" fares, which are available on student, yearly, or excursion fares.

**5.** Many of these fares require a change of plane at an intermediate point, and a stopover may be permitted, or even obligatory, depending on schedules. Simply because a flight stops at a given airport does not mean you can break your journey there – the airline must have traffic rights to pick up or set down passengers between points A and B before it will be permitted. This is where dealing with a specialized agency (like Journey Latin America!) will really pay dividends. There are dozens of agencies that offer the simple returns to Lima at roughly the same (discounted) fare. On multi-stop itineraries, the specialized agencies can often save clients hundreds of pounds.

**6.** Although it's a little more complicated, it's possible to sell tickets in London for travel originating in Latin America at substantially cheaper fares than those available locally. This is useful for the traveller who doesn't know where he will end up, or who plans to travel for more than a year. Because of high local taxes a one-way ticket from Latin America is more expensive than a one-way in the other direction, so it's always best to buy a return. Taxes are calculated as a percentage of the full IATA fare; on a discounted fare the tax can therefore make up as much as 30-50% of the price.

**7.** There are several cheap French charters to Peru, but no-one in the UK sells them (although AOM tickets are available through Journey Latin America).

Travellers starting their journey in continental Europe may try: Uniclam-Voyages, 63 rue Monsieur-le Prince, 75006 Paris for charters. The Swiss company, Balair (owned by Swissair) has regular charter flights to South America. For cheap flights in Switzerland, Globetrotter Travel Service, Renweg, 8001 Zürich, has been recommended. Also try Nouvelles Frontières, Paris, T (1) 41-41-58-58; Hajo Siewer Jet Tours, Martinstr 39, 57462 Olpe, Germany, T (02761) 924120. The German magazine *Reisefieber* is useful.

**8.** If you buy discounted air tickets *always* check the reservation with the airline concerned to make sure the flight still exists. Also remember the IATA airlines' schedules change in March and October each year, so if you're going to be away a long time it's best to leave return flight coupons open.

In addition, check whether you are entitled to any refund or re-issued ticket if you lose, or have stolen, a discounted air ticket. Some airlines require the repurchase of a ticket before you can apply for a refund, which will not be given until after the validity of the original ticket has expired. The Iberia group and Air France, for example, operate this costly system. Travel insurance in some cases covers lost tickets.

**9.** Note that some South American carriers change departure times of short-haul or domestic flights at short notice and, in some instances, schedules shown in the computers of transatlantic carriers differ from those ac-

tually flown by smaller, local carriers. If you book, and reconfirm, both your transatlantic and onward sectors through your transatlantic carrier you may find that your travel plans have been based on out of date information. The surest solution is to reconfirm your outward flight in an office of the onward carrier itself.

## BY SEA

Enquiries regarding passages should be made through agencies in your own country, or through John Alton of Strand Cruise and Travel Centre, Charing Cross Shopping Concourse, The Strand, London WC2N 4HZ, T 0171-836 6363, F 0171-497 0078. In Switzerland, contact Wagner Frachtschiffreisen, Stadlerstrasse 48, CH-8404 Winterthur, T (052) 242 14 42, F 242 14 87. In the USA, contact Freighter World Cruises, 180 South Lake Ave, Pasadena, CA 91101, T (818) 449-3106, or Travltips Cruise and Freighter Travel Association, 163-07 Depot Road, PO Box 188, Flushing, NY 11358, T (800) 872-8584. The *Nordwoge* Shipping Company carries 7 passengers on a 70-day round trip Felixstowe, Bilbao, Panama Canal, Buenaventura, Guayaquil, Callao, Arica (or Iquique), San Antonio, Valparaíso, Talcahuano, Antofagasta, Guayaquil, Buenaventura, Panama Canal, Bilbao, various N European ports, Felixstowe, £5,300 pp. Chilean Line's *Laja* and *Lircay*, New Orleans, Houston, Tampico, Cristóbal, Panama Canal, Guayaquil, Callao, Antofagasta, San Antonio, Arica, Callao, Buenaventura, Panama Canal, Cristóbal, New Orleans, 48-day round trip, US$4,800-5,280 pp.

## CUSTOMS

**● Duty free allowance**

400 cigarettes or 50 cigars or 500 grams of tobacco, 2 litres of alcoholic drinks, new articles for personal use or gifts up to value US$200.

**● Export ban**

No object of archaeological interest may be taken out of Peru.

## ON ARRIVAL

### ● Clothing

Most Latin Americans, if they can afford it, devote great care to their clothes and appearance; it is appreciated if visitors do likewise. How you dress is mostly how people will judge you. Buying clothing locally can help you to look less like a tourist. A medium weight shawl with some wool content is recommended for women: it can double as pillow, light blanket, bathrobe or sunscreen as required. For men, a smart jacket can be very useful.

### ● Courtesy

Remember that politeness – even a little ceremoniousness – is much appreciated. In this connection professional or business cards are useful. Men should always remove any headgear and say "con permiso" when entering offices, and be prepared to shake hands; always say "Buenos días" (until midday) or "Buenas tardes" and wait for a reply before proceeding further. Always remember that the traveller from abroad has enjoyed greater advantages in life than most Latin American minor officials, and should be friendly and courteous in consequence. Never be impatient; do not criticize situations in public: the officials may know more English than you think and they can certainly interpret gestures and facial expressions. Politeness can be a liability, however, in some situations; most Latin Americans are disorderly queuers. In commercial transactions (buying a meal, goods in a shop, etc) politeness should be accompanied by firmness, and always ask the price first.

Politeness should also be extended to street traders; saying "No, gracias " with a smile is better than an arrogant dismissal. Whether you give money to beggars is a personal matter, but your decision should be influenced by whether a person is begging out of need or trying to cash in on the tourist trail. In the former case, local people giving may provide an indication. Giving money to children is a separate issue, upon which most agree: don't do it. There are occasions where giving food in a restaurant may be appropriate, but first inform yourself of local practice.

### ● Hours of business

*Shops*: 0900 or 1000-1230 and 1500 or 1600-2000. In the main cities, supermarkets do not close for lunch and Lima has some that are open 24 hrs. Some are closed on Sat; most are closed on Sun. *Banks*: most are open 0900-1230, 1500-1800 the year round. Closed Sat. Some banks in Lima open from 0900-1600 and do not close for lunch. **NB** All banks close on 30 June and 31 Dec for balancing; if it falls on Sat or Sun, banks may close 1 day before or after. This does not apply to the banks at Jorge Chávez international airport which are open 24 hrs every day. *Offices*: 0830-1230, 1500-1800 the year round; some have continuous hours 0900-1700; most close on Sat. *Government Offices*: Jan to Mar, Mon-Fri 0830-1130. Rest of year: Mon-Fri 0900-1230, 1500-1700, but this changes frequently.

### ● Official time

5 hrs behind GMT.

### ● Police

Whereas in Europe and North America we are accustomed to law enforcement on a systematic basis, in general, enforcement in Latin America is achieved by periodic campaigns. The most typical is a round-up of criminals in the cities just before Christmas. In Dec, therefore, you may well be asked for identification at any time, and if you cannot produce it, you will be jailed. If a visitor is jailed his/her friends should provide food every day. This is especially important for people on a diet, such as diabetics. In the event of a vehicle accident in which anyone is injured, all drivers involved are automatically detained until blame has been established, and this does not usually take less than 2 weeks.

Never offer a bribe unless you are fully conversant with the customs of the country. Wait until the official makes the suggestion, or offer money in some form which is apparently not bribery, eg "In our country we have a system of on-the-spot fines (*multas de inmediato*). Is there a similar system here?" Do not assume that an official who accepts a bribe is prepared to do anything else that is illegal. You bribe him to persuade him to do his job, or to persuade him not to do it, or to do it more quickly, or more slowly. You do not bribe him to do something which is against the law. The mere suggestion would make him very upset. If an official suggests that a bribe must be paid before you can proceed on your way, be patient (assuming you have the time) and he may relent.

## ● Safety

The following notes on personal safety should not hide the fact that most Peruvians, particularly outside those areas affected by crime or terrorism, are hospitable and helpful.

**General tips** Keep all documents secure; hide your main cash supply in different places or under your clothes: extra pockets sewn inside shirts and trousers, pockets closed with a zip or safety pin, moneybelts (best worn below the waist rather than outside or at it or around the neck), neck or leg pouches, a thin chain for attaching a purse to your bag or under your clothes and elasticated support bandages for keeping money and cheques above the elbow or below the knee have been repeatedly recommended (the last by John Hatt in *The Tropical Traveller*). Keep cameras in bags (preferably with a chain or wire in the strap to defeat the slasher) or briefcases; take spare spectacles (eyeglasses); don't wear wrist-watches or jewellery. If you wear a shoulder-bag in a market, carry it in front of you. Backpacks are vulnerable to slashers: a good idea is to cover the pack with a sack (a plastic one will also keep out rain and dust) with maybe a layer of wire netting between, or make an inner frame of chicken wire. Use a pack which is lockable at its base.

Ignore mustard smearers and paint or shampoo sprayers, and strangers' remarks like "what's that on your shoulder?" or "have you seen that dirt on your shoe?" Furthermore, don't bend over to pick up money or other items in the street. These are all ruses intended to distract your attention and make you easy for an accomplice to steal from. If someone follows you when you're in the street, let him catch up with you and "give him the eye". While you should take local advice about being out at night, do not assume that daytime is safer than nighttime. If walking after dark, walk in the road, not on the pavement/sidewalk.

Be wary of "plainclothes policemen"; insist on seeing identification and on going to the police station by main roads. Do not hand over your identification (or money – which he should not need to see anyway) until you are at the station. On no account take them directly back to your lodgings. Be even more suspicious if he seeks confirmation of his status from a passer-by. If someone tries to bribe you, insist on a receipt. If attacked, remember your assailants may well be armed, and try not to resist.

It is best, if you can trust your hotel, to leave any valuables you don't need in safe-deposit there, when sightseeing locally. Always keep an inventory of what you have deposited. If you don't trust the hotel, lock everything in your pack and secure that in your room (some people take eyelet-screws for padlocking cupboards or drawers). If you lose valuables, always report to the police and note details of the report – for insurance purposes.

Take care everywhere, even during festivals when streets are crowded. Be especially careful when arriving in or leaving a town at night by bus or train; in fact, it is better to travel by day whenever possible. Take taxis to stations, when carrying luggage, before 0800 and after dark (look on it as an insurance policy). Never accept food, drink, sweets or cigarettes from unknown fellow travellers on buses or trains. They may be drugged, and you would wake up hours later without your belongings. Avoid staying in hotels too near to bus companies, as drivers who stay overnight are sometimes in league with thieves; avoid restaurants near bus terminals if you have all your luggage with you, it is hard to keep an eye on all your gear when eating. On trains, one large bag is easier to watch, and lock to a rack (more than once), than lots of small ones. In poor areas of cities be on your guard as this is where most theft takes place. Try to find a travel companion if alone, as this will reduce the strain of watching your belongings all the time. Outside the July-Aug peak holiday period, there is less tension, less risk of crime, and more friendliness. A friendly attitude on your part, smiling even when you've thwarted a thief's attempt, can help you out of trouble. In addition, do not be discourteous to officials.

**Drugs** Although certain illegal drugs are readily available anyone carrying any is almost automatically assumed to be a drug trafficker. If arrested on any charge the wait for trial in prison can take a year and is particularly unpleasant. Unfortunately, we have received reports of drug-planting, or mere accusation of drug-trafficking by the PNP on foreigners in Lima, with US$1,000 demanded for release. If you are asked by the narcotics police to go to the toilets to have your bags searched, insist on taking a witness. **Drugs use or purchase is punishable by up to 15 years' imprisonment**.

Tricks employed to get foreigners into trouble over drugs include slipping a packet of cocaine into the money you are exchanging, being invited to a party or somewhere involving a taxi ride, or simply being asked on the street if you want to buy cocaine. In all cases, a plain clothes 'policeman' will discover the planted cocaine, in your money, at your feet in the taxi, and will ask to see your passport and money. He will then return them, minus a large part of your cash. Do not get into a taxi, do not show your money, and try not to be intimidated. Being in pairs is no guarantee of security, and single women may be particularly vulnerable. Beware also thieves dressed as policemen asking for your passport and wanting to search for drugs; searching is only permitted if prior paperwork is done.

**Insurgency** It remains hard to tell how many followers and sympathizers Sendero Luminoso has, but the military now seems to have taken control of most departments. The Central Highlands suffered much of the violence and, until 1992, it was not safe to travel in that region. With the reestablishment of military control, there has been much improvement. People have been travelling through the area, mostly with favourable reports. It is still essential to inform yourself of the latest situation before going. There are many checkpoints, which present no problem. Travel only by day. Avoid the Huallaga Valley because of drug trafficking and terrorism.

Keep yourself informed before going and while travelling. For up-to-date information contact the Tourist Police, T Lima 476-9896, F 476-7708, your embassy or consulate, fellow travellers, the South American Explorers Club, who issue the pamphlet 'How Not to Get Robbed in Peru' (T Lima 425-0142, or in Quito) and, also in Quito, *The Latin American Travel Advisor* (published by Latin American Travel Consultants, PO Box 17-17-908, Quito, F 593-2-562-566, E-Mail LATA@pi.pro.ec on Internet).

## ● Shopping

Pre-paid Kodak slide film cannot be developed in South America; it is also very hard to find. Kodachrome is almost impossible to buy. Some travellers (but not all) have advised against mailing exposed films home; either take them with you, or have them developed, but not printed, once you have checked the laboratory's quality. Note that postal authorities may use less sensitive equipment for X-ray screening than the airports do. Modern controlled X-ray machines are supposed to be safe for any speed of film, but it is worth trying to avoid X-ray as the doses are cumulative. Many airport officials will allow film to be passed outside X-ray arches; they may also hand-check a suitcase with a large quantity of film if asked politely.

Developing black and white film is a problem. Often it is shoddily machine-processed and the negatives are ruined. Ask the store if you can see an example of their laboratory's work and if they hand-develop.

Exposed film can be protected in humid areas by putting it in a balloon and tying a knot. Similarly keeping your camera in a plastic bag may reduce the effects of humidity.

## ● Tipping

Restaurants: service is included in the bill (see below), but if someone goes out of his way to serve tips can be given. Taxi drivers, none (in fact, bargain the price down, then pay extra for good service if you get it). Cloakroom attendants and hairdressers (very high class only), US$0.50-$1. Railway or airport porters, US$0.50. **NB** Anyone who as much as touches your bag will expect a tip. Usherettes, none. Car wash boys, US$0.30, car 'watch' boys, US$0.20.

## ● Travelling alone

First time exposure to a country where sections of the population live in extreme poverty or squalor and may even be starving can cause odd psychological reactions in visitors. So can the exceptional curiosity extended to visitors, especially women. Simply be prepared for this and try not to over-react. The following hints have mainly been supplied by women, but most apply to any single traveller. When you set out, err on the side of caution until your instincts have adjusted to the customs of a new culture. If, as a single woman, you can befriend a local woman, you will learn much more about the country you are visiting. Unless actively avoiding foreigners like yourself, don't go too far from the beaten track; there is a very definite "gringo trail" which you can join, or follow, if seeking company. This can be helpful when looking for safe accommodation, especially if arriving after dark (which is best avoided). Remember that for a single woman a taxi at night can be as dangerous as wandering around on her own. At borders dress as smartly as possible. Travelling by train is a good way to meet locals, but buses are much easier for a person alone; on major routes your seat is often reserved and your luggage can usually be locked in the hold. It is easier for men to take the friendliness of locals at face value; women may be subject to much unwanted attention. To help minimize this, do not wear suggestive clothing and, advises Alex Rossi of Jawa Timur, Indonesia, do not flirt. By wearing a wedding ring, carrying a photograph of your "husband" and "children", and saying that your "husband" is close at hand, you may dissuade an aspiring suitor. If politeness fails, do not feel bad about showing offence and departing. When accepting a social invitation, make sure that someone knows the address and the time you left. Ask if you can bring a friend (even if you do not intend to do so). A good rule is always to act with confidence, as though you know where you are going, even if you do not. Someone who looks lost is more likely to attract unwanted attention.

## ● Voltage

220 volts AC, 60 cycles throughout the country, except Arequipa (50 cycles).

## ● Weights & measures

The metric system of weights and measures is compulsory.

## ● What to take

Everybody has his/her own list, but those most often mentioned include air cushions for slatted seats, inflatable travel pillow for neck support, strong shoes (and remember that footwear over 9½ English size, or 42 European size, is difficult to obtain); a small first-aid kit and handbook, fully waterproof top clothing, waterproof treatment for leather footwear, wax earplugs (which are almost impossible to find outside large cities) and airline-type eye mask to help you sleep in noisy and poorly curtained hotel rooms, sandals (rubber-thong Japanese-type or other – can be worn in showers to avoid athlete's foot), a polyethylene sheet 2m x 1m to cover possibly infested beds and shelter your luggage, polyethylene bags of varying sizes (up to heavy duty rubbish bag size) with ties, a toilet bag you can tie round your waist, if you use an electric shaver, take a rechargeable type, a sheet sleeping-bag and pillow-case or separate pillow-case – in some countries they are not changed often in cheap hotels; a 1½-2m piece of 100% cotton can be used as a towel, a bedsheet, beach towel, makeshift curtain and wrap; a mosquito net (or a hammock with a fitted net), a straw hat which can be rolled or flattened and reconstituted after 15 mins soaking in water, a clothes line, a nailbrush (useful for scrubbing dirt off clothes as well as off oneself), a vacuum flask, a water bottle, a small dual-voltage immersion heater, a small dual-voltage (or battery-driven) electric fan, a light nylon waterproof shopping bag, a universal bath- and basin-plug of the flanged type that will fit any waste-pipe (or improvise one from a sheet of thick rubber), string, velcro, electrical insulating tape, large penknife preferably with tin and bottle openers, scissors and corkscrew – the famous Swiss Army range has been repeatedly recommended (for knife sharpening, go to a butcher's shop), alarm clock or watch, candle, torch (flashlight) – especially one that will clip on to a pocket or belt, pocket mirror, pocket calculator, an adaptor and flex to enable you to take power from an electric-light socket (the Edison screw type is the most commonly used). Remember not to throw away spent batteries containing mercury or cadmium; take them home to be disposed of, or recycled properly.

Useful medicaments are given at the end of the 'Health' section, page 458); to these might be added some lip salve with sun protection, and pre-moistened wipes (such as 'Wet Ones'). Always carry toilet paper. Natural fabric sticking plasters, as well as being long-lasting, are much appreciated as gifts. Dental floss can be used for backpack repairs, in addition to its original purpose. **Never** carry firearms. Their possession could land you in serious trouble.

A note for **contact lens wearers**: lens solution can be difficult to find, especially outside major cities. Ask for it in a chemist/pharmacy, rather than an optician's.

## ON DEPARTURE

### ● Airport departure taxes

There is a US$25 airport tax on international flight departures, payable in dollars or soles. For non-Peruvians, there is a security tax of US$4-5 and an airport tax of US$3.50-4 (depending on the airport) on domestic flights (if you are working in Peru, carry a letter stating this and insist you are 'residente' and pay local tax of US$2). 18% VAT is charged on air tickets.

## WHERE TO STAY

### ● Hotels

All de luxe and 1st class hotels charge 28% in taxes, which includes VAT and service charges; lower category hotels charge 20-23% (similarly restaurants). Most hotels have this surcharge included in their prices, but best check first. By law all places that offer accommodation now have a plaque outside bearing the letters H (Hotel), Hs (Hostal), HR (Hotel Residencial) or P (Pensión) according to type. A hotel has 51 rooms or more, a hostal 50 or fewer; the categories do not describe quality or facilities. Many hotels have safe parking for motor cycles. All hotels seem to be crowded at the end of July, Independence celebrations. Reception areas may be misleading; it is a good idea to see the room before booking. Hotels tend to be more expensive in the N than in the S. When booking a hotel from an airport, or station by phone, always talk to the hotel yourself; do not let anyone do it for you (except an accredited hotel booking service). You will be told the hotel of your choice is full and be directed to a more expensive one. **NB** Hotels are checked by the police for drugs, especially the rooms of foreigners. Make sure they do not remove any of your belongings. You do not need to show them money. Cooperate, but be firm about your rights. Note that in the text "with bath" usually means "with shower and toilet", not "with bath tub". Remember, cheaper hotels don't always supply soap, towels and toilet paper; in colder (higher) regions they may not supply enough blankets, so take your own or a sleeping bag.

## Hotel prices

Our hotel price ranges, including taxes and service charges but without meals unless stated, are as follows:

| | | | | | |
|---|---|---|---|---|---|
| **L1** | Over US$200 | **L2** | US$151-200 | **L3** | US$101-150 |
| **A1** | US$81-100 | **A2** | US$61-80 | **A3** | US$46-60 |
| **B** | US$31-45 | **C** | US$21-30 | **D** | US$12-20 |
| **E** | US$7-11 | **F** | US$4-6 | **G** | Up to US$3 |

**NB** Prices are for double rooms, except in **F** and **G** ranges where the price is almost always per person.

Other abbreviations used in the book (apart from pp = per person; a/c = air conditioned; rec = recommended; T = telephone; TCs = travellers' cheques; s/n = "sin número", no street number; p = piso – floor, in Spanish-speaking countries) should be self-explanatory.

**NB** The electric showers used in innumerable hotels should be checked for obvious flaws in the wiring; try not to touch the rose while it is producing hot water.

**Cockroaches** These are ubiquitous and unpleasant, but not dangerous. Take some insecticide powder if staying in cheap hotels; Baygon (Bayer) has been recommended. Stuff toilet paper in any holes in walls that you may suspect of being parts of cockroach runs.

**Toilets** Many hotels, restaurants and bars have inadequate water supplies. **Almost without exception used toilet paper should not be flushed down the pan, but placed in the receptacle provided**. This applies even in quite expensive hotels. Failing to observe this custom will block the pan or drain, a considerable health risk. It is quite common for people to stand on the toilet seat (facing the wall – easier to balance), as they do in Asia. If you are concerned about the hygiene of the facility, put paper on the seat.

### • Camping

Easy in Peru, especially along the coast. There can be problems with robbery when camping close to a small village. Avoid such a location, or ask permission to camp in a backyard or *chacra* (farmland). Most Peruvians are used to campers, but in some remote places, people have never seen a tent. Be casual about it, do not unpack all your gear, leave it inside your tent (especially at night) and never leave a tent unattended. Obey the following rules for "wild" camping: (1) arrive in daylight and pitch your tent as it gets dark; (2) ask permission to camp from the parish priest, or the fire chief, or the police, or a farmer regarding his own property; (3) never ask a group of people – especially young people; (4) never camp on a beach (because of sandflies and thieves). If you can't get information from anyone, camp in a spot where you can't be seen from the nearest inhabited place, or road, and make sure no one saw you go there.

Camping gas in little blue bottles is available in the main cities. Those with stoves designed for lead-free gasoline should use *ron de quemar*, available from hardware shops (*ferreterías*). White gas is called *bencina*, also available from hardware stores.

### • Youth hostels

Information on youth hostels and student accommodation can be obtained from INTEJ, Av San Martín 240, Barranco, Lima, T 477-4105. Also Asociación Peruana de Albergues Turísticos Juveniles, Av Casimiro Ulloa 328, Miraflores, Lima, T 446-5488, F 444-8187. Always take a torch and candles, especially in remoter regions.

# FOOD AND DRINK

## FOOD

The high-class hotels and restaurants serve international food and, on demand, some native dishes, but the taverns (*chicherías*) and the local restaurants (*picanterías*) supply the highly seasoned native food at its best. Soups tend to be very good, and a meal in themselves. In the Lima area the most popular fish dishes are the *ceviche* – raw fish, seasoned with lemons, onions and red peppers (see **Health**); the *escabeche* – fish with onions, hot green pepper, red peppers, prawns (*langostinos*), cumin, hard eggs, olives, and sprinkled with cheese, and *chupe de camarones*, a shrimp stew made with varying and somewhat surprising ingredients. *Parihuela* is a popular bouillabaisse which includes *yuyo de mar*, a tangy seaweed. *Yacu-chupe*, or green soup, has a basis of potato, with cheese, garlic, coriander leaves, parsley, peppers, eggs, onions, and mint. *Causa* and *carapulca* are two good potato dishes; *papa a la huancaina* is another potato dish, topped with a spicy sauce made with milk and cheese; *causa* is made with yellow potatoes, lemons, pepper, hard-boiled eggs, olives, lettuce, sweet cooked corn, sweet cooked potato, fresh cheese, and served with onion sauce. Favourite meat dishes are *ollucos con charqui* (a kind of potato with dried meat), *caucau*, made with tripe, potatoes, peppers, and parsley and served with rice, *anticuchos*, hearts of beef with garlic, peppers, cumin seeds and vinegar; *estofado de carne*, a stew which often contains wine; *carne en adobo*, a cut and seasoned steak; *fritos*, fried pork, usually eaten in the morning; *sancochado*, meat and all kinds of vegetables stewed together and seasoned with ground garlic; *lomo a la huancaína*, beef with egg and cheese sauce; *lomo saltado* is a beef stew with onions, vinegar, ginger, chilli, tomatoes and fried potatoes, served with rice; and *sopa a la criolla* containing thin noodles, beef heart, bits of egg and vegetables and pleasantly spiced. *Cuy* is guinea pig; *chicharrones*, deep fried chunks of pork ribs and chicken; *lechón*, suckling pig. Any dish described as *arequipeño* can be expected to be hot and spicy. *Mondonguito* is a boiled small intestine. The best beef is imported from Argentina and is expensive. Duck is excellent. *Rocoto relleno* is spicy bell pepper stuffed with beef and vegetables. Corn dishes: *choclo con queso*, corn on the cob with cheese; *tamales*, boiled corn dumplings filled with meat and wrapped in banana leaf; *cancha*, toasted corn. For snacks, Peruvian *empanadas* are good. *Palta rellena* is avocado filled with chicken salad.

Among the desserts and confections are *cocada al horno* – coconut, with yolk of egg, sesame seed, wine and butter; *picarones* – frittered cassava flour and eggs fried in fat and served with honey; *mazamorra morada* – purple maize, sweet potato starch, lemons, various dried fruits, sticks of ground cinnamon and cloves and perfumed pepper; *manjar blanco* – milk, sugar and eggs; *maná* – an almond paste with eggs, vanilla and milk; *alfajores* – shortbread biscuit with *manjar blanco*, pineapple, peanuts, etc; *pastelillos* – yucas with sweet potato, sugar and anise fried in fat and powdered with sugar and served hot; and *zango de pasas*, made with maize, syrup, raisins and sugar. *Turrón*, the Lima nougat, is worth trying. *Tejas* are sugar candies wrapped in wax paper; the pecan-flavoured ones are tastiest. The various Peruvian fruits are of good quality: they include bananas, the citrus fruits, pineapples, dates, avocados (*paltas*), eggfruit (*lúcuma*), the custard apple (*chirimoya*) which can be as big as your head, quince, *papaya*, mango, guava, the passion-fruit (*maracuyá*) and the soursop (*guanábana*).

The tea hour starts about 1800 at the good hotels. If asked to a party ask the hostess what time you are *really* expected unless the time is specified on the invitation card as *hora inglesa* – English time; Peruvians tend to ask guests for dinner at 2000.

A normal lunch or dinner costs US$5-8, but can go up to about US$80 in a first-class restaurant, with drinks and wine included. Middle and high-class restaurants add 11% tax and 17% service to the bill (sometimes 18% and 13% respectively); this is not shown on the price list or menu, check in advance. Lower class restaurants charge only 5% tax, while cheap, local restaurants charge no taxes. Lunch is the main meal: dinner in restaurants is normally about 1900 onwards, but choice may be more limited than lunchtime. There are plenty of cheap and good restaurants around the centre of Lima and most offer a 'business lunch' called *menú* for US$1.30-3 for a 3-course meal. There are many Chinese restaurants (*chifas*) in Peru which serve good food at reasonable prices. For really economically-minded people the *Comedores populares* in most cities of Peru offer a standard 3-course meal US$1. Meals at this price, or little more, can be found under name of *menú económico* at many restaurants throughout Peru.

Vegetarians should be able to list all the foods they cannot eat; saying "Soy vegetariano/a" (I'm a vegetarian) or "no como carne" (I don't eat meat) is often not enough.

## DRINK

The usual international drinks with several very good local ones: *pisco*, a brandy made in the Ica valley, from which pisco sour is made; *chilcano*, a longer refreshing drink also made with *guinda*, a local cherry brandy; and *algarrobina*, a sweet cocktail made with the syrup from the bark of the carob tree, egg whites, milk, pisco and cinnamon. Wine is acidic and not very good, the best of a poor lot are the Ica wines Tacama and Ocucaje; both come in red, white and rosé, sweet and dry varieties. Tacama blancs de blancs and brut champagne have been rec, also Gran Tinto Reserva Especial. Viña Santo Tomás, from Chincha, is reasonable and cheap. Casapalca is not rec. Beer is best in lager and porter types, especially the Cusco and Arequipa brands (lager) and Trujillo Malta (porter). In Lima only Cristal and Pilsener (not related to true Pilsen) are readily available, others have to be sought out. Look out for the sweetish 'maltina' brown ale, which makes a change from the ubiquitous pilsner – type beers. *Chicha de jora* is a maize beer, usually homemade and not easy to come by, refreshing but strong, and *chicha morada* is a soft drink made with purple maize. Coffee is often brought to the table in a small jug accompanied by a mug of hot water to which you add the coffee essence. If you want coffee with milk, a mug of milk is brought. There are many different kinds of herb tea: the commonest are *manzanilla* (camomile) and *hierbaluisa* (lemon grass).

## GETTING AROUND

### AIR TRANSPORT

Air services link towns which are often far apart and can only be reached otherwise with difficulty. The three main companies are Faucett, AeroPerú and Americana. Aero Continente flies mostly the same routes as these three, for about the same fares, but with better service. Americana and Continente share planes on some routes, Americana taking the routes to the N, Aero Continente those to the S and jungle. Expreso Aéreo fly to towns in the mountains and the jungle using smaller aircraft (not very reliable). Aero Cóndor links some of the smaller coastal, mountain and jungle towns. The airforce runs some commercial flights to jungle areas, only a few times a month, not reliable, but half the price of other airlines. Since the privatization of AeroPerú, competition is hard and there are often substantial discounts with all the airlines. Tickets are not interchangeable between the companies, but may be permitted in the case of cancelled flights. See under Lima (page 118) for airline addresses, towns served, and above for taxes. Note that flight schedules and departure times change often, and that delays are common. In the rainy season cancellations occur, sometimes for 2 days. There are also unannounced route changes and poor time-keeping (Americana seems to be the most reliable of the three main companies). Always allow an extra day between national and international flights, especially in the rainy season. Internal flight prices are fixed in US dollars (but can be paid in soles) and have 18% tax added. It is possible to buy AeroPerú domestic tickets more cheaply outside Peru, but the offer changes frequently. You cannot alter the destinations in Peru, only the date. (If you fly Cusco-Juliaca you go via Arequipa and can stop over, completing the Juliaca leg later.) If you fly to Peru with AeroPerú from Miami, you are given one free internal flight and any other routes for US$50 each. AeroPerú, Faucett and Americana offer 2, 3 4 or 5-stop tickets for US$99, US$149, US$179 or US$209 if bought outside Peru; also an unlimited ticket for US$269, valid for 30 days. If you have a choice, remember time-keeping tends to be better early am than later. When buying an internal flight, check with travel agencies for occasional special deals, but scrutinize the ticket carefully. Also check with the different airlines; even though they maintain the same set price, they sometimes do promotions on flights.

**NB** If possible travel with hand luggage only (48 cm x 24 cm x 37 cm) so there is more chance of you and your baggage arriving at the same destination. Unpredictable weather contributes to poor time-keeping, but companies are also criticized for their passenger service, especially as regards information and overbooking. Note that flights into the mountains may well be put forward 1 hr if there are reports of bad weather. Neither AeroPerú or Faucett has enough aircraft and both are in financial difficulties. Flights to jungle regions are also unreliable. See also warning on page 323.

Flights must be reconfirmed in the town you will be leaving from 24 hrs in advance, but 72 hrs is advised. 20 mins before departure, the clerk is allowed by law to let standby passengers board, taking the reserved seats of those who haven't turned up. AeroPerú offers senior citizen discounts (40%) but some offices may not grant them. Tickets can be bought through travel agencies (but check them carefully), or direct through the airline; the price is the same.

**Air Freight** Luggage, packets, etc, are not handled with care; make sure there are no loose parts, or put your rucksack in a separate bag. Always lock your luggage when possible. Check that the correct destination label has been attached. Never put valuables into luggage to be checked in.

## LAND TRANSPORT

### ● Trains

There are passenger services on the following lines, which are often quicker and more comfortable than buses: Huancayo-Huancavelica, Arequipa-Juliaca-Puno, Puno-Juliaca-Cusco, and Cusco-Machu Picchu-Quillabamba. Details of services in the text. Good cheap meals are usually served on trains. **NB** Train schedules are cut in the rainy season, sometimes to 2-3 times a week, occasionally they are cancelled for weeks or months. The train from Lima, via La Oroya, to Huancayo has not run since 1991.

### ● Road

Major and minor roads are given in the text. The two roads to Cusco, one by the Central Andes and the other by Arequipa and Puno, make a most spectacular circuit of 2,400 km possible. Preferably it should be done clockwise: there would be less driving on the outsides of precipices; it would be downhill on the poor stretch between Puno and Arequipa, and the return to Lima would be by a good road. Most of the high Sierra roads are narrow, unsurfaced and liable to landslides; many accidents. Surfaces are usually very rough, and this makes for slow travel and frequent breakdowns. If you have to drive at night, do not go fast; many local vehicles have poor lights and street lighting is bad. Be sure to check with the Peruvian Touring and Automobile Club regarding road conditions before driving in the Sierra.

Few roads in Peru, except for the Pan-American and Central Highways, the roads connecting Huaraz and Caraz with Pativilca, and Pacasmayo with Cajamarca, and the Puno-Desaguadero road to Bolivia are paved. Toll roads in Peru include Aguas Verdes-Tumbes, many on the Pan-American Highway between Tumbes and Lima, Pativilca-Huaraz, Lima-Pucusana, Ica-Nasca, Lima (highway around city), Variante-Pacasmayo, which vary from US$1.50 to US$0.50. Ecuador to Chile/Bolivia on main roads comes to about US$17. (Motorcycles are exempt from road tolls: use the extreme righthand lane at toll gates.)

### ● Motoring

**Road information** The Touring y Automóvil Club del Perú, Av César Vallejo 699, Lince, Lima (T 403270, F 419652), with offices in most provincial cities, gives news about the roads and hotels along the way (although for the most up-to-date information try the bus and colectivo offices). It sells a very good road map at US$5 (Mapa Vial del Perú, 1:3,000,000, Ed 1980, reliable information about road conditions) and route maps covering most of Peru (Hoja de Ruta, detail maps 1:1,000,000, very good but no information on road conditions). Good maps are available from the South American Explorers Club, who will give good advice on road conditions. Buy maps separately or in packages of 8. Cuadernos de Viaje are travel notebooks covering all Peru with valuable information and maps, in Spanish. Other maps can be bought from street vendors in Colmena and Plaza San Martín, Lima. 'Westermanns Monatshefte; folio Ecuador, Peru, Bolivien' has excellent maps of Peru, especially the archaeological sites.

**Fuel** Gasoline is sold as: 'extra' (84 octane), US$2.05 a gallon, and 'importada' (95 octane), US$2.50-2.75 a gallon, found in Lima, the coastal towns and Arequipa; unleaded fuel (90 and 97 octane SP) is sold on the coast, US$2.25-US$2.55. Fuel in remote jungle areas can be double the price of urban areas. Diesel costs US$1.15 a gallon. Filling stations are called *grifos*. Always make sure your fuel tank is full when branching off a major highway, fill up whenever possible and make sure you do not receive diesel or kerosene.

**Traffic and parking** In Lima never trust the green light; Peruvian drivers tend to regard traffic lights as recommendations, at most. No-parking signs are painted at the roadside: illegally parked cars are towed away. Do not leave your vehicle on the street in Lima, always put it in a car park (called *playa*, usual charge US$0.50/hr). If you want to sleep in your car, check with the local tourist police first. They may allow you to park near their office.

**General hints** Roads go to very high altitudes in Peru – make sure that the spark is properly adjusted and consider use of smaller carburettor jets if driving much at altitude. Avoid mountain travel between Nov and April. Take two planks of wood in case car gets stuck in soft soil when allowing other vehicles to pass. Never travel off the main roads without being self-sufficient. If you need mechanical assistance in the mountains ask for the nearest mining or road construction camp. 4WD is not necessary, but it does give you greater flexibility in mountain and jungle territory, although you may not get far in Amazonas, where roads are frequently impassable. Wherever you travel you should expect from time to time to find roads that are badly maintained, damaged or closed during the wet season, and delays because of floods, landslides and huge potholes. Don't plan your schedules too tightly. Disadvantages of travelling in your own vehicle include the difficulties of getting insurance, theft, finding guarded parking lots, maintenance on appalling roads and nervous exhaustion, which may outweigh the advantages of mobility and independence.

**Spares** Imported car spares available and cheaper than in neighbouring countries. Makes with well-established dealerships are easiest to obtain (eg Volvo, Peugeot, VW). VW Beetles, Toyota Coronas and Datsun Stanzas are assembled in Peru and are therefore easier to get spares and service for. Most towns can supply a mechanic of sorts, and probably parts for Bosch fuel injection equipment. Watch the mechanics like a hawk, since there's always a brisk market in spares, and some of yours may be highly desirable. That apart, they enjoy a challenge, and can fix most things, eventually.

**Preparation** Preparing the car for the journey is largely a matter of common sense: obviously any part that is not in first class condition should be replaced. It's well worth installing extra heavy-duty shock-absorbers (such as Spax or Koni) before starting out, because a long trip on rough roads in a heavily laden car will give heavy wear. Fit tubes on "tubeless" tyres, since air plugs for tubeless tyres are hard to find, and if you bend the rim on a pothole, the tyre will not hold air. Take spare tubes, and an extra spare tyre. Also take spare plugs, fan-belts, radiator hoses and headlamp bulbs; even though local equivalents can easily be found in cities, it is wise to take spares for those occasions late at night or in remote areas when you might need them. You can also change the fanbelt after a stretch of long, hot driving to prevent wear (eg after 15,000 km/10,000 miles). If your vehicle has more than one fanbelt, always replace them all at the same time (make sure you have the necessary tools if doing it yourself). If your car has sophisticated electrics, spare "black boxes" for the ignition and fuel injection are advisable, plus a spare voltage regulator or the appropriate diodes for the alternator, and elements for the fuel, air and oil filters if these are not a common type. (Some drivers take a spare alternator of the correct amperage, especially if the regulator is incorporated into the alternator.) Dirty fuel is a frequent problem, so be prepared to change filters more often than you would at home: in a diesel car you will need to check the sediment bowl often, too. An extra in-line fuel filter is a good idea if feasible (although harder to find, metal canister type is preferable to plastic), and for travel on dusty roads an oil bath air filter is best for a diesel car. It is wise to carry a spade, jumper cables, tow rope and an air pump. Fit tow hooks to both sides of the vehicle frame. A 12 volt neon light for camping and repairs will be invaluable. Spare fuel containers should be steel and not plastic, and a siphon pipe is essential for those places where fuel is sold out of the drum. Take a 10 litre water container for self and vehicle.

**Security** Apart from the mechanical aspects, spare no ingenuity in making your car secure. Use heavy chain and padlocks to chain doors shut, fit security catches on windows, remove interior window winders (so that a hand reaching in from a forced vent cannot open the window). All these will help, but none is foolproof. Anything on the outside – wing mirrors, spot lamps, motifs etc – is likely to be stolen too. So are wheels if not secured by locking nuts. Try never to leave the car unattended except in a locked garage or guarded parking space. Remove all belongings and leave the empty glove compartment open when the car is unattended. Also lock the clutch or accelerator to the steering wheel with a heavy, obvious chain or lock. Street children will generally protect your car fiercely in exchange for a tip. Be sure to note down key numbers and carry spares of the most important ones (but don't keep all spares inside the vehicle).

**Documents** You must have an international driving licence – especially with a number. If you don't have a number on your licence, improvise. (It has been reported that a UK driving licence is acceptable.) You also need the registration document in the name of the driver, or, in the case of a car registered in someone else's name, a notarized letter of authorization. A great deal of conflicting information surrounds what documents are required in addition to the vehicle's registration. According to the RAC in the UK there are three recognized documents for taking a vehicle into South America: a *carnet de passages* issued by the Fedération Internationale de l'Automobile (FIA – Paris), a *carnet de passages* issued by the Alliance Internationale de Tourisme (AIT-Geneva), and the *Libreta de Pasos por Aduana* issued by the Federación Interamericana de Touring y Automóvil Clubs (FITAC). Officially, Peru requires either *carnet*, the *libreta* and, for caravans and trailers, an inventory (the consulate in London says that a *libreta* is necessary, but if you cannot obtain one a written declaration that the car will leave Peru, authorized at a Peruvian consulate before leaving your home country, will do instead). Motorists report that a 90-day transit permit for vehicles is available at land borders without a *carnet de passages*, contrary to what officials may say. *Formulario 015*, which can be requested at the border, entitles visitors to bring a vehicle into Peru duty free for 3 months, it is not extendable, but it is free (one correspondent was charged US$35 anyway). In view of this confusion, contact the Peruvian automobile club and get their advice. In general, motorists in South America seem to fare better with a *carnet de passages* than without it.

The *libreta*, a 10-page book of three-part passes for customs, should be available from any South American automobile club member of FITAC; cost seems to be US$200, half refundable. The *carnet de passages* is issued only in the country where the vehicle is registered (in the UK it costs £65 for 25 pages, £55 for 10 pages, valid 12 months, either bank indemnity or insurance indemnity, half of the premium refundable value of the vehicle and countries to be visited required), available from the RAC or the AA. In the USA the AAA seems not to issue the *carnet*, although the HQ in Washington DC may give advice. It is available from the Canadian Automobile Association (1775 Courtwood Crescent, Ottawa, K2C 3JZ, T 613-226-7631, F 613-225-7383) for Canadian and US citizens, cost C$450; full details obtainable from the CAA.

**Insurance** for the vehicle against accident, damage or theft is best arranged in the country of origin, but it is getting increasingly difficult to find agencies who offer this service. It is very expensive to insure against accident and theft, especially as you should take into account the value of the car increased by duties calculated in real (ie non devaluing) terms. If the car is stolen or written off you will be required to pay very high import duty on its value. Get the legally required minimum cover, not expensive, as soon as you can, because if you should be involved in an accident and are uninsured, your car could be confiscated. If anyone is hurt, do not pick them up (you may become liable). Seek assistance from the nearest police station or hospital if you are able to do so.

## ● Car hire

The minimum age for renting a car is 25. Car hire companies are given in the text; they do tend to be very expensive, reflecting the high costs and accident rates. Hotels and tourist agencies will tell you where to find cheaper rates, but you will need to check that you have such basics as spare wheel, toolkit and functioning lights etc.

**Car hire insurance** Check exactly what the hirer's insurance policy covers. In many cases it will only protect you against minor bumps and scrapes, not major accidents, nor "natural" damage (eg flooding). Ask if extra cover is available. Also find out, if using a credit card, whether the card automatically includes insurance. Beware of being billed for scratches which were on the vehicle before you hired it.

## ● Motorcycling

People are generally very amicable to motorcyclists and you can make many friends by returning friendship to those who show an interest in you.

**The machine** It should be off road capable: my choice would be the BMW R80/100/GS for its rugged and simple design and reliable shaft drive, but a Kawasaki KLR 650s, Honda Transalp/Dominator, or the ubiquitous Yamaha XT600 Tenere would also be suitable. A road bike can go most places an off road bike can go at the cost of greater effort.

**Preparations** Fit heavy duty front fork springs and the best quality rebuildable shock absorber you can afford (Ohlins, White Power). Fit lockable luggage such as Krausers (reinforce luggage frames) or make some detachable aluminium panniers. Fit a tank bag and tank panniers for better weight distribution. A large capacity fuel tank (Acerbis), +300 mile/480 km range is essential if going off the beaten track. A washable air filter is a good idea (K&N), also fuel filters, fueltap rubber seals and smaller jets for high altitude Andean motoring. A good set of trails-type tyres as well as a high mudguard are useful. Get to know the bike before you go, ask the dealers in your country what goes wrong with it and arrange a link whereby you can get parts flown out to you. If riding a chain driven bike, a fully enclosed chaincase is useful. A hefty bash plate/sump guard is invaluable.

**Spares** Reduce service intervals by half if driving in severe conditions. A spare rear tyre is useful but you can buy modern tyres in Lima at least. Take oil filters, fork and shock seals, tubes, a good manual, spare cables (taped into position), a plug cap and spare plug lead. A spare electronic ignition is a good idea, try and buy a second hand one and make arrangements to have parts sent out to you. A first class tool kit is a must and if riding a bike with a chain then a spare set of sprockets and an 'o' ring chain should be carried. Spare brake and clutch levers should also be taken as these break easily in a fall. Parts are few and far between, but mechanics are skilled at making do and can usually repair things. Castrol oil can be bought everywhere and relied upon.

Take a puncture repair kit and tyre levers. Find out about any weak spots on the bike and improve them. Get the book for international dealer coverage from your manufacturer, but don't rely on it. They frequently have few or no parts for modern, large machinery.

**Clothes and equipment** A tough waterproof jacket, comfortable strong boots, gloves and a helmet with which you can use glass goggles (Halycon) which will not scratch and wear out like a plastic visor. The best quality tent and camping gear that you can afford and a petrol stove which runs on bike fuel is helpful.

**Security** Try not to leave a fully laden bike on its own. An Abus D or chain will keep the bike secure. A cheap alarm gives you peace of mind if you leave the bike outside a hotel at night. Most hotels will allow you to bring the bike inside. Look for hotels that have a courtyard or more secure parking and never leave luggage on the bike overnight or whilst unattended.

**Documents** Passport, International Driving Licence, bike registration document are necessary. Riders fare much better with a *carnet de passages* than without it.

## ● Cycling

At first glance a bicycle may not appear to be the most obvious vehicle for a major journey, but given ample time and reasonable energy it most certainly is the best. It can be ridden, carried by almost every form of transport from an aeroplane to a canoe, and can even be lifted across one's shoulders over short distances. Cyclists can be the envy of travellers using more orthodox transport, since they can travel at their own pace, explore more remote regions and meet people who are not normally in contact with tourists.

**Choosing a bicycle** The choice of bicycle depends on the type and length of expedition being undertaken and on the terrain and road surfaces likely to be encountered. Unless you are planning a journey almost exclusively on paved roads – when a high quality touring bike such as a Dawes Super Galaxy would probably suffice – a mountain bike is strongly recommended. The good quality ones (and the cast iron rule is **never** to skimp on quality) are incredibly tough and rugged, with low gear ratios for difficult terrain, wide tyres with plenty of tread for good road-holding, cantilever brakes, and a low centre of gravity for improved stability. Although touring bikes, and to a lesser extent mountain bikes, and spares are available in the larger cities, remember that most indigenous manufactured goods are shoddy and rarely last. Buy everything you possibly can before you leave home.

**Bicycle equipment** A small but comprehensive tool kit (to include chain rivet and crank removers, a spoke key and possibly a block remover), a spare tyre and inner tubes, a puncture repair kit with plenty of extra patches and glue, a set of brake blocks, brake and gear cables and all types of nuts and bolts, at least 12 spokes (best taped to the chain stay), a light oil for the chain (eg Finish-Line Teflon Dry-Lube), tube of waterproof grease, a pump secured by a pump lock, a Blackburn parking block (a most invaluable accessory, cheap and virtually weightless), a cyclometer, a loud bell, and a secure lock and chain. *Richard's Bicycle Book* makes useful reading for even the most mechanically minded.

**Luggage and equipment** Strong and waterproof front and back panniers are a must. When packed these are likely to be heavy and should be carried on the strongest racks available. Poor quality racks have ruined many a journey for they take incredible strain on unpaved roads. A top bag cum rucksack (eg Carradice) makes a good addition for use on and off the bike. A Cannondale front bag is good for maps, camera, compass, altimeter, notebook and small tape-recorder. (Other rec panniers are Ortlieb – front and back – which is waterpoof and almost "sandproof", Mac-Pac, Madden and Karimoor.) "Gaffa" tape is excellent for protecting vulnerable parts of panniers and for carrying out all manner of repairs.

All equipment and clothes should be packed in plastic bags to give extra protection against dust and rain. (Also protect all documents, etc carried close to the body from sweat.) Always take the minimum clothing. It's better to buy extra items en route when you find you need them. Generally it is best to carry several layers of thin light clothes than fewer heavy, bulky ones. Always keep one set of dry clothes, including long trousers, to put on at the end of the day. The incredibly light, strong, waterproof and wind resistant goretex jacket and overtrousers are invaluable. Training shoes can be used for both cycling and walking.

**Useful tips** Wind, not hills is the enemy of the cyclist. Try to make the best use of the times of day when there is little; mornings tend to be best but there is no steadfast rule. Take care to avoid dehydration, by drinking regularly. In hot, dry areas with limited supplies of water, be sure to carry an ample supply. For food, carry the staples (sugar, salt, dried milk, tea, coffee, porridge oats, raisins, dried soups, etc) and supplemented these with whatever local foods can be found in the markets. Give your bicycle a thorough daily check for loose nuts or bolts or bearings. See that all parts run smoothly. A good chain should last 2,000 miles, 3,200 km or more but be sure to keep it as clean as possible – an old toothbrush is good for this – and to oil it lightly from time to time. Remember that thieves are attracted to towns and cities, so when sight-seeing, try to leave your bicycle with someone such as a café owner or a priest. Country people tend to be more honest and are usually friendly and very inquisitive. However, don't take unnecessary risks; always see that your bicycle is secure (most hotels will allow bikes to be kept in rooms). In more remote regions dogs can be vicious; carry a stick or some small stones to frighten them off. Traffic on main roads can be a nightmare; it is usually far more rewarding to keep to the smaller roads or to paths if they exist. Most towns have a bicycle shop of some description, but it is best to do your own repairs and adjustments whenever possible.

The Expedition Advisory Centre, administered by the Royal Geographical Society, 1, Kensington Gore, London SW7 2AR has published a useful monograph entitled *Bicycle Expeditions*, by Paul Vickers. Published in March 1990, it is available direct from the Centre, price £6.50 (postage extra if outside the UK). (In the UK there is also the Cyclist's Touring Club, CTC, Cotterell House, 69 Meadrow, Godalming, Surrey, GU7 3HS, T 01483-417217, e-mail cycling@ctc.org.uk, for touring, and technical information.)

Most cyclists agree that the main danger comes from other traffic. A rearview mirror has been frequently recommended to forewarn you of vehicles which are too close behind. You also need to watch out for oncoming, overtaking vehicles, unstable loads on trucks, protruding loads etc. Make yourself conspicuous by wearing bright clothing and a helmet.

## ● Bus

Services along the coast and to Arequipa are usually quite good, but try to avoid travel at night, assaults on buses have occurred; buses in the mountain areas generally are small, old, crowded and offer little comfort; Ormeño and Cruz del Sur thought generally to be the best. The larger companies are usually the best as they tend not to cancel services; the smaller companies will cancel if they do not have enough passengers. The main companies (and some others) have luxury services on the coastal routes, with toilet, video and reclining seats. Tickets cost 30% more than normal. For bus lines, see Lima, **Bus companies**. For long journeys take a water bottle. Blankets and emergency food are a *must* in the mountains. Always possible to buy food on the roadside, as buses stop frequently. Luggage can be checked in on a bus, but it is your own responsibility to look after it when the bus stops. Backpacks can be protected by a rice sack, for further security use chicken wire as well. Always carry your valuables with you, even when leaving the bus at a stop. If your bus breaks down and you are transferred to another line and have to pay extra, keep your original ticket for refund from the first company. If possible, on country buses avoid the back seats because of the bumpiness, and the left side because of exhaust fumes. Prices given in the text are the minimum for the route. Colectivos usually charge twice the bus fare. They leave only when full. They go almost anywhere in Peru; most firms have offices. Book 1 day in advance. They pick you up at your hotel or in the main plaza. Trucks are not always much cheaper than buses; they charge ¾ bus fare, but wholly unpredictable, not for long hops, and comfort depends on the load. Always try to arrive at your destination in daylight: much safer.

**NB** Prices of bus tickets are raised by 50-75%, 2-3 days before 28 July (Independence Day) and Christmas. Tickets are sold out 2-3 days in advance at this time and transport is hard to come by.

## ● Hitchhiking

Hitchhiking is difficult. Freight traffic has to stop at the police *garitas* outside each town and these are the best places to try (also toll points, but these are further from towns). Drivers usually ask for money but don't always expect to get it. In mountain and jungle areas you usually have to pay drivers of lorries, vans and even private cars; ask the driver first how much he is going to charge, and then recheck with the locals. Private cars are very few and far between. Readers report that mining trucks are especially dirty to travel in, avoid if possible.

## ● Taxi

Taxi prices are fixed in the mountain towns, about US$0.80 in the urban area. Fares are not fixed in Lima even though there are standard fares (see under Lima). Most taxi drivers will try to charge more for foreigners, so ask locals. The main cities have taxis which can be hired by phone, which charge a little more, but are reliable and safe.

Many taxi drivers work for commission from hotels. Choose your own hotel and get a taxi driver who is willing to take you there.

Taxis at airports are always more expensive; seek advice about the price in advance and do not use the taxis in front of the airport.

## COMMUNICATIONS

### ● Language

Spanish. Quechua, the language of the Inca empire, has been given some official status and there is much pride in its use; it is spoken by millions of Sierra Indians who have little or no knowledge of Spanish. Another important Indian language is Aymara, used in the area around Lake Titicaca.

### ● Newspapers

Lima has several morning papers: *La Nación*, *El Comercio* (good international news), *La República* (liberal-left), *Expreso*, *Ojo*, *El Mundo*; *El Peruano* (with parliamentary gazette); *Síntesis* and *Gestión* are business dailies. Weekly magazines are *Caretas* and *Sí*; monthlies include *Business*, *Proceso Económico*, *Debate* and *Idede*. There is a monthly magazine in English, the *Lima Times*, with useful information and articles, and a weekly economic and political report, the *Andean Report*. The main provincial cities have at least one newspaper each.

### ● Postal services

Sending parcels abroad must be done at Centro de Clasificación de Correos, Tomás Valle, block 600, Lima (take bus 128, direction San Germán); open Mon-Fri 0900-1330, Sat 0800-1300. Staff in the post office help with all checking and then sew parcels into sacks for US$1. It can cost about US$20/kg to send a parcel abroad. To avoid paying a tax of US$0.20/kg on parcels sent abroad, take your passport and onward ticket, plus a photocopy of each to the post office. To send a letter anywhere in the Americas costs US$0.80, to the rest of the world US$0.90. For US$0.50 extra letters can be sent 'con certificado', which is rec. A Dutch company called EMS are reliable for sending smaller packages, eg film, home. Expensive US$34/kilo (to Europe). More expensive still is UPS; see under Lima, **Air Freight**.

To receive mail, letters can be sent to Poste Restante/General Delivery (*lista de correos*), your embassy, or, for cardholders, American Express offices. Remember that there is no W in Spanish; look under V, or ask. For the smallest risk of misunderstanding, use title, initial and surname only. If having items sent to you by courier (eg DHL), do not use poste restante, but an address such as a hotel: a signature is required on receipt. Try not to have articles sent by post to Peru; taxes can be 200% of the value.

### ● Radio

**World Band Radio** South America has more local and community radio stations than practically anywhere else in the world; a shortwave (world band) radio offers a practical means to brush up on the language, sample popular culture and absorb some of the richly varied regional music. International broadcasters such as the BBC World Service, the Voice of America, Boston (Mass)-based Monitor Radio International (operated by *Christian Science Monitor*) and the Quito-based Evangelical station, HCJB, keep the traveller abreast of news and events, in both English and Spanish.

Compact or miniature portables are recommended, with digital tuning and a full range of shortwave bands, as well as FM, long and medium wave. Detailed advice on radio models (£150 for a decent one) and wavelengths can be found in the annual publication, *Passport to World Band Radio* (Box 300, Penn's Park, PA 18943, USA). Details of local stations is listed in *World TV and Radio Handbook* (WTRH), PO Box 9027, 1006 AA Amsterdam, The Netherlands, US$19.95. Both of these, free wavelength guides and selected radio sets are available from the BBC World Service Bookshop, Bush House Arcade, Bush House, Strand, London WC2B 4PH, UK, T 0171-257 2576.

### ● Telephone services

The state company, Entel, has been privatized and is now called Telefónica del Perú. There are offices in all large and medium-sized towns. Overseas calls made through the operator cost on average US$12 for 3 mins (minimum). Collect calls can now be made (most of the time) to North America and some European countries at the CPT office on Plaza San Martín, Lima, or elsewhere from Telefónica offices. The best place to try is Lima. Local, national and international calls can be made from public phone boxes with coins or phone cards which can be bought at Telefónica offices (though cards don't work everywhere). Telephone directories found in most hotel rooms have a useful map of Lima and show itineraries of the buses. Fax and telex abroad can be sent from major Telefónica offices, US$4-5/page/minute. (See also Lima, **Telecommunication**.)

**NB** At the end of 1994 an extra digit was added to Lima phone numbers, which now have 7 digits. Throughout the rest of the country, all phone numbers are being changed and should have 6 digits. Visitors to Peru are advised to check numbers when they are in the country.

## SPORT

Association football is the most popular. Basketball and other sports are also played on the coast, particularly around Lima and Callao. Golf clubs and racecourses are mentioned in the text. Riding is a favourite recreation in the Sierra, where horses can be hired at reasonable rates. Cricket is played at the Lima Cricket Club. Bullfights and cockfights are held throughout the country. There is excellent deep-sea fishing off Ancón, N of Lima, and at the small port of Cabo Blanco, N of Talara (see text). In that part of the Andes easily reached from La Oroya, the lakes and streams have been stocked with trout, and fly fishing is quite good.

For details about the best rainbow trout fishing in Peru (near Juliaca and in Lakes Arapa and Titicaca) write to Sr José Bernal Paredes, Casilla 874, Arequipa.

**Swimming** Between Dec and April the entire coast of Peru offers good bathing, but during the rest of the year only the northern beaches near Tumbes provide pleasantly warm water. There are many bathing resorts near Lima (do not swim at, or even visit, these beaches alone). The current off the coast can be very strong, making it too dangerous to swim in places. A Foptur brochure lists the many surfing beaches.

**Walking** The South American Explorers Club has good information and advice on trekking and sells books. Serious walkers are advised to get *Backpacking and Trekking in Peru and Bolivia* (Bradt Publications, T/F (UK) 01494-873478) which describes 3-5 day treks in the Cordilleras Blanca, Vilcabamba and Vilcanota (Cusco region), and in the Cajamarca area (6th edition, 1995). *The Peruvian Andes*, by Philipe Béaud, is a good guide, describing 100 climbs and 40 treks in Spanish, French and English. John Richter's *Yurak Yunka* can be obtained from the South American Explorers' Club or from *Lima 2000* bookshop, J Bernal 271, Lima. For an account of the Andean Inca road, see Christopher Portway, *Journey Along the Andes* (Impact Books, London, 1993).

The popular trekking routes in Peru are becoming damaged because of over use. Little is done by the government to maintain the trails and less is done by locals. Trekkers are given no information and no guards control the routes. A few conservation groups are trying to combat this problem, but with very little success. Please give everyone a good example by not dropping litter and by picking up that left by others. Point out the importance of this to guides and porters.

## HOLIDAYS AND FESTIVALS

1 Jan: New Year. Mar or April: Maundy Thursday (pm). Good Friday. 1 May: Labour Day. 29 June: Saints Peter and Paul. 28, 29 July: Independence (when all prices go up). 30 Aug: Santa Rosa de Lima. 7 Oct: Battle of Angamos. 1 Nov: All Saints. 8 Dec: Immaculate Conception. 25 Dec: Christmas.

**NB** Everything closes on New Year's Eve, Christmas Eve, and other holidays designated 'family holidays', especially July-Aug. At these times, expect prices to rise. Also note that the Fujimori administration has decreed that when a public holiday falls on a day in mid-week it will be moved to the following Mon.

Between mid-July and the beginning of Sept is the Peruvian tourist season: prices rise, transport can be difficult and hotels are heavily booked. The big national holidays are Dec, Jan and Feb.

# Rounding up



## ACKNOWLEDGEMENTS


For their help and hospitality in Peru in Oct/Nov 1995, during the preliminary research for this Handbook, Alan Murphy wishes to thank the following (in chronological order): Jaime Acevedo of Casa de Jaime restaurant, Iquitos; Carlos Manco Aedo, Ayacucho; Alberto and Haydeé Cafferata of Pony's Travel, Caraz; Lucio Canicoba, Yungay; Cumbe Mayo Tours in Cajamarca; Clara Bravo Díaz and Michael White, Trujillo; Felipe Díaz, Caraz; Victor Echeverray and Mariano Araya of the Archaeology Museum, Caraz; Richard Elgar and Bill Glick of the South American Explorers' Club, Lima; Henry and Carlos at Hostal de las Artes, Lima; Peter Jensen, Explorama Tours, Iquitos; Kaly Tours, Chiclayo; Cecilia Kamiche of Ideal Travels and James Vreeland, Arequipa; Edwin Medina Latorre, Puerto Maldonado; Rosana Martínez, Lima; Julio Olazo of Mountain Bike Adventures, Huaraz; Edwin Godoy Pérez, Iquitos; 'Pocho de los Andes' of Monttrek, Huaraz; Francisco Guillén Valencia, Ayacucho; Prof René Valencia, director of Huascarán National Park; Selio Villón of Casa de Guías, Huaraz; Maggy Yncio of Indiana Tours, Chiclayo.

Ben Box who visited Peru in Sept/Oct 1995, would like to thank the following: Richard Elgar and Bill Glick; Nieves de la Cruz de Kaufer, Stephen Kaufer, Rubén de la Cruz Llanos and Rubén de la Cruz Vilches, Lima and Lunahuaná; Alcalde Daniel de la Cruz, Lunahuaná; Nicholas Asheshov and family and Ana María Burga, Hotel Valle Sagrado de los Inkas, Urubamba; Alfonso Amaut, Cusco; Ken Duncan, Huayllabamba; Efraín Alegría, Nasca; Dra María Judith de Chusiwaccha, Pisco; María Lazarte (Foptur), Rosa Sheen Ortega (Canatur) and the staff and participants of the Peru Travel Mart; Carlos Rosell, Apavit, Lima; George Nicholson Árias and Carmen Azurin of the Peruvian Consulate, London.

For their invaluable help in the preparation of the text of this Handbook, thanks in addition go to Robert and Daisy Kunstaetter (Latin American Travel Consultants, Quito): for their support and friendship and help in researching the Callejón de Huaylas and Northern Coast.

Richard Elgar and Bill Glick at South American Explorers Club, Lima: for their support and hospitality and help in researching Chachapoyas region, Mantaro Valley, Huancayo, Tacna and Juliaca, and, of course, Lima's seafood restaurants.

Simon Harvey and Mark Duffy: for writing the introductory article on Adventure Sports, and for travelling to and researching

Pucallpa, the Huallaga Valley, Cotahuasi Canyon, the Callejón de Huaylas and the Mantaro Valley.

Michael White and Clara Bravo Díaz, Trujillo.

Cecilia Kamiche and James Vreeland in Arequipa.

"Pocho de los Andes" at MontTrek in Huaraz.

Jaime Acevedo for help in researching Iquitos.

Rubén de la Cruz Llanos, Rubén de la Cruz Vilches and Nieves de la Cruz de Kaufer in Lima and Lunahuaná.

Mariella Bernasconi for help with the Cusco section.

Efraín Alegría for help with the Nasca section.

Nicholas Asheshov, Urubamba, for assistance with the Sacred Valley section.

Peter Pollard and Charlie Nurse for their contributions.

Also Valerie Fraser and Nigel Dunstone, and Mo Fini and Lucy Davies at Tumi. Peter Frost for his contributions in the Cusco chapter. John Forrest of TreeS for his article on Tambopata. George Nicholson at the Peruvian Consulate in London. And not forgetting Ben Box!

Thanks are also due to all the travellers and correspondents who contributed to the 1997 edition of the *South American Handbook*.

## FURTHER READING

*The Ancient Civilizations of Peru*, J. Alden Mason, 1991.

*The Prehispanic Cultures of Peru*, Justo Caceres Macedo, 1988.

*Chachapoyas; The Cloud People*, Morgan Davis, 1988.

*The Conquest of the Incas*, John Hemming, 1972.

*The City of Kings: A guide to Lima*, Carolyn Walton, 1987.

*Lima monumental*, Margarita Cubillas Soriano, 1993.

*Exploring Cusco*, Peter Frost.

*Cut Stones and Crossroads: a Journey in Peru*, Ronald Wright, 1984.

For information on the Nasca Lines, see the Box 'Mystery of the lines'.

Many general books contain information on Peru (for instance *The Cambridge Encylopedia of Latin America and the Caribbean*, edited by Simon Collier, Thomas E Skidmore and Harold Blakemore, 2nd edition 1992, and *The Penguin History of Latin America*, Edwin Williamson, 1992) and there are many periodicals which specialize in Peru: consult a good library for those which cover your particular interest. Consistently interesting is *South American Explorer*, published quarterly by the South American Explorers Club, 126 Indian Creek Road, Ithaca, NY 14850, T (607) 277-0488.

See the **Literature** section for recommendations. Mentioned in the source list is the *Peru Reader*, which, besides literature, also contains history, culture and politics and is an excellent introduction to these topics; the anthology ranges from the precolonial to the present.

See the **Adventure tourism** section for various relevant bibliographies.

Business travellers are advised to get *Hints to Exporters: Peru*, from DTI Export Publications, PO Box 55, Stratford-upon-Avon, Warwickshire, CV37 9GE.

## MAPS AND GUIDE BOOKS

Several good maps are mentioned in the **Maps** section in the Lima chapter and the **Motoring** section of **Information for travellers**. It is also a good idea to get as many as possible in your home country before leaving, especially if travelling by land. A recommended series of general maps is that published by International Travel Map Productions (ITM), 345 West Broadway, Vancouver BC, V5Y 1P8, Canada, T (604) 879-3621, F (604) 879-4521, compiled with historical notes, by the late Kevin Healey. Relevant to this Handbook are South America North West (1:4M) and Amazon Basin (1:4M). Another map series that has been mentioned is that of New World Edition, Bertelsmann, Neumarkter Strasse 18, 81673 München, Germany, *Südamerika Nord*, *Südamerika Sud* (both 1:4M). For information on Bradt Publications' Backpacking Guide Series, other titles and imported maps and guides, contact 41 Norloft Road, Chalfont St Peter, Bucks, SL9 0LA, UK, T/F 01494 873478. Relevant to this Handbook are *Backpacking and Trekking in Peru and Bolivia*, by Hilary Bradt, 6th edition 1995, and *Central and South America by Road*, by Pam Ascanio, 1996.

A very useful book, highly recommended, aimed specifically at the budget traveller is *The Tropical Traveller*, by John Hatt (Penguin Books, 3rd edition, 1993).

**The Latin American Travel Advisor** is a quarterly news bulletin with up-to-date detailed and reliable information on countries throughout South and Central America. The publication focuses on public safety, health, weather and natural phenomena, travel costs, the economy and politics in each country. Annual airmail subscriptions US$39, a single current issue US$15, information transmitted by fax or e-mail US$10 per country. Payment by US$ cheque, Mastercard or Visa (no money orders, credit card payments by mail or fax with card number, expiry date, cardholder's name and signature). Contact PO Box 17-17-908, Quito, Ecuador, F 593-2-562-566. Internet LATA@pi.pro.ec, World Wide Web http://www.amerispan.com/latc or http://www.greenarrow.com/latc.htm.

# Useful addresses

## EMBASSIES AND CONSULATES

**Australia**
9 Floor, 197 London Circuit, Canberra City, ACT 2601, T (61-62) 2572953, F (61-62) 25775198

**Argentina**
Av del Libertador 1720; 1425 Capital Federal, T (54-1) 8022000, F (54-1) 8025887; Consulates: Córdoba, La Plata

**Bolivia**
Edificio Alianza, Mezanine, Fernando Guachalla y 6 de Agosto, Sopocachi, La Paz, T (591-2) 353550, F (591-2) 367640; Consulate: Santa Cruz

**Brazil**
Av Das Naçes, Lote 43, 70428 900 Brasília DF, T (55-61) 2429933, F (55-61) 2435677; Consulates: Rio de Janeiro, So Paulo, Manaus

**Canada**
130 Albert Street, Suite 1901 Ottawa, Ontario KAIP 5G4, T 1-(613) 288-1777, F: 1-(613) 2323062; Consulates: Toronto, Montreal and Vancouver

**Chile**
Av Andrés Bello 1751, Providencia, Santiago, T (56-2) 2356451, F (56-2) 2358139

**Colombia**
Carrera 10 No 93-48, Bogotá, T (57-1) 2189212, F (57-1) 6235102

**Costa Rica**
Del Auto Mercado de los Yoses 300 mts, Sur y 75 mts, Oeste, San José, T (506) 2259145, F (506) 2530457

**Ecuador**
Av Amazonas No 1429 esq Colón, Edificio España. Penthouse, Quito, T (593-2) 554161, F (593-2) 562349

**France**
50, Av. Kleber, Paris 75116, T (33-1) 47043453, F (33-1) 47559830

**Germany**
Godesberger Allee 125-127, 53175 Bonn, T (49-228) 373045, F (49-228) 379475; Consulate in Berlin, Schadowtrasse, 6, 10117 Berlin, T (49-30) 2291455, F ( 49-30) 2292857

**Guatemala**
Segunda Avenida 9-67 Zona 9, Guatemala, Guatemala 01009, T (502-2) 318558, F (502-2) 343744

**Hong Kong**
10th Floor Wong Chung Ming Commercial House, 16 Wyndham Street, Central Hong Kong, T (852) 28682622, F (852) 28400733

**Israel**
37, Revov Ha-Marganit Shikun Vatikim, 52 584 Ramat Gan, T (972-3) 6135591, F (972-3) 7512286

**Italy**
Via Po, 22, 00198 Roma, T (39-6) 8416556, F (39-6) 85354447; Consulate in Milan, Via Giacosa 31; 20127 Milan, T (39-2) 26821276, F (39-2) 26821752

**Japan**
4-4-27 Higashi, Shibuya-Ku, Tokio 150, T (81-3) 34064240, F (81-3) 34097589

**Korea**
Namhan Building, Sixth Floor, 76-42 Hannam Dong, Yongsan-Ku, Se£l, T (82-2) 7935810, F (82-2) 7973736

### Malaysia
Peti Nro. 18, Wisma, Selangor Dredoing, 6th, Floor, South Block 142 - A Jalan Ampang, 50450 Kuala Lumpur, Post box No. 18, T (603) 2633034/26330, F (603) 2633039

### Mexico
Paseo de la Reforma 2601, Lomas Reforma, CP 11020 Mexico DF, T (52-5) 5702443, F (52-5) 2590530

### Singapore
390, Orchard Road No 12-03, Singapore 0923, Palais Renaissance, T (65) 7388595/7388740, F (65) 7388601

### South Africa
Infotech Building, Suite 202, 1090 Arcadia Street 0083, Hatfield, Pretoria, T (27-12) 3422390, F (27-12) 3424449

### Spain
Principe de Vergara No. 36, 5o Derecha, 28001 Madrid, T (34-1) 4314242, 4314424, F (34-1) 5776861; Consulate in Barcelona, Av Diagonal Nro 441, Barcelona 08036, T (34-3) 4103833, F (34-3) 4192847

### Sweden
Brunnsgatan 21-B, 111 38 Estocolmo, T (46-8) 4110019, F (46-8) 205592

### Switzerland
Thunstrasse No 36, CH-3005, Berne, T (41-31) 3518555, F (41-31) 3518570

### UK
52 Sloane Street, London SW1X 9SP, T 0171 235 1917, F 0171 235 4463

### Uruguay
Soriano 1124, Montevideo, T (598-2) 921046, F (598-2) 921194

### USA
1700 Massachusetts Avenue, NW, Washington DC 200036, T 1-(202) 833-9860 al 833-9869, F 1-(202) 785-0933; Consulates: Chicago, Houston, Los Angeles, Miami, New York, Paterson, Puerto Rico, San Francisco.

### Venezuela
Centro Empresarial Andrés Bello, Torre Oeste, Piso 7, Sector Maripérez, Caracas, T (58-2) 793-7974, F (58-2) 7936705

## TOURIST BOARD

***Promperú*** (tourism promotion and information), Calle 1 Oeste s/n, Edificio MITINCI, piso 13 (Urb Corpac), Lima 27, Peru. T (1) 224-3279/224-3125/224-3271, F (1) 224-3323. URL: http://www.rcp.net.pe/promperu; e-mail postmaster@promperu.gob.pe.

24-hour hotline for travellers' complaints, (1) 224-7888, or toll-free 0-800-4-2579.

**Ministerio de Industria, Comercio, Comercio, Turismo e Integración**, Calle 1 Oeste, Corpac, piso 14, F 442-9280.

Outside Peru, tourism matters are handled by the embassies and consulates of Peru.

## SPECIALIST TOUR COMPANIES

### Journey Latin America
16 Devonshire Road, Chiswick, London W4 2HD, T 0181-747 3108. Long established company running escorted tours throughout the region. They also offer a wide range of flight options.

### Trailfinders
48 Earl's Court Road, London W8 6EJ, T 0171-938 3366.

### South American Experience
47 Causton Street, Pimlico, London SW1P 4AT, T 0171 976 5511, F 0171 986 6908. Apart from booking flights and accommodation, also offer tailor-made trips.

### Last Frontiers
Swan House, High Street, Long Crendon, Buckinghamshire, HP18 9AF, T 01844 208405

### Passage to South America
Fovant Mews, 12 Nonya Road, London SW17 7PH, T 0181-767 8989. Wide range of tailor-made packages throughout the region including the lost kingdom of the Incas.

### STA Travel
Priory House, 6 Wrights Lane, London W8 6TA, T 0171-938 4711

### Cox & Kings Travel
St James Court, 45 Buckingham Gate, London, T 0171-873 5001

**Ladatco Tours**
Based in Miami, run "themed" explorer tours based around the Incas, mysticism etc. T USA (305) 854-8422 or F (305) 285-0504.

**Hayes & Jarvis**
152 King Street, London W6, T 0171 222 7844. Long established operator. Offers tailor-made itineries as well as packages.

**Adventure Travel Centre**
131-135 Earls Court Road, London, SW5 9RH, organises short tours as well as longer expeditions.

**Explore Worldwide**
1 Frederick Street, Aldershot, Hants GU11 1LQ, T 01252 344161, F 01252 343170. Highly respected operator with offices in Eire, Australia,New Zealand, USA and Canada who run 2-5 week tours in more than 90 countries worldwide including Peru.

# Useful words and phrases

NO AMOUNT of dictionaries, phrase books or word lists will provide the same enjoyment as being able to communicate directly with the people of the country you are visiting. Learning Spanish is an important part of the preparation for any trip to Peru and you are encouraged to make an effort to grasp the basics before you go. As you travel you will pick up more of the language and the more you know, the more you will benefit from your stay. The following section is designed to be a simple point of departure.

## General pronunciation

The stress in a Spanish word conforms to one of three rules: 1) if the word ends in a vowel, or in **n** or **s**, the accent falls on the penultimate syllable (*vent**a**na, vent**a**nas*); 2) if the word ends in a consonant other than **n** or **s**, the accent falls on the last syllable (*habl**a**r*); 3) if the word is to be stressed on a syllable contrary to either of the above rules, the acute accent on the relevant vowel indicates where the stress is to be placed (*pantal**ó**n, met**á**fora*). Note that adverbs such as *cuando*, 'when', take an accent when used interrogatively: *¿cuándo?*, 'when?'

## Vowels

**a** not quite as short as in English 'cat'

**e** as in English 'pay', but shorter in a syllable ending in a consonant

**i** as in English 'seek'

**o** as in English 'shop', but more like 'pope' when the vowel ends a syllable

**u** as in English 'food'; after 'q' and in 'gue', 'gui', **u** is unpronounced; in 'güe' and 'güi' it is pronounced

**y** when a vowel, pronounced like 'i'; when a semiconsonant or consonant, it is pronounced like English 'yes'

**ai, ay** as in English 'ride'

**ei, ey** as in English 'they'

**oi, oy** as in English 'toy'

Unless listed below **consonants** can be pronounced in Spanish as they are in English.

**b, v** their sound is interchangeable and is a cross between the English 'b' and 'v', except at the beginning of a word or after 'm' or 'n' when it is like English 'b'

**c** like English 'k', except before 'e' or 'i' when it is as the 's' in English 'sip'

**g** before 'e' and 'i' it is the same as **j**

**h** when on its own, never pronounced

**j** as the 'ch' in the Scottish 'loch'

**ll** as the 'g' in English 'beige'; sometimes as the 'lli' in 'million'

**ñ** as the 'ni' in English 'onion'

**rr** trilled much more strongly than in English

**x** depending on its location, pronounced as in English 'fox', or 'sip', or like 'gs'

**z** as the 's' in English 'sip'

## GREETINGS, COURTESIES

**hello**
hola
**good morning**
buenos días
**good afternoon/evening/night**
buenas tardes/noches
**goodbye**
adiós/chao
**see you later**
hasta luego
**how are you?**
¿cómo está?/¿cómo estás?
**pleased to meet you**
mucho gusto/encantado/encantada
**please**
por favor
**thank you (very much)**
(muchas) gracias
**yes**
sí
**no**
no
**excuse me/I beg your pardon**
permiso
**I do not understand**
no entiendo
**please speak slowly**
hable despacio por favor
**what is your name**
¿cómo se llama?
**Go away!**
¡Váyase!

## BASIC QUESTIONS

**where is_?**
¿dónde está_?
**how much does it cost?**
¿cuánto cuesta?
**how much is it?**
¿cuánto es?
**when?**
¿cuándo?
**when does the bus leave?**
¿a qué hora sale el autobus?
**- arrive?**
- llega -
**why?**
¿por qué?
**what for?**
¿para qué?
**what time is it?**
¿qué hora es?
**how do I get to_?**
¿cómo llegar a_?
**is this the way to the church?**
¿la iglesia está por aquí?

## BASICS

**bathroom/toilet**
el baño
**police (policeman)**
la policía (el policía)
**hotel**
el hotel (la pensión,el residencial, el alojamiento)
**restaurant**
el restaurante
**post office**
el correo
**telephone office**
el centro de llamadas
**supermarket**
el supermercado
**bank**
el banco
**exchange house**
la casa de cambio
**exchange rate**
la tasa de cambio
**notes/coins**
los billetes/las monedas
**travellers' cheques**
los travelers/los cheques de viajero
**cash**
el efectivo
**breakfast**
el desayuno
**lunch**
el almuerzo
**dinner/supper**
la cena
**meal**
la comida
**drink**
la bebida

**mineral water**
el agua mineral
**soft fizzy drink**
la gaseosa/cola
**beer**
la cerveza
**without sugar**
sin azúcar
**without meat**
sin carne

**Getting around**
**on the left/right**
a la izquierda/derecha
**straight on**
derecho
**second street on the left**
la segunda calle a la izquierda
**to walk**
caminar
**bus station**
la terminal (terrestre)
**train station**
la estación (de tren/ferrocarril)
**bus**
el bus/el autobus/ la flota/el colectivo/ el micro etc
**train**
el tren
**airport**
el aeropuerto
**aeroplane/airplane**
el avión
**first/second class**
primera/segunda clase
**ticket**
el boleto
**ticket office**
la taquilla
**bus stop**
la parada

## ACCOMMODATION

**room**
el cuarto/la habitación
**single/double**
sencillo/doble
**with two beds**
con dos camas
**with private bathroom**
con baño
**hot/cold water**
agua caliente/fría
**noisy**
ruidoso
**to make up/clean**
limpiar
**sheets**
las sábanas
**blankets**
las mantas
**pillows**
las almohadas
**clean/dirty towels**
toallas limpias/sucias
**toilet paper**
el papel higiénico
**Chemist**
farmacia
**(for) pain**
(para) dolor
**stomach**
el estómago
**head**
la cabeza
**fever/sweat**
la fiebre/el sudor
**diarrhoea**
la diarrea
**blood**
la sangre
**altitude sickness**
el soroche
**doctor**
el médico
**condoms**
los preservativos
**contraceptive (pill)**
anticonceptivo (la píldora anticonceptiva)
**period/towels**
la regla/las toallas
**contact lenses**
las lentes de contacto
**aspirin**
la aspirina

## TIME

**at one o'clock**
a la una
**at half past two/ two thirty**
a las dos y media
**at a quarter to three**
a cuarto para las tres
or a las tres menos quince
**it's one o'clock**
es la una

**it's seven o'clock**
son las siete
**it's twenty past six/ six twenty**
son las seis y veinte
**it's five to nine**
son cinco para las nueve/ son las nueve menos cinco
**in ten minutes**
en diez minutos
**five hours**
cinco horas
**does it take long?**
¿tarda mucho?
**Monday** lunes
**Tuesday** martes
**Wednesday** miercoles
**Thursday** jueves
**Friday** viernes
**Saturday** sábado
**Sunday** domingo
**January** enero
**February** febrero
**March** marzo
**April** abril
**May** mayo
**June** junio
**July** julio
**August** agosto
**September** septiembre
**October** octubre
**November** noviembre
**December** diciembre

## NUMBERS

**one** uno/una
**two** dos
**three** tres
**four** cuatro
**five** cinco
**six** seis
**seven** siete
**eight** ocho
**nine** nueve
**ten** diez
**eleven** once
**twelve** doce
**thirteen** trece
**fourteen** catorce
**fifteen** quince
**sixteen** dieciseis
**seventeen** diecisiete
**eighteen** dieciocho
**nineteen** diecinueve
**twenty** veinte
**twenty one, two** veintiuno, veintidos etc
**thirty** treinta
**forty** cuarenta
**fifty** cincuenta
**sixty** sesenta
**seventy** setenta
**eighty** ochenta
**ninety** noventa
**hundred** cien or ciento
**thousand** mil

## KEY VERBS

**To Go**
ir
I go voy; you go (familiar singular) vas; he, she, it goes, you (unfamiliar singular) go va; we go vamos; they, you (plural) go van.

**To Have** (possess)
tener
tengo; tienes; tiene; tenemos; tienen (also used as To Be, as in 'I am hungry' tengo hambre)
(**NB** haber also means to have, but is used with other verbs, as in 'he has gone' ha ido. he; has; ha; hemos; han.
Hay means 'there is'; perhaps more common is No hay meaning 'there isn't any')

**To Be** (in a permanent state)
ser
soy (profesor - I am a teacher); eres; es; somos; son

**To Be (positional or temporary state)**
estar
estoy (en Londres - I am in London); estás; está (contenta - she is happy); estamos; están.

*This section has been compiled on the basis of glossaries compiled by André de Mendonça and David Gilmour of South American Experience, London, and the Latin American Travel Advisor, No 9, March 1996.*

# Health in Latin America

WITH the following advice and precautions you should keep as healthy as you do at home. Most visitors return home having experienced no problems at all apart from some travellers' diarrhoea. In Latin America the health risks, especially in the lowland tropical areas, are different from those encountered in Europe or the USA. It also depends on where and how you travel. There are clear health differences between the countries of Latin America and in risks for the business traveller, who stays in international class hotels in large cities, the backpacker trekking from country to country and the tourist who heads for the beach. There is huge variation in climate, vegetation and wildlife from the deserts of Chile to the rain forests of Amazonia and from the icy remoteness of Andean peaks, to the teeming capital cities. There are no hard and fast rules to follow; you will often have to make your own judgment on the healthiness or otherwise of your surroundings. There are English (or other foreign language) speaking doctors in most major cities who have particular experience in dealing with locally-occurring diseases. Your Embassy representative will often be able to give you the name of local reputable doctors and most of the better hotels have a doctor on standby. If you do fall ill and cannot find a recommended doctor, try the Outpatient Department of a hospital – private hospitals are usually less crowded and offer a more acceptable standard of care to foreigners.

## BEFORE TRAVELLING

Take out medical insurance. Make sure it covers all eventualities especially evacuation to your home country by a medically equipped plane, if necessary. You should have a dental check up, obtain a spare glasses prescription, a spare oral contraceptive prescription (or enought pills to last) and, if you suffer from a chronic illness (such as diabetes, high blood pressure, ear or sinus troubles, cardio-pulmonary disease or nervous disorder) arrange for a check up with your doctor, who can at the same time provide you with a letter explaining the details of your disability in English and if possible Spanish and/or Portuguese. Check the current practice in countries you are visiting for malaria prophylaxis (prevention). If you are on regular medication, make sure you have enough to cover the period of your travel.

### Children

More preparation is probably necessary for babies and children than for an adult and perhaps a little more care should be taken when travelling to remote areas where health services are primitive. This is because children can be become more rapidly ill than adults (on the other hand they often recover more quickly). Diarrhoea and vomiting are the most common problems, so take the usual precautions, but more intensively. Breastfeeding is best and most convenient for babies, but powdered milk is generally available and so are baby foods in most countries. Papaya, bananas and avocados are all nutritious and can be cleanly prepared. The treatment of diarrhoea is the same for adults, except that it should start earlier and be continued with more persistence. Children get dehydrated very quickly in hot countries and can become drowsy and uncooperative unless cajoled to drink water or juice plus salts. Upper respiratory infections, such as colds, catarrh and middle ear infections are also common and if your child suffers from these normally take some antibiotics against the possibility. Outer ear infections after swimming are also common and antibiotic eardrops will help. Wet wipes are always useful and sometimes difficult to find in South America, as, in some places are disposable nappies.

## MEDICINES AND WHAT TO TAKE

There is very little control on the sale of drugs and medicines in South America. You can buy any and every drug in pharmacies without a prescription. Be wary of this because pharmacists can be poorly trained and might sell you drugs that are unsuitable, dangerous or old. Many drugs and medicines are manufactured under licence from American or European companies, so the trade names may be familiar to you. This means you do not have to carry a whole chest of medicines with you, but remember that the shelf life of some items, especially vaccines and antibiotics, is markedly reduced in hot conditions. Buy your supplies at the better outlets where there are refrigerators, even though they are more expensive and check the expiry date of all preparations you buy. Immigration officials occasionally confiscate scheduled drugs (Lomotil is an example) if they are not accompanied by a doctor's prescription.

**Self-medication** may be forced on you by circumstances so the following text contains the names of drugs and medicines which you may find useful in an emergency or in out-of-the-way places. You may like to take some of the following items with you from home:

**Sunglasses**
ones designed for intense sunlight

**Earplugs**
for sleeping on aeroplanes and in noisy hotels

**Suntan cream**
with a high protection factor

**Insect repellent**
containing DET for preference

**Mosquito net**
lightweight, permethrin-impregnated for choice

**Tablets**
for travel sickness

**Tampons**
can be expensive in some countries in Latin America

**Condoms**

**Contraceptives**

**Water sterilising tablets**

**Antimalarial tablets**

**Anti-infective ointment** eg Cetrimide

**Dusting powder** for feet etc containing fungicide

**Antacid tablets** for indigestion

**Sachets of rehydration salts** plus anti-diarrhoea preparations

**Painkillers** such as Paracetamol or Aspirin

**Antibiotics** for diarrhoea etc

**First Aid kit** Small pack containing a few sterile syringes and needles and disposable gloves. The risk of catching hepatitis etc from a dirty needle used for injection is now negligible in Latin America, but some may be reassured by carrying their own supplies – available from camping shops and airport shops.

## Vaccination and immunisation

Smallpox vaccination is no longer required anywhere in the world. Neither is cholera vaccination recognised as necessary for international travel by the World Health Organisation – it is not very effective either. Nevertheless, some immigration officials are demanding proof of vaccination against cholera in Latin America and in some countries outside Latin America, following the outbreak of the disease which originated in Peru in 1990-91 and subsequently affected most surrounding countries. Although very unlikely to affect visitors to Latin America, the cholera epidemic continues making its greatest impact in poor areas where water supplies are polluted and food hygiene practices are insanitary.

Vaccination against the following diseases are recommended:

**Yellow Fever**

This is a live vaccination not to be given to children under 9 months of age or persons allergic to eggs. Immunity lasts for 10 years, an International Certificate of Yellow Fever Vaccination will be given and should be kept because it is sometimes asked for. Yellow fever is very rare in Latin America, but the vaccination is practically without side effects and almost totally protective.

**Typhoid**

A disease spread by the insanitary preparation of food. A number of new vaccines against this condition are now available; the older TAB and monovalent typhoid vaccines are being phased out. The newer, eg Typhim Vi, cause less side effects, but are more expensive. For those who do not like injections, there are now oral vaccines.

**Poliomyelitis**

Despite its decline in the world this remains a serious disease if caught and is easy to protect against. There are live oral vaccines and in some countries injected vaccines. Whichever one you choose it is a good idea to have booster every 3-5 years if visiting developing countries regularly.

**Tetanus**

One dose should be given with a booster at 6 weeks and another at 6 months and 10 yearly boosters thereafter are recommended. Children should already be properly protected against diphtheria, poliomyelitis and pertussis (whooping cough), measles and HIB all of which can be more serious infections in Latin America than at home. Measles, mumps and rubella vaccine is also given to children throughout the world, but those teenage girls who have not had rubella (german measles) should be tested and vaccinated. Hepatitis B vaccination for babies is now routine in some countries. Consult your doctor for advice on tuberculosis inoculation: the disease is still widespread in Latin America.

**Infectious Hepatitis**

Is less of a problem for travellers than it used to be because of the development of two extremely effective vaccines against the A and B form of the disease. It remains common, however, in Latin America. A combined hepatitis A & B vaccine is now licensed and will be available in 1997 – one jab covers both diseases.

**Other vaccinations:**

Might be considered in the case of epidemics eg meningitis. There is an effective vaccination against rabies which should be considered by all travellers, especially those going through remote areas or if there is a

particular occupational risk, eg for zoologists or veterinarians.

## FURTHER INFORMATION

Further information on health risks abroad, vaccinations etc may be available from a local travel clinic. If you wish to take specific drugs with you such as antibiotics these are best prescribed by your own doctor. Beware, however, that not all doctors can be experts on the health problems of remote countries. More detailed or more up-to date information than local doctors can provide are available from various sources. In the UK there are hospital departments specialising in tropical diseases in London, Liverpool, Birmingham and Glasgow and the Malaria Reference Laboratory at the London School of Hygiene and Tropical Medicine provides free advice about malaria, T 0891 600350. In the USA the local Public Health Services can give such information and information is available centrally from the Centre for Disease Control (CDC) in Atlanta, T (404) 3324559.

There are additional computerised databases which can be assessed for destination-specific up-to-the-minute information. In the UK there is MASTA (Medical Advisory Service to Travellers Abroad), T 0171 631 4408, F 0171 436 5389, Tx 8953473 and Travax (Glasgow, T 0141 946 7120, ext 247). Other information on medical problems overseas can be obtained from the book by Dawood, Richard (Editor) (1992) *Travellers' Health: How to stay healthy abroad*, Oxford University Press 1992, £7.99. We strongly recommend this revised and updated edition, especially to the intrepid traveller heading for the more out of the way places. General advice is also available in the UK in *Health Information for Overseas Travel* published by the Department of Health and available from HMSO, and *International Travel and Health* published by WHO, Geneva.

# STAYING HEALTHY

## INTESTINAL UPSETS

The thought of catching a stomach bug worries visitors to Latin America but there have been great improvements in food hygiene and most such infections are preventable. Travellers' diarrhoea and vomiting is due, most of the time, to food poisoning, usually passed on by the insanitary habits of food handlers. As a general rule the cleaner your surroundings and the smarter the restaurant, the less likely you are to suffer.

**Foods to avoid:** uncooked, undercooked, partially cooked or reheated meat, fish, eggs, raw vegetables and salads, especially when they have been left out exposed to flies. Stick to fresh food that has been cooked from raw just before eating and make sure you peel fruit yourself. Wash and dry your hands before eating – disposable wet-wipe tissues are useful for this.

**Shellfish** eaten raw are risky and at certain times of the year some fish and shellfish concentrate toxins from their environment and cause various kinds of food

### Water purification

There are a number of ways of purifying water in order to make it safe to drink. Dirty water should first be strained through a filter bag (camping shops) and then boiled or treated. Bringing water to a rolling boil at sea level is sufficient to make the water safe for drinking, but at higher altitudes you have to boil the water for longer to ensure that all the microbes are killed.

There are sterilising methods that can be used and there are proprietary preparations containing chlorine (eg Puritabs) or iodine (eg Pota Aqua) compounds. Chlorine compounds generally do not kill protozoa (eg giardia).

There are a number of water filters now on the market available in personal and expedition size. They work either on mechanical or chemical principles, or may do both. Make sure you take the spare parts or spare chemicals with you and do not believe *everything* the manufacturers say.

poisoning. The local authorities notify the public not to eat these foods. Do not ignore the warning. **Heat treated milk** (UHT) pasteurised or sterilised is becoming more available in Latin America as is pasteurised cheese. On the whole matured or processed cheeses are safer than the fresh varieties and fresh unpasteurised milk from whatever animal can be a source of food poisoning germs, tuberculosis and brucellosis. This applies equally to icecream, yoghurt and cheese made from unpasteurised milk, so avoid these homemade products – the factory made ones are probably safer.

**Tap water** is rarely safe outside the major cities, especially in the rainy season. Stream water, if you are in the countryside, is often contaminated by communities living surprisingly high in the mountains. Filtered or bottled water is usually available and safe, although you must make sure that somebody is not filling bottles from the tap and hammering on a new crown cap. If your hotel has a central hot water supply this water is safe to drink after cooling. Ice for drinks should be made from boiled water, but rarely is so stand your glass on the ice cubes, rather than putting them in the drink. The better hotels have water purifying systems.

## TRAVELLERS' DIARRHOEA

This is usually caused by eating food which has been contaminated by food poisoning germs. Drinking water is rarely the culprit. Sea water or river water is more likely to be contaminated by sewage and so swimming in such dilute effluent can also be a cause.

Infection with various organisms can give rise to travellers' diarrhoea. They may be viruses, bacteria, eg Escherichia coli (probably the most common cause worldwide), protozoal (such as amoebas and giardia), salmonella and cholera. The diarrhoea may come on suddenly or rather slowly. It may or may not be accompanied by vomiting or by severe abdominal pain and the passage of blood or mucus when it is called dysentery.

How do you know which type you have caught and how to treat it?

If you can time the onset of the diarrhoea to the minute ("acute") then it is probably due to a virus or a bacterium and/or the onset of dysentery. The treatment in addition to rehydration is Ciprofloxacin 500 mg every 12 hrs; the drug is now widely available and there are many similar ones.

If the diarrhoea comes on slowly or intermittently ("sub-acute") then it is more likely to be protozoal, ie caused by an amoeba or giardia. Antibiotics such a Ciprofloxacin will have little effect. These cases are best treated by a doctor as is any outbreak of diarrhoea continuing for more than 3 days. Sometimes blood is passed in ameobic dysentery and for this you should certainly seek medical help. If this is not available then the best treatment is probably Tinidazole (Fasigyn) 1 tablet four times a day for 3 days. If there are severe stomach cramps, the following drugs may help but are not very useful in the management of acute diarrhoea: Loperamide (Imodium) and Diphenoxylate with Atropine (Lomotil) They should not be given to children.

Any kind of diarrhoea, whether or not accompanied by vomiting, responds well to the replacement of water and salts, taken as frequent small sips, of some kind of rehydration solution. There are proprietary preparations consisting of sachets of powder which you dissolve in boiled water or you can make your own by adding half a teaspoonful of salt (3.5 gms) and 4 tablespoonsful of sugar (40 gms) to a litre of boiled water.

Thus the lynch pins of treatment for diarrhoea are rest, fluid and salt replacement, antibiotics such as Ciprofloxacin for the bacterial types and special diagnostic tests and medical treatment for the amoeba and giardia infections. Salmonella infections and cholera, although rare, can be devastating diseases and it would be wise to get to a hospital as soon as possible if these were suspected.

Fasting, peculiar diets and the consumption of large quantities of yoghurt have not been found useful in calming travellers' diarrhoea or in rehabilitating inflamed bowels. Oral rehydration has on the other hand, especially in children, been a life saving technique and should always be practised, whatever other treatment you use. As there is some evidence that alcohol and milk might prolong diarrhoea they should be avoided during and immediately after an attack.

Diarrhoea occurring day after day for long periods of time (chronic diarrhoea) is notoriously resistent to amateur attempts at treatment and again warrants proper diagnostic tests (most towns with reasonable sized hospitals have laboratories for stool samples). There are ways of preventing travellers' diarrhoea for short periods of time by taking antibiotics, but this is not a foolproof technique and should not be used other than in exceptional circumstances. Doxycycline is possibly the best drug. Some preventatives such as Enterovioform can have serious side effects if taken for long periods.

Paradoxically **constipation** is also common, probably induced by dietary change, inadequate fluid intake in hot places and long bus journeys. Simple laxatives are useful in the short-term and bulky foods such as maize, beans and plenty of fruit are also useful.

## HIGH ALTITUDE

Spending time at high altitude in South America, especially in the tropics, is usually a pleasure – it is not so hot, there are no insects and the air is clear and spring like. Travelling to high altitudes, however, can cause medical problems, all of which can be prevented if care is taken.

On reaching heights above about 3,000m, heart pounding and shortness of breath, especially on exertion are a normal response to the lack of oxygen in the air. A condition called acute mountain sickness (*Soroche* in South America) can also affect visitors. It is more likely to affect those who ascend rapidly, eg by plane and those who over-exert themselves (teenagers for example). Soroche takes a few hours or days to come on and presents with a bad headache, extreme tiredness, sometimes dizziness, loss of appetite and frequently nausea and vomiting. Insomnia is common and is often associated with a suffocating feeling when lying in bed. Keen observers may note their breathing tends to wax and wane at night and their face tends to be puffy in the mornings – this is all part of the syndrome. Anyone can get this condition and past experience is not always a good guide: the author, having spent years in Peru travelling constantly between sea level and very high altitude never suffered symptoms, then was severely affected whilst climbing Kilimanjaro in Tanzania.

The treatment of acute mountain sickness is simple – rest, painkillers, (preferably not aspirin based) for the headache and anti sickness pills for vomiting. Oxygen is actually not much help, except at very high altitude. Various local panaceas – Coramina glucosada, Effortil, Micoren are popular in Latin America and mate de coca (an infusion of coca leaves widely available and perfectly legal) will alleviate some of the symptoms.

To **prevent** the condition: on arrival at places over 3,000m have a few hours rest in a chair and avoid alcohol, cigarettes and heavy food. If the symptoms are severe and prolonged, it is best to descend to a lower altitude and to reascend slowly or in stages. If this is impossible because of shortage of time or if you are going so high that acute mountain sickness is very likely, then the drug Acetazolamide (Diamox) can be used as a preventative and continued during the ascent. There is good evidence of the value of this drug in the prevention of soroche, but some people do experience peculiar side effects. The usual dose is 500 mg of the slow release preparation each night, starting the night before ascending above 3,000m.

Watch out for **sunburn** at high altitude. The ultraviolet rays are extremely powerful. The air is also excessively dry at high altitude and you might find that your skin dries out and the inside of your nose becomes crusted. Use a moisturiser for the skin and some vaseline wiped into the nostrils. Some people find contact lenses irritate because of the dry air. It is unwise to ascend to high altitude if you are pregnant, especially in the first 3 months, or if you have a history of heart, lung or blood disease, including sickle cell.

A more unusual condition can affect mountaineers who ascend rapidly to high altitude – **acute pulmonary oedema**. Residents at altitude sometimes experience this when returning to the mountains from time spent at the coast. This condition is often preceded by acute mountain sickness and comes on quite rapidly with severe breathlessness, noisy breathing, cough, blueness of the lips and frothing at the mouth. Anybody who develops this must be brought down as soon as possible, given oxygen and taken to hospital.

A rapid descent from high places will make sinus problems and middle ear infections worse and might make your teeth ache. Lastly, don't fly to altitude within 24 hrs of SCUBA diving. You might suffer from 'the bends'.

## HEAT AND COLD

Full acclimatisation to high temperatures takes about 2 weeks. During this period it is normal to feel a bit apathetic, especially if the relative humidity is high. Drink plenty of water (up to 15 litres a day are required when working physically hard in the tropics), use salt on your food and avoid extreme exertion. Tepid showers are more cooling than hot or cold ones. Large hats do not cool you down, but do prevent sunburn. Remember that, especially in the highlands, there can be a large and sudden drop in temperature between sun and shade and between night and day, so dress accordingly. Warm jackets or woollens are essential after dark at high altitude. Loose cotton is still the best material when the weather is hot.

## INSECTS

These are mostly more of a nuisance than a serious hazard and if you try, you can prevent yourself entirely from being bitten. Some, such as mosquitos are, of course, carriers of potentially serious diseases, so it is sensible to avoid being bitten as much as possible. Sleep off the ground and use a mosquito net or some kind of insecticide. Preparations containing Pyrethrum or synthetic pyrethroids are safe. They are available as aerosols or pumps and the best way to use these is to spray the room thoroughly in all areas (follow the instructions rather than the insects) and then shut the door for a while, re-entering when the smell has dispersed. Mosquito coils release insecticide as they burn slowly. They are widely available and useful out of doors. Tablets of insecticide which are placed on a heated mat plugged into a wall socket are probably the most effective. They fill the room with insecticidal fumes in the same way as aerosols or coils.

You can also use insect repellents, most of which are effective against a wide range of pests. The most common and effective is diethyl metatoluamide (DET). DET liquid is best for arms and face (care around eyes and with spectacles – DET dissolves plastic). Aerosol spray is good for clothes and ankles and liquid DET can be dissolved in water and used to impregnate cotton clothes and mosquito nets. Some repellents now contain DET and Permethrin, insecticide. Impregnated wrist and ankle bands can also be useful.

If you are bitten or stung, itching may be relieved by cool baths, antihistamine tablets (care with alcohol or driving) or mild corticosteroid creams, eg. hydrocortisone (great care: never use if any hint of infection). Careful scratching of all your bites once a day can be surprisingly effective. Calamine lotion and cream have limited effectiveness and antihistamine creams are not recommended – they can cause allergies themselves.

Bites which become infected should be treated with a local antiseptic or antibiotic cream such as Cetrimide, as should any infected sores or scratches.

When living rough, skin infestations with body lice (crabs) and scabies are easy to pick up. Use whatever local commercial preparation is recommended for lice and scabies.

Crotamiton cream (Eurax) alleviates itching and also kills a number of skin parasites. Malathion lotion 5% (Prioderm) kills lice effectively, but avoid the use of the toxic agricultural preparation of Malathion, more often used to commit suicide.

## TICKS

They attach themselves usually to the lower parts of the body often after walking in areas where cattle have grazed. They take a while to attach themselves strongly, but swell up as they start to suck blood. The important thing is to remove them gently, so that they do not leave their head parts in your skin because this can cause a nasty allergic reaction some days later. Do not use petrol, vaseline, lighted cigarettes etc to remove the tick, but, with a pair of tweezers remove the beast gently by gripping it at the attached (head) end and rock it out in very much the same way that a tooth is extracted. Certain tropical flies which lay their eggs under the skin of sheep and cattle also occasionally do the same thing to humans with the unpleasant result that a maggot grows under the skin and pops up as a boil or pimple. The best way to remove these is to cover the boil with oil, vaseline or nail varnish so as to stop the maggot breathing, then to squeeze it out gently the next day.

## SUNBURN

The burning power of the tropical sun, especially at high altitude, is phenomenal.

Always wear a wide brimmed hat and use some form of suncream lotion on untanned skin. Normal temperate zone sun tan lotions (protection factor up to 7) are not much good; you need to use the types designed specifically for the tropics or for mountaineers or skiers with protection factors up to 15 or above. These are often not available in Latin America. Glare from the sun can cause conjunctivitis, so wear sunglasses especially on tropical beaches, where high protection factor sunscreen should also be used.

## PRICKLY HEAT

A very common intensely itchy rash is avoided by frequent washing and by wearing loose clothing. Cured by allowing skin to dry off through use of powder and spending two nights in an airconditioned hotel!

## ATHLETES FOOT

This and other fungal skin infections are best treated with Tolnaftate or Clotrimazole.

## OTHER RISKS AND MORE SERIOUS DISEASES

Remember that rabies is endemic throughout Latin America, so avoid dogs that are behaving strangely and cover your toes at night from the vampire bats, which also carry the disease. If you are bitten by a domestic or wild animal, do not leave things to chance: scrub the wound with soap and water and/or disinfectant, try to have the animal captured (within limits) or at least determine its ownership, where possible, and seek medical assistance at once. The course of treatment depends on whether you have already been satisfactorily vaccinated against rabies. If you have (this is worthwile if you are spending lengths of time in developing countries) then some further doses of vaccine are all that is required. Human diploid vaccine is the best, but expensive: other, older kinds of vaccine, such as that derived from duck embryos may be the only types available. These are effective, much cheaper and interchangeable generally with the human derived types. If not already vaccinated then anti rabies serum (immunoglobulin) may be required in addition. It is important to finish the course of treatment whether the animal survives or not.

## AIDS

In South America AIDS is increasing but is not wholly confined to the well known high risk sections of the population, ie homosexual men, intravenous drug abusers and children of infected mothers. Heterosexual transmission is now the dominant mode and so the main risk to travellers is from casual sex. The same precautions should be taken as with any sexually transmitted disease. The Aids virus (HIV) can be passed by unsterilised needles which have been previously used to inject an HIV positive patient, but the risk of this is negligible. It would, however, be sensible to check that needles have been properly sterilised or disposable needles have been used. If you wish to take your own disposable needles, be prepared to explain what they are for. The risk of receiving a blood transfusion with blood infected with the HIV virus is greater than from dirty needles because of the amount of fluid exchanged. Supplies of blood for transfusion should now be screened for HIV in all reputable hospitals, so again the risk is very small indeed. Catching the AIDS virus does not always produce an illness in itself (although it may do). The only way to be sure if you feel you have been put at risk is to have a blood test for HIV antibodies on your return to a place where there are reliable laboratory facilities. The test does not become positive for some weeks.

## MALARIA

In South America malaria is theoretically confined to coastal and jungle zones, but is now on the increase again. Mosquitos do not thrive above 2,500m, so you are safe at altitude. There are different varieties of malaria, some resistant to the normal drugs. Make local enquiries if you intend to visit possibly infected zones and use a prophylactic regime. Start taking the tablets a few days before exposure and continue to take them for 6 weeks after leaving the malarial zone. Remember to give the drugs to babies and children also. Opinion varies on the precise drugs and dosage to be used for protection. All the drugs may have some side effects and it is important to balance the risk of catching the disease against the albeit rare side effects. The increasing complexity of the subject is such that as the malarial parasite becomes immune to the new generation of drugs it has made concentration on the physical prevention from being bitten by mosquitos more important. This involves the use of long sleeved shirts or blouses and long trousers, repellants and nets. Clothes are now available impregnated with the insecticide Permethrin or Deltamethrin or it is possible to impregnate the clothes yourself. Wide meshed nets impregnated with Permethrin are also available, are lighter to carry and less claustrophobic to sleep in.

### Prophylaxis and treatment

If your itinerary takes you into a malarial area, seek expert advice before you go on a suitable prophylactic regime. This is especially true for pregnant women who are particularly prone to catch malaria. You can still catch the disease even when sticking to a proper regime, although it is unlikely. If you do develop symptoms (high fever, shivering, headache, sometimes diarrhoea), seek medical advice immediately. If this is not possible and there is a great likelihood of malaria, the treatment is:

Chloroquine, a single dose of 4 tablets (600 mg) followed by 2 tablets (300 mg) in 6 hrs and 300 mg each day following.

Falciparum type of malaria or type in doubt: take local advice. Various combinations of drugs are being used such as Quinine, Tetracycline or Halofantrine. If falciparum type malaria is definitely diagnosed, it is wise to get to a good hospital as treatment can be complex and the illness very serious.

## INFECTIOUS HEPATITIS (JAUNDICE)

The main symptoms are pains in the stomach, lack of appetite, lassitude and yellowness of the eyes and skin. Medically speaking there are two main types. The less serious, but more common is Hepatitis A for which the best protection os the careful preparation of food, the avoidance of contaminated drinking water and scrupulous attention to toilet hygiene. The other, more serious, version is Hepatitis B which is acquired usually as a sexually transmitted disease or by blood transfusions. It can less commonly be transmitted by injections with unclean needles and possibly by insect bites. The symptoms are the same as for Hepatitis A. The incubation period is much longer (up to 6 months compared with 6 weeks) and there are more likely to be complications.

Hepatitis A can be protected against with gamma globulin. It should be obtained from a reputable source and is certainly useful for travellers who intende to live rough. You should have a shot before leaving and have it repeated every 6 months. The dose of gamma globulin depends on the concentration of the particular preparation used, so the manufacturer's advice should be taken. The injection should be given as close as possible to your departure and as the dose depends on the likely time you are to spend in potentially affected areas, the manufacturer's instructions should be followed. Gamma globulin has really been superceded now by a proper vaccination against Hepatitis A (Havrix) which gives immunity lasting up to 10 years. After that boosters are required. Havrix monodose is now widely available as is Junior Havrix. The vaccination has negligible side effects and is extremely effective. Gamma globulin injections can be a bit painful, but it is much cheaper than Havrix and may be more available in some places.

Hepatitis B can be effectively prevented by a specific vaccine (Engerix) – 3 shots over 6 months before travelling. If you have had jaundice in the past it would be worthwhile having a blood test to see if you are immune to either of these two types, because this might avoid the necessity and costs of vaccination or gamma globulin. There are other kinds of viral hepatitis (C, E etc) which are fairly similar to A and B, but vaccines are not available as yet.

## TYPHUS

Can still occur carried by ticks. There is usually a reaction at the site of the bite and a fever. Seek medical advice.

## INTESTINAL WORMS

These are common and the more serious ones such as hookworm can be contracted from walking barefoot on infested earth or beaches.

Various other tropical diseases can be caught in jungle areas, usually transmitted by biting insects. They are often related to African diseases and were probably introduced by the slave labour trade. Onchocerciasis (river blindness) carried by black flies is found in parts of Mexico and Venezuela. Leishmaniasis (Espundia) is carried by sandflies and causes a sore that will not heal or a severe nasal infection. Wearing long trousers and a long sleeved shirt in infected areas protects against these flies. DET is also effective. Epidemics of meningitis occur from time-to-time. Be careful about swimmimg in piranha or caribe infested rivers. It is a good idea not to swim naked: the Candiru fish can follow urine currents and become lodged in body orifices. Swimwear offers some protection.

## LEPTOSPIROSIS

Various forms of leptospirosis occur throughout Latin America, transmitted by a bacterium which is excreted in rodent urine. Fresh water and moist soil harbour the organisms which enter the body through cuts and scratches. If you suffer from any form of prolonged fever consult a doctor.

## SNAKE BITE

This is a very rare event indeed for travellers. If you are unlucky (or careless) enough to be bitten by a venomous snake, spider, scorpion or sea creature, try to identify the creature, but do not put yourself in further danger. Snake bites in particular are very frightening, but in fact rarely poisonous – even venomous snakes bite without injecting venom. What you might expect if bitten are: fright, swelling, pain and bruising around the bite and soreness of the regional lymph glands, perhaps nausea, vomiting and a fever. Signs of serious poisoning would be the following symptoms: numbness and tingling of the face, muscular spasms, convulsions, shortness of breath and bleeding. Victims should be got to a hospital or a doctor without delay. Commercial snake bite and scorpion kits are available, but usually only useful for the specific type of snake or scorpion for which they are designed. Most serum has to be given intravenously so it is not much good equipping yourself with it unless you are used to making injections into veins. It is best to rely on local practice in these cases, because the particular creatures will be known about locally and appropriate treatment can be given.

**Treatment of snake bite** Reassure and comfort the victim frequently. Immobilise the limb by a bandage or a splint or by getting the person to lie still. Do not slash the bite area and try to suck out the poison because this sort of heroism does more harm than good. If you know how to use a tourniquet in these circumstances, you will not need this advice. If you are not experienced do not apply a tourniquet.

### Precautions

Avoid walking in snake territory in bare feet or sandals – wear proper shoes or boots. If you encounter a snake stay put until it slithers away, and do not investigate a wounded snake. Spiders and scorpions may be found in the more basic hotels, especially in the Andean countries. If stung, rest and take plenty of fluids and call a doctor. The best precaution is to keep beds away from the walls and look inside your shoes and under the toilet seat every morning. Certain tropical sea fish when trodden upon inject venom into bathers' feet. This can be exceptionally painful. Wear plastic shoes when you go bathing if such creatures are reported. The pain can be relieved by immersing the foot in extremely hot water for as long as the pain persists.

## DENGUE FEVER

This is increasing worldwide including in South and Central American countries and the Caribbean. It can be completely prevented by avoiding mosquito bites in the same way as malaria. No vaccine is available. Dengue is an unpleasant and painful disease, presenting with a high temperature and body pains, but at least visitors are spared the more serious forms (haemorrhagic types) which are more of a problem for local people who have been exposed to the disease more than once. There is no specific treatment for dengue – just pain killers and rest.

## CHAGAS' DISEASE (SOUTH AMERICAN TRYPANOSOMIASIS)

This is a chronic disease, very rarely caught by travellers and difficult to treat. It is transmitted by the simultaneous biting and excreting of the Reduvid bug, also known as the Vinchuca or Barbeiro. Somewhat resembling a small cockroach, this nocturnal bug lives in poor adobe houses with dirt floors often frequented by opossums. If you cannot avoid such accommodation, sleep off the floor with a candle lit, use a mosquito net, keep as much of your skin covered as possible, use DET repellent or a spray insecticide. If you are bitten overnight (the bites are painless) do not scratch them, but wash thoroughly with soap and water.

## DANGEROUS ANIMALS

Apart from mosquitos the most dangerous animals are men, be they bandits or behind steering wheels. Think carefully about violent confrontations and wear a seat belt if you are lucky enough to have one available to you.

## WHEN YOU RETURN HOME

Remember to take your antimalarial tablets for 6 weeks after leaving the malarial area. If you have had attacks of diarrhoea it is worth having a stool specimen tested in case you have picked up amoebas. If you have been living rough, blood tests may be worthwhile to detect worms and other parasites. If you have been exposed to bilharzia (*schistosomiasis*) by swimming in lakes etc, check by means of a blood test when you get home, but leave it for 6 weeks because the test is slow to become positive. Report any untowards symptoms to your doctor and tell the doctor exactly where you have been and, if you know, what the likelihood of disease is to which you were exposed.

The above information has been compiled for us by Dr David Snashall, who is presently Senior Lecturer in Occupational Health at the United Medical Schools of Guy's and St Thomas' Hospitals in London and Chief Medical Adviser to the British Foreign and Commonwealth Office. He has travelled extensively in Central and South America, worked in Peru and in East Africa and keeps in close touch with developments in preventative and tropical medicine.

# Travelling with children

People contemplating overland travel in South America with children should remember that a lot of time can be spent waiting for buses, trains, and especially for aeroplanes. On bus journeys, if the children are good at amusing themselves, or can readily sleep while travelling, the problems can be considerably lessened. If your child is of an early reading age, take reading material with you as it is difficult, and expensive to find. A bag of, say 30 pieces, of Duplo or Lego can keep young children occupied for hours. Travel on trains, while not as fast or at times as comfortable as buses, allows more scope for moving about. Some trains provide tables between seats, so that games can be played. Beware of doors left open for ventilation especially if air-conditioning is not working.

## Food

Food can be a problem if the children are not adaptable. It is easier to take biscuits, drinks, bread etc with you on longer trips than to rely on meal stops where the food may not be to taste. Avocados are safe, easy to eat and nutritious; they can be fed to babies as young as 6 months and most older children like them. A small immersion heater and jug for making hot drinks is invaluable, but remember that electric current varies. Try and get a dual-voltage one (110v and 220v).

## Fares

On all long-distance buses you pay for each seat, and there are no half-fares if the children occupy a seat each. For shorter trips it is cheaper, if less comfortable, to seat small children on your knee. Often there are spare seats which children can occupy after tickets have been collected. In city and local excursion buses, small children generally do not pay a fare, but are not entitled to a seat when paying customers are standing. On sightseeing tours you should *always* bargain for a family rate – often children can go free. (In trains, reductions for children are general, but not universal.)

All civil airlines charge half for children under 12, but some military services don't have half-fares, or have younger age limits. Note that a child travelling free on a long excursion is not always covered by the operator's travel insurance; it is adviseable to pay a small premium to arrange cover.

## Hotels

In all hotels, try to negotiate family rates. If charges are per person, always insist that two children will occupy one bed only, therefore counting as one tariff. If rates are per bed, the same applies. In either case you can almost always get a reduced rate at cheaper hotels. Occasionally when travelling with a child you will be refused a room in a hotel that is "unsuitable". On river boat trips, unless you have very large hammocks, it may be more comfortable and cost effective to hire a 2-berth cabin for 2 adults and a child. (In restaurants, you can normally buy children's helpings, or divide one full-size helping between two children.)

Travel with children can bring you into closer contact with Latin American families and, generally, presents no special problems – in fact the path is often smoother for family groups. Officials tend to be more amenable where children are concerned and they are pleased if your child knows a little Spanish. Moreover, even thieves and pickpockets seem to have some of the traditional respect for families, and may leave you alone because of it!

# Tinted boxes

# Illustrations



# Advertisers

# Index

## D

## J



## K



## L



## M

# The Footprint list

**Andalucía Handbook**
**Cambodia Handbook**
**Caribbean Islands Handbook**
**Chile Handbook**
**East Africa Handbook**
**Ecuador Handbook** with the Galápagos
**Egypt Handbook**
**India Handbook**
**Indonesia Handbook**
**Laos Handbook**
**Malaysia & Singapore Handbook**
**Mexico & Central America Handbook**
**Morocco Handbook** with Mauritania
**Myanmar (Burma) Handbook**
**Namibia Handbook**
**Pakistan Handbook**
**eru Handbook**
**outh Africa Handbook**
**outh American Handbook**
**i Lanka Handbook**
**ailand Handbook**
**et Handbook**
**isia Handbook** with Libya
**tnam Handbook**
**babwe & Malawi Handbook** th Botswana, Moçambique & mbia

New in Autumn 1997
**Israel Handbook**
**Nepal Handbook**

In the pipeline
**Argentina Handbook**
**Brazil Handbook**
**Colombia Handbook**
**Cuba Handbook**
**Jordan, Syria & Lebanon Handbook**
**Venezuela Handbook**

## Footprint T shirt

The Footprint T-shirt is available in 100% cotton in various colours.

## Mail Order

Footprint Handbooks are available worldwide in good bookstores. They can also be ordered directly from us in Bath (see below for address). Please contact us if you have difficulty finding a title.

The Footprint Handbook website will be coming to keep you up to date with all the latest news from us (http://www.footprint-handbooks.co.uk). For the most up-to-date information and to join our mailing list please contact us at:

**Footprint Handbooks**
6 Riverside Court
Lower Bristol Road
Bath BA2 3DZ, England
T +44(0)1225 469141
F +44(0)1225 469461
E Mail handbooks@footprint.cix.co.uk



# Maps

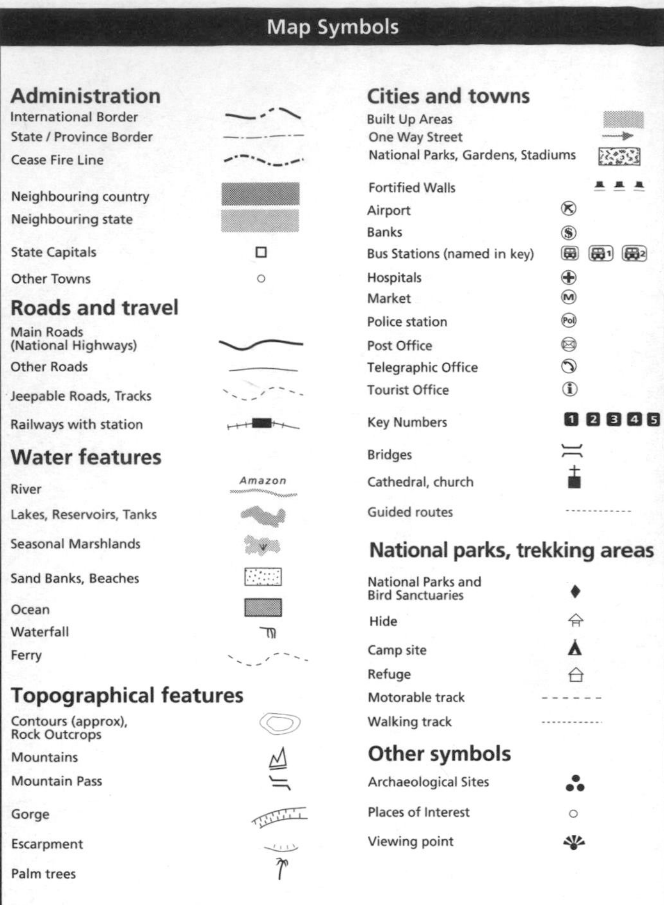


# Footprint Handbooks

All of us at Footprint Handbooks hope you have enjoyed reading and travelling with this Handbook, one of the first published in the new Footprint series. Many of you will be familiar with us as Trade & Travel, a name that has served us well for years. For you and for those who have only just discovered the Handbooks, we thought it would be interesting to chronicle the story of our development from the early 1920's.

It all started 75 years ago in 1921, with the publication of the Anglo-South American Handbook. In 1924 the South American Handbook was created. This has been published each year for the last 73 years and is the longest running guidebook in the English language, immortalised by Graham Greene as "the best travel guide in existence".

One of the key strengths of the South American Handbook over the years, has been the extraordinary contact we have had with our readers through their hundreds of letters to us in Bath. From these letters we learnt that you wanted more Handbooks of the same quality to other parts of the world.

In 1989 my brother Patrick and I set about developing a series modelled on the South American Handbook. Our aim was to create the ultimate practical guidebook series for all travellers, providing expert knowledge of far flung places, explaining culture, places and people in a balanced, lively and clear way. The whole idea hinged, of course, on finding writers who were in tune with our thinking. Serendipity stepped in at exactly the right moment: we were able to bring together a talented group of people who know the countries we cover inside out and whose enthusiasm for travelling in them needed to be communicated.

The series started to grow. We felt that the time was right to look again at the identity that had brought us all this way. After much searching we commissioned London designers Newell & Sorrell to loo at all the issues. Their solution was a ne identity for the Handbooks represent the books in all their aspects, looking a all the good things already achieved taking us into the new millennium.

The result is Footprint Handbo new name and mark, simple yet as bold, stylish and instantly recog The images we use conjure up the of real travel and communicate ties of the Handbooks in a straig and evocative way.

For us here in Bath, it h exciting exercise working t dramatic change. Already the like our favourite travelling we cannot wait to get m Footprint Handbooks o shelves and out onto the

James Dawson